MW01531281

IBM

International Technical Support Organization

**IBM @server i5 and iSeries System Handbook
IBM i5/OS Version 5 Release 3   October 2004**

March 2005

GA19-5486-26

Note: Before using this information and the product it supports, read the information in "Notices" on page xix.

Twenty-seventh edition (March 2005)

This edition applies to IBM i5/OS Version 5 Release 3 (product number 5722-SS1).

Contents

Notices

This information was developed for products and services offered in the U.S.A.

IBM may not offer the products, services, or features discussed in this document in other countries. Consult your local IBM representative for information on the products and services currently available in your area. Any reference to an IBM product, program, or service is not intended to state or imply that only that IBM product, program, or service may be used. Any functionally equivalent product, program, or service that does not infringe any IBM intellectual property right may be used instead. However, it is the user's responsibility to evaluate and verify the operation of any non-IBM product, program, or service.

IBM may have patents or pending patent applications covering subject matter described in this document. The furnishing of this document does not give you any license to these patents. You can send license inquiries, in writing, to:
IBM Director of Licensing, IBM Corporation, North Castle Drive Armonk, NY 10504-1785 U.S.A.

The following paragraph does not apply to the United Kingdom or any other country where such provisions are inconsistent with local law: INTERNATIONAL BUSINESS MACHINES CORPORATION PROVIDES THIS PUBLICATION "AS IS" WITHOUT WARRANTY OF ANY KIND, EITHER EXPRESS OR IMPLIED, INCLUDING, BUT NOT LIMITED TO, THE IMPLIED WARRANTIES OF NON-INFRINGEMENT, MERCHANTABILITY OR FITNESS FOR A PARTICULAR PURPOSE. Some states do not allow disclaimer of express or implied warranties in certain transactions, therefore, this statement may not apply to you.

This information could include technical inaccuracies or typographical errors. Changes are periodically made to the information herein; these changes will be incorporated in new editions of the publication. IBM may make improvements and/or changes in the product(s) and/or the program(s) described in this publication at any time without notice.

Any references in this information to non-IBM Web sites are provided for convenience only and do not in any manner serve as an endorsement of those Web sites. The materials at those Web sites are not part of the materials for this IBM product and use of those Web sites is at your own risk.

IBM may use or distribute any of the information you supply in any way it believes appropriate without incurring any obligation to you.

Any performance data contained herein was determined in a controlled environment. Therefore, the results obtained in other operating environments may vary significantly. Some measurements may have been made on development-level systems and there is no guarantee that these measurements will be the same on generally available systems. Furthermore, some measurement may have been estimated through extrapolation. Actual results may vary. Users of this document should verify the applicable data for their specific environment.

Information concerning non-IBM products was obtained from the suppliers of those products, their published announcements or other publicly available sources. IBM has not tested those products and cannot confirm the accuracy of performance, compatibility or any other claims related to non-IBM products. Questions on the capabilities of non-IBM products should be addressed to the suppliers of those products.

This information contains examples of data and reports used in daily business operations. To illustrate them as completely as possible, the examples include the names of individuals, companies, brands, and products. All of these names are fictitious and any similarity to the names and addresses used by an actual business enterprise is entirely coincidental.

COPYRIGHT LICENSE:
This information contains sample application programs in source language, which illustrates programming techniques on various operating platforms. You may copy, modify, and distribute these sample programs in

xix

any form without payment to IBM, for the purposes of developing, using, marketing or distributing application programs conforming to the application programming interface for the operating platform for which the sample programs are written. These examples have not been thoroughly tested under all conditions. IBM, therefore, cannot guarantee or imply reliability, serviceability, or function of these programs. You may copy, modify, and distribute these sample programs in any form without payment to IBM for the purposes of developing, using, marketing, or distributing application programs conforming to IBM's application programming interfaces.

Trademarks

The following terms are trademarks of the International Business Machines Corporation and the Rational Software Corporation, in the United States, other countries, or both:

@server®	DB2 Connect™	NetView®
eServer™	DB2 OLAP Server™	NetVista™
ibm.com®	DB2 Universal Database™	Notes®
iNotes™	DB2®	Open Class®
iSeries™	DRDA®	Operating System/400®
i5/OS™	Electronic Service Agent™	OS/2®
pSeries®	Enterprise Storage Server®	OS/390®
xSeries®	Everyplace®	OS/400®
z/OS®	ESCON®	Passport Advantage®
zSeries®	FlashCopy®	Power Architecture™
Advanced Function	FICON®	Power Everywhere™
Presentation™	GDDM®	Power PC®
Advanced Function Printing™	Hypervisor™	PowerPC®
Advanced Peer-to-Peer	Infoprint®	Print Services Facility™
Networking®	Integrated Language	POWER™
AnyNet®	Environment®	POWER4™
AD/Cycle®	Intelligent Miner™	POWER5™
AFCCU™	Intelligent Printer Data Stream™	QuickPlace®
AFP™	IntelliStation®	QMF™
AIX 5L™	IBM®	Rational®
AIX®	IMS™	Redbooks (logo) 🖉 ™
AS/400e™	IPDS™	Redbooks™
AS/400®	Language Environment®	RPG/400®
BCOCA™	Lotus Enterprise Integrator®	RS/6000®
C/400®	Lotus Notes®	S/370™
ClearCase®	Lotus Workflow™	S/390®
ClusterProven®	Lotus®	Sametime®
CICS®	LPDA®	SecureWay®
COBOL/400®	Magstar®	SmartSuite®
DataPropagator™	MQSeries®	System/36™
Distributed Relational Database	MVS™	System/370™
Architecture™	Net.Data®	System/38™
Domino Designer®	Netfinity®	Systems Application
Domino.Doc®	Network Station®	Architecture®
Domino®	NetServer™	SAA®

SANergy®	Virtualization Engine™	Workplace™
Tivoli®	VisualAge®	
TotalStorage®	WebSphere®	

The following terms are trademarks of other companies:

Intel, Intel Inside (logos), MMX, and Pentium are trademarks of Intel Corporation in the United States, other countries, or both.

Microsoft, Windows, Windows NT, and the Windows logo are trademarks of Microsoft Corporation in the United States, other countries, or both.

Java and all Java-based trademarks and logos are trademarks or registered trademarks of Sun Microsystems, Inc. in the United States, other countries, or both.

UNIX is a registered trademark of The Open Group in the United States and other countries.

SET, SET Secure Electronic Transaction, and the SET Logo are trademarks owned by SET Secure Electronic Transaction LLC.

Other company, product, and service names may be trademarks or service marks of others.

Preface

The new IBM® @server i5 servers extend the IBM @server iSeries™ family. They are the first servers in the industry based on the leading-edge IBM POWER5™ 64-bit microprocessor. Today's @server i5 servers give the flexibility to move from one generation of technology to another without disrupting a company's business. IBM i5/OS™ Version 5 Release 3, the next generation of OS/400®, features support for multiple operating systems and application environments on a single, simplified platform. @server i5 servers do more with less.

This twenty-seventh edition of the *IBM @server i5 and iSeries System Handbook*, distributed and respected worldwide, supports these latest iSeries announcements. It provides a product and feature overview of the newest @server i5 Models 520, 550, 570, and 595. It describes the newest release of operating system software, i5/OS V5R3, as well as iSeries Models 800, 810, 825, 870, and 890. Information is featured to present all aspects of today's @server i5 servers, from the architectural foundation to performance considerations.

This Handbook is written for IBM System Specialists, Marketing Representatives, Business Partners, and Clients to answer first-level questions. It offers a comprehensive guide to iSeries models, associated hardware, and OS/400-related software currently marketed by IBM representatives.

This IBM Redbook is one of several books produced by the IBM International Technical Support Organization (ITSO) to highlight the iSeries product line. Use this handbook as a reference for the options that are available. Then, refer to the companion manual *IBM @server i5, iSeries, and AS/400e System Builder*, SG24-2155, for more detailed information and configuration rules. You may also refer to *IBM @server iSeries Migration: System Migration and Upgrades at V5R1 and V5R2*, SG24-6055, for details about upgrading to the iSeries 800, 810, 820, 825, 830, 840, 870, and 890 servers. The Hardware Service Manager is described in *Logical Partitions on the IBM PowerPC: A Guide to Working with LPAR on POWER5 for IBM @server i5 Servers*, SG24-8000.

Refer to IBM online publications and systems, such as ViewBlue and PartnerInfo (or their equivalent outside of the United States), and your IBM marketing and support representative for final confirmation.

To order a copy or copies of this handbook, see "Related publications" on page 785.

xxiii

The team that wrote this redbook

This redbook was produced by a worldwide team of specialists working at the ITSO, Rochester Center.

Matthew Bedernjak is an Advisory I/T Specialist in Toronto, Canada. He has six years of experience in IBM TotalStorage® and UNIX® (IBM RS/6000® servers and AIX®) platforms, supporting the Americas. He holds a bachelor degree in civil engineering and is currently completing a master degree in mechanical and industrial engineering from the University of Toronto. His expertise is in tape storage systems (open and large systems), storage area networks (SANs), Tivoli® Storage Management, AIX and IBM @server pSeries® and disaster recovery. He has written extensively about disaster recovery and IBM TotalStorage products.

Celia Burke is a Senior IT Specialist with IBM Australia. She has 18 years of midrange systems experience and currently provides pre-sales technical support to IBM business partners across Australia.

Mary Cheever, Senior iSeries Techline Specialist, has been with IBM for 27 years. She has experience as an iSeries Systems Engineer and currently provides iSeries pre-sales technical marketing support.

Louis Cuypers, iSeries Technical Support Specialist, has been with IBM Belgium for 29 years. He specializes in technical support and problem determination hardware and software for the iSeries server. His previous experience includes working with the System/32, System/34, System/36™, System/38™, and AS/400® system. Louis has participated in many ITSO residencies since the release of OS/400 V4R1. He is recognized worldwide as an advocate for iSeries products and delivery.

Harold Distler is an iSeries Product Specialist involved with pre- and post-sales support for iSeries hardware, operating system, and software for Sirius Computing Solutions. He is also familiar with other platforms and networking. His 25-year career in the computing industry includes 17 years with IBM. He was an IBM Customer Engineer for office products, unit record, System/32, System/34, System/36, and System/38 systems. He also provided Level 2 support for PC hardware and AIX. He was involved in RT/PC development before he moved into the field as an open systems system engineer.

Greg Hidalgo is an Advisory Techline Specialist on iSeries on the Western Area team in Dallas, Texas. Before joining Techline, he was with Level 2 support for OnDemand/Visual Info and OV/400. Greg joined IBM as a systems engineer in Houston and has 25 years of service with the company.

Miroslav Iwachow is Business Development Manager and iSeries support specialist working in Avnet in Czech Republic, a distributor of IBM. Miroslav previously worked for six years for IBM in the Czech Republic as the AS/400e™ product manager and team leader. Presently he specializes in supporting IBM Business Partners across Europe. He teaches courses that prepare Business Partners for IBM certifications.

Axel Lachman is a Project Manager and Senior Systems Engineer for FoxCom, an iSeries Business Partner in Germany. He has 12 years of experience in the OS/400 field. He is an IBM Certified Solutions Expert - iSeries Technical Solutions. His areas of expertise include On Demand Business enablement of line of business (LOB) applications, application modernization, Server Consolidation with logical partitions (LPARs), Microsoft® Windows® integration, and Linux planning and implementation. Axel also teaches On Demand Business-related topics and technical certification courses extensively for IBM Learning Services in Germany.

Henry Matos is a Senior iSeries System Specialist for IBM in Atlanta, Georgia. He joined IBM in 1976 as a computer operator trainee with the Program Information Department (PID) in Hawthorne, New York. After various computer-related assignments with internal IBM, he became a field AS/400 Systems Engineer in 1988 working out of the Manhattan, Midtown Branch office in New York. Henry later joined the IBM Techline organization and became the first Latin America Techline Specialist from Atlanta, Georgia.

Glen McClymont is a Senior AS/400 Techline Specialist with IBM in Canada. Since 1988, he has worked with the iSeries server in customer hardware support, software support, and most recently in pre-sales marketing support. Glen has 30 years with IBM. He is an alumni resident for the ITSO from previous Handbook and Builder residencies, providing expertise between updates.

Lori O'Dell is an iSeries Solution Design Specialist with Avnet Hall-Mark IBM Division. She is also an IBM Certified Solutions Expert - iSeries Technical Solutions. She provides both pre- and post-sales technical support to several key IBM Business Partners. Lori has four years of experience with the iSeries product line and currently holds seven IBM Certifications.

Susan Powers is a Consulting I/T Specialist at the ITSO, Rochester Center. Prior to joining the ITSO in 1997, she was an AS/400® Technical Advocate in the IBM Support Center with a variety of communications, performance, and work management assignments. Her IBM career began as a program support representative and systems engineer in Des Moines, Iowa. She holds a degree in mathematics, with an emphasis in education, from St. Mary's College of Notre Dame. She is the project manager for the iSeries Handbook and System Builder suite of IBM Redbooks™.

Samit Saliceti is an iSeries Solutions Design Specialist for Avnet Partner Solutions, IBM Americas. He has two years experience in pre- and post-sales technical support of IBM Business Partners for Avnet. Samit is the team lead assistant. He holds six IBM certifications.

Jerry Watson, iSeries Systems Specialist, has been with IBM United Kingdom for 18 years. After ten years as an AS/400 Systems Engineer working with clients in the London area, he moved to iSeries EMEA Techline and is now based in Leeds. His direct participation in the Handbook and System Builder began with the OS/400 V4R1 residency.

We appreciate contributions from the iSeries Information Center. And we thank the following developers, engineers, and product managers who provided technical validation, consultation, and information about the content and message of this handbook:

► For input on iSeries processors and features:

Gerald Allen
Denis Nizinski
Jeff Trachy
Jesus Villarreal
Dave Wells, team leader

► For input on iSeries migration and placement rules:

Dave Dosch
Mike Fallenstein, I/O Configuration
Mark Olson

► For product coordination:

Bill Shaffer, iSeries Product Manager, Printing and E-output
Mark Olson, IBM @server iSeries Brand Manager

► For input on hardware and software products, and other assistance:

Bill Armstrong	Steve Hank	Ray Perkins
Taylor Bliese	Jay Hansen	Ron Peterson
Jim Cook	Dwight Harrison	Brian Podrow
Amit Dave	Jamie Haverman	Mike Prochaska
Sharon Davidson	Tonya Holt	Gene Rentz
Terri Dudek	Chad Inglett	Linda Robinson
Clair Ewert	Ian Jarman	Van Sammons
Barbara Foss	Craig E. Johnson	Doug Schilling
Jim Fritsch	Charlie Jones	Craig Schmitz
Les Fullem	Debbie Landon	Jenifer Servais
Mark Funk	Kevin Larsen	Art Snyder
Tim Fynskov	Nancy Lowe	Mike Snyder
Jose Francisco Gazga	Kyle Lucke	Greg Vande Corput
Mark Gennrich	Edith Lueke	Jeff Van Heuklon
Bob Gintowt	Mark Manges	Jeff Waldbillig
Jim Gosack	Scott Maxson	Larry C. Walsh
Thomas Gray	Mark McDonnell	Deb Ward
Chuck Grimm	Hilary Melville	Ron Wesely
Randy Grimm	Brian Noordyke	Larry Whitley
Duane Grosz	Roger Olson	Janet Y Willis
Beth Hagemeister	Bob Padzieski	Joe Writz
IBM Rochester	**IBM Rochester**	**IBM Rochester**
Mark A. Freeman	David Slater	Nan Ni
Bill Shaffer	Jenny Wong	Aurora Ritter
IBM Boulder	**IBM Canada**	**IBM Austin**

Become a published author

Join us for a two- to six-week residency program! Help write an IBM Redbook dealing with specific products or solutions, while getting hands-on experience with leading-edge technologies. You'll team with IBM technical professionals, Business Partners and/or customers.

Your efforts will help increase product acceptance and customer satisfaction. As a bonus, you'll develop a network of contacts in IBM development labs, and increase your productivity and marketability.

Find out more about the residency program, browse the residency index, and apply online at:

ibm.com/redbooks/residencies.html

Comments welcome

Your comments are important to us!

We want our Redbooks to be as helpful as possible. Send us your comments about this or other Redbooks in one of the following ways:

► Use the online **Contact us** review redbook form found at:

   ibm.com/redbooks

► Send your comments in an Internet note to:

   redbook@us.ibm.com

► Mail your comments to:

   IBM Corporation, International Technical Support Organization
   Dept. JLU Building 107-2
   3605 Highway 52N
   Rochester, Minnesota 55901-7829

1

The next generation iSeries

IBM @server i5 servers extend the iSeries family by offering excellent scalability of IBM POWER5 servers. The @server i5 servers exhibit excellence in design and development and manufacturing. They are the first servers in the industry based on the IBM game-changing POWER5 64-bit microprocessor. Today's @server i5 servers give you the flexibility to move from one generation of technology to another without disrupting your business.

IBM also announces IBM i5/OS V5R3, the next generation of Operating System/400® (OS/400). Featuring support for multiple operating systems and application environments on a single, simplified platform, the @server i5 helps you do more with less. This is what you need to simplify your infrastructure, drive down costs, and drive up productivity in today's on demand world.

These highly integrated, powerful servers offer an on demand computing environment for i5/OS (the latest generation of IBM OS/400), IBM AIX 5L™, IBM WebSphere®, Microsoft Windows, Linux, Lotus® Domino®, and Java™ solutions. Flexible growth options, resource virtualization, and intuitive management tools mean that @server i5 servers can provide the power and capacity to run core business applications. They also provide the freedom and scalability to add new applications for On Demand Business on the same server.

3

Today's iSeries announcements allow you to:

▶ Simplify your infrastructure

- Run i5/OS, Linux, AIX 5L, and Windows on a single server
- Share resources, maximize utilization with IBM Virtualization Engine™, and manage infrastructure with IBM Director Multiplatform

▶ Integrate to innovate

- Exploit i5/OS integration with IBM software
- Personalize application access with WebSphere Portal
- Foster interaction and collaboration with IBM Lotus Team Workplace™

▶ Deliver without disruption

- Extend Capacity on Demand (CoD) leadership with memory and reserve CoD
- Strive for continuos operations with fault tolerant technologies
- Deliver robust, open database solutions with IBM DB2® Universal Database™ (UDB)

Simplicity in an on demand world

Today's on demand world is high-pressure and fast moving. Business demands change constantly. To gain a competitive edge, companies, regardless of how big or small, must be able to react instantly to clients' changing needs. It means having a flexible IT infrastructure that can grow and dynamically adapt to these demands. All too frequently, this adaptation can mean running multiple servers, which often means greater complexity and increased management costs. Because complex infrastructures are not agile and do not respond well to rapid change, it may also mean lost business opportunities.

But it doesn't have to. The iSeries server demonstrates a unique design that delivers the benefits of today's innovative technology without complexity. It is a highly integrated, reliable server platform that allows businesses to run multiple operating environments simultaneously. It dynamically adjusts to the changing requirements of an On Demand Business.

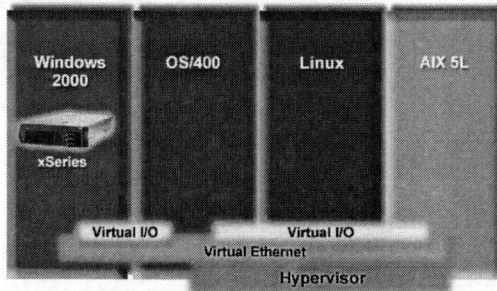

The iSeries offers an integrated architecture combined with legendary availability, high security, easy management, and mainframe-class technology. Because of this, the iSeries is uniquely positioned to play a leadership role in this new way of computing, providing simplicity in an on demand world.

Simplify your infrastructure

@server i5 servers are designed to reduce complexity, streamline your infrastructure, and enhance productivity through server consolidation. They can also dynamically adjust resources to meet your computing needs, without adding an extra server every time you accept a new business challenge. The features that are designed to help simplify your infrastructure include:

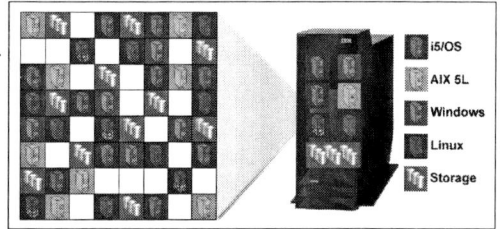

- ► **Support for multiple operating systems** facilitate server consolidation. This helps to decrease complexity, enhance manageability, and promote low total cost of ownership (TCO).

- ► **Dynamic, even automatic, distribution of processing resources** help raise server utilization rates and improve productivity.

- ► **Dynamic logical partitioning**, part of IBM Virtualization Engine Systems Technologies, is designed to pool resources and optimize their use across up to 254 partitions running multiple application environments and operating systems.

Integrate to innovate

To deliver new value to your business, you need to integrate. Staying competitive in an on demand world requires that companies react at the pace of On Demand Business and deploy applications quickly. This is why @server i5 servers include a suite of tools to support integrated Web enablement. By integrating applications and data across different databases that run on multiple servers or a diverse operating system, @server i5 servers can help your company unite people, processes, and information more effectively.

The features that are designed to promote integration and innovation in your business include:

- ► **A vast array of available applications** from a global network of independent software vendors to simplify deployment and help lower TCO
- ► **Integrated middleware** including security and workload management tools: IBM DB2 UDB software with i5/OS V5R3 enhancements, IBM Lotus Domino software, IBM WebSphere Application Server - Express for iSeries, and IBM HTTP Server (powered by Apache)
- ► **Easy-to-use, graphical management tools** built into iSeries Navigator to help streamline administration of multiple operating systems

Deliver without disruption

Even the most comprehensive, powerful system requires simple management tools to be effective. Application requirements grow as companies expand. Businesses need intuitive, optimized management facilities every step of the way. The following features of @server i5 servers are designed to enable your company to deliver key data and applications without disruption:

- ► **Clear upgrade paths from earlier servers** to enable businesses to seamlessly upgrade their servers between technology generations while helping to build on their investments in storage and networking
- ► **IBM @server On/Off Capacity on Demand** designed to dynamically add and then remove extra processor or memory capacity to handle spikes in demand, without permanently activating the processors or memory or requiring an upgrade purchase
- ► **Scalable POWER5 performance** that offers a highly scalable, upgradable, industry-standard and rack-optimized building-block architecture to help support balanced growth

Looking toward the future

As we move into the on demand world, the need for businesses to move faster, improve flexibility, and bolster collaboration on a global level will grow. For this reason, the adoption of optimized IT infrastructures based on integration, virtualization, open standards, and autonomic computing will become more critical to business success. The iSeries server possesses all attributes of such an environment, forming a solid technology foundation for on demand IT solutions. Thanks to the iSeries, the on demand computing world of tomorrow is rapidly becoming a reality today.

This Handbook provides an overview of the hardware and software for Models 520, 550, 570, and 595 supported by i5/OS V5R3, as well as Models 890, 870, 825, 810, and 800 supported by i5/OS V5R3 and OS/400 V5R2.

2

iSeries architecture: Fundamental strength of the eServer i5 and iSeries

The accelerating rate of change of both hardware and software technologies necessitates that the server you select is designed with the future in mind. The iSeries accommodates inevitable, rapid, and dramatic technology changes with relatively minimal effort required by clients, to allow them to meet their on demand requirements.

Paradoxically, the characteristic of the most advanced design and technology is that you do not notice it; you are not meant to do so. It accommodates rapidly-changing hardware and software technologies in stride, permitting you to fully exploit the latest technologies on demand.

iSeries servers and the supporting software offer important advanced capabilities in key areas such as On Demand Business, Java, Web serving, Lotus Domino, integration with Windows, managed availability, database, and Business Intelligence solutions. To gain an appreciation of these technologies and of the particular strength of the iSeries server in delivering them, this chapter provides a summary of each prime element.

7

With well over 750,000 systems shipped worldwide, the success of the iSeries is realized with the highest customer satisfaction index in the industry, as measured by IBM internal studies. The foundation of success starts with the design of the system, the architecture. Those components are also described in this chapter.

In brief, success factors for the iSeries are that it:

► Offers state-of-the-art 64-bit relational database processing

► Supports an object-based design that makes it highly virus resistant

► Has proven it can deliver over 99.9% availability on a single system

► Has operated for more than one year without requiring a re-initial program load (IPL), in hundreds of client shops

► Can have up to 60 Windows servers in a single system while sharing host systems disk storage, tape, and CD-ROM resources

► Directly (natively) supports different file structures, such as PC files, UNIX files, NetWare files, Domino files (Network File System (NSF)), ASCII files, and EBCDIC files

► Allows the deployment of Java, ported UNIX applications, Windows, Domino-based applications, and Linux on a single server

► Integrates leading edge technology

  The iSeries server was the first server with Silicon-On-Insulator (SOI) technology. The POWER4™ and POWER5 technology-based processors are an extension of that technology at 0.18 and 0.13 micron level.

► Offers Capacity on Demand (permanent or temporary) upgrades to support immediate and future processor utilization

► Supports up to 254 partitions running i5/OS and IBM AIX 5L or Linux

► With micropartitioning, allows up to 10 partitions per processor

► Can ship with over 650 processor chips under the covers of a "single" large system

► Incorporates many autonomic self-healing capabilities

System concepts

iSeries servers are designed and built as a *total system*, fully integrating the hardware and system software components that a business demands. As a general-purpose business and network system, it is optimized for the required environment with these unique benefits:

► The iSeries architecture is a brilliant, technology-neutral architecture. It enables businesses to readily exploit the latest hardware and software technologies, typically without causing disruption to existing application software. See "iSeries architecture" on page 9.

► The single purpose pervading each aspect of the iSeries architecture is to *empower a business* with the most advanced technology available, *without encumbering it* with the complexities that such technologies inevitably contain. The iSeries allows you to rapidly deploy advanced business applications and facilitates business growth.

► Clients typically decide on the required application software first and then select an environment in which to run it. iSeries models have thousands of client/server applications written by IBM Business Partners across the globe. In addition, the iSeries server provides excellent platforms for Windows, Lotus Domino, and Linux applications. iSeries models have national language support for over 50 languages, available in 140 countries or regions. IBM support across the world is provided by an impressive network of global partners.

A concise and expanded explanation of the iSeries server architecture is contained in the renowned book *Fortress Rochester: The Inside Story of the IBM @server iSeries* written by AS/400 and iSeries Chief Architect, Dr. Frank G. Soltis.

iSeries architecture

This section describes aspects of the iSeries server architecture that contribute most to the server's success as the *server of choice.*

Single-level storage

Application programs on an iSeries server are unaware of the underlying hardware characteristics, because of the iSeries layered architecture approach, Technology Independent Machine Interface (TIMI). TIMI frees application code from worrying about processor technology, such as moving from 48- to 64-bit or Complex Instruction Set Computing (CISC) to Reduced Instruction Set Computing (RISC).

Note: CISC addressing is 48 bits. All other processing is 32-bits wide.

The concept of single-level storage means that an application does not deal with storage device specifics. The knowledge of the underlying characteristics of hardware devices (in this case, main storage and disk storage) reside in the

System Licensed Internal Code (SLIC). All of the storage is automatically managed by the system. No user intervention is ever needed to take full advantage of any storage technology. Programs work with objects. Objects are accessed by name, not by address.

iSeries servers are commercial servers designed to handle many programs and users running simultaneously. Single-level storage enables high-speed switching between active and idle programs and users as compared to other operating system architectures. It contributes directly to iSeries high performance characteristics.

The iSeries server address size is vast. iSeries models can address the number of bytes that 64 bits allows it to address. The value 2^{64} is equal to 18,446,744,073,709,551,616. Therefore, the iSeries models can address 18,446,744,073,709,551,616 bytes, or 18.4 quintillion bytes. To put this into more meaningful terms, it is twice the number of millimeters in a light year. Light travels at approximately 6,000,000,000,000 miles in one year.

Single-level storage also enables another extremely important iSeries client benefit, *object persistence*. Object persistence means that the object continues to exist in single-level storage (unless purposely deleted by the client). Memory access is extremely fast. A typical server requires that information be stored in a separate file system if the information is to be shared or retained for a long time. The maintenance and awareness of the separate location can impact the total cost of ownership of the application.

Persistence of objects is important for support of object-oriented databases for data accessibility and recovery. Objects continue to exist even after their creator goes away. iSeries models are uniquely positioned to exploit this characteristic of object persistence. Customary systems use a less elegant mechanism that requires them to store their persistent objects in a separate file system, with all the attendant performance implications of application and operating system implementation.

Technology Independent Machine Interface

iSeries servers are atypical in that they are defined by software, not by hardware. When a program presents instructions to the machine interface for execution, it *thinks* that the interface is the system hardware, but it is not. This interface is known as Technology Independent Machine Interface. The instructions presented to TIMI pass through a layer of microcode before they are "understood" by the hardware itself.

This comprehensive design insulates application programs and their users from changing hardware characteristics. When a different hardware technology is

deployed, IBM rewrites sections of the microcode to absorb the fluctuations in hardware characteristics. As a result, the interface presented to the client remains the same.

The microcode layer is known as the System Licensed Internal Code. Many of the frequently-executed routines run in SLIC. Supervisory resource management functions in SLIC include validity and authorization checks. On a customary system, these routines reside in the operating system. Because SLIC is closer to the silicon, routines performed there are faster than routines placed "higher" in the machine.

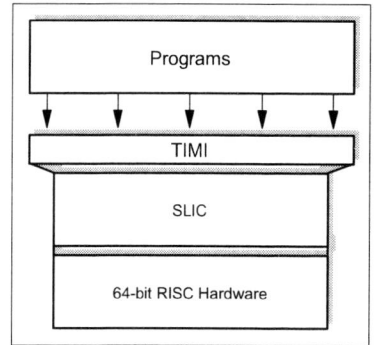

The brilliance of this design was dramatically illustrated when the AS/400 system changed its processor technology from CISC processors to 64-bit RISC processors in 1995. With any other system, the move from CISC to RISC would involve recompiling (and possibly some rewriting) programs. Even then, with other systems, the programs would run in 32-bit mode on the newer 64-bit hardware.

This is not so with the iSeries server, because of TIMI. Clients could *save* programs off their CISC AS/400 systems and *restore* them on their RISC AS/400e models. The programs run as 64-bit programs. As soon as they made this transition, clients had *64-bit application programs* that ran on a *64-bit operating system,* containing a *64-bit relational database* that fully exploited the *64-bit RISC hardware.*

TIMI and SLIC take technology in stride. New architectural features are exploited to fully accommodate post-RISC technologies, which may incorporate 96-bit or 128-bit processors or shifts to different processor technologies. TIMI helps condition the iSeries to bring new technology to market.

You can find further information about TIMI on the Web at:

`http://www-1.ibm.com/servers/enable/site/porting/iseries/overview/overview.html`

POWER Hypervisor

@server i5 servers work with a different structure when compared to the previous technologies used with the iSeries servers. Above the POWER5 technology-based hardware is a new code layer called the *POWER™ Hypervisor™*.

This code is part of the firmware shipped with the @server i5 hardware. The POWER Hypervisor resides in flash memory on the Service Processor. This firmware performs the initialization and configuration of the @server i5 hardware, as well as the virtualization support required to run up to 254 partitions concurrently on the @server i5 servers.

The layers above the POWER Hypervisor are different for each supported operating system.

For i5/OS, TIMI and the layers above the POWER Hypervisor are still in place. SLIC, however, is changed and enabled for interfacing with the POWER Hypervisor. The POWER Hypervisor code is based on the iSeries Partition Licensed Internal Code (PLIC)

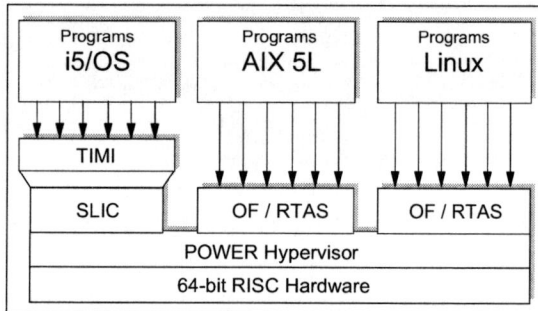

Programs	Programs	Programs
i5/OS	**AIX 5L**	**Linux**
TIMI		
SLIC	OF / RTAS	OF / RTAS
POWER Hypervisor		
64-bit RISC Hardware		

code that is enhanced for use with the @server i5 hardware. The PLIC is now part of the POWER Hypervisor.

For the AIX 5L and Linux operating systems, the layers above the POWER Hypervisor are similar, but their content is characteristic for each operating system. The layers of code supporting Linux and AIX 5L consist of System Firmware and Run-Time Abstraction Services (RTAS).

System Firmware is composed of Low Level Firmware and Open Firmware. *Low Level Firmware* is code that performs server unique input/output (I/O) configurations such as high-speed link (HSL)-2/RIO-G loops and PCI-X bridges. *Open Firmware* contains the boot time drivers (for example, SCSI, SSA, token ring, and Ethernet), the boot manager, and the device drivers required to initialize the PCI adapters and attached devices. The Run-Time Abstraction Services consist of code that supplies platform dependent accesses and can be called from the operating system. These calls are passed to the POWER Hypervisor that handles all I/O interrupts.

The @server i5 layered code structure makes the @server i5 platform more flexible. It also enables easy accommodation of different operating systems.

The POWER Hypervisor allows for multiple operating systems to run on the new hardware. i5/OS, Linux, and AIX 5L V5.3 and v5.2 are supported in logical partitions (LPARs) on the @server i5 server. No additional investment is

required to bring existing applications running on the iSeries today, with an earlier supported OS/400 release, to i5/OS or to the new @server i5 hardware.

Hierarchy of microprocessors

iSeries servers are designed for business computing. One of the fundamental characteristics of that environment is that it is I/O-intensive, rather than compute-intensive. In addition to outstanding performance in the business environment, the microprocessor design hierarchy gives the iSeries server an elegant method of integrating diverse environments into a single, harmonious client solution.

The microprocessors that look after a particular I/O device are accommodated on I/O cards that fit into slots on the system buses. One of these cards may be the Integrated xSeries® Server. This is a PC on a card that enables the iSeries server to run a Windows server, for example.

The following figure shows a highly simplified view of the balanced architecture of the iSeries systems. The maximum configuration values in the diagram represent a 1.65 GHz 64-way Model 595.

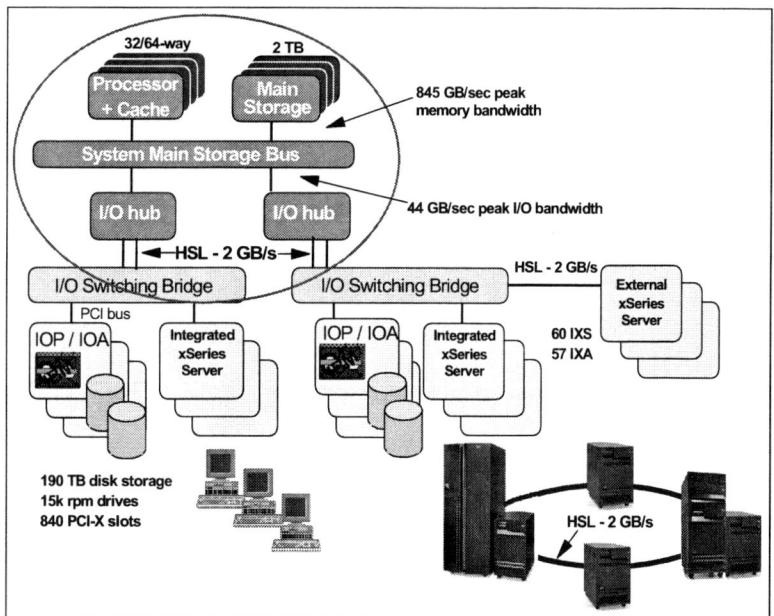

High performance on an iSeries server is achieved by using many individual high performance microprocessors, I/O devices, and interconnect technologies. Key to the iSeries high performance is the POWER5 distributed switch that supports enormous bandwidth between processors, cache, memory, and I/O. While programs run on POWER5 microprocessors, movement of data is handled by high performance I/O adapters and I/O processors. Data moves between I/O towers and to Integrated xSeries Adapter PC servers across HSL at 2 GB/s and storage area network (SAN) disk and tape devices are supported at 2 Gbps over Fibre Channel.

The multichip modules (MCMs) contain eight processors each. In such an MCM, there are four physical copper SOI chips with two processor cores. Each core is capable of running symmetric multi-threading that to the operating system looks like two separate processors. Each chip contains 276 million transistors forming two processors running at a speed in excess of 1.5GHz. The 8-way MCM is the building block for the system. It is only available with four chips, each with its attached L3 cache. A single processor on a chip has all of the L2 and L3 cache resources attached to the module (144 MB per MCM).

On an iSeries Model 595, a 64-way symmetric multiprocessing (SMP) configuration is implemented with eight MCMs, with each MCM containing four dual core POWER5 chips running at speeds greater than 1.5 GHz.

A single large iSeries configuration can have well over 650 processors. The main system processor complex (can be comprised of 64 separate processors) can encounter a request for data to be read from or written to any I/O device. That request for data is delegated to the particular microprocessor dedicated to that I/O device. Meanwhile, the main system processor continues executing another application program. Nanoseconds (10^{-9} second) is the unit of time used to measure main storage access times. I/O operations are measured in milliseconds (10^{-3} second).

Technology in stride

The iSeries server delivers tremendous capacity growth in its product line. The iSeries Layer (also known as Technology Independent Machine Interface) has made it possible to completely change the underlying hardware with minimum, if any, impact to iSeries applications. TIMI helps condition the iSeries to bring new technology to market.

The first AS/400e models based on the 64-bit RISC PowerPC® AS processors were announced in June 1995. In 1997, the 12-way AS/400e system was delivered using Power PCA35 microprocessors. Known as Apache technology, the Power PCA35 microprocessors provided a growth of 4.6 times. In September 1998, a 12-way AS/400e system was delivered using the Power PCA50

microprocessor. Known as code name Northstar, the Power PCA50 microprocessors nearly doubled the high-end capacity. This set of processors provided the fourth generation since the AS/400 system's inception in 1988 with 64-bit AS/400 Power PC® microprocessors. The latest generation of POWER5 processors is 4.4 times as powerful as its predecessor POWER4 generation of microprocessors.

The following figure shows the advance in processor technology.

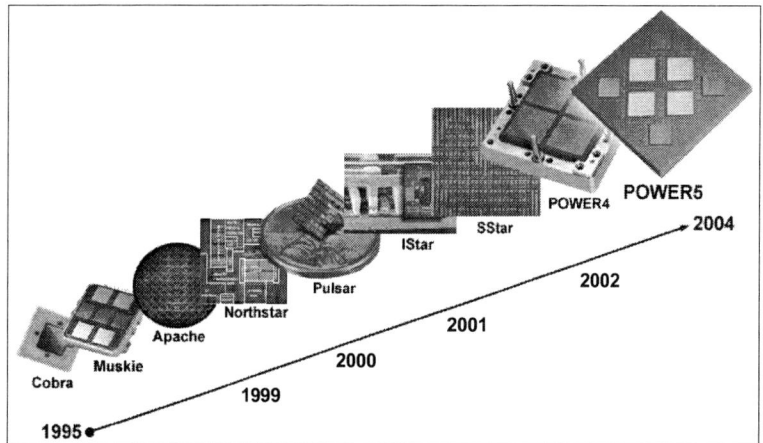

Pulsar, ISTAR, and SSTAR processors use on-chip copper-wiring technology. The Pulsar processors integrate IBM CMOS7S technology. ISTAR and SSTAR processors integrate CMOS8S technology. Previously, Northstar technology used aluminum for on-chip wiring. Copper's better conductivity permits thinner wires to be used, which enables the transistors to be packed closer together. The denser new technology permits additional micro-architecture methods to improve performance.

Delivered in 2002, the next evolution of IBM @server microprocessors was POWER4 fabricated in CMOS8S technology. Keeping multiple levels of high speed cache is still necessary to keep the processors busy. Denser processor technology permits more on-chip cache.

Continuing this industry-leading technology is POWER5 in CMOS9S today. The improved density with CMOS9S technology allows for larger caches, and for cache-controllers and memory controllers to be on-chip, resulting in higher processor performance.

This growth and implementation of new technology is possible because of the iSeries TIMI layer. TIMI allows the system to incorporate significant new hardware technology quickly and transparently. The ease with which clients have migrated to these powerful systems is a testimony to the fundamental strength of the server's architecture.

The following figure shows this change of hardware processor technology and previews what is planned in future generations.

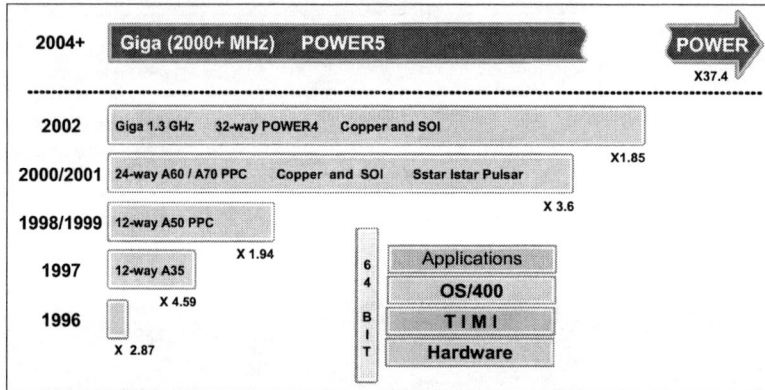

The summary charts in "Summary of today's iSeries" on page 79 indicate the processor technology used in each @server i5 and iSeries server.

Microprocessor excellence

This section features the technology that contributes to @server i5 and iSeries microprocessor excellence.

Multithreading

Multithreading minimizes the processor wait or idle time. In general, multithreading allows a single processor to process multiple threads in a different fashion than a single processor without this capability. There are several distinct differences between different types of multithreading implemented in the industry. We restrict our discussion to IBM technologies only.

Testing indicates a major performance improvement over the multithreading algorithm used in the hardware multithreading (HMT) of the SSTAR technology processors. Internal laboratory testing indicates that commercial applications see a 25% to 35% throughput improvement compared to no multithreading

implementation and about 10% for HMT (controlled by setting the QPRCMLTTSK system value). The 130 nanometer (nm) chip circuit technology is used.

POWER4

POWER4 cannot be considered only a chip, but rather an architecture of how a set of chips is designed together to build a system. As such, POWER4 can be considered a technology in its own right. The interconnect topology, referred to as a *Distributed Switch*, is new to the industry with POWER4. In that light, systems are built by interconnecting POWER4 chips to form up to 32-way symmetric multiprocessors. The reliability, availability, and serviceability (RAS) design incorporated into POWER4 is pervasive throughout the system and is as much a part of the design. POWER4 is the chip technology used in the iSeries Model 825, 870, and 890.

The POWER4 design can handle a varied and robust set of workloads. This is especially important as the On Demand Business world evolves and data intensive demands on systems merge with commercial requirements. The need to satisfy high performance computing requirements with its historical high bandwidth demands and commercial requirements, along with data sharing and SMP scaling requirements, dictate a single design to address both environments.

POWER5

POWER5 technology is the ninth generation of 64-bit architecture. Although the hardware is based on POWER4, POWER5 is much more than an improvement in processor or chip design. It is a complete architectural change, creating a much more efficient superscalar processor complex. For example, the high performance distributed switch is enhanced. POWER5 technology is implemented in the @server i5 Model 520, 550, 570, and 595.

As with previous hardware technology, POWER5 technology-based processors have two load/store, two arithmetic, and one branch unit. The *processor complex* design is built in such a way that it can most efficiently execute multiple instruction streams concurrently. With simultaneous multithreading (SMT) active, instructions of two different threads can be issued per single cycle.

The POWER5 concept is a step further into autonomic computing. Several enhanced reliability and availability enhancements are implemented. Along with increased redundant components, it incorporates new technological high standards, such as special ways to reduce junction temperatures to reach a high level of availability. The full system design approach is required to maintain

balanced utilization of hardware resources and high availability of the new @server i5 systems.

Memory and CPU sharing, a dual clock, and dual service processors with failover capability are examples of the full system design approach for high availability. IBM designed the @server i5 system processor, caching mechanisms, memory allocation methods, and the HSL-2/RIO-2 adapters for performance and availability. In addition, advanced error correction and low power consumption circuitry are improved with thermal management.

Multiprocessor POWER5 technology-based servers have multiple autonomic computing features for higher availability compared with single processor servers. If a processor is running, but is experiencing a high rate of correctable soft errors or is failing a periodic floating point self test, it can be *deconfigured dynamically*. Its workload can be picked up automatically by the remaining processor or processors without an IPL. If there is an unused IBM @server Capacity Upgrade on Demand (CUoD) processor or if one processor unit of unused capacity in a shared processor pool is available, the deconfigured processor can be replaced dynamically by the unused processor capacity to maintain the same level of processor performance.

The future

> "Power Architecture™ is more than just a technology, but rather a movement for change. It's time for architecture that enables innovation to flourish. It's time for Power Everywhere™."
>
> *– Nick Donofrio, IBM Senior VP*

For the future, Power Architecture microprocessors are being designed to keep running through many hard processor failures. The processor state will be maintained and switched to a hot standby processor. Reliability and availability characteristics associated only with IBM @server zSeries® class machines will be incorporated into the @server i5 systems.

Silicon On Insulator

In 2000, the iSeries led the industry by delivering the first server with the new Silicon-On-Insulator technology. SOI represents a fundamental advance in the way chips are built. The unique IBM SOI process alters the design of transistors, essentially "turbo charging" them, so they run faster and use less power. For example, a microprocessor designed to operate at a given speed can instead be built using SOI technology to achieve higher speeds. At the same time, if

performance levels are held constant, SOI chips can require as little as one-third the power of today's microchips.

The transistors are built within and on top of a thin layer of silicon that is on top of an insulating layer. The insulating layer is fabricated by implanting a thin layer of oxide beneath the primary silicon surface of the wafer. AS/400e and iSeries processors use SOI with ISTAR, SSTAR, POWER4, and POWER5 technology.

On-chip copper-wiring technology

Northstar technology used in prior AS/400e processors deploys aluminum for on-chip wiring. Pulsar, ISTAR, SSTAR, POWER4 and POWER5 processors use on-chip copper-wiring technology. Pulsar processors integrate IBM CMOS 7S technology. ISTAR and SSTAR processors integrate IBM CMOS 8S technology. POWER4 processors integrate CMOS 8S3 technology and POWER5 processors integrate CMOS9S3 technology.

Copper's better conductivity permits thinner wires to be used, which enables the transistors to be packed closer together. This denser technology permits additional micro architecture methods to improve performance. Denser processor technology also permits more on-chip cache. Keeping multiple levels of high-speed cache enables efficient utilization of the processors.

Powerful processor features based on the IBM industry leading copper and SOI technology were added in 2002.

Advanced I/O architecture

AS/400 and iSeries servers have a tremendously powerful and flexible I/O architecture, from the main processor or microprocessor all the way to the disk drive, tape device, local area network (LAN) or wide area network (WAN), or other I/O device. Focusing on one component of this architecture, the I/O cards which are inserted into the iSeries servers, are a combination of an I/O processor card (IOP) and an I/O adapter card (IOA).

The IOP and IOA are a mainframe-inspired implementation. Other midrange or PC servers use only an IOA. Using the combined IOP and IOA architecture gives the iSeries several advantages. The architecture offloads cycles from the main processor, isolates the main processor from the adapter and network errors, and manages, configures, and services the IOAs.

Note: For historical reasons, disk, tape, and workstation IOAs are called *controllers* on the AS/400 and iSeries.

When the first AS/400 systems where announced, a set of IBM proprietary I/O standards called System Products Division (SPD) were used. In the late 1990s, IBM started the movement to the emerging industry I/O standards called Peripheral Component Interconnect (PCI). PCI standards can refer to the I/O bus, the I/O card slots, and the I/O cards themselves. Vendors can, and do, implement extensions to these standards where the standard hasn't evolved to cover the function, or other client benefits are seen. IBM tends to implement the standards, adding extensions for function, performance, and reliability.

Like any good set of standards in a dynamic environment, PCI standards continue to evolve. A second generation of PCI standards was implemented in 2000 on the iSeries Model 270, 820, 830, and 840 I/O, and the I/O towers, such as the #5074 PCI Expansion Tower. A number of new PCI I/O cards (IOAs) were also introduced. Excellent investment leverage was provided, as most of the first generation PCI cards worked in the new PCI slots. Most second generation PCI cards worked in the first PCI slots.

PCI-X

In 2002 and 2003, the third generation of PCI standards for iSeries was implemented, called *PCI-X*. PCI-X is a higher speed version of the conventional PCI standard and enables function and performance for iSeries servers beyond that of PCI. This new standard keeps pace with the demands of high-bandwidth business-critical applications such as Fibre Channel, RAID, networking and SCSI. PCI-X adapters also run in PCI slots, but at a slower PCI speed.

Several PCI-X IOAs are introduced with i5/OS, again providing an excellent investment leverage. PCI-X slots are provided in iSeries Models 520, 550, 570, 595, 825, 870, and 890 and in I/O towers such as the #5094 and #5095 PCI-X Expansion Towers. Second generation PCI cards work in the PCI-X slots, and some of the first generation PCI cards work in the PCI-X slots. PCI-X cards can work in the second generation PCI slots.

Hot-plugging

Hot-plugging is an industry phrase, which can apply to either I/O devices such as disk, tape, or optical drives, or I/O cards. Hot-plugging allows a client to remove or add an I/O device or card without taking the server down. This improves availability of the system and allows you to perform upgrades, maintenance, or repair without impacting the users of the system.

Driven by the demand for the highest possible availability, the iSeries advanced technology enables concurrent install of new IOPs, adapters, and devices by allowing the user to select a specific device, powering it down and removing it safely from the system. The server can add hardware to deactivated slots or bays and after insertion and powerup recognize this new hardware, load the correct

internal code, and make the functions of the newly installed hardware available without interrupting normal operations.

iSeries and AS/400 servers have supported disk hot-plugging on all but the smallest servers for many years. Disk hot-plugging capability is available on @server i5 Models 520, 550, 570, and 595, and iSeries Models 800, 810, 825, 870, and 890. The in-use disk drive must be protected by RAID or mirroring before removing the drive.

PCI hot-plugging was first introduced in 2000 on the iSeries Models 820, 830, and 840, and the 2-way Model 270. It was introduced at the same time the second generation PCI technology was introduced. Hot-plug PCI is supported on @server i5 Models 520, 550, 570, and 595, and iSeries Models 825, 870, and 890, and 2-way Model 810.

PCI hot-plugging in the iSeries models is made possible by power control to individual card slots. In most cases, IOA configurations can be changed while other IOAs on the same IOP remain operational.

Removing the IOP or IOA associated with a running load source disk drive is an obvious example of something which is not hot-pluggable unless the IOP or IOA has been mirrored. The operator interface controlling hot-plugging uses the Hardware Service Manager in the System Service Tools (SST), or a subset of Dedicated Service Tools (DST), depending on which tool you have started.

Refer to the individual PCI card feature descriptions in Chapter 18, "iSeries I/O adapters and controllers" on page 337, and a description of the server models to determine if *hot swapping* of a specific PCI card is supported.

High-speed links

First introduced in the year 2000 on the iSeries servers, a new bus structure using HSL provided a faster data transportation mechanism running at 1 GB/s. As faster processors, larger caches, faster memory, super fast cross-bar switch complex, faster direct access storage device (DASD), and much faster IOPs and IOAs emerged, it was clear the earlier AS/400 infrastructure needed more speed, capacity, and function as IBM made the transition to iSeries.

In 2004, IBM announced POWER5 technology for iSeries servers. These are Models 520, 550, 570, and 595, which use the second generation of HSL technology called HSL-2/RIO-2. Although the POWER5 technology-based processors for iSeries use the same physical HSL-2 connections as used on iSeries Models 825, 870, and 890, Models 520, 550, 570, and 595 can run the RIO-G loop at up to 2 GB/s.

Note: HSL loops can be either copper or optical cable.

The HSL-2/RIO-2 structure provides performance improvements and future system growth. HSL-2/RIO-2 architecture is flexible and powerful. An HSL-2/RIO-2 design provides:

► 2 GB/s technology

► A simplified and flexible implementation that supports:

- Loop technology for redundancy

- Multiple towers per loop: Mix and match the HSL-attached I/O towers on the loop

- Migration to PCI I/O and HSL-attached I/O towers

- Migration of HSL to HSL-2 attached I/O towers

- Switchable I/O towers with independent auxiliary storage pools (IASPs)

- Expanded Windows capability with attached 1- to 8-way servers using Integrated xSeries Adapters which add the servers to the HSL

- Complex HSL clusters (three iSeries servers and no I/O towers on a loop) (OS/400 V5R2 or later)

- Simple HSL clusters (two iSeries servers and up to four towers) (V5R1 or later)

Refer to "HSL fabric" on page 297 for additional information about HSL-2/RIO-2.

iSeries integration with the Windows Server

iSeries servers include the ability to manage Intel®-based Windows servers via the Integrated xSeries Server or the Integrated xSeries Adapter. Up to 60 Integrated xSeries Servers are supported on selected iSeries models. iSeries servers support the attachment of external 1-way to 8-way IBM @server xSeries servers via the high-speed link.

With the Integrated xSeries Adapter, selected xSeries servers running a Windows Server can help to extend Windows application scalability. At the same time, they can retain the same storage consolidation and systems management advantages of the Integrated xSeries Server has on the iSeries.

Virtual storage management enables an administrator to dynamically add storage to a running Windows server without a reboot.

User administration features include the ability to synchronize user accounts, user profiles, and passwords between i5/OS and Windows.

Virtual Ethernet can provide a secure, high-performance bus interconnect between Windows, Linux and OS/400 without an external LAN.

Flexible server deployment and testing features include the ability to store multiple Windows server images on the iSeries (for example, different service packs of applications), and then boot only the server required on an Integrated xSeries Server. A single backup methodology for all Windows servers and OS/400 provides a robust disaster recover solution. Microsoft Cluster Service supports dynamically switching virtual storage spaces (disks) between Windows servers.

The Integrated xSeries Server features a 2.0 GHz Intel Xeon processor with a 512 KB L2 cache, a 400 MHz front side bus (FSB), an on-board 10/100 Mbps Ethernet controller, and four USB ports.

The Integrated xSeries Adapter is a PCI adapter that connects xSeries servers to the iSeries HSL bus, and provides the server virtual storage and Ethernet. The Integrated xSeries Adapter is supported with a range of xSeries servers, including the xSeries 235, 255, 360, and 440.

Refer to "1519-100, 1519-200 Integrated xSeries Adapter for iSeries (direct attach)" on page 307 for additional information about Integrated xSeries Adapters for the iSeries.

Reliable, managed availability

The iSeries server has a reliable history of designing key functions into the hardware and software. High availability is one reason to select a managed availability approach. Other reasons include minimal disruptive backup solutions, and the ability to nondisruptively install and pre-test new versions, releases, or software fixes to make optimum use of all company and system resources.

Hallmarks of iSeries availability include redundant internal hardware features, such as RAID-5 and mirroring. The robustness and stability of OS/400 extends into its multiple, subsystem support (batch, interactive, multi-language, and applications). The iSeries server offers managed availability to ensure that it is ready to do business when you are.

iSeries managed availability software is also called *cross-system mirroring*. It provides:

► The ability to have one system act as a hot backup system to one or more primary systems

   The primary and secondary systems do not have to be the same size or model.

► A rapid switchover to the secondary machine in the event of an emergency

► The ability to apply new software versions and releases (OS/400 and associated software), or fixes on the secondary system, while the primary system continues to function

   Testing can occur on the secondary system before nondisruptively updating the primary system.

iSeries servers offer superior technology, service, and support in each of five critical components of availability:

► **Single system reliability**: Architecture and baseline design make the iSeries server one of the most reliable servers in the world. From its inception, the iSeries architecture inherits a design where reliability and availability are equivalent to features such as processor speed, memory capability, and number of disk arms when planning for reliability.

   The iSeries design and development resources that enable high levels of availability in a single system environment are useful for prevention of unplanned outages. The single-system iSeries remains the core building block to repeat and extend functions into other areas of the business.

► **Single-system availability management**: iSeries servers have high-availability facilities that are not only fast and automated, but are easy to use. Planned and unplanned outages are reduced with high availability facilities which include:

   – Automated journal management
   – Access path protection
   – Batch journal caching
   – Save-while-active
   – Parallel save and restore
   – Backup Recovery and Media Services (BRMS) for iSeries
   – RAID-5 disk parity protection
   – Disk mirroring protection

► **Clusters**: Cluster technology is implemented to reduce downtime caused by planned outages and site disasters. System availability during planned outages contributes to an increase coverage of unplanned outage. Refer to "iSeries clustering" on page 540.

- **Cluster-enabled applications**: A high availability solution for the iSeries server involves an active participation of cluster middleware providers. IBM Business Partners provide advanced cluster management and data resiliency tools. Solution developers design applications to maintain the state of an application across an outage.

- **Availability services and support**: As a world-leading enterprise computing vendor, IBM has a collection of products and services to assist the client to develop and maintain a high availability environment. The on demand capabilities of the Model 825, 870, and 890 servers include High Availability and Capacity BackUp business continuity offerings.

Clustering with switchable DASD and IASP

i5/OS V5R3, OS/400 V5R2 and V5R1 with HSL OptiConnect provide switchable disk capability between two servers. V5R2 or later allows three systems on an HSL loop. IASPs and switched disk clusters provide the ability to access content on a set of disk units from a second system. Support for both planned and unplanned outages is improved when the system currently using a switchable disk experiences an outage. Operations are continued on a system even when an isolated controller or disk unit fails.

Data availability is improved with IASPs or switched disk clustering. Upon an outage within a cluster, users can be switched to an alternate node in the cluster (another iSeries server). Integrated file system (IFS) data and operating system library objects residing in an IASP can be switched to another iSeries server without an IPL. This enables one iSeries to take over data and an I/O controller in a disk tower from another iSeries.

The primary function in the early stages of clustering is to offer coverage for planned upgrades and maintenance on the production system without affecting users accessing data from the switched disk towers, for the user-defined file system (UDFS) only. Cluster management middleware, shipped as part of OS/400 option 41 (HA Switchable Resources), manages the switchover. For high availability purposes, it ensures that no two systems access the disks (data) at the same time.

A properly designed switched disk cluster can offer advantages over a data replication cluster. Because a switched disk cluster does not use data replication, there is less overhead on the systems and, therefore, more resource available to process transactions. A switched disk cluster can be simpler to operate. The application is critical to the design of a true continuously available environment.

Domino takes advantage of this support and uses the switched disk architecture to enable clustering. Switched disks do not remove the requirement to have application resiliency.

Cross-site mirroring

Cross-site mirroring (XSM), sometimes called *geographic mirroring*, enables you to mirror data on disks at sites that can be separated by a significant geographic distance. You use this technology to extend the functionality of a device cluster resource group (CRG) beyond the limits of physical component connection.

Geographic mirroring provides the ability to replicate changes made to the production copy of an independent disk pool to a mirror copy of that independent disk pool. As data is written to the production copy of an independent disk pool, the operating system mirrors that data to a second copy of it through another system. This process keeps multiple identical copies of the data.

Through the device CRG, should a failover or switchover occur, the backup node can seamlessly take on the role of the primary node. The server or servers that act as backups are defined in the recovery domain. The backup nodes can be at the same or different physical location as the primary.

When an outage occurs on the server defined as the primary node in the recovery domain and a switchover or failover is initiated, the node designated as the backup in the recovery domain becomes the primary access point for the resource and then owns the production copy of the independent disk pool. Therefore, you can gain protection from the single point of failure associated with switchable resources.

Virtualization technology

Virtual technology enables resource sharing in an integrated, flexible computing environment on a single server. This section discusses key virtual technologies that are available with each iSeries server.

Virtualization Engine

Virtualization Engine is the name for a technology that describes the ability to see and manage system and storage resources across a computing environment. A set of system services includes workload management, integrated grid services, and a set of tools to help monitor the computing resource. Services have the capability of workload balancing across different operating systems within a single server and across the computing network.

Refer to "Product Previews: Closed" on page 66 for a preview of this service.

Dynamic logical partitioning

Logical partitioning enhances the role of the iSeries as a consolidated server. With LPAR, companies have both the power and flexibility to address multiple system requirements in a single machine.

Server virtualization, a term often used with partitioning, is accomplished on the iSeries through the use of Hypervisor technology. Hypervisor encompasses a combination of both hardware features and control code. @server i5 servers use POWER Hypervisor, as described in "POWER Hypervisor" on page 11, to deliver this virtualization support.

LPAR, as implemented on the iSeries, extends the original architectural design concept of application execution by allowing OS/400, Linux or AIX to run in a given partition. Extensive dynamic and granular resource sharing is allowed across processors (SMP configurations), memory, disk, tape, and other devices, including Virtual Ethernets, which are covered in the next section. Multiple partitions are supported for selected iSeries uni-processor models. The following figure illustrates resource sharing across partitions.

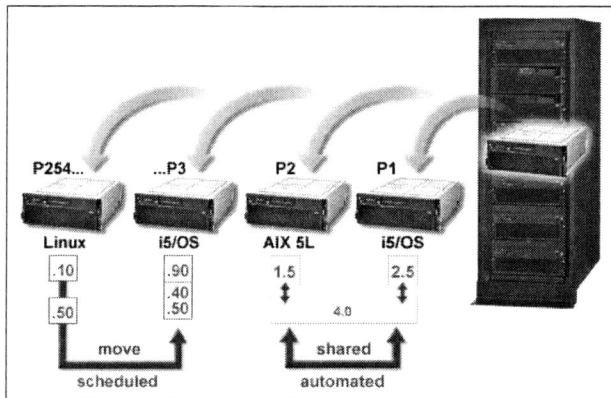

With i5/OS, partitions can be defined as capped or uncapped. Capped partitions cannot exceed their assigned processor resources. Uncapped partitions can use automatically extra unused processing power in a shared pool. For a detailed description, refer to "LPAR capped and uncapped partitions" on page 48.

For more details about LPAR, see "Logical partitions" on page 534.

Virtual Ethernet

Virtual Ethernet (also referred to as Virtual LAN (VLAN)) provides the ability to provide multiple communication paths between applications that are executed in each LPAR. More importantly, Virtual Ethernet allows high-speed bus-to bus communication between *selected* OS/400 partitions and Linux partitions. It is possible to tie in each of the multiple communication paths between partitions to a specific application. OS/400 V5R2 introduced the capability to connect Integrated xSeries Servers and Integrated xSeries Adapters via Virtual Ethernet.

@server i5 hardware provides an IEEE 802.1Q VLAN Virtual Ethernet switch as part of the POWER Hypervisor. Up to 4094 VLANs are available with i5/OS V5R3 running on @server i5 hardware. For systems prior to the POWER5 technology-based models, up to 16 independent high-speed internal bus-to-bus communication paths are supported between LPARs.

The enablement and setup of Virtual Ethernet is easy and does not require an IPL or any special hardware or software. When a virtual communications port is enabled for a given partition, a communication resource (CMNxx) is created for that partition. The user can then create a high-speed 1 Gb Ethernet line description over this resource and set up TCP/IP configuration appropriately to start communicating to another partition. A maximum of 16 virtual ports can be enabled for high-speed communications per partition for systems prior to the POWER5 technology-based models. For i5/OS V5R3 partitions running on @server i5 hardware, thousands of virtual ports can be created per partition.

AIX 5L for eServer i5

AIX 5L is rapidly emerging as the preferred platform for UNIX users and independent software vendors. AIX 5L delivers industrial strength UNIX reliability, availability and security while offering flexible system administration and ease of integration with Linux. With innovative virtualization and micro-partitioning, AIX 5L helps you avoid compromises and accept no limits in the on demand world.

AIX 5L is an open standards-based operating system. It is designed to conform with the Open Group's Single UNIX Specification Version 3. It provides fully integrated support for 32- and 64-bit applications running concurrently, in their range of scalability. It also supports IBM @server i5, p5, pSeries, and RS/6000 server product lines, and IntelliStation® POWER and RS/6000 workstations.

The benefits of AIX on the @server i5 enable you to:

- ► Simplify your infrastructure
  - − Consolidate UNIX servers
  - − Extend i5/OS with complementary AIX 5L applications
- ► Optimize your investments
  - − Share processor and memory resources
  - − Move resources to where they are needed
  - − Exploit i5/OS storage subsystem
  - − Leverage skills and best practices

With the support of AIX on @server i5 servers, comparisons of @server i5 to p5 servers is inevitable. In general, the @server i5 servers offer an integrated approach, while @server p5 servers provide a la carte functionality. Some functions integrated in the @server i5 or i5/OS are either add-ons or not available for @server p5 servers, for example:

- ► DB2 Universal Database (DB2 UDB)
- ► Micro partitioning
- ► Virtual storage hosting
- ► Virtual Ethernet hosting
- ► Virtual CD/DVD and tape hosting

For additional information about AIX 5L on @server i5, refer to this Web site:

`http://www-1.ibm.com/servers/eserver/iseries/aix/`

AIX 5L Version 5.3

The latest version of AIX 5L takes on demand computing to the next level. AIX 5L Version 5.3 offers simultaneous multi-threading on POWER5 systems to deliver industry leading throughput and performance levels. With support for advanced virtualization, AIX 5L V5.3 helps you to dramatically increase your server utilization and consolidate workloads for more efficient management. AIX 5L V5.3 represents the latest advance in a long record of IBM operating system innovation and helps clients to accelerate their On Demand Business.

For additional information about AIX 5L Version 5.3, go to:

`http://www-1.ibm.com/servers/aix/os/53desc.html`

AIX 5L Version 5.2

AIX 5L Version 5.2 integrates innovative technologies to achieve outstanding performance, reliability and flexibility in today's On Demand Business environment. Client-validated enhancements, such as dynamic logical partitioning and CUoD, differentiate the AIX 5L platform from competitors.

For additional information about AIX 5L V5.2, refer to the following Web site:

`http://www-1.ibm.com/servers/aix/os/52desc.html`

AIX 5L and logical partitions

AIX 5L V5.3 and V5.2 are supported in LPARs on the @server i5. AIX 5L V5.3 leverages advanced virtualization technologies. The following table lists the virtual partition characteristics of AIX 5L V5.2 and V5.3 on the @server i5.

	AIX 5L V5.2	AIX 5L V5.3
Dynamic LPAR (processors, memory and I/O)	Y	Y
Micro-partitions (up to 10 partitions per processor)	N	Y
Uncapped partitions (automatic movement of processor resources)	N	Y
Virtual storage and Ethernet (through i5/OS)	N	Y
Direct I/O (managed by AIX 5L)	Y	Y

We recommend that you use the LPAR Validation Tool (LVT) to help you understand and plan for deploying AIX partitions on the @server i5. The LVT guides you through the supported I/O options including which direct I/O adapters are supported in AIX 5L partitions.

In addition, when planning to run AIX 5L on @server i5, it is also important to obtain licenses for AIX 5L and corresponding Software Maintenance (SWMA).

AIX 5L is licensed by processor and by processor group on the @server i5. AIX 5L V5.2 licenses for a pSeries system can be transferred to the @server i5. AIX 5L SWMA is required for each AIX 5L license. One-year and three-year options are available.

To estimate the amount of server capacity needed to run AIX 5L applications on logically partitioned @server i5 servers, refer to the paper *Sizing IBM @server i5 Servers for AIX 5L Applications* at:

`http://www-1.ibm.com/servers/eserver/iseries/aix/pdf/sizing_for_aix5l_apps.pdf`

Linux for iSeries and eServer i5

One of the most important developments in business computing in recent years is the arrival of Linux. Linux, an open-source implementation of UNIX, is rapidly becoming the de facto standard for such fundamental infrastructure applications as Web servers, firewalls, file servers, and e-mail servers. Now, thanks to the powerful combination of the scalability, reliability and manageability of @server i5 servers and the flexibility of Linux, businesses can take advantage of a new way to simplify their IT infrastructure and expand their application environment, with the potential to greatly reduce cost.

Taking advantage of advanced LPAR technologies, clients can consolidate multiple stand-alone infrastructure servers on a single @server i5 server. This enables clients to automatically move processor and dynamically add storage resources between individual partitions to support changing business demands. Linux supports an array of open source solutions to run your infrastructure. In addition, IBM is working with leading Linux solution providers to expand the set of business applications and solutions available for @server i5.

The iSeries family of servers can combine business applications and solutions for On Demand Business with Linux applications on a single server. A Linux server can be set up with as little as 10% of an iSeries processor. Each partition supports its own independent operating system image and can be isolated from other partitions. This allows business applications to run securely alongside Internet solutions. With an OS/400 V5R2, processor resources can be dynamically moved between partitions to support changing business demands. @server i5 supports automatic processor movement.

The iSeries award-winning Linux implementation exploits the i5/OS advanced storage architecture by leveraging the storage resources in the i5/OS partition. The 64-bit environments can offer more scalability through larger memory and address more spaces than traditional 32-bit Linux environments. Up to 10 Linux partitions per processor are supported, with a system maximum of 254 partitions running on POWER5 technology-based servers, and 31 on POWER4 and SSTAR processors. Linux distributions from Novell, Inc. and Red Hat, Inc. support the iSeries family of servers.

See "Linux for iSeries" on page 503 for further information about Linux.

IBM i5/OS

One of the single, most dramatic points about the iSeries server is that the operating system, i5/OS, is a single entity. This section describes the meaning of this concept.

Note: IBM i5/OS for V5R2 and earlier versions is called OS/400.

After you buy an iSeries server, you do not have to continue shopping for system software components before the server is ready to run your business. All of the software factors for a relational database, comprehensive security, communications with a broad range of diverse systems, including Internet capabilities, and many more components are already in the operating system. Each is fully integrated into i5/OS, and fully tested too. All components and prerequisites for running business applications in the new century work together and are fully tested together. i5/OS operates as a single entity.

On the iSeries servers, high-level machine instructions execute only on what they are designed for. Only a program (an object) can be executed. Data (also an object) can be read, updated, or deleted, but cannot be executed (a common technique for introducing viruses on other architectures).

Object-based

An object is a container. Everything the system uses (user and system data structures) is packaged in one of these containers. The objects are encapsulated, which means that you cannot see inside. The list of valid ways in which that object can be used is inseparable from an object.

There are two important consequences of an object-based design. The first is that a system built around an object model supports machine independence. This means that technology changes can be made in the environment without affecting application programs. The second consequence is that an object-based design delivers an inherently high level of system integrity and security.

All objects are structured with a common object header and a functional portion dependent on object type. Therefore, on the iSeries servers, instructions work on only what they are supposed to work. Data cannot be treated as executable code. Executable code cannot be treated as data by having something written into the middle of it.

OS/400 distinguishes between user and system programs. Certain instructions apply to all objects, while other instructions work only on specific types of objects. Therefore, it is not possible for valid programs to misuse an object, unlike

the situation that exists for non-iSeries systems without an object-based approach. The iSeries remains virus-resistant with such features as this. And i5/OS is one of the lowest cost systems to operate in a secure manner.

DB2 Universal Database

DB2 UDB for iSeries offers state-of-the-art database functions and open systems and standards-based technology. It also provides the maturity, stability, and ease of use that has become the trademark of the iSeries server. It is fully integrated into the i5/OS operating system software and is not a separate product.

DB2 has been enhanced over the years to include many new and emerging standards. The integrated database is a full function database with features competitive to other widely used databases. The fact that the database is integrated allows the operating system to control some of its management functions and makes it easier to maintain than competitive database from other vendors reducing the need for a dedicated database administrator. Its security functions are integrated into the operating system. These functions allow a better security model than other databases where additional tools may need to be purchased to provide these functions.

Many iSeries clients have the need for applications that access both DB2 UDB for iSeries data and data on other databases platforms such as Oracle or Sybase. The SQL Client Integration application programming interface (API) allows providers of gateways and client/server solutions to integrate their products with DB2 UDB for iSeries.

See "DB2 Universal Database for iSeries" on page 516 for further information about i5/OS for DB2 UDB, and Chapter 26, "IBM licensed programs: Database accessories" on page 597, for associated database products.

Java and On Demand Business for iSeries

Java is the environment of choice for programming in today's network computing environment. It allows true portability of applications between platforms without modification or recompiling. iSeries servers are uniquely positioned to leverage Java as it evolves from its current Web focus to a full commercial application environment. The strengths of the iSeries server are combined with Java's object-oriented, network computing technology to provide solutions in this millennium.

See "IBM Java for iSeries" on page 508 for more information.

iSeries Web serving

i5/OS contains a complete set of base products and features that can be used to create a Web presence. Included are TCP/IP, Java, virtual private networking (VPN), cryptographic services, Secure Sockets Layer (SSL), certificate management, HTTP server, and much more. The IBM WebSphere family of products offered by IBM for the iSeries server allows you to build a complete On Demand Business Web site that is secure, easy to develop and maintain, and scale based on your needs.

For Web serving with the iSeries servers, network computing is supported with IBM HTTP Server for iSeries. See "HTTP Server for iSeries (5722-DG1)" on page 554.

See Chapter 27, "WebSphere and On Demand Business for iSeries" on page 609, and "IBM WebSphere Development Studio for iSeries (5722-WDS)" on page 642 for more information.

Lotus Domino for iSeries

Lotus Domino for iSeries is the leading groupware solution available for the iSeries server. It provides unparalleled capability for iSeries clients to use their business data in collaborative solutions for On Demand Business, both within their organizations and with their partners over the Internet. Lotus Domino for iSeries provides a critical foundation as companies begin to move from "information overload" into organizational learning and knowledge management. No competitive product offers the ease of use, low cost of ownership, tight integration, and positioning for the future that Lotus Domino for iSeries delivers. Lotus Domino for iSeries is offered with familiar iSeries and AS/400e terms and conditions for purchase, services, and support.

iSeries for Domino offerings, supported by Models 810, 825 and 550, are targeted specifically for Lotus Domino workloads. They provide continual growth to support business needs. They have full iSeries functionality, including full database capability.

Refer to Chapter 3, "Workload, capacity, and performance" on page 39, for more information about Domino servers, and Chapter 28, "Lotus products for iSeries" on page 623, for associated software.

iSeries advanced user interface

The iSeries serves the small business client with minimal skill or resource to manage complex environments. OS/400 delivers advanced graphical user interface (GUI) functions to iSeries clients. iSeries Navigator is enriched with industry-leading integrated systems management via an easy-to-use GUI.

iSeries Navigator

The systems management function is delivered via the easy-to-use iSeries Navigator GUI. iSeries Navigator includes:

► Work management (active jobs, subsystems, job queues, memory pools)

► Backup and Recovery (BRMS GUI plug-in)

► LPAR

► System values, including a system comparison and update via Management Central

► Distributed user and group administration via Management Central

► Licensed program and fix creation, distribution, and installation via Management Central

► Enhancements to performance monitors and collection services to graph events over extended time periods

► New monitors and events for managing jobs and messages

► Complete DASD management: Disk balancing, compression, management of disk pools, and units

► Simple two-node and complex three-node cluster configuration

► Integrated xSeries Server: Windows user and group and disk administration

► Database Navigator: Provides a pictorial view of the database showing the relationships between objects

► Graphical command prompting

► TaskPads: A user-interface extension that allows easy access to key administrative tasks

Other ease-of-use initiatives for OS/400 V5R2 include the addition of numerous GUI extensions to existing iSeries Navigator functions, for the creation of numerous configuration and administration wizards (many of which are in the new GUI areas listed in the previous list), and a new plug-in for performance management. Extensive automation for workload management with new file and business-to-business (B2B) transaction monitors, systems and storage management, backup and media policies, and network management including

support for IPv6. Also supported is DB2 UDB transaction management, switched disk cluster management, Linux dynamic partition management, and enterprise identity mapping security.

Management Central-Pervasive

Management Central-Pervasive (MC-Pervasive) allows iSeries network administrators to keep an eye on their iSeries servers while they are away from their workstation or office. Using an Internet capable cellular phone, personal digital assistant (PDA) with a wireless modem, or a Web browser, the administrator can monitor and manage their iSeries server status and performance metrics on the iSeries servers.

As of V5R1, functions for Management Central-Pervasive include:

► Additional support for system performance monitoring
► Monitor specific jobs and servers on multiple systems
► Monitor message queues on multiple systems
► Hold, release, or end a job on any endpoint system
► Run commands on any system or group of systems
► Manage Integrated xSeries Servers

    – View status of Integrated xSeries Servers
    – Startup and shutdown of Integrated xSeries Servers
    – Run Windows commands
    – Monitor Integrated xSeries events (routed to an iSeries message queue)

► Read only mode for selected users

These additional V5R1 functions are available via an English-only PTF. Refer to the iSeries Navigator for Wireless Web site to find the PTF numbers to load the code for Management Central-Pervasive:

`http://www-1.ibm.com/servers/eserver/iseries/navigator/pervasive.html`

EZ-Setup

EZ-Setup is an application intended to simplify the setup of a new iSeries server by having users answer questions in an *interview*. The answers to these questions are then used to produce a customized list of tasks. The tasks include wizards and step-by-step information for completing a server setup, including tasks to:

- Configure security settings
- Create a TCP/IP interface
- Set up iSeries for the Internet
- Install and configure Domino
- Configure Operations Console
- Install Information Center

Summary

The iSeries server architecture has been extremely successful in delivering on its design goals. However, it is an extensible architecture. It will continue to evolve to exploit technology for the benefit of the commercial IT marketplace in an on demand world.

3

Workload, capacity, and performance

Workload and performance are critical considerations in selecting a computing system. The performance that users see with their @server i5 and iSeries servers depends on many factors that often involve:

- ► The type and number of disk devices
- ► The amount of memory
- ► The system model and processor
- ► The application being run

We recommend that you order sufficient memory to balance memory across processors. For sizing recommendations for the @server i5 and iSeries servers, consult your IBM Marketing Representative and service provider. You can find detailed performance information in *iSeries Performance Capabilities Reference*, SC41-0607.

This chapter discusses some of the performance measurements to consider. This includes workload ratings and processor positioning. This chapter also discusses the tools that are available to measure and size the workload.

39

Server structure and terminology

The @server i5 520, 550, 550, 570, and 595 servers, and the iSeries 810, 825, 870, and 890 servers, include a Processor feature and an Edition feature:

- **Processor feature**: Feature code by which the *processor* is ordered
- **Edition feature**: Feature code by which the *package* of features is ordered
- **Server feature**: Feature code by which the processor *configuration* is ordered

@server i5 and iSeries models offer two commercial processing workload (CPW) ratings:

- **Processor CPW**: Represents maximum relative performance running commercial processing workloads (CPWs) for a processor configuration

  Use this value to compare relative performance between models with the same or different number of processors.

- **5250 CPW**: Represents the relative performance available to perform 5250 online transaction processing (OLTP, interactive) workloads

Important: Limited 5250 CPW is always available for a system administrator to use 5250 display device input/output (I/O) to manage various aspects of the server. Multiple administrative jobs quickly exceed this limited 5250 capacity.

Commercial processing workload

The performance capacity of all @server i5 and iSeries servers is represented by a workload measurement called commercial processing workload. CPW values are given to all @server i5 and iSeries processors. They are derived by performing various monitored and measured workloads on @server i5 and iSeries servers. The results (reported values) can be used to compare relative performance characteristics of processor features offered for @server i5 and iSeries servers. The reported values for CPW do not represent a guaranteed level of capacity to perform a given workload. They can serve as a quick means to compare performance.

With the addition of the Model 595 to the IBM @server product line, the CPW figures are represented in the following chart.

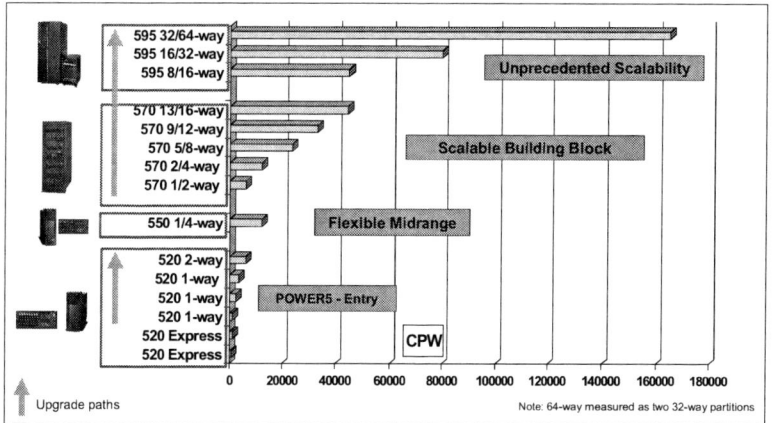

Chart labels:
- 595 32/64-way
- 595 16/32-way
- 595 8/16-way
- Unprecedented Scalability
- 570 13/16-way
- 570 9/12-way
- 570 5/8-way
- 570 2/4-way
- 570 1/2-way
- Scalable Building Block
- 550 1/4-way
- Flexible Midrange
- 520 2-way
- 520 1-way
- 520 1-way
- 520 1-way
- 520 Express
- 520 Express
- POWER5 - Entry
- CPW
- 0 20000 40000 60000 80000 100000 120000 140000 160000 180000

Upgrade paths

Note: 64-way measured as two 32-way partitions

Several IBM and non-IBM tools are available to do performance analysis and sizing. IBM tools include the IBM Performance Tools for iSeries licensed program product (LPP) (5722-PT1) for analysis and sizing and the IBM @server Workload Estimator (WLE) that can be found on the support Web site. Refer to "IBM Performance Tools for iSeries (5722-PT1)" on page 690 and "IBM eServer Workload Estimator" on page 51 for further information.

5250 CPW

5250 CPW is an approximate value that represents the amount of processing power to be used to perform 5250 OLTP work.

> **Note:** 5250 CPW is known as Interactive CPW on earlier servers.

Remember that:

▶ A system administration job submitted to *batch* is not considered 5250 OLTP work.

▶ The use of iSeries Navigator (graphical user interface (GUI) administration functions) is not considered 5250 OLTP work.

▶ Any task that uses a 5250 data stream is considered 5250 OLTP work and requires some amount of 5250 CPW to process regardless of how the task is started.

▶ A task submitted through a 5250 session (5250 device or 5250 emulation) that does display or printer I/O requires 5250 CPW.

► A task submitted through a 5250 session (5250 device or 5250 emulation) as a *batch* job is not considered 5250 OLTP work and does not require any 5250 CPW unless the task does display or printer I/O.

5250 OLTP applications no longer require 5250 CPW after being WebFaced by using the IBM WebFacing Tool of IBM WebSphere Development Studio for iSeries (5722-WDS).

To learn more about how these features influence system performance, see "Refacing options for the iSeries client" on page 53. This referenced section includes some of the @server i5 and iSeries products available to support 5250 OLTP applications. Also, refer to *Aiming for Zero Interactive on iSeries*, which discusses 5250 OLTP:

`http://www.ibm.com/servers/eserver/iseries/perfmgmt/pdf/ZeroInteractive.pdf`

Refer to "5250 OLTP considerations" on page 313 for upgrade considerations.

5250 devices

The @server i5, iSeries and AS/400e servers support a family of displays and emulation adapters that are known as *5250*. The supported data stream is known as a *5250 data stream*. Throughput considerations for these workstations account for the flow of the character stream, as discussed in the following section.

A 5250 twinaxial device or 5250 emulation adapter in a PC can support a single address, multiple addresses, or shared sessions on a single address. Whenever a device is powered on or when the 5250 emulation software is started on a PC, any addresses defined respond to the workstation controller polls. These addresses count as an active address, even though no device description may exist on the @server i5 and iSeries server. This occurs when the system value QAUTOCFG is set to *NO.

► When a device has *multiple addresses* defined for multiple sessions to support jump screen or an attached printer, each session counts toward the maximum active addresses supported by that workstation controller.

► When a device has a *single address* defined with shared sessions, that device counts as one of the maximum active addresses. There can be up to four shared sessions on a single device.

There is a maximum of 300 shared sessions per I/O processor (IOP).

Refer to Technote *Twinaxial Attached Device Throughput for Twinaxial Devices*, TIPS-0358, to determine the types of sessions that count toward the maximum. It

also discusses the 5250 Express Data Stream capabilities relative to twinaxial workstation adapters.

pSeries performance

iSeries POWER5 server models that run AIX can be expected to produce the same performance as eqivalent pSeries models given the same memory, disk, I/O, and workload configurations.

The capacity of pSeries servers is often expressed in terms of *rPerf.* You can find the definition of rPerf and the performance ratings for @server p5 and pSeries servers on the Web at:

`http://www-1.ibm.com/servers/eserver/pseries/hardware/rperf.html`

iSeries for Domino performance terminology

iSeries for Domino models are specially priced and configured for Domino workloads. iSeries for Domino separates mail, instant messaging, and collaborative applications while automatically balancing and adjusting performance. With iSeries for Domino servers, you can run non-Domino workloads without restriction, even when the Domino server is not active.

Note: This is unlike the Dedicated Server for Domino servers (now *withdrawn from marketing*), which have restrictions on non-Domino workloads.

Performance on the iSeries for Domino servers is calculated using a Mail and Calendar User (MCU) measurement.

Mail and Calendar Users

MCU is a relative performance measurement derived by performing mail and calendar functions using Domino and Notes® clients. The MCU workload is significantly more complex than the Simple Mail Users (SMU) measured workload.

The MCU workload represents concurrent users on a Notes client who are reading, updating, or deleting documents in an e-mail database. It also represents users who are performing lookups in the Domino Directory, and scheduling calendar appointments and invitations. Reported values reflect 70% processor utilization to allow for growth and peak loads in excess of client workload estimates.

See "Summary of today's iSeries" on page 79 for a listing of the MCU rating for each iSeries for Domino server.

Capacity on Demand

@server i5 and iSeries Capacity on Demand (permanent or temporary) offers the ability to nondisruptively activate one or more additional central processors on the @server i5 550, 570 and 595 and iSeries 825, 870, and 890 servers. Any and all of the inactive processors installed in the server can be activated as additional permanent or temporary capacity. This is of significant value for clients who want to add capacity without disruption.

There are differences in the Capacity on Demand implementation for the different models. For example, @server i5 570 and 595 models have the ability to activate memory on demand. To take advantage of Capacity on Demand and On Demand Memory, you must purchase a configuration that includes the inactive processor capacity or memory. See "Capacity on Demand upgrades" on page 317 for considerations involving Capacity on Demand upgrades. For additional information about IBM @server resource functions available with i5/OS V5R3, see "LPAR capped and uncapped partitions" on page 48.

All @server i5 550, 570 and 595 and certain iSeries 825, 870, or 890 servers come with extra processor capacity built into the server. This extra capacity, known as *inactive* (or *standby*) *processors*, can be activated permanently or temporarily.

Appropriately configured @server i5 570 and 595 models also have extra memory capacity that can be activated permanently or temporarily

For more information about Capacity on Demand, refer to:

http://www.ibm.com/servers/eserver/iseries/ondemand/cod/

Capacity Upgrade on Demand (permanent capacity)

IBM @server Capacity Upgrade on Demand (CUoD) is the iSeries offering for permanently activate processors or memory. When one or more activation features are ordered, an activation code is generated and shipped to the client (mailed and posted on the Web). The activation code (think of it as a capacity key) must be entered on the proper server screen, and the newly activated processors are ready to use. No initial program load (IPL) is required. The permanently activated capacity needs to be assigned to a partition prior to use, regardless of whether the server is configured for logical partitioning.

To enable permanent activation of the inactive processors, a quantity of activation features and license entitlements is ordered. IBM manufacturing then generates an activation code (capacity key) unique to the server and the required additional OS/400 license key or keys. The activation code is mailed to the client and is posted at the following Web site:

http://www.ibm.com/servers/eserver/iseries/ondemand/cod/

Activating additional processors also requires an additional OS/400 license entitlement to be purchased for every processor or part of processor used by OS/400. This is ordered via a chargeable feature of OS/400 (5722-SS1). Processors activated solely for Linux, AIX 5L, or both do not require an OS/400 license entitlement.

The OS/400 license key is mailed to the client and is posted on the Web at:

http://www.ibm.com/servers/eserver/iseries/wwkms

Refer to "OS/400 terms and conditions changes" on page 589 for more information about OS/400 and license entitlements.

On/Off Capacity on Demand (temporary capacity)

On/Off Capacity on Demand is the iSeries offering to temporarily activate capacity and memory. It is used to temporarily activate capacity for the @server i5 Model 570, and the iSeries Model 825, 870, and 890 servers. Temporary capacity can be turned on and off to match peak periods. It allows a variable number of days and processors to be requested (processor days). The capacity is effective immediately. An IPL is not required.

Before requesting temporary capacity on the server, the server must be enabled. To do this, an enablement feature (Miscellaneous Equipment Specification (MES) only feature) must be ordered and the required contracts signed. An enablement code allows up to 360 processor days of temporary capacity for the @server i5 550, 570 or 595 server, or 192 processor days on other servers.

This means that requests for temporary capacity can be made over the life of the machine as long as the processor day limits are not exceeded. When the limit is reached, a new enablement feature must be ordered, and a new enablement code entered. Every time a new enablement code is entered, the limit of processor days that can be requested is reset.

When temporary capacity is needed, the OS/400 temporary capacity screen on the server is used to specify the memory or number of inactive processors that are required to be temporarily activated, and the number of days. That is, the processor day is equal to the number of processors multiplied by the number of days. The activated processors simply need to be assigned to a partition prior to use, regardless of whether the server is configured for LPAR. Activating

additional processors does not require any additional OS/400 license entitlement to be purchased for the temporarily activated processors.

Note: Additional licensing charges may apply for software that is priced by processor. Refer to the software vendor for further information.

It is important that the processors are assigned to a partition as soon as they are activated to achieve the full benefit of the temporary capacity.

Note: At the end of the temporary period (processor days requested), the temporarily activated processors must be made available to be reclaimed by the server, or unreturned processor days are billed (per the signed contract).

The contract, signed by the client before receiving the enablement code, requires the client to report billing data at least once a month, regardless of whether there is activity. This data is used to determine the proper amount to bill the client at the end of each billing period (calendar quarter).

Processor days of credit are then applied against any requested or unreturned processor days of temporary capacity. This happens automatically, until they are used up.

Failure to report billing data during a billing quarter results in a bill for 90 days of temporary capacity. The sales channel is notified of client requests for temporary capacity. As a result, the sales channel is required to place an order for a quantity of billing features (one feature equals one processor day).

The client pays for activated processor days after or before activation. Billing features are ordered afterward (one feature per processor day). For Model 825, 870, and 890, a Prepaid feature provides additional budget flexibility. A block of 30 processor days can be bought at a discounted price if purchased in advance. The 30 processor days are credit days and are applied by IBM at the end of the billing period. Credit days cannot be transferred to a server with a different type and serial number. Credit days are not transferred if a client sells the server. Credit days not used in one quarter "roll over" into the next quarter.

Reserve Capacity on Demand (prepaid capacity)

IBM @server Reserve Capacity on Demand delivers great flexibility in meeting peak demands. This option is also ideal for spikes in needed capacity (peak loads). But unlike On/Off CoD, a Prepaid Activation Feature is purchased up-front that sets a value on the server representing the number of processor days that

can be used as reserve CoD capacity. No contract and no reporting to IBM is required when paying for the reserve capacity ahead of time.

Reserve CoD represents an automatic way to activate temporary capacity. Reserve CoD enables the user to place a quantity of inactive processors into the server's shared processor pool, which then becomes available to the pool's resource manager. When the server recognizes that the number of base (purchased/active) processors assigned across uncapped partitions has been 100% used, and at least 10% of an additional processor is needed (based on multiple hits over the measured period), then a processor day is charged against the reserve CoD account balance. The processor day is good for 24 hours. Another processor day is charged for each additional processor put into use based on the 10% utilization rule. No charging occurs when the 24-hour clock expires and there is no longer a need for additional processors.

Reserve CoD is an effective way to handle peak loads that occur on a limited basis. Unlike On/Off CoD, contracts and reporting to IBM is not required. The purchase of reserve CoD activation time is prepaid in blocks of 30 processor days. Multiple blocks of activations can be loaded at a time.

Reserve processor days are transferred with the machine if the server is transferred to a different client. Any remaining reserve processor days are lost when upgrading to a different model, or physically adding processors. For example, if upgrading from a 2/4-way to a 5/8-way, the reserve processor days are set to zero.

Note: The break-even pricing for processor days on @server i5 servers is approximately 90 processor days. You can permanently activate a processor for the same price it costs to prepay for 90 processor days of reserve CoD capacity.

Trial Capacity on Demand (no charge capacity)

IBM @server Trial Capacity on Demand is quick, easy, and ready when you are. Use it for trial processor capacity or trial memory capacity, or for both. Trial capacity is offered at no additional charge.

IBM provides you with a code (a *key*) to start the trial. The code is good for 30 consecutive powered-on days, after it is entered at the server console. A request for trial processor or memory capacity can be made after initial installation, after a processor upgrade, or after the purchase of one or more permanent processor activations.

You must make the trial capacity available to be reclaimed by the server at the end of the trial period.

To request or start a trial, go to:

`http://www.ibm.com/servers/eserver/iseries/ondemand/cod`

Note: The Model 890 #2487 and #2488 processors, the Model 840 #2416, #2417, #2419, #2352, #2353, and #2354 processors, and the Model 830 #2349 processor each come with inactive capacity that can be permanently activated (CoD). These models offer trial capacity, which is a means of "trying" on demand capacity before buying it. Trial capacity allows 100% of the inactive processors to be activated for a period of 7 by 24 hours of system operation. If powered off, the clock does not increment.

Each model offers a number of *startup processors* that are in *active* status and a set of *inactive processors* that are in *standby* status. To permanently activate one or more inactive processor, place an MES order for the desired quantity of the model-specific activation code, as follows:

- ▶ #1604 CUoD Activation for the Model 840*
- ▶ #1605 CUoD Activation for the Model 830*
- ▶ #1610 890 CUoD Activation for the Model 890*

*The 830, 840, and 890 processors (#2487 and #2488) are *withdrawn from marketing*.

Ordering a CoD activation feature generates an activation code, which is posted on a Web site and mailed to the client. This activation code must be entered on the @server i5 or iSeries server console.

For further details, refer to the planning guides for CUoD or On/Off Capacity on Demand on the Web at:

`http://www.ibm.com/servers/eserver/iseries/ondemand/cod`

LPAR capped and uncapped partitions

Partitions use processing resources. Dedicated processing resources cannot be used by any other partition while the partition is active. However, with i5/OS V5R3 on the Model 520 and 570, when the partition is shut down, its processors become available by any partition using the uncapped sharing mode.

Partitions in a shared processing pool can have a sharing mode of capped or uncapped. A *capped partition* indicates that the logical partition (LPAR) will never exceed its assigned processing capacity. *Uncapped partitions* increase the processing power for a partition and the workload demand needed at a particular time assuming you have free resources in a shared pool.

Use capped mode when a software application never requires more than a certain amount of processing power. Any unused processing resource is used only by the uncapped partitions in the shared processing pool.

Shared and capped partitions

Processors using the capped shared mode are assigned from the shared processor pool. A partition using processors in this mode is guaranteed the use of the total processor capacity assigned to it if the workload requires it. This is similar to how shared processors are currently implemented.

Uncapped capacity

Uncapped capacity is limited to the minimum of the number of virtual processors assigned to the partition and the capacity of the shared pool. If two partitions need additional resources at the same time to complete a job, the server can distribute the unused processing resources to both partitions. This distribution process is determined by the uncapped weight of each of the partitions.

Uncapped weight is a number that you set for each uncapped partition in the shared processing pool. By setting the uncapped weight, any available unused capacity is distributed to contending LPARs in proportion to the established value of the uncapped weight.

For a discussion about partitions in a shared processing pool, see:

```
http://publib.boulder.ibm.com/infocenter/eserver/v1r2s/en_US/index.htm?info/
iphat/iphatsharedproc.htm
```

See the table on page 539 for partition limitations.

Shared uncapped processors

Processors using the uncapped sharing mode are also assigned from the shared pool. The partition is guaranteed the use of the total processor capacity assigned to it if it needs it (such as shared capped). However, if the workload requires it, the shared uncapped partition can acquire additional processing capacity. This additional processor capacity can be taken from the shared processor pool from which that partition is using resources.

A processor using uncapped mode can always use its assigned capacity. Partitions using uncapped processors can *weigh* the importance of a partition to give importance to one uncapped partition over another.

For more information about, and a demonstration for, uncapped processors, see the Capacity on Demand section in the iSeries Information Center at:

```
http://publib.boulder.ibm.com/infocenter/eserver/v1r2s/en_US/index.htm?info/
iphat/iphatsharedproc.htm
```

Memory

Memory used by the POWER5 technology-based processors is moved in blocks known as a *logical memory block* (LMB). Also regarded as a memory region, an LMB is the smallest memory unit managed by the POWER5 processors. The LMB size on Models 520, 550, 570 and 595 is 16 MB. The LMB size on Models 800, 810, 825, 870, and 890 is 1 MB. Dynamic memory movement between LPARs is on LMB boundaries (1 MB or 16 MB depending on the model).

Workload measurement and sizing tools

Capacity planning and performance management tools, which are available to work with IBM i5/OS V5R3 and OS/400 V5R2, include:

► IBM @server Workload Estimator
► IBM Performance Management for iSeries
► IBM Performance Tools for iSeries
► PATROL for iSeries – Predict
► IBM WebFacing Tool
► IBM Disk Magic for Windows

The IBM @server Workload Estimator is a Web-based estimation tool. It recommends a system that best fits overall system needs. It is described in the following section.

Use PM @server iSeries (formerly called PM/400) to gather performance information and pass the performance statistics to the IBM eServer Workload Estimator for projecting future needs of installed workloads.

For more information about PM @server iSeries, see:

http://www.ibm.com/servers/eserver/iseries/pm/

You can use Performance Tools for iSeries to measure resource utilization. Refer to "IBM Performance Tools for iSeries (5722-PT1)" on page 690 for more information.

Use PATROL for iSeries – Predict to perform detailed capacity planning and "what-if" scenarios. For more information, see "PATROL for iSeries – Predict (5620-FIF)" on page 690.

Use the IBM WebFacing Tool to convert 5250 source applications to applications to run with the WebSphere Application Server. The IBM WebFacing Tool is discussed in "IBM WebFacing Tool" on page 54.

Use Disk Magic for iSeries when IBM TotalStorage Enterprise Storage Server®
(ESS) disk drives are in the configuration. See "Disk Magic for iSeries" on
page 53 for more information.

IBM eServer Workload Estimator

The IBM @server Workload Estimator is a Web-based estimation tool that
automates the manual calculations previously required from paper sizers. It
allows the user the option to enter data for multiple workloads, from which a
machine recommendation is made that best fits overall system needs.

Workloads supported by IBM @server Workload Estimator include:

- Installed system
- PM @server iSeries
- Web serving
- Java
- WebSphere Commerce Suite
- IBM WebFacing Tool
- WebSphere Portal Server
- WebSphere Commerce Payments
- Traditional
- Generic computing resources
- Domino
- Linux file serving
- Linux Web serving
- Non-IBM workload

You can learn more about IBM @server Workload Estimator on the Web at:

`http://www-912.ibm.com/supporthome.nsf/document/16533356`

When you reach this site, select **Sizing Tools**.

Disk arm requirements

A physical disk drive (and the processing through the disk controller) performs a
specific number of disk accesses each second. The configuration of disk units
influences the overall performance of the system. Newer disk arms and
controllers provide better performance than previous disk drives. Therefore,
fewer disk drives (disk arms or actuators) can typically be used, yet provide
comparable performance.

You can provide for the best obtainable disk subsystem performance and enable
the best possible overall system performance. To do so, it is important to size an

iSeries server with an appropriate number of disk arms. The white paper *iSeries Disk Arm Requirements* discusses this concept. You can find it on the Web at:

http://www.ibm.com/servers/eserver/iseries/perfmgmt/pdf/V5R2FiSArmct.pdf

PM @server iSeries and IBM @server Workload Estimator include disk arm statistics and arm requirements for sizing. Use PM @server iSeries or IBM eServer Workload Estimator to help size the minimum number of disk arms required for a given iSeries processor. Performance Tools for iSeries provides detailed reports on collected performance data.

Solution developers and other application solution providers also have recommendations for a minimum configuration as it relates to their solution.

To ensure that you have sufficient disk arms to meet the needed workload, it is best to have performance runs from your current system run at a time when the disk workload is heavy. These can then be used as input to various tools including the IBM @server Workload Estimator and PATROL for iSeries – Predict.

You can also use the reports to determine the number of disk requests/second that are happening on your current system, as reported in the System Performance Report and other Performance Tools reports.

Disk workload is measured in terms of operations/second. Depending on the speed or vintage of the disk drives and controllers, average service time should be somewhere in the 3.5 to 10 millisecond range (lower for newer, higher for old 7200 rpm disks). Numbers higher than these can indicate a disk bottleneck and therefore stored demand. Use such tools as PATROL for iSeries – Predict to determine the stored demand. Note that the tools assume a properly tuned system. If a bottleneck exists, the system cannot be properly tuned.

The number of disk arms required can be determined from the number of disk accesses that must be performed each second.

If upgrading to a larger or newer system, the new system typically can perform more disk requests each second. In addition, more memory acts like a read cache and can reduce the number of physical disk accesses that must occur.

Note: There is no substitute for proper modeling.

The following general rules apply in many cases. These rules assume an average disk access size of between 6k and 10k in size (shown in the performance report). If you are in the over 25k range, lower the values by 20%. This also assumes that *all* disks are the same size and use the same type of controller.

Historically 10k rpm disk drives on #2748/#2778/#4727/#4778 disk unit
controllers (with 15 drives attached to the controller) could do about 20 disk
operations/second with adequate or good performance. By the time you reached
25 disk operations per second, you could feel the controller slowing down. Any
more than that and the controller started to bottleneck.

Using 10k rpm drives and replacing the above controller with a #2757 PCI-X
Ultra RAID Disk Controller meant that you could go up to about 50 disk
operations/second/disk with a possibility of still handling peaks at 60 operations
per second (after which the disk drive started to bottleneck). With 15k disk drives
and a #2757 (15 drives per controller), you could go up to 50 disk operations per
second per drive.

For disk-related performance information, refer to Chapter 14, "DASD
Performance Management," in *iSeries Performance Capabilities Reference*,
SC41-0607.

Disk Magic for iSeries

The IBM Disk Magic for iSeries product is intended for modeling ESS disk drives
on iSeries servers. Configuration and workload details are entered into the tool.
Algorithms support calibration, configuration changes, workload changes, and
automatic cache modeling. The output is available in tabular and graphic reports.

Performance analysis is based on limited measurement data. Disk Magic for
iSeries is most useful to obtain rough performance estimates of ESS drives on
iSeries servers.

You can find the tool on the Web at:

```
http://w3.ibm.com/sales/systems/portal
https://www-1.ibm.com/partnerworld/sales/systems/portal
```

Refacing options for the iSeries client

Several products are available for the iSeries to reface (browser-enable) 5250
application software. Some of the products available from IBM include:

► IBM WebFacing Tool: Part of WebSphere Development Studio (5722-WDS)

► Host Access Transformation Services Toolkit: Part of WebSphere
  Development Studio (5722-WDS)

► WebSphere Host Access Transformation Server (HATS Studio): Part of Host
  Access Client Package for iSeries (5733-A78)

► WebSphere Host Access Transformation Server Limited Edition (HATS LE):
  Part of iSeries Access Family (5722-XW1)

- ▶ iSeries Access for Web: Part of iSeries Access Family (5722-XW1)
- ▶ WebSphere Host on Demand: Part of Host Access Client Package for iSeries (5733-A78)
- ▶ WebSphere Host Publisher: Part of iSeries Access Family and WebSphere Integration Offering V1.0 (5722-XW1 and 5733-A53)

> **Note:** The iSeries Access Family product (5722-XW1) no longer includes WebSphere Host Publisher as of 6 August 6 2004. Users are encouraged to migrate to WebSphere HATS.

The unique requirements of the client application determine the best solution for a client environment. You can find a comparison of functions for many of the IBM products on the Web at:

```
http://www-1.ibm.com/servers/eserver/iseries/access/web/
web_to_host_comparisons.html
```

IBM WebFacing Tool

The IBM WebFacing Tool, provided in the IBM WebSphere Development Studio for iSeries, creates a Web-ready GUI to 5250 applications. The applications can then be made available in a familiar GUI format recognized by any Web user to anyone with a browser.

To create the interface, the IBM WebFacing Tool works from Data Description Specification (DDS) display files and User Interface Manager (UIM) help files. The interface which is generated consists of Java Servlets, JavaServer Pages (JSPs), JavaBeans, and JavaScript. The interface runs under WebSphere - Express for iSeries, WebSphere Application Server V5, or WebSphere Application Server V4. These WebFaced applications do not require 5250 CPW capacity when run on the Model 520, 550, 570, 595, 800, 810, 825, 870, or 890.

Applications that are Web-enabled using the IBM WebFacing Tool generally perform better than applications refaced with other tools. Most other tools convert the 5250 data stream to a Web interface in a run-time conversion. This impacts the execution performance of these refaced applications.

With the IBM WebFacing Tool, the Web interface is created at development time. During application execution, the data from the application is redirected to the Web interface created by the IBM WebFacing Tool. No 5250 data stream is created and there is no run-time conversion. This up-front resource investment pays off with more efficient production operations.

The 5250 data stream and 5250 OLTP are efficient and have been fine-tuned over many years. 5250 applications running with the GUI take significantly more CPU resource than if they run with the original green-screen interface under a 5250 OLTP environment. The magnitude of the increase in resource depends upon the application. The larger the percentage of time is spent doing screen I/O in a 5250 application, the larger the CPW increases when running with a GUI. Typically the application requires several times the processor resource.

> **Tip:** Understand the 5250 application functions being brought to the Web, and pilot those parts of the application.

For additional tips and considerations, refer to Chapter 14, "DASD Performance Management", in *iSeries Performance Capabilities Reference*, SC41-0607. Also see *Aiming for Zero Interactive on iSeries*, which discusses 5250 OLTP and is available on the Web at:

```
http://www.ibm.com/servers/eserver/iseries/perfmgmt/pdf/ZeroInteractive.pdf
```

Use IBM @server Workload Estimator to help predict the system characteristics for these applications that are enhanced by the IBM WebFacing Tool. You can access the tool on the Web at:

```
http://www-912.ibm.com/wle/EstimatorServlet
```

Refer to "IBM WebSphere Development Studio for iSeries (5722-WDS)" on page 642 to read more about the IBM WebFacing Tool and WebSphere.

Editions

iSeries Editions are flexible-options packages that help simplify choices and maximize business value. @server i5 and iSeries servers are offered with Editions that provide you with some of IBM's most popular middleware in an integrated package, yet have the ability to run traditional OLTP applications that require 5250 CPW. Each iSeries edition incorporates a set of software licensing and hardware features designed to help meet the specific demands of small, medium, and large enterprises.

The editions offered for today's iSeries servers include:

► **Enterprise Edition**: The Enterprise Edition is designed for clients who require the highest level of flexibility. It is designed as a total system, fully integrating and exploiting all of the fundamental hardware and software all On Demand Businesses need. The Enterprise Edition is featured for clients with dynamic business environments who need to respond immediately to fluctuating, unpredictable On Demand Business needs.

The Enterprise Edition offering includes everything in the Standard Edition and more. The Enterprise Edition leverages the widest range of IBM middleware while still having the ability to run traditional OLTP applications without first being WebFaced by the IBM WebFacing Tool of WebSphere Development Studio.

The Enterprise Edition provides maximum 5250 CPW for 5250 OLTP workloads. The Enterprise also provides support for Capacity on Demand (permanent and temporary).

► **Standard Edition**: The Standard edition is attractively priced to drive new workloads that do not require 5250 OLTP CPW on the @server i5 models. The Standard Edition is featured for a wide variety of solutions for On Demand Business and client server.

> **Note:** 5250 OLTP applications modernized (WebFaced) using the IBM WebFacing Tool of IBM WebSphere Development Studio can be used with the Standard Edition.

► **Value Edition**: The Value Edition for iSeries Model 520 edition is tailored specifically to small enterprises and is available on select @server i5 520 servers. Minimum hardware requirements apply.

► **Express Edition**: The @server i5 520 Express Edition offers a choice of five pre-packaged offerings that provide small and medium enterprises with the basic infrastructure for running their core business applications. The 520 Express Edition simplifies your decision process by delivering the key elements of your IT infrastructure in a single server with supporting hardware, software, maintenance, and support at an aggressive price.

All @server i5 520 Express Edition offerings include hardware and i5/OS. The #7392, #7392 and #7393 Editions feature mirrored disk protection while editions #7394 and #7395 feature RAID disk protection. All offerings are available at initial order as deskside servers, however they can later be converted to a rack-mount configuration or additional features can be added by chargeable upgrade orders. All @server i5 520 Express Editions are shipped from IBM with the system console on twinax workstation controller as the default setting.

> **Note:** The @server i5 9405 520 Express Edition is packaged under machine type 9405.

► **Domino Edition**: The @server i5 Domino Edition is designed for organizations of all sizes, where e-mail and electronic collaboration are

increasingly becoming important applications with the same requirements for availability and security as line-of-business applications.

The Domino Edition continues the tradition established by the iSeries Dedicated Server for Domino (the DSD) and the iSeries for Domino. That is, the price and performance are targeted for Lotus workloads combined with the reliability, manageability, and low cost of ownership that have made iSeries a highly successful Domino server. In addition to the two processors that are standard on the @server i5 Domino Edition, you have the option to activate one or two more processors with built-in Capacity on Demand. Optionally, you can create LPARs and run Linux or AIX on the additional processors.

► **Solution Edition**: The Solution Edition is designed for clients with qualifying ISV solutions to provide a more attractively priced total solution. Like the Enterprise Edition, one Enterprise Enablement feature is included, providing one processor authorization of 5250 CPW.

The Solution Edition leverages IBM middleware and can run traditional OLTP applications without first being WebFaced by the IBM WebFacing Tool of WebSphere Development Studio.

The Solution Edition supports multiple operating systems (i5/OS, AIX 5L, and Linux), Web modernization with enhanced refacing support, up to 10 partitions per processor (LPAR), 5250 OLTP, and Capacity on Demand (including CoD and On/Off Capacity on Demand). Additional hardware and software are included with the Solution Edition.

Capacity BackUp Edition (CBU): The Capacity BackUp Edition is designed for clients who require an off-site disaster recovery system. It provides everything the Enterprise Edition provides, except it is shipped with a minimal set of software content because IBM software licensing can allow the primary iSeries server's licensing to be transferred to a backup iSeries server in case the primary server is out of production. The server has a minimum set of startup processors that can be used for any purpose and a large number of inactive processors that can be activated temporarily at no charge in the event of a disaster. The inactive processors cannot be permanently activated.

The Capacity BackUp (CBU) Edition is offered for the @server i5 570, and iSeries Models 825, 870, and 890.

> **Note:** The Capacity BackUp server is not intended for a backup server for 24 x 7 high availability solutions that require day-to-day full operation of the backup server. Such utilization can require a significant number of chargeable processor days.
>
> On demand memory features are not activated for no-charge during a disaster.

► **High Availability Edition (HA)**: The High Availability Edition provides everything the Enterprise Edition provides (including hardware that is physically identical to the equivalent Enterprise Edition hardware), except it is shipped with less software content. It is designed for clients who require 24 x 7 availability.

You can connect multiple @server i5 and iSeries systems together with high-function third-party software for role swapping and running production on both primary and secondary servers. In this multiple iSeries server environment, the @server i5 or iSeries for high availability is an attractively priced model linked with a model of equal or higher CPW.

The High Availability Edition provides maximum 5250 CPW for 5250 OLTP workloads. The High Availability Edition also provides support for Capacity on Demand (permanent and temporary).

Notes:

► On/Off Capacity on Demand is used to temporarily activate capacity for the @server i5 Model 570 and the iSeries Model 825, 870, and 890 servers.

► POWER5 partitioning implementation requires a minimum of 240 CPW worth of processor power per partition. Therefore the maximum number of partitions for the editions with 500 CPW is two, and the maximum for partitions for the editions with 1000 CPW is four. This implementation applies to all Editions.

For information that is unique to the edition offering of each iSeries model, see the appropriate model chapter in this Handbook.

All iSeries Editions include:

► Support for multiple operating systems (i5/OS or OS/400), Linux, IBM AIX 5L)

► Support for Web modernization with enhanced IBM WebFacing Tool support (the ability to deploy IBM WebFaced applications without 5250 OLTP CPW)

► Support for Virtualization Engine Systems Technologies, including dynamic logical partitioning

► Licensing for i5/OS (WebSphere Express is integrated with i5/OS as part of i5/OS V5R3)

Some editions support 5250 OLTP applications. Each edition offers a different level of capacity, power, and functionality.

Note: Enterprise Editions ordered for iSeries 825, 870, and 890 servers at OS/400 V5R2 include licenses for DB2 DataPropagator™, WebSphere Application Server Express, Lotus Instant Messaging and Web Conferencing (Sametime®), and Lotus Team Workplace (QuickPlace®).

The tables in the following sections reflect the specific components that are included with each iSeries edition and @server i5 and iSeries models shipped with V5R3 of i5/OS.

Components for Enterprise, Standard, Solution, Domino, High Availability and Capacity BackUp editions

	Standard						Enterprise						Domino	Solution	HA			CBU
	520[7]	550	570	595	810	825/870/890	520	550	570	595	810	825/870/890	550	550	520	810	570/825/870/890	570/825/870/890
Features																		
Support for multiple operating systems	Y	Y	Y	Y	Y	Y	Y	Y	Y	Y	Y	Y	Y	Y	Y		Y	Y
Support for Web modernization	Y	Y	Y	Y	Y	Y	Y	Y	Y	Y	Y	Y	Y	Y	Y		Y	Y
Support for LPAR	Y	Y	Y	Y	Y	Y	Y	Y	Y	Y	Y	Y	Y	Y	Y		Y	Y
Support for Capacity on Demand		Y	Y	Y		Y		Y	Y	Y		Y		Y	Y	Y	Y	Y
Support for 5250 OLTP							Y	Y	Y	Y	Y	Y		Y		Y	Y	Y
Installation Assistant using VMI							Y	Y	Y			Y		Y				
Software license or licenses																		
IBM i5/OS V5R3	Y	Y	Y	Y	Y	Y	Y	Y	Y	Y	Y	Y	Y	Y	Y	Y	Y	Y
On Demand Business solution tool licenses																		
WebSphere Portal Express Plus [2]							Y	Y	Y	Y				Y				
DB2 Query Manager & Development Toolkit [3]							Y	Y	Y	Y	Y	Y		Y	Y	Y	Y	
DB2 symmetric multiprocessor (SMP) [3]							Y	Y	Y			Y					Y	
DB2 UDB Extenders [3]							Y	Y	Y			Y						
XML Toolkit							Y	Y	Y			Y						

	Standard						Enterprise						Domino	Solution	HA			CBU
	520[7]	550	570	595	810	825/870/890	520	550	570	595	810	825/870/890	550	550	520	810	570/825/870/890	570/825/870/890
Datacenter management tools licenses																		
Performance Tools [3,4]							Y	Y	Y	Y	Y	Y			Y	Y	Y	
Backup Recovery and Media Services [3,5]							Y	Y	Y			Y					Y	
HA Switchable Resources [3]							Y	Y	Y			Y					Y	
Media and Storage Extensions [3]							Y	Y	Y			Y					Y	
Tivoli Monitoring for Web							Y	Y	Y			Y						
Tivoli Storage Manager Extended Edition [1]							Y	Y	Y			Y						
Virtualization Engine for iSeries, Enterprise Workload Manager							Y	Y	Y									
Education and services																		
IBM ILS Education Credits							1	3	5			5 \ 3 \ 1	1					
IBM Service Voucher(s) [8]							1	1	1	1	1	1				1		1
Hardware																		
Processor activation [6]							Y	Y	Y									
Integrated xSeries Server							Y	Y	Y									

1. One license per start-up processor and five client licenses
2. Per user license
3. Includes one server license
4. Includes a Manager option
5. Includes Network option
6. For Linux or AIX 5L (if used by i5/OS, one i5/OS processor license required)
7. Standard Editions of Model 520 do not have 5250 OLTP. Value and Express editions do have a limited preset value. See the following table.
8. Services vary with model.

Components for Express, Value, Standard and Advanced editions

	Value 800 #2463	Standard 800 #2463	Advanced 800 #2464	Value 520 #7450	Value 520 #7451	Express 520 #7390	Express 520 #7391	Express 520 #7392	Express 520 #7393	Express 520 #7394
Features										
Support for multiple operating systems	Y	Y	Y	Y	Y	Y	Y	Y	Y	Y
Support for Web modernization	Y	Y	Y	Y	Y	Y	Y	Y	Y	Y
Support for LPAR	Y	Y	Y	Y	Y	Y	Y	Y	Y	Y
Support for 5250 OLTP	Y	Y	Y	Y	Y	Y	Y	Y	Y	Y
Software										
IBM i5/OS V5R3	Y	Y	Y	Y	Y	Y	Y	Y	Y	Y
WebSphere-Express V5 for iSeries		Y	Y							
Performance Tools [4]		Y	Y							
DB2 Query Manager & Development Toolkit		Y	Y				Y	Y	Y	Y
iSeries Access							Y	Y	Y	Y
Query for iSeries							Y	Y	Y	Y
WebSphere Development Studio							Y	Y	Y	Y
Virtualization Engine for iSeries (7333-VE1)						Y	Y	Y	Y	Y
Cryptographic Access Provider 128 bit						Y	Y	Y	Y	Y
Client Encryption 128 bit						Y	Y	Y	Y	Y
Web Enablement (5722- WE1)						Y	Y	Y	Y	Y
Twinax adapter (included)	-				-					
Hardware										
Tape/disk controller (included)	1	1	1	1	1	1	1	1	1	1
RAID disk controller (included)	Op	Op	Op	Op	Op	Op	Op	Op	1	1
Disk drives (included) minimum	1	2	2	1	1	2	2	2	4	4
30 GB QIC tape (included)	Op	1	1	1	1	1	1	1	1	1
DVD-ROM (included)	1	1	1	1	1	1	1	1	1	1
Main memory (included) GB	.25	.5	2	.5	.5	1	1	2	1	2

	Value	Standard	Advanced	Value	Value	Express				
	800 #2463	800 #2463	800 #2464	520 #7450	520 #7451	520 #7390	520 #7391	520 #7392	520 #7393	520 #7394
Ethernet LAN ports (card or embedded)	1	1	1	2	2	2	2	2	2	2
2-line comm. adapter (included)	1	1	1	1	1	1	1	1	1	1
Twinax adapter (included)	-	1	1	Op	Op	1	1	1	1	1

1. One license per start-up processor and five client licenses
2. Per user license
3. Includes one server license
4. Includes a Manager option
5. Includes a Network option
6. For Linux or AIX 5L (if used by i5/OS, one i5/OS processor license is required)
7. Standard Editions of Model 520 do not have 5250 OLTP. Value and Express editions do have a limited preset value.
8. Services vary with model.
9. Op = optional

See "Edition upgrades" on page 317 for considerations when upgrading editions.

For current information and more details about each edition for the @server i5 and iSeries models, see:

http://www.ibm.com/servers/eserver/iseries/hardware/editions

You can find product brochures for the @server i5 editions at:

http://www.ibm.com/servers/eserver/iseries/literature/index.html

Simultaneous multithreading explained

Although an operating system gives the impression that it is concurrently executing a large number of tasks, each processor in a symmetric multiprocessor (SMP) traditionally executes a single task's instruction stream at any moment.

The QPRCMLTTSK system value controls whether to enable the individual SMP processors to concurrently execute multiple instruction streams. Each instruction stream belongs to separate tasks or threads. When enabled, each individual processor concurrently executes multiple tasks at the same time. The effect of its use will likely increase the performance capacity of a system or improve the responsiveness of a multithreaded application.

Running multiple instruction streams at the same time does not improve the performance of any given task. Since this is the case with any performance recommendations, results vary in different environments.

The way that multithreading is done depends on the hardware model, and therefore, the performance capacity gains vary. @server i5 Models 520, 550, 570, and 595 support this approach through a concept called simultaneous multithreading (SMT). There are several distinct differences between different types of multithreading implemented in the industry. You may find articles discussing Intel's Hyper-Threading, Superthreading, and other multitasking techniques from several sources.

Older iSeries processors use an approach called *hardware multithreading* (HMT). In the hardware multithreading approach, the hardware automatically switches between the tasks on any long processing delay event, for example, a cache miss. Some models do not support any form of multithreading, which means the QPRCMLTTSK system value has no performance effect. Because the QPRCMLTTSK system value enables the parallel use of shared processor resources, the performance gains depend highly on the application and the model. Refer to the *iSeries Performance Capabilities Reference*, SC41-0607, for guidelines about what performance gains you may expect through its use.

In some exceptional cases, some applications are better served by disabling simultaneous multithreading.

4

iSeries direction

This chapter outlines both future and present directions of the iSeries platform. It discusses product previews, statements of direction, and general planning information. Products, features, and software that are withdrawn are identified with announced dates when support is to be discontinued. By communicating these future plans, IBM intends to help our clients plan for better use of their system.

You can find further information about product previews, statements of direction, and plans for products that are no longer supported on a release, on the iSeries planning information Web site at:

`http://www.ibm.com/servers/eserver/iseries/support/planning/v5r3direct.html`

Product Previews

Product Previews identify specific functions that IBM has committed to incorporate into future iSeries hardware or software releases. Understanding them can provide insight into IBM plans and directions for future iSeries hardware or software releases. The information released represents the current intent of IBM. They represent goals and objectives only. All statements regarding the plans, directions, and intent of IBM are subject to change or withdrawal without notice.

IBM has announced an intention to provide an update of OS/400 and enhancements to server hardware that include the following enhancements. The previews that are listed are separated into fulfilled and non-fulfilled categories at the time of each incremental announcement through October 2004.

Product Previews: Closed

No Product Previews are open at the time of the October 2004 iSeries announcements. This section presents those Product previews that have closed since August 2004.

As part of the iSeries announcements made on 27 August 2004, the following Product Preview was closed:

▶ **Virtualization Engine Systems Services**: IBM plans to provide Virtualization Engine Systems Services across the following functional categories in second half 2004:

- *IBM Director Multiplatform*: A consistent systems management infrastructure allows heterogeneous systems and their resources to be managed in a homogeneous way. It leverages proven technologies from IBM Director. Coupled with the Virtualization Engine console, which provides a common Web-based console for monitoring and managing the overall health of your on demand operating environment, you have a set of powerful system management capabilities.

- *Systems Provisioning*: Automated change management allows you to deploy and re-purpose (commission and decommission) IT resources to react to changing business demands. Extending the current logical partitioning and integrated Windows attachment capabilities of the @server i5 servers, it allows for the virtualization of resource pools to be redeployed on an as-needed basis.

- *IBM Enterprise Workload Manager*: This allows you to identify work requests based on service class definitions and track performance of those requests against stated business goals. It provides problem isolation

and workload optimization of a heterogeneous multitier workload through a set of self-managing capabilities.

- *IBM Grid Toolbox V3 for Multiplatforms*: Provides the infrastructure that clients and independent software vendors (ISVs) need to develop, deploy, and manage distributed workloads with greater ease. It enables you to capitalize on IBM @server and IBM middleware Qualities of Service. The toolbox is based on the Open Grid Services Architecture. This version of the toolbox is best leveraged by businesses that are responsible for deploying and managing grids or for ISVs that develop products designed to assist in the management or deployment of grids.

As part of the iSeries announcements made on 31 August 2004, the following Product Previews were closed:

- ▶ **@server i5 570 growth plans:** Leveraging a new building block architecture, the Model 570 can cover an extremely broad capacity range. You can start with a 1/2-way server in a single building block and eventually grow to a 16-way server using four building blocks. The building block architecture enables balanced growth for the Model 570. When building blocks are added, the processor, memory, and input/output (I/O) capacities are increased. Extending the Model 570 to a 16-way server is planned to be available in second half 2004.

- ▶ **9402 and 9404 upgrades**: Upgrades from iSeries Models 810, 820, 825, and 830 that use the 9406 machine type designation, into the @server i5 Models 520, 550 or 570, are announced and available in June 2004. For Models 810, 820, 825, and 830 that use the less common 9402 and 9404 machine type designators, upgrades are planned to be available starting third quarter 2004.

There is no pricing difference planned between the 9402/9404 upgrades and 9406 upgrades, since there is no physical difference between the machine types for these models. During the 9402/9404 upgrade, the machine type designator is changed to 9406 to allow IBM to better support the server.

For additional information, see:

`http://www.ibm.com/servers/eserver/support/iseries/planning/nav.html`

- ▶ **Linux on Integrated xSeries solutions (Integrated xSeries Server/Integrated xSeries Adapter):** IBM intends to provide support for Linux on selected Integrated xSeries Servers and xSeries servers attached to iSeries via the Integrated xSeries Adapter. This support is planned to be available in second half 2004 as a program temporary fix (PTF) to iSeries Integration for Windows Server (5722-WSV).

- **Capacity on Demand**: IBM plans to enhance Capacity on Demand by adding the following capabilities:
  - Ability to purchase activations for inactive memory on an @server i5 570

    IBM will make the memory available for use when permanent or temporary activation codes are applied to an iSeries server.
  - Ability to prepurchase reserve processor capacity, perfect for unplanned business workload peaks

    A quantity of inactive processors can be placed in the server's shared processor pool as reserve processors. When the server recognizes that additional capacity is needed by a partition, a processor day is subtracted from the prepurchased total.
  - Ability to request trial processor or memory capacity that can be used for a predetermined consecutive number of days

    A trial activation code can be requested at a Capacity on Demand Web site to activate the no-charge capacity for a business workload peak, for a benchmark, or to try a new workload.
- **Additional High Availability options**: IBM plans to announce and deliver, in the second half of 2004, additional high-availability options:
  - iSeries for High Availability offerings for the @server i5 520, 550 and 570
  - An iSeries for Capacity BackUp offering for the @server i5 570
  - Support for the attachment of more than one Hardware Management Console (HMC) per server

With the release of PTFs SI13704 and MF33158 on 31 August 2004, the following Product Preview was closed:

- **OS/400 support for higher capacity optical libraries**: For the IBM @server i5 and iSeries, IBM plans to enhance i5/OS V5R3 to support Plasmon's next generation of Ultra Density Optical (UDO) drives in the Plasmon G-series libraries for IBM OS/400 optical libraries. For more information, see:

  http://www-1.ibm.com/servers/eserver/iseries/optical/

As part of the iSeries announcements made on 31 August 2004 and 30 September 2004, the following Product Preview was closed:

- **Linux on @server i5 servers:** IBM is working with Novell, Inc. and Red Hat, Inc. to certify Linux distributions for @server i5 servers. These distributions, the next version of SUSE LINUX Enterprise Server, and the next quarterly update of Red Hat Enterprise Linux 3, are expected to be available from the Linux distributors in third quarter 2004.

Hardware features used with Linux can be ordered for the Model 520, 550 and 570 servers. These features require a POWER5 Linux distribution. For more information about Linux distributions available for iSeries, see:

```
http://www.ibm.com/servers/eserver/iseries/linux/dist.html
```

As part of the iSeries announcements made on 15 October 2004, the following Product Preview was closed:

▶ **pSeries support for i5/OS:** IBM plans to extend the capabilities of the @server p5 product line by introducing support for the i5/OS operating system. i5/OS support will provide additional flexibility for large-scale server consolidation where AIX 5L or Linux is the primary operating system. i5/OS support is planned to be limited to one processor on selected @server p5 570 servers and up to two processors on future high-end @server p5 systems. This capability is planned to be available in the first half of 2005.

> **Note:** The 9411-100 type model number is available to enable the ordering of i5/OS supported devices on @server p5 systems. It is added to the @server p5 systems and all items unique to the iSeries (towers) are added as features to this type. For details see, "9411-100 eServer p5 I/O Subsystem for i5/OS" on page 306.

As part of the IBM announcements made on 29 October 2004, the following Product Preview was closed:

▶ **Integrated xSeries Server based on Intel Pentium® M processor technology**: The current Integrated xSeries Server is supported within selected iSeries I/O towers attached to the @server i5. In the second half of 2004, iSeries plans to provide a new Integrated xSeries Server, based on Intel Pentium M processor technology, for installation in the system unit or I/O towers of new @server i5 servers.

With successful testing completed in October 2004, the following Product Preview was closed:

▶ **Switched I/O tower clustering support:** Support for the #5094, #5294, #5095, and #5095 PCI-X I/O towers and drawers to be installed as switched I/O towers in clusters consisting of @server i5 servers and installed earlier iSeries servers is planned for third quarter 2004. At that time, @server i5 servers will support the attachment of these I/O towers and drawers, which have not been enhanced with the faster high-speed link (HSL)-2 hardware. Prior to third quarter 2004, the #5074, #5079, #5088, and #0588 towers and drawers can be used as switched I/O towers in these mixed server clusters. Switching I/O towers is a function of OS/400 that is typically used to increase the iSeries server's availability.

Statement of Direction

Statements of Direction identify the commitment of IBM to direct iSeries servers toward a given design or technology. Understanding them can provide insight into the design and technology plans of IBM. All statements regarding IBM plans, directions, and intent are subject to change or withdrawal without notice.

Statement of Direction: Open

The following Statements of Direction remain open at the time of the October 2004 announcement:

- **Enterprise Extender:** IBM intends to deliver Enterprise Extender for iSeries with a future i5/OS software release. Enterprise Extender provides a mechanism for integrating Systems Network Architecture (SNA) applications with an Internet Protocol (IP) network. Enterprise Extender is a recommended alternative for AnyNet® as the solution for transporting SNA traffic over an IP network.

- **Subcapacity pricing**: To continue to lead the industry in developing solutions for On Demand Business, IBM intends to provide flexible pricing and financing that enables you to exploit new technology. IBM has already taken important steps in this area with our announcement of complementary On/Off Capacity on Demand offerings for hardware and software.

  IBM considers subcapacity licensing to be a strategic offering within the on demand portfolio. Subcapacity licensing enables the licensing of the on demand portfolio. Subcapacity licensing enables the licensing of software products for use on less than the full capacity (in processors) of the machine when used within a logical partition. IBM currently offers subcapacity licensing for selected software, including WebSphere Application Server running on iSeries.

  IBM intends to announce subcapacity licensing terms and conditions for additional middleware products, such as WebSphere Application Server and DB2 Enterprise Server Edition, on other platforms such as AIX 5L, i5/OS, OS/400, and Linux on POWER. IBM also plans to deliver license management tools to assist you in tracking and reporting your software assets to take advantage of these flexible pricing models.

Statement of Direction: Closed

As part of the iSeries announcements made on 11 June 2004 and 31 August 2004, IBM fulfilled our commitment to the following Statement of Direction:

- ► **Future iSeries management environment**: IBM plans to deliver an integrated management environment with services such as partitioning, hardware virtualization, and workload management for OS/400, AIX, and Linux applications on an IBM @server. The new management environment will integrate OS/400, middleware, and enhancements from research and development to deliver dramatically enhanced partitioning, optimized asset utilization, and on-demand resource allocation for heterogeneous operating environments.

As part of the iSeries announcements made in May 2004, IBM fulfilled our commitment of the following Statement of Direction:

- ► **Support for AIX on iSeries**: With the availability of i5/OS V5R3 in August 2004, IBM has further extended the self-managing systems initiative of the IBM autonomic computing initiative with self-optimizing and configuring capabilities that include native support for AIX in logical partitions alongside OS/400 partitions on the iSeries product line. This allows clients to leverage a broader range of application environments including OS/400, Windows, Linux, and now AIX on a single IBM @server. With this capability, a common set of resources can be managed and shared across a total client solution, made up of applications targeted to different operating environments. This extends the self-optimization capabilities of iSeries to meet the needs of clients in a simple, low-cost, and efficient manner.

Planning information

As business grows, the information systems needs of a business change, and technology changes to allow more efficient and cost-effective methods to solve business problems. As the iSeries and OS/400 are enhanced, new technology is introduced. Other technology reaches a point where no further enhancements, functions, or maintenance is planned. This section helps clients to plan for these changes and to protect their investment as their business needs change:

- ► **OS/400 support of selected AS/400 and iSeries models**: OS/400 V5R2 is the final release to support AS/400e Models 150, 600, 620, 640, 650, S10, S20, S30, S40, and SB1. IBM plans for i5/OS V5R3 to be the final release to be supported on AS/400e Models 170, 250, 720, 730, and 740.

  The next release of OS/400 is planned to be supported on Models 270, 520, 550, 570, 800, 810, 820, 825, 830, 840, 870, 890, SB2, and SB3.

▶ **Systems Product Division (SPD) I/O**: IBM plans for i5/OS V5R3 to be the final release to support the attachment of SPD towers or SPD Migration towers. Clients must complete the migration or conversion of I/O attached to their iSeries Model 820, 830, or 840 via SPD towers or migration towers before upgrading beyond i5/OS V5R3.

Any SPD I/O cards in these towers or older I/O devices which can only be attached to SPD cards must be replaced by newer I/O. SPD-attached #5065 or #5066 PCI I/O towers must be converted to the #5074 or #5079 PCI HSL-attached Expansion Towers or replaced with newer generation #5094 or #5294 PCI-X towers. The PCI-X towers offer a higher speed HSL connection and the ability to support 15k rpm disk drives.

The following functions provided by SPD cards do not have equivalent function PCI cards:

– ASCII Adapter

– V.25 Autocall cable

– Select standby mode

– X.21 switched WAN dial-up or shorthold mode WAN

– Asynchronous communication speeds of less than 300 bps

– Data Rate Select signal on the EIA 232/V.24 interface: This function is used by some older 2400 bps modems to reduce the speed to 1200 bps.

– Link Problem Determination Aids (LPDA®)-1: This is a diagnostic function supported by some modems.

– V.54 local and remote loopback: This is a diagnostics functions supported by some modems.

PCI adapters also do not support X.21 switched WAN dial-up or shorthold mode WAN.

▶ **iSeries Access**: IBM plans to remove the support of the Windows 98 and Windows Me operating systems from the iSeries Access for Windows client. iSeries Access for Windows on Windows 98 and Me continues to be supported in OS/400 V5R2. In subsequent releases, iSeries Access for Windows will not install on the Windows 95, 98, or Me operating systems.

The removal of Windows 98 and Windows Me applies to all of the functions shipped with iSeries Access for Windows, including EZ-Setup, iSeries Navigator, Management Central, and Operations Console. iSeries Access for Windows will continue to be supported on the Windows NT® 4.0, Windows 2000, and Windows XP operating systems. In addition, migration from Client Access for Windows 95 or NT and Client Access Enhanced for Windows 3.1 to iSeries Access for Windows will continue to be supported in OS/400 V5R2 but will be removed in subsequent releases.

- **iSeries Support for Windows Network Neighborhood (iSeries NetServer™)**: IBM plans to remove the support of the Windows 98 and Windows Me operating systems from iSeries NetServer. Windows 98 and Me continue to be supported in OS/400 V5R2, but not in subsequent releases. iSeries NetServer will continue to support the Windows NT 4.0, Windows 2000, Windows XP, and Linux (running Samba) operating systems.

- **IBM HTTP Server**: OS/400 V5R2 is the final release to support HTTP Server (original). With IBM i5/OS, IBM HTTP Server (powered by Apache) includes the generally available version of the Apache Software Foundation's Apache 2.0 Web server. For more information, including migrating HTTP Server (original) configurations to HTTP Server (powered by Apache), see:

  http://www.ibm.com/eserver/iseries/software/http

- **XML Parsers**: OS/400 V5R2 is the final release to ship the XML for C++ and procedural parsers as part of OS/400. These parsers are service programs QXML4C310 and QXML4PR310 in library QSYS. Comparable XML for C++ and procedural parsers are now available via LPO 5733-XT1 (XML Toolkit for iSeries).

- **Open Class® Library**: OS/400 V5R2 is the final release to ship the Open Class Library, part of WebSphere Development Studio for iSeries and OS/400. For documentation to assist in migrating from IBM Open Class to the C++ Standard Library, see:

  http://www.ibm.com/servers/eserver/iseries/support/planning/nav.html

  Suggested replacements: All applications that use the Open Class Headers and Service Programs need to be refreshed using the C++ Standard Library provided with 5722-WDS and 5722-SS1. When discontinued, IBM Open Class Headers shipped in library QSYSINC with a descriptive text of "IOC HEADER" and the IBM Open Class Service Programs, QYPPOC370 and QYPPOC510 are no longer shipped in library QSYS with OS/400.

  For assistance in migration from IBM Open Class to the C++ Standard Library, see:

  http://www.ibm.com/servers/eserver/iseries/support/planning/pdf/iocmigrwp.pdf

- **Distributed Computing Environment (DCE)**: OS/400 V5R2 is the final release to support DCE Base Services for AS/400 (5769-DC1) and DCE Data Encryption Standard Library Routines for AS/400 (5769-DC3).

  For a suggested replacement, we recommend that our clients build their distributed applications using the functions provided by MQSeries®, IBM Toolbox for Java, WebSphere Application Server, or Lotus Domino technologies for iSeries.

- **Ultimedia System Facility (USF)**: OS/400 V5R2 is the final release for the USF application programming interfaces (APIs) to be shipped or supported with iSeries Access for Windows.

  For suggested replacements, clients have chosen to develop multimedia applications using more standard means such as DB2 UDB for iSeries binary large object (BLOB) support or the integrated file system (IFS).

- **Access Class Libraries**: OS/400 V5R2 is the final release to support the Access Class Libraries in OS/400. The Access Class Libraries are C++ classes that provide access to OS/400 resources, including DB2 UDB for iSeries.

  For suggested replacements, IBM recommends that current users of the Access Class Libraries use the appropriate C language APIs to access OS/400 resources. Current users should also consider using Java and the corresponding IBM Toolbox for Java interfaces to access OS/400 resources.

- **OS/400 Language Feature - English Uppercase**: IBM plans for i5/OS V5R3 to be the last release to support the English Uppercase language features (#2950 and #5550) for OS/400 (5722-SS1).

- **S/36 and S/38 migration**: OS/400 V5R2 is the final release to support:
  - OS/400 Option 4: S/36 and S/38 Migration
  - OS/400 Option 11: S/36 Migration Assistant
  - RSTS36FLR command within OS/400 used to restore S/36 folders

- **Application Development Manager and Application Dictionary Services**: There were two priced features in WebSphere Development Studio for iSeries:
  - Application Development Manager (ADM)
  - Application Dictionary Services (ADS)

  IBM discontinued marketing these products in i5/OS V5R3. This should not be construed as a lack of interest in source and library control, and impact analysis. The importance of source-control management and impact analysis has increased greatly in the last several years since the introduction of the Integrated Language Environment® (ILE) to promote modular programming and to encourage code reuse. In recent years, the introduction of Web and Java development and the IBM WebFacing Tool have dramatically increased the number of Java components to manage.

  For more information, see the white paper *A Case for Source Control Management* on the Web at:

  `http://www.ibm.com/servers/enable/tools/pdf/scmpaper.pdf`

- **Cryptographic Support for AS/400** (5722-CR1): IBM plans to support this product for one release beyond i5/OS V5R3, after which it will be discontinued. Clients looking for a cryptographic API set should consider the following alternatives:

  - IBM i5/OS Cryptographic Services API

  - Common Cryptographic Architecture (CCA) API for the iSeries Cryptographic Coprocessor feature

  - Java Cryptography Extension (JCE)

Withdrawn products

When products and features are withdrawn from IBM marketing, they are removed from this Handbook. You can find information about earlier iSeries and AS/400e products and features by referencing the *IBM @server i5, iSeries, and AS/400e System Builder*, SG24-2155, or searching for a legacy editions of the *IBM @server i5 and iSeries System Handbook*, GA19-5486, which are available on the following Web site:

`http://publib.boulder.ibm.com/pubs/html/as400/online/chgfrm.htm`

Refer to "Products and features no longer marketed by IBM" on page 755 for a list of the recommended replacements for many withdrawn features and products.

Features and devices not supported with i5/OS V5R3

iSeries Models 600, 620, 640, 650, 650, S10, S20, S30, S40, SB1, 150, and earlier generations of AS/400 systems are not supported with i5/OS V5R3. Also the following features are not supported with IBM i5/OS V5R3:

- #2811 PCI 25 Mbps UTP ATM
- #2812 PCI 45 Mbps Coax T3/DS3 ATM
- #2815 PCI 155 Mbps UTP OC3 ATM
- #2816 PCI 155 Mbps MMF ATM
- #2817 PCI 155 Mbps MMF ATM IOA
- #2818 PCU 155 Mbps SMF OC3 ATM
- #2819 PCI 34 Mbps Coax E3 ATM
- #4815 PCI ATM 155 Mbps UTP OC3
- #4816 PCI ATM 155 Mbps MMF
- #4818 PCI ATM 155 Mbps SMF OC3
- #2761 and #4761 PCI Integrated Analog Modem

The other input/output adapters (IOAs) and controllers, which are supported with OS/400 V5R2 on Models 800, 810, 825, 870, and 890, are supported with i5/OS V5R3 on the Model 520, 550 and 570.

Some hardware features are supported with i5/OS V5R3 but are not supported on all iSeries models. Refer to the Planning Web site for more information:

http://www.ibm.com/servers/eserver/iseries/support/planning/v5r3hardware.html

Features and devices not supported with OS/400 V5R2

AS/400 Models 4xx and 5xx are not supported with OS/400 V5R2 or later. Also the following features are not supported with V5R2 or later:

► #2750/#4750 PCI ISDN BRI U IOA
► #2751/#4751 ISDN adapters
► #4800 PCI Cryptographic Processor
► #6385/#6485 QIC-5010 13 GB ¼-inch Cartridge Tape

The #2761/#4761 PCI Integrated Analog Modem supports the fax function only with OS/400 V5R2. The IPX protocol is not supported with V5R2. The NetVista™ Thin Clients device is not supported with V5R2.

> **Note:** Some hardware features are supported with OS/400 V5R2, but are not supported on all iSeries models.

For a list of features, devices, and products not supported or marketed by IBM, refer to "Products and features no longer marketed by IBM" on page 755, and "Features and devices not supported with OS/400 V5R1" on page 754.

Refer to the Planning Web sites for more information:

http://www.ibm.com/servers/eserver/iseries/support/planning/v5r2hardware.html
http://www.ibm.com/servers/eserver/iseries/support/planning/v5r1hardware.html
http://www.ibm.com/servers/eserver/iseries/support/planning/v4r5hardware.html

Hardware

Hardware

5

Summary of today's iSeries

The tables in this chapter summarize the resource capabilities and performance characteristics of all processors in the current product line of iSeries servers. Processor and performance characteristics are included, along with the maximum capacities for main storage, disk, local area network (LAN), communication lines, workstations, tape devices, CD devices, and other input/output (I/O) components.

The following graphic depicts the commercial processing workload (CPW) ratings of each of the currently marketed @server i5 servers. The characteristics of each of these @server i5 processors are summarized in this chapter.

595 32/64-way
595 16/32-way
595 8/16-way

Unprecedented Scalability

570 13/16-way
570 9/12-way
570 5/8-way
570 2/4-way
570 1/2-way

Scalable Building Block

550 1/4-way

Flexible Midrange

520 2-way
520 1-way
520 1-way
520 1-way
520 Express
520 Express

POWER5 - Entry

CPW

0   20000   40000   60000   80000   100000   120000   140000   160000   180000

↑ Upgrade paths

Note: 64-way measured as two 32-way partitions

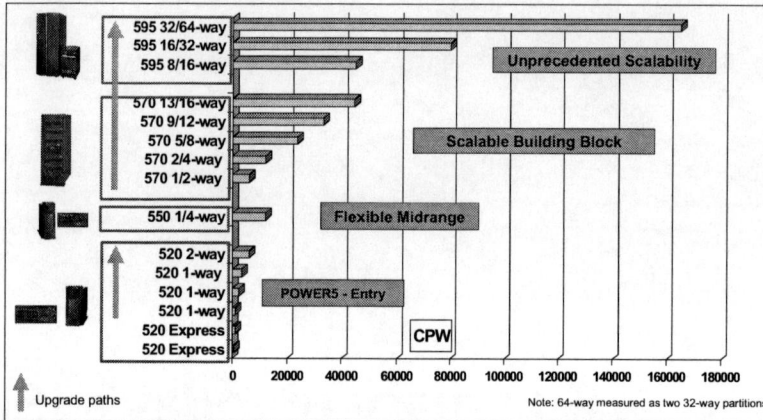

The capacities of iSeries and AS/400e processors that are no longer marketed are summarized in Chapter 34, "Summary of earlier AS/400, AS/400e, and iSeries models" on page 711, and in the *IBM @server i5, iSeries, and AS/400e System Builder*, SG24-2155. You can find information about i5/OS V5R3 operating system limits, such as the maximum members in a database file, maximum objects in a library, and jobs on the system, in the iSeries Information Center at:

http://www.ibm.com/eserver/iseries/infocenter

Under Systems Management, select the **Availability** topic, and then click **OS/400 Maximum Capacities**.

You can find information about OS/400 V5R2 operating system limits in *OS/400 Maximum Capacities V5R2*, REDP-0204.

Note: In the following tables, the values in the columns with the darker shaded heading represent the base configuration of the system. The capacities shown may require prerequisites. Some combinations of features are not valid.

Table 1: Summary of the eServer i5 Model 520

The following table provides the Model 520 system minimum and maximum capacities.

	Model 520					
Processor feature	**#8950**	**#8951**	**#8952**	**#8953**	**#8954**	**#8955**
Server feature[9]	**#0900**	**#0901**	**#0902**	**#0903**	**#0904**	**#0905**
Relative system						
Processor CPW	500	1000	1000	2400	3300	6000
Mail and Calendar Users [2a]	---	2300	2300	5500	7300	13300
5250 CPW [5]						
Value[6a]	30	60	-	-	-	-
Express[6a]	-	60	-	-	-	-
Standard[6a]	-	-	0	0	0	0
Enterprise[6a]	-	-	1000	2400	3300	6000
High Availability[6a]	-	-	1000	2400	3300	6000
Number/type/ speed of processor	1/POWER5/ 1.5 GHz	1/POWER5/ 1.5 GHz	1/POWER5/ 1.5 GHz	1/POWER5/ 1.5 GHz	1/POWER5/ 1.65 GHz	2/POWER5/ 1.65 GHz
L2 Cache (MB)	1.88	1.88	1.88	1.88	1.88	1.88
L3 Cache (MB)	0	0	0	0	36	36
Main storage (GB min/max)	0.5/32	0.5/32	1/32	1/32	1/32	1/32
Main storage DIMMs (minimum/maximum)	8	8	8	8	8	8
Logical partitions (LPAR)	2	4	4	10	10	20
Minimum i5/OS level	V5R3	V5R3	V5R3	V5R3	V5R3	V5R3
Software group[6a]	P05	P10	P10	P10	P20	P20

Numbers are for all 520 processor features	Base system	System maximum
Disk storage (GB)		
Integrated minimum	35.16 / 70.2	-
Integrated maximum	564.48	19615.68
External maximum[7]	-	18929.44
Total maximum	19000	19000
DASD arms maximum	8	278
Internal arms	8	278
External LUNs	-	277
Physical packaging		
Rack design - EIA units	4	4
External HSL-2/RIO-2 ports	2	2
External HSL-2/RIO-2 loops	1	1
PCI/PCI-X Expansion Tower	-	6
External xSeries Servers	8	8
PCI card slots[10]	6	90
Diskette (8 or 5 ¼-inch)	0	0
Communication lines[3]	8	192
LAN ports (includes embedded)	5	36
Integrated xSeries Servers	-	18
Twinaxial workstation controllers	3	48
Twinaxial workstations	120	1920
Internal CD/DVD/tape[4]	2	12
External tape/optical/CD/DVD	-	36
Cryptographic coprocessor	-	8
Cryptographic accelerator	-	8

Table 2: Summary of the eServer i5 Model 550

The following table provides the Model 550 system minimum and maximum capacities.

	Model 550
Processor feature	**#8958**
Server feature[9]	**#0915**
Relative system performance[1, 2]	
Processor CPW	3300/12000
Mail and Calendar Users [2a]	7300/26600
5250 CPW [5]	
Standard[6b]	0
Enterprise[6b]	Maximum
Solution[6b]	
Solution Edition for PeopleSoft Enterprise EO[6b]	
Domino[6b]	
Number/type/speed of processor	1/4/POWER5/1.65 GHz
L2 Cache (MB)	1.9
L3 Cache (MB)	36
Main storage (GB min/max)	2/64
Main storage DIMMs (minimum/maximum)	4/16
LPAR	40
Minimum i5/OS level	V5R3
Software group[6b]	P20

Numbers are for all 550 processor features	Base system	System maximum
Disk storage (GB)		
Integrated minimum	35.16	35.16
Integrated maximum	564.48	38102.4
External maximum[7]	-	-
Total maximum	-	-
DASD arms maximum		
Internal arms	8	548
External LUNs	-	547
Physical packaging		
Rack design - EIA units	4	4
External HSL-2/RIO-2 ports	2	4
External HSL-2/RIO-2 loops	1	2
PCI/PCI-X Expansion Tower	6	12
External xSeries Servers	8	16
PCI card slots[10]	5	172
Diskette (8 or 5 ¼-inch)	-	-
Communication lines[3]		320
LAN ports (includes embedded)	5	96
Integrated xSeries Servers	1	36
Twinaxial workstation controllers	2	133
Twinaxial workstations	80	5320
Internal CD/DVD/tape[4]	2	26
External tape/optical/CD/DVD (LPAR)		18 (36)
Cryptographic coprocessor		8
Cryptographic accelerator		4

Table 2a: Summary of the eServer i5 Model 550 On Demand features

The following table summarizes the On Demand feature codes for the Model 550. Features included with each Model 550 (base features) are shaded in gray.

| Model 550 1/4-way | | | | | Processor activations | | | | Enterprise Enablement (5250 OLTP) | | |
| | | | | | On Demand | | | | | | |
Server feature	Edition feature	Edition type	Base i5/OS Licenses (5722-SS1)	#8450 Base Processors	CoD purchased	On/Off CoD Enablement 360 days	On/Off CoD (Billing) 1 day	Reserve CoD (Prepaid) 90 days	#9286 Base 5250	Additional 5250 (per processor)	100% CPU (initial order only)
Standard Edition											
#0915	#7462		1	2	#7871	#7930	#7931	#7934	N/A	N/A	N/A
Enterprise Edition											
#0915	#7463		1	2	#7871	#7930	#7931	#7934	1	#7576	N/A
Domino Edition											
#0915	#7462		2	2	#7871	#7930	#7931	#7934	N/A	N/A	N/A
Solution Edition											
#0915	#7558		1	2	#7871	#7930	#7931	#7934	1 x #9286	#7576	N/A

Table 3: Summary of the eServer i5 Model 570 (Part 1)

The following table provides the Model 570 system minimum and maximum capacities.

	Model 570	
Processor feature	#8961	#8961 (x2)
Server feature	#0919	#0920
Relative system performance[1, 2]		
Processor CPW	3300/6000	6350/12000
Mail and Calendar Users [2a]	7300/13300	14100/26600
5250 CPW [5]		
Standard[6c]	0	0
Enterprise[6c]	Maximum	Maximum
Number/type/speed of processor	0/2/POWER5/1.65 GHz	2/4/POWER5/1.65 GHz
L2 Cache (MB per processor)	1.88	1.88
L3 Cache (MB per processor)	36	36
Main storage (GB minimum/maximum)	2/65	2/128
Main storage DIMMs (minimum/maximum)	4/8	8/16
LPAR	10/20	20/40
Minimum i5/OS level [8]	V5R3	V5R3
Software group [6c]	P30	P30
Disk storage (GB)		
Integrated minimum	35.16	35.16
Integrated maximum	19474.56	38525.76
External maximum [7]	19439.40	38490.60
Total maximum	19474.56	38525.76
DASD arms maximum	276	546
Internal arms	276	546
External LUNs	275	545
Physical packaging		
Rack design - EIA units	4	4
External HSL-2/RIO-2 ports	2	4
External HSL-2/RIO-2 loops	1	2
PCI/PCI-X Expansion Tower	6	12
External xSeries Servers (IXA)	8	16
PCI card slots [10]	90	173
Diskette (8 or 5 ¼-inch)	0	0
Communication lines [3]	278	320
LAN ports (includes embedded)	71	96
Integrated xSeries Servers	19	36
Twinaxial workstation controllers	69	133

	Model 570	
Processor feature	**#8961**	**#8961 (x2)**
Server feature	**#0919**	**#0920**
Twinaxial workstations	2760	5360
Internal DVD-ROM/DVD-RAM [4]	1	1
Internal CD-ROM/Tape	0	0
Feature I/O Tower CD-ROM/Tape	12	24
External tape (LPAR)	18 (36)	18 (36)
External optical/CD/DVD (LPAR)	18 (36)	18 (36)
Cryptographic coprocessor	8	8
Cryptographic accelerator (combined system partition maximum)	4 (8)	4 (8)

Table 4: Summary of the eServer i5 Model 570 (Part 2)

	Model 570					
Processor feature	**#8971**	**#8971**	**#8971**	**#8971**	**#8971**	**#8971**
Server feature	**#0930**	**#0921**	**#0922**	**#0924**	**#0926**	**#0928**
Relative system performance[1, 5a]						
Processor CPW	3300/ 6000	6350/ 12000	15200/ 23650	25500/ 33400	36300/ 44700	6350/ 44700
Mail and Calendar Users [9]	7300/ 13300	14100/ 26600	33600/ 52500	57300 77000	83600/ 102000	14100/ 102000
5250 CPW [5]						
Standard	0	0	0	0	0	
Enterprise	Maximum	Maximum	Maximum	Maximum	Maximum	
High Availability	Maximum	Maximum	Maximum	Maximum	Maximum	
Capacity BackUp						Maximum
Number/type/speed of processor	1/2/ POWER5/ 1.65 GHz	2/4/ POWER5/ 1.65 GHz	5/8/ POWER5/ 1.65 GHz	9/12/ POWER5/ 1.65 GHz	13/16/ POWER5/ 1.65 GHz	2/16/ POWER5/ 1.65 GHz
L2 Cache (MB)/chip	1.88	1.88	1.88	1.88	1.88	1.88
L3 Cache (MB)/processor card	36	36	36	36	36	36
Main storage (GB minimum/maximum)	2/64	4/128	8/256	12/384	16/512	16/512

	Model 570					
Processor feature	#8971	#8971	#8971	#8971	#8971	#8971
Server feature	#0930	#0921	#0922	#0924	#0926	#0928
Main storage DIMMs (minimum/maximum)	4/8	8/16	16/32	24/48	32/64	32/64
LPAR	10/20	20/40	50/80	90/120	120/160	20/160
Minimum i5/OS level [8]	i5/OS V5R3	i5/OS V5R3	i5/OS V5R3	i5/OS V5R3	i5/OS V5R3	i5/OS V5R3
Software group [6c]	P30	P30	P40	P40	P40	P30
Disk storage (GB)						
Integrated minimum	35.16	35.16	35.16	35.16	35.16	35.16
Integrated maximum	19474.56	38525.76	5800.32	77474.88	96949.44	96949.44
External maximum [7]	19439.40	38490.60	57929.76	77404.32	96878.88	96878.88
Total maximum	19474.56	38525.76	5800.32	77474.88	96949.44	96949.44
DASD arms maximum	276	546	822	1098	1374	1374
Internal arms	276	546	822	1098	1374	1374
External LUNs	275	545	821	1097	1373	1373
Physical packaging						
Rack design - EIA units	4	4	8	12	16	16
External HSL-2/RIO-2 ports	2	4	8	12	16	16
External HSL-2/RIO-2 loops	1	2	4	6	8	8
PCI/PCI-X Expansion Tower	6	12	18	24	30	30
External xSeries Servers (IXA)	8	16	32	48	57	57
PCI card slots [12]	90	173	266	353	443	443
Diskette drive (8-inch or 5 ¼- inch)	0	0	0	0	0	0
Communication lines [3]	278	320	480	480	480	480

	Model 570					
Processor feature	#8971	#8971 x 2	#8971 x 4	#8971 x 6	#8971 x8	#8971
Server feature	#0930	#0921	#0922	#0924	#0926	#0928
Relative system						
Processor CPW	3300/6000	6350/ 12000	15200/ 2350050	25500/ 33400	36300/ 44700	6350/ 44700
Mail and Calendar Users[2a]	14100/ 26600	14100/ 25900	33600/ 52500	57300/ 77000	83600/ 102000	14100/ 102000
5250 CPW [5]	6000	12000	12000/235	12000/4470	12000/44700	6350/44700
Standard[6c]	0	0	0	0	0	0
Enterprise[6c]	Maximum	Maximum	Maximum	Maximum	Maximum	-
High Availability[6c]	Maximum	Maximum	Maximum	Maximum	Maximum	-
Capacity BackUp[6c]	Maximum	-	-	-	-	Maximum
Number/type/speed of processor	1/2/ POWER5/ 1.65 GHz	2/4/ POWER5/ 1.65 GHz	5/8/ POWER5/ 1.65 GHz	9/12/ POWER5/ 1.65 GHz	13/16/ POWER5/ 1.65 GHz	2/16/ POWER5/ 1.65 GHz
L2 Cache (MB) per processor	1.88	1.88	1.88	1.88	1.88	1.88
L3 Cache (MB) per processor	36	36	36	36	36	36
Main storage (GB minimum/maximum)	2/64	4/128	8/256	12/384	16/512	16/512
Main storage DIMMs (minimum/maximum)	4/8	8/16	16/32	24/48	32/64	32/64
Logical partitions (LPAR)	10/20	20/40	50/80	90/120	120/160	20/160
Minimum i5/OS level [8]	V5R3	V5R3	V5R3	V5R3	V5R3	V5R3
Software group [6c]	P30	P30	P40	P40	P40	P40
Disk storage (GB)						
Integrated minimum	35.16	35.16	35.16	35.16	35.16	35.16
Integrated maximum	19474.56	38525.76	5800.32	77474.88	96949.44	96949.44
External maximum [7]	19439.40	38490.60	57929.76	77404.32	96878.88	96878.88
Total maximum	19474.56	38525.76	5800.32	77474.88	96949.44	96949.44
DASD arms maximum	276	546	822	1098	1374	1374
Internal arms	276	546	822	1098	1374	1374
External LUNs	275	545	821	1097	1373	1373
Physical packaging						
Rack Design - EIA units	4	4	8	12	16	16
External HSL-2/ RIO-2 ports	2	4	8	12	16	16
External HSL-2/ RIO-2 loops	1	2	4	6	8	8

	Model 570					
Processor feature	**#8971**	**#8971 x 2**	**#8971 x 4**	**#8971 x 6**	**#8971 x8**	**#8971**
Server feature	**#0930**	**#0921**	**#0922**	**#0924**	**#0926**	**#0928**
PCI/PCI-X Expansion Tower	6	12	18	24	30	30
External xSeries Servers (IXA)	8	16	32	48	57	57
PCI card slots [10]	90	173	266	353	443	443
Diskette drive (8 inch or 5-¼ inch)	0	0	0	0	0	0
Communication lines [3]	278	320	480	480	480	480
LAN ports (includes embedded)	74	96	128	128	128	128
Integrated xSeries Servers	18	36	48	48	48	48
Twinaxial workstation controllers	69	134	204	274	334	334
Twinaxial workstations	2760	5360	7200	7200	7200	7200
Internal DVD-ROM/ DVD-RAM [4]	1	1	2	3	4	4
Internal CD-ROM/Tape	0	0	0	0	0	0
Feature I/O Tower CD-ROM/Tape	12	24	36	48	48	48
External tape (LPAR)	18 (36)	18 (36)	26 (48)	26 (48)	26 (48)	26 (48)
External optical/CD/DVD (LPAR)	18 (36)	18 (36)	26 (48)	26 (48)	26 (48)	26 (48)
Cryptographic coprocessor (combined system partition max)	8	8	8 (32)	8 (32)	8 (32)	8 (32)
Cryptographic accelerator (combined system partition max)	4 (8)	4 (8)	4 (8)	4 (8)	4 (8)	4 (8)

Table 4a: Summary of the eServer i5 Model 570 On Demand features

The following table summarizes the On Demand feature codes for the Model 570. Features included with each Model 570 (base features) are shaded in gray.

Model 570			i5/OS		Processor activations					Enterprise Enablement (5250 OLTP)		
						On Demand						
Server feature	Edition feature	n-way	Licenses per CPU 5722-SS1	Base Processors	Capacity Upgrade on Demand	on Demand Enablement 360 days	Billing (per CPU-day) 1 day	Reserve prepaid (per CPU-day) 90 days		Base	Additional CPU	All CPU (initial order only)
Standard Edition												
#0919	#7488	1/2	1	1 x #8452	#7897	#7951	#7952	#7956		N/A	N/A	N/A
#0920	#7469	2/4	2	2 x #8452								
#0930	#7490	1/2	1	1 x #8452								
#0921	#7494	2/4	1	2 x #8452								
#0922	#7471	5/8	4	5 x #8452								
#0924	#7473	9/12	4	9 x #8452								
#0926	#7475	13/16	4	13 x #8452								
Enterprise and High Availability Editions												
#0919	#7489	1/2	1	2 x #8452	#7897	#7951	#7952	#7956		Max	N/A	N/A
#0920	#7470	2/4	2	3 x #8452						Max		
#0930	#7491/ #7559	1/2	1	2 x #8452						2 x #9286	#7577	#7597
#0921	#7495/ #7560	2/4	1	3 x #8452						4 x #9286		
#0922	#7472/ #7561	5/8	4	6 x #8452						4 x #9286		

| Model 570 | | | i5/OS | Processor activations | | | | | Enterprise Enablement (5250 OLTP) | | |
| | | | | | | On Demand | | | | | |
Server feature	Edition feature	n-way	Licenses per CPU 5722-SS1	Base Processors	Capacity Upgrade on Demand	on Demand Enablement 360 days	Billing (per CPU-day) 1 day	Reserve prepaid (per CPU-day) 90 days	Base	Additional CPU	All CPU (initial order only)
Enterprise and High Availability Editions (cont.)											
#0924	#7474/ #7562	9/12	4	10 x #8452					4 x #9286		
#0926	#7476/ #7563	13/ 16	4	14 x #8452					4 x #9286		
Capacity Backup Edition											
#0928	#7570	2/16	2	2 x #8452	N/A	#7951	#7952	#7956	2 x #9286	Max	Max

Table 5: Summary of the eServer i5 Model 595

The Model 595 system minimum and maximum capacities are provided in the following table.

	Model 595			
Processor feature	#8981	#8981x2	#8981x4	#8981x2
Server feature	#0946	#0947	#0952	#0948
Relative system performance[1, 2]				
Processor CPW	24500/45500	46000/85000	86000/165000	46000/85000
Mail and Calendar Users [2a]	104000	194000	375000	
5250 CPW [5]				
Standard[6d]	0	0	0	0
Enterprise[6d]	Maximum	Maximum	Maximum	
High Availability[6d]	Maximum	Maximum	Maximum	-
Capacity BackUp[6]	-	-	-	Maximum
Number/type/speed of processor	8/16 /POWER5/ 1.65 GHz	16/32 /POWER5/ 1.65 GHz	32/64 /POWER5/ 1.65 GHz	32/POWER5/ 1.65 GHz
L2 Cache (MB per processor) MCM	1.88	1.88	1.88	1.88
L3 Cache (MB per processor) MCM	36	36	36	36
Main storage (GB minimum/maximum)[11]	8(16)/512	16(32)/1024	32(64)/2048	16(32)/1024
Main storage DIMMs (minimum/maximum)	4/16	4/32	4/64	4/32
Logical partitions (LPAR)	160	254	254	254
Minimum i5/OS level [8]	V5R3	V5R3	V5R3	V5R3
Software group [6d]	P50	P50	P560	P50
Disk storage (GB)				
Integrated minimum	70	70	70	70
Integrated maximum				
External maximum [7]	116736	194560	194560	194560
Total maximum	116736	194560	194560	194560
DASD arms maximum	1620	2700	2700	2700
Internal arms	1620	2700	2700	2700
External LUNs	1619	2699	2699	2699
Physical packaging				
Rack design - EIA units				
External HSL-2/RIO-2 ports	6	12	24	12
External HSL-2/RIO-2 loops	12	24	48	24

	Model 595			
Processor feature	#8981	#8981x2	#8981x4	#8981x2
Server feature	#0946	#0947	#0952	#0948
PCI/PCI-X Expansion Tower	36	59	59	60
External xSeries Servers (IXA)	48	57	57	57
PCI card slots [10]	504	840	840	840
Diskette (8 or 5 ¼-inch)	0	0	0	0
Communication lines [3]	600	600	600	600
LAN ports (includes embedded)	160	160	160	160
Integrated xSeries Servers	60	60	60	60
Twinaxial workstation controllers	180	180	180	180
Twinaxial workstations	7200	7200	7200	7200
Internal DVD-ROM/DVD-RAM [4]	2	2	2	2
Internal CD-ROM/Tape				
Feature I/O Tower CD-ROM/Tape	64	120	120	120
External tape				
External optical/CD/DVD				
Cryptographic coprocessor (combined system partition maximum)	8 (32)	8 (32)	8 (32)	9
Cryptographic accelerator (combined system partition maximum)	4 (16)	4 (16)	4 (16)	

Table 5a: Summary of the eServer i5 Model 595 Editions

	Model 595		
Processor feature	#0946	#0947	#0652
Server feature	#8981	#8981	#8981
Standard	#7496	#7498	#7984
Enterprise	#7497	#7499	#7985

Table 5b: Summary of the eServer i5 Model 595 On Demand features

The following table summarizes the On Demand feature codes for the Model 595. Features included with each Model 595 (base features) are shaded in gray.

Model 595			i5/OS		Base Processors	Processor activations				Enterprise Enablement (5250 OLTP)		
			Licenses per CPU			Capacity Upgrade on Demand	On Demand			Base	Additional CPU	All CPU (initial order only)
Server feature	Edition feature	n-way					on Demand Enablement	Billing (per CPU-day)	Reserve prepaid (per CPU-day)			
			5722-SS1				360 days	1 day	90 days			
Standard Edition												
#0946	#7496	8/16	4		8 x #8461	#7925	#7839	#7993	#7926	N/A	N/A	N/A
#0947	#7489	16/32	4		16 x #8461							
#0952	#7984	32/64	4		32 x #8461							
Enterprise Edition												
#0946	#7497	8/16	4		9 x #8461	#7925	#7839	#7993	#7926	4 x #9286	#7579	#7598
#0947	#7499	16/32	4		17 x #8461					4 x #9286		
#0952	#7985	32/64	4		33 x #8461					4 x #9286		

Notes for eServer i5 Models 520, 550, 570, and 595

Note 1	CPW is used to measure the performance of all iSeries and AS/400e processors announced from September 1996 onward. The CPW value is measured on maximum configurations. The type and number of disk devices, the number of workstation controllers, the amount of memory, the system model, other factors, and the application running determine what performance is achievable.
Note 2	Processor performance represents the relative performance (maximum capacity) of a processor feature running CPW in a client/server environment. Processor capacity is achievable when the commercial workload is not constrained by main storage and direct access storage device (DASD). Performance of the 5250 CPW represents the relative performance available to perform host-centric workloads. The amount of 5250 CPW capacity consumed reduces the available processor capacity by the same amount.
Note 2a	Mail and Calendar Users (MCU) is a relative performance measurement derived by performing mail and calendar functions using Domino and Notes clients. The MCU workload represents users on a Notes client who are reading, updating or deleting documents in an e-mail database. It also represents users who are performing lookups in the Domino directory and scheduling calendar appointments and invitations. Reported values reflect 70% processor utilization to allow for growth and peak loads in excess of client workload estimates.
Note 3	One line is used if #5544 System Console on Operations Console is used. One line might be used if #5546 System Console on 100 Mbps Token Ring or #5548 System Console on 100 Mbps Ethernet is selected and the #0367 Operations Console PCI Cable must be connected. The numbers include the ECS line.
Note 4	There must be one DVD-ROM or DVD-RAM per system. For Models 870 and 890, there must be one DVD-RAM or DVD-ROM in the #9094 Base PCI I/O Enclosure.
Note 5	5250 CPW (Interactive) is an approximate value that reflects the amount of Processor CPW that can be used for workloads performing 5250-based tasks. Remember that: ▶ The iSeries Enterprise Edition provides maximum 5250 CPW support (up to 100% of the capacity of the active processor CPW). ▶ The iSeries Standard Edition provides zero CPW for 5250 work. Limited 5250 CPW is available for a system administrator to use 5250 display device I/O to manage various aspects of the server. Multiple administrative jobs exceed this capability. ▶ A task submitted through a 5250 session (5250 device or 5250 emulation) that does display or printer I/O requires 5250 CPW. ▶ A task submitted through a 5250 session (5250 device or 5250 emulation) as a "batch" job is not considered 5250 OLTP work and does not require any 5250 CPW unless the task does display or printer I/O. ▶ Maximum 5250 CPW is equivalent to the Processor CPW for the active processor.

Note 6a **Model 520**	Software group is determined by the combination of processor feature and edition feature. Display the QPRCFEAT system value or DSPHDWRSC TYPE(*AHW) to display the processor feature code value. This value is also shown for the Capacity Card CCIN value when using SST to perform a Capacity Upgrade on Demand. This table provides a cross reference. For Model 520 2-way processors shipped prior to 10 December 2004 that have keyed products installed, update the server firmware to accept the lower P20 software tier. ▶ Apply PTF MH00199 on servers using i5/OS to apply the firmware. ▶ Apply SF222_075 on servers using HMC to apply the firmware. Order PTF MH00201 to receive a CD that can be applied via the HMC. Update HMC code to the latest V4R3 level before updating the server firmware. See the following Web site for the latest HMC updates: `http://techsupport.services.ibm.com/server/hmc/power5`

Processor	Server feature	Edition feature	Software group	Processor feature code or QPRCFEAT value
#8950	#0900	#7450 Value	P05	7450
#8951	#0901	#7392 Express	P05	7392
		#7394 Express	P05	7394
		#7451 Value	P10	7451
#8952	#0902	#7458 Standard	P10	7458
		#7459 Enterprise	P10	7459
		#7552 High Availability	P10	7459
#8953	#0903	#7452 Standard	P10	7452
		#7453 Enterprise	P10	7453
		#7553 High Availability	P10	7453
#8954	#0904	#7454 Standard	P20	7454
		#7455 Enterprise	P20	7455
		#7554 High Availability	P20	7455
#8955	#0905	#7456 Standard	P20	7456
		#7457 Enterprise	P20	7457
		#7555 High Availability	P20	7457

Note 6b Model 550	Software group is determined by the combination of processor feature and edition feature. Display the QPRCFEAT system value or DSPHDWRSC TYPE(*AHW) to display the processor feature code value. This value is also shown for the Capacity Card CCIN value when using SST to perform a Capacity Upgrade on Demand. This table provides a cross reference.				
	Processor	**Server feature**	**Edition feature**	**Software group**	**Processor feature code or QPRCFEAT value**
	#8958	#0915	#7462 Standard	P20	7462
			#7463 Enterprise	P20	7463
			#7530 Domino	P20	7530
			#7558 Solution	P20	7463
			#7531 Solution Edition for PeopleSoft Enterprise EO	P20	7463

Note 6c Model 570	Software group is determined by the combination of processor feature and edition feature. Display the QPRCFEAT system value or DSPHDWRSC TYPE(*AHW) to display the processor feature code value. This value is also shown for the Capacity Card CCIN value when using SST to perform a Capacity Upgrade on Demand. This table provides a cross reference.				
	Processor	**Server feature**	**Edition feature**	**Software group**	**Processor feature code or QPRCFEAT value**
	#8961	#0919	#7488 Standard	P30	7450
			#7489 Enterprise	P30	7451
	#8961	#0920	#7469 Standard	P30	7458
			#7470 Enterprise	P30	7459
	#8971	#0921	#7494 Standard	P30	7494
			#7495 Enterprise	P30	7495
			#7460 High Availability	P40	7495
	#8971	#0922	#7471 Standard	P40	7441
			#7472 Enterprise	P40	7442
			#7561 High Availability	P40	7472
	#8971	#0924	#7473 Standard	P40	7473
			#7474 Enterprise	P40	7474
			#7562 High Availability	P40	7474

Note 6c Model 570 (cont.)	#8971	#0926	#7475 Standard	P40	7475
			#7476 Enterprise	P40	7476
			#7563 High Availability	P40	7476
	#8971	#0928	#7570 Capacity BackUp	P40	7570
	#8971	#0930	#7490 Standard	P30	7490
			#7491 Enterprise	P30	7491
			#7559 High Availability	P30	7491

Note 6d Model 595	Software group is determined by the combination of processor feature and edition feature. Display the QPRCFEAT system value or DSPHDWRSC TYPE(*AHW) to display the processor feature code value. This value is also shown for the Capacity Card CCIN value when using SST to perform a Capacity Upgrade on Demand. This table provides a cross reference.

Processor	Server feature	Edition feature	Software group	Processor feature code or QPRCFEAT value
#8981	#0946	#7496 Standard	P50	7496
		#7497 Enterprise	P50	7497
	#0947	#7498 Standard	P50	7489
		#7499 Enterprise	P50	7499
	#0952	#7984 Standard	P60	7984
		#7985 Enterprise	P60	7985

Note 7	External DASD capacity assumes 70.56 GB LUNs (logical unit numbers). External DASD cannot exceed the maximum system capacity or the maximum number of disk arms.
Note 8	i5/OS V5R3 with the (month) 2004 level of LIC and Cumulative PTF package C4nnn530. For the latest information, refer to Informational APAR II13365 on the Web at: http://www.ibm.com/support/us/
Note 9	The Server features used for iSeries for Domino specify the minimum amount of disk, memory, and Domino licenses required for an initial order.
Note 10	When a second HSL-2/RIO-2 loop is required, one PCI card slot is used for the HSL-2/RIO-2 adapter.
Note 11	One terabyte (TB) of memory can be ordered after 28 October 2004. Two TB are planned to be available in 2005.

Table 6: Summary of the iSeries Model 800

	Model 810			
Processor feature	**#2465**	**#2466**	**#2467**	**#2469**
Server feature	**#0868**	**#0866**	**#0867**	**#0869**
Relative system performance[1, 2]				
Processor CPW	750	1020	1470	2700
5250 CPW[5a]				
Standard[6d]	0	0	0	0
Enterprise[6d]	750	1020	1470	2700
High Availability[6d]	750	1020	1470	2700
Number/type/speed of processor	1/SStar/540 MHz	1/SStar/540 MHz	1/SStar/750 MHz	2/SStar/ 750 MHz
L2 Cache (MB) per processor	2	2	4	4
Main storage (MB minimum to maximum)	512 to 16384	512 to 16384	512 to 16384	512 to 16384
Main storage DIMMs (minimum/maximum)	1/8	1/8	1/8	2/16
Minimum operating system level[8b]	V5R2	V5R2	V5R2	V5R2
Software group[6a]	P10	P10	P10	P20

Numbers are for all 800 processor features	Base system	#7116 System Expansion	#5095/#0595 PCI-X Expansion	#5094 PCI-X Expansion Tower	Total system maximum
Disk storage (GB)					
Integrated minimum	17.5	17.5	17.5	17.5	
Integrated maximum	423.3	846.7	846.7	3175.2	4445
External maximum[7]	-	-	-	-	4375
Total maximum	-	-	-	-	4445
DASD arms maximum	6	12	12	45	63
Internal arms	6	12	12	45	63
External LUNs	-	-	-	-	62
Physical packaging					
External HSL ports	2	-	-	-	2
External HSL loops	1	-	-	-	1
PCI-X Expansion Tower	1	-	-	-	1
External xSeries Servers	3	-	-	-	3
Embedded IOP	1	-	-	-	1
PCI card slots	7	-	7	14	21
Maximum PCI IOA cards	6	-	5	11	17
Communication lines[3]	18	-	20	44	60
LAN ports	3	-	5	8	11
Integrated xSeries Servers[10a]	1	-	1	3	4
Twinaxial workstation	4	-	5	11	15
Twinaxial workstations	160	-	200	440	600
Internal CD/DVD/tape[4]	2	-	-	2	4
External tape	4	-	5	11	15
External optical/CD/DVD	4	-	5	11	15
Cryptographic coprocessor	4	-	3	4	4
Cryptographic accelerator	2	-	2	2	2

Table 7: Summary of the iSeries Model 810

	Model 810			
Processor feature	**#2465**	**#2466**	**#2467**	**#2469**
Server feature	**#0868**	**#0866**	**#0867**	**#0869**
Relative system performance[1, 2]				
Processor CPW	750	1020	1470	2700
5250 CPW[5a]				
Standard[6d]	0	0	0	0
Enterprise[6d]	750	1020	1470	2700
High Availability[6d]	750	1020	1470	2700
Number/type/speed of processor	1/SStar/540 MHz	1/SStar/540 MHz	1/SStar/750 MHz	2/SStar/ 750 MHz
L2 Cache (MB) per processor	2	2	4	4
Main storage (MB minimum to maximum)	512 to 16384	512 to 16384	512 to 16384	512 to 16384
Main storage DIMMs (minimum/maximum)	1/8	1/8	1/8	2/16
Minimum operating system level[8b]	V5R2	V5R2	V5R2	V5R2
Software group[6b]	P10	P10	P10	P20

The Model 810 iSeries for Domino system minimum and maximum capacities are provided in the following table.

	Model 810 iSeries for Domino		
Processor feature	**#2466**	**#2467**	**#2469**
Server feature[9c]	**#0769**	**#0770**	**#0771**
Relative system performance[1, 2]			
Processor CPW	1020	1470	2700
Mail and Calendar Users (MCU)[2a]	3100	4200	7900
5250 CPW[5a]			
Domino[6d]	0	0	0
Number/type/speed of processor	1/SStar/540 MHz	1/SStar/750 MHz	2/SStar/750 MHz
L2 Cache (MB) per processor	2	4	4
Main storage (GB minimum to maximum)[9b]	1.5 to 16	3.5 to 16	5.5 to 16
Main storage DIMMs (maximum)	8	8	16
Minimum operating system level[8b]	V5R2	V5R2	V5R2
Software group[6d]	P10	P10	P20

Numbers are for all 810 processor features	Base system	#7116 System Expansion Unit	#5095/#0595 PCI-X Expansion Tower	#5094 PCI-X Expansion Tower	Total system maximum
Disk storage (GB)					
Integrated minimum	17.5	17.5	17.5	17.5	
Integrated maximum	423.3	846.7	846.7	3172.5	13971
External maximum[7]	-	-	-	-	13901
Total maximum	-	-	-	-	13971
DASD arms maximum	6	12	12	45	198
Internal arms	6	12	12	45	198
External LUNs	-	-	-	-	197
Physical packaging					
External HSL ports	2	-	-	-	-
External HSL loops	1	-	-	-	1
PCI/PCI-X Expansion Tower	4	-	-	-	4
External xSeries Servers	7	-	-	-	7
Embedded IOP	1	-	-	1	5
PCI card slots	7	-	7	14	63
Maximum PCI IOA cards	6	-	5	11	50
Communication lines[3]	18	-	20	44	192
LAN ports	3	-	5	11	36
Integrated xSeries Servers	1	-	1	3	13
Twinaxial workstation controllers	4	-	5	11	48
Twinaxial workstations	160	-	200	440	1920
Internal CD/DVD/tape[4]	2	-	-	2	10
External tape	4	-	5	11	18
External optical/CD/DVD	4	-	5	11	18
Cryptographic coprocessor	4	-	3	8	8
Cryptographic accelerator	2	-	2	2	2

Table 8: Summary of the iSeries Model 825

The Model 825 system minimum and maximum capacities are provided in the following table.

	Model 825			
Processor feature	**#2473**			**#2495**
Server feature[7]	**#0873**	-	-	**#0890**
Server feature for Domino[9c]	-	**#0772**	**#0773**	-
Relative system performance[1, 2]				
Processor CPW	3600/6600	-	-	1250/6600
Mail and Calendar Users (MCU)[2a]	-	11600	17400	-
5250 CPW[5b]				
Standard and Domino[6d]	-	0	0	-
Enterprise[6d]	Maximum	-	-	-
High Availability[6d]	Maximum	-	-	-
Capacity Backup[6d]	-	-	-	Maximum
Number/type/speed of processor	3/6/POWER4/ 1.1 GHz	4/POWER4/ 1.1 GHz	6/POWER4 1.1 GHz	1/6/POWER4/ 1.1 GHz
L3 Cache (MB per processor)	16	16	16	16
L2 Cache (MB per processor)	0.72	0.72	0.72	0.72
Main storage (GB minimum to maximum)[9b]	2 to 48	6 to 48	12 to 48	2 to 48
Main storage DIMMs (minimum/maximum)	8/24	8/24	8/24	8/24
Minimum operating system level[8b]	V5R2	V5R2	V5R2	V5R2
Software group[6c]	P30	P30	P30	P30

Numbers are for all 825 processor features	Base system	#5095/#0595 PCI-X Expansion Tower	#5094 PCI-X Expansion Tower	Total maximum
Disk storage (GB)[9b]				
Integrated minimum	17.5	-	-	17.5
Integrated maximum	1058.4	846.7	3175.2	58216
External maximum[7]	-	-	-	58145
Total maximum	-	-	-	58216
DASD arms maximum				
Internal arms	15	12	45	825
External LUNs	-	-	-	824
Physical packaging				
External HSL-2 ports	6	-	-	6
External HSL-2 loops	3	-	-	3
PCI Expansion Towers	16	-	-	16
PCI-X Expansion Towers	18	-	-	18
External xSeries Servers	18	-	-	18
Embedded IOP	1	-	1	19
Embedded IOA	1	-	-	1
PCI card slots	10	7	14	262
Maximum PCI IOA cards	8	5	11	205
Communication lines[3a]	30	20	44	320
LAN ports	6	5	11	96
Integrated xSeries Servers	1	1	3	36
Twinaxial workstation controllers	5	5	11	135
Twinaxial workstations	200	200	440	5400
Internal CD-ROM/DVD-RAM/tape[4]	2	-	2	18
External tape/optical/CD/DVD	5	5	11	18
Cryptographic coprocessor	5	3	8	8
Cryptographic accelerator	4	4	4	4

The following table summarizes the On Demand feature codes for the Model 825. Features included with each Model 825 (base features) are shaded in gray.

Model 825			i5/OS	Processor activations				
						On Demand		
Server feature	Edition feature	n-way	Licenses per CPU / 5722-SS1	Base Processors	Capacity Upgrade on Demand	on Demand Enablement / 360 days	Billing (per CPU-day) / 1 day	Reserve prepaid (per CPU-day) / 90 days
Standard Edition								
825	#7416	3/6	3	3	#1609	#1773	#1782	#1682
Enterprise Edition								
825	#7418	3/6	3	3	#1609	#1773	#1783	#1683
High Availability Edition								
#0873	#7434	3/6	3	3	#1609	#1773	#1783	#1683
Capacity Backup Edition								
#0890	#7439	1/6	3	3	N/A	#1779	#1797	#1697

Table 9: Summary of the iSeries Model 870

The Model 870 system minimum and maximum capacities are provided in the following table.

	Model 870		
Processor feature	**#2486**	**#2489**	**#2496**
Server feature	**#0886**	**#0889**	**#0891**

Relative system performance[1, 2]
  Processor CPW
  5250 CPW[5c]
  Standard[6f]
  Enterprise[6f]
  High Availability[6f]
  Capacity BackUp[6f]
	
	11500/20000
	--
	0
	Maximum
	Maximum
	--
		
		7700/11500
		
		0
		Maximum
		Maximum
		--
			
			3200/20000
			--
			0
			Maximum
			Maximum
			Maximum

Number/type/speed of processor	8/16/POWER4/ 1.3 GHz	5/8/POWER4/ 1.3 GHz	2/16/POWER4/ 1.3 GHz
L2 and L3 Cache (MB/processor)	16.72	16.72	16.72
Main storage (GB minimum to maximum)	8 to 128	8 to 64	8 to 128
Main storage cards (minimum/maximum)	2/4	2/2	2/4
Minimum operating system level[8b]	V5R2	V5R2	V5R2
Software group[6d]	P40	P40	P40

Numbers are for all 870 processor features	#9094 Base Tower	#5095/#0595 PCI-X Expansion Tower	#5094 PCI-X Expansion Tower	Total system maximum
Disk storage (GB)				
Integrated minimum	17.5	17.5	17.5	
Integrated maximum	3175.2	846.7	3175.2	144446
External maximum[7]	-	-	-	144375
Total maximum	-	-	-	144446
DASD arms maximum				
Internal arms	45	12	45	2047
External LUNs	-	-	-	2046
Physical packaging				
External HSL/HSL-2 ports	-/16	-	-	-/16
External HSL/HSL-2 loops	-/8	-	-	-/8
PCI/PCI-X Expansion Towers	47	-	-	47
External xSeries Servers	60	-	-	60
Embedded IOP	-	-	-	-
Embedded IOA	-	-	-	-
PCI card slots	14	7	14	672
Maximum PCI IOA cards	11	5	11	528
Communication lines[3]	38	20	44	480
LAN ports	7	5	8	128
Integrated xSeries Servers	2	1	3	48
Twinaxial workstation controllers	9	5	11	180
Twinaxial workstations	360	200	440	7200
Internal CD/DVD/tape[4a]	2	-	2	26
External tape/optical/CD/DVD	9	5	11	26
Cryptographic coprocessor	8	3	8	32
Cryptographic accelerator	4	4	4	8

The following table summarizes the On Demand feature codes for the Model 870. Features included with each Model 870 (base features) are shaded in gray.

Model 870			i5/OS	Processor activations				
						On Demand		
Server feature	Edition feature	n-way	Licenses per CPU	Base Processors	Capacity Upgrade on Demand	on Demand Enablement	Billing (per CPU-day)	Reserve prepaid (per CPU-day)
			5722-SS1			360 days	1 day	90 days
Standard Edition								
870	#7419	8/16	4	8	#1611	#1776	#1785	#1685
870	#7431	5/8		5	#1614	#1774	#1784	#1684
Enterprise Edition								
870	#7421	8/16	4	8	#1611	#1776	#1786	#1686
870	#7433	5/8		5	#1614	#1774	#1795	#1695
High Availability Edition								
#0889	#7435	5/8		5	#1614	#1774	#1795	#1695
#0886	#7436	8/16		8	#1611	#1776	#1786	#1686
Capacity Backup Edition								
#0891	#7440	2/16		2	N/A	#1780	#1798	#1698

Table 10: Summary of the iSeries Model 890

The following tables provide the Model 890 system minimum and maximum capacities.

	Model 890		
Processor feature	**#2497**	**#2498**	**#2499**
Server feature	**#0897**	**#0898**	**#0892**

Relative system performance[1, 2]
  Processor CPW
  5250 CPW[5c]
  Standard[6g]
  Enterprise[6g]
  High Availability[6g]
  Capacity Backup[6g]
	
	20000/29300
	
	0
	Maximum
	Maximum
	-
		
		29300/37400
		
		0
		Maximum
		Maximum
		-
			
			5600/37400
			
			0
			-
			-
			Maximum

Number/type/speed of processor	16/24/POWER4/ 1.3 GHz	24/32/POWER4/ 1.3 GHz	4/32/POWER4/ 1.3 GHz
L2 and L3 Cache (MB/processor)	16.72	16.72	16.72
Main storage (GB minimum to maximum)	8 to 192	16 to 256	16 to 256
Main storage cards (minimum/maximum)	2/6	4/8	4/8
Minimum operating system level[8b]	V5R2	V5R2	V5R2
Software group[6e]	P50	P50	P50

Processor feature	Model 890			
	#2487	**#2488**	**#0197**	**#0198**
Relative system performance[1, 2]				
Processor CPW	20200 - 29300	29300 - 37400	29300	37400
5250 CPW[5]			0	0
#1576 (Base)	120	120	-	-
#1577	240	240	-	-
#1578	560	560	-	-
#1579	1050	1050	-	-
#1581	2000	2000	-	-
#1583	4550	4550	-	-
#1585	10000	10000	-	-
#1587	16500	16500	-	-
#1588	20200	20200	-	-
#1591	-	37400	-	-
Number/type/speed of processor	16/24/POWER4/ 1.3 GHz	24/32/POWER4/ 1.3 GHz	24/POWER4/ 1.3 GHz	32/POWER4/ 1.3 GHz
L2 Cache (MB)	1.5 MB/chip set	1.5 MB/chip set	1.5 MB/chip set	1.5 MB/chip set
L2 and L3 Cache (MB/processor)	16.72	16.72	16.72	16.72
Main storage (GB minimum to maximum)	16 to 192	24 to 256	16 to 192	24 to 256
Main storage cards (minimum/maximum)	2/6	4/8	2/6	4/8
Minimum operating system level[8b]	V5R2	V5R2	V5R2	V5R2
Software group[6e]	P50 or P60	P50 or P60	P50	P50

Numbers are for all 890 processor features	#9094 Base Tower	#5095/#0595 PCI-X Expansion Tower	#5094 PCI-X Expansion Tower	Total maximum
Disk storage (GB)				
Integrated minimum	17.5	17.5	17.5	
Integrated maximum	3172.5	846.7	3175.2	144446
External maximum[7]	11290	3175	13548	144375
Total maximum	14462	4021	16720	144446
DASD arms maximum				
Internal arms	45	12	45	2047
External LUNs	160	127	192	2046
Physical packaging				
External HSL/HSL-2 ports	-/24	-	-	-/24
External HSL/HSL-2 loops	-/12	-	-	-/12
PCI/PCI-X Expansion Towers	47	-	-	47
External xSeries Servers	60	-	-	60
Embedded IOP	-	-	-	-
Embedded IOA	-	-	-	-
PCI card slots	14	7	14	672
Maximum PCI IOA cards	11	5	11	528
Communication lines[3]	38	20	44	480
LAN ports	7	5	8	128
Integrated xSeries Servers	2	1	3	48
Twinaxial workstation controllers	9	5	11	180
Twinaxial workstations	360	200	440	7200
Internal CD-ROM/DVD-RAM/tape[4a]	2	-	2	26
External tape/optical/CD/DVD	9	5	11	26
Cryptographic coprocessor	8	3	8	32
Cryptographic accelerator	4	4	4	8

The following table summarizes the On Demand feature codes for the Model 890. Features included with each Model 890 (base features) are shaded in gray.

Model 890			i5/OS	Processor activations				
				Base Processors	On Demand			
Server feature	Edition feature	n-way	Licenses per CPU		Capacity Upgrade on Demand	on Demand Enablement	Billing (per CPU-day)	Reserve prepaid (per CPU-day)
			5722-SS1			360 days	1 day	90 days
Standard Edition								
890	#7422	16/24		16	#1612	#1777	#1788	#1688
890	#7425	24/32		24	#1613	#1778	#1791	#1691
Enterprise Edition								
890	#7424	16/24		16	#1612	#1777	#1789	#1689
890	#7427	24/32		24	#1613	#1778	#1792	#1692
High Availability Edition								
#0897	#7437	16/24		16	#1612	#1777	#1789	#1689
#0898	#7438	24/32		24	#1613	#1778	#1792	#1692
Capacity Backup Edition								
#0892	#7441	4/32		4	N/A	#1781	#1799	#1699

Notes for iSeries Models 800, 810, 825, 870, and 890 overview

Note 1	CPW is used to measure the performance of all iSeries and AS/400e processors announced from September 1996 onward. The CPW value is measured on maximum configurations. The type and number of disk devices, the number of workstation controllers, the amount of memory, the system model, other factors, and the application running determine what performance is achievable.
Note 2	Processor performance represents the relative performance (maximum capacity) of a processor feature running CPW in a client/server environment. Processor capacity is achievable when the commercial workload is not constrained by main storage and direct access storage device (DASD). Performance of the 5250 CPW represents the relative performance available to perform host-centric workloads. The amount of in 5250 CPW capacity consumed reduces the available processor capacity by the same amount.
Note 2a	Mail and Calendar Users (MCU) is a relative performance measurement derived by performing mail and calendar functions using Domino and Notes clients. The MCU workload represents concurrent users on a Notes client who are reading, updating, or deleting documents in an e-mail database. It also represents users who are performing lookups in the Domino Directory, and scheduling calendar appointments and invitations. Reported values reflect 70% processor utilization to allow for growth and peak loads in excess of client workload estimates.
Note 3	One line is used if #5544 System Console on Operations Console is used. One line can be used if #5546 System Console on 100 Mbps Token Ring or #5548 System Console on 100 Mbps Ethernet is selected and the #0367 Operations Console PCI Cable is connected.
Note 3a	One line is used if #5544 System Console on Operations Console is used. One line can be used if #5548 System Console on 100 Mbps Ethernet is selected and the #0367 Operations Console PCI Cable is connected.
Note 4	There must be one DVD-ROM or DVD-RAM per system.
Note 4a	There must be one DVD-RAM or DVD-ROM in the #9094 Base PCI I/O Enclosure.
Note 5a Model 810	5250 CPW (Interactive) is an approximate value that reflects the amount of Processor CPW that can be used for workloads performing 5250-based tasks. Remember that: ▶ The iSeries Enterprise Edition provides maximum 5250 CPW support (up to 100% of the capacity of the active processor CPW). The iSeries Standard Edition provides zero CPW for 5250 work. ▶ Any task that uses a 5250 data stream is considered 5250 online transaction processing (OLTP) work and requires some amount of 5250 CPW to process no matter how the task was started. ▶ A task submitted through a 5250 session (5250 device or 5250 emulation) that does display or printer input/output (I/O) requires 5250 CPW. ▶ A task submitted through a 5250 session (5250 device or 5250 emulation) as a "batch" job is not considered 5250 OLTP work and does not require any 5250 CPW unless the task does display or printer I/O. ▶ Limited 5250 CPW is available with the Standard Edition for a system administrator to use 5250 display device I/O to manage various aspects of the server. Multiple administrative jobs exceed this capability.

Note 5b **Model** **825**	5250 CPW (Interactive) is an approximate value that reflects the amount of Processor CPW that can be used for workloads performing 5250-based tasks. Remember that: ▸ The iSeries Enterprise Edition provides maximum 5250 CPW support (up to 100% of the capacity of the active processor CPW). The iSeries Standard Edition provides limited CPW for 5250 work. ▸ Any task that uses a 5250 data stream is considered 5250 OLTP work and requires some amount of 5250 CPW to process no matter how the task was started. ▸ A task submitted through a 5250 session (5250 device or 5250 emulation) that does display or printer I/O requires 5250 CPW. ▸ A task submitted through a 5250 session (5250 device or 5250 emulation) as a "batch" job is not considered 5250 OLTP work and does not require any 5250 CPW unless the task does display or printer I/O. ▸ Limited 5250 CPW is available with the Standard Edition for a system administrator to use 5250 display device I/O to manage various aspects of the server. Multiple administrative jobs exceed this capability. ▸ Maximum 5250 CPW is equivalent to the processor CPW for the active processor.
Note 5c **Model** **870 and** **890**	5250 CPW (Interactive) is an approximate value that reflects the amount of Processor CPW that can be used for workloads performing 5250-based tasks. Remember that: ▸ The iSeries Enterprise Edition provides maximum 5250 CPW support (up to 100% of the capacity of the active processor CPW). The iSeries Standard Edition provides zero CPW for 5250 work. ▸ Any task that uses a 5250 data stream is considered 5250 OLTP work and requires some amount of 5250 CPW to process no matter how the task was started. ▸ A task submitted through a 5250 session (5250 device or 5250 emulation) that does display or printer I/O requires 5250 CPW. ▸ A task submitted through a 5250 session (5250 device or 5250 emulation) as a "batch" job is not considered 5250 OLTP work and does not require any 5250 CPW unless the task does display or printer I/O. ▸ Limited 5250 CPW is available with the Standard Edition for a system administrator to use 5250 display device I/O to manage various aspects of the server. Multiple administrative jobs exceed this capability. ▸ Maximum 5250 CPW is equivalent to the processor CPW for the active processor.
Note 6a **Model** **800**	Software group is determined by the combination of Processor feature and Edition feature. This table provides a cross reference. Display the QPRCFEAT system value on DSPHDWRSC TYPE(*AHW) to display the processor feature code value.

Processor	Server feature	Edition feature	Software group	Processor feature code or QPRCFEAT value
#2463	#0863	#7400 Value	P05	7400
	#0864	#7400 Standard	P05	7400
#2464	#0865	#7408 Advanced	P10	7408

Note 6b Model 810	Software group is determined by the combination of Processor feature and Edition feature. This table provides a cross reference. Display the QPRCFEAT system value on DSPHDWRSC TYPE(*AHW) to display the processor feature code value.				
	Processor	**Server feature**	**Edition feature**	**Software group**	**Processor feature code or QPRCFEAT value**
	#2465	#0868	#7404 Standard	P10	7404
			#7406 Enterprise	P10	7406
			#7445 High Availability	P10	7406
	#2466	#0866	#7407 Standard	P10	7407
			#7409 Enterprise	P10	7409
			#7446 High Availability	P10	7409
		#0769	#7407 Domino	P10	7407
	#2467	#0867	#7410 Standard	P10	7410
			#7412 Enterprise	P10	7412
			#7447 High Availability	P10	7412
		#0770	#7410 Domino	P10	7410
	#2469	#0869	#7428 Standard	P20	7428
			#7430 Enterprise	P20	7430
			#7448 High Availability	P20	7430
		#0771	#7428 Domino	P20	7428
Note 6c Model 825	Software group is determined by the combination of Processor feature and Edition feature. This table provides a cross reference. Display the QPRCFEAT system value on DSPHDWRSC TYPE(*AHW) to display the processor feature code value. This value is also shown for the Capacity Card CCIN value when using SST to display system capacity information.				
	Processor feature	**Server feature**	**Edition feature**	**Software group**	**Processor feature code or QPRCFEAT value**
	#2473	#0873	#7416 Standard	P30	7416
			#7418 Enterprise	P30	7418
			#7434 High Availability	P30	7418
		#0772	#7416 Domino	P30	7416
		#0773	#7416 Domino	P30	7416
	#2495	#0890	#7439 Capacity BackUp	P30	7439

Note 6d Model 870	Software group is determined by the combination of Processor feature and Edition feature. This table provides a cross reference. Display the QPRCFEAT system value on DSPHDWRSC TYPE(*AHW) to display the processor feature code value. This value is also shown for the Capacity Card CCIN value when using SST to display system capacity information.				
	Processor feature	**Server feature**	**Edition feature**	**Software group**	**Processor feature code or QPRCFEAT value**
	#2486	#0886	#7419 Standard	P40	7419
			#7421 Enterprise	P40	7421
			#7436 High Availability	P40	7421
	#2489	#0889	#7431 Standard	P40	7431
			#7433 Enterprise	P40	7433
			#7435 High Availability	P40	7433
	#2496	#0891	#7440 Capacity BackUp	P40	7440
Note 6e Model 890	Software group is determined by the combination of processor feature and edition feature. Display the QPRCFEAT system value or DSPHDWRSC TYPE(*AHW) to display the processor feature code value. This value is also shown for the Capacity Card CCIN value when using SST to perform a Capacity Upgrade on Demand.				
	Processor feature	**Server feature**	**Interactive feature**	**Software group**	**Processor feature code or QPRCFEAT value**
	#0197		N/A	P50	0197
	#0198		N/A	P50	0198
	#2487		#1576	P50	2AF0
			#1577	P60	2AF1
			#1578	P60	2AF2
			#1579	P60	2AF3
			#1581	P60	2AF5
			#1583	P60	2AF7
			#1585	P60	2AF9
			#1587	P60	2AFB
			#1588	P60	2AFC

Note 6e Model 890 (cont.)	Processor feature	Server feature	Interactive feature	Software group	Processor feature code or QPRCFEAT value
	#2488		#1576	P50	2AD0
			#1577	P60	2AD1
			#1578	P60	2AD2
			#1579	P60	2AD3
			#1581	P60	2AD5
			#1583	P60	2AD7
			#1585	P60	2AD9
			#1587	P60	2ADB
			#1588	P60	2ADC
			#1591	P60	2ADF
	#2497	#0897	#7422 Standard	P50	7422
			#7424 Enterprise	P50	7424
			#7437 High Availability	P50	7424

Processor feature	Server feature	Edition feature	Software group	Processor feature code or QPRCFEAT value
#2498	#0898	#7425 Standard	P50	7425
		#7427 Enterprise	P50	7427
		#7438 High Availability	P50	7427
#2499	#0892	#7441 Capacity BackUp	P50	7441

Note 7	External DASD capacity assumes 70.56 GB LUNs. External DASD cannot exceed maximum system capacity or the maximum number of disk arms.
Note 8a	OS/400 V5R2 with February 2003 level of Licensed Internal Code (LIC) and Cumulative PTF Package C3021520.
Note 8b	Hardware upgrades to iSeries Model 810, 825, 870, or #2497 or #2498 Model 890 processors require the February 2003 level of Licensed Internal Code (LIC), OS/400 operating system, and the most current Cumulative PTF package. For more information, see: http://www.ibm.com/eserver/iseries/support
Note 9a	System can run with 256 MB, but the #0864 and #0865 Server features requires 512 MB of main storage.

Note 9b Model 810 and 825	The Domino Edition servers require a minimum disk and memory capacity as follows.		
	Server feature	Disk	Memory
	#0769	105 GB	1.5 GB
	#0770	315 GB	3.5 GB
	#0771	525 GB	5.5 GB
	#0772	560 GB	6 GB
	#0773	945 GB	12 GB
Note 9c	The Server features used for iSeries for Domino specify the minimum amount of disk, memory, and Domino licenses required for an initial order.		
Note 10a	Not supported in the #5094 by the IBM marketing configurator.		

Summary of the iSeries expansion units and towers

This section identifies the maximum capacities of expansion units and towers supported by Models 520, 550, 570, 595, 800, 810, 825, 870, and 890.

	#5094	#5095	#5088	#5294	0588	0595	#5790
Disk storage							
DASD arms maximum	45	12	N/A	2x 45	N/A	12	N/A
Disk grouping	5	6	N/A	2x 5	N/A	6	N/A
# of supported Controllers	9		N/A	2x 9	N/A		N/A
Maximum Disk storage GB	3164.4	843.84	N/A	6328.8	N/A	843.84	N/A
Physical packaging	Tower	Tower	Tophat	Rack	Drawer	Drawer	Drawer
Rackable			No		Yes	Yes	Yes
EIA Units	18	N/A	8	36	8	5	4
Internal CD/DVD/tape	2		N/A		N/A		0
Dual Power Cords	#5115	optional	yes	#5116	yes		yes
Redundant Power Supply	yes	#5138		yes	yes	#5138	yes
Slim line media bays	N/A	N/A	N/A	N/A	N/A	N/A	N/A
Number of busses							
Base IOP	1	1	0	2	0	1	
PCI Slots	14	7	14	2x 14	14	7	6
Integrated xSeries Server	2		2	4			2
Minimum OS	i5/OS V5R3	i5/OS V5R3	i5/OS V5R3	i5/OS V5R3	i5/OS V5R3	i5/OS V5R3	i5/OS V5R3
Copper HSL-2/RIO-2 Adapters	#9517	#9517	#9877	#9517		#9517	#9531
Optical HSL-2/RIO-2	#9876	#9876	#9876	#9876	#9876	#9876	

6

eServer i5 Model 520

The @server i5 520 server is designed for small to mid-sized businesses. These are businesses that need power and capacity to run traditional core business applications and need the freedom and scalability to add new applications for On Demand Business to the same server. The 520 is the industry's first POWER5 technology-based server. It has the capability to simultaneously run multiple operating environments and dynamically distribute processing resources.

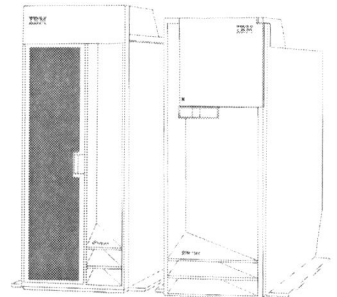
@server i5 Model 520 System Unit
(rack and stand-alone configuration)

The Model 520 is offered as a deskside tower and rack mounted configuration. It provides an integrated set of hardware capabilities including two integrated 1 Gbps Ethernet ports and an integrated Small Computer System Interface (SCSI) controller. An optional redundant power supply is available. Hot-plugging is supported for PCI-X card slots, disk slots, and redundant fans. Hot-plugging of removable media devices is not supported.

Model overview

This section takes a closer look at the minimum functional server, required features, and optional features.

Minimum functional server

A minimum functional server consists of the base server unit and selected priced features. The base server includes:

► Physical package and power elements

► Six hot-plug PCI-X card slots

► Operator panel (mounting hardware is different between the rack mount system and the deskside system)

> **Note:** A Hardware Management Console (HMC) is required to manage specific configurations. See "Hardware Management Console" on page 679 for more information.

► Base 850W (100-127/200-240V) Power Supply (CCIN 51B6)

► Base direct access storage device (DASD) cage (CCIN 28D2) (four hot-plug internal disk slots)

► Base SCSI controller (CCIN 570B)

This controller is integrated with the backplane and does not take up one of the PCI-X slots. It provides support for up to eight disk units (four in the base DASD cage and four in the#6574 4-Disk Slot Exp - Base Controller), the required internal DVD feature, internal feature DVDs, and feature tapes. This controller does not support Redundant Array of Independent Disks (RAID) or hardware data compression. A #5709 RAID Enabler Card (CCIN 5709) controller must be added if the system data protection is RAID.

The #5709 RAID Enabler Card (CCIN 5709) plugs into the backplane and does not take up one of the PCI-X slots. It provides support for up to eight disk units, the required internal DVD feature, internal feature DVDs, and feature tapes. This controller supports RAID but does not support hardware data compression. The #5709 has a 16 MB write cache.

► Three media bays and one operator panel bay

   – The three media bays consist of one half-height (5 ¼-inch wide x 1-inch high, top bay) and two slimline bays. The half-height bay is for SCSI media devices. (Half-high optical devices are not supported in this bay.) The top slimline bay is usable by IBM i5/OS for the required DVD-ROM and

DVD-RAM. The second slimline bay is straight IDE and is usable only with AIX 5L or Linux partitions on 9406 systems.

- In the rack drawer configuration, the bottom bay is for the operator panel. With a deskside configuration, the operator panel is mounted in a separate bracket attached to the top of the system. The bottom bay in a deskside configuration is left empty and is covered by a plate insert.

► Two serial ports and two USB 2.0 ports

These ports are not usable by i5/OS.

► Two 1 Gb, 100 Mb, and 10 Mb Ethernet ports

These ports are not usable for a local area network (LAN) console.

► Base Service Processor (CCIN 28D7) (plugs in slot P1-C7)

► Two HMC ports and two SPCN ports

► Two high-speed loop (HSL)-2/RIO-G ports

► #9844 Base PCI IOP (plugs in slot P1-C6)

This provides support for up to two IOAs (slots P1-C3 and P1-C5).

Required features

Notes: In the following list, the asterisk (*) indicates that the item is supported for conversion only.

The *required* features for the 520 system unit include:

► Specific combinations of the Processor feature, Edition feature, and Server feature are allowed as shown in the following table.

Processor	Server feature	Edition feature	Software group	Processor feature code or QPRCFEAT value
#8950	#0900	#7390, #7391, #7393 Express #7450 Value	P05	7450
#8951	#0901	#7392, #7394 Express #7451 Value	P10	7451
#8952	#0902	#7458 Standard	P10	7458
		#7459 Enterprise	P10	7459
#8953	#0903	#7452 Standard	P10	7452
		#7453 Enterprise	P10	7453
#8954	#0904	#7454 Standard	P20	7454
		#7455 Enterprise	P20	7455
#8955	#0905	#7456 Standard	P20	7456
		#7457 Enterprise	P20	7457
		#7555 High Availability	P20	7457

- The #7390, #7391 and #7393 Express Editions for the @server i5 Model 520 provide 30 5250 OLTP workloads while the #7392 and #7394 Express Editions provide 60 CPW.

- The Value Edition for the #7450 and #7451 @server i5 Model 520 provides 30 and 60 CPW respectively for 5250 OLTP workloads.

- The Standard Edition for the Model 520 processors provides limited 5250 CPW for 5250 OLTP workloads. The Standard Edition also provides support for Capacity on Demand (permanent and temporary).

- The Enterprise and High Availability Editions provide maximum 5250 CPW for 5250 OLTP workloads. The Enterprise and High Availability Editions also provide support for Capacity on Demand (permanent and temporary).

Edition content varies by the processor and server features that are selected. For more information, see "Editions" on page 55.

Refer to the Model 520 summary chart in "Table 1: Summary of the eServer i5 Model 520" on page 81 to determine the processor feature code and QPRCFEAT value.

- Internal disk units - 10k or 15k rpm only
  - #4317 8.58 GB 10k RPM Disk Unit*
  - #4318 17.54 GB 10k RPM Disk Unit*
  - #4319 35.16 GB 10k RPM Disk Unit
  - #4326 35.16 GB 15k RPM Disk Unit
  - #4327 70.56 GB 15k RPM Disk Unit

  One of the following load source specify codes is required:
  - #0829 - #4318 Load Source Specify*
  - #0830 - #4319 Load Source Specify
  - #0834 - #4326 Load Source Specify
  - #0835 - #4327 Load Source Specify
- DVD-ROM or DVD-RAM
  - #2640 DVD-ROM
  - #5751 DVD-RAM
- System console attachment adapter
  - #5540 System Console on Twinaxial Workstation IOA
    - #4746 PCI Twinaxial IOA (can be placed in either slot P1-C5 or P1-C2)
  - #5544 System Console on Operations Console
    - #0367 Operations Console PCI Cable (attaches to #9793)
  - #5546 System Console on 100 Mbps Token Ring
    - #2744 PCI 100 Mbps Token Ring IOA (can be placed in either slot P1-C5 or P1-C2)
    - #0367 Operations Console PCI Cable
  - #5548 System Console on 100 Mbps Ethernet
    - #2849 10/100 Mbps Ethernet Adapter (can be placed in either slot P1-C5 or P1-C2)
    - #0367 Operations Console PCI Cable
  - #5550 System Console on HMC

    The HMC is required for systems using logical partitions (LPARs), IBM @server Capacity Upgrade on Demand (CUoD) and redundant Service Processor operations.
- #7884 520 Rack Mount (4 EIA Units. Includes 28-inch rack mounting rails) or #7885 520 Deskside.

Optional features

The *optional* features for the 520 system unit include:

► The 520 deskside can be converted to a rack mount
   (available 31 March 2005)

► If a Peripheral Component Interconnect (PCI) disk controller is required in the
   system unit, choose one of the following controllers:

   – #5715 PCI-X Tape/DASD Controller

     Provides support for up to four disk units. This controller supports data
     mirroring. It does not support RAID-5 or data compression.

   – #5703 PCI-X RAID Disk Unit Controller

     Provides support for up to four disk units. This controller supports RAID
     but does not support hardware data compression.

► Internal tape unit

   – #1889 80 GB VXA-2 Tape Device
   – #5753 30 GB ¼-inch Cartridge Tape Device
   – #5754 50 GB ¼-inch Cartridge Tape Device
   – #6134 60 GB 8mm Tape Device (supported in Linux and AIX partitions
     only)
   – #8754 Optional Base 50 GB ¼-inch Cartridge Tape Device

► #5158 850W AC Power Supply

   – Requires an additional linecord
   – Enables hot-plugging of either power supply

► #6574 4-Disk Slot Exp - Base Controller

   – This provides the disk unit backplane for attachment of up to four
     additional disk units.

   – Disk units in the #6574 are controlled by the integrated base disk controller
     or by the #5709 if it is installed.

► #6584 4-Disk Slot Expansion (*withdrawn from marketing* on
   19 November 2004)

   – It can be driven by a #5715 (non-RAID) or #5703 (RAID) disk controller in
     a PCI slot of the system unit.

   – It cannot be controlled by the integrated base disk controller or by the
     #5709 if it is installed.

   – The disk controller cannot be supported by a second IOP. This means that
     you cannot have a second i5/OS partition in just the CEC. You can have a
     partition where the disk controller was owned by Linux or AIX (not using
     the virtual disk option).

- #6594 4-Disk Slot Expansion
  - It can be driven by a #5715 (non-RAID) or #5703 (RAID) disk controller in a PCI slot of the system unit.
  - It cannot be controlled by the integrated base disk controller or by the #5709 if it is installed.
  - With #6594 the disk controller can be controlled by a second IOP. This means that you can have a second i5/OS partition in the CEC only or you can have a partition where the disk controller is owned by Linux or AIX (not using the virtual disk option).
  - The #6594 repositions the SCSI cable connector so that a long card can be placed in card slot 4 and forces card slot 5 to be a short card. Therefore, you cannot have #4811PCI Integrated xSeries Server in the 520 system unit if you also have a #6594.
- Uninterruptible power supply

  We recommend that you have an external uninterruptible power supply to protect the system unit and any external components against utility power outages.

  Note: A #1827 Serial-UPS conversion cable is required to provide uninterruptible power supply control/feedback information for the @server i5 Model 520. This does not impact the ability of the uninterruptible power supply to provide power in case of an outage. Its absence prevents the uninterruptible power supply from alerting the Model 520 that it is under the uninterruptible power supply and from advising the server to the amount of remaining uninterruptible power supply battery power.

The Model 520 initial installation is Customer Setup (CSU). IBM Service Representatives perform the processor upgrades within models.

Processor features

- The #8950 Model 520 POWER5 1.5 GHz Uni processor (CCIN 522A) includes:
  - Eight Dual Inline Memory Module (DIMM) memory positions (plug into the processor, direct attach)
  - No L3 cache
  - #7450 Processor Capacity Card (CCIN 7450) required with this processor feature

- The #8951 Model 520 POWER5 1.5 GHz Uni Processor (CCIN 522A) includes:

  - Eight DIMM memory positions (plug into the processor, direct attach)
  - No L3 cache
  - #7451 Processor Capacity Card (CCIN 7451) required with this processor feature

- The #8952 Model 520 POWER5 1.5 GHz Uni processor (CCIN 522A) includes:

  - Eight DIMM memory positions (plug into the processor, direct attach)
  - No L3 cache
  - #7458 or #7459 Processor Capacity Card (CCIN 7458/7459) required with this processor feature

- The #8953 Model 520 POWER5 1.5G Hz Uni processor (CCIN 522A) includes:

  - Eight DIMM memory positions (plug into the processor, direct attach)
  - No L3 cache
  - #7452 or #7453 Processor Capacity Card (CCIN 7452/7453) required with this processor feature

- The #8954 Model 520 POWER5 1.65 GHz Uni processor (CCIN 5228) includes:

  - Eight DIMM memory positions (plug into processor, direct attach)
  - 36 MB L3 cache
  - #7454 or #7455 Processor Capacity Card (CCIN 7454/7455) required with this processor feature

- The #8955 Model 520 POWER5 1.65 GHz 2-way processor (CCIN 5229) includes:

  - Eight DIMM memory positions (plug into the processor, direct attach)
  - 36 MB L3 cache
  - #7456 or #7457 Processor Capacity Card (CCIN 7456/7457) required with this processor feature

Refer to "Table 1: Summary of the eServer i5 Model 520" on page 81 to find Processor CPW, Mail and Calendar Users (MCU), and 5250 CPW, and to determine the processor feature code and QPRCFEAT value.

Main storage

Supported memory features for the Model 520 are:

> **Note**: In the following list, the double asterisk (**) indicates that the feature is supported for migration only. Plugging rules must be followed.

- ► #3093 - 512 MB Main Storage (DIMM DDR 256 Mb technology)**
- ► #3094 - 1 GB Main Storage (DIMM DDR 256 Mb technology)**
- ► #3096 - 2 GB Main Storage (DIMM DDR 256 Mb technology)**
- ► #4444 - 1 GB DDR Main Storage (DDR1 - 256 Mb technology, CCIN 309B)
  Ships four 256 MB DIMMs for a total of 1 GB
- ► #4445 - 4 GB DDR Main Storage (DDR1 - 128 Mb technology, CCIN 30D3)
  Ships four 1 GB DIMMs for a total of 4 GB
- ► #4447 - 2 GB DDR Main Storage (DDR1 - 64 Mb technology, CCIN 30D2)
  Ships four 512 MB DIMMs for a total of 2 GB
- ► #4449 - 8 GB DDR Main Storage (DDR1 - 128 Mb technology, stacked, CCIN 30D5)
  Ships four 2 GB DIMMs for a total of 8 GB
- ► #4450 - 16 GB DDR Main Storage (DDR1 - 1 Gb technology, stacked, CCIN 30AC)
  Ships four 4 GB DIMMs for a total of 16 GB

Configuration considerations for memory include:

- ► A minimum of 2 GB of memory is required.
- ► Memory must be on both processors.
- ► DIMMs must be installed in sets of four (quads) with one exception. A single pair of 256 MB DIMMs is allowed on the #8950 processor. Whenever more DIMMs are added, an additional pair of 256MB DIMMs must be added to the original pair (to make a quad). Then one additional quad of DIMMs may be added to the system.
- ► For processor #8950, the first DIMM pair goes into DIMM slots J0A and J2A. The second pair of DIMMs goes into slots J0C and J2C.
- ► The first quad of DIMMs is plugged into DIMM slots J0A, J2A, J0C, and J2C.
- ► The second quad of DIMMs is plugged into DIMM slots J0B, J2B, J0D, and J2D.

The following table shows allowable main storage capacities in MB for the Model 520 processors.

512*	1024	2048	3072
4096	5120	6144	8192
9216	10240	12288	16384
17408	18432	20480	24576
32768			
* 512 MB is allowed on the #8950 only.			

9406 Model 520 schematics

The following diagrams show the slot and feature card arrangement of the Model 520 system unit, processor, memory cards, and supported expansion units. You can find schematics of any supported expansion units in Chapter 15, "Towers, racks, and high-speed link" on page 261.

9406 Model 520 system unit: Top, front, and rear views

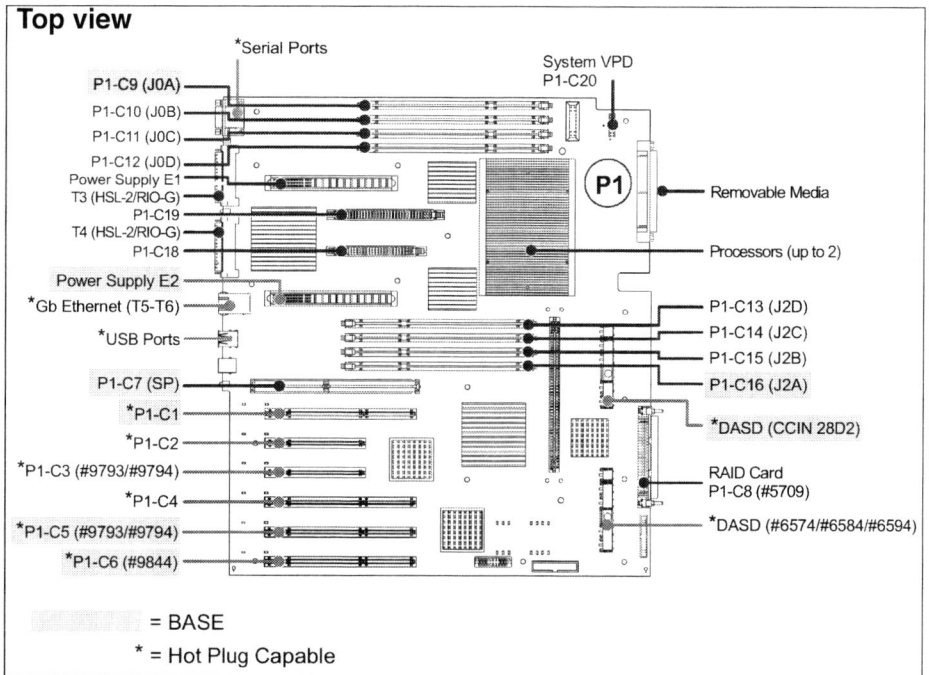

Top view

P1-C9 (J0A)
P1-C10 (J0B)
P1-C11 (J0C)
P1-C12 (J0D)
Power Supply E1
T3 (HSL-2/RIO-G)
P1-C19
T4 (HSL-2/RIO-G)
P1-C18
Power Supply E2
*Gb Ethernet (T5-T6)
*USB Ports
P1-C7 (SP)
*P1-C1
*P1-C2
*P1-C3 (#9793/#9794)
*P1-C4
*P1-C5 (#9793/#9794)
*P1-C6 (#9844)

*Serial Ports

System VPD
P1-C20

P1

Removable Media

Processors (up to 2)

P1-C13 (J2D)
P1-C14 (J2C)
P1-C15 (J2B)
P1-C16 (J2A)

*DASD (CCIN 28D2)

RAID Card
P1-C8 (#5709)

*DASD (#6574/#6584/#6594)

= BASE
* = Hot Plug Capable

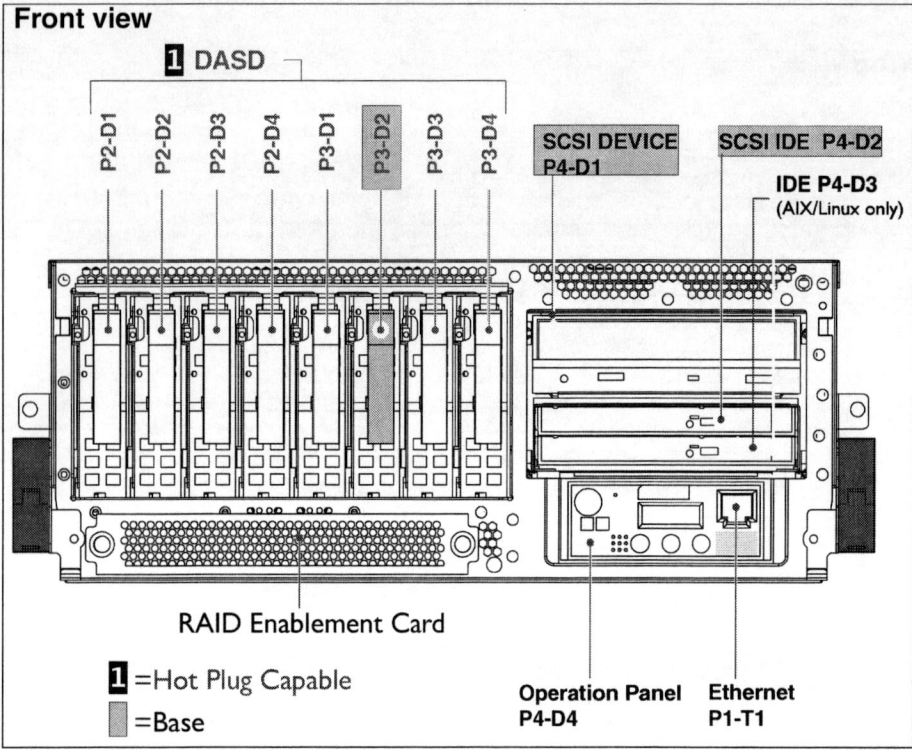

Front view

1 DASD

P2-D1 P2-D2 P2-D3 P2-D4 P3-D1 P3-D2 P3-D3 P3-D4

SCSI DEVICE
P4-D1

SCSI IDE P4-D2

IDE P4-D3
(AIX/Linux only)

RAID Enablement Card

1 =Hot Plug Capable

=Base

Operation Panel
P4-D4

Ethernet
P1-T1

Rear view

*Power Supply E1 *Power Supply E2 P1 - C7 HMC 1 C7 - T1 HMC 2 C7 - T2

Serial Port
T3 [HSL-2/RIO-G] 1
T4 [HSL-2/RIO-G] 0
Gb Ethernet T5
Gb Ethernet T6
USB0 T7
USB1 T8
RackInd T9

*P1 - C6
*P1 - C5
*P1 - C4
*P1 - C3
*P1 - C2
*P1 - C1

SPCN 0 C7-T3
SPCN 1 C7-T4
IP

Serial Port — An #1827 Serial-UPS Conversion Cable connects to the top serial port on a rack mounted system or the right-hand serial port to a deskside system.

▓ = BASE

* = Hot Plug Capable

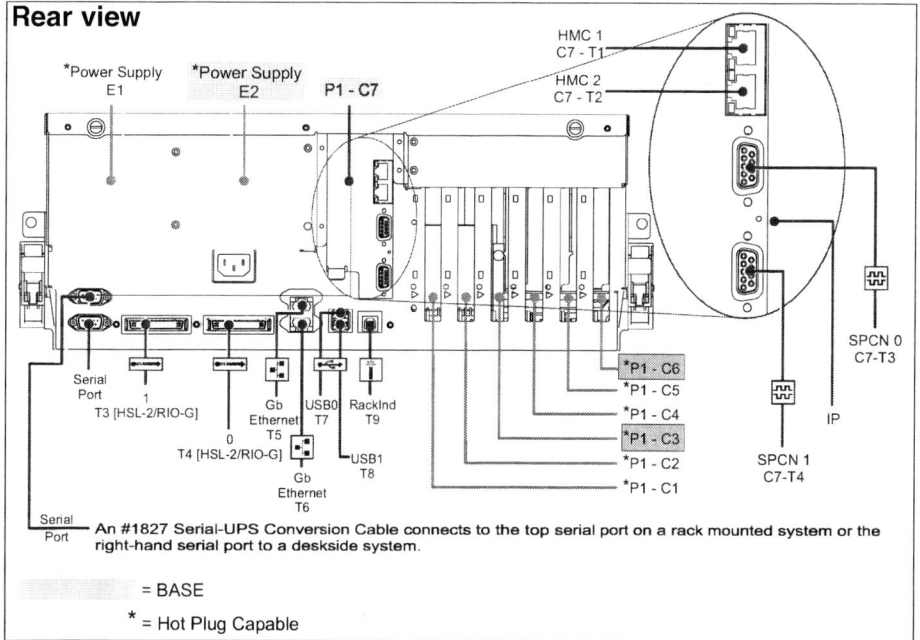

Note: You can find line cord and power receptacle specification information on the Web at:

http://www.ibm.com/eserver/iseries/infocenter

High-speed link for Model 520

The Model 520 supports a single HSL-2/RIO-2 loop. The maximum rated speed of the HSL-2/RIO-2 is 2 GB/s, which is double the speed of the previous HSL/HSL-2 adapters. The following rules apply to towers that are supported at these speeds:

► The #5094, #5294, #0595, and #5095 come with a #9517 HSL-2/RIO-2 adapter. The #5790 PCI Expansion Drawer comes with a #9531 HSL-2/RIO-2 adapter.

► HSL-2 adapters in existing #5094, #5294, #0595, and #5095 towers must be replaced with a #6417 HSL-2/RIO-G Bus Adapter.

► Mixing HSL and HSL-2 towers is allowed with the correct combination of cables.

Rack mounted Model 520 system units can only attach to HSL-2/RIO-2 cables 2.5m or longer and can only attach to SPCN cables 3m or longer. Shorter cable lengths do not allow the system unit to be pulled out from the rack far enough for concurrent maintenance.

> **Note:** The #6587 Model 520 Rear Cover should only be used with deskside configurations which have do not have HSL cables. No rear cover is associated with the rack mounted 520.
>
> Do not use the #6587 if you have an HSL-attached Integrated xSeries Adapter, #5074, #5079, #5095/#0595, #5094, #5294, or #5088/#0588 tower. The #6587 is not deep enough to allow HSL cables to bend gradually enough to ensure the cables will not be damaged.

See "HSL fabric" on page 297 for information about supported HSL cables and HSL loop maximums. You can find more information in *High-speed Link Loop Architecture for the IBM @server iSeries Server: OS/400 Version 5 Release 2*, REDP-3652, and in the HSL Rules presentation available at:

http://www-1.ibm.com/servers/eserver/iseries/ha/systemdesign.html

Model 520 PCI cards and features

The Model 520 is a PCI-based technology system. The number of PCI cards that can be supported in a Model 520 depends on whether an input/output (I/O) tower is attached and the number of PCI slots. PCI card placement rules and LPAR configuration considerations also affect the number of slots supported.

See the table on page 82 for the number of maximum features supported by the total system and in the Model 520 system unit. See Chapter 17, "iSeries PCI I/O processors" on page 323, and Chapter 18, "iSeries I/O adapters and controllers" on page 337, for full descriptions of the features that are supported. See "AIX and Linux Direct Attach features overview" on page 340 for supported Linux Direct Attach features.

> **Note:** The placement of PCI cards follows special rules. Refer to "PCI card technology" on page 338 and *PCI Card Placement Rules for the IBM @server iSeries Server Version 5 Release 2*, REDP-3638, before you propose any configuration.

External towers

Migration towers are not supported on the Model 520. PCI towers are supported with upgrades for migration only.

Refer to Chapter 15, "Towers, racks, and high-speed link" on page 261, for information about supported towers for the Model 520, and "Summary of the iSeries expansion units and towers" on page 119 for a table of configuration maximums.

Model 520 upgrades

See Chapter 16, "Upgrades to eServer i5 and i5/OS" on page 311, for general upgrade considerations and server-to-server upgrade possibilities. Supported model upgrades for the Model 520 are identified in the *Upgrade* topic of the Find and Compare Tool (FACT) at:

http://www-919.ibm.com/servers/eserver/fact/

7

eServer i5 Model 550

The @server i5 Model 550 is a mid-sized IBM POWER5 technology-based server. It has the capability to simultaneously run multiple operating environments and dynamically distribute processing resources. This server is designed for small to mid-sized businesses. These businesses need power and capacity to run traditional core business applications and to support IBM i5/OS applications together with Linux, Windows, AIX applications, or all three.

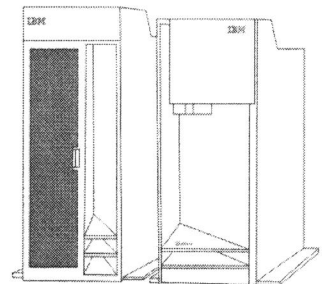

@server *i5 Model 550 System Unit* (rack configuration)

The Model 550 is offered as a deskside tower and a rack mounted configuration. It provides an integrated set of hardware capabilities including two integrated 1 Gbps Ethernet ports and an integrated Small Computer System Interface (SCSI) controller. An optional redundant power supply is available. Hot-plugging is supported for PCI-X card slots, disk slots, and redundant fans. In addition, @server i5 servers can hot-plug into input/output (I/O) towers or drawers, or they can be xSeries attached by Integrated xSeries Adapters. Hot-plugging of removable media devices is not supported.

Model overview

This section takes a closer look at the minimum functional server, required features, and optional features.

Minimum functional server

A minimum functional server consists of the base server unit and selected priced features. The base server includes:

► Physical package and power elements

► Five hot-plug PCI-X card slots

► Operator panel

Mounting hardware is different between the rack mount system and the deskside system.

► Base 1475W Power Supply (CCIN 51BA)

► Base DASD cage (four hot-plug disk slots) (CCIN 28F6)

► Base SCSI controller (CCIN 570B)

This controller is integrated with the backplane and does not take up one of the PCI-X slots. It provides support for up to eight disk units (four in the Base DASD cage (CCIN 28F6) and four in the #6592 4-Disk Slot Expansion Base Controller), the required internal DVD feature, internal feature DVDs, and feature tapes. The base controller does not support Redundant Array of Independent Disks (RAID) or hardware data compression. A #5709 RAID Enabler Card (CCIN 5709) controller must be added if the system data protection is RAID.

The #5709 RAID Enabler Card (CCIN 5709) plugs into the backplane and does not take up one of the PCI-X slots. It provides support for up to eight disk units, the required internal DVD feature, internal feature DVDs, and feature tape devices. This controller supports RAID. It does not support hardware data compression. The #5709 has a 16 MB write cache.

► Three media bays and one operator panel bay

 – The three media bays consist of one half-height (5 ¼-inch wide x 1-inch high, top bay) and two slimline bays. The half-height bay is for SCSI media devices. (Half-high optical devices are not supported in this bay.) The top slimline bay is usable by i5/OS for the required DVD-ROM and DVD-RAM. The second slimline bay is straight integrated development environment (IDE) and is usable only with AIX 5L V5.2 or Linux partitions on 9406 systems.

- In the rack drawer configuration, the bottom bay is for the operator panel. With a deskside configuration, the operator panel is mounted in a separate bracket attached to the top of the system. The bottom bay in a deskside configuration is left empty and is covered by a plate insert.

► Two serial ports and two USB 2.0 ports

These ports are not usable by i5/OS.

► Two 1000/100/10 Mb Ethernet ports

These ports are not usable for a local area network (LAN) console.

► Base Service Processor (CCIN 28D7) (plugs in slot P1-C7)

► Two Hardware Management Console (HMC) ports and two SPCN ports

► Two high-speed link (HSL)-2/RIO-G ports

► #9844 Base PCI IOP (plugs in slot P1-C1)

Provides support for Peripheral Component Interconnect (PCI) slot P1-C2 only.

Required features

Note: In the lists of features that follow, the asterisk (*) indicates that the feature is supported for conversion only.

The *required* features for the 550 system unit include:

► Specific combinations of the Processor feature, Edition feature, and Server feature are allowed as shown in the following table.

Processor	Server feature	Edition feature	Software group	Processor feature code or QPRCFEAT value
#8958 (3000/12000 CPW)	#0915	#7462 Standard	P20	7462
		#7463 Enterprise	P20	7463
		#7530 Domino	P20	7650
		#7531 Solution for PeopleSoft EnterpriseOne	P20	
		#7558 Solution	P20	

Note: Standard and Enterprise Editions for the #8958 processor provide limited and maximum 5250 CPW respectively for 5250 OLTP workloads.

Edition content varies by processor and server features selected. For more information, see "Editions" on page 55.

► Internal disk units - 10k or 15k rpm only

- #4317 8.58 GB 10k RPM Disk Unit*
- #4318 17.54 GB 10k RPM Disk Unit*
- #4319 35.16 GB 10k RPM Disk Unit
- #4326 35.16 GB 15k RPM Disk Unit
- #4327 70.56 GB 15k RPM Disk Unit

One of the following load source specify codes is required:

- #0829 - #4318 Load Source Specify*
- #0830 - #4319 Load Source Specify
- #0834 - #4326 Load Source Specify
- #0835 - #4327 Load Source Specify

► DVD-ROM or DVD-RAM

- #2640 DVD-ROM
- #5751 DVD-RAM

► System console attachment adapter

- #5540 System Console on Twinaxial Workstation IOA

  • #4746 PCI Twinaxial IOA (placed in slot P1-C4)

- #5544 System Console on Operations Console

  • #0367 Operations Console PCI Cable (attaches to #9793 in slot P1-C2)

- #5546 System Console on 100 Mbps Token Ring

  • #2744 PCI 100 Mbps Token Ring IOA (can be placed in slot P1-C4)
  • #0367 Operations Console PCI Cable

- #5548 System Console on 100 Mbps Ethernet

  • #2849 10/100 Mbps Ethernet Adapter (can be placed in slot P1-C4)
  • #0367 Operations Console PCI Cable

- #5550 System Console on HMC

  The HMC is required for systems using logical partitions (LPARs), IBM @server Capacity Upgrade on Demand (CUoD) upgrade operations, and redundant Service Processor operations.

► #7886 IBM Rack Mount (four EIA Units, includes fixed length rack mounting rails) or #7887 Deskside

Optional features

The *optional* features for the @server i5 Model 550 system unit include:

► If a PCI disk controller is required in the system unit, choose one of the following controllers:

- #5703 PCI-X RAID Disk Unit Controller

  Provides support for up to four disk units. This controller supports RAID but does not support hardware data compression.

- #5715 PCI-X Tape/DASD Controller

  Provides support for up to four disk units. This controller supports RAID but does not support hardware data compression.

- #6592 4-Disk Slot Expansion - Base Controller

  This controller is a disk backplane feature that enables the second set of four hot-plug internal disk slots. Disk units plugged into the #6592 are controlled by the integrated base disk controller or by the #5709 (if present).

► Internal tape unit

- #1889 80 GB VXA-2 Tape Device
- #5753 30 GB ¼-inch Cartridge Tape Device
- #5754 50 GB ¼-inch Cartridge Tape Device
- #6134 60 GB 8mm Tape Device (supported in Linux and AIX partitions only)
- #6258 36 GB 4mm Tape Unit (supported in Linux and AIX 5L V5.2 partitions only)
- #8754 Optional Base 50 GB ¼-inch Cartridge Tape Device (withdrawn July 2004)

► #7889 1475W Power Supply

- Requires an additional linecord
- Enables hot-plugging of either power supply

► #6593 4-Disk Slot Expansion PCI-X Controller

- The #6593 can be driven by a disk controller in a PCI slot of the system unit.
- The #6593 cannot be controlled by the integrated base disk controller or by the #5709 if it is installed.

- The #6593 repositions the SCSI cable connector so that a long card can be placed in card slot 4 and forces card slot 5 to be a short card.

- The #6593 can be used to obtain disk mirroring protection

► #7798 non-IBM Rack Mount

The #7798 is identical to #7886 IBM Rack Mount, except an adjustable set of mounting rails/slides is shipped instead of the fixed length rails/slides used in IBM racks.

► Uninterruptible power supply

We recommend that you have an external uninterruptible power supply to protect the system unit and any external components against utility power outages.

> **Note:** A #1827 Serial-UPS conversion cable is required to provide uninterruptible power supply control/feedback information for the @server i5 Model 550. This does not impact the ability of the uninterruptible power supply to provide power in case of an outage. Its absence prevents the uninterruptible power supply from alerting the Model 550 that it is under the uninterruptible power supply and from advising the server to the amount of remaining uninterruptible power supply battery power.

The Model 550 initial installation is IBM installed. Processor upgrades within models are performed by IBM Service Representatives.

Processor features

► #8958 Model 550 Processor (POWER5 1/4-way 1.65 GHz DCM)

- The #8958 supports eight Dual Inline Memory Module (DIMM) memory positions (plug into the processor, direct attach).

- The Model 550 has 1.9 MB of L2 cache and 36 MB of L3 cache.

Main storage

Supported memory features for the Model 550 are:

► #4443 - 512 MB DDR Main Storage (DDR1 - 256 Mb technology, CCIN 309B)

- Ships two 256 MB DIMMs for a total of 512 MB

- Only orderable on #8950 processor with a maximum of two of these features per system

- ► #4444 - 1 GB DDR Main Storage (DDR1 - 256 Mb technology, CCIN 309B)

  Ships four 256 MB DIMMs for a total of 1 GB
- ► #4445 - 4 GB DDR Main Storage (DDR1 - 128 Mb technology, CCIN 30D3)

  Ships four 1 GB DIMMs for a total of 4 GB
- ► #4447 - 2 GB DDR Main Storage (DDR1 - 64 Mb technology, CCIN 30D2)

  Ships four 512 MB DIMMs for a total of 2 GB
- ► #4449 - 8 GB DDR Main Storage (DDR1 - 128 Mb technology, stacked, CCIN 30D5)

  Ships four 2 GB DIMMs for a total of 8 GB
- ► #4450 - 16 GB DDR Main Storage (DDR1 - 1 Gb technology, stacked, CCIN 30AC)

  Ships four 4 GB DIMMs for a total of 16 GB

Configuration considerations for memory include:

- ► DIMMs must be installed in sets of four (quads).
- ► The first quad of DIMMs is plugged into DIMM slots J0A, J0B, J0C, and J0D.
- ► The second quad of DIMMs is plugged into DIMM slots J1A, J1B, J1C, and J1D.

9406 Model 550 schematics

The following diagrams show the slot and feature card arrangement of the Model 550 system unit, processor, memory cards, and supported expansion units. You can find schematics of any supported expansion units in Chapter 15, "Towers, racks, and high-speed link" on page 261.

9406 Model 550 system unit: Top, front, and rear views

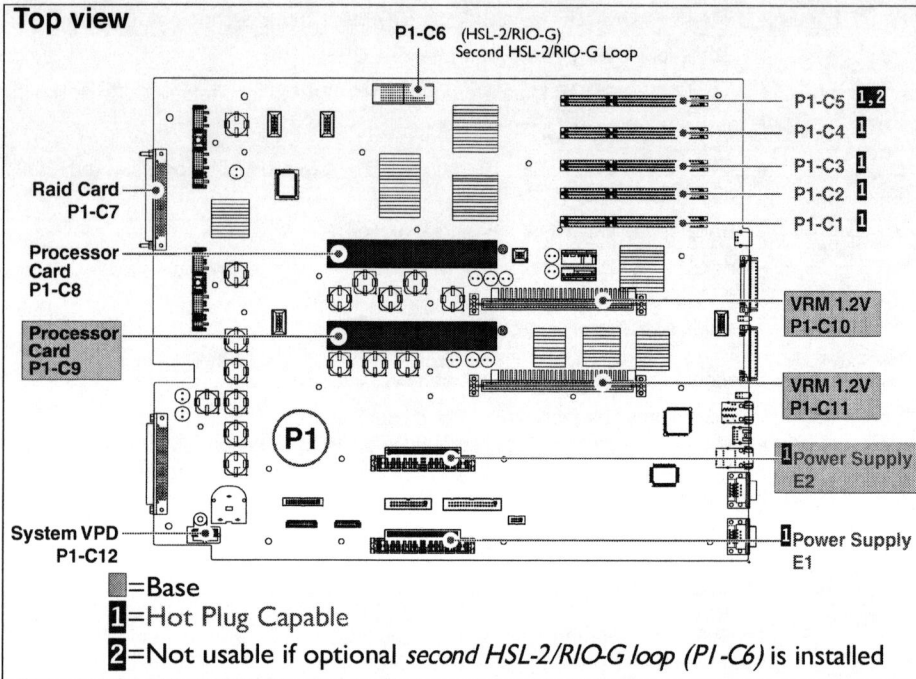

Top view

P1-C6 (HSL-2/RIO-G)
Second HSL-2/RIO-G Loop

P1-C5 **1, 2**
P1-C4 **1**
P1-C3 **1**
P1-C2 **1**
P1-C1 **1**

Raid Card
P1-C7

Processor
Card
P1-C8

Processor
Card
P1-C9

VRM 1.2V
P1-C10

VRM 1.2V
P1-C11

P1

1 Power Supply
E2

System VPD
P1-C12

1 Power Supply
E1

█=Base
1=Hot Plug Capable
2=Not usable if optional *second HSL-2/RIO-G loop (P1-C6)* is installed

Front view

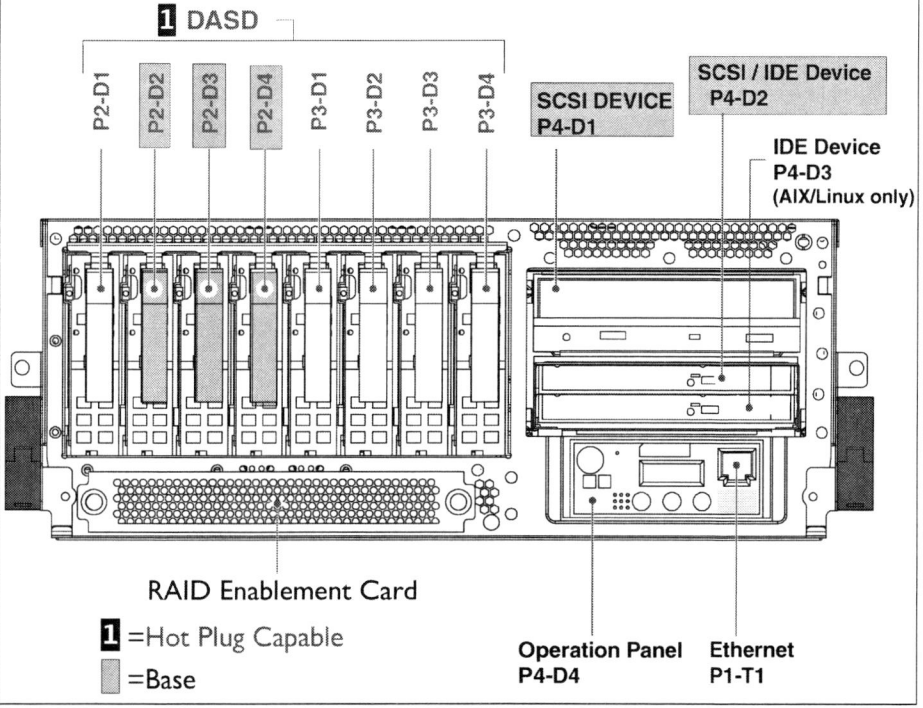

1 DASD

P2-D1
P2-D2
P2-D3
P2-D4
P3-D1
P3-D2
P3-D3
P3-D4

SCSI DEVICE
P4-D1

SCSI / IDE Device
P4-D2

IDE Device
P4-D3
(AIX/Linux only)

RAID Enablement Card

1 =Hot Plug Capable

=Base

Operation Panel
P4-D4

Ethernet
P1-T1

Rear view

Power Supply **1** E1   Power Supply **1** E2

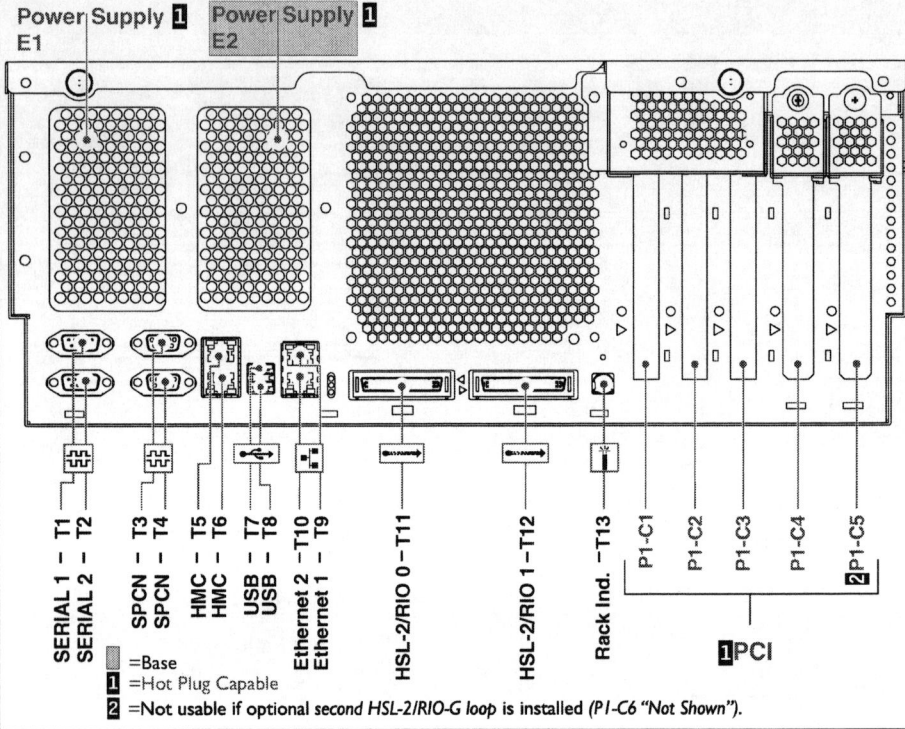

SERIAL 1 – T1
SERIAL 2 – T2
SPCN – T3
SPCN – T4
HMC – T5
HMC – T6
USB – T7
USB – T8
Ethernet 2 – T10
Ethernet 1 – T9
HSL-2/RIO 0 –T11
HSL-2/RIO 1 –T12
Rack Ind. –T13
P1-C1
P1-C2
P1-C3
P1-C4
2 P1-C5

1 PCI

▨ =Base
1 =Hot Plug Capable
2 =Not usable if optional *second HSL-2/RIO-G loop* is installed *(P1-C6 "Not Shown")*.

Note: You can find line cord and power receptacle specification information on the Web at:

http://www.ibm.com/eserver/iseries/infocenter

550 and 570 processor card

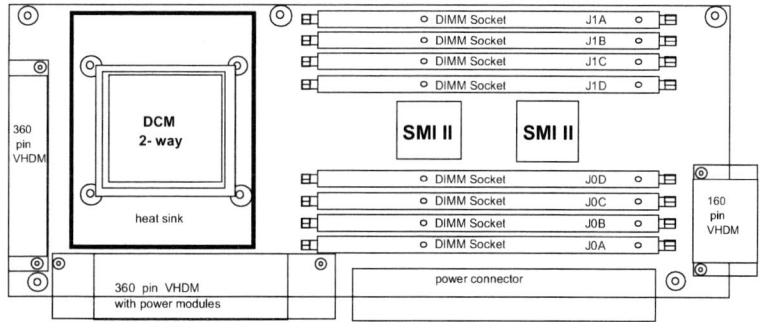

```
┌─────────────────────────────────────────────────────────────────────────────┐
│ (○)        ┌──────────┐  (○)  ┌─┐ ┌────── ○ DIMM Socket      J1A  ○ ─┐ ┌─┐ (○) │
│            │          │       ├─┤ ├────── ○ DIMM Socket      J1B  ○ ─┤ ├─┤     │
│  ┌─────────┼──────────┼────┐  ├─┤ ├────── ○ DIMM Socket      J1C  ○ ─┤ ├─┤     │
│  (○)  (○)──┼──────────┼──(○)  ├─┤ ├────── ○ DIMM Socket      J1D  ○ ─┤ ├─┤     │
│            │          │                                                       │
│ 360        │   DCM    │            ┌────────┐   ┌────────┐                    │
│ pin        │  2- way  │            │ SMI II │   │ SMI II │                    │
│ VHDM       │          │            └────────┘   └────────┘                    │
│            │          │                                                       │
│  (○)  (○)──┼──────────┼──(○)  ├─┤ ├────── ○ DIMM Socket      J0D  ○ ─┤ ├─┤ (○) │
│            └──────────┘       ├─┤ ├────── ○ DIMM Socket      J0C  ○ ─┤ ├─┤     │
│              heat sink        ├─┤ ├────── ○ DIMM Socket      J0B  ○ ─┤ ├─┤ 160 │
│                               ├─┤ ├────── ○ DIMM Socket      J0A  ○ ─┤ ├─┤ pin │
│ (○)(○)                  (○)                                            VHDM    │
│ (○)       360  pin  VHDM              ┌──── power connector ────┐  (○)         │
│           with power modules                                                  │
└─────────────────────────────────────────────────────────────────────────────┘
```

High-speed link for Model 550

The Model 550 supports two HSL-2/RIO-2 loops. The maximum rated speed of the HSL-2/RIO-2 is 2 GB/s, which is double the speed of the previous HSL/HSL-2 adapters. The following rules apply to towers that are supported at these speeds:

▶ New #5094, #5294, #0595, and #5095s come with a #9517 HSL-2/RIO-2 adapter. The #5790 PCI-X Expansion Drawer includes a #9531 HSL-2/RIO-2 adapter.

▶ HSL-2 adapters in existing #5094, #5294, #0595, and #5095 towers must be replaced with a #6417 HSL-2/RIO-G Bus Adapter.

▶ Mixing of HSL and HSL-2 towers is permitted with the correct combination of cables.

See "HSL fabric" on page 297 for information about supported HSL cables and HSL loop maximums. You can find more information in *High-speed Link Loop Architecture for the IBM @server iSeries Server: OS/400 Version 5 Release 2*, REDP-3652, and in the HSL Rules presentation available at:

http://www-1.ibm.com/servers/eserver/iseries/ha/systemdesign.html

Model 550 PCI cards and features

The Model 550 is a PCI-based technology system. The number of PCI cards that can be supported in a Model 550 depends on whether an I/O tower is attached and on the number of PCI slots. PCI card placement rules and LPAR configuration considerations also affect the number of slots that are supported.

See the table on page 82 for the number of maximum features supported by the total system and in the Model 550 system unit. See Chapter 17, "iSeries PCI I/O processors" on page 323, and Chapter 18, "iSeries I/O adapters and controllers" on page 337, for full descriptions of the features that are supported. See "AIX and Linux Direct Attach features overview" on page 340 for supported Linux Direct Attach features.

> **Note:** The placement of PCI cards follows special rules. Refer to "PCI card technology" on page 338 and *PCI Card Placement Rules for the IBM @server iSeries Server Version 5 Release 2*, REDP-3638, before you propose any configuration.

External towers

Migration towers are not supported on the Model 550. PCI towers are supported with upgrades for migration only.

Refer to Chapter 15, "Towers, racks, and high-speed link" on page 261, for information about supported towers for the Model 550, and "Summary of the iSeries expansion units and towers" on page 119 for a table of configuration maximums.

Model 550 upgrades

See Chapter 16, "Upgrades to eServer i5 and i5/OS" on page 311, for general upgrade considerations and server-to-server upgrade possibilities. Supported model upgrades for the Model 550 are identified in the *Upgrade* topic of the Find and Compare Tool (FACT) at:

http://www-919.ibm.com/servers/eserver/fact/

Model 550 Capacity on Demand

The @server i5 Model 550 offers Capacity on Demand options that make it possible to activate additional processor resource. CUoD, On/Off Capacity on Demand, Reserve Capacity on Demand, and Trial Capacity on Demand are available for the Model 550. On Demand features are described in this section.

► Capacity Upgrade on Demand (Permanent)

Purchase processor activation features when needed. Requires the purchase of operating system licenses.

► On/Off Capacity on Demand (Temporary)

Pay for processor day billing features at the end of each billing period. Additional i5/OS licenses are not required.

► Reserve Capacity on Demand (Prepaid)

Buy blocks of processor days ahead of time. Additional i5/OS licenses are not required.

► Trial Capacity on Demand

Request trial capacity from CoD Web site for special purposes. Additional i5/OS licenses not required.

Refer to the table on page 85 to see the feature codes associated with the Model 550 Capacity on Demand options. See the following Web site for more information about Capacity on Demand:

`http://www-1.ibm.com/servers/eserver/iseries/ondemand/cod/`

eServer i5 Model 570

The @server i5 Model 570 is the industry's first POWER5 technology-based server. It has the capability to simultaneously run multiple operating environments with an integrated infrastructure that's simpler, more productive, and more resilient than ever before. The 16-way @server i5 Model 570 delivers 20% more performance than the previous high-end iSeries server, the 32-way @server 1.3 GHz POWER4 processors.

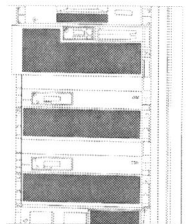

@server i5 Model 570 System Unit

The Model 570 is offered as a rack mounted configuration. It provides an integrated set of hardware capabilities that include two integrated 1 Gbps Ethernet ports and an integrated Small Computer System Interface (SCSI) controller. Also incorporated are hot-plug PCI-X card slots and disk slots, redundant hot-plug power supplies, dual power cords, redundant hot-plug cooling fans, and an optional redundant CPU power regulator. Hot-plugging of removable media devices is not supported.

Model overview

This section takes a closer look at the minimum functional server, required features, and optional features.

Minimum functional server

A minimum functional server consists of the base server unit and selected priced features. The base server includes:

► Physical package and power elements

► Base CEC enclosure (CCIN 788A)

► I/O Backplane (CCIN 28DA), which includes:

  – Two USB Type A

    Not supported on IBM i5/OS V5R3; are supported by specific releases of AIX 5L and specific Linux distributions

  – Two 10/100/1000 Mbps UTP Ethernet ports

    Not supported by i5/OS V5R3 for local area network (LAN) console

  – Two high-speed link (HSL)-2/RIO-G ports

    Enables 1 HSL-2/RIO-2 loop

  – One system connection port (for Service Processor flex cable connection)

  – Six hot-plug PCI-X card slots

    Slots 1 through 5 are long slots. Slot 6 is a short slot. Slot 6 volume may also be used for HSL-2/RIO-2 input/output (I/O) port expansion.

► Serial Port card (CCIN 25F8)

  – Two serial ports provide a full-duplex serial interface to support communications with serial peripheral devices. Configured as RS232 serial.

  – It is not supported by i5/OS V5R3 but are supported by specific releases of AIX 5L and specific Linux distributions.

► System Serial number, VPD, capacity card

► Blindswap cassettes

  – Manufacturing installs empty blindswap cassettes in all empty PCI-X slots. PCI-X slots 1 to 5 require #7862, and PCI-X slot 6 requires #7861. The Integrated xSeries Adapter, if installed, requires blindswap cassette #7863.

  – Additional restrictions may apply, based on specific cards.

- Direct access storage device (DASD) backplane (CCIN 28DB)
  - One 6-pack DASD cage supports up to six 1-inch disk drives.
  - The load source disk installs in card slot 4.
- Removable media backplane (CCIN 28DC)
  - Two removable media slots are available.
  - CCIN 180A converts a slimline slot from integrated development environment (IDE) to SCSI and blocks the second slot.
  - 9406 Model 570 only supports one slimline removable media slot for the required #2640 DVD-ROM (default) or the #5751 DVD-RAM.

  > **Note:** The 9406 Model 570 does not support a removable magnetic media device in the base CEC. A tower and associated support or an external tape or DVD-RAM device is required.

- Power and cooling
  - Power Supply Distribution backplane (CCIN 28DD)
  - System midplane (CCIN 28D9)
    - Supports two hot-plug power supplies (CCIN 51B7)
    - Two fans or blowers for temperature regulation purposes
- Two base 1400W 240V power supplies (CCIN 51B7)
- CEC backplane (CCIN 27AE)
- CPU Regulator (CCIN 28E8)
  - A system with one 0/2 way processor cards includes one CPU Regulator.
  - A system with two 0/2 way processor cards (a 2/4-way system) includes two CPU Regulators.
- Base I/O adapters (IOAs) or I/O processors (IOPs)
  - #5709 RAID Enabler Card (CCIN 5709)

    The required card fits into a dedicated slot on the backplane and does not use a PCI-X adapter slot. The #5709 provides RAID capability for the embedded disk controller.

  - #9793 or #9794 Two-Line IOA with Modem: PCI-X Slot 2
  - #9844 Base PCI IOP: One in PCI-X Slot 1

► #1846 Operator Panel (CCIN 28D4)

A minimally configured stand-alone system requires a single operator panel for operation.

> **Note:** A Hardware Management Console (HMC) is required to manage specific configurations. See "Hardware Management Console" on page 679 for more information.

► Service processor (CCIN 28EA) contains:
  – One Rack Indicator Port
  – Two SPCN (RS485) control for attached I/O subsystems
  – Two Ethernet or HMC ports

> **Note:** If two or more 570 are stacked together, the second Service Processor in the second unit can perform redundant Service Processor functions. The planned availability of the microcode is in 2005.

► VPD card
► Rack Rail Kit

Should be considered part of the base CEC hardware.

Required features

> **Note:** In the following list, a single asterisk (*) indicates that the feature is supported for conversion only.

The *required* features for the 570 system unit include:

► Specific combinations of the Processor feature, Edition feature, and Server feature are allowed as shown in the following table.

Processor	Server feature	Edition feature	Software group	Processor feature code or QPRCFEAT value
#8961 (3300/6000 CPW)	#0919	#7488 Standard	P30	7488
		#7489 Enterprise	P30	7489
#8961 (6350/11700 CPW)	#0920	#7469 Standard	P30	7469
		#7470 Enterprise	P30	7470
#8971 (6350/12000 CPW)	#0921	#7494 Standard	P30	7494
		#7495 Enterprise	P30	7495
		#7560 High Availability	P30	7560
#8971 (15200/23500 CPW)	#0922	#7471 Standard	P40	7471
		#7472 Enterprise	P40	7472
		#7561 High Availability	P40	7561
#8971 (25500/33400 CPW)	#0924	#7473 Standard	P40	7473
		#7474 Enterprise	P40	7474
		#7562 High Availability	P40	7562
#8971 (36300/44700 CPW)	#0926	#7475 Standard	P40	7475
		#7476 Enterprise	P40	7476
		#7563 High Availability	P40	7563
#8971 (6000/44700 CPW)	#0928	#7570 Capacity BackUp	P40	7570
#8971 (3000/6000 CPW)	#0930	#7490 Standard	P30	7490
		#7491 Enterprise	P30	7491
		#7559 High Availability	P30	

Note: The Standard Edition for the Model 570 processors provides limited 5250 CPW for 5250 OLTP workloads. The Enterprise, High Availability, and Capacity BackUp Editions for the Model 570 processors provide maximum 5250 CPW for 5250 OLTP workloads if activated.

The Standard, Enterprise and High Availability Editions also provide support for Capacity on Demand (permanent and temporary). The Capacity on Demand Edition provides support for temporary capacity only.

Edition content varies by processor and server features selected. For more information, see "Editions" on page 55.

► Main storage

All main storage on the Model 570 is feature main storage.

► DVD-ROM or DVD-RAM

- #2640 DVD-ROM
- #5751 DVD-RAM

► Internal disk units - 10k or 15k rpm only

- #4317 8.58 GB 10k RPM Disk Unit*
- #4318 17.54 GB 10k RPM Disk Unit*
- #4319 35.16 GB 10k RPM Disk Unit
- #4326 35.16 GB 15k RPM Disk Unit
- #4327 70.56 GB 15k RPM Disk Unit

One of the following load source specify codes is required:

- #0828 - #4317 Load Source specify*
- #0829 - #4318 Load Source Specify*
- #0830 - #4319 Load Source Specify
- #0834 - #4326 Load Source Specify
- #0835 - #4327 Load Source Specify

► Disk protection specify codes (one must be specified)

- #0040 Mirrored System Disk Level
- #0041 RAID Protection - All
- #0042 Mirrored System IOP Level
- #0043 Mirrored System Bus Level

The #0041 is the default for disk data protection.

► Internal tape

The Model 570 only supports one slimline removable media slot for the required #2640 DVD-ROM (default) or the #5751 DVD-RAM. The 9406 Model 570 does not support a removable magnetic media device in the base CEC. A tower and associated support or an external tape or DVD-RAM device is required.

► System console attachment adapter

- #5540 System Console on Twinaxial Workstation IOA

  • #4746 PCI Twinaxial IOA

- #5544 System Console on Operations Console

  • #0367 Operations Console PCI Cable (attaches to #9793 or #9794)

- #5546 System Console on 100 Mbps Token Ring
  - #2744 PCI 100 Mbps Token Ring IOA
  - #0367 Operations Console PCI Cable
- #5548 System Console on 100 Mbps Ethernet
  - #2849 10/100 Mbps Ethernet Adapter
  - #0367 Operations Console PCI Cable
- #5550 System Console on HMC

  The HMC is required for systems using logical partitions (LPARs), IBM @server Capacity Upgrade on Demand (CUoD) upgrade operations, and redundant Service Processor operations.

Optional features

The *optional* features for the 570 system unit include:

▶ #1800 HSL-2 Ports - 2 Copper

Adds capacity for second HSL-2/RIO-2 loop

▶ #1801 Optical Bus Expansion Card - 2 port

Adds capacity for an optical HSL loop

▶ #7875 Redundant CPU Regulator

▶ Uninterruptible power supply

We recommend that you have an external uninterruptible power supply to protect the system unit and any external components against utility power outages.

> **Note:** A #1827 Serial-UPS conversion cable is required to provide uninterruptible power supply control or feedback information for the @server i5 Model 570. It does not impact the ability of the uninterruptible power supply to provide power in case of an outage. Its absence prevents the uninterruptible power supply from alerting the Model 570 that it is under the uninterruptible power supply and from advising the server to the amount of remaining uninterruptible power supply battery power.

The Model 570 initial installation is IBM installed. Processor upgrades within models are performed by IBM Service Representatives.

Processor features

► The #8961 POWER5, 0/2-way, 1.65 GHz processor (CCIN 26EA) includes:
  - 36 MB L3 cache per processor card
  - 1.88 MB L2 cache chip
  - Eight main memory Dual Inline Memory Module (DIMM) slots per processor card

> **Note:** The #8961 was withdrawn from marketing on 01 October 2004.

► The #8971 POWER5, 0/2-way, 1.65 GHz processor (CCIN 26F2) includes:
  - 36 MB L3 cache per processor card
  - 1.88 MB L2 cache per chip
  - Eight main memory Dual Inline Memory Module (DIMM) slots per processor card

► The #0919 Server feature represents a 1/2-way processor. This is one #8961 0/2-way processor and one #8452 Base Processor Activation.

► The #0920 Server feature represents a 2/4-way processor. This is two #8961 0/2-way processors and two #8452 Base Processor Activations. (The #0920 was withdrawn from marketing on 01 October 2004.)

► The #0930 Server feature represents a 1/2-way processor. This is one #8971 0/2-way processors and one #8452 Base Processor Activation.

► The #0921 Server feature represents a 2/4-way processor. This is two #8971 0/2-way processors and two #8452 Base Processor Activations.

► The #0922 Server feature represents a 5/8-way processor. This is four #8971 0/2-way processors and five #8452 Base Processor Activations.

► The #0924 Server feature represents a 9/12way processor. This is six #8971 0/2-way processors and nine #8452 Base Processor Activations.

► The #0926 Server feature represents a 13/16-way processor. This is eight #8971 0/2-way processors and thirteen #8452 Base Processor Activations.

► The #09208 Server feature represents a 2/16way processor. This is eight #8971 0/2-way processors and two #8452 Base Processor Activations.

> **Note:** The #0919, #0920, #7469, #7488, #7489 and #8961 processors were withdrawn from marketing on 01 October 2004.

Refer to "Table 3: Summary of the eServer i5 Model 570 (Part 1)" on page 86 to find Processor CPW, Mail and Calendar Users (MCU), 5250 CPW, and to determine the processor feature code and QPRCFEAT value.

Main storage

Supported memory features for the Model 570 are:

- ▶ #3043 - 512 MB Main Storage DIMM (DDR - 256 Mb technology, unstacked, CCIN 3043) - four are required *
- ▶ #3044 - 1 GB Main Storage DIMM (DDR - 256 Mb technology, stacked, CCIN 3044) four are required *
- ▶ #3046 - 2 GB Main Storage DIMM (DDR - 256 Mb technology, stacked, CCIN 3046) four are required *
- ▶ #4452 - 2 GB DDR Main Storage (DDR1 CCIN 309D)

  Ships four 512 MB DIMMs for a total of 2 GB
- ▶ #4454 - 8 GB DDR Main Storage (DDR1 CCIN 30AA)

  Ships four 2 GB DIMMs for a total of 8 GB
- ▶ #4490 - 4 GB DDR Main Storage (DDR1 CCIN 309E)

  Ships four 1 GB DIMMs for a total of 4 GB
- ▶ #4491 - 16 GB DDR Main Storage (DDR1 CCIN 30B3)

  Ships four 4 GB DIMMs for a total of 16 GB
- ▶ #4492 - 32 GB DDR Main Storage (DDR1 CCIN 30F7)

  Ships four 8 GB DIMMs for a total of 32GB

  Only supported on #8971 Processor (CCIN 26F2)

The Model 570 offers pluggable DIMMs for memory. Each 0/2-way processor card contains eight slots for up to eight pluggable DIMMs. The minimum memory for a 9406 Model 570 is 2 GB. The maximum memory capacity depends on the number of processors ordered for the system and on the type of memory and functionality required.

The main storage cards are installed according to the following rules. There are no restrictions for mixing and matching DIMMs other than:

- ▶ Memory DIMMs must be installed in quads.
- ▶ Quads must all be the same DIMM.

DIMMs are plugged, by quad, in either of the following sequences:

- ▶ J0A, J0C, J1A, J1C
- ▶ J0B, J0D, J1B, J1D

Note: We recommend that you perform memory balancing. You must order sufficient memory to balance memory across processors.

Memory spreading and balancing

Performance measurements have determined that optimal performance requires both spreading of memory across processors and balancing memory across processors. The following rules should be followed for Model 570 memory.

▶ **Memory minimums**: Each processor card must have at least one set of memory DIMM placed on it. Memory is ordered in feature codes of quads. The following table lists the minimum memory requirements.

n-way Processor	Minimum memory	#4452
1/2-way	2GB	#4452 x1
2/4-way	4GB	#4452 x 2
5/8-way	8GB	#4452 x 4
9/12-way	12GB	#4452 x 6
13/16-way	16GB	#4452 x 8

▶ **Balancing**: Each 0/2 way processor card must have a minimum of 2 GB memory on it.

▶ **Spreading**: Memory should be spread across the processor cards. Memory DIMMs should be selected to enable equal memory configurations across processors in an n-way unit. If memory greater than the minimum is ordered, the selection of memory features should be based on driving the most number of DIMM quads onto the system, as evenly distributed across the processors as possible.

▶ **#4492 8 GB DIMMs**: The 8 GB DIMMs carry the following restrictions:

  – 8 GB DIMMs cannot be placed on a processor card with another size DIMM.

  – 8 GB DIMMs slow the system memory clock down from 266 MHz to 200 MHz.

  As a result, the #4492 can only be placed on a processor card by itself, with another #4492 or with a #7935.

▶ **Processor additions or enclosure additions**: Existing memory should be spread onto the new processor cards or the additional processors should ship with memory.

9406 Model 570 schematics

You can find schematics of any supported expansion units in Chapter 15, "Towers, racks, and high-speed link" on page 261.

Note: The Model 570 system schematics are under construction at the time of publication. The following diagrams show a view of the front, rear, and top of the Model 570. Look for the latest diagrams with card slot placement in *IBM @server i5, iSeries, and AS/400e System Builder*, SG24-2155.

9406 Model 570 system unit: Top, front, and rear views

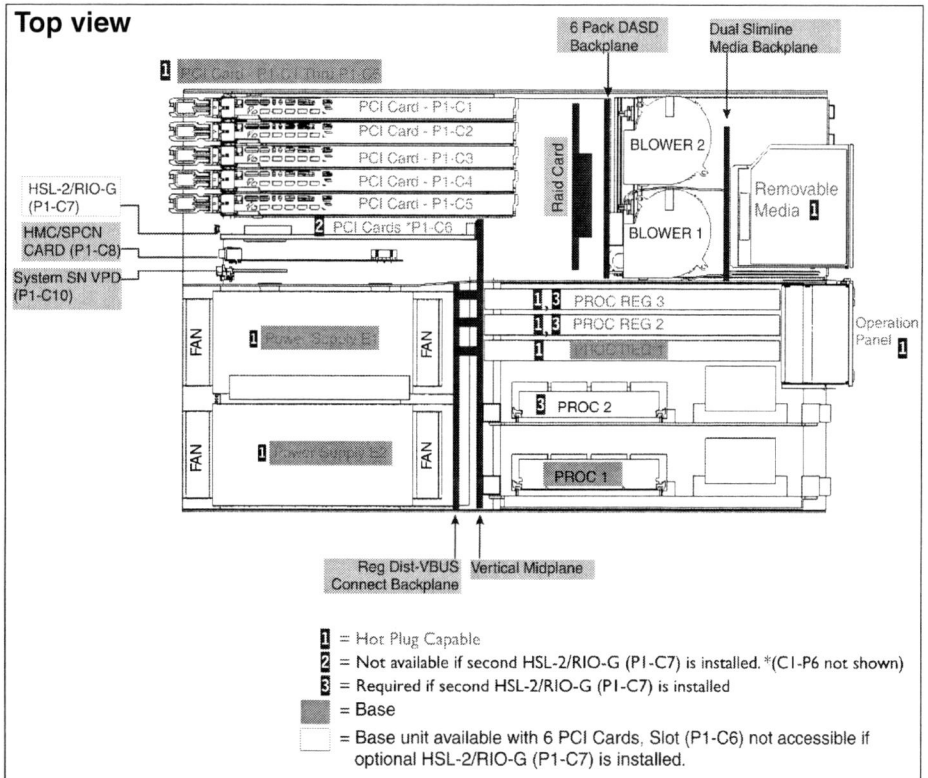

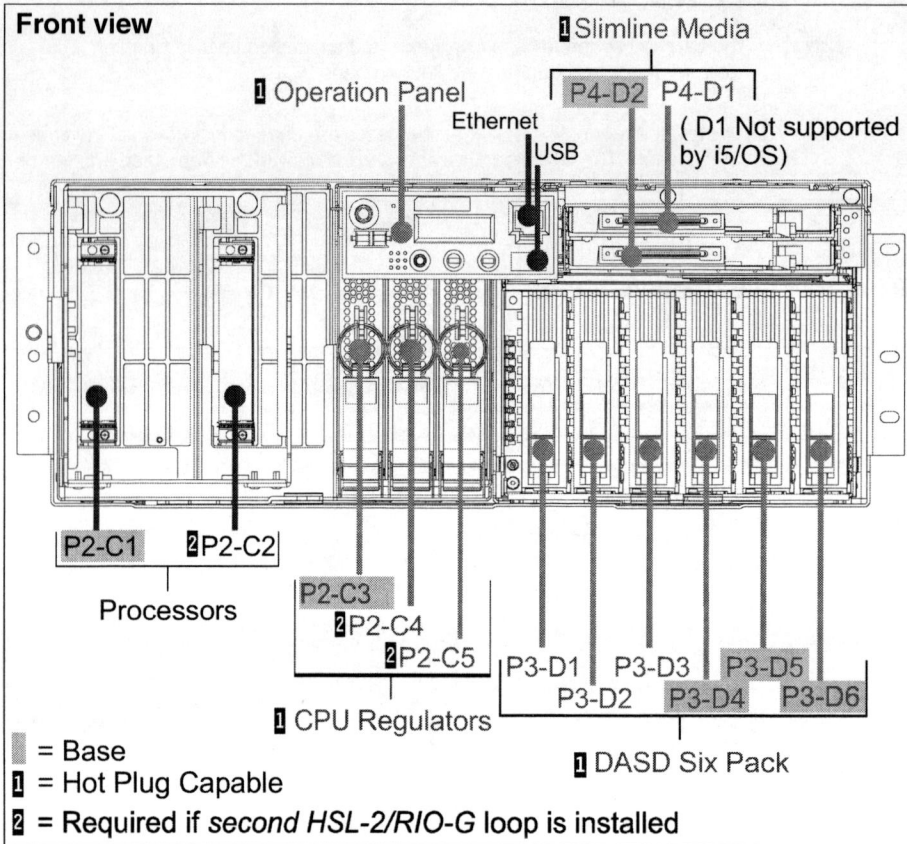

Front view

1 Slimline Media

1 Operation Panel

P4-D2   P4-D1

Ethernet
USB

(D1 Not supported
by i5/OS)

P2-C1   **2** P2-C2

Processors

P2-C3
2 P2-C4
2 P2-C5

1 CPU Regulators

P3-D1   P3-D3   P3-D5
P3-D2   P3-D4   P3-D6

1 DASD Six Pack

■ = Base
1 = Hot Plug Capable
2 = Required if *second HSL-2/RIO-G* loop is installed

Rear view

Multi-adapter Bridge 1

2 P1-C6

1 P1-C5

1 P1-C4

1 P1-C3

1 P1-C2

1 P1-C1

Multi-adapter Bridge 2

Service Processor Card (P1-C8)

P1-C8-T1 (HMC1)

P1-C8-T2 (HMC2)

P1-C8-T3 SPCN0

P1-C8-T4 SPCN1

P1-C10 - S/N VPD Card

I2C

P1-T1 - Serial Port (P2) **4**

P1-T2 - Serial Port (P1)

1 P1-E1   **1** P1-E2

(HSL-2/RIO-G) P1-C7-T1(1)
               P1-C7-T2(0)

3 *Second HSL-2/RIO-G Loop*

P1-T8(0) P1-T9(1) P1-T10
                    System Connect

(HSL-2/RIO-G)

P1-T5 -USB(1) Not usable i5/OS

P1-T3 - RI

(Rack Ind Port)

P1-T7 - Ethernet(1)

P1-T6 - Ethernet(0)

P1-T4- USB(0) Not usable i5/OS

= Base

1 = Hot Plug Capable

2 = Not usable if optional *second HSL-2/RIO-G loop (P1-C7)* is installed

3 = If optional *second HSL-2/RIO-G loop (P1-C7)* is installed, Proc. 2 and both Proc. Reg. 2 and 3 are required

4 = #1827 Serial-UPS Conversion Cable connects to the (P2) serial port

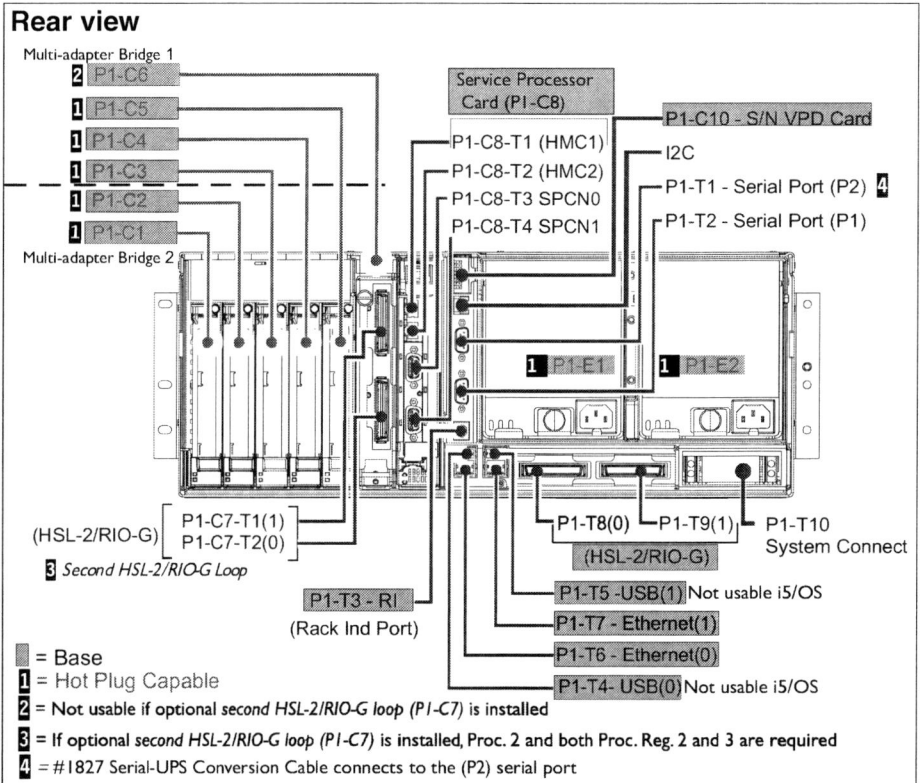

Note: You can find line cord and power receptacle specification information on the Web at:

http://www.ibm.com/eserver/iseries/infocenter

Model 570 processor card

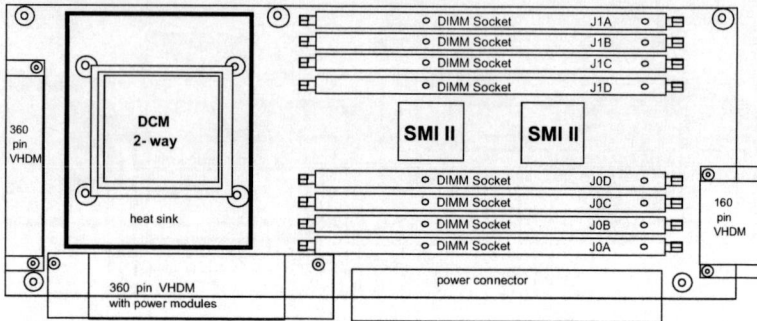

High-speed link for Model 570

HSL configuration considerations for the Model 570 include:

► The Model 570 1/2-way system supports a single HSL-2/RIO-2 loop with a maximum of six towers across the loop.

► The 2/4-way system supports two HSL-2/RIO-2 loops with a maximum of 12 towers across both loops.

► The 5/8-way supports four HSL-2/RIO-2 loops with a maximum of 18 towers across all loops.

► The 9/12-way supports four six HSL-2/RIO-2 loops with a maximum of 24 towers across all loops.

► The 13/16-way supports eight HSL-2/RIO-2 loops with a maximum of 30 towers across all loops.

The speed of the HSL-2/RIO-2 is doubled to 2 GB/s. compared to the previous HSL-2 adapters operating at 1 GB/s. The following rules apply to towers that are supported at these speeds:

► The #5094, #5294, #0595, and #5095 come with a #9517 HSL-2/RIO-2 adapter. The #5790 PCI-X Expansion Drawer includes a #9531 HSL-2/RIO-2 adapter

► HSL-2 adapters in existing #5094, #5294, #0595, and #5095 towers must be replaced with a #6417 HSL-2/RIO-G Bus Adapter.

► Mixing of HSL and HSL-2 towers is permitted with the correct combination of cables.

See "HSL fabric" on page 297 for information about supported HSL cables and HSL loop maximums. You can find more information in *High-speed Link Loop Architecture for the IBM @server iSeries Server: OS/400 Version 5 Release 2*, REDP-3652, and in the HSL Rules presentation available at:

`http://www-1.ibm.com/servers/eserver/iseries/ha/systemdesign.html`

Model 570 PCI cards and features

The Model 570 is a Peripheral Component Interconnect (PCI)-based technology system. The number of PCI cards that can be supported in a Model 570 depends on whether an I/O tower is attached and the number of PCI slots. PCI card placement rules and LPAR configuration considerations also affect the number of slots supported.

See the table on page 86 for the number of maximum features supported by the total system and in the Model 570 system unit. See Chapter 17, "iSeries PCI I/O processors" on page 323, and Chapter 18, "iSeries I/O adapters and controllers" on page 337, for full descriptions of the features that are supported. See "AIX and Linux Direct Attach features overview" on page 340 for the supported Linux Direct Attach features.

> **Note:** The placement of PCI cards follows special rules. Refer to "PCI card technology" on page 338 and *PCI Card Placement Rules for the IBM @server iSeries Server Version 5 Release 2*, REDP-3638, before you propose any configuration.

External towers

Migration towers are not supported on the Model 570. PCI towers are supported with upgrades for migration only.

Refer to Chapter 15, "Towers, racks, and high-speed link" on page 261, for information about supported towers for the Model 570, and "Summary of the iSeries expansion units and towers" on page 119 for a table of configuration maximums.

Model 570 upgrades

See Chapter 16, "Upgrades to eServer i5 and i5/OS" on page 311, for general upgrade considerations and server-to-server upgrade possibilities. Supported model upgrades for the Model 570 are identified in the *Upgrade* topic of the Find and Compare Tool (FACT) at:

http://www-919.ibm.com/servers/eserver/fact/

Model 570 Capacity on Demand

The @server i5 Model 570 offers Capacity on Demand options that make it possible to activate additional processor resource. CUoD, On/Off Capacity on Demand, Reserve Capacity on Demand, and Trial Capacity on Demand are available for the Model 570. On Demand features are described in this section.

On Demand features may have some base activations. The following options are available to activate additional resources:

► Capacity upgrade on Demand (Permanent)

   Purchase processor activation features when needed. Requires the purchase of operating system licenses.

► On/Off Capacity on Demand (Temporary)

   Pay for processor day billing features at the end of each billing period. Additional i5/OS licenses are not required.

► Reserve Capacity on Demand (Prepaid)

   Buy blocks of processor days ahead of time. Additional i5/OS licenses are not required.

► Trial Capacity on Demand

   Request trial capacity from CoD Web site for special purposes. Additional i5/OS licenses are not required.

Refer to the table on page 91 to see the feature codes associated with the Model 570 Capacity on Demand options. See the following Web site for more information about Capacity on Demand:

http://www-1.ibm.com/servers/eserver/iseries/ondemand/cod/

9

eServer i5 Model 595

The @server i5 Model 595 is the newest member of the POWER5 technology-based servers. It is an 8 to 64-way processor with performance of up to 165,000 commercial processing workload (CPW). A highly scalable, upgradable industry-standard architecture helps support balanced growth. IBM Capacity on Demand features enable extra power at a moment's notice to handle surges in demand of CPU or memory to meet constantly shifting business priorities.

Supported by advanced virtualization technologies, Model 595 servers are designed to run multiple operating systems simultaneously, including IBM i5/OS, Linux, IBM AIX 5L, Microsoft Windows (via an Integrated xSeries Adapter (IXA) or an Integrated xSeries Server (IXS).

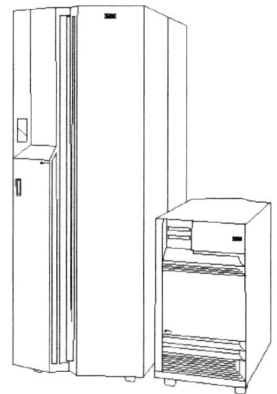

@server *i5 Model 595*

The Model 595 is offered as either a Standard or Enterprise Edition, each with four i5/OS processor licenses. Extensive on demand capabilities and dynamic partitioning for up to a total of 254 partitions of i5/OS, Linux, and AIX 5L are supported.

The Model 595 is built using a processor book structure. Each 16-way processor book has two 8-way multichip modules (MCM) with state-of-the-art, 64-bit,

167

POWER5 processors. Each processor book has sixteen memory slots. Each book also provides attachment capability for up to six HSL-2/RIO-2 loops on which HSL-2/RIO-2 input/output (I/O) drawers and towers can be attached.

The Model 595 consists at a minimum of two enclosures: a two-meter system unit enclosure and an I/O tower about one meter in height.

Model overview

This section takes a closer look at the minimum functional server, required features, and optional features.

Minimum functional server

A minimum functional server consists of the base server unit and selected priced features. The Model 595 supports hot plug and concurrent add of PCI cards, disk units, and removable media devices.

Included in the base server are the physical package and power elements as follows:

► System unit (also known as the Central Electronics Complex or CEC)
► #9194 Base PCI-X Expansion Tower or #8294 Optional Base 1.8M Rack
► Line cord features

  Two line cord features should be specified for the 595 system unit, with two additional line cord features for the #9194 Base PCI-X Expansion Tower as well as two HSL-2/RIO-2 cables. Three (the default) or four HSL-2/RIO-2 cables are needed for the #8294 Optional Base 1.8M Rack and two additional line cords for the top tower.

► Power Assembly
  – #182x

    One or more of these features provide redundant power cabling.

  – #6186 Bulk Power Regulator

    • Two are required with a 8/16-way processor feature.
    • Four are required with a 16/32-way processor feature.
    • Six are required with a 32/64-way processor feature.

  – Bulk Power Controller (CCIN 275D)

    Two are required with all processor features.

- #7837 Bulk Power Distribution
  - Two are required with a 8/16-way processor feature.
  - Four are required with 16/32-way and 32/64-way processor features.
- Distributed Converter Assembly (DCA)
  - Three DCAs are included as a base feature with the 8/16-way processor.
  - Six DCAs are included as a base feature with the 16/32-way processor.
  - Twelve DCAs are included as a base feature with the 32/64-way processor.

▶ CEC Rack Front and Rear Doors
- One feature includes both a front door and a rear door for the system unit.
- Choose either #6251 Slim Line Doors or #6252 Acoustic Doors.

▶ #3757 Service Shelf Toolkit
- Every installation location must have access to one Service Tool Kit.
- The IBM Marketing Configurator defaults to one. It can be removed in multi-system orders to prevent multiple quantities shipped to the same installation.

▶ One Multiplexer Card included in every processor book (CCIN 28E6)

▶ One System Unit backplane

▶ Two Clock Cards (CCIN 28E4)

▶ One Front Indicator Light Strip (CCIN 291A) and one Rear Indicator Light Strip (CCIN 291B)

▶ Up to four 16-way processor books with each two 8-way MCMs

▶ Sixteen main storage card slots in each processor book

▶ Six slots for feature HSL-2/RIO-2 adapters in each processor book

▶ Two #7818 HSL-2/RIO-2 2-port Copper (CCIN 28D8) are compulsory per system

▶ #9844 Base PCI IOP provides support for:
- The required SCSI IOA which controls up to 15 disk units, the required DVD-RAM/DVD-ROM, and an internal tape feature or a DVD-RAM/DVD-ROM feature

- A base Console/Workstation IOA

  The IBM marketing configurator determines which feature combinations are placed on the order based on the #5540, #5544, #5546, #5548 or #5550 System Console specify code.

- The #9771/#9793/#9794 Base PCI Two-Line WAN with integrated modem

> **Note:** A Hardware Management Console (HMC) is required to manage specific configurations. See "Hardware Management Console" on page 679 for more information.

► Two Service Processors (CCIN 28DE). Each contains:
  – One SPCN (RS485) control for attached I/O subsystems
  – Two Ethernet ports for connection to HMC through Bulk Power Controller
  – Two ports for connection to Front and Rear Light Strips

> **Note:** Redundant Service Processor function is planned to be available with new microcode in 2005.

► Anchor card

The Anchor card is considered part of the base system unit hardware.

Required features

> **Note:** The features listed in this section that are not orderable as new features are marked as follows:
>
>   * Supported as migration feature only
> ** Supported in system unit for upgrades only
> *** Miscellaneous Equipment Specification (MES) only

The *required* features for the 595 system unit include:

► Supported specific combinations of the Processor feature, Edition feature, and Server feature, as shown in the following table.

Processor feature	Server feature	Edition feature	Software group	Processor feature or QPRCFEAT value
#8981	#0946	#7496 Standard	P50	7496
		#7497 Enterprise	P50	7497
	#0947	#7498 Standard	P50	7498
		#7499 Enterprise	P50	7499
	#0952	#7984 Standard	P60	7984
		#7985 Enterprise	P60	7985

Note: The Standard Edition for the Model 595 processors provides limited 5250 CPW for 5250 OLTP workloads. The Enterprise Edition for the Model 595 processors provides up to maximum 5250 CPW for 5250 OLTP workloads if activated and support for Capacity on Demand (permanent and temporary).

► Main storage

All main storage on the Model 595 is feature main storage. See the main storage on page "Main storage" on page 174 for a list of supported memory features and configuration considerations.

► PCI disk controller (SCSI IOA)

The SCSI IOA supports the DVD-ROM, DVD-RAM, migrated CD-ROM, internal tape, and disk units in the base PCI enclosure.

 – #2757 PCI-X Ultra RAID Disk Controller
 – #2780 PCI-X Ultra RAID Disk Controller (the base default)
 – #4748 PCI RAID Disk Unit Controller*
 – #4778 PCI RAID Disk Unit Controller*

► Removable optical device (one must be specified)

 – #4425 CD-ROM*
 – #4430 DVD-RAM*
 – #4625 CD-ROM***
 – #4630 DVD-RAM*
 – #4631 DVD-ROM
 – #4633 DVD-RAMBO

► Internal disk units - 10k or 15k rpm only

 – #4317 8.58 GB 10k RPM Disk Unit**
 – #4318 17.54 GB 10k RPM Disk Unit**
 – #4319 35.16 GB 10k RPM Disk Unit
 – #4326 35.16 GB 15k RPM Disk Unit
 – #4327 70.56 GB 15k RPM Disk Unit

One of the following load source specify codes is required:

 – #0829 - #4318 Load Source Specify*
 – #0830 - #4319 Load Source Specify*
 – #0834 - #4326 Load Source Specify
 – #0835 - #4327 Load Source Specify

- ► Disk protection specify codes (one must be specified)
    - – #0040 Mirrored System Disk Level
    - – #0041 RAID Protection - All
    - – #0042 Mirrored System IOP Level
    - – #0043 Mirrored System Bus Level

  #0042 is the default for disk data protection.
- ► System console/communications adapter

  The console on LAN options requires a dedicated LAN adapter.
    - – #5540 System Console on Twinaxial Workstation IOA
      - • #4746 PCI Twinaxial IOA
    - – #5544 System Console on Operations Console
      - • #0367 Operations Console PCI Cable
    - – #5546 System Console on 100 Mbps Token Ring
      - • #2744 PCI 100 Mbps Token Ring IOA
      - • #0367 Operations Console PCI Cable
    - – #5548 System Console on 100 Mbps Ethernet
      - • #0367 Operations Console PCI Cable
      - • #2849 10/100 Mbps Ethernet Adapter or
      - • #4838 PCI 100/10 Mbps Ethernet IOA
    - – #5550 System Console on HMC

  An #0367 Operations Console PCI Cable is added to the order by the IBM marketing configurator.

Optional features

The *optional* features for the @server i5 Model 595 include these internal tape devices:

- ► #4482 4 GB ¼-inch Cartridge Tape Device*
- ► #4483 16 GB ¼-inch Cartridge Tape Device*
- ► #4486 25 GB ¼-inch Cartridge Tape Device*
- ► #4487 50 GB ¼-inch Cartridge Tape Device*
- ► #4682 4 GB ¼-inch Cartridge Tape Device
- ► #4684 30 GB ¼-inch Cartridge Tape Device
- ► #4685 80 GB VXA-2 Tape Device
- ► #4686 25 GB ¼-inch Cartridge Tape Device*
- ► #4687 50 GB ¼-inch Cartridge Tape Device

We recommend that you have an external uninterruptible power supply to protect the system unit and any external components against utility power outages.

IBM Service Representatives perform the Model 595 initial installation and model upgrades.

IBM is offering a service to aid in configuring partitioned systems. Clients can order the charged #8453 Base Customer Placement. Configurations are built with hardware components using placement information from the LPAR Verification Tool (LVT). The client is responsible for submitting LVT information. The #8453 Base Customer Placement option is supported on new system builds.

Processor features

The processor features for the Model 595 include:

- ▶ #8981 Model 595 Processor book (POWER5 1.65 GHZ 0/16-way CCIN 52A4)
  - – Two 8-way MCMs
  - – Sixteen DDR1 memory card slots (cards plug into processor book planar)
  - – Six HSL-2/RIO-2 adapter slots
- ▶ #8461 Base activations for 16-way, 32-way, and 64-way systems
  - – Eight required with 16-way systems
  - – Sixteen required with 32-way systems
  - – Thirty-two required with 64-way systems
- ▶ Additional single processor activations are orderable with #7925

Refer to "Model 595 Capacity on Demand" on page 186 for a cross-reference of the processor and CoD features.

Refer to "Table 5: Summary of the eServer i5 Model 595" on page 93 to find Processor CPW, Mail and Calendar Users (MCU), and 5250 CPW, and to determine the processor feature code.

Main storage

Supported memory features for the Model 595 are:

- ▶ #7828 -16 GB Main Storage (DDR1 memory card CCIN 304E)
  Ships one fully activated memory card

- ▶ #7829 - 32 GB Main Storage (DDR1 memory card CCIN 30F9)
  Ships one fully activated memory card

> **Note:** The #7829 is planned to be available in second quarter 2005.

- ▶ #7816- 2/4 GB CoD Main Storage (DDR1 memory card CCIN 303E)

  Ships one memory card.

  2 GB system memory is activated. An additional two GB of system memory is available for activation in increments of one GB (#7970)

- ▶ #7835- 4/8 GB CoD Main Storage (DDR1 memory card CCIN 303F)

  Ships one memory card.

  4 GB system memory is activated. An additional four GB of system memory is available for activation in increments of one GB (#7970).

- ▶ #8195 - 256 GB Main Storage (32 x 8 GB)

  The #8395 provides 32 fully activated 8 GB memory card features for a total of 256 GB of active DDR1 system memory. The #8195 feature is shown on the order and in the install records, not 32 #7835 features.

- ▶ #8197 - 512 GB Main Storage (32 x 16 GB)

  The #8197 provides 32 fully activated memory features for a total of 512 GB of active DDR1 system memory. The #8198 feature is shown on the order and in the install records, not 32 #7828 features.

- ▶ #8198 - 512 GB Main Storage (16 x 32 GB)

  The #8198 provides 16 #7829 32 GB fully activated memory features for a total of 512 GB of active DDR1 system memory. The #8198 feature is shown on the order and in the install records, not 16 #7829 features.

The Model 595 offers pluggable DDR1 memory cards. Each processor book has 16 slots for memory cards. The minimum memory for a Model 595 is four memory cards with 8 GB of memory activated. The maximum memory capacity depends on the number of processor books ordered for the system and on the type of memory and functionality required.

Memory placement

Follow these rules for Model 595 memory.

► Use the recommended amount of minimum memory.

> **Note:** For best performance, order sufficient memory to balance memory across MCM and processor books.

Each processor book must have at least two pairs of memory cards (one pair for each MCM). The recommended minimum memory is shown in the following table.

Offering	Minimum activated	Minimum physical	Orientation feature code x quantity
8/16-way	8 GB	16 GB	#7816 x 4
16/32-way	16 GB	32 GB	#7816 x 8
32/64-way	32 GB	64 GB	#7816 x 16

► Memory must be ordered in identical pairs.

► Each processor book must have a minimum of four memory cards on it.

► Spread memory across the processor books.

Select memory cards to enable equal memory configurations across processors in an n-way unit. If memory greater than the minimum is ordered, select memory features to drive the most number of memory cards onto the system, as evenly distributed across the processors as possible.

► Spread existing memory onto the new processor cards in any new processor and enclosure additions.

Memory increments are handled by the IBM marketing configurator.

#9194 Base PCI-X Expansion Tower

The #9194 Base PCI-X Expansion Tower is the base PCI I/O enclosure shipped with a Model 595 server. The #9194 is attached to the Model 595 system unit with two HSL-2/RIO-2 cables (an HSL-2/RIO-2 loop) through a #9517 Base HSL-2/RIO-G Bus Adapter. The #9517 is the base feature code and is required on the order. Two SPCN cables are required to form an SPCN loop with Service Processors in the system unit. The #9194 has dual line cord capability. A #5164 Dual Power Cords - #8294/#9194 must be ordered.

The #9194 has 15 disk unit slots, with an additional 30 slots available with a #5168 30-Disk Expansion for #9194 Tower. The #9194 has two removable media slots and 14 PCI card slots. A #9844 Base PCI IOP is included. (The feature code is required). A #2780 PCI-X Ultra RAID Disk Controller is required. The #2780 drives the disk units in the base 15 disk unit slots and the removable media devices in the two removable media slots. An additional #2780 PCI-X Ultra RAID Disk Controller is required to drive the disk units in the 30 feature disk unit slots. The disk unit slots (both base and feature) are partitioned in groups of 15. Each group of 15 is further partitioned into three groups of five. Each group of five is on a separate Ultra4 SCSI bus from the ##2780 PCI-X Ultra RAID Disk Controller.

The 11 PCI IOAs are supported (driven) by the #9844 Base PCI IOP, by a feature #2844 PCI IOP or IOPs and by #4810/#4812 PCI Integrated xSeries Servers.

Two (any combination) of the following HSL cables must be ordered:

- ► #1307 -1.75m Copper HSL-2 Cable
- ► #1308 -2.5m Copper HSL-2 Cable
- ► #1482 - 3.5m HSL-2 Cable
- ► #1483 - 10m HSL-2 Cable
- ► #1481 - 1m HSL-2 Cable
- ► #1485 - 15m HSL-2 Cable

Two line cords and two SPCN cables for the #9194 Base PCI-X Expansion Tower must be ordered.

#5168 30-Disk Expansion for #9194 Tower

The #5168 30-Disk Expansion for #9194 Tower is a disk unit expansion enclosure feature for the #9194 Base PCI-X Expansion Tower The #5168 includes two 15 disk unit enclosures, one power supply, backplanes, and cables.

A disk controller is required to support the disk units in each of the two disk unit enclosures included with #5168. Each group of 15 disk units is further divided into three groups of five disk units with each group of five disk units supported on a separate SCSI bus. A minimum of two disk unit controllers and a maximum of six are required to support 30 disk units.

#8294 Optional Base 1.8M Rack

The #8294 Optional Base 1.8M Rack is a racking option for a Model 595. It supports up to 90 disk units, has 28 PCI-X slots and has four removable media slots.

The #8294 consists of a 1.8m rack with two enclosures; a bottom enclosure and a top enclosure. The bottom enclosure is essentially a #9194 Base PCI-X Expansion Tower with side covers and casters removed and with a 30-disk expansion feature included as base (no feature code required). The top enclosure is essentially a #5094 PCI-X Expansion Tower with side covers and casters removed and a 30-disk expansion feature included as base (no feature code required).

Included with the bottom enclosure is a #9517 Base HSL-2/RIO-G Bus Adapter and a #9844 Base PCI IOP. A #2780 PCI-X Ultra RAID Disk Controller is required to drive the load source DASD and the removable media devices.

Included with the top enclosure is a #9517 Base HSL-2/RIO-G Bus Adapter or a #9876 Base Optical Bus Adapter (select one), a #9844 Base PCI IOP and a #0694 #5094 Equivalent specify code.

Each enclosure supports 45 disk units for a total of 90 disk units. The 45 disk unit positions are partitioned into groups of 15. Each group of 15 requires support by one #2780 PCI-X Ultra RAID Disk Controller. Each group of 15 is further divided into groups of five disk units, with each group of five disk units supported on a separate Ultra4 SCSI bus from the #2780 PCI-X Ultra RAID Disk Controller.

The #8294 also supports up to four removable media devices. These removable media devices are supported by the two #2780 PCI-X Ultra RAID Disk Controllers which support the first group of 15 disk units in each enclosure.

The two enclosures in the #8294 are separately attached to the system unit via HSL cables as though they are stand-alone #9194 and #5094 units. The bottom enclosure must be on the first HSL loop of the system unit. The top enclosure may be on this same HSL loop or a separate HSL loop. The top enclosure may be attached via HSL to a different system than the bottom enclosure, but cannot be ordered that way. Once the system is received, use an Record Purpose Only (RPO) to remove the #0694 from the records of the original ordered system and add it to the records of the other system.

The lower enclosure of the #8294 is connected to the system unit via two HSL-2/RIO-2 cables. An additional HSL-2/RIO-2 cable is required if the top enclosure is on the same HSL loop. One or two HSL cables are required if the top enclosure is on a separate HSL loop or connected to a different system unit. An HSL loop uses all optical or all copper ports/cables. A copper loop can

intermix I/O towers/units with copper HSL and copper HSL-2 ports. Select the appropriate cable based on the type of HSL ports to which it is attached, and the cable length required.

Both the top and bottom enclosures in the #8294 must be connected via SPCN cables. They must be in an SPCN cable loop. Three SPCN cables are required to connect both enclosures of the #8294 to the service processor ports of the system unit. If the top enclosure of the #8294 is attached to a different system unit, then the top enclosure is connected to the SPCN cable loop of that system and one or two SPCN cables are required.

Dual line cord capability is required with the bottom enclosure of the #8294. A #5164 Dual Power Cords - #8294/#9194 is required on the order. Dual line cord capability is also required on the top enclosure of the #8294, with feature #5165 Dual Power Cords - #8294, if the top enclosure is attached to the same system unit as the bottom enclosure. If the top enclosure is attached to a different system unit, then the #5165 is optional. An additional line cord (for a total of four) must be ordered when a #5165 is installed. Plugging in the second line cord, even if to the same outlet, enables the AC power modules to be redundant.

#8294 Optional Base 1.8M Rack schematic

The following figure shows a schematic of the #8294 Optional Base 1.8M Rack.

Note: The total number of disk bays is 2 x 45.

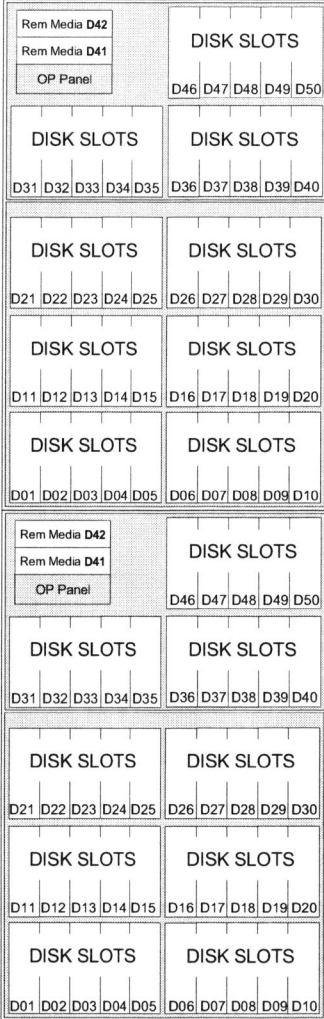

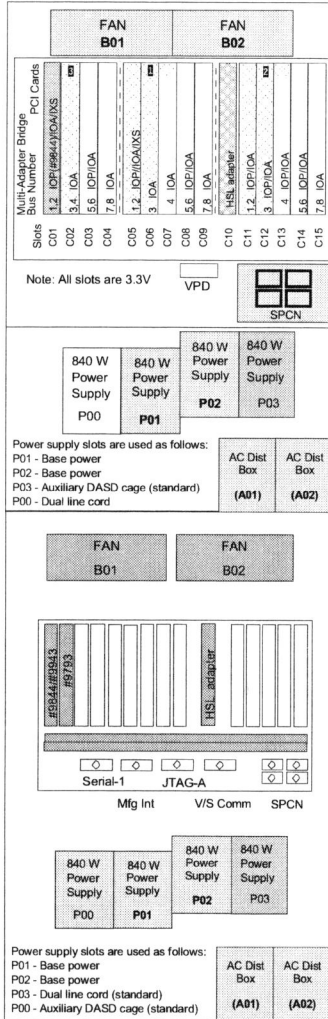

Rem Media **D42**	DISK SLOTS	
Rem Media **D41**		
OP Panel	D46 D47 D48 D49 D50	

| DISK SLOTS | DISK SLOTS |
| D31 D32 D33 D34 D35 | D36 D37 D38 D39 D40 |

| DISK SLOTS | DISK SLOTS |
| D21 D22 D23 D24 D25 | D26 D27 D28 D29 D30 |

| DISK SLOTS | DISK SLOTS |
| D11 D12 D13 D14 D15 | D16 D17 D18 D19 D20 |

| DISK SLOTS | DISK SLOTS |
| D01 D02 D03 D04 D05 | D06 D07 D08 D09 D10 |

Rem Media **D42**	DISK SLOTS	
Rem Media **D41**		
OP Panel	D46 D47 D48 D49 D50	

| DISK SLOTS | DISK SLOTS |
| D31 D32 D33 D34 D35 | D36 D37 D38 D39 D40 |

| DISK SLOTS | DISK SLOTS |
| D21 D22 D23 D24 D25 | D26 D27 D28 D29 D30 |

| DISK SLOTS | DISK SLOTS |
| D11 D12 D13 D14 D15 | D16 D17 D18 D19 D20 |

| DISK SLOTS | DISK SLOTS |
| D01 D02 D03 D04 D05 | D06 D07 D08 D09 D10 |

FAN B01   FAN B02

Multi-Adapter Bridge Bus Number / PCI Cards

| Slots | C01 | C02 | C03 | C04 | C05 | C06 | C07 | C08 | C09 | C10 | C11 | C12 | C13 | C14 | C15 |

1,2 IOP/(#9844)/IOA/IXS
3,4 IOA
5,6 IOP/IOA
7,8 IOA
1,2 IOP/IOA/IXS
3 IOA
4 IOA
5,6 IOP/IOA
7,8 IOA
HSL adapter
1,2 IOP/IOA
3 IOP/IOA
4 IOP/IOA
5,6 IOP/IOA
7,8 IOA

Note: All slots are 3.3V   VPD   SPCN

| 840 W Power Supply P00 | 840 W Power Supply **P01** | 840 W Power Supply **P02** | 840 W Power Supply P03 |

Power supply slots are used as follows:
P01 - Base power
P02 - Base power
P03 - Auxiliary DASD cage (standard)
P00 - Dual line cord

| AC Dist Box **(A01)** | AC Dist Box **(A02)** |

FAN B01   FAN B02

#9844/#9943 /#9793   HSL adapter

| Serial-1 | JTAG-A | |
| Mfg Int | V/S Comm | SPCN |

| 840 W Power Supply P00 | 840 W Power Supply **P01** | 840 W Power Supply **P02** | 840 W Power Supply P03 |

Power supply slots are used as follows:
P01 - Base power
P02 - Base power
P03 - Dual line cord (standard)
P00 - Auxiliary DASD cage (standard)

| AC Dist Box **(A01)** | AC Dist Box **(A02)** |

Legend

Base Feature

Required Feature

Unavailable if Integrated Netfinity Server is installed

Note 1: If C05 has an Integrated xSeries Server, slot C06 is unavailable, and slot C07 is available only as a short slot. A #2792 does not reduce a third slot to a short slot.

Note 2: If C11 has an Integrated xSeries Server, slot C12 is unavailable, and slot C13 is available only as a short slot. A #2792 does not reduce a third slot to a short slot.

Note 3: Integrated xSeries Server placement is not supported from the plant. Only a #2792 is allowed in this position.

See the #9094 PCI Card Enclosure for card placement details.

#5164 Dual Power Cords - #8294/#9194

The #5164 Dual Power Cords - #8294/#9194 is a required feature that provides dual line cord support for the #9194 Base PIC I/O Enclosure on the Model 595. With the #5164, the enclosure requires two #14xx line cords and has two AC input boxes.

9406 Model 595 schematics

You can find schematics of any supported expansion units in Chapter 15, "Towers, racks, and high-speed link" on page 261.

9406 Model 595 system unit: Front, rear, and memory views

Front view

PBA (Base)

PBD 7837
PBC (Base)
PBR(6186)

Upper blowers

System Unit

Lower Blowers

Air Plenum

NODE DC/DC CONVERTER ASSEMBLY
NODE DC/DC CONVERTER ASSEMBLY
NODE DC/DC CONVERTER ASSEMBLY
NODE DC/DC CONVERTER ASSEMBLY
NODE DC/DC CONVERTER ASSEMBLY
NODE DC/DC CONVERTER ASSEMBLY
BASE DC/DC CONVERTER ASSEMBLY
BASE DC/DC CONVERTER ASSEMBLY

NODE 3   NODE 2   NODE 1   NODE 0

DASD plug sequence for optimum performance: D31, D36, D46, D32, D37, D47, ... D50, (add 2nd adaptor), D01, D11, D21, D02, ... D25, (add 3rd adaptor), D06, D16, D26, D07, ... D30.

Legend

W = DSCard Address
X = IOA number
Y = SCSI bus number
Z = AS/400 Drive Addres
Kn = Physical Aaddresss

#9194 Base PCI-X I/O Enclosure

(1-x-0-7)
Rem Media D42
Rem Media D41
OP Panel

(1-x-2-3) (1-x-2-4) (1-x-2-5) (1-x-2-6) (1-x-2-7)
D46 D47 D48 D49 D50

(1-x-0-1) (1-x-0-2) (1-x-0-3) (1-x-0-4) (1-x-0-5)   (1-x-1-3) (1-x-1-4) (1-x-1-5) (1-x-1-6) (1-x-1-7)
D31 D32 D33 D34 D35   D36 D37 D38 D39 D40

(2-x-2-3) (2-x-2-4) (2-x-2-5) (2-x-2-6) (2-x-2-7)   (3-x-2-3) (3-x-2-4) (3-x-2-5) (3-x-2-6) (3-x-2-7)
D21 D22 D23 D24 D25   D26 D27 D28 D29 D30

(2-x-1-3) (2-x-1-4) (2-x-1-5) (2-x-1-6) (2-x-1-7)   (3-x-1-3) (3-x-1-4) (3-x-1-5) (3-x-1-6) (3-x-1-7)
D11 D12 D13 D14 D15   D16 D17 D18 D19 D20

(2-x-0-3) (2-x-0-4) (2-x-0-5) (2-x-0-6) (2-x-0-7)   (3-x-0-3) (3-x-0-4) (3-x-0-5) (3-x-0-6) (3-x-0-7)
D01 D02 D03 D04 D05   D06 D07 D08 D09 D10

(#5168)

Rear view

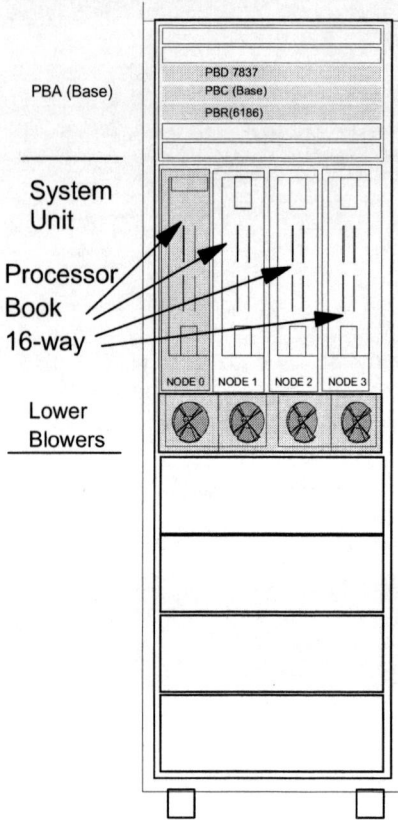

PBA (Base)

PBD 7837
PBC (Base)
PBR(6186)

System
Unit

Processor
Book
16-way

NODE 0 NODE 1 NODE 2 NODE 3

Lower
Blowers

Legend

W = DS Card address
X = IOA number
Y = SCSI bus number
Z = i5 drive address
Kn = Physical address

#9194 Base PCI-X
I/O enclosure

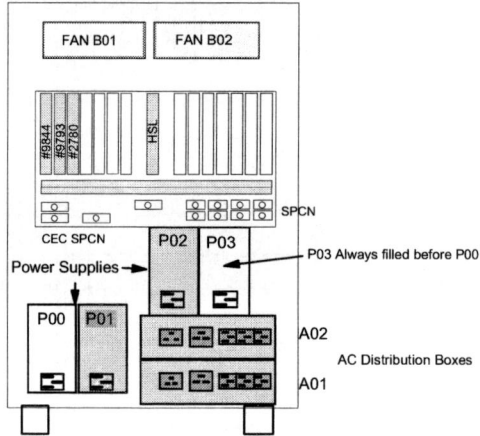

FAN B01   FAN B02

#9844
#9793
#2780

HSL

SPCN

CEC SPCN

Power Supplies →

P02   P03

P03 Always filled before P00

P00   P01

A02

AC Distribution Boxes

A01

Single Model 505 processor book and memory (node)

HSL2/RIO-G

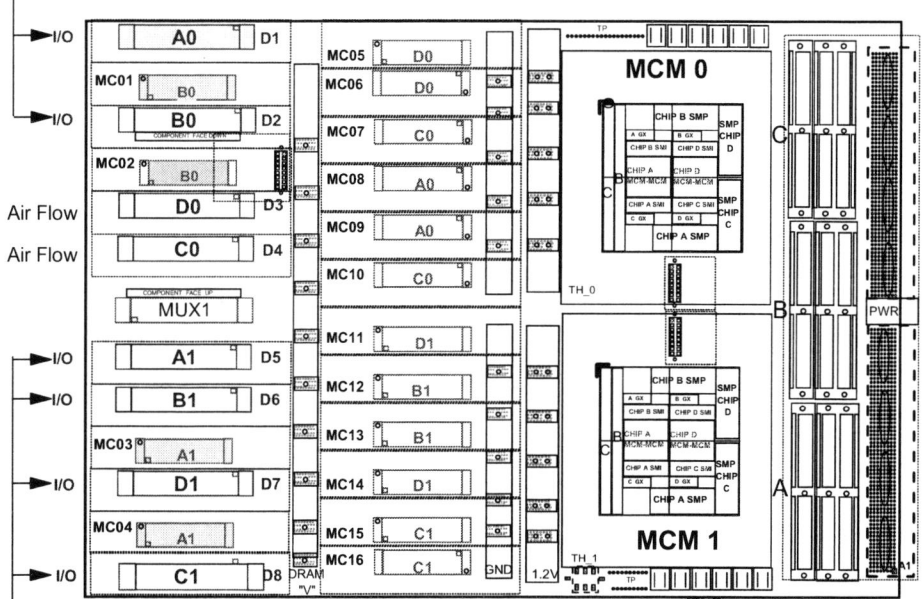

HSL2/RIO-G

595 memory cards for processor book

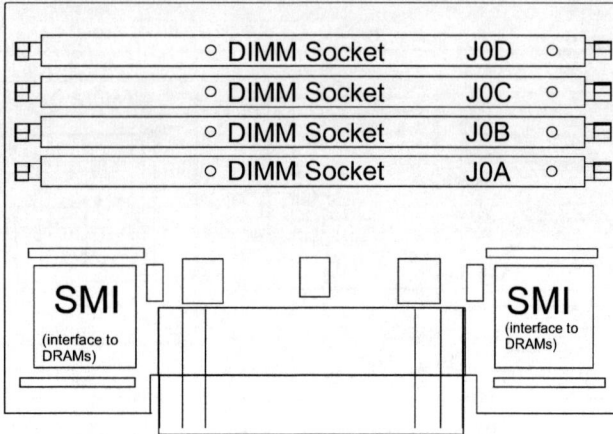

○ DIMM Socket	J0D ○
○ DIMM Socket	J0C ○
○ DIMM Socket	J0B ○
○ DIMM Socket	J0A ○

SMI
(interface to DRAMs)

SMI
(interface to DRAMs)

Note: You can find line cord and power receptacle specification information on the Web at:

`http://www.ibm.com/eserver/iseries/infocenter`

High-speed link for Model 595

The following number of loops are supported:

► The Model 595 8/16-way supports six HSL-2/RIO-2 loops on one processor book with a maximum of 36 I/O towers across all loops.

► The Model 595 16/32-way supports twelve HSL-2/RIO-2 loops across two processor books with a maximum of 60 I/O towers across all loops.

► The Model 595 32/6-way supports four processor books with a total of twenty four HSL-2/RIO-2 loops with a maximum of 60 I/O towers across all loops.

The speed of the HSL-2/RIO-2 is 2 GB/s compared to the previous HSL-2 adapters operating at 1 GB/s.

The following rules apply to towers that are supported at these higher speeds:

► New #5094, #5294, #0595, and #5095 come with a #9517 Base HSL-2/RIO-G Bus Adapter.

- HSL-2 adapters in existing #5094, #5294, #0595, and #5095 towers must be replaced with a #6417 HSL-2/RIO-G Bus Adapter.
- Mixing of HSL and HSL-2 towers is permitted with the correct combination of cables.

See "HSL fabric" on page 297 for information about supported HSL cables and HSL loop maximums.

You can find more information in *High-speed Link Loop Architecture for the IBM @server iSeries Server: OS/400 Version 5 Release 2*, REDP-3652, and in the HSL Rules presentation available at:

`http://www-1.ibm.com/servers/eserver/iseries/ha/systemdesign.html`

Model 595 PCI cards and features

The Model 595 is a Peripheral Component Interconnect (PCI)-based technology system. The number of PCI cards that can be supported in a Model 595 depends on the number of I/O tower is attached and the number of PCI slots. PCI card placement rules and LPAR configuration considerations also affect the number of slots supported.

See the Summary table on page 167 for the number of maximum features supported by the total system and in the Model 595 system unit. See Chapter 17, "iSeries PCI I/O processors" on page 323, and Chapter 18, "iSeries I/O adapters and controllers" on page 337, for full descriptions of the features that are supported. See "AIX and Linux Direct Attach features overview" on page 340 for the supported Linux Direct Attach features.

> **Note:** The placement of PCI cards follows special rules. Refer to "PCI card technology" on page 338 and *PCI Card Placement Rules for the IBM @server iSeries Server Version 5 Release 2*, REDP-3638, before you propose any configuration.

External towers

SPD Migration towers are not supported on the Model 595. PCI towers are supported with upgrades for migration only. Refer to Chapter 15, "Towers, racks, and high-speed link" on page 261, for details about supported towers for the Model 595, and "Summary of the iSeries expansion units and towers" on page 119 for a table of configuration maximums.

Model 595 upgrades

See Chapter 16, "Upgrades to eServer i5 and i5/OS" on page 311, for general upgrade considerations and server-to-server upgrade possibilities. Supported model upgrades for the Model 595 are identified in the *Upgrade topic* of the Find and Compare Tool (FACT) at:

http://www-919.ibm.com/servers/eserver/fact/

Model 595 Capacity on Demand

The @server i5 Model 595 offers Capacity on Demand options that make it possible to activate additional processor resource. IBM @server Capacity Upgrade on Demand (CUoD), On/Off Capacity on Demand, Reserve Capacity on Demand, and Trial Capacity on Demand are available for the Model 595. On Demand features are described in this section.

On Demand features may have some base activation features. The following options are available to activate additional processor or memory resources:

► Capacity upgrade on Demand (Permanent)

   Purchase processor activation features when needed. Requires a purchase of operating system licenses.

► On/Off Capacity on Demand (Temporary)

   Pay for processor day billing features at the end of each billing period. Additional i5/OS licenses are not required.

► Reserve Capacity on Demand (Prepaid)

   Buy blocks of processor days ahead of time. Additional i5/OS licenses are not required.

► Trial Capacity on Demand

   Request trial capacity from CoD Web site for special purposes. Additional i5/OS licenses are not required.

Refer to the table on page 95 to see the feature codes associated with the Model 595 Capacity on Demand options. See the following Web site for more information about Capacity on Demand:

http://www-1.ibm.com/servers/eserver/iseries/ondemand/cod/

iSeries Model 800

The Model 800 server delivers the performance, reliability, and security needed for applications that incorporate traditional processor workloads typical for a small business. Model 800 configurations offer a competitive entry point for clients who are still interested in 5250 performance, but who do not need the processor performance required to run a full On Demand Business implementation.

The Model 800 offers up to 63 disk units, a high-performance Peripheral Component Interconnect (PCI) bus and hot plug PCI disk slots, a high-speed link, and V.90 integrated modem. Options include a 1 Gb high-speed Ethernet LAN adapter and 100 Mbps high-speed token-ring adapter. The Model 800 supports the 1.6 GHz and 2.0 GHz Integrated xSeries Servers. Options to rack mount the Model 800 are available.

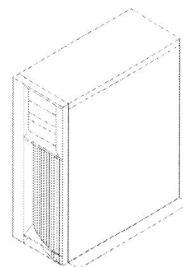

iSeries Model 800 System Unit

Model overview

This section takes a closer look at the minimum functional server, required features, and optional features.

Minimum functional server

A minimum functional server consists of the base server unit and selected priced features. The base server includes:

- Physical package and power elements
- Seven PCI card slots
- Operator panel
- Base direct access storage device (DASD) cage (six internal disk slots)

  - The base DASD cage for #2463 supports concurrent maintenance when a #7137 DASD Concurrent Maintenance Cage is installed.

  - The #2464 has a concurrent maintenance cage shipped with the processor.

- Two removable media slots (for base DVD-ROM/DVD-RAM)
- Embedded Base 32 MB PCI IOP (CCIN 286C)

  Provides support for a maximum of up to four input/output adapters (IOAs), including:

  - Up to two disk controllers

  - Up to six disk units, the required DVD-ROM/DVD-RAM, and either an internal tape or additional DVD-ROM/DVD-RAM

  - Base console/workstation IOA

    The IBM marketing configurator determines which feature combinations are placed on the order based on the #5540, #5544, #5546, or #5548 System Console specify code.

- Optional Base feature

  - #9746 PCI Twinaxial IOA

    - #0864 iSeries 800 Standard Edition
    - #0865 iSeries 800 Advanced Edition

  - #9749 Base PCI 100/10 Ethernet IOA

Required features

Note: In the following section, the single asterisk (*) indicates that the feature is supported for conversion only.

The *required* features include:

► Specific combinations of the Processor feature, Edition feature, and Server feature are allowed as shown in the following table.

Processor feature	Server feature	Edition feature	Software group	Processor feature code or QPRCFEAT value
#2463 (300 CPW)	#0863	#7400 Value	P05	7400
	#0864	#7400 Standard	P05	7400
#2464 (950 CPW)	#0865	#7408 Enterprise	P10	7409

Note: iSeries 800 servers have the ability to process 5250 online transaction processing (OLTP) workloads. Each 800 server has a fixed amount of 5250 commercial processing workload (CPW). The Value and Standard Editions for the #2463 processor provide 25 CPW and the Advanced Edition on the #2464 processor provides 50 CPW for 5250 OLTP workloads.

Edition content varies by processor and server features selected. For more information, see "Editions" on page 55.

► Main storage

All main storage on the Model 800 is feature main storage. See "Main storage" on page 193 for a list of supported memory features and configuration considerations.

► PCI disk controller (one must be specified)
- #2757 PCI-X Ultra RAID Disk Controller
- #4778 PCI RAID Disk Unit Controller*
- #5703 PCI-X RAID Disk Unit Controller
- #5705 PCI-X Tape/DASD Controller
- #2780 PCI-X Ultra4 RAID Disk Controller

The system unit supports up to two disk unit controllers to control disks in the system unit and #7116 System Unit Expansion (if installed).

Note: A #7137 DASD Concurrent Maintenance Cage is required when placing a #2757 or #2780 in the #2463 processor system unit.

You must specify one integrated optical device:

- #4530 DVD-RAM
- #4531 DVD-ROM

► Internal disk units

- #4318 17.54 GB 10k RPM Disk Unit*
- #4319 35.16 GB 10k RPM Disk Unit
- #4326 35.16 GB 15k RPM Disk Unit
- #4327 70.56 GB 15k RPM Disk Unit
- #4327 70.56 GB 15k RPM Disk Unit

One of the following load source specify codes is required:

- #0829 - #4318 Load Source Specify*
- #0830 - #4319 Load Source Specify
- #0834 - #4326 Load Source Specify
- #0835 - #4327 Load Source Specify

► Internal tape device

- #4582 4 GB ¼-inch Cartridge Tape Device
- #4584 30 GB ¼-inch Cartridge Tape Device
- #4585 80 GB VXA-2 Tape Device
- #4587 50 GB ¼-inch Cartridge Tape Device
- #8287 Opt Base 50 GB ¼-inch Cartridge Tape Device
- #9284 30 GB ¼-inch Cartridge Tape Device
- #9285 Base 80 GB VXA-2 Tape Device

► System console attachment adapter

- #5540 System Console on Twinaxial Workstation IOA

    • #4746/#9746 PCI Twinaxial IOA

- #5544 System Console on Operations Console

    • #0367 Operations Console PCI Cable (attaches to #9793)

- #5546 System Console on 100 Mbps Token Ring

    • #2744 PCI 100 Mbps Token Ring IOA
    • #0367 Operations Console PCI Cable

- #5548 System Console on 100 Mbps Ethernet
  - #9749 Base PCI 100/10 Ethernet IOA/#2849 10/100 Mbps Ethernet Adapter
  - #0367 Operations Console PCI Cable

Optional features

The *optional* features include:

▶ Internal tape device

- #4582 4 GB ¼-inch Cartridge Tape Device
- #4584 30 GB ¼-inch Cartridge Tape Device
- #4585 80 GB VXA-2 Tape Device
- #4587 50 GB ¼-inch Cartridge Tape Device
- #8287 Opt Base 50 GB ¼-inch Cartridge Tape Device
- #9284 30 GB ¼-inch Cartridge Tape Device
- #9285 Base 80 GB VXA-2 Tape Device

▶ #0551 iSeries Rack

- Up to two Model 800s may be installed in an #0551 rack.

- Any Model 800 mounted in an #0551 must have the #7116 System Unit Expansion.

- Specify codes and features supported when used in conjunction with a Model 800 include the #0133 Plant Install in Rack and #0137 Field Install in Rack.

See "#0551 iSeries Rack" on page 290 for a complete description of the #0551 iSeries Rack and supported features and specify codes.

▶ #7002 HSL Enabler

- The #7002 is an high-speed link (HSL) internal flex cable, which enables HSL capability to allow connection to one PCI or PCI-X expansion tower.

- This cable connects the processor with a right angle bus connector to the back of the machine. Two HSL cables (#14XX) are required to connect the CEC to the expansion tower.

▶ #7116 System Unit Expansion

- The system unit expansion supports up to an additional 12 disk units.

- The #7116 has no PCI card slots and no removable media slots.

- The #7116 supports six disk units.

- Disk units are driven by up to two disk unit controllers located in the CEC.

- A #7137 DASD Concurrent Maintenance Cage is required.

- A #7136 DASD Expansion Unit - 6 slot is required to support more than six disk units.
- The #7116 requires a separate power cord.
- If installed in an #0551 iSeries Rack, the #7116 may be powered by a PDU by ordering #1422 PDU Line Cord.

► #7136 DASD Expansion Unit - 6 slot

- DASD six-position expansion unit
- Supports an additional six disk units (for a total of 12) in the #7116
- Requires a #7116 System Unit Expansion

► #7137 DASD Concurrent Maintenance Cage

- DASD six-pack cage for the Model 800
- Supports concurrent disk maintenance and replaces the standard non-concurrent maintenance DASD six-pack cage
- Provides a higher speed interface for drives, more than double the bandwidth of the base DASD cage
- Recommended for 15k rpm disk drives
- Required if a #2757 PCI-X Ultra RAID Disk Controller, #7116 System Unit Expansion, or #4326 35.16 GB 15k RPM Disk Unit is installed

► Uninterruptible power supply

We recommend that you have an external uninterruptible power supply to protect the system unit and any external components against utility power outages.

The Model 800 initial installation is Customer Setup (CSU). Processor upgrades within models are performed by IBM Service Representatives.

Processor features

The #2463 Model 800 SSTAR Uni processor (CCIN 25B9) includes:

► Eight Dual Inline Memory Modules (DIMM) memory positions (plug into the processor, direct attach)
► Embedded Base IOP (CCIN 286C)
► Common Service Processor (CSP) (CCIN 25B9)

The #2464 Model 800 SSTAR Uni processor (CCIN 25BA) includes:

► Eight DIMM memory positions (plug into the processor, direct attach)
► Embedded Base IOP (CCIN 286C)
► Common Service Processor (CSP) (CCIN 25B9)

The iSeries for Domino processors include a regular processor feature and a special server feature. The server feature is used for pricing and for initial order placement. Upgrades are supported in the normal way based on the Processor and Edition feature.

Refer to "Table 6: Summary of the iSeries Model 800" on page 100, to find Processor CPW, Mail and Calendar Users (MCU), 5250 CPW, and to determine the processor feature code and QPRCFEAT value.

Main storage

Supported memory features for the Model 800 are:

- ► #3092 - 256 MB Main Storage (DIMM DDR 128 Mb technology)
- ► #3093 - 512 MB Main Storage (DIMM DDR 256 Mb technology)
- ► #3094 - 1 GB Main Storage (DIMM DDR 256 Mb technology)
- ► #3096 - 2 GB Main Storage (DIMM DDR 256 Mb technology)

Configuration considerations for memory include:

- ► A single main storage DIMM is allowed.

- ► When additional memory is required, the existing memory card must be paired with a card of similar capacity. Additional DIMMs must be added in pairs of the same capacity and technology.

- ► Eight slots are available in the base system for main storage DIMMs, which plug into the backplane.

- ► The #0864 and #0865 Server features require a minimum of 512 MB.

The following table shows the allowable main storage capacities in MB for the Model 800 processors.

256*	512*	1024	1536
2048	2560	3072	3584
4096	4608	5120	5632
6144	6656	7168	7680
8192			
* The #0864 and #0865 Server features require a minimum of 512 MB.			

9406 Model 800 schematics

The following diagrams show the slot and feature card arrangement of the Model 800 system unit, processor, memory cards, and supported expansion units. You can find schematics of any supported expansion units in Chapter 15, "Towers, racks, and high-speed link" on page 261.

9406 Model 800 system unit

#2463 and #2464 Processors

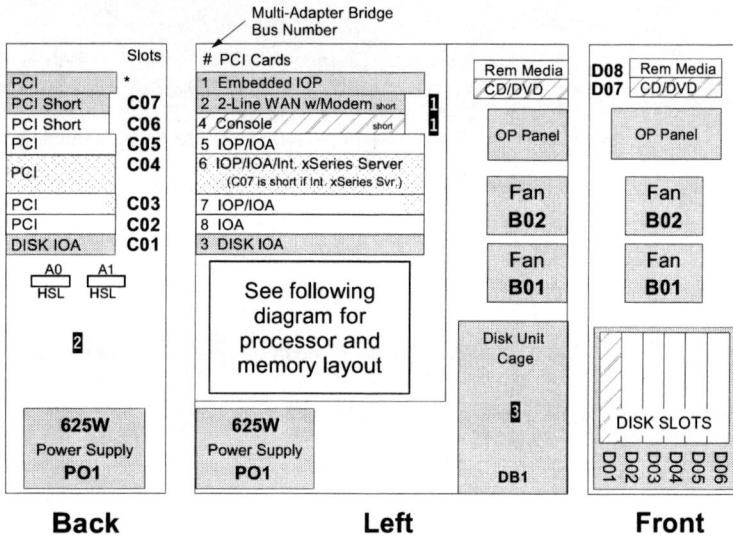

Back   **Left**   **Front**

Note 1: Cards may be reversed depending on choice of console.

Note 2: Card slots do not support hot plugging with #2463 processor.

Note 3: Non-concurrent maintenance cage shipped with #2463 processor.
Concurrent maintenance cage shipped with #2464 processor.

* Embedded

Legend

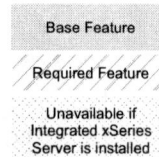

Base Feature

Required Feature

Unavailable if Integrated xSeries Server is installed

Model 800 Processor and Memory

#2463 and #2464

Processor w/o Cache

DIMM CONN - J3H	H
DIMM CONN - J0L	A
DIMM CONN - J2H	F
DIMM CONN - J1L	C
DIMM CONN - J1H	D
DIMM CONN - J2L	E
DIMM CONN - J0H	B
DIMM CONN - J3L	G

Memory Controller

Processor Regulator

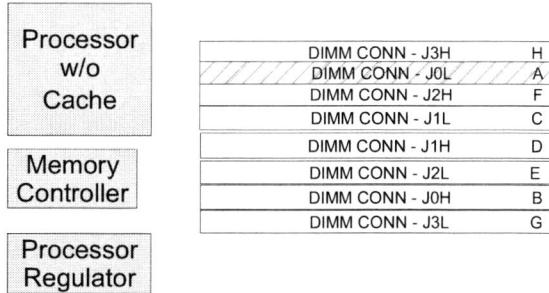

Model 800 #7116 System Unit Expansion DASD Sidecar

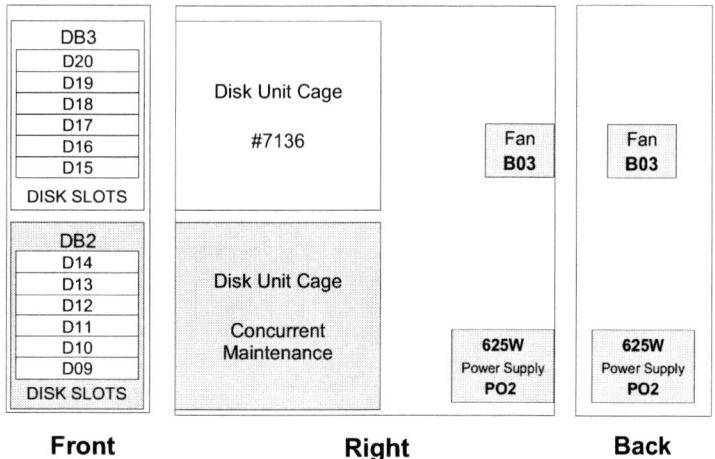

DB3
D20
D19
D18
D17
D16
D15
DISK SLOTS

Disk Unit Cage

#7136

DB2
D14
D13
D12
D11
D10
D09
DISK SLOTS

Disk Unit Cage

Concurrent Maintenance

Fan B03

Fan B03

625W Power Supply PO2

625W Power Supply PO2

Front   **Right**   **Back**

For information about the #5075 PCI Expansion Tower, see "#5075 PCI Expansion Tower" on page 268.

Note: For line cord and power receptacle specification information, go to:
http://www.ibm.com/eserver/iseries/infocenter

High-speed link on Model 800

The Model 800 supports a single HSL loop. See "HSL fabric" on page 297 for information about supported HSL cables and HSL loop maximums.

You can find further information in *High-speed Link Loop Architecture for the IBM @server iSeries Server: OS/400 Version 5 Release 2*, REDP-3652, and in the HSL Rules presentation available on the Web at:

`http://www-1.ibm.com/servers/eserver/iseries/ha/systemdesign.html`

Model 800 PCI cards and features

The Model 800 is a PCI-based technology system. The number of PCI cards that can be supported in a Model 800 depends on whether an I/O tower is attached and the number of PCI slots. PCI card placement rules and logical partition (LPAR) configuration considerations also affect the number of slots supported. PCI hot plugging is not allowed.

See the table on page 102 for the number of maximum features supported by the total system and in the Model 800 system unit. See Chapter 17, "iSeries PCI I/O processors" on page 323, and Chapter 18, "iSeries I/O adapters and controllers" on page 337, for full descriptions about the features that are supported. See "AIX and Linux Direct Attach features overview" on page 340 for supported Linux Direct Attach features.

> **Note:** The placement of PCI cards follows special rules. Refer to "PCI card technology" on page 338 and *PCI Card Placement Rules for the IBM @server iSeries Server Version 5 Release 2*, REDP-3638, before you propose any configuration.

External towers

Refer to Chapter 15, "Towers, racks, and high-speed link" on page 261, for information about supported towers for the Model 800.

Model 800 upgrades

See Chapter 16, "Upgrades to eServer i5 and i5/OS" on page 311, for general upgrade considerations and processor upgrades within the Model 800. Supported model upgrades for the Model 800 are identified in the *Upgrade* topic of the Find and Compare Tool (FACT) at:

`http://www-919.ibm.com/servers/eserver/fact/`

iSeries Model 810

The iSeries 810 is an integrated, reliable server that supports multiple operating environments. It can run a variety of applications simultaneously. The Model 810 offers small to medium-size companies legendary iSeries security and availability. It also offers the power and capacity to run traditional core business applications while providing the freedom and scalability to add new On Demand Business technologies.

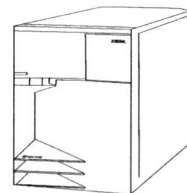

iSeries Model 810 System Unit

The Model 810 memory can be increased up to a maximum of 16 GB. There is a maximum of 198 disk units from four expansion towers, all based on a system unit that includes a high-performance PCI bus and hot plug Peripheral Component Interconnect (PCI) disk slots, a high-speed link (HSL), and V.90 integrated modem. Options include a 1 Gb high-speed Ethernet LAN adapter and 100 Mbps high-speed token-ring adapter. The Model 810 supports the 1.6 GHz and 2.0 GHz Integrated xSeries Servers. Options to rack mount the Model 810 are available. The Model 810 provides an external connection to expansion towers and xSeries servers.

Model overview

This section takes a closer look at the minimum functional server, required features, and optional features.

> **Note:** In the Required features and Optional features sections, note the following descriptions:
>
> * Supported for conversion only
> **Supported on upgrade

Minimum functional server

A minimum functional server consists of the base server unit and selected priced features. The base server includes:

► Physical package and power elements

► Seven PCI card slots

  – No hot plugging of PCI cards with #2465, #2466, and #2467 processors
  – Hot plugging of PCI cards supported with the #2769 processor

► Operator panel

► Base direct access storage device (DASD) cage (six internal disk slots)

► Supports concurrent maintenance

► Two removable media slots

► Embedded Base PCI IOP (CCIN 286D, CCIN 286E)

Provides support for a maximum of up to four input/output adapters (IOAs), including:

  – A PCI disk controller (Small Computer System Interface (SCSI) IOA)
  – #9749 Base PCI 100/10 Ethernet IOA
  – #9771/#9793/#9794 Base PCI Two-Line WAN with integrated modem
  – Base console/workstation IOA

  The IBM marketing configurator determines which feature combinations are to be on the order based on the #5540, #5544, #5546, or #5548 System Console specify code.

Required features

The *required* features include:

► Specific combinations of the Processor feature, Edition feature, and Server feature are allowed as shown in the following table.

Processor feature	Server feature	Edition feature	Software group	Processor feature code or QPRCFEAT value
#2465 (750 CPW)	#0868	#7404 Standard #7406 Enterprise	P10 P10	7404 7406
#2466 (1020 CPW)	#0866	#7407 Standard	P10	7407
		#7409 Enterprise	P10	7409
	#0769	#7407 Domino	P10	7407
#2467 (1470 CPW)	#0867	#7410 Standard	P10	7410
		#7412 Enterprise	P10	7412
	#0770	#7410 Domino	P10	7410
#2469 (2700 CPW)	#0869	#7428 Standard	P20	7428
		#7430 Enterprise	P20	7430
	#0771	#7428 Domino	P20	7428

Note: The Standard Edition for the Model 810 processors provides limited 5250 CPW for 5250 OLTP workloads. The Enterprise and High Availability Editions for the Model 810 processors provide maximum 5250 CPW for 5250 OLTP workloads.

Edition content varies by processor and server features selected. For more information, see "Editions" on page 55.

The Server feature used for iSeries for Domino specifies the minimum amount of disk, memory, and Domino licenses required for an initial order, as noted in the following table.

Server feature	Processor feature	Edition feature	Min. DASD (GB)	Min. Memory (GB)	Required Domino licenses		MCU rating*
					Server	Client	
#0769	#2466	#7407	105	1.5	1	100	3100
#0770	#2467	#7410	315	3.5	1	100	4200
#0771	#2469	#7428	525	5.5	1	400	7900
* The Mail and Calendar User (MCU) ratings cannot be achieved using the minimum configurations described in the preceding table.							

► Main storage

All main storage on the Model 810 is feature main storage. See "Main storage" on page 205 for a list of supported memory features and configuration considerations.

► PCI disk unit controller (one must be specified)
  – #2757 PCI-X Ultra RAID Disk Controller
  – #2763 PCI RAID Disk Unit Controller *
  – 2780 PCI-X Ultra4 RAID Disk Controller
  – #2782 PCI-X RAID Disk Unit Controller
  – #4748 PCI RAID Disk Unit Controller *
  – #4778 PCI RAID Disk Unit Controller *
  – 5703 PCI-X RAID Disk Unit Controller
  – #5705 PCI-X Tape/DASD Controller

The system unit supports up to two disk unit controllers to control disks in the system unit and #7116 System Unit Expansion (if installed).

► Internal disk units
  – #4308 4.19 GB Disk Unit*
  – #4314 8.58 GB Disk Unit*
  – #4317 8.58 GB 10k RPM Disk Unit*
  – #4318 17.54 GB 10k RPM Disk Unit*
  – #4319 35.16 GB 10k RPM Disk Unit
  – #4324 17.54 GB Disk Unit*
  – #4326 35.16 GB 15k RPM Disk Unit
  – #4327 70.56 GB 15k RPM Disk Unit
  – #4331 1.6 GB Read Cache Device**

- ► Integrated optical
  - – #4525 CD-ROM *
  - – #4530 DVD-RAM
  - – #4531 DVD-ROM
- ► System console attachment adapter
  - – #5540 System Console on Twinaxial Workstation IOA
    - • #4746 PCI Twinaxial IOA
  - – #5544 System Console on Operations Console
    - • #0367 Operations Console PCI Cable
  - – #5546 System Console on 100 Mbps Token Ring
    - • #2744 PCI 100 Mbps Token Ring IOA
    - • #0367 Operations Console PCI Cable
  - – #5548 System Console on 100 Mbps Ethernet
    - • #2849 10/100 Mbps Ethernet Adapter
    - • #0367 Operations Console PCI Cable

Optional features

The *optional* features include:

- ► Internal tape device
  - – #4582 4 GB ¼-inch Cartridge Tape Device
  - – #4583 16 GB ¼-inch Cartridge Tape Device
  - – #4584 30 GB ¼-inch Cartridge Tape Device
  - – #4585 80 GB VXA-2 Tape Device
  - – #4586 25 GB ¼-inch Cartridge Tape Device
  - – #4587 50 GB ¼-inch Cartridge Tape Device
- ► #0551 iSeries Rack
  - – Up to two Model 810s may be installed in a #0551 iSeries Rack.
  - – Any iSeries Model 810 mounted in a #0551 must have the #7116 System Unit Expansion.
  - – Specify codes and features supported when used in conjunction with an iSeries Model 810 are the #0133 Plant Install in Rack and #0137 Field Install in Rack.

  See "#0551 iSeries Rack" on page 290 for a complete description of the #0551 iSeries Rack and supported features and specify codes.

- ► #7116 System Unit Expansion
  - – The #7116 is a feature system unit expansion that allows up to an additional 12 disk units to be added. It has no PCI card slots and no removable media slots.
  - – Supports six disk units (standard). Requires a #7136 to support more than six disk units.
  - – The #7116 disk units are driven by a disk unit controller located in the CEC.
  - – A separate power cord is required.
  - – If installed in a #0551 iSeries Rack, it may be powered by a PDU by ordering feature #1422 PDU Line Cord.
- ► #7136 DASD Expansion Unit - 6 slot
  - – The #7136 is a concurrent maintenance DASD six-position expansion feature, which may be ordered to support an additional six disk units (for a total of 12) in the #7116.
  - – The #7116 is required.
- ► Uninterruptible power supply

  We recommend that you have an external uninterruptible power supply to protect the system unit and any external components against utility power outages.

The Model 810 initial installation is Customer Setup (CSU). IBM Service Representatives perform processor upgrades within models.

Processor features

- ► The #2465 SSTAR Uni processor (CCIN 25BA) includes:
  - – 2 MB L2 cache
  - – Eight Dual Inline Memory Module (DIMM) memory positions (plug into the processor, direct attach)
  - – Embedded Base IOP (CCIN 286D)
  - – Common Service Processor (CSP) (CCIN 25BA)
- ► The #2466 Processor SSTAR Uni processor (CCIN 25BA) includes:
  - – 2 MB L2 cache
  - – Eight DIMM memory positions (plug into the processor, direct attach)
  - – Embedded Base IOP (CCIN 286D)
  - – Common Service Processor (CSP) (CCIN 25BA)

- ► The #2467 Processor SSTAR Uni processor (CCIN 25F0) includes:
    - − 4 MB L2 cache
    - − Eight DIMM memory positions (plug into the processor, direct attach)
    - − Embedded Base IOP (CCIN 286E)
    - − Common Service Processor (CSP) (CCIN 25F0)
- ► The #2469 SSTAR 2-way processor (CCIN 25EB) includes:
    - − 4 MB L2 cache per processor
    - − Sixteen DIMM memory positions via the memory riser card (CCIN 2884)
    - − Base I/O backplane (CCIN 282F)
    - − Embedded Base IOP (CCIN 284E)
    - − Common Service Processor (CSP) (CCIN 282F)

The iSeries for Domino processors include a regular processor feature and a special server feature. The server feature is used for pricing and for initial order placement. Upgrades are supported in the normal way based on the Processor and Edition feature.

Refer to "Table 7: Summary of the iSeries Model 810" on page 102 to find Processor CPW, Mail and Calendar Users (MCU), 5250 CPW, and to determine the processor feature code and QPRCFEAT value.

Main storage

Supported memory features for the #2465, #2466, and #2467 processors are:

- ► #3092 - 256 MB Main Storage (DIMM DDR 128 Mb technology) (Unstacked)
- ► #3093 - 512 MB Main Storage (DIMM DDR 256 Mb technology) (Unstacked)
- ► #3094 - 1 GB Main Storage (DIMM DDR 256 Mb technology) (Stacked)
- ► #3096 - 2 GB Main Storage (DIMM DDR 256 Mb technology) (Stacked)

Configuration considerations include:

- ► A single main storage DIMM is allowed.
- ► Additional DIMMs must be added in pairs of the same capacity and technology.
- ► Eight slots are available in the base system for main storage DIMMs, which plug into the backplane.

Supported memory features for the #2469 processor are:

- ► #3022 - 128 MB Main Storage (64 Mb technology)

    Support can be ordered only up to the minimum number of DIMMs required to meet a pairing or quad system memory requirement.

- ► #3024 - 256 MB Main Storage (128 Mb technology) (unstacked)
- ► #3025 - 512 MB Main Storage (128 Mb technology) (stacked)

  Cannot be mixed with #3026 for pairing or quadding.
- ► #3026 - 512 MB Main Storage (256 Mb technology) (unstacked)

  Cannot be mixed with #3025 for pairing or quadding.
- ► #3027 - 1 GB Main Storage (256 Mb technology) (stacked)
- ► #3029 - 128 MB Main Storage (128 Mb technology) (unstacked)
  - – Cannot be mixed with #3022 for pairing or quadding
  - – Maximum of eight #3029 allowed on a system

Memory in the #2469 Model 810 is not compatible and does not migrate to the Model 870.

Configuration considerations include:

- ► A base CCIN 2884 Memory Expansion Card with 16 DIMM slots is included. All main storage DIMM features plug into this card.
- ► A minimum of two DIMMS (same feature code and technology) must be selected. If more than two DIMMs are required, all memory features must be in sets of four (quads), including making a quad out of the initial pair. Each DIMM in the set of four must be of the same feature code and technology.
- ► All DIMMs must be plugged in quads starting from the outer four corners going toward the center (for example A, B, C, D, then E, F, G, H). The exception allows a single set of two main storage DIMMs if these are the only two on the system.
- ► Mixing quad "groups" on the same riser card is allowed, including mixing stacked (#3025) and unstacked (#3024) memory technology.

9406 Model 810 schematics

The following diagrams show the slot and feature card arrangement of the Model 810 system unit, processor, memory cards, and supported expansion units. You can find schematics of any supported expansion units in Chapter 15, "Towers, racks, and high-speed link" on page 261.

9406 Model 810 system unit

#2465, #2466, #2467, and #2469 Processors

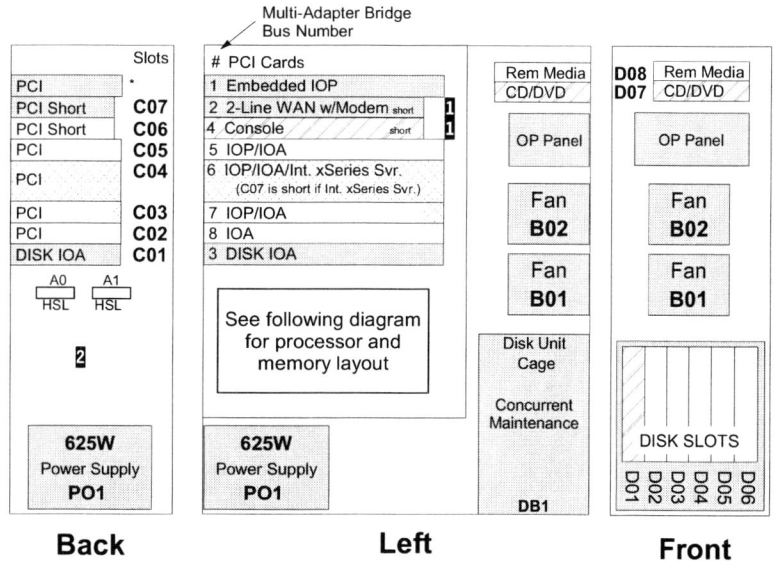

Multi-Adapter Bridge
Bus Number

Slots		#	PCI Cards
PCI	*	1	Embedded IOP
PCI Short	C07	2	2-Line WAN w/Modem short
PCI Short	C06	4	Console short
PCI	C05	5	IOP/IOA
PCI	C04	6	IOP/IOA/Int. xSeries Svr.
			(C07 is short if Int. xSeries Svr.)
PCI	C03	7	IOP/IOA
PCI	C02	8	IOA
DISK IOA	C01	3	DISK IOA

A0   A1
HSL HSL

2

See following diagram
for processor and
memory layout

Rem Media	D08	Rem Media
CD/DVD	D07	CD/DVD
OP Panel		OP Panel
Fan B02		Fan B02
Fan B01		Fan B01

Disk Unit
Cage

Concurrent
Maintenance

DISK SLOTS

D01 D02 D03 D04 D05 D06

625W	625W
Power Supply	Power Supply
PO1	PO1

DB1

Back   Left   Front

Note 1: Cards may be reversed depending on choice of console.

Note 2: Card slots do not support hot plugging with #2466 and #2467 processors.

* Embedded

Legend

Base Feature

Required Feature

Unavailable if
Integrated xSeries
Server is installed

Model 810 Processor and Memory

#2465, #2466, #2467

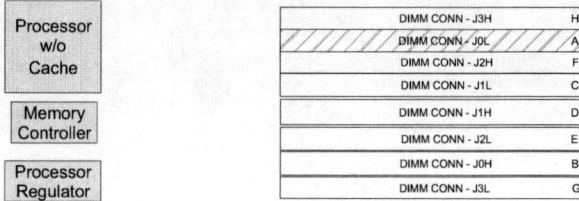

Processor w/o Cache	
Memory Controller	
Processor Regulator	

DIMM CONN - J3H	H
DIMM CONN - J0L	A
DIMM CONN - J2H	F
DIMM CONN - J1L	C
DIMM CONN - J1H	D
DIMM CONN - J2L	E
DIMM CONN - J0H	B
DIMM CONN - J3L	G

#2469

M02	Processor
Regulator	CPU

| M01 | Memory Riser Card | ← |

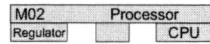

CCIN 2884 Memory Riser Card

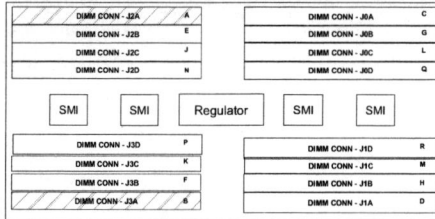

DIMM CONN - J2A	A
DIMM CONN - J2B	E
DIMM CONN - J2C	J
DIMM CONN - J2D	N

DIMM CONN - J0A	C
DIMM CONN - J0B	G
DIMM CONN - J0C	L
DIMM CONN - J0D	Q

SMI	SMI	Regulator	SMI	SMI

DIMM CONN - J3D	P
DIMM CONN - J3C	K
DIMM CONN - J3B	F
DIMM CONN - J3A	B

DIMM CONN - J1D	R
DIMM CONN - J1C	M
DIMM CONN - J1B	H
DIMM CONN - J1A	D

Model 810 #7116 System Unit Expansion DASD Sidecar

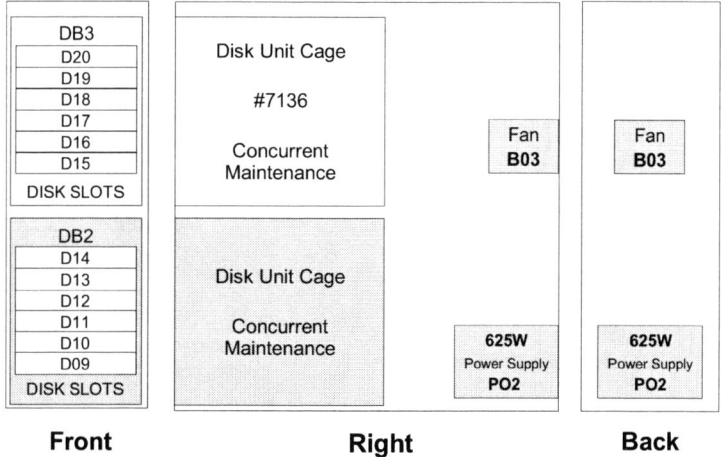

DB3				
D20	Disk Unit Cage			
D19				
D18	#7136			
D17			Fan	Fan
D16			**B03**	**B03**
D15	Concurrent			
DISK SLOTS	Maintenance			
DB2				
D14				
D13	Disk Unit Cage			
D12				
D11	Concurrent		**625W**	**625W**
D10	Maintenance		Power Supply	Power Supply
D09			**PO2**	**PO2**
DISK SLOTS				

Front　　　　　　**Right**　　　　　　**Back**

Note: You can find line cord and power receptacle specification information on the Web at:

http://www.ibm.com/eserver/iseries/infocenter

High-speed link on Model 810

The Model 810 supports a single HSL loop. See "HSL fabric" on page 297 for information about supported HSL cables and HSL loop maximums.

You can learn more in *High-speed Link Loop Architecture for the IBM @server iSeries Server: OS/400 Version 5 Release 2*, REDP-3652, and in the HSL Rules presentation that is available on the Web at:

http://www-1.ibm.com/servers/eserver/iseries/ha/systemdesign.html

Model 810 PCI cards and features

The Model 810 is a PCI-based technology system. See the table on page 102 for the number of maximum features supported by the total system and in the Model 810 system unit. See Chapter 17, "iSeries PCI I/O processors" on page 323, and Chapter 18, "iSeries I/O adapters and controllers" on page 337, for full descriptions of the features that are supported.

See "AIX and Linux Direct Attach features overview" on page 340 for the supported Linux Direct Attach features.

Note: The placement of PCI cards follows special rules. Refer to "PCI card technology" on page 338 and *PCI Card Placement Rules for the IBM @server iSeries Server Version 5 Release 2*, REDP-3638, before you propose any configuration.

External towers

Refer to Chapter 15, "Towers, racks, and high-speed link" on page 261, for information about supported towers for the Model 810.

Model 810 upgrades

See Chapter 16, "Upgrades to eServer i5 and i5/OS" on page 311, for general upgrade considerations and server upgrade possibilities within the Model 810.

Supported model upgrades for the Model 810 are identified in the *Upgrade* topic of the Find and Compare Tool (FACT) at:

http://www-919.ibm.com/servers/eserver/fact/

iSeries Model 825

The iSeries 825 is a powerful server that is designed for medium to large enterprises that need high versatility in a world of On Demand Business. The Model 825 supports multiple operating environments and can run a variety of applications simultaneously. It provides excellent scalability and large input/output (I/O) capacity for server consolidation. Capacity on Demand capabilities and a choice of Editions provide outstanding flexibility to respond to changing business needs.

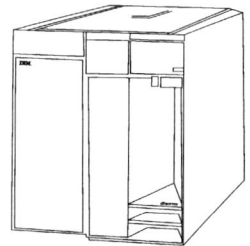

iSeries Model 825

The Model 825 is offered as a deskside tower. It provides space for 15 disks attached with a Small Computer System Interface (SCSI) controller. An optional redundant power supply is available. Hot-plugging is supported for PCI-X card slots, disk slots, and redundant fans. It can attach Integrated xSeries Adapters. Hot-plugging of removable media devices is not supported.

Model overview

This section takes a closer look at the minimum functional server, required features, and optional features.

> **Note:** In the Required features and Optional features sections, the single asterisk (*) indicates that the feature is supported for conversion only.

Minimum functional server

A minimum functional server consists of the base server unit and selected priced features. The base server includes:

▶ Physical package and power elements

▶ System unit (CEC)

▶ Active backplane (CCIN 25CA)

- 10 PCI-X card slots
- Hot plug PCI capability
- Two high-speed link (HSL) slots/connectors
- Integrated/embedded 10/100 Mbps Ethernet IOA (CCIN 288E)

▶ Operator panel (CCIN 250A)

▶ #9793/#9794 Base PCI Two-Line WAN with integrated modem

▶ Base direct access storage device (DASD) cage

Concurrent disk maintenance is supported. One base DASD Cage (CCIN 28BC) is included in the base system unit and provides five disk unit slots. Up to two additional #7124 DASD Expansion Unit - 5 slot cages can be added, for a maximum of three DASD cages and up to 15 disk units in the base system (CEC).

▶ HSL bus adapters

- #9787 Base HSL-2 Ports - 2 Copper (CCIN 28B3)

- In addition to the #9787, one of the following HSL adapters must be specified:

  • #9785 Base HSL-2 Ports - 2 Copper
  • #9786 Base HSL Ports - 2 Optical

▶ Two 1040 W Power Supply (two line cords required)

- Power supply and fan hot plugging is supported.

▶ #9844 Base PCI IOP

Provides support for the Converged Service Processor and up to four input/output adapters (IOAs).

Required features

The *required* features include:

► Specific combinations of the Processor feature, Edition feature, and Server feature are allowed as shown in the following table.

Processor feature	Server feature	Edition feature	Software group	Processor feature code or QPRCFEAT value
#2473	#0873	#7416 Standard	P30	7416
		#7418 Enterprise	P30	7418
		#7434 High Availability	P30	7418
	#0772	#7416 Domino	P30	7416
	#0773	#7416 Domino	P30	7416
#2495	#0890	#7439 Capacity BackUp	P30	7439

Note: The Standard Edition for the Model 825 processors provides limited 5250 CPW for 5250 OLTP workloads. The Enterprise, High Availability, and Capacity BackUp Editions for the Model 825 processors provide maximum 5250 CPW for 5250 OLTP workloads.

The Enterprise and High Availability Editions also provide support for Capacity on Demand (permanent and temporary). The Capacity on Demand Edition provides support for temporary capacity only.

Edition content varies by processor and server features selected. For more information, see "Editions" on page 55.

The Domino servers have minimum requirements for the number of processors, DASD, memory, and Domino server and client licenses.

The following table lists the Domino measurements for the iSeries Model 825.

Model	Server feature	Processor feature	Edition feature	MCU rating*
825	#0772	#2473	#7416	11600
	#0773	#2473	#7416	17400
* The MCU ratings cannot be achieved using minimum configurations.				

▶ Main storage

See "Main storage" on page 217 for a list of supported memory features, and configuration considerations.

▶ PCI disk controller (Small Computer System Interface (SCSI) IOA)

The SCSI IOA supports the DVD-ROM, DVD-RAM, migrated CD-ROM, internal tape, and disk units (in the CEC).

The Model 825 system unit supports three disk unit cages (five-pack) and two removable media bays.

- #2757 PCI-X Ultra RAID Disk Controller
- #2780 PCI-X Ultra4 RAID Disk Controller
- #2782 PCI-X RAID Disk Unit Controller
- #4778 PCI RAID Disk Unit Controller
- #5703 PCI-X RAID Disk Unit Controller

Note: The PCI SCSI Disk Controller must have its SCSI bus 0 cabled to the base (upper) DASD cage. The Load Source DASD must be placed in the base DASD cage.

▶ Removable optical device (one must be specified)

- #4630 DVD-RAM
- #4631 DVD-ROM (Default)

▶ Internal disk units

- #4317 8.58 GB 10k RPM Disk Unit*
- #4318 17.54 GB 10k RPM Disk Unit*
- #4319 35.16 GB 10k RPM Disk Unit
- #4326 35.16 GB 15k RPM Disk Unit
- #4327 70.56 GB 15k RPM Disk Unit

One of the following load source specify codes is required:

- #0829 - #4318 Load Source Specify*
- #0830 - #4319 Load Source Specify
- #0834 - #4326 Load Source Specify
- #0835 - #4327 Load Source Specify

► Disk protection specify codes (one must be specified)

- #0040 Mirrored System Disk Level
- #0041 RAID Protection - All
- #0042 Mirrored System IOP Level
- #0043 Mirrored System Bus Level

#0041 is the default for disk data protection.

► System console attachment adapter

The console on LAN options require a dedicated LAN adapter. A #0367 Operations Console PCI Cable is added to the order by the IBM marketing configurator.

- #5540 System Console on Twinaxial Workstation IOA
  - #4746 PCI Twinaxial IOA
- #5544 System Console on Operations Console
  - #0367 Operations Console PCI Cable
- #5548 System Console on 100 Mbps Ethernet
  - Embedded 10/100 Mbps Ethernet IOA (CCIN 288E)
  - #0367 Operations Console PCI Cable

Note: The #5546 System Console on 100 Mbps Token Ring is not supported.

Optional features

The *optional* features include:

► #0551 iSeries Rack

Up to two Model 825s may be installed in an #0551 rack. See "#0551 iSeries Rack" on page 290 for a complete description of the #0551 iSeries Rack and supported features and specify codes.

► #7124 DASD Expansion Unit - 5 slot

The #7124 is a 5-pack DASD cage for the Model 825 system unit. The #7124 includes the DASD cage, DASD backplane, and associated SCSI cables. A maximum of two may be ordered on a Model 825 system.

▶ Internal tape devices

   – #4682 4 GB ¼-inch Cartridge Tape Device
   – #4684 30 GB ¼-inch Cartridge Tape Device
   – #4685 80 GB VXA-2 Tape Device
   – #4687 50 GB ¼-inch Cartridge Tape Device

The Model 825 initial installation and model upgrades are performed by an IBM Service Representative.

Processor features

The #2473 3/6-way (POWER4 1.1 GHz) includes:

▶ Three processor cards (CCIN 25DC)
▶ 96 MB L3 Cache (16 MB L3/ processor)
▶ Smart Chip Processor VPD Card (CCIN 2473)
▶ Base I/O backplane (CCIN 25CA)
▶ #9787 CCIN 28B3 Expansion Card (provides two HSL-2 ports)
▶ CCIN 289D Connector Card

Specify one #1609 825 CUoD Activation feature for each additional standby processor activated (maximum of three). Specify one #1773 TCoD Enablement feature for each additional standby processor when approaching limit of usable on/off processor days.

The #2495 1/6-way (POWER4 1.1 GHz) includes:

▶ Three processor cards (CCIN 25DC)
▶ 96 MB L3 Cache (16 MB L3/ processor)
▶ Smart Chip Processor VPD Card (CCIN 2473)
▶ Base I/O backplane (CCIN 25CA)
▶ #9787 CCIN 28B3 Expansion Card (provides two HSL-2 ports)
▶ CCIN 289D Connector Card

Select one #1779 On/Off Capacity on Demand enablement feature for each additional standby processor when approaching the limit of usable on/off processor days.

> **Note:** The Capacity on Demand (permanent and temporary) capabilities, including activation, enablement, and billing features, are described in "Capacity on Demand" on page 44.

Refer to "Table 8: Summary of the iSeries Model 825" on page 104 to find Processor CPW, Mail and Calendar Users (MCU), and 5250 CPW, and to determine the processor feature code and QPRCFEAT value.

Main storage

The following memory features are available on the Model 825:

- ▶ #3042 - 256 MB Main Storage DIMM DDR - 128 Mb Technology (Unstacked)
- ▶ #3043 - 512 MB Main Storage DIMM DDR - 256 Mb Technology (Unstacked)
- ▶ #3044 - 1024 MB Main Storage DIMM DDR - 256 Mb Technology (Stacked)
- ▶ #3046 - 2048 MB Main Storage DIMM DDR - 512 Mb Technology (Stacked)

For the Model 825, the main storage Dual Inline Memory Modules (DIMMs) are installed directly onto the processor cards. Each processor card has eight DIMM slots. The eight slots are arranged in two sets of four. The DIMMs must be installed in sets of four (quads). Each set of four DIMMs must be the same memory capacity and technology. Each system order must have at least one set of three main storage DIMM quads (12 DIMMs total) installed. An exception is the 2 GB memory capacity point, where two quads (eight DIMMs total) are allowed.

Three processor cards (three multichip modules (MCMs)) are installed in the Model 825 system. There is a total of 24 DIMM slots, in which 8, 12, 16, 20, or 24 memory DIMMs may be installed.

The following main storage requirements apply:

- ▶ The marketing configurator defaults to 3 GB of memory. If 2 GB of total main storage is specified, a message is issued indicating this memory configuration is not recommended by IBM.
- ▶ Except on systems with 2 GB of memory capacity, no Single Chip Model (SCM) board is allowed to contain more than twice the memory capacity of any other processor.

The marketing configurator determines the correct number and combination of memory features to fulfill a chosen increment. It is based on the minimum number of memory features required to meet the increment within the requirements of one quad per SCM board. No SCM board having more than two times the total memory of any other SCM board is allowed.

9406 Model 825 schematics

The following diagrams show the slot and feature card arrangement of the Model 825 system unit, base enclosure, and rack. You can find schematics of any supported expansion units in Chapter 15, "Towers, racks, and high-speed link" on page 261.

9406 Model 825 system unit

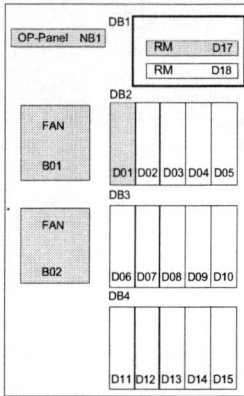

Front

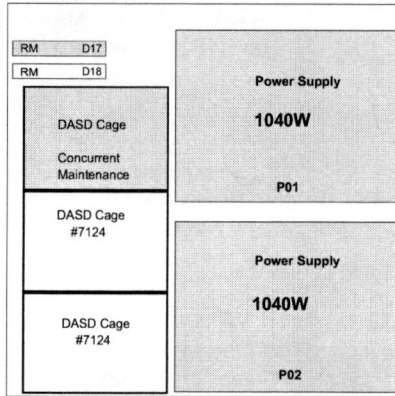

Right

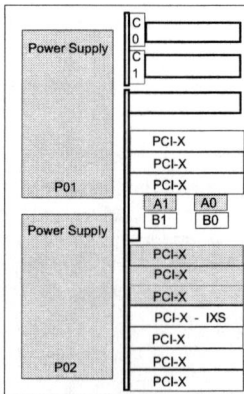

Back

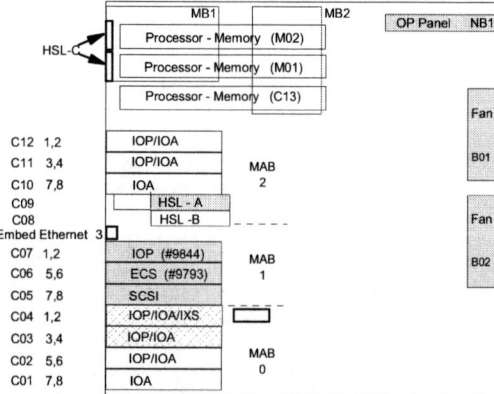

Left

Note: Hot plug and concurrent add of the following items are supported:

Note: Hot plug and concurrent add of the following items are supported:

▶ PCI cards
▶ Disk units
▶ Removable media
▶ Power supplies
▶ Fans

9406 Model 825 Processor and Memory

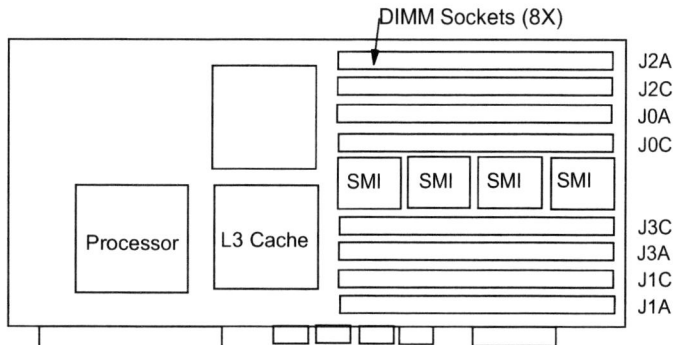

DIMM Sockets (8X)

J2A
J2C
J0A
J0C

SMI SMI SMI SMI

Processor   L3 Cache

J3C
J3A
J1C
J1A

Note: DIMM quad plugging is J1A, J3A, J0A, J2A, and then J1C, J3C, J0C, J2C

Note: You can find line cord and power receptacle specification information on the Web at:

http://www.ibm.com/eserver/iseries/infocenter

High-speed link on Model 825

The Model 825 supports up to three HSL loops, two of which can be optical fiber HSL loops. The optical fiber HSL loop extends the distance between the Model 825 system unit and the I/O units from a limit of 15 meters prior to OS/400 V5R2, to a maximum of 250 meters. The extra length can help to improve data reliability and protection. See "HSL fabric" on page 297 for information about supported HSL cables and HSL loop maximums.

You can find further information in *High-speed Link Loop Architecture for the IBM @server iSeries Server: OS/400 Version 5 Release 2*, REDP-3652, and in the HSL Rules presentation, which is available on the Web at:

http://www-1.ibm.com/servers/eserver/iseries/ha/systemdesign.html

> **Important:** The Model 825 has a unique set of rules that influence the maximum number of components on a HSL loop. As such, rules specific to the Model 825 warrant a more detailed description than what is presented in *High-speed Link Loop Architecture for the IBM @server iSeries Server: OS/400 Version 5 Release 2*, REDP-3652. TechNote *iSeries Model 825 High-speed Link Loop*, TIPS-0297, complements this Redpaper.

Model 825 PCI cards and features

The Model 825 is a PCI-based technology system. Since migration towers cannot attach to the Model 825, System Products Division (SPD) cards in systems or towers migrating to the Model 825 must be replaced with PCI card equivalents. Refer to "Hardware no longer marketed by IBM" on page 755 for a list of SPD functions not supported by PCI adapters.

See the table on page 104 for the number of maximum features supported by the total system and in the Model 825 system unit. See Chapter 17, "iSeries PCI I/O processors" on page 323, and Chapter 18, "iSeries I/O adapters and controllers" on page 337, for full descriptions of the features that are supported. See "AIX and Linux Direct Attach features overview" on page 340 for supported Linux Direct Attach features.

> **Note:** The placement of PCI cards follows special rules. Refer to "PCI card technology" on page 338 and *PCI Card Placement Rules for the IBM @server iSeries Server Version 5 Release 2*, REDP-3638, before you propose any configuration.

External towers

Migration towers are not supported on the Model 825. PCI towers are supported with upgrades for migration only.

Refer to Chapter 15, "Towers, racks, and high-speed link" on page 261, for information about supported towers for the Model 825, and "Table 8: Summary of the iSeries Model 825" on page 104 for a table of configuration maximums.

Model 825 upgrades

See Chapter 16, "Upgrades to eServer i5 and i5/OS" on page 311, for general upgrade considerations and server-to-server upgrade possibilities. Supported model upgrades for the Model 825 are identified in the *Upgrade* topic of the Find and Compare Tool (FACT) at:

`http://www-919.ibm.com/servers/eserver/fact/`

Model 825 Capacity on Demand

The iSeries Model 825 offers several Capacity on Demand options that make it possible to activate additional processor resource. IBM @server Capacity Upgrade on Demand (CUoD) and On/Off Capacity on Demand are available for the Model 825. On Demand features are described in this section.

On Demand features may have base activations. The following options are available to activate additional resources:

▶ Capacity upgrade on Demand (Permanent)

Purchase processor activation features when needed. This requires the purchase of operating system licenses.

▶ On/Off Capacity on Demand (Temporary)

Pay for processor day billing features at the end of each billing period. Additional i5/OS licenses are not required.

Refer to the table on page 106 to see the feature codes associated with the Model 825 Capacity on Demand options. See the following Web site for more information about Capacity on Demand:

`http://www-1.ibm.com/servers/eserver/iseries/ondemand/cod/`

13

iSeries Model 870

The iSeries 870 is a mainframe-class server that is built to handle the needs of large enterprises. This server includes IBM @server Capacity Upgrade on Demand (CUoD) features to provide tremendous power and maximum flexibility to run mixed, multiple workloads.

The Model 870 delivers outstanding response times for mainstay 5250 online transaction processing (OLTP) applications, high performance for Web and applications for On Demand Business, plus a wide array of integrated management tools that can help you respond to business needs in an instant.

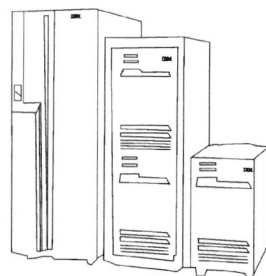

iSeries Model 870

The 5/8-way and 8/16-way are IBM POWER4 processors. Configurations range from 7700 to 20000 CPW, up to 128 GB of memory and up to 37 TB of disk.

223

Model overview

This section takes a closer look at the minimum functional server, required features, and optional features.

> **Note:** In the Required features and Optional features sections, note the following descriptions:
>
> * Supported for conversion/migration only
> **MES only

Minimum functional server

A minimum functional server consists of the base server unit and selected priced features. The Model 870 supports hot plug and concurrent add of Peripheral Component Interconnect (PCI) cards, disk units, and removable media devices. Included in the base server are the physical package and power elements as follows:

► System unit (CEC)

► #9094 Base PCI I/O Enclosure (with #5114) or #8094 Optional 1.8 M I/O Rack

► Line cord features: Two line cord features should be specified for the 870 CEC, with two additional line cord features for the #9094. If the #8094 Optional 1.8 M I/O Rack is ordered instead of the #9094 Base PCI I/O Enclosure, then two line cords are needed for the lower tower as well as one or two line cords for the upper tower.

► Bulk Power Regulator (CCIN CQ02)

- Two required with 24-way processor feature
- Four required with 32-way processor feature

► Bulk Power Controller (CCIN RGA1)

- Two required with all processor features
- Bulk Power Distribution (CCIN RGA2)
- Two required with 24-way and 32-way processor features

► Distributed Converter Assembly (CCIN DCA1)

- Two DCAs are "base"
- Two DCAs added with 24-way processor feature (total of four DCAs)
- Three DCAs added with 32-way processor features (total of five DCAs)

► Capacitor Card (CCIN 274F): One is "base"

One Capacitor Card is added with 24-way and 32-way processor features (total of two).

- ► Clock card (CCIN 25C1)
- ► Pass-through card (CCIN 272D): Two on the #2486 processor
- ► PCI and Common Service Processor (CSP) card (CCIN 28AA)
- ► Operator Panel with key stick (CCIN 247A)
- ► #9730 Base HSL-2 Ports - 4 Copper (CCIN 273B)
- ► #9771/#9793/#9794 Base PCI Two-Line WAN with integrated modem
- ► #9844 Base PCI IOP provides support for:
  - – The required Small Computer System Interface (SCSI) input/output adapter (IOA), which controls up to 15 disk units, the required DVD-RAM/DVD-ROM, and a feature internal tape or a feature DVD-RAM/DVD-ROM
  - – A base console/workstation IOA

    The IBM marketing configurator determines which feature combinations are to be on the order based on the #5540, #5544, #5546, or #5548 System Console specify code.

  - – The #9771/#9793/#9794 Base PCI Two-Line WAN with integrated modem

    Note: In countries (or regions) where #9771/#9793/#9794 is not homologated, the marketing configurator adds a #4745 PCI Two-Line WAN IOA or a #2742 PCI Two-Line WAN IOA, a #0032 modem feature, and a #0348 cable to the order. The #4745/#2742 is mandatory and cannot be removed from the system until the #9793/#9794 homologation is completed. The #0032 and #0348 features may be removed from the order or system at any time.

Required features

The *required* features include:

- ► Specific combinations of the Processor feature, Edition feature, and Server feature are allowed as shown in the following table.

Processor feature	Server feature	Edition feature	Software group	Processor feature code or QPRCFEAT value
#2486	#0886	#7419 Standard	P40	7419
		#7421 Enterprise	P40	7421
		#7436 High Availability	P40	7421
#2489	#0889	#7431 Standard	P40	7431
		#7433 Enterprise	P40	7433
		#7435 High Availability	P40	7433
#2496	#0891	#7440 Capacity BackUp	P40	7440

Note: The Standard Edition for the Model 870 processors provides limited 5250 CPW for 5250 OLTP workloads. The Enterprise, High Availability, and Capacity BackUp Editions for the Model 870 processors provide maximum 5250 CPW for 5250 OLTP workloads.

The Enterprise and High Availability Editions also provide support for Capacity on Demand (permanent and temporary). The Capacity on Demand Edition provides support for temporary capacity only.

Edition content varies by processor and server features selected. For more information, see "Editions" on page 55.

▶ Main storage

See "Main storage" on page 229 for a list of supported memory features, and configuration considerations.

▶ PCI disk controller (SCSI IOA)

The SCSI IOA supports the DVD-ROM, DVD-RAM, migrated CD-ROM, internal tape, and disk units in the base PCI enclosure.

- #2757 PCI-X Ultra RAID Disk Controller
- #2780 PCI-X Ultra4 RAID Disk Controller
- #4748 PCI RAID Disk Unit Controller
- #4778 PCI RAID Disk Unit Controller

▶ Removable optical device (one must be specified)

- #4425 CD-ROM*
- #4430 DVD-RAM*
- #4625 CD-ROM**
- #4630 DVD-RAM
- #4631 DVD-ROM

- Internal disk units
  - #4317 8.58 GB 10k RPM Disk Unit*
  - #4318 17.54 GB 10k RPM Disk Unit*
  - #4319 35.16 GB 10k RPM Disk Unit
  - #4326 35.16 GB 15k RPM Disk Unit
  - #4327 70.56 GB 15k RPM Disk Unit

  One of the following load source specify codes is required:
  - #0829 - #4318 Load Source Specify*
  - #0830 - #4319 Load Source Specify
  - #0834 - #4326 Load Source Specify
  - #0835 - #4327 Load Source Specify

- Disk protection specify codes (one must be specified)
  - #0040 Mirrored System Disk Level
  - #0041 RAID Protection - All
  - #0042 Mirrored System IOP Level
  - #0043 Mirrored System Bus Level

  #0041 is the default for disk data protection.

- System console/communications adapter

  The console on LAN options require a dedicated LAN adapter. A #0367 Operations Console PCI Cable is added to the order by the marketing configurator.
  - #5540 System Console on Twinaxial Workstation IOA
    - #4746 PCI Twinaxial IOA
  - #5544 System Console on Operations Console
    - #0367 Operations Console PCI Cable
  - #5546 System Console on 100 Mbps Token Ring
    - #2744 PCI 100 Mbps Token Ring IOA
    - #0367 Operations Console PCI Cable
  - #5548 System Console on 100 Mbps Ethernet
    - #2849 10/100 Mbps Ethernet Adapter
    - #4838 PCI 100/10 Mbps Ethernet IOA
    - #0367 Operations Console PCI Cable

Optional features

The *optional* features include the following internal tape devices:

- ▶ #4482 4 GB ¼-inch Cartridge Tape Device*
- ▶ #4483 16 GB ¼-inch Cartridge Tape Device
- ▶ #4486 25 GB ¼-inch Cartridge Tape Device
- ▶ #4487 50 GB ¼-inch Cartridge Tape Device*
- ▶ #4682 4 GB ¼-inch Cartridge Tape Device
- ▶ #4684 30 GB ¼-inch Cartridge Tape Device
- ▶ #4685 80 GB VXA-2 Tape Device
- ▶ #4686 25 GB ¼-inch Cartridge Tape Device
- ▶ #4687 50 GB ¼-inch Cartridge Tape Device

IBM Service Representatives perform the Model 870 initial installation and model upgrades.

Processor features

The #2486 8/16-way (POWER4 1.3 GHz) includes:

- ▶ Processor Capacity Card (CCIN 7419 or CCIN 7421)
- ▶ Processor 0 (CCIN 25D3)
- ▶ Processor 1 (CCIN 25D3)

The #2486 Model 870 has two processor modules. Each processor module has eight processors. The system comes with a minimum of eight processors activated. Specify one #1611 870 CUoD Activation feature for each additional standby processor activated (maximum of eight). Specify one #1776 TCoD Enablement feature for each additional standby processor when approaching the limit of usable on/off processor days.

The #2489 5/8-way (POWER4 1.3 GHz) includes:

- ▶ Processor Capacity Card (CCIN 7431 or CCIN 7433)
- ▶ Processor 0 (CCIN 25D3)

The #2489 Model 870 has one processor module. Each processor module has eight processors. For #2489, the processor module should be plugged in plug/slot 0. The system comes with a minimum of five processors activated.

Specify one #1614 POD Activation feature for each additional standby processor activated (maximum of eight). Specify one #1776 TCoD Enablement feature for each additional standby processor when approaching limit of usable on/off processor days.

The #2496 2/16-way (POWER4 1.3 GHz) includes:

▶ Processor Capacity Card (CCIN 7440)
▶ Processor 0 (CCIN 25D3)
▶ Processor 1 (CCIN 25D3)

The #2496 Model 870 has two processor modules. Each processor module has eight processors. The system comes with a minimum of two processors activated.

Specify one #1780 TCoD Enablement feature for each additional standby processor when approaching the limit of usable on/off processor days.

Note: The Capacity on Demand (permanent and temporary) capabilities, including activation, enablement and billing features, are described in "Capacity on Demand" on page 44.

Refer to "Table 8: Summary of the iSeries Model 825" on page 104 to find Processor CPW, Mail and Calendar Users (MCU), 5250 CPW, and to determine the processor feature code and QPRCFEAT value.

Main storage

Eight main storage card sockets exist on the backplane of the Model 870. A maximum of four of the following main storage cards can be placed in the system:

▶ #3015 - 8192 MB Main Storage Card
▶ #3017 - 32768 MB Main Storage Card
▶ #3020 - 4096 GB Main Storage Card
▶ #3035 - 16384 MB Main Storage Card

A minimum of two main storage cards of equal capacity are required. The main storage cards are installed according to the following rules:

▶ The cards must be installed in pairs of equal capacity.

▶ The pairs of must plug into memory card slots under the same multichip modules (MCM) (slots 0 and 1, slots 2 and 3).

▶ Mixed main storage cards must be of the adjacent capacity. For example, 4 GB and 8 GB are allowed, but 4 GB and 16 GB are not allowed.

▶ There is no requirement when mixed main storage cards are used, for cards of higher capacity to precede or follow those of smaller capacity.

The following table shows the allowable main storage capacities and slot positioning for the #2489 Model 870 processor.

Allowable memory capacity (GB)	Memory card slot 0	Memory card slot 1	Memory card slot 2	Memory card slot 3	Memory card slots 4 to 7
8	#3020 4 GB	#3020 4 GB	Empty	Empty	Empty
16	#3015 8 GB	#3015 8 GB	Empty	Empty	Empty
32	#3035 16 GB	#3035 16 GB	Empty	Empty	Empty
64	#3017 32 GB	#3017 32 GB	Empty	Empty	Empty

The next table shows the allowable main storage capacities and slot positioning for the #2486 and #2496 Model 870 processors.

Allowable memory capacity (GB)	Memory card slot 0	Memory card slot1	Memory card slot 2	Memory card slot 3	Memory card slots 4 to 7
8	#3020 4 GB	#3020 4 GB	Empty	Empty	Empty
16	#3020 4 GB	#3020 4 GB	#3020 4 GB	#3020 4 GB	Empty
24	#3015 8 GB	#3015 8 GB	#3020 4 GB	#3020 4 GB	Empty
24	#3020 4 GB	#3020 4 GB	#3015 8 GB	#3015 8 GB	Empty
32	#3015 8 GB	#3015 8 GB	#3015 8 GB	#3015 8 GB	Empty
48	#3035 16 GB	#3035 16 GB	#3015 8 GB	#3015 8 GB	Empty
48	#3015 8 GB	#3015 8 GB	#3035 16 GB	#3035 16 GB	Empty
64	#3035 16 GB	#3035 16 GB	#3035 16 GB	#3035 16 GB	Empty
96	#3017 32 GB	#3017 32 GB	#3035 16 GB	#3035 16 GB	Empty
96	#3035 16 GB	#3035 16 GB	#3017 32 GB	#3017 32 GB	Empty

Allowable memory capacity (GB)	Memory card slot 0	Memory card slot1	Memory card slot 2	Memory card slot 3	Memory card slots 4 to 7
128	#3017 32 GB	#3017 32 GB	#3017 32 GB	#3017 32 GB	Empty

#9094 Base PCI I/O Enclosure

The #9094 Base PCI I/O Enclosure is the base PCI-X I/O enclosure shipped with the Model 870 and 890 system units. A #9094 is attached to the system unit via an high-speed link (HSL) cable through a #9887 Base HSL-2 Bus Adapter. One JTAG cable and one V/S Communication cable (VPD and SPCN combined) are included for the attachment of the #9094 to the system unit. The #5114 Dual Line Cords - Tower is a required feature. Specify two line cords for the #9094.

The #9094 has 15 disk unit slots, with an additional 30 slots available when using feature #5107 30 Disk Expansion. The 45 disk unit positions are in three groups of 15. Each group of 15 disk units is further divided into three groups of five disk units with each group of five disk units supported on a separate SCSI bus.

The #9094 also has two removable media slots and 14 PCI-X card slots. A #9844 Base PCI IOP is included in the base. A #2757 PCI-X Ultra RAID Disk Controller or #4748/#4778 PCI RAID Disk Unit Controller is required to drive the disk units in the base 15 disk unit slots and the removable media devices in the two removal media slots.

The #9094 Base PCI I/O Enclosure supports up to nine OS/400 or Linux controlled #2757/#4748/#4778/#5703 disk controllers (up to nine in total). The #5703 PCI-X RAID Disk Unit Controller can be used after three #2757/#4748/#4778 controllers are installed. The #0143 Disk Controller Placement Exception is a prerequisite for this configuration when the #5703 is the only disk unit controller ordered.

A maximum of three #2757 PCI-X Ultra RAID Disk Controller or #4748/#4778 PCI RAID Disk Unit Controllers are allowed per #9094. Up to 15 disk units per #2757 are supported in a #9094.

The 11 PCI IOAs are supported by the #9844 Base PCI IOP, by feature #2844 PCI IOPs, and by the #2791, #2792/#9792, #4710/#9710, or #2799 PCI Integrated xSeries Server.

Two cables must be ordered to attach to the HSL or HSL-2 ports. When ordering cables to connect to the HSL interface, optical HSL, copper HSL, copper HSL-2, or copper HSL to HSL-2 cables are required. An HSL loop uses all optical or all copper ports and cables. A copper loop can intermix I/O towers or units with

copper HSL and copper HSL-2 ports. Select the appropriate cable based on the type of HSL ports to which it is being attached, and the cable length required.

One SPCN cable is required for each tower.

#5107 30 Disk Expansion

The #5107 is a disk unit expansion enclosure feature for the #9094 Base PCI I/O Enclosure. The #5107 includes two 15 disk unit enclosures, one 840-watt power supply, backplanes, and cables.

A #2757 PCI-X Ultra RAID Disk Controller or #4748/#4778 PCI RAID Disk Unit Controller or #5703 PCI-X RAID Disk Unit Controller is required to support disk units in each of the two disk unit enclosures included with #5107. Each group of 15 disk units is further divided into three groups of five disk units with each group of five disk units supported on a separate SCSI bus. A minimum of two disk unit controllers and a maximum of six are required to support 30 disk units.

#8094 Optional 1.8 M I/O Rack

The #8094 is a optional base I/O rack shipped on the Model 870 instead of the #9094 Base PCI I/O Enclosure. The #8094 supports up to 90 disk units, up to 22 PCI IOAs, and up to three additional removable media units. A #8094 is a 1.8 M rack with two enclosures.

▸ The bottom enclosure is a #9094 Base PCI I/O Enclosure with side covers and casters removed and a #5107 30 Disk Expansion included in the base (no feature code required). The #5114 Dual Line Cords - Tower is a mandatory feature for the #9094.

▸ The top enclosure is a #5094 PCI-X Expansion Tower with side covers and casters removed, and a #5108 30-Disk Expansion Feature (no feature code required) included in the base. The #5115 Dual Line Cords - Tower feature code is required for dual line cords in the top enclosure.

The #0694 - (#5094 Equivalent) is a prerequisite.

Included with the bottom enclosure is one JTAG cable and one VPD-S cable, required to attach the bottom enclosure to the system unit. Also included is the #9887 Base HSL-2 Bus Adapter and #9844 Base PCI IOP.

The #8094 also supports up to four removable media devices (internal tape, CD-ROM, and DVD). These removable media devices are supported by the two #2757 PCI-X Ultra RAID Disk Controller, #4748/#4778 PCI RAID Disk Unit Controller, or #9778 Base PCI RAID Disk Unit Controller that support the first group of 15 disk units in each enclosure.

The two enclosures in the #8094 are separately attached to the system unit via HSL cables as though they were a stand-alone #9094 and #5094. They are also treated as separate units for HSL loop plugging and configuration rules and recommendations. As such, the bottom enclosure must be attached to the system unit's first HSL loop.

A bus adapter is included to provide the HSL interface to the top enclosure. Select one of the following types:

▶ #9886 - Base Optical Bus Adapter, to specify four optical HSL ports
▶ #9887 Base HSL-2 Bus Adapter, to specify four copper HSL-2 ports

Three or four cables must be ordered to attach to the HSL or HSL-2 ports. When ordering cables to connect to the HSL interface, optical HSL, copper HSL, copper HSL-2, or copper HSL to HSL-2 cables are required. An HSL loop uses all optical or all copper ports and cables. A copper loop can intermix I/O towers and units with copper HSL and copper HSL-2 ports. Select the appropriate cable based on the type of HSL ports to which it is being attached and the cable length required.

Specify three or four line cords for the #8094 Optional 1.8 M I/O Rack.

If the top enclosure is to be attached to a different system than what was initially ordered, remove for Record Purpose Only (RPO) the #0694 - #5094 Equivalent specify code from the initially ordered system and add it to the target system.

A schematic of the #8094 Optional 1.8 M I/O Rack can be found on page 252.

#5114 Dual Line Cords - Tower

The required #5114 feature provides dual line cord support for the #9094 Base PCI I/O Enclosure on the Model 870 and 890 and for the lower enclosures of the #8093 and #8094 towers. With the #5114, the enclosure requires two #14xx line cords and has two AC input boxes.

9406 Model 870 schematics

The following diagrams show slot and feature card arrangement of the Model 870 system unit, base enclosure, and rack. You can find schematics of any supported expansion units in Chapter 15, "Towers, racks, and high-speed link" on page 261.

9406 Model 870 system unit

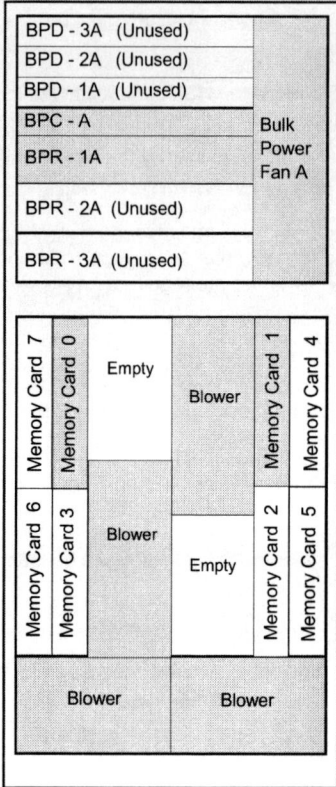

Front

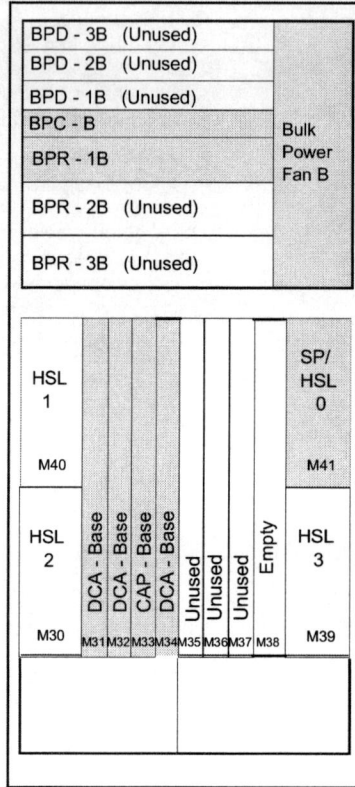

Back

Model 870 CEC Backplane

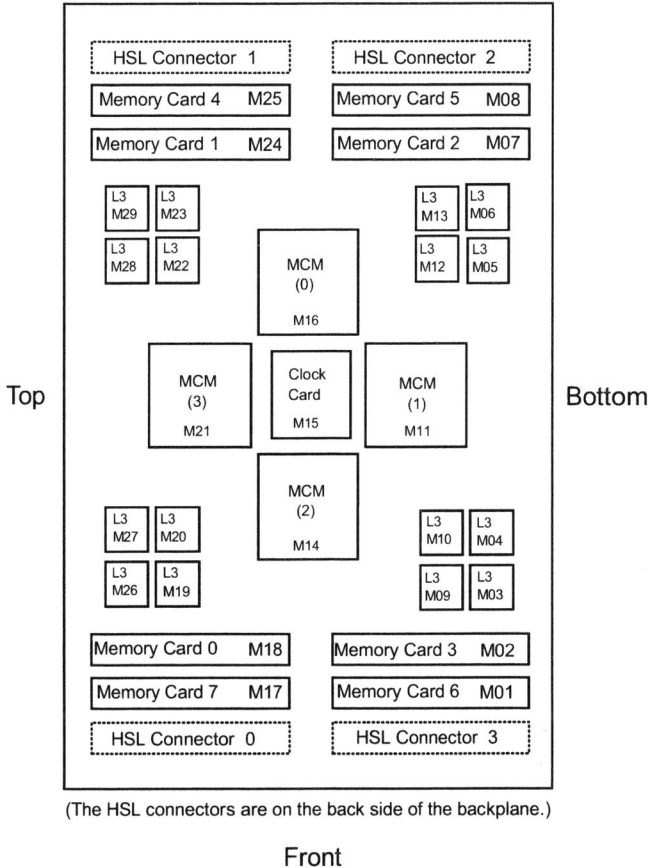

```
                    ┌─────────────────────┐   ┌─────────────────────┐
                    ┆ HSL Connector  1    ┆   ┆ HSL Connector  2    ┆
                    └─────────────────────┘   └─────────────────────┘
                    ┌─────────────────────┐   ┌─────────────────────┐
                    │ Memory Card 4   M25 │   │ Memory Card 5   M08 │
                    └─────────────────────┘   └─────────────────────┘
                    ┌─────────────────────┐   ┌─────────────────────┐
                    │ Memory Card 1   M24 │   │ Memory Card 2   M07 │
                    └─────────────────────┘   └─────────────────────┘

                    ┌────┐┌────┐                      ┌────┐┌────┐
                    │ L3 ││ L3 │                      │ L3 ││ L3 │
                    │M29 ││M23 │                      │M13 ││M06 │
                    └────┘└────┘          ┌────────┐  └────┘└────┘
                    ┌────┐┌────┐          │  MCM   │  ┌────┐┌────┐
                    │ L3 ││ L3 │          │  (0)   │  │ L3 ││ L3 │
                    │M28 ││M22 │          │        │  │M12 ││M05 │
                    └────┘└────┘          │  M16   │  └────┘└────┘
                                          └────────┘
                              ┌────────┐ ┌──────┐ ┌────────┐
                              │  MCM   │ │Clock │ │  MCM   │
          Top                 │  (3)   │ │Card  │ │  (1)   │        Bottom
                              │        │ │ M15  │ │        │
                              │  M21   │ └──────┘ │  M11   │
                              └────────┘          └────────┘
                                          ┌────────┐
                                          │  MCM   │
                    ┌────┐┌────┐          │  (2)   │  ┌────┐┌────┐
                    │ L3 ││ L3 │          │        │  │ L3 ││ L3 │
                    │M27 ││M20 │          │  M14   │  │M10 ││M04 │
                    └────┘└────┘          └────────┘  └────┘└────┘
                    ┌────┐┌────┐                      ┌────┐┌────┐
                    │ L3 ││ L3 │                      │ L3 ││ L3 │
                    │M26 ││M19 │                      │M09 ││M03 │
                    └────┘└────┘                      └────┘└────┘

                    ┌─────────────────────┐   ┌─────────────────────┐
                    │ Memory Card 0   M18 │   │ Memory Card 3   M02 │
                    └─────────────────────┘   └─────────────────────┘
                    ┌─────────────────────┐   ┌─────────────────────┐
                    │ Memory Card 7   M17 │   │ Memory Card 6   M01 │
                    └─────────────────────┘   └─────────────────────┘
                    ┌─────────────────────┐   ┌─────────────────────┐
                    ┆ HSL Connector  0    ┆   ┆ HSL Connector  3    ┆
                    └─────────────────────┘   └─────────────────────┘
```

(The HSL connectors are on the back side of the backplane.)

Front

Note: MCM slots 0 and 2 contain processor modules. MCM slots 1 and 3 have pass-through cards (CCIN 272D) installed.

#9094 Base PCI I/O Enclosure

Dual Line Cord

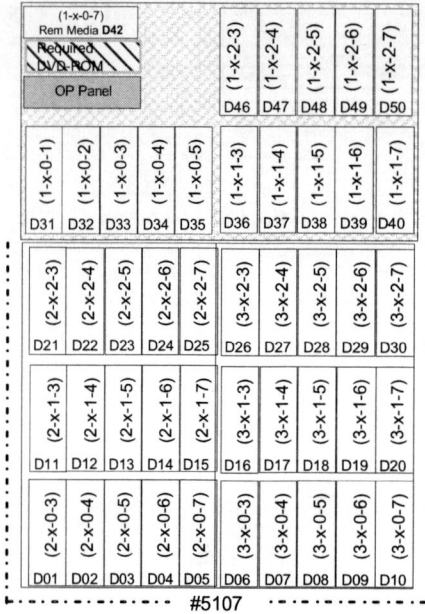

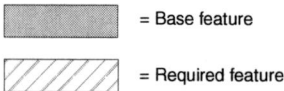

Front

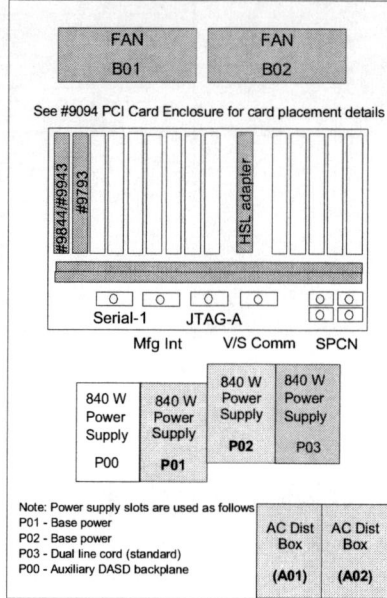

Back

Note: Hot plug and concurrent add of PCI cards, disk units, and removable media devices are supported.

#9094 PCI Card Enclosure

Slots	Multi-Adapter Bridge PCI Bus Number	Cards
C01	1,2	#9844 / #9943 [3]
C02	3,4	#9793
C03	5,6	IOP/IOA
C04	7,8	IOA
C05	1,2	IOP/IXS [1]
C06	3	IOA
C07	4	IOA
C08	5,6	IOP/IOA
C09	7,8	IOA
C10		HSL adapter
C11	1,2	IOP/IXS [2]
C12	3	IOA
C13	4	IOA
C14	5,6	IOP/IOA
C15	7,8	IOA

(Multi-Adapter Bridge Boundary after C04 and after C09)

Legend

Base Feature	Required Feature	Unavailable if Integrated xSeries Server is installed

Note 1: If C05 has an Integrated xSeries Server, slot C06 is unavailable, and slot C07 is available only as a short slot. A #2792 does not reduce a third slot to a short slot.

Note 2: If C11 has an Integrated xSeries Server, slot C12 is unavailable, and slot C13 is available only as a short slot. A #2792 does not reduce a third slot to a short slot.

Note 3: Slot C01 in the #9094 for a Model 870 has a #9844, and a #9844 or #9943 for a Model 890.

#8094 Optional 1.8 M I/O Rack

Note: The total number of disk bays is 2 x 45.

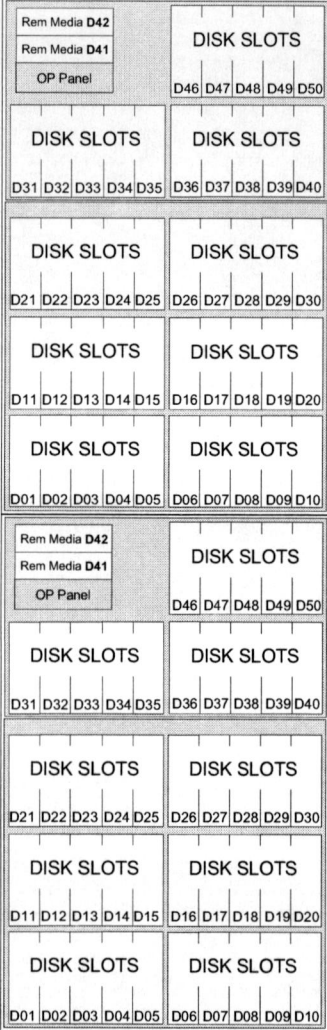

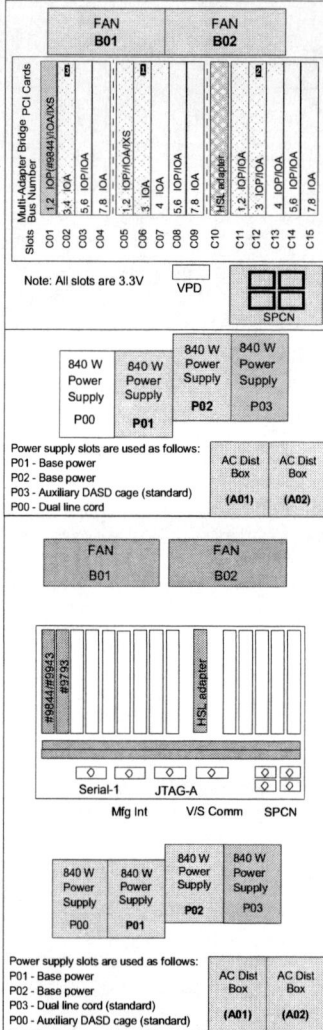

Left section (disk slots):

Rem Media D42	DISK SLOTS
Rem Media D41	
OP Panel	D46 D47 D48 D49 D50

| DISK SLOTS | DISK SLOTS |
| D31 D32 D33 D34 D35 | D36 D37 D38 D39 D40 |

| DISK SLOTS | DISK SLOTS |
| D21 D22 D23 D24 D25 | D26 D27 D28 D29 D30 |

| DISK SLOTS | DISK SLOTS |
| D11 D12 D13 D14 D15 | D16 D17 D18 D19 D20 |

| DISK SLOTS | DISK SLOTS |
| D01 D02 D03 D04 D05 | D06 D07 D08 D09 D10 |

Rem Media D42	DISK SLOTS
Rem Media D41	
OP Panel	D46 D47 D48 D49 D50

| DISK SLOTS | DISK SLOTS |
| D31 D32 D33 D34 D35 | D36 D37 D38 D39 D40 |

| DISK SLOTS | DISK SLOTS |
| D21 D22 D23 D24 D25 | D26 D27 D28 D29 D30 |

| DISK SLOTS | DISK SLOTS |
| D11 D12 D13 D14 D15 | D16 D17 D18 D19 D20 |

| DISK SLOTS | DISK SLOTS |
| D01 D02 D03 D04 D05 | D06 D07 D08 D09 D10 |

Middle section (first card enclosure):

FAN B01   FAN B02

Multi-Adapter Bridge PCI Cards / Bus Number

Slots: C01 C02 C03 C04 C05 C06 C07 C08 C09 C10 C11 C12 C13 C14 C15

1,2 IOP/#9844/IOA/XS
3,4 IOA
5,6 IOP/IOA
7,8 IOA
1,2 IOP/IOA/XS
3 IOA
4 IOA
5,6 IOP/IOA
7,8 IOA
HSL adapter
1,2 IOP/IOA
3 IOP/IOA
4 IOP/IOA
5,6 IOP/IOA
7,8 IOA

Note: All slots are 3.3V   VPD

SPCN

| 840 W Power Supply P00 | 840 W Power Supply **P01** | 840 W Power Supply **P02** | 840 W Power Supply P03 |

Power supply slots are used as follows:
P01 - Base power
P02 - Base power
P03 - Auxiliary DASD cage (standard)
P00 - Dual line cord

AC Dist Box **(A01)**   AC Dist Box **(A02)**

Middle section (second card enclosure):

FAN B01   FAN B02

#9844/#9943   #37793   HSL adapter

Serial-1   JTAG-A
Mfg Int   V/S Comm   SPCN

| 840 W Power Supply P00 | 840 W Power Supply **P01** | 840 W Power Supply **P02** | 840 W Power Supply P03 |

Power supply slots are used as follows:
P01 - Base power
P02 - Base power
P03 - Dual line cord (standard)
P00 - Auxiliary DASD cage (standard)

AC Dist Box **(A01)**   AC Dist Box **(A02)**

Legend

Base Feature

Required Feature

Unavailable if Integrated Netfinity Server is installed

Note 1: If C05 has an Integrated xSeries Server, slot C06 is unavailable, and slot C07 is available only as a short slot. A #2792 does not reduce a third slot to a short slot.

Note 2: If C11 has an Integrated xSeries Server, slot C12 is unavailable, and slot C13 is available only as a short slot. A #2792 does not reduce a third slot to a short slot.

Note 3: Integrated xSeries Server placement is not supported from the plant. Only a #2792 is allowed in this position.

See the #9094 PCI Card Enclosure for card placement details.

Note: For line cord and power receptacle specification information, go to:
`http://www.ibm.com/eserver/iseries/infocenter`

High-speed link on Model 870

The Model 870 supports up to eight HSL loops, six of which can be optical fiber HSL loops. The optical fiber HSL loop extends the distance between the Model 870 system unit and the I/O units from a limit of 15 meters prior to OS/400 V5R2, to a maximum of 250 meters. The extra length can help to improve data reliability and protection.

See "HSL fabric" on page 297 for information about supported high-speed link (HSL) cables and HSL loop maximums. You can find further information in *High-speed Link Loop Architecture for the IBM @server iSeries Server: OS/400 Version 5 Release 2*, REDP-3652, and in the HSL Rules presentation, which is available at:

`http://www-1.ibm.com/servers/eserver/iseries/ha/systemdesign.html`

Model 870 PCI cards and features

The Model 870 is a PCI-based technology system. Since migration towers cannot attach to the Model 870, System Products Division (SPD) cards in systems or towers migrating to the Model 870 must be replaced with PCI card equivalents. Refer to "Hardware no longer marketed by IBM" on page 755 for a list of SPD functions not supported by PCI adapters.

See the table on page 107 for the number of maximum features supported by the total system and in the Model 870 system unit. See Chapter 17, "iSeries PCI I/O processors" on page 323, and Chapter 18, "iSeries I/O adapters and controllers" on page 337, for full descriptions of the features that are supported. See "AIX and Linux Direct Attach features overview" on page 340 for supported Linux Direct Attach features.

Note: The placement of PCI cards follows special rules. Refer to "PCI card technology" on page 338 and *PCI Card Placement Rules for the IBM @server iSeries Server Version 5 Release 2*, REDP-3638, before you propose any configuration.

External towers

Migration towers are not supported on the Model 870. PCI towers are supported with upgrades for migration only.

Refer to Chapter 15, "Towers, racks, and high-speed link" on page 261, for information about supported towers for the Model 825, and "Summary of the iSeries expansion units and towers" on page 119 for a table of configuration maximums.

Model 870 upgrades

See Chapter 16, "Upgrades to eServer i5 and i5/OS" on page 311, for general upgrade considerations and server-to-server upgrade possibilities. Supported model upgrades for the Model 870 are identified in the *Upgrade* topic of the Find and Compare Tool (FACT) at:

http://www-919.ibm.com/servers/eserver/fact/

Model 870 Capacity on Demand

The iSeries Model 870 offers Capacity on Demand options that make it possible to activate additional processor resource. CUoD and On/Off Capacity on Demand are available for the Model 870. On Demand features are described in this section.

On Demand features may have base activations. The following options are available to activate additional resources:

► Capacity upgrade on Demand (Permanent)

Purchase processor activation features when needed. Requires purchase of operating system licenses.

► On/Off Capacity on Demand (Temporary)

Pay for processor day billing features at the end of each billing period. Additional i5/OS licenses not required.

Refer to the table on page 109 to see the feature codes associated with the Model 870 Capacity on Demand options. See the following Web site for more information about Capacity on Demand:

http://www-1.ibm.com/servers/eserver/iseries/ondemand/cod/

14

iSeries Model 890

The iSeries 890 is a 16-way and 32-way server based on IBM POWER4 technology. The Model 890 can support thousands of users and deliver top-end performance for Web, On Demand Business, and mainstay 5250 online transaction processing (OLTP) applications. With IBM @server Capacity Upgrade on Demand (CUoD) and multi-platform and application support, this server delivers maximum function and adaptability for business in an on demand world.

The 16-way and 32-way POWER4 processors range from 20000 to 37400 CPW, up to 256 GB of memory and up to 144 TB of disk.

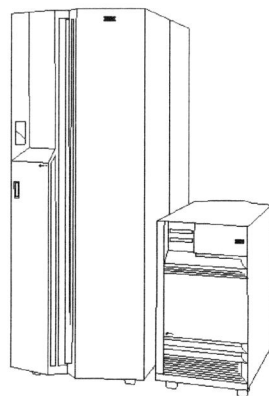

iSeries Model 890

Model overview

This section takes a closer look at the minimum functional server, required features, and optional features.

> **Note:** In the Required features and Optional features sections, note the following descriptions:
>
> * Supported for conversion/migration only
> **MES only

Minimum functional server

A minimum functional server consists of the base server unit and selected priced features. The Model 890 supports hot plug and concurrent add of PCI cards, disk units, and removable media devices. Included in the base server are the physical package and power elements as follows:

- ► System unit (CEC)

- ► #9094 Base PCI I/O Enclosure or #8094 Optional 1.8 M I/O Rack

- ► Line cord features

  Two line cord features should be specified for the 890 CEC, with two additional line cord features for the #9094. Three or four are needed for the #8094.

- ► Bulk Power Regulator (CCIN CQ02)

  - – Two required with 24-way processor feature
  - – Four required with 32-way processor feature

- ► Bulk Power Controller (CCIN RGA1)

  - – Two required with all processor features

- ► Bulk Power Distribution (CCIN RGA2)

  - – Two required with 24-way and 32-way processor features

- ► Distributed Converter Assembly (CCIN DCA1)

  - – Two DCAs are "base"
  - – Two DCAs added with 24-way processor feature (total of four DCAs)
  - – Three DCAs added with 32-way processor features (total of five DCAs)

- ► Capacitor Card (CCIN 274F): One is "base"

  - – One Capacitor Card is added with 24-way and 32-way processor features (total of two).

- ► CEC Backplane (CCIN 25C0)

- Clock card (CCIN 25C2)
- Pass-through card (CCIN 272D)
  - One is installed with the 24-way processor to fill empty multichip modules (MCM) slot.
- Peripheral Component Interconnect (PCI) and Common Service Processor (CSP) card (CCIN 28AA)
- Operator Panel (CCIN 247A)
- Four MCM sockets for up to four processor modules
- Eight main storage card sockets
- Four slots for base and feature high-speed link (HSL)-2 adapters
- #9730 Base HSL-2 Ports - 4 Copper (CCIN 273B)
- #9771/#9793/#9794 Base PCI Two-Line WAN with integrated modem
- #9844 Base PCI IOP provides support for:
  - The required SCSI IOA which controls up to 15 disk units, the required DVD-RAM/DVD-ROM, and a feature internal tape or a feature DVD-RAM/DVD-ROM
  - A base Console/Workstation IOA

    The IBM marketing configurator determines which feature combinations are placed on the order based on the #5540, #5544, #5546, or #5548 System Console specify code.
  - The #9771/#9793/#9794 Base PCI Two-Line WAN with integrated modem

> **Note:** In countries (or regions) where #9771/#9793/#9794 is not homologated, the marketing configurator adds a #4745 PCI 2-line WAN IOA or a #2742 Two-Line WAN IOA, a #0032 modem feature, and a #0348 cable to the order. The #4745/#2742 is mandatory and cannot be removed from the system until the #9793/#9794 homologation is completed. The #0032 and #0348 features may be removed from the order or system at any time.

Required features

The *required* features include:

► Specific combinations of the Processor feature, Edition feature, and Server feature are allowed as shown in the following table.

Processor feature	Server feature	Edition feature	Software group	Processor feature code or QPRCFEAT value
#2497 (20000/29300 CPW)	#0897	#7422 Standard	P50	7422
		#7424 Enterprise	P50	7424
		#7437 High Availability	P50	7424
#2498 (29300/37400 CPW)	#0898	#7425 Standard	P50	7425
		#7427 Enterprise	P50	7427
		#7438 High Availability	P50	7427
#2499 (5600/37400 CPW)	#0892	#7441 Capacity BackUp	P50	7441

> **Note:** The Standard Edition for the Model 890 processors provides limited 5250 CPW for 5250 OLTP workloads. The Enterprise, High Availability, and Capacity BackUp Editions for the Model 890 processors provide maximum 5250 CPW for 5250 OLTP workloads.
>
> The Enterprise and High Availability Editions also provide support for Capacity on Demand (permanent and temporary). The Capacity on Demand Edition provides support for temporary capacity only.

Edition content varies by processor and server features selected. For more information, see "Editions" on page 55.

► Main storage

See "Main storage" on page 247 for a list of supported memory features and configuration considerations.

► PCI disk controller (SCSI IOA)

The SCSI IOA supports the DVD-ROM, DVD-RAM, migrated CD-ROM, internal tape, and disk units in the base PCI enclosure.

- #2757 PCI-X Ultra RAID Disk Controller
- 2780 PCI-X Ultra4 RAID Disk Controller
- #4748 PCI RAID Disk Unit Controller*
- #4778 PCI RAID Disk Unit Controller*

- ▶ Removable optical device (one must be specified)
  - − #4425 CD-ROM*
  - − #4430 DVD-RAM*
  - − #4625 CD-ROM**
  - − #4630 DVD-RAM
  - − #4631 DVD-ROM
- ▶ Internal disk units
  - − #4317 8.58 GB 10k RPM Disk Unit*
  - − #4318 17.54 GB 10k RPM Disk Unit*
  - − #4319 35.16 GB 10k RPM Disk Unit
  - − #4326 35.16 GB 15k RPM Disk Unit
  - − #4327 70.56 GB 15k RPM Disk Unit

  One of the following load source specify codes is required:
  - − #0829 - #4318 Load Source Specify*
  - − #0830 - #4319 Load Source Specify
  - − #0834 - #4326 Load Source Specify
  - − #0835 - #4327 Load Source Specify
- ▶ Disk protection specify codes (one must be specified)
  - − #0040 Mirrored System Disk Level
  - − #0041 RAID Protection - All
  - − #0042 Mirrored System IOP Level
  - − #0043 Mirrored System Bus Level

  The #0041 is the default for disk data protection.
- ▶ System console/communications adapter

  The console on LAN options requires a dedicated LAN adapter. A #0367 Operations Console PCI Cable is added to the order by the marketing configurator.
  - − #5540 System Console on Twinaxial Workstation IOA
    - • #4746 PCI Twinaxial IOA
  - − #5544 System Console on Operations Console
    - • #0367 Operations Console PCI Cable
  - − #5546 System Console on 100 Mbps Token Ring
    - • #2744 PCI 100 Mbps Token Ring IOA
    - • #0367 Operations Console PCI Cable

– #5548 System Console on 100 Mbps Ethernet

- #2849 10/100 Mbps Ethernet Adapter
- #4838 PCI 100/10 Mbps Ethernet IOA
- #0367 Operations Console PCI Cable

Optional features

The *optional* features include the following internal tape devices:

- #4482 4 GB ¼-inch Cartridge Tape Device*
- #4483 16 GB ¼-inch Cartridge Tape Device
- #4486 25 GB ¼-inch Cartridge Tape Device
- #4487 50 GB ¼-inch Cartridge Tape Device*
- #4682 4 GB ¼-inch Cartridge Tape Device
- #4684 30 GB ¼-inch Cartridge Tape Device
- #4685 80 GB VXA-2 Tape Device
- #4686 25 GB ¼-inch Cartridge Tape Device
- #4687 50 GB ¼-inch Cartridge Tape Device

IBM Service Representatives perform the Model 890 initial installation and model upgrades.

Processor features

- The #2497 16/24-way POWER4 1.3 GHz processor includes:

  – Processor Capacity Card (CCIN 2487)
  – Processor 0 (CCIN 25D3)
  – Processor 1 (CCIN 25D3)
  – Processor 2 (CCIN 25D3)

  Specify one #1612 POD Activation feature for each additional standby processor activated (maximum of eight). Specify one #1777 TCoD Enablement feature for each additional standby processor when approaching the limit of usable on/off processor days.

- The #2498 24/32-way POWER4 1.3 GHz processor includes:

  – Processor Capacity Card (CCIN 2488)
  – Processor 0 (CCIN 25D3)
  – Processor 1 (CCIN 25D3)
  – Processor 2 (CCIN 25D3)
  – Processor 3 (CCIN 25D3)

  Specify one #1613 POD Activation feature for each additional standby processor activated (maximum of eight). Specify one #1778 TCoD

Enablement feature for each additional standby processor when approaching the limit of usable on/off processor days.

► The #2499 4/32-way POWER4 1.3 GHz processor includes:
  – Processor Capacity Card (CCIN 7441)
  – Processor 0 (CCIN 25D3)
  – Processor 1 (CCIN 25D3)
  – Processor 2 (CCIN 25D3)
  – Processor 4 (CCIN 25D3)

Specify one #1781 TCoD Enablement feature for each additional standby processor when approaching limit of usable on/off processor days.

Note: The Capacity on Demand (permanent and temporary) capabilities, including activation, enablement and billing features, are described in "Capacity on Demand" on page 44.

Refer to "Table 10: Summary of the iSeries Model 890" on page 110, to find Processor CPW, Mail and Calendar Users (MCU), 5250 CPW, and to determine the processor feature code and QPRCFEAT value.

Main storage

The available main storage features are:

► #3015 - 8 GB Main Storage Card (inside) (DRAM)
► #3016 - 8 GB Main Storage Card (outside) (DRAM)
► #3017 - 32 GB Main Storage Card (inside) (DRAM)
► #3018 - 32 GB Main Storage Card (outside) (DRAM)
► #3020 - 4 GB Main Storage Card (inside) (DRAM)
► #3021 - 4 GB Main Storage Card (outside) (DRAM)
► #3035 - 16 GB Main Storage Card (inside) (DRAM)
► #3036 - 16 GB Main Storage Card (outside) (DRAM)

Add all main storage cards on the Model 890 in pairs of the same capacity and technology. Six slots are available for main storage cards in the #2487, #2497 and #0197 processors. Eight slots are available for main storage cards in the #2488, #2498, #2499 and #0198 processors. The slots are arranged in groups of "inner" and "outer" slots. The 24-way has four inner slots and two outer slots. The 32-way has four inner and four outer slots. Inner slots are filled first.

Important: Fill all slots. An exception is allowed for 16 GB on a 24-way processor and for 24 GB on a 32-way processor.

The main storage cards are installed according to the following rules:

▶ Main storage cards are installed in pairs of equal capacity.

▶ The pairs of main storage cards must plug into slots under the same MCM (slots 0 and 1, slots 2 and 3, slots 4 and 5, slots 6 and 7).

▶ Mixed memory pairs must be adjacent capacities (4 GB with 8 GB is allowed; 4 GB with 16 GB is not allowed).

▶ There is a maximum of two card sizes on each Model 890.

The following table shows the allowable main storage capacities in MB for the Model 890 processors.

Processor Memory increment	#2497	#2498/#2499
8 GB	Y *	Y *
16 GB	Y	Y *
24 GB	Y	Y
32 GB	Y	Y
40 GB	Y	Y
48 GB	Y	Y
56 GB	-	Y
64 GB	Y	Y
80 GB	Y	Y
98 GB	Y	Y
112 GB	-	Y
160 GB	Y	Y
192 GB	Y	Y
224 GB	-	Y
256 GB	-	Y
* Not recommended for most configurations.		

#9094 Base PCI I/O Enclosure

The #9094 Base PCI I/O Enclosure is the base PCI-X I/O enclosure shipped with the Model 870 and 890 system units. A #9094 is attached to the system unit via an high-speed link (HSL) cable through a #9887 Base HSL-2 Bus Adapter. One JTAG cable and one V/S Communication cable (VPD and SPCN combined) are included for the attachment of the #9094 to the system unit. The #5114 Dual Line Cords - Tower is a required feature. Specify two line cords for the #9094.

The #9094 has 15 disk unit slots, with an additional 30 slots available when using feature #5107 30 Disk Expansion. The 45 disk unit positions are in three groups of 15. Each group of 15 disk units is further divided into three groups of five disk units with each group of five disk units supported on a separate SCSI bus.

The #9094 also has two removable media slots and 14 PCI-X card slots. A #9844 Base PCI IOP is included in the base. A #2757 PCI-X Ultra RAID Disk Controller or #4748/#4778 PCI RAID Disk Unit Controller is required to drive the disk units in the base 15 disk unit slots and the removable media devices in the two removal media slots.

The #9094 Base PCI I/O Enclosure supports up to nine OS/400 or Linux controlled #2757/#4748/#4778/#5703 disk controllers (up to nine in total). The #5703 PCI-X RAID Disk Unit Controller can be used after three #2757/#4748/#4778 controllers are installed. The #0143 Disk Controller Placement Exception is a prerequisite for this configuration when the #5703 is the only disk unit controller ordered.

A maximum of three #2757 PCI-X Ultra RAID Disk Controllers or #4748/#4778 PCI RAID Disk Unit Controllers are allowed per #9094. Up to 15 disk units per #2757 are supported in a #9094.

The 11 PCI IOAs are supported by the #9844 Base PCI IOP, by feature #2844 PCI IOPs, and by the #2791, #2792/#9792, #4710/#9710, or #2799 PCI Integrated xSeries Server.

Two cables must be ordered to attach to the HSL or HSL-2 ports. When ordering cables to connect to the HSL interface, optical HSL, copper HSL, copper HSL-2, or copper HSL to HSL-2 cables are required. An HSL loop uses all optical or all copper ports and cables. A copper loop can intermix I/O towers or units with copper HSL and copper HSL-2 ports. Select the appropriate cable based on the type of HSL ports to which it is being attached, and the cable length required.

One SPCN cable is required for each tower.

#5107 30 Disk Expansion

The #5107 is a disk unit expansion enclosure feature for the #9094 Base PCI I/O Enclosure. The #5107 includes two 15 disk unit enclosures, one 840-watt power supply, backplanes, and cables.

A #2757 PCI-X Ultra RAID Disk Controller or #4748/#4778 PCI RAID Disk Unit Controller or #5703 PCI-X RAID Disk Unit Controller is required to support the disk units in each of the two disk unit enclosures included with #5107. Each group of 15 disk units is further divided into three groups of five disk units with each group of five disk units supported on a separate SCSI bus. A minimum of two disk unit controllers and a maximum of six are required to support 30 disk units.

#8094 Optional 1.8 M I/O Rack

The #8094 is a optional base I/O rack shipped on the Model 890 instead of the #9094 Base PCI I/O Enclosure. The #8094 supports up to 90 disk units, up to 22 PCI IOAs, and up to three additional removable media units. A #8094 is a 1.8 M rack with two enclosures.

► The bottom enclosure is a #9094 Base PCI I/O Enclosure with side covers and casters removed and a #5107 30 Disk Expansion included in the base (no feature code required). The #5114 Dual Line Cords - Tower is a mandatory feature for the #9094.

► The top enclosure is a #5094 PCI-X Expansion Tower with side covers and casters removed and a #5108 30-Disk Expansion Feature (no feature code required) included in the base. (#5115 Dual Line Cords - Tower feature code is required for dual line cords in the top enclosure).

► The #0694 #5094 Equivalent is a prerequisite.

Included with the bottom enclosure is one JTAG cable and one VPD-S cable required to attach the bottom enclosure to the system unit. Also included are the #9887 Base HSL-2 Bus Adapter and #9844 Base PCI IOP.

Each enclosure supports 45 disk unit positions, for a total of 90. The 90 disk unit positions are in groups of 15, each supported by a minimum of one separate disk controller.

The #8094 also supports up to four removable media devices (internal tape, CD-ROM, DVD). These removable media devices are supported by the two #2757 PCI-X Ultra RAID Disk Controllers, #4748/#4778 PCI RAID Disk Unit Controllers, or #9778 Base PCI Raid Disk Unit Controllers that can support the first group of disk units in each enclosure.

The two enclosures in the #8094 are separately attached to the system unit via HSL cables as though they were a stand-alone #9094 and #5094. They are also treated as separate units for HSL loop plugging and configuration rules and recommendations. As such, the bottom enclosure must be attached to the system unit's first HSL loop.

A bus adapter is included to provide the HSL interface to the top enclosure. Select one of the following options:

► #9886 Base Optical Bus Adapter, to specify four optical HSL ports
► #9887 Base HSL-2 Bus Adapter, to specify four copper HSL-2 ports

Three or four cables must be ordered to attach to the HSL or HSL-2 ports.

When ordering cables to connect to the HSL interface, optical HSL, copper HSL, copper HSL-2, or copper HSL to HSL-2 cables are required. An HSL loop uses all optical or all copper ports/cables. A copper loop can intermix I/O towers or units with copper HSL and copper HSL-2 ports. Select the appropriate cable based on the type of HSL ports to which it is being attached, and the cable length required.

Specify three or four line cords for the #8094 Optional 1.8 M I/O Rack.

If the top enclosure is to be attached to a different system than what was initially ordered, remove for Record Purpose Only (RPO) the #0694 #5094 Equivalent specify code from the initially ordered system and add it to the target system.

#8094 Optional 1.8 M I/O Rack schematic

The following figure shows a schematic of the #8094 Optional 1.8 M I/O Rack.

Note: The total number of disk bays is 2 x 45.

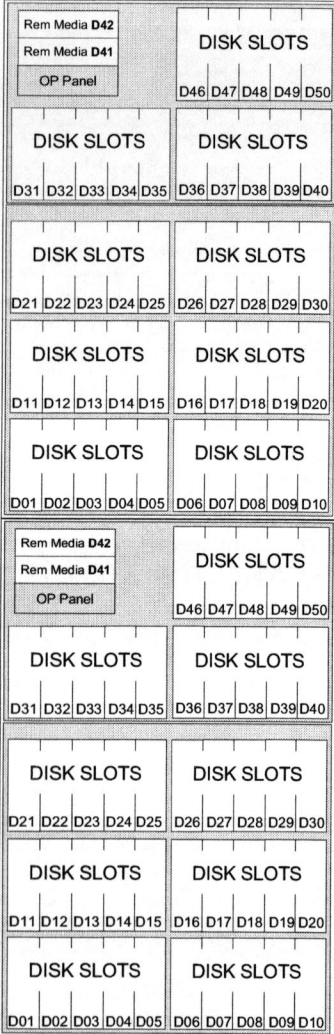

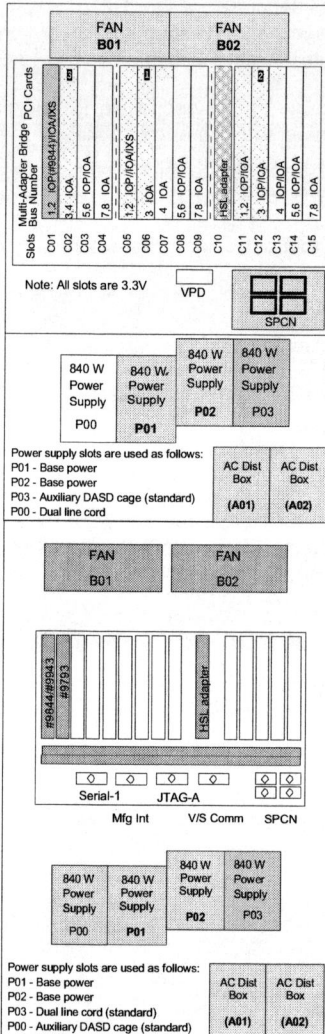

Disk slot layout (top enclosure):

- Rem Media **D42**
- Rem Media **D41**
- OP Panel
- DISK SLOTS D46 D47 D48 D49 D50
- DISK SLOTS D31 D32 D33 D34 D35
- DISK SLOTS D36 D37 D38 D39 D40
- DISK SLOTS D21 D22 D23 D24 D25
- DISK SLOTS D26 D27 D28 D29 D30
- DISK SLOTS D11 D12 D13 D14 D15
- DISK SLOTS D16 D17 D18 D19 D20
- DISK SLOTS D01 D02 D03 D04 D05
- DISK SLOTS D06 D07 D08 D09 D10

Disk slot layout (bottom enclosure):

- Rem Media **D42**
- Rem Media **D41**
- OP Panel
- DISK SLOTS D46 D47 D48 D49 D50
- DISK SLOTS D31 D32 D33 D34 D35
- DISK SLOTS D36 D37 D38 D39 D40
- DISK SLOTS D21 D22 D23 D24 D25
- DISK SLOTS D26 D27 D28 D29 D30
- DISK SLOTS D11 D12 D13 D14 D15
- DISK SLOTS D16 D17 D18 D19 D20
- DISK SLOTS D01 D02 D03 D04 D05
- DISK SLOTS D06 D07 D08 D09 D10

Center enclosure (top):

FAN **B01**   FAN **B02**

Multi-Adapter Bridge PCI Cards Bus Number

Slots	Card description
C01	1,2 IOP/(#9844)/IOA/XS
C02	3,4 IOA
C03	5,6 IOP/IOA
C04	7,8 IOA
C05	1,2 IOP/IOA4/XS
C06	3 IOA
C07	4 IOA
C08	5,6 IOP/IOA
C09	7,8 IOA
C10	HSL adapter
C11	1,2 IOP/IOA
C12	3 IOA
C13	4 IOP/IOA
C14	5,6 IOP/IOA
C15	7,8 IOA

Note: All slots are 3.3V   VPD   SPCN

Power supplies:
840 W Power Supply P00 | 840 W Power Supply P01 | 840 W Power Supply P02 | 840 W Power Supply P03

Power supply slots are used as follows:
P01 - Base power
P02 - Base power
P03 - Auxiliary DASD cage (standard)
P00 - Dual line cord

AC Dist Box **(A01)**   AC Dist Box **(A02)**

Center enclosure (bottom):

FAN **B01**   FAN **B02**

#9844/#9843   #9793   HSL adapter

Serial-1   JTAG-A
Mfg Int   V/S Comm   SPCN

Power supplies:
840 W Power Supply P00 | 840 W Power Supply P01 | 840 W Power Supply P02 | 840 W Power Supply P03

Power supply slots are used as follows:
P01 - Base power
P02 - Base power
P03 - Dual line cord (standard)
P00 - Auxiliary DASD cage (standard)

AC Dist Box **(A01)**   AC Dist Box **(A02)**

Legend

Base Feature

Required Feature

Unavailable if Integrated Netfinity Server is installed

Note 1: If C05 has an Integrated xSeries Server, slot C06 is unavailable, and slot C07 is available only as a short slot. A #2792 does not reduce a third slot to a short slot.

Note 2: If C11 has an Integrated xSeries Server, slot C12 is unavailable, and slot C13 is available only as a short slot. A #2792 does not reduce a third slot to a short slot.

Note 3: Integrated xSeries Server placement is not supported from the plant. Only a #2792 is allowed in this position.

See the #9094 PCI Card Enclosure for card placement details.

#5114 Dual Line Cords - Tower

The #5114 required feature provides dual line cord support for the #9094 Base PCI I/O Enclosure on the Model 870 and 890 and for the lower enclosures of the #8093 and #8094 towers. With the #5114, the enclosure requires two #14xx line cords and has two AC input boxes.

9406 Model 890 schematics

The following diagrams show the slot and feature card arrangement of the Model 890 system unit, base enclosure, and rack. You can find schematics of any supported expansion units in Chapter 15, "Towers, racks, and high-speed link" on page 261.

9406 Model 890 system unit

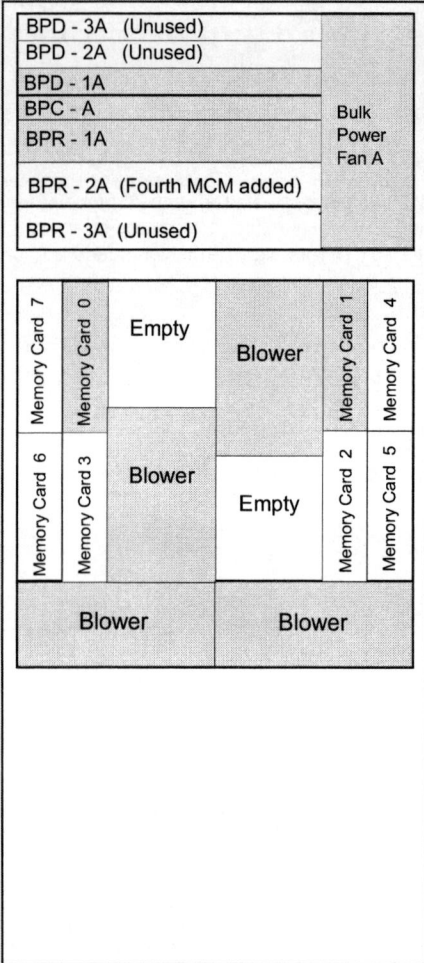

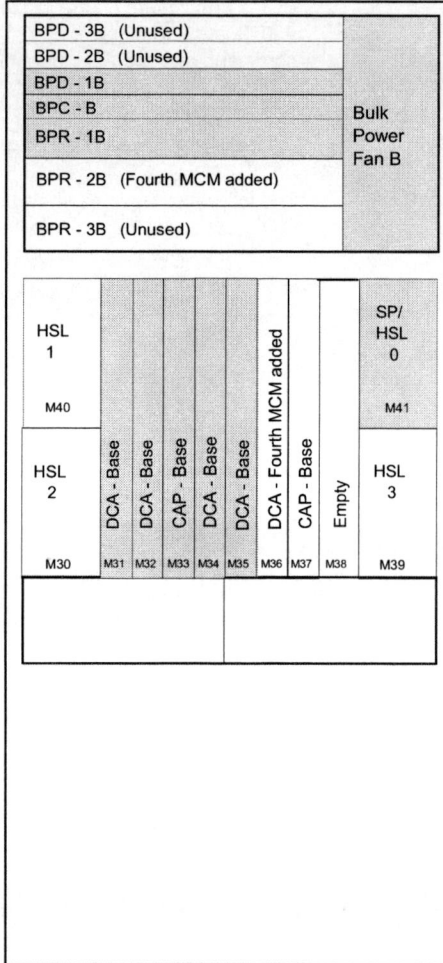

Front

Back

Model 890 CEC Backplane

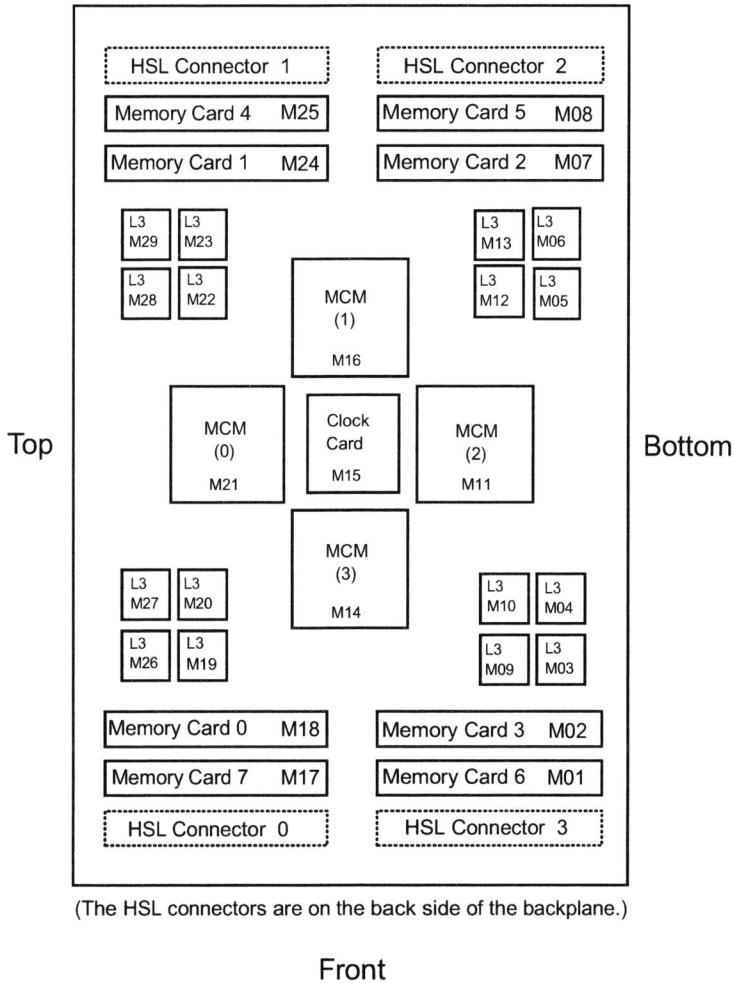

HSL Connector 1	HSL Connector 2
Memory Card 4 M25	Memory Card 5 M08
Memory Card 1 M24	Memory Card 2 M07

| L3 M29 | L3 M23 | | L3 M13 | L3 M06 |
| L3 M28 | L3 M22 | MCM (1) M16 | L3 M12 | L3 M05 |

Top

MCM (0) M21   Clock Card M15   MCM (2) M11

Bottom

MCM (3) M14

| L3 M27 | L3 M20 | | L3 M10 | L3 M04 |
| L3 M26 | L3 M19 | | L3 M09 | L3 M03 |

Memory Card 0 M18	Memory Card 3 M02
Memory Card 7 M17	Memory Card 6 M01
HSL Connector 0	HSL Connector 3

(The HSL connectors are on the back side of the backplane.)

Front

Note: One pass-through card (CCIN 272D) is installed with the 24-way processor to fill empty MCM slot 1.

#9094 Base PCI I/O Enclosure

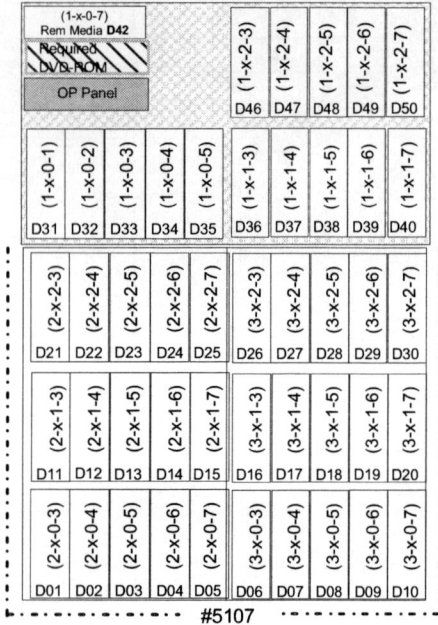

Front

Dual Line Cord

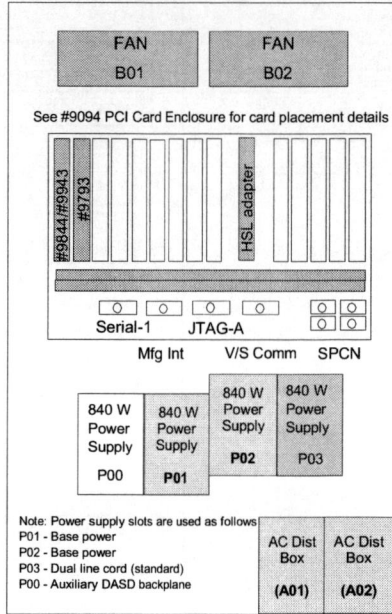

PCI

Back

LEGEND

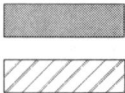

= Base feature

= Required feature

(W-X-Y-Z)	
	Kn

W = DS Card Address
X = IOA number
Y = SCSI bus number
Z = AS/400 Drive Address
Kn = Physical Address

Note: Hot plug and concurrent add of PCI cards, disk units, and removable media devices are supported.

#9094 PCI Card Enclosure

Slots	Multi-Adapter Bridge Bus Number	PCI Cards
C01	1,2	#9844 / #9943 **[3]**
C02	3,4	#9793
C03	5,6	IOP/IOA
C04	7,8	IOA
		Multi-Adapter Bridge Boundary
C05	1,2	IOP/IXS **[1]**
C06	3	IOA
C07	4	IOA
C08	5,6	IOP/IOA
C09	7,8	IOA
		Multi-Adapter Bridge Boundary
C10		HSL adapter
C11	1,2	IOP/IXS **[2]**
C12	3	IOA
C13	4	IOA
C14	5,6	IOP/IOA
C15	7,8	IOA

Legend

Base Feature   Required Feature   Unavailable if Integrated xSeries Server is installed

Note 1: If C05 has an Integrated xSeries Server, slot C06 is unavailable, and slot C07 is available only as a short slot. A #2792 does not reduce a third slot to a short slot.

Note 2: If C11 has an Integrated xSeries Server, slot C12 is unavailable, and slot C13 is available only as a short slot. A #2792 does not reduce a third slot to a short slot.

Note 3: Slot C01 in the #9094 for a Model 870 has a #9844, and a #9844 or #9943 for a Model 890.

#8094 Optional 1.8 M I/O Rack

Note: The total number of disk bays is 2 x 45.

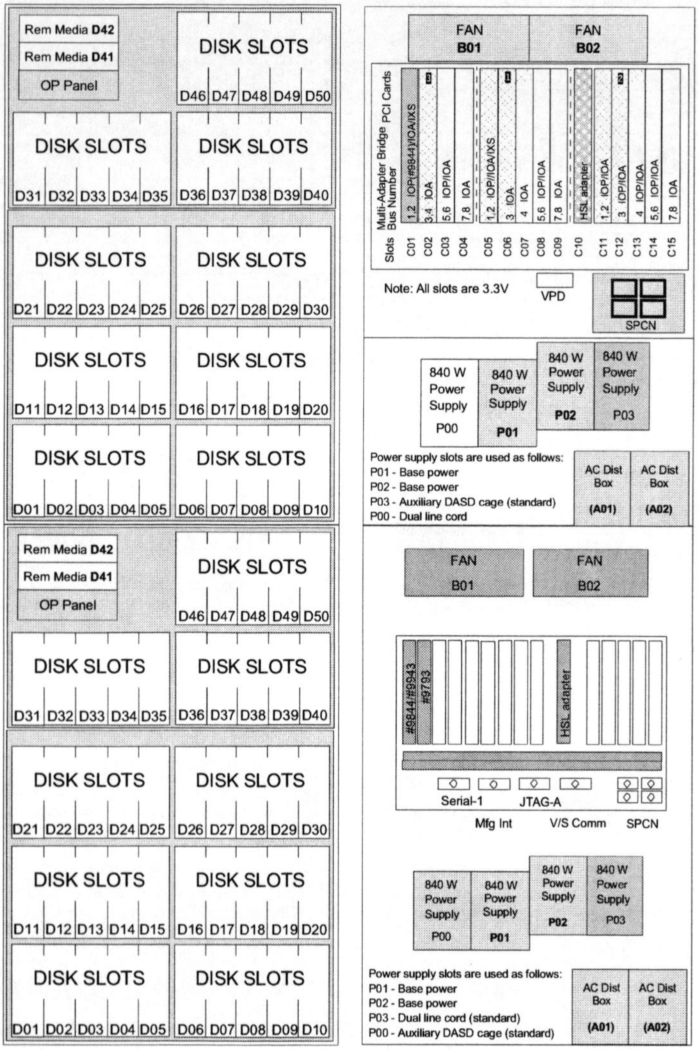

Rem Media D42
Rem Media D41
OP Panel
DISK SLOTS
D46 D47 D48 D49 D50
D31 D32 D33 D34 D35
D36 D37 D38 D39 D40
D21 D22 D23 D24 D25
D26 D27 D28 D29 D30
D11 D12 D13 D14 D15
D16 D17 D18 D19 D20
D01 D02 D03 D04 D05
D06 D07 D08 D09 D10
FAN B01
FAN B02
Multi-Adapter Bridge Bus Number
PCI Cards
Slots
1,2 IOP(#9844)/IOA/IXS
3,4 IOA
5,6 IOP/IOA
7,8 IOA
1,2 IOP/IOA/IXS
3 IOA
4 IOA
5,6 IOP/IOA
7,8 IOA
HSL adapter
1,2 IOP/IOA
3 IOP/IOA
4 IOP/IOA
5,6 IOP/IOA
7,8 IOA
C01 C02 C03 C04 C05 C06 C07 C08 C09 C10 C11 C12 C13 C14 C15
Note: All slots are 3.3V
VPD
SPCN
840 W Power Supply P00
840 W Power Supply P01
840 W Power Supply P02
840 W Power Supply P03
Power supply slots are used as follows:
P01 - Base power
P02 - Base power
P03 - Auxiliary DASD cage (standard)
P00 - Dual line cord
AC Dist Box (A01)
AC Dist Box (A02)
#9844/#9943
#9793
HSL adapter
Serial-1
JTAG-A
Mfg Int
V/S Comm
SPCN
Power supply slots are used as follows:
P01 - Base power
P02 - Base power
P03 - Dual line cord (standard)
P00 - Auxiliary DASD cage (standard)

Legend

Base Feature

Required Feature

Unavailable if Integrated Netfinity Server is installed

Note 1: If C05 has an Integrated xSeries Server, slot C06 is unavailable, and slot C07 is available only as a short slot. A #2792 does not reduce a third slot to a short slot.

Note 2: If C11 has an Integrated xSeries Server, slot C12 is unavailable, and slot C13 is available only as a short slot. A #2792 does not reduce a third slot to a short slot.

Note 3: Integrated xSeries Server placement is not supported from the plant. Only a #2792 is allowed in this position.

See the #9094 PCI Card Enclosure for card placement details.

High-speed link on Model 890

The Model 890 (24- and 32-way models) supports up to 14 HSL loops, 12 of which can be optical fiber HSL loops. The 16- and 24-way models support up to 12 HSL loops, 10 of which can be optical fiber HSL loops. The optical fiber HSL loop extends the distance between the Model 890 system unit and the I/O units from a limit of 15 meters prior to OS/400 V5R2, to a maximum of 250 meters. The extra length can help to improve data reliability and protection.

See "HSL fabric" on page 297 for information about supported high-speed link (HSL) cables and HSL loop maximums. Find more information in *High-speed Link Loop Architecture for the IBM @server iSeries Server: OS/400 Version 5 Release 2*, REDP-3652, and in the HSL Rules presentation, which is available on the Web at:

http://www-1.ibm.com/servers/eserver/iseries/ha/systemdesign.html

Model 890 PCI cards and features

The Model 890 is a PCI-based technology system. Since migration towers cannot attach to the Model 890, System Products Division (SPD) cards in systems or towers migrating to the Model 890 must be replaced with PCI card equivalents. Refer to "Hardware no longer marketed by IBM" on page 755 for a list of SPD functions not supported by PCI adapters.

See the summary table on page 110 for the number of maximum features supported by the total system and in the Model 890 system unit. See Chapter 17, "iSeries PCI I/O processors" on page 323, and Chapter 18, "iSeries I/O adapters and controllers" on page 337, for full descriptions. See "AIX and Linux Direct Attach features overview" on page 340 for supported Linux Direct Attach features.

Note: The placement of PCI cards follows special rules. Refer to "PCI card technology" on page 338 and *PCI Card Placement Rules for the IBM @server iSeries Server Version 5 Release 2*, REDP-3638, before you propose any configuration.

External towers

Migration towers are not supported on the Model 890. PCI towers are supported with upgrades for migration only.

Refer to Chapter 15, "Towers, racks, and high-speed link" on page 261, for information about supported towers for the Model 890, and "Summary of the iSeries expansion units and towers" on page 119 for a table of configuration maximums.

Model 890 upgrades

See Chapter 16, "Upgrades to eServer i5 and i5/OS" on page 311, for general upgrade considerations and server-to-server upgrade possibilities. Supported model upgrades for the Model 890 are identified in the *Upgrade* topic of the Find and Compare Tool (FACT) at:

http://www-919.ibm.com/servers/eserver/fact/

Model 890 Capacity on Demand

The iSeries Model 890 offers Capacity on Demand options that make it possible to activate additional processor resource. CUoD and On/Off Capacity on Demand are available for the Model 890. On Demand features are described in this section.

On Demand features may have base activations. The following options are available to activate additional resources:

► Capacity upgrade on Demand (Permanent)

Purchase processor activation features when needed. Requires purchase of operating system licenses.

► On/Off Capacity on Demand (Temporary)

Pay for processor day billing features at the end of each billing period. Additional i5/OS licenses not required.

Refer to the Capacity on Demand table on page 113 to see the feature codes associated with the Model 890 Capacity on Demand options. See the following Web site for more information about Capacity on Demand:

http://www-1.ibm.com/servers/eserver/iseries/ondemand/cod/

15

Towers, racks, and high-speed link

To house components beyond the capability of the system unit, towers are added. Expansion towers are offered for new or migrated PCI features. Rack mounting options are available for select systems and towers. Towers and rack-mounted devices are connected to each other using high-speed links (HSL), either HSL or HSL-2/RIO-2.

For information about the software required to support towers and input/output (I/O) on iSeries servers, refer to Informational APAR II13440 on the Web at:

`http://www-912.ibm.com/n_dir/nas4apar.nsf/nas4aparhome`

To learn about planning for iSeries racks, including PDU specifications, the number of PCI cards supported, and the number of EIA units, refer to the iSeries racking presentation at:

`http://www-1.ibm.com/servers/eserver/support/iseries/planning/pdf/iseriesracking.pdf`

Migration towers

Migration towers (#5033, #5034, #5035, and #5077) are the result of an upgrade from an AS/400e Model 600, 620, 640, 650, 720, 730, 740, or Sxx to an iSeries Model 820, 830, or 840, as follows:

- ► #5033 Migration Tower I (600/S10 System Unit)
- ► #5034 Migration Tower I (10 disk S20/620, 720 system)
- ► #5035 Migration Tower I (15 disk S20/620, 720 system)
- ► #5077 Migration Tower II

SPD expansion towers attach to iSeries 820, 830, and 840 models via the #5034 or #5035, and #5077 Migration Towers. The I/O and disk units in the former system unit and any attached towers remain accessible to the upgraded system through the connection of the migration tower to the HSL loop.

For configuration rules for tower and migration, see *IBM @server iSeries Migration: System Migration and Upgrades at V5R1 and V5R2*, SG24-6055, and *IBM @server iSeries Migration: A Guide to Upgrades and Migrations to POWER Technology*, SG24-7200. Refer to the *IBM @server i5, iSeries, and AS/400e System Builder*, SG24-2155, for detailed information about each migration tower.

> **Note:** The @server i5 520, 550, 570, and 595, and iSeries 800, 810, 825, 870, and 890 models do not support migration towers or SPD hardware. Migration towers are *withdrawn from IBM marketing*.

Migration tower IOAs

The following PCI and SPD IOAs are supported in migration towers.

> **Note:** Some or all of the IOAs listed are *withdrawn from marketing*. This list is included for reference purposes to assist in planning system upgrades.

- ► #2699/#9699 Base Two-Line WAN IOA
- ► #2718 PCI Magnetic Media Controller
- ► #2720/#9720 Base PCI WAN/Twinaxial IOA
- ► #2721/##9721 Base PCI Two-Line WAN IOA
- ► #2722 Twinaxial Workstation IOA
- ► #2723/#9723 PCI Ethernet IOA (10 Mbps)
- ► #2724/#9724 PCI Token Ring IOA
- ► #2726 PCI RAID Disk Unit Controller Ultra SCSI
- ► #2729 PCI Magnetic Media Controller
- ► #2740 PCI RAID Disk Unit Controller
- ► #2741 PCI RAID Disk Unit Controller

- ▶ #2745/#9745 PCI Two-Line WAN IOA
- ▶ #2746 PCI Twinaxial Workstation IOA
- ▶ #2748 PCI RAID Disk Unit Controller
- ▶ #2750 PCI ISDN BRI U Adapter
- ▶ #2751 PCI ISDN BRI S/T IOA
- ▶ #2761 Integrated Analog Modem
- ▶ #2838/#9738 PCI 100/10 Mbps Ethernet IOA
- ▶ #6149 16/4 Mbps Token Ring IOA
- ▶ #6180/#9280 Twinaxial Workstation IOA
- ▶ #6181/#9381 Base Ethernet IEEE 802.3 IOA
- ▶ #6501 Tape/Disk Device Controller (SPD)
- ▶ #6513 Internal Tape Device Controller (SPD)
- ▶ #6533 RAID Disk Unit Controller Ultra SCSI (SPD)
- ▶ #6534 Magnetic Media Controller (SCSI SPD)
- ▶ CCIN 671A MFIOP with RAID
- ▶ #9728 Base Disk Unit Controller

For a more complete list of withdrawn features, see "Products and features no longer marketed by IBM" on page 755.

See the iSeries Planning site for a discussion about replacement features and for SPD to PCI migration considerations:

http://www.ibm.com/servers/eserver/support/iseries/planning

Refer to the *IBM @server iSeries and AS/400e System Builder*, SG24-2155, for feature descriptions.

Migration tower IOPs

The following PCI and SPD IOPs are supported in migration towers.

> **Note:** Some or all of the IOPs listed are *withdrawn from marketing*. This list is included for reference purposes to assist in planning system upgrades.

- ▶ #2629 LAN/WAN/Workstation IOP
- ▶ #2809 PCI LAN/WAN/Workstation IOP
- ▶ #2810 LAN/WAN IOP
- ▶ #2824 PCI Feature Controller
- ▶ #2838 PCI 100/10 Mbps Ethernet IOA
- ▶ #2865 PCI Integrated Netfinity Server
- ▶ #6618 Integrated Netfinity Server

For a more complete list of withdrawn features, see "Products and features no longer marketed by IBM" on page 755.

See the iSeries Planning site for a discussion about replacement features and for SPD to PCI migration considerations.

http://www.ibm.com/servers/eserver/support/iseries/planning

Refer to the *IBM @server iSeries and AS/400e System Builder*, SG24-2155, for feature descriptions.

PCI and PCI-X expansion towers

Expansion towers provide iSeries servers with the ability to support additional I/O and disk units. For information about the number and types of towers supported by each iSeries server, see Chapter 5, "Summary of today's iSeries" on page 79.

#5074 PCI Expansion Tower

The #5074 is attached to Models 520, 550, 570, 595 810, 820, 825, 830, 840, 870, and 890 for adding up to 45 disk units, up to 11 Peripheral Component Interconnect (PCI) input/output adapters (IOAs), and up to two removable media units. The #5074 includes the #9691 Base Bus Adapter or the #9739 Base Optical Bus Adapter to provide the HSL interface to the system. The IBM marketing configurator adds one #9691 Base Bus Adapter (copper) bus adapter interface or #9739 Base Optical Bus Adapter (optical) to the order. The #5074 contains two buses.

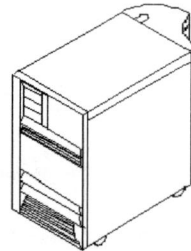

#5074 PCI Expansion Tower

Select any two HSL cable features for the first or only tower of an HSL loop. For additional towers on the HSL loop, select one HSL cable per tower. A list of the supported HSL cables is shown in the table on page 304. A list of the supported SPCN cables is shown in the table on page 301.

The #5074 has a #9943 Base PCI IOP. It also has PCI slots for up to 11 PCI IOAs, space for up to 45 disk units (15 are "base", 30 additional with #5101), space for two removable media devices (internal tape, CD-ROM, or DVD-RAM), one battery backup, and redundant or hot swap power supplies.

The 11 PCI IOAs are supported (driven) by a #2843 PCI IOP, #2844 PCI IOP, #9943 Base PCI IOP, #2790 PCI Integrated Netfinity Server, or the #2791/#2792/#2799 or #4710 PCI Integrated xSeries Server.

The #5074 can contain Ultra2 SCSI disk units that are controlled by a #2757/#4748/#4778 PCI RAID Disk Unit Controller. The removable media

devices are supported by the same #2757/#4748/#4778 which supports the first set of 15 disk units. A maximum of three #2757/#4748/#4778 PCI RAID Disk Unit Controllers (any combination) are supported.

The #5074 PCI Expansion Tower supports four 32-bit and seven 32/64-bit PCI slots.

The mounting for the first 15 disk units is included in the #5074 PCI Expansion Tower (base). The mounting for the next 30 disk units is optional by ordering a #5101 30 Disk Unit Expansion.

The #5074 also supports up to two removable media devices (internal tape, CD-ROM, or DVD-RAM). On new orders, select one line cord with each #5074 PCI Expansion Tower.

#5105 Dual Line Cords - I/O Tower

The #5105 Dual Line Cords - I/O Tower provides dual line cord capability for a #5074 and the top units in an #8079 or #8093. Two #14XX line cords must be ordered for each tower with a #5105, or top unit when ordered as an initial order. No batteries are shipped, and two 840W power supplies are shipped with this configuration. When ordering a #5105 as a simple Miscellaneous Equipment Specification (MES) against an existing #5074 or #8079/#8093 top unit, one additional #14XX line cord is required to be ordered (for a total of two line cords). Existing batteries are removed, and the 765W power supplies are removed and replaced with two 840W power supplies.

The #5074s mounted in an #0551 rack (withdrawn from marketing in first half 2002) support the #5101 30 Disk Unit Expansion feature. If the #5074 has a #5101 30 Disk Unit Expansion installed, the #5101 must be converted to a #5111 (no parts required).

OS/400 V5R1 or later and supporting PTFs are required. Refer to Informational APAR II12950 at:

http://as400service.rochester.ibm.com/supporthome.nsf/document/10000035

IBM marketing configurator users can refer to this Web site for ordering information:

http://w3.ibm.com/sales/systems/portal/_s.155/253

#5101 30 Disk Unit Expansion

The #5101 is a disk unit expansion enclosure feature for the #5074 PCI Expansion Tower, the #9074 Base I/O Tower, and the #9079 Base I/O Tower. The #5101 includes two 15 disk unit enclosures, one 765-watt power supply, backplanes, and cables. One #2757/#4748/#4778 PCI RAID Disk Unit Controller is required to support the 15 disk units in each of the two disk unit enclosures included with #5101. Two #2757/#4748/#4778 PCI RAID Disk Unit Controllers are required to support 30 disk units.

#5111 30 Disk Expansion with Dual Line Cord

The #5111 is a disk unit expansion enclosure for systems and towers that are dual line cord enabled. It includes two 15 disk unit enclosures, backplanes, and cables. Two #2757/#4748/#4778 PCI RAID Disk Unit Controllers are required to support 30 disk units.

The prerequisites are:

► #5103 when ordered for a Model 830 system unit (#9074 Base I/O Tower)
► #5104 when ordered for a Model 840 system unit (#9079 Base I/O Tower)
► #5105 when ordered for a stand-alone #5074 or the top unit in a #8079

OS/400 V5R1 or later and supporting PTFs are required. Refer to Informational APAR II12950 at:

http://as400service.rochester.ibm.com/supporthome.nsf/document/10000035

#5074 PCI Expansion Tower schematic

Note: The total number of disk bays is 45.

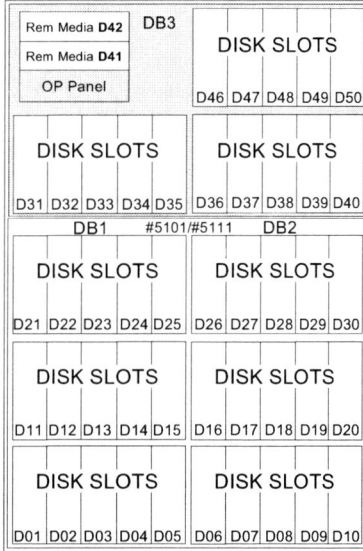

Front

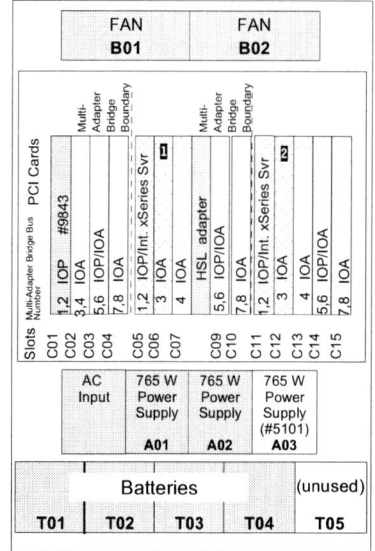

Back

Legend

Base Feature	Required Feature	Unavailable if Integrated xSeries Server is installed

Note 1: If C05 has an Integrated xSeries Server, slot C06 is unavailable, and slot C07 is available only as a short slot.

Note 2: If C11 has an Integrated xSeries Server, slot C12 is unavailable, and slot C13 is available only as a short slot.

#5075 PCI Expansion Tower

The #5075 PCI Expansion Tower is attached to Models 270, 810, 820, and 825 for adding up to six disk units and up to seven PCI IOAs. The #5075 has a 32 MB PCI IOP (CCIN 284B) embedded on the backplane. The #2842 PCI IOP (when attached to a Model 270), the #2843 PCI IOP (when attached to a Model 820) PCI IOP or the #2844 PCI IOP may be added. A #4748/#4778 PCI RAID Disk Unit Controller, #2757 PCI-X Ultra RAID Disk Controller, a #2763 PCI RAID Disk Unit Controller, #2782 PCI-X RAID Disk Unit Controller, or a #9767 Base PCI Disk Unit Controller may be installed in PCI slot C01 to control the disk units. The #9767 supports up to four disk units when installed in the #5075. The #5075 contains two buses.

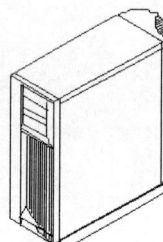

#5075 PCI Expansion Tower

The #5075 PCI Expansion Tower contains a 32 MB PCI IOP (CCIN 284B) embedded on its backplane.

Select any two of the supported HSL cables. A list of the supported HSL cables is shown in the table on page 304.

Select one of the following SPCN cables per Model 270 or 820:

► #1463 - 2m SPCN Cable
► #1464 - 6m SPCN Cable
► #1465 - 15m SPCN Cable

A list of the supported SPCN cables is shown in the table on page 301.

The #5075 can control Ultra2 SCSI disk units. A maximum of one disk unit controller is allowed within a #5075.

On new orders, specify one line cord with each #5075 PCI Expansion Tower. Marketing configurators default to the line cord type of the system.

When the #5075 is attached to the Model 270 or 810, the seven PCI IOAs are supported (driven) by an embedded 32 MB PCI IOP and by the #2842 PCI IOP, #2844 PCI IOP, the #2890 PCI Integrated Netfinity Server, or the #2891/#2892/#2899 PCI Integrated xSeries Servers.

When the #5075 is attached to the Models 810, 820, and 825, the seven PCI IOAs are supported (driven) by an embedded 32 MB PCI IOP and by a #2843 PCI IOP, #2844 PCI IOP, the #2790 PCI Integrated Netfinity Server, or the #2791/#2792/#2799 PCI Integrated xSeries Servers.

The #5075 PCI Expansion Tower is not supported on Models 520, 550, 570, 595, 830, 840, 870, or 890. When performing upgrades, the #5075 can be converted to a #5074. Some features in the #5075 are migrated or converted to the #5074 at no charge. Other features allowed in the #5075 are not supported in the #5074 and must be replaced. See "Upgrade options for expansion towers" on page 318 for a discussion about the #5075 to #5074 feature conversion.

The #5075 is not supported on Models 520, 550, 570, and 595. The #5075 was *withdrawn from marketing* on 21 November 2003.

#5075 PCI Expansion Tower schematic

		Multi-Adapter Bridge Bus Number				
OP Panel	OP Panel	PCI Cards		Slots		
		7,8 IOA	Short	C08	PCI Short	
	Multi-Adapter Bridge Boundary	5,6 IOP/IOA	1	C07	PCI	Multi-Adapter Bridge Boundary
Fan #5156 B02	Fan #5156 B02	3,4 IOP/IOA		C06	PCI	
		1,2 IOP/IOA/Int. xSeries Svr		C05	PCI	
		7,8 IOA	2	C04	PCI	
		5,6 IOP/IOA		C03	PCI	
Fan B01	Fan B01	3,4 IOP/IOA/Int. xSeries Svr		C02	PCI	
		2 DISK IOA		C01	DISK IOA	
		1 Embedded IOP		EMBED	PCI	

Front	Right	Back
OP Panel	Disk Unit Cage	575W Power Supply #5156 PO2
Fan #5156 B02		575W Power Supply #5156 PO2
Fan B01	DB1	575W Power Supply PO1
DISK SLOTS D01 D02 D03 D04 D05 D06		575W Power Supply PO1

Legend

Base Feature   Required Feature   Unavailable if Integrated xSeries Server is installed

Note 1: If C05 has an Integrated xSeries Server, slot C06 is unavailable, and slot C07 is available only as a short slot.

Note 2: If C02 has an Integrated xSeries Server, slot C03 is unavailable, and slot C04 is available only as a short slot.

Note 3: If #5700/#5701 is installed in C01 then move Disk IOA to next available slot.

Restriction: #5700/#5701 must be placed in a 32-bit slot

#7002 HSL Enabler

The #7002 is a feature HSL internal flex cable, which enables connection to a #5075 PCI Expansion Tower. It can be ordered only on the #2248, #2250, #2422, and #2431 processors of the Model 270. This cable connects the processor using a right-angle bus connector to the back of the machine. Two #14xx HSL cables are required to connect the system unit to the expansion tower.

On processor upgrades from #2248, #2250, #2422, or #2431 to other processor features, the marketing configurator removes for Record Purpose Only (RPO) the #7102 from the inventory records.

#5156 Redundant Power and Cooling

The #5156 adds an additional 575-watt power supply for redundancy and an additional cooling fan to the #5075 PCI Expansion Tower, which attaches to Models 270 and 820.

Marketing configurators default, on a Model 820, to a #5156 for any added #5075 when the system unit contains a #5155 575-watt power supply. If a #5155 is ordered as an MES to an existing Model 820, default one #5156 for each #5075 present or ordered. The #5156s are not mandatory and can be removed from an order.

#5078 PCI Expansion Unit

The #5078 is a "top hat" that installs on the top of the #9079 Base I/O Tower (Model 840 only), #5074 PCI Expansion Tower, or #5094 PCI-X Expansion Tower to allow PCI IOAs to be installed. The #5078 may be ordered with a #5074 PCI Expansion Tower or #9079 Base I/O Tower or added at a later time. If the #5078 is ordered with the #5074/#9079, the #5074/#5079 ships with the #5078 installed.

The #5078 includes the #9691 Base Bus Adapter or the #9739 Base Optical Bus Adapter to provide the HSL interface to the system. The IBM marketing configurator adds the #9691 to the order automatically.

The #5078 contains two buses. PCI cards are supported using the same rules as the #5074/#9079. Internal disk and removable media devices are not supported in the #5078. The #5078 may be on the same HSL loop on which the #5074/#9079 is mounted, or it may be on a separate HSL loop.

Select any two of the supported HSL cable features for the first or only tower of an HSL loop. For additional towers on the HSL loop, select one HSL cable per tower. A list of the supported HSL cables is shown in the table on page 304. When the #5078 is on the same HSL loop as the #5074/#9079 on which it is mounted, the #1461 3m Copper HSL cable is sufficient.

Select one SPCN cable per tower. A list of the supported SPCN cables is shown in the table on page 301.

The #5078 includes two electrical cables to connect to a #5074/#9079 power source.

The #5078 PCI Expansion Unit supports four 32-bit and seven 32/64-bit PCI slots. The 11 PCI IOAs are supported (driven) by feature #2843 PCI IOPs, #2844 PCI IOPs, the #2790 PCI Integrated Netfinity Server, or the #2791/#2792/#2799 or #4710 PCI Integrated xSeries Servers.

The #5078 can also be mounted in an #0550 and #0551 iSeries Rack by ordering feature code #0578 instead of #5078. See page "Racks" on page 290 for information about the #0550, #0551, and #0578. The #5078 PCI Expansion Unit counts as one tower for HSL loop rules.

The #5078/#0578 is not supported on Models 520, 550, 570, and 595.

#5078 PCI Expansion Unit schematic

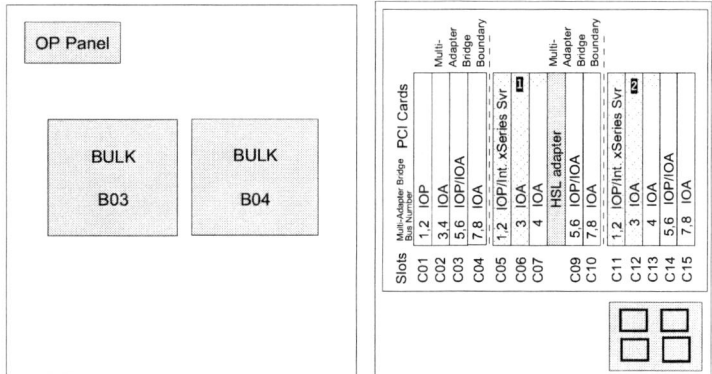

OP Panel			Slots	Multi-Adapter Bridge Bus Number	PCI Cards
			C01	1,2	IOP
			C02	3,4	IOA
BULK B03	BULK B04		C03	5,6	IOP/IOA
			C04	7,8	IOA
			C05	1,2	IOP/Int. xSeries Svr [1]
			C06	3	IOA
			C07	4	IOA
					HSL adapter
			C09	5,6	IOP/IOA
			C10	7,8	IOA
			C11	1,2	IOP/Int. xSeries Svr [2]
			C12	3	IOA
			C13	4	IOA
			C14	5,6	IOP/IOA
			C15	7,8	IOA

Multi-Adapter Bridge Boundary

Front   **Back**

Legend

Base Feature   Required Feature   Unavailable if Integrated xSeries Server is installed

Note 1: If C05 has an Integrated xSeries Server, slot C06 is unavailable, and slot C07 is available only as a short slot.

Note 2: If C11 has an Integrated xSeries Server, slot C12 is unavailable, and slot C13 is available only as a short slot.

Note 3: If #5700/#5701 is installed in C01 then move Disk IOA to next available slot.

Restriction: #5700/#5701 must be placed in a 32-bit slot

#5079 1.8 M I/O Tower

The #5079 1.8 M I/O Tower is essentially two #5074 PCI Expansion Towers, with side covers and casters removed, placed in a 1.8 M tower. Each #5079 tower counts as two #5074s toward the system model maximum number of towers.

The #5079 is attached to Models 520, 550, 570, 595, 810, 820, 825, 830, 840, 870, and 890 for adding up to 90 disk units, up to 22 PCI IOAs, and up to four removable media units. The #5079 includes two #9691 Base Bus Adapters, two #9739 Base Optical Bus Adapters, or one each of #9691 and #9739, to provide the HSL interface to the system.

The #5079 can control Ultra2 SCSI disk units and supports up to four removable media devices (internal tape, CD-ROM, or DVD-RAM). These devices are supported by two #2757/#4748/#4778 PCI RAID Disk Unit Controllers, which support the first two groups of 15 disk units. Up to six #2757/#4748/#4778s are supported per #5079.

The upper and lower enclosures (#5074s) in the #5079 are not connected with an HSL cable. If both enclosures of the #5079 are to be placed in the same HSL loop, a #1460 - 3m Copper HSL Cable must be ordered to connect the upper and lower enclosures. Or, if both enclosures of the #5079 are to be placed in the same optical HSL loop, a #1470 - 6m Optical HSL Cable must be ordered to connect the upper and lower enclosures.

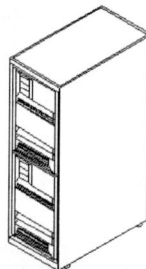

#5079 1.8 M PCI I/O Expansion Tower

The #5074 is the default when a PCI IOP or IOA is ordered that requires a PCI expansion unit. The #5079 may be specified on the extra controllers screen. For each #5079 ordered, a quantity of two #0574 (#5074 equivalent) specify codes is added to the order. If a #5079 is to be shared between two systems, one #0574 must be removed from the original ordering system and added to the sharing system, using an RPO change.

Select any two to four of the supported HSL cables for each additional tower. For a list of supported HSL cables, see the table on page 304. And select two SPCN cables per tower. See the table on page 304 for a list of supported SPCN cables.

A #5079 has two #9943 Base PCI IOPs. It also has PCI slots for up to 22 PCI IOAs, and space for up to 90 disk units. The 22 PCI IOAs are supported (driven) by feature #2843 PCI IOPs, #2844 PCI IOPs, the #2790 PCI Integrated Netfinity Server, or the #2791/#2792/#2799 or #4710 PCI Integrated xSeries Servers.

On new orders, select two line cords with each #5079 1.8 M PCI I/O Expansion Tower. Order at least one #0574 specify feature for any #5079 initial order.

#5079 1.8 M I/O Tower schematic

Note: Total number of disk bays is 2 x 45

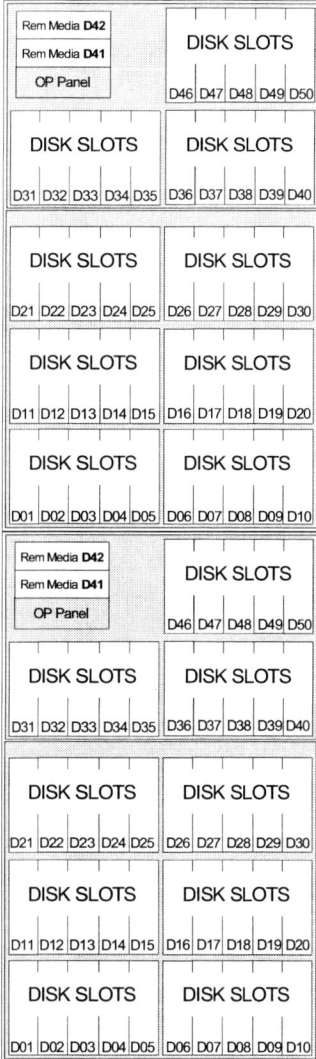

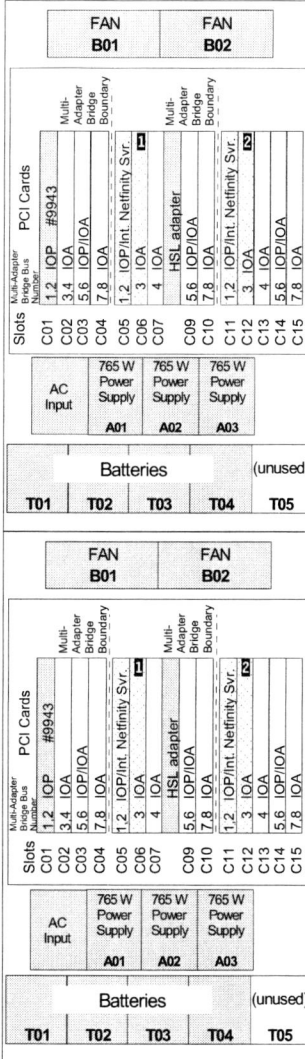

Left tower (disk slots, top unit):

Rem Media **D42**	DISK SLOTS	
Rem Media **D41**		
OP Panel	D46 D47 D48 D49 D50	

DISK SLOTS	DISK SLOTS
D31 D32 D33 D34 D35	D36 D37 D38 D39 D40

DISK SLOTS	DISK SLOTS
D21 D22 D23 D24 D25	D26 D27 D28 D29 D30

DISK SLOTS	DISK SLOTS
D11 D12 D13 D14 D15	D16 D17 D18 D19 D20

DISK SLOTS	DISK SLOTS
D01 D02 D03 D04 D05	D06 D07 D08 D09 D10

Left tower (disk slots, bottom unit):

Rem Media **D42**	DISK SLOTS	
Rem Media **D41**		
OP Panel	D46 D47 D48 D49 D50	

DISK SLOTS	DISK SLOTS
D31 D32 D33 D34 D35	D36 D37 D38 D39 D40

DISK SLOTS	DISK SLOTS
D21 D22 D23 D24 D25	D26 D27 D28 D29 D30

DISK SLOTS	DISK SLOTS
D11 D12 D13 D14 D15	D16 D17 D18 D19 D20

DISK SLOTS	DISK SLOTS
D01 D02 D03 D04 D05	D06 D07 D08 D09 D10

PCI Cards / Slots (top unit):

FAN B01　FAN B02

Slots	Multi-Adapter Bridge Bus Number	
C01	1,2	IOP #9943
C02	3,4	IOA
C03	5,6	IOP/IOA
C04	7,8	IOA
C05	1,2	IOP/Int. Netfinity Svr. [1]
C06	3	IOA
C07	4	IOA
C09	5,6	IOP/IOA — HSL adapter
C10	7,8	IOA
C11	1,2	IOP/Int. Netfinity Svr. [2]
C12	3	IOA
C13	4	IOA
C14	5,6	IOP/IOA
C15	7,8	IOA

Multi-Adapter Bridge Boundary

AC Input	765 W Power Supply A01	765 W Power Supply A02	765 W Power Supply A03

Batteries				(unused)
T01	T02	T03	T04	T05

PCI Cards / Slots (bottom unit):

FAN B01　FAN B02

Slots	Multi-Adapter Bridge Bus Number	
C01	1,2	IOP #9943
C02	3,4	IOA
C03	5,6	IOP/IOA
C04	7,8	IOA
C05	1,2	IOP/Int. Netfinity Svr. [1]
C06	3	IOA
C07	4	IOA
C09	5,6	IOP/IOA — HSL adapter
C10	7,8	IOA
C11	1,2	IOP/Int. Netfinity Svr. [2]
C12	3	IOA
C13	4	IOA
C14	5,6	IOP/IOA
C15	7,8	IOA

Multi-Adapter Bridge Boundary

AC Input	765 W Power Supply A01	765 W Power Supply A02	765 W Power Supply A03

Batteries				(unused)
T01	T02	T03	T04	T05

Legend

Base Feature

Required Feature

Unavailable if Integrated Netfinity Server is installed

Note 1: If C05 has an Integrated Netfinity Server, slot C06 is unavailable, and slot C07 is available only as a short slot.

Note 2: If C11 has an Integrated Netfinity Server, slot C12 is unavailable, and slot C13 is available only as a short slot.

#5106 Dual Line Cord - I/O Tower

The #5106 Dual Line Cords - #5079 Tower provides dual line cord capability for a single unit in a #5079 tower. Two #14XX line cords must be ordered for each #5106 present when a #5106 is ordered on an initial order of a #5079. No batteries are shipped, and two 840W power supplies are shipped with this configuration. When ordering a #5106 as a simple MES against an existing #5079, one additional #14XX line cord is required to be ordered with each #5106 ordered. Existing batteries are removed, and the 765W power supplies are removed and replaced with two 840W power supplies.

The marketing configurator defaults a quantity of two #5106s for each #5079 ordered, on a system that has dual line cords on the CEC.

OS/400 V5R1 (with PTFs) or later is required. Refer to Informational APAR II12950 at:

http://as400service.rochester.ibm.com/supporthome.nsf/document/10000035

IBM marketing configurator users can refer to this Web site for ordering information:

http://w3-1.ibm.com/sales/systems/portal/_s.155/253

#5088 PCI-X Expansion Unit

The #5088 is an eight-EIA-unit-high "top hat" installed on top of a #5074/#5094 expansion tower, or on top of a #9079 Base I/O Tower or #9094 Base PCI I/O Enclosure. The #5088 has 14 PCI-X slots for PCI IOPs and IOAs. Disk units and removable media are not supported by the #5088.

The #5088 has two redundant 575W power supplies and two internal power connectors that attach to the AC distribution box in the #5074/#5094/#9079/#9094. The #5074/#5094/#9079 may have one or two line cords, so the #5088 may or may not have dual line cord capability depending on the configuration of the #5074, #5094 or #9079. The #9094 has dual line cord included.

If the #5088 is ordered together with a #5094/#9094, the #5094/#9094 ships with the #5088 installed. The #5088 may also be ordered for field install on an existing #5074/#5094/#9094. The #5088 may not be installed on a #5294 1.8m I/O Tower or #8094 Optional 1.8 M I/O Rack.

PCI IOAs are supported by feature #2843/#2844 PCI IOPs, feature #2790, #2890 PCI Integrated Netfinity® Servers, feature #2791, #2792, #2799, #2891, #2892, #2899 PCI Integrated xSeries Servers, and the #4710 PCI Integrated xSeries Server. A #9844 can be used in a #5088. It cannot be ordered with or on a #5088.

A bus adapter to provide the HSL interface to the system is included. Select one of the following options:

- ▶ #9876 Base Optical Bus Adapter (replacement for #9886)
- ▶ #9877 - Base HSL-2 Bus Adapter (replacement for #9887)
- ▶ #9886 Base Optical Bus Adapter to specify two optical HSL ports
- ▶ #9887 Base HSL-2 Bus Adapter to specify two copper HSL-2 ports

One or two cables must be ordered to attach to the HSL or HSL-2 ports. When ordering cables to connect to the HSL interface, optical HSL, copper HSL, copper HSL-2, or copper HSL to HSL-2 cables are required. An HSL loop uses all optical or all copper ports and cables. A copper loop can intermix I/O towers and units with copper HSL and copper HSL-2 ports. Select the appropriate cable based on the type of HSL ports to which it is being attached, and the cable length required.

- ▶ Copper HSL to HSL-2 (HSL on one end and HSL-2 on the other end)
    - – #1474 - 6m HSL to HSL-2 Cable
    - – #1475 - 10m HSL to HSL-2 Cable
- ▶ Copper HSL-2 (HSL-2 on both ends of the cable)
    - – #1482 - 3.5m HSL-2 Cable
    - – #1483 - 10m HSL-2 Cable
    - – #1485 - 15m HSL-2 Cable
- ▶ Optical HSL
    - – #1470 - 6m Optical HSL Cable
    - – #1471 - 30m Optical HSL Cable
    - – #1472 - 100m Optical HSL Cable
    - – #1473 - 250m Optical HSL Cable

For each I/O tower or unit, select one SPCN cable. A list of the supported SPCN cables is shown in the table on page 304.

A maximum of one per #5074, #5094, #9079, or #9094 is allowed.

This feature requires OS/400 V5R2, plus PTFs. Refer to Informational APAR II13440 at the following Web site:

http://www-912.ibm.com/n_dir/nas4apar.nsf/nas4aparhome

#5088 PCI-X Expansion Unit schematic

Front

OP Panel

POWER P01 (B01)

POWER P02 (B02)

Back

Slots	Multi-Adapter Bridge Bus Number	PCI Cards
C01	1,2	IOP/IOA/IXS
C02	3,4	IOA
C03	5,6	IOP/IOA
C04	7,8	IOA
C05	1,2	IOP/IOA/IXS
C06	3	IOA
C07	4	IOA
C08	5,6	IOP/IOA
C09	7,8	IOA
C10		HSL adapter
C11	1,2	IOP/IOA/IXS
C12	3	IOP/IOA
C13	4	IOP/IOA
C14	5,6	IOP/IOA
C15	7,8	IOA

Multi-Adapter Bridge Boundary (after C04, C09)

Note: All slots are 3.3V

VPD

SPCN

Legend

Base Feature

Required Feature

Unavailable if Integrated xSeries Server is installed

Note 1: If C05 has an Integrated xSeries Server, slot C06 is unavailable, and slot C07 is available only as a short slot. A #2792 does not reduce a third slot to a short slot.

Note 2: If C11 has an Integrated xSeries Server, slot C12 is unavailable, and slot C13 is available only as a short slot. A #2792 does not reduce a third slot to a short slot.

Note 3: IXS placement is not supported from plant. Only a #2792 is allowed in this position.

#0588 PCI-X Expansion Unit in Rack

The #0588 is the equivalent of a #5088 PCI-X Expansion Unit, but the #0588 is mounted in an #0551 or #0550 rack. A #0588 is eight EIA units high and has 14 PCI-X slots for PCI IOPs and IOAs. Disk units and removable media are not supported by the #0588. An #0588 can be on initial, upgrade, or MES orders, but cannot be converted to a #5088.

PCI IOAs are supported by feature #2843/#2844 PCI IOPs, feature #2790, #2890 PCI Integrated Netfinity Servers, feature #2791, #2792, #2799, #2891, #2892, #2899 PCI Integrated xSeries Servers, and the #4710 PCI Integrated xSeries Server. A #9844 may be used in an #0588. It cannot be ordered with or for a #0588.

The #0588 has two redundant 575W power supplies and two integrated power distribution units (PDU) compatible line cords. The line cords may be connected

to the same PDU or separate PDUs in the #0550 or #0551 rack. When the line cords are connected to separate PDUs, and those PDUs are connected to two different power sources, the #0588 has dual line cord capability.

Up to four #0588s can be mounted in an #0551, and one #0588 may be mounted in an #0550. A PDU is required when one, two, or three #0588s are to be installed in the same #0551. A minimum of two PDUs are required if four #0588s are ordered for the same #0551. One PDU (or two for dual line cords) is required for an #0588 in an #0550.

A bus adapter to provide the HSL interface to the system is included. Select one of the following options:

▶ #9876 - Base Optical Bus adapter (replacement for #9886)
▶ #9877 - Base HSL-2 Bus Adapter (replacement for #9887)
▶ #9886 Base Optical Bus Adapter to specify two optical HSL ports
▶ #9887 Base HSL-2 Bus Adapter to specify two copper HSL-2 ports

One or two cables must be ordered to attach to the HSL or HSL-2 ports. When ordering cables to connect to the HSL interface, optical HSL, copper HSL, copper HSL-2, or copper HSL to HSL-2 cables are required. An HSL loop uses all optical or all copper ports and cables. A copper loop can intermix I/O towers and units with copper HSL and copper HSL-2 ports. Select the appropriate cable based on the type of HSL ports to which it is being attached, and the cable length required:

▶ Copper HSL to HSL-2 (HSL on one end and HSL-2 on the other end)
▶ Copper HSL-2 (HSL-2 on both ends of the cable)
▶ Optical HSL

A list of the supported HSL cables is shown in the table on page 304.

For each I/O tower or unit, select one SPCN cable. A list of the supported SPCN cables is shown in the table on page 304.

This feature requires OS/400 V5R2, plus PTFs. Refer to Informational APAR II13440 at the following Web site:

http://www-912.ibm.com/n_dir/nas4apar.nsf/nas4aparhome

#5094 PCI-X Expansion Tower

The #5094 PCI-X Expansion Tower has 15 disk unit slots, with an additional 30 slots available when using feature #5108 Disk Unit Expansion. The 45 disk unit positions are in groups of 15. Each group of 15 disk units is further divided into three groups of five disk units with each group of five disk units supported on a separate SCSI bus.

The #5094 also has two removable media slots and 14 PCI-X card slots. A #9844 Base PCI IOP is included in the base. A #2757 PCI-X Ultra RAID Disk Controller or #4748/#4778 PCI RAID Disk Unit Controller is required to drive the disk units in the base 15 disk unit slots and the removable media devices in the two removable media slots.

For Models 270, 800, 810, 820, 825, 830, 840, 870, and 890, up to nine disk controllers can be used in one tower driven by OS/400 or Linux. Each disk controller can then be attached to one or more disk unit enclosures which contain five disks each. The #5703 PCI-X RAID Disk Unit Controller can be used after three #2757/#4748/#4778 controllers are installed. The #0143 Disk Controller Placement Exception is a prerequisite for the #5703. Up to 18 disk units per #2757 are supported in the system unit or external tower disk cage of the Model 270, 800, and 810. Up to 15 disk units per #2757 are supported in a #9094 Base PCI I/O Enclosure attached to a Model 870 or 890.

For Models 520, 550, 570, and 595, a maximum of nine #5703/#5715 (any combination) are supported per #5094. There is no requirement for a #2757/#4748/#4778 controller to be installed. The number of #2757/#4748/#4778 installed in a #5094 is limited to a maximum of three.

Up to 20 disk units per #2757 are supported in a #5094 PCI-X Expansion Tower attached to a Model 520, 550, 570, or 595.

A bus adapter to provide the HSL interface to the system is included. Select one of the following options:

- ▶ #6417 HSL-2/RIO-G Bus Adapter (for upgrades only)
- ▶ #9517 Base HSL-2/RIO-G Bus Adapter (copper) for attachment to 520, 550, 570, and 595
- ▶ #9876 Base Optical Bus Adapter (replacement for #9886)
- ▶ #9877 - Base HSL-2 Bus Adapter (replacement for #9887)
- ▶ #9886 Base Optical Bus Adapter to specify two optical HSL ports
- ▶ #9887 Base HSL-2 Bus Adapter to specify two copper HSL-2 ports

One or two cables must be ordered to attach to the HSL or HSL-2 ports.

When ordering cables to connect to the HSL interface, optical HSL, copper HSL, copper HSL-2, or copper HSL to HSL-2 cables are required. An HSL loop uses all optical or all copper ports and cables. A copper loop can intermix I/O towers and units with copper HSL and copper HSL-2 ports. Select the appropriate cable based on the type of HSL ports to which it is being attached, and the cable length required.

- ▶ Copper HSL to HSL-2 (HSL on one end and HSL-2 on the other end)
- ▶ Copper HSL-2 (HSL-2 on both ends of the cable)
- ▶ Optical HSL

A list of the supported HSL cables is shown in the table on page 304.

For each I/O tower or unit, select one SPCN cable. A list of the supported SPCN cables is shown in the table on page 304.

This feature requires OS/400 V5R2, plus PTFs. Refer to Informational APAR II13440 at the following Web site:

`http://www-912.ibm.com/n_dir/nas4apar.nsf/nas4aparhome`

Note: A #9877 - Base HSL-2 Bus Adapter is shipped with new orders of a #5094 for Models 800, 810, 820, 825, 830, 840, 870, and 890. A #9517 Base HSL-2/RIO-G Bus Adapter is shipped for Models 520, 550, 570, and 595.

#5108 30-Disk Expansion Feature

The #5108 is a disk unit expansion enclosure feature for a #5094 Base I/O Expansion Tower and the #9094 Base PCI I/O Enclosure. It includes two 15 disk unit enclosures, one 840-watt power supply, backplanes, and cables.

The #2757 PCI-X Ultra RAID Disk Controller, #2780 PCI-X Ultra RAID Disk Controller, #4748/#4778 PCI RAID Disk Unit Controller, or #5703 PCI-X RAID Disk Unit Controller is required to support the disk units in each of the two disk unit enclosures included with #5108. Each group of 15 disk units is further divided into three groups of five disk units with each group of five disk units supported on a separate SCSI bus. A minimum of two disk unit controllers and a maximum of six are required to support 30 disk units.

A schematic of the #5094 PCI-X Expansion Tower follows.

Note: The total number of disk bays is 45.

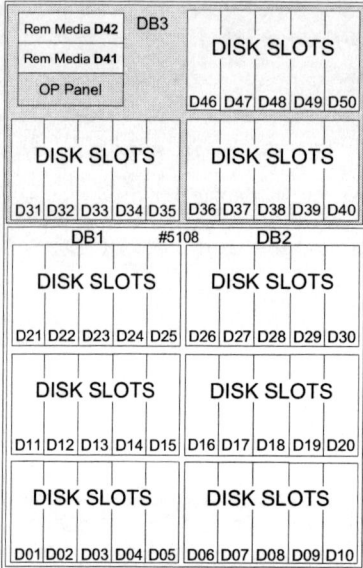

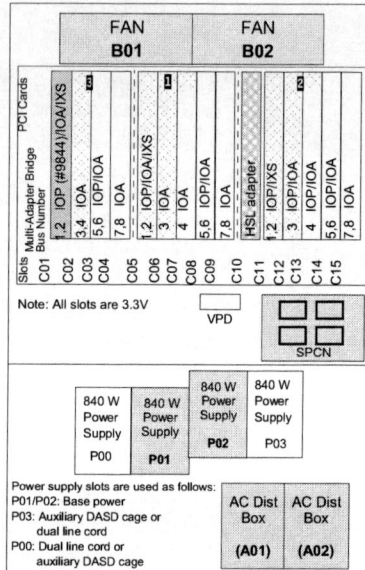

Front   Back

Legend

| Base Feature | Required Feature | Unavailable if Integrated xSeries Server is installed |

Note 1: If C05 has an Integrated xSeries Server, slot C06 is unavailable, and slot C07 is available only as a short slot. A #2792 does not reduce a third slot to a short slot.

Note 2: If C11 has an Integrated xSeries Server, slot C12 is unavailable, and slot C13 is available only as a short slot. A #2792 does not reduce a third slot to a short slot.

Note 3: IXS placement is not supported from plant. Only a #2792 is allowed in this position.

#5115 Dual Line Cords - Tower

The #5115 is a dual line cord enabler for the upper unit in a #8094 Optional 1.8 M I/O Rack, and for the #5094 PCI-X Expansion Tower. The #5115 includes two AC input boxes. An additional line cord must be specified.

#5094 PCI-X Expansion Tower schematic

The #5094 PCI-X Expansion Tower is supported by Models 800, 810, 820, 825, 830, 840, 870, and 890.

Note: The total number of disk bays is 45.

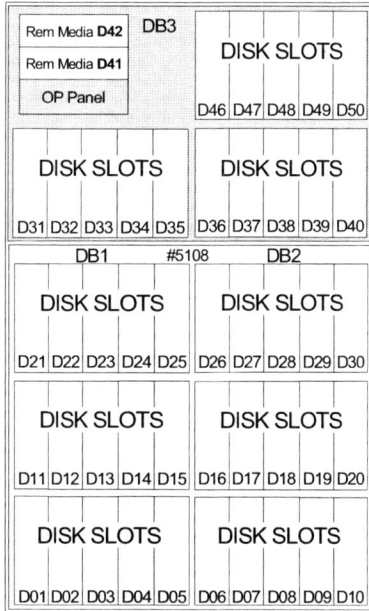

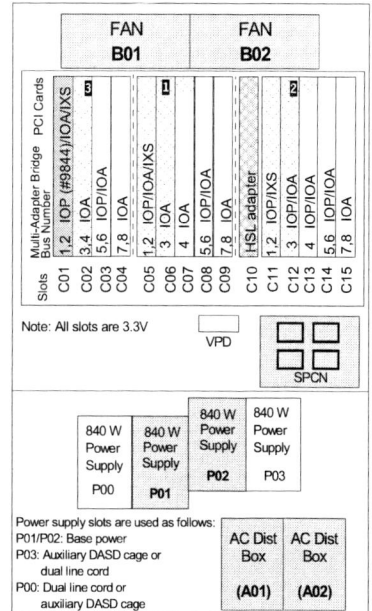

Front   Back

Legend

Base Feature | Required Feature | Unavailable if Integrated xSeries Server is installed

Note 1: If C05 has an Integrated xSeries Server, slot C06 is unavailable, and slot C07 is available only as a short slot. A #2792 does not reduce a third slot to a short slot.

Note 2: If C11 has an Integrated xSeries Server, slot C12 is unavailable, and slot C13 is available only as a short slot. A #2792 does not reduce a third slot to a short slot.

Note 3: IXS placement is not supported from plant. Only a #2792 is allowed in this position.

#5095 PCI-X Expansion Tower

The #5095 has seven PCI-X IOP/IOA slots and supports up to 12 disk units. A #9844 Base PCI IOP is included.

A bus adapter to provide the HSL interface to the system is included. Select one of the following options:

► #6417 HSL-2/RIO-G Bus Adapter (for upgrades only)
► #9517 Base HSL-2/RIO-G Bus Adapter (copper) (for new towers only)
► #9876 Base Optical Bus Adapter (replacement for #9886)
► #9877 - Base HSL-2 Bus Adapter (replacement for #9887)
► #9886 Base Optical Bus Adapter to specify two optical HSL ports
► #9887 Base HSL-2 Bus Adapter to specify two copper HSL-2 ports

One or two cables must be ordered to attach to the HSL or HSL-2 ports. When ordering cables to connect to the HSL interface, optical HSL, copper HSL, copper HSL-2, or copper HSL to HSL-2 cables are required. An HSL loop uses all optical or all copper ports and cables. A copper loop can intermix I/O towers and units with copper HSL and copper HSL-2 ports. Select the appropriate cable based on the type of HSL ports to which it is being attached, and the cable length required.

► Copper HSL to HSL-2 (HSL on one end and HSL-2 on the other end)
► Copper HSL-2 (HSL-2 on both ends of the cable)
► Optical HSL

A list of the supported HSL cables is shown in the table on page 304.

For each I/O tower or unit, select one SPCN cable. A list of the supported SPCN cables is shown in the table on page 304.

The #5095 has redundant power when feature #5138 Redundant Power and Cooling is specified. The #5138 includes a second 435W power supply, and a second line cord must also be ordered to provide dual line cord capability.

This feature requires OS/400 V5R2, plus PTFs. Refer to Informational APAR II13440 at the following Web site:

`http://www-912.ibm.com/n_dir/nas4apar.nsf/nas4aparhome`

> **Note:** A #9877 - Base HSL-2 Bus Adapter is shipped with new orders of a #5095 for Models 800, 810, 820, 825, 830, 840, 870, and 890. A #9517 Base HSL-2/RIO-G Bus Adapter is shipped for Models 520, 550, 570, and595.

#5095 PCI-X Expansion Tower schematic

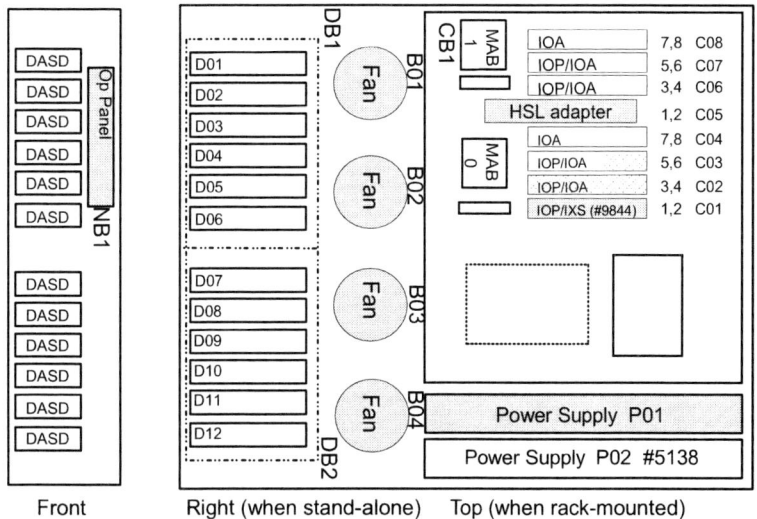

Front   Right (when stand-alone)   Top (when rack-mounted)

#0595 PCI-X Tower Unit in Rack

#0595 PCI-X Expansion Unit in Rack is the racked version of the #5095 PCI-X Expansion Tower which provides I/O capability for iSeries servers. The #0595 has functional capabilities identical to the #5095. The #0595 has seven PCI-X IOP/IOA slots and supports up to 12 disk units. A #9844 Base PCI IOP is included. The #0595 uses five EIA units of space in the tower and up to seven #0595 may be installed in a #0551 iSeries Rack.

The #0595 has redundant power when feature #5138 is specified. Feature #5138 includes a second 435W power supply and a second line cord must also be ordered to provide dual line cord capability.

A bus adapter to provide the HSL interface to the system is included. Select one of the following options:

- ▸ #6417 HSL-2/RIO-G Bus Adapter (for upgrades only)
- ▸ #9517 Base HSL-2/RIO-G Bus Adapter (copper) (for new towers only)
- ▸ #9876 Base Optical Bus Adapter (replacement for #9886)
- ▸ #9877 - Base HSL-2 Bus Adapter (replacement for #9887)
- ▸ #9886 Base Optical Bus Adapter to specify two optical HSL ports
- ▸ #9887 Base HSL-2 Bus Adapter to specify two copper HSL-2 ports

One or two cables must be ordered to attach to the HSL or HSL-2 ports. When ordering cables to connect to the HSL interface, optical HSL, copper HSL, copper HSL-2, or copper HSL to HSL-2 cables are required. An HSL loop uses all optical or all copper ports and cables. A copper loop can intermix I/O towers and units with copper HSL and copper HSL-2 ports. Select the appropriate cable based on the type of HSL ports to which it is being attached, and the cable length required.

- ► Copper HSL to HSL-2 (HSL on one end and HSL-2 on the other end)
- ► Copper HSL-2 (HSL-2 on both ends of the cable)
- ► Optical HSL

A list of the supported HSL cables is shown in the table on page 304. Also, for each I/O tower or unit, select one SPCN cable. A list of the supported SPCN cables is shown in the table on page 304.

This feature requires OS/400 V5R2, plus PTFs. Refer to Informational APAR II13440 at the following Web site:

http://www-912.ibm.com/n_dir/nas4apar.nsf/nas4aparhome

> **Note:** A #9877 - Base HSL-2 Bus Adapter is shipped with new orders of a #0595 for Models 800, 810, 820, 825, 830, 840, 870, and 890. A #9517 Base HSL-2/RIO-G Bus Adapter is shipped for Models 520, 550, 570, and 595.

#5097 1.8m I/O Tower

The #5097 1.8m I/O Tower is a I/O expansion tower that can contain up to 90 disk units. It has 28 PCI slots and four removable media bays. The #5097 is the result of a conversion from a #8093 Optional 1.8 M I/O Rack to the #5097.

Each #5097 is essentially a #5094 PCI-X Expansion Tower(bottom enclosure) and a #5074 PCI Expansion Tower (top enclosure) with side covers and casters removed and then placed in a 1.8M rack. Each #5097 counts as one #5094 and one #5074 towards the system model maximums.

#5294 1.8m I/O Tower

The #5294 1.8m I/O Tower has space for up to 90 disk units, 28 PCI-X IOA/IOP slots, and up to four removable media units. Two #9844 Base PCI IOPs are included. A #5294 is equivalent to two #5094 PCI-X Expansion Towers with side covers and casters removed, and with two 30-disk expansion included (no feature required) and placed in a 1.8 M tower.

The 90 disk unit positions are controlled by up to 18 OS/400 or Linux controlled disk controllers.

The #5294 also supports up to four removable media devices (internal tape or CD-ROM/DVD). These removable media devices are supported by the two #2757/#4748/#4778 PCI RAID Disk Unit Controllers that support the first two groups of disk units.

A bus adapter to provide the HSL interface to the system is included. Select two of the following options:

- #6417 HSL-2/RIO-G Bus Adapter (for upgrades only)
- #9517 Base HSL-2/RIO-G Bus Adapter (copper) (for new towers only)
- #9876 Base Optical Bus Adapter (replacement for #9886)
- #9877 - Base HSL-2 Bus Adapter (replacement for #9887)
- #9886 Base Optical Bus Adapter to specify two optical HSL ports
- #9887 Base HSL-2 Bus Adapter to specify two copper HSL-2 ports

Two to four cables must be ordered to attach to the HSL or HSL-2 ports. When ordering cables to connect to the HSL interface, optical HSL, copper HSL, copper HSL-2, or copper HSL to HSL-2 cables are required. An HSL loop uses all optical or all copper ports and cables. A copper loop can intermix I/O towers and units with copper HSL and copper HSL-2 ports. Select the appropriate cable based on the type of HSL ports to which it is being attached, and the cable length required.

- Copper HSL to HSL-2 (HSL on one end and HSL-2 on the other end)
- Copper HSL-2 (HSL-2 on both ends of the cable)
- Optical HSL

A list of the supported HSL cables is shown in the table on page 304. Also, for each I/O tower or unit, select one SPCN cable. A list of the supported SPCN cables is shown in the table on page 304.

The prerequisite is the #0694 #5094 Equivalent. This feature requires OS/400 V5R2, plus PTFs. Refer to Informational APAR II13440 at the following Web site:

`http://www-912.ibm.com/n_dir/nas4apar.nsf/nas4aparhome`

> **Note:** A #9877 - Base HSL-2 Bus Adapter is shipped with new orders of a #5294 for Models 800, 810, 820, 825, 830, 840, 870, and 890. A #9517 Base HSL-2/RIO-G Bus Adapter is shipped for Models 520, 550, 570, and 595.

#5116 Dual Line Cords - #5294 Tower

The #5116 provides dual line cord capability for a single enclosure in a #5294 tower. Two line cords must be specified for each #5116 ordered with a #5294. When ordering a #5116 for an installed #5294, an additional line cord must be specified for each #5116. One power supply is shipped with each #5116.

The marketing configurator defaults two #5116s for each #5294 ordered, with a system that has dual line cords on the system unit.

#5294 1.8m I/O Tower schematic

Note: The total number of disk bays is 2 x 45.

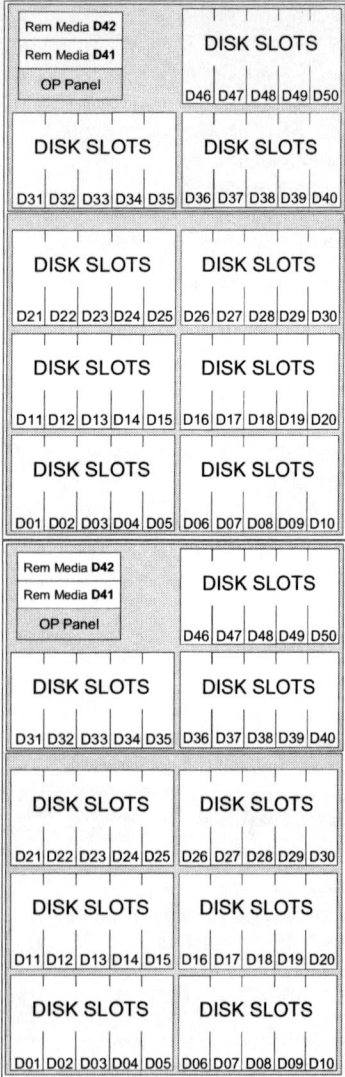

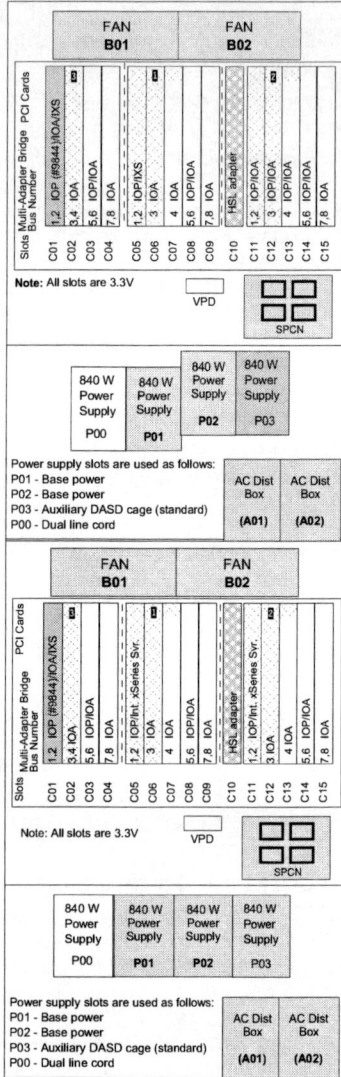

First tower (top)

Rem Media **D42**
Rem Media **D41**
OP Panel

DISK SLOTS
D46 D47 D48 D49 D50

DISK SLOTS
D31 D32 D33 D34 D35

DISK SLOTS
D36 D37 D38 D39 D40

DISK SLOTS
D21 D22 D23 D24 D25

DISK SLOTS
D26 D27 D28 D29 D30

DISK SLOTS
D11 D12 D13 D14 D15

DISK SLOTS
D16 D17 D18 D19 D20

DISK SLOTS
D01 D02 D03 D04 D05

DISK SLOTS
D06 D07 D08 D09 D10

FAN **B01** | FAN **B02**

PCI Cards

Slots / Multi-Adapter Bridge / Bus Number

C01	1,2 IOP (#9844)/IOA/IXS
C02	3,4 IOA
C03	5,6 IOP/IOA
C04	7,8 IOA
C05	1,2 IOP/IXS
C06	3 IOA
C07	4 IOA
C08	5,6 IOP/IOA
C09	7,8 IOA
C10	HSL adapter
C11	1,2 IOP/IOA
C12	3 IOA
C13	4 IOA
C14	5,6 IOP/IOA
C15	7,8 IOA

Note: All slots are 3.3V

VPD

SPCN

840 W Power Supply P00
840 W Power Supply **P01**
840 W Power Supply **P02**
840 W Power Supply **P03**

Power supply slots are used as follows:
P01 - Base power
P02 - Base power
P03 - Auxiliary DASD cage (standard)
P00 - Dual line cord

AC Dist Box **(A01)**
AC Dist Box **(A02)**

Second tower (bottom)

Rem Media **D42**
Rem Media **D41**
OP Panel

DISK SLOTS
D46 D47 D48 D49 D50

DISK SLOTS
D31 D32 D33 D34 D35

DISK SLOTS
D36 D37 D38 D39 D40

DISK SLOTS
D21 D22 D23 D24 D25

DISK SLOTS
D26 D27 D28 D29 D30

DISK SLOTS
D11 D12 D13 D14 D15

DISK SLOTS
D16 D17 D18 D19 D20

DISK SLOTS
D01 D02 D03 D04 D05

DISK SLOTS
D06 D07 D08 D09 D10

FAN **B01** | FAN **B02**

PCI Cards

Slots / Multi-Adapter Bridge / Bus Number

C01	1,2 IOP (#9844)/IOA/IXS
C02	3,4 IOA
C03	5,6 IOP/IOA
C04	7,8 IOA
C05	1,2 IOP/Int. xSeries Svr.
C06	3 IOA
C07	4 IOA
C08	5,6 IOP/IOA
C09	7,8 IOA
C10	HSL adapter
C11	1,2 IOP/Int. xSeries Svr.
C12	3 IOA
C13	4 IOA
C14	5,6 IOP/IOA
C15	7,8 IOA

Note: All slots are 3.3V

VPD

SPCN

840 W Power Supply P00
840 W Power Supply **P01**
840 W Power Supply **P02**
840 W Power Supply **P03**

Power supply slots are used as follows:
P01 - Base power
P02 - Base power
P03 - Auxiliary DASD cage (standard)
P00 - Dual line cord

AC Dist Box **(A01)**
AC Dist Box **(A02)**

Legend

Base Feature

Required Feature

Unavailable if Integrated Netfinity Server is installed

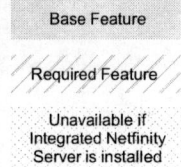

Note 1: If C05 has an Integrated xSeries Server, slot C06 is unavailable, and slot C07 is available only as a short slot. A #2792 does not reduce a third slot to a short slot.

Note 2: If C11 has an Integrated xSeries Server, slot C12 is unavailable, and slot C13 is available only as a short slot. A #2792 does not reduce a third slot to a short slot.

Note 3: IXS placement is not supported from plant. Only a #2792 is allowed in this position.

#5790 PCI-X Expansion Unit

The #5790 PCI Expansion Drawer is a rack mounted, four EIA, half-wide unit that has six full-length 64bit PCI-X slots requiring four units of vertical space in the rack. The #5790 comes standard with two redundant power supplies, dual power cords and hot-plug PCI adapter slots. Blind swap cassettes are used to enclose and insert each PCI adapter.

Two #5790 units can fit side by side within a #7311 Unit Enclosure providing a total of 12 PCI-X slots in four units of rack space.

One #7311 Unit Enclosure supports two #5790 drawers, but may also be used for one drawer. A PDU in the rack is optional.

The #5790 includes a #9531 Base HSL-2 Bus Adapter which provides the HSL-2 interface to the system. The IBM marketing configurator automatically adds the #9531 to the order.

One or two of the following cables must be ordered to attach to the HSL or HSL-2 ports.

- #1307 -1.75m Copper HSL-2 Cable (cannot be plugged into a racked model 520 or 550 system unit)
- #1308 -2.5m Copper HSL-2 Cable
- #1474 - 6m HSL to HSL-2 Cable
- #1475 - 10m HSL to HSL-2 Cable
- #1481 - 1m HSL-2 Cable (cannot be plugged into a racked model 520 or 550 system unit)
- #1482 - 3.5m HSL-2 Cable
- #1483 - 10m HSL-2 Cable

Two of the following line cords must be ordered for use with each #5790:

- #6459 - 12-ft. 250V/10A, Right Angle, Drawer to IBM PDU
- #6470 - 6-ft. 125V/15A Line Cord United States/Canada
- #6471 - 9-ft. 125V/15A Line Cord Brazil
- #6472 - 9-ft. 250V/10A Line Cord EU/Asia
- #6473 - 9-ft. 250V/10A Line Cord Denmark
- #6474 - 9-ft. 250V/10A Line Cord UK
- #6475 - 9-ft. 250V/10A Line Cord Israel
- #6476 - 9-ft. 250V/10A Line Cord Switzerland
- #6477 - 9-ft. 250V/10A Line Cord South Africa/Pakistan
- #6478 - 9-ft. 250V/10A Line Cord Italy/Chile
- #6479 - 9-ft. 250V/10A Line Cord Australia/NZ/Argentina
- #6487 - 6-ft. 250V/15A Line Cord Thailand
- #6488 - 9-ft. 125V/15A or 250V/10A Uruguay and Brazil
- #6493 - 9-ft. 250V/10A Line Cord China

- ▶ #6494 - 9-ft. 250V/10A Line Cord India
- ▶ #6496 - 9-ft. 250V/10A Line Cord Korea
- ▶ #6497 - 6-ft. 250V/15A Line Cord OEM PDU
- ▶ #6498 - 6-ft. 250V/15A Line Cord OEM PDU

Select an appropriate number of the following SPCN cables for use with a #5790:

- ▶ #0369 100m Optical SPCN Cable (not supported on Model 520)
- ▶ #1468 - 250m Optical SPCN Cable (not supported on Model 520)
- ▶ #6001 Power Control Cable - 2M (cannot be plugged into a racked Model 520 or 550 system unit)
- ▶ #6006 Power Control Cable - 3M
- ▶ #6007 Power Control Cable - 15M
- ▶ #6008 Power Control Cable - 6M
- ▶ #6029 Power Control Cable - 30M

The #5790 PCI-X Expansion Unit is supported on @server i5 Models 520, 550 and 570. The #5790 requires i5/OS V5R3.

#5790 PCI Expansion Drawer schematic

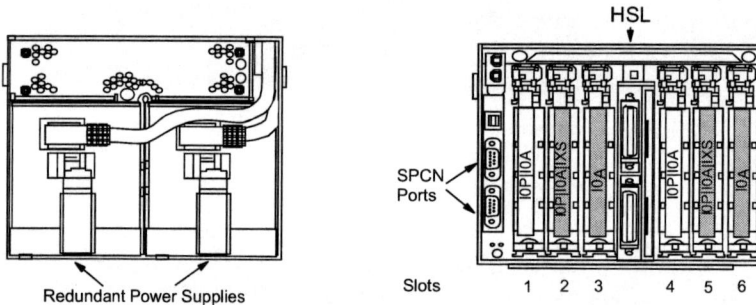

Note: A #4812 PCI Integrated xSeries Server consumes two slots.

#8093 Optional 1.8 M I/O Rack

The #8093 Optional 1.8 M I/O Rack is the 1.8 meter optional base I/O rack for the Model 870 and 890.

Note: The total number of disk bays is 2 x 45.

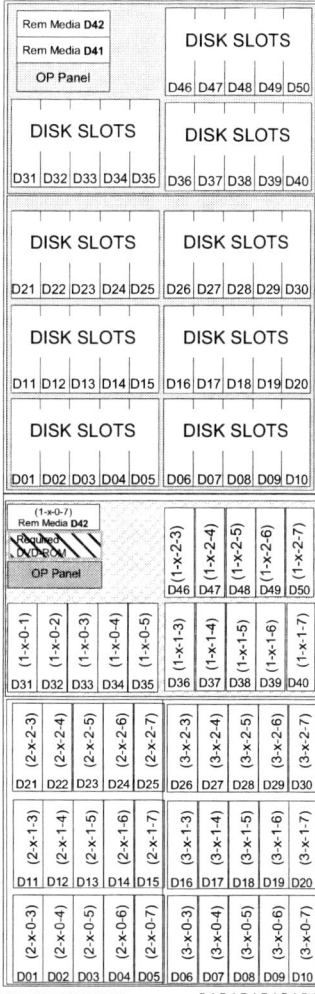

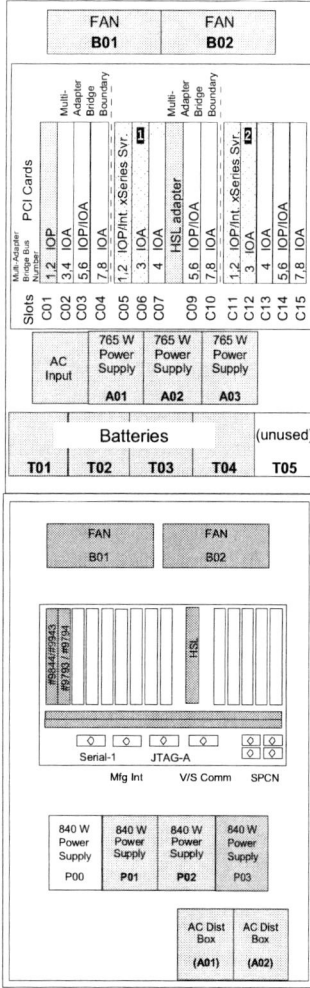

Rem Media **D42**
Rem Media **D41**
OP Panel

DISK SLOTS
D46 D47 D48 D49 D50

DISK SLOTS
D31 D32 D33 D34 D35

DISK SLOTS
D36 D37 D38 D39 D40

DISK SLOTS
D21 D22 D23 D24 D25

DISK SLOTS
D26 D27 D28 D29 D30

DISK SLOTS
D11 D12 D13 D14 D15

DISK SLOTS
D16 D17 D18 D19 D20

DISK SLOTS
D01 D02 D03 D04 D05

DISK SLOTS
D06 D07 D08 D09 D10

(1-x-0-7)
Rem Media **D42**
Required DVD-ROM
OP Panel

(1-x-2-3) D46
(1-x-2-4) D47
(1-x-2-5) D48
(1-x-2-6) D49
(1-x-2-7) D50

(1-x-0-1) D31
(1-x-0-2) D32
(1-x-0-3) D33
(1-x-0-4) D34
(1-x-0-5) D35

(1-x-1-3) D36
(1-x-1-4) D37
(1-x-1-5) D38
(1-x-1-6) D39
(1-x-1-7) D40

(2-x-2-3) D21
(2-x-2-4) D22
(2-x-2-5) D23
(2-x-2-6) D24
(2-x-2-7) D25

(3-x-2-3) D26
(3-x-2-4) D27
(3-x-2-5) D28
(3-x-2-6) D29
(3-x-2-7) D30

(2-x-1-3) D11
(2-x-1-4) D12
(2-x-1-5) D13
(2-x-1-6) D14
(2-x-1-7) D15

(3-x-1-3) D16
(3-x-1-4) D17
(3-x-1-5) D18
(3-x-1-6) D19
(3-x-1-7) D20

(2-x-0-3) D01
(2-x-0-4) D02
(2-x-0-5) D03
(2-x-0-6) D04
(2-x-0-7) D05

(3-x-0-3) D06
(3-x-0-4) D07
(3-x-0-5) D08
(3-x-0-6) D09
(3-x-0-7) D10

FAN **B01**
FAN **B02**

PCI Cards

Multi-Adapter Bridge Bus Number

Multi-Adapter Bridge Boundary

Multi-Adapter Bridge Boundary

HSL adapter

Int. xSeries Svr. **1**
Int. xSeries Svr. **2**

Slots
C01 — 1,2 IOP
C02 — 3,4 IOA
C03 — 5,6 IOP/IOA
C04 — 7,8 IOA
C05 — 1,2 IOP/Int. xSeries Svr.
C06 — 3 IOA
C07 — 4 IOA
C09 — 5,6 IOP/IOA
C10 — 7,8 IOA
C11 — 1,2 IOP/Int. xSeries Svr.
C12 — 3 IOA
C13 — 4 IOA
C14 — 5,6 IOP/IOA
C15 — 7,8 IOA

AC Input

765 W Power Supply **A01**
765 W Power Supply **A02**
765 W Power Supply **A03**

Batteries
T01 T02 T03 T04 (unused) T05

FAN B01
FAN B02

#9844/#943 #9793 / #9794

HSL

Serial-1   JTAG-A
Mfg Int   V/S Comm   SPCN

840 W Power Supply P00
840 W Power Supply **P01**
840 W Power Supply **P02**
840 W Power Supply P03

AC Dist Box **(A01)**
AC Dist Box **(A02)**

Legend

Base Feature

Required Feature

Unavailable if Integrated xSeries Server is installed

Note 1: If C05 has an Integrated xSeries Server, slot C06 is unavailable, and slot C07 is available only as a short slot.

Note 2: If C11 has an Integrated xSeries Server, slot C12 is unavailable, and slot C13 is available only as a short slot.

Note 3: The position of the cards may change depending on the console and other features selected.

See the #9094 PCI Card Enclosure for card placement details.

Racks

Options are available to rack mount selected iSeries server models and towers. Rack mounting allows multiple components to be mounted in a rack, conserving floor space and providing a secure environment for the devices.

#0550 iSeries Rack

The #0550 iSeries Rack is a 1.8-meter rack with an iSeries 830 model installed. The #0550 is ordered as a feature to allow a Model 830 to be installed in the rack. The Model 830 occupies the lower 26 EIA units of the rack, leaving 10 EIA units available for installation of other devices. When an #0550 is ordered, a #5101 30 Disk Unit Expansion is included in the 830 server.

The marketing configurator does not manage rack space in the #0550 rack.

> **Note:** The #0550 is only valid on an initial order. Existing 830 servers cannot be installed in a rack due to weight restrictions.

Up to two PDUs may be installed in the #0550. The PDUs may be ordered as part of the initial order or added at a later time. Each PDU has six power sockets that provide power for devices that support the #1422 PDU Line Cord. A country (region)-specific line cord must be ordered for each PDU to connect to external power. The supported PDUs are:

- #5160 Power Distribution Unit - 1 Phase NEMA
- #5161 Power Distribution Unit - 1 Phase IEC
- #5162 Power Distribution Unit - 2 of 3 Phase

The Model 830 does not support the #1422 PDU Line Cord and cannot be powered by a PDU. A country (region)-specific line cord must be ordered for the 830 installed in the #0550 iSeries Rack.

#0551 iSeries Rack

The #0551 iSeries Rack is an empty 1.8-meter rack that provides a total of 36 EIA units of space. The #0551 can be ordered as a feature of an iSeries server as part of an initial order or added at a later time. The following features specify the means of populating the #0551:

- #0121 Lower Unit in Rack Specify (270) (*withdrawn from marketing* on 21 November 2003)
- #0122 Upper Unit in Rack Specify (270) (*withdrawn from marketing* on 21 November 2003)

- #0123 - #5074 Lower Unit in Rack (810, 820, 825, 830, 840, 870, 890) (*withdrawn from marketing* on 3 December 2002)
- #0125 - #9079 Lower Unit in Rack (840) (*withdrawn from marketing* on 21 November 2003)
- #0127 - 270 Field Install in Rack (270) (*withdrawn from marketing* on 7 May 2003)
- #0133 Plant Install in Rack (270, 800, 810)
- #0134 Field Install in Rack (HD) (825) (*withdrawn from marketing* on 21 November 2003)
- #0137 Field Install in Rack (270, 800, 810)
- #0138 Field Install in Rack (825)
- #0578 PCI Expansion Unit in Rack (810, 820, 825, 830, 840, 870, 890)
- #0588 PCI-X Expansion Unit in Rack (800, 810, 820, 825, 830, 840, 870, 890)
- #0595 PCI-X Expansion Unit in Rack (270, 800, 810, 820, 830, 840, 870, 890)
- #7884 520 Rack Mount

The following features are optional for the #0551 rack:

- #6580 Optional Rack Security Kit
- #7840 Side-by-Side for 1.8m Racks:

One of the following features is required on the #0551:

- #6068 Front Door (black/flat)
- #6246 1.8m Rack Trim

EIA units in a #0551

The marketing configurator does not manage rack space in the #0551 iSeries Rack. Use the following table to determine the number of EIA units required in the #0551 for each iSeries system unit or expansion tower.

System unit or expansion tower	EIA units
3581- xx3, xx7	5
3581- L28	2
3582	4
3583	14
3590	12
3592	10

System unit or expansion tower	EIA units
Model 270 System Unit	16 EIA units (includes one for #0127, 2 for #0133 and #0137)
Model 520 System Unit	4
Model 550 System Unit	4
Model 570 Processor 0/4-way	4
Model 570 Processor 5/8-way	8
Model 570 Processor 9/12-way	12
Model 570 Processor 13/16-way	16
Model 595 Processor Way	18 EIA in a 24-inch Enterprise Rack
Model 800 System Unit	16 EIA units (includes 2 EIA for #0133 and #0137)
Model 810 System Unit	16 EIA units (includes 2 EIA for #0133 and #0137)
Model 825 System Unit	16 EIA units (includes 2 EIA for #0134 and #0138)
Model 870 System Unit	17 EIA in a 24-inch Enterprise Rack
Model 890 System Unit	17 EIA in a 24-inch Enterprise Rack
#0551 iSeries Rack	36
#0578 PCI Expansion Unit in Rack	8
#0588 PCI-X Expansion Unit in Rack	8
#5094 PCI-X Expansion Tower	14
#0595 PCI-X Expansion Unit in Rack	5
#5790 PCI-X Expansion drawer	4 (two can be mounted side by side)
7210-025 External DVD RAM Drive	2 EIA (includes the #8723 rack shelf)
7210-030 External DVD RAM Drive	2 EIA (includes the #8723 rack shelf
7212-102 Tape/Optical Rack Enclosure	1
7310-CR2 HMC rack mountable console	1

For more information about the EIA units used in a rack or tower, refer to the following Web site:

http://www-1.ibm.com/servers/eserver/support/iseries/planning/index.html

Up to four power distribution units may be installed in the #0551. The PDUs may be ordered as part of the initial order or added at a later time. Each PDU has six power sockets that provide power for devices that support the #1422 PDU Line Cord. A country (region)-specific line cord must be ordered for each PDU to connect to external power.

The supported PDUs are:

- #5160 Power Distribution Unit - 1 Phase NEMA
- #5161 Power Distribution Unit - 1 Phase IEC
- #5162 Power Distribution Unit - 2 of 3 Phase
- #5163 Power Distribution Unit - 3 Phase
- #7188 Power Distribution Unit - 1 or 3 Phase

The supported specify codes are:

- #0121 Lower Unit in Rack Specify (270) (*withdrawn from marketing* on 21 November 2003)

- #0122 Upper Unit in Rack Specify (270) (*withdrawn from marketing* on 21 November 2003)

- #0133 Plant Install in Rack

  - The #0133 Plant Install in Rack feature is used to mount a Model 270, 800 or 810 system unit (sidecar feature must be present) in a #0551 rack either in the plant or in the field.

  - The #0133 Plant Install in Rack is IBM installed in the plant or client installed in the field.

  - The #0133 can be ordered on initial orders, MES orders, or model upgrades into the Model 810.

  - If the system order received at the plant contains a system unit, sidecar feature (#7104 or #7116), #0551 rack, and the #0133, the system is mounted in the #0551 at the plant. If any of these four components are missing from the order, the system is *not* mounted in the #0551 at the plant.

  - It the system is not installed in a #0551 in the plant, the #0133 feature provides the hardware components: a set of "slides", cable management arm, a heavy duty tray, a 270/800/810 adapter plate, and a pair of 270/800/810 lift covers. The #0133 is client installed in the field.

  - A line cord is required for both the system unit and system unit expansion.

  > **Note:** For system units being mounted in the upper portions of a rack and *not* using the #1422 PDU cord, be sure the line cord (and SPCN cable, if present) is of sufficient length.

- An #0551 iSeries Rack is required for mounting a Model 270, 800, or 810, but the #0551 is not required on the order or on the inventory records for the system that is ordering an #0133 Plant Install in Rack.

► #0134 Field Install in Rack (HD)

- The #0134 is used to mount a Model 825 system unit in a #0551 iSeries Rack.

- The #0134 was *withdrawn from marketing* on 21 November 2003.

► #0137 Field Install in Rack

- The #0137 Field Install in Rack is an IBM installed feature.

- The #0137 Field Install in Rack feature is used to mount a Model 270, 800 or 810 system unit (sidecar feature #7104 or #7116 must be present) in a #0551 rack in the field. This feature provides a set of "slides", cable management "arm", a heavy duty ray, a 270, 800, or 810 adapter plate, and a pair of 270/800/810 lift covers.

- The #0137 may be specified on any type of order (initial, model upgrades into a Model 810 or simple MES).

- A line cord is required for both the system unit and system unit expansion.

> **Note:** For system units being mounted in the upper portions of a rack and not using the #1422 PDU cord, be sure the line cord (and SPCN cable, if present) is of sufficient length.

- An #0551 iSeries Rack is required for mounting a Model 270, 800 or 810, but the #0551 is not required on the order or on the inventory records for the system that is ordering a #0137 Field Install in Rack.

► #0138 Field Install in Rack

- The #0138 Field Install in Rack is an IBM installed feature.

- The #0138 Field Install in Rack feature is used to mount a Model 825 system unit in a #0551 rack. This feature provides a set of "slides", cable management "arm", a tray, an 825 adapter plate and a pair of 825 lift covers.

- The #0138 may be specified on any type of order (initial, model upgrade or simple MES).

> **Note:** For system units being mounted in the upper portions of a rack and not using the #1422 PDU cord, be sure the line cord (and SPCN cable, if present) is of sufficient length.

- An #0551 iSeries Rack is required for mounting a Model 825, but the #0551 is not required on the order or on the inventory records for the system that is ordering a #0138 Field Install in Rack.

► #0123 - #5074 Lower Unit in Rack Specify (*withdrawn from marketing* on 03 December 2002)

► #0125 - #9079 Lower Unit in Rack Specify (*withdrawn from marketing* on 07 May 2003)

► #0127 270 Field Install in Rack Specify (*withdrawn from marketing* on 07 May 2003)

#0553 2.0m Rack

The #0553 2.0m Rack is a 19-inch wide two meter high rack which contains 42 EIA units of space. The #0553 can be ordered as a feature of an @server i5 or iSeries server as part of an initial order or added at a later time.

The following features specify the means of populating the #0553 rack:

► #0133 Plant Install in Rack
► #0137 Field Install in Rack
► #0138 Field Install in Rack
► #0578 PCI Expansion Unit in Rack
► #0588 PCI-X Expansion Unit in Rack
► #0595 PCI-X Tower Unit in Rack
► #7884 520 Rack Mount

One of the following features is required on the #0553:

► #6069 - Optional Front Door for 2.0m Rack
► #6247 - Enhanced No Door Trim Kit
► #6249 - 2.0m Rack Acoustic Door

The optional features for the #0553 rack are:

► #6580 - Optional Rack Security Kit
► #7780 - 2.0m Rack Side Attach Kit
► #7841 - Ruggedize Rack Kit (Brace, Bolt Down Hardware, Metal Filler Panels)

The IBM marketing configurator does not manage rack space in the #0553 iSeries Rack. Use the table on page 276 to determine the number of EIA units required in the #0553 for each @server i5 or iSeries system unit and expansion towers. Mixing of different system models within a single #0553 is not allowed on initial order systems.

The #0553 can support up to nine power distribution units (PDU), four mounted vertically and five mounted horizontally. The PDUs may be ordered on initial

orders, model upgrades, or on MES orders. Each #5160, #5161, #5162 and #5163 PDU has six power sockets and the #7188 PDU has 12 power sockets that can be used to provide power for devices rack mounted in the #0553 iSeries rack using the #1422 or #6458 PDU Line Cord. Only #7188 PDUs can be mixed with other PDU features, otherwise, no mixing of PDU features within a #0553 or on a system is allowed. Horizontally mounted PDUs occupy 1EIA of rack space.

The PDUs that are supported on the #0553 are:

► #5160 Power Distribution Unit 1 Phase NEMA

These line cords are supported on the #5160 for connection to utility power:

- #1424 - 200V 6-ft. Locking Line Cord
- #1425 - 200V 6-ft. Watertight Line Cord
- #1426 - 200V 14-ft. Locking Line Cord
- #1427 - 200V 14-ft. Watertight Line Cord
- #1446 - 4.3m 200V/30A Power Cord Korea
- #1447 - 4.3m 200V/30A Power Cord AU
- #1448 - 4.3m 200V/30A Power Cord NZ

► #5161 Power Distribution Unit 1 Phase

This line cord is supported on the #5161 for connection to utility power:

- #1449 - 4.3m 200V/32A Power Cord EU 1-Phase

► #5162 Power Distribution Unit 2 of 3 Phase

This line cord is supported on the #5162 for connection to utility power:

- #1450- 4.3m 200V/16A Power Cord EU 2-Phase

► #5163 Power Distribution Unit 3 of 3 Phase

This line cord is supported on the #5163 for connection to utility power:

- #1477 - 200V 16A 14ft. IEC309/46 Line Cord

► #7188 Power Distribution Unit 1 Phase NEMA

The #7188 PDU is the replacement for the #5160, #5161, #5162 and #5163. These line cords are supported on the #7188 to connect to utility power:

- #6489 - 14-ft. 3PH/24A Power Cord
- #6491 - 14-ft. 1PH/63A Power Cord
- #6492 - 14-ft. 1PH/48-60A Power Cord
- #6653 - 14-ft. 3PH/16A Power Cord
- #6654 - 14-ft. 1PH/24-30A Power Cord
- #6655 - 14-ft. 1PH/24-30A Watertight Power Cord
- #6656 - 14-ft. 1PH/32A Power Cord
- #6657 - 14-ft. 3PH/24A Power Cord
- #6658 - 14-ft. 3PH/16A Power Cord Korea

All racked units plugging into a PDU require a PDU line cord, #1422 or #6458. Mixing of different system models within a single #0553 iSeries Rack is not allowed on initial order systems.

PDU features can be ordered without a #0553 rack being ordered or present on the system.

Note: For system units being mounted in the upper portions of a rack and not using the #1422 or #6458 PDU cord, be sure the line cord (and SPCN cable, if present) is of sufficient length.

IBM 9309 Rack Enclosure

The 9309 Rack Enclosures provide operator control panels, acoustic noise reduction, power control to all units within the rack (under the control of the System Unit), and power control to the next rack SPCN chain. All additional racks attached to the system unit are termed "secondary" racks.

iSeries 9406 models support the 9309 Rack Enclosures. External I/O devices, such as direct access storage device (DASD), magnetic tapes, and diskette units, can be accommodated in these 1.6 M racks.

The following 9309 Rack and System Unit Rack Enclosures are supported:

▶ **9309 #9171**: General Purpose I/O Rack with SPCN
▶ **9406 #5044**: System Unit Expansion Rack (9406-5X0 (old models), 620, 640, and 650 models only)

HSL fabric

HSL loops provide redundancy to all attached towers. In addition, the implementation of HSL and OS/400 provide data flow balancing across the loop by assigning communication paths during an initial program load (IPL) to optimize loop throughput based upon loop and tower configurations.

HSL loops can be either copper or optical. Optical provides longer distance, but offers a lower data rate.

▶ With iSeries Models 825, 870, and 890, and with I/O towers, such as the #5094 PCI-X Expansion Tower, #0595/#5095 PCI-X Expansion Tower, and #0588/#5088 PCI-X Expansion Unit, a different copper HSL port is used.

▶ There is no change to the optical HSL loop on Models 825, 870, and 890.

Considerations for loop configurations include:

► Rack mounted Model 520 system units can only attach to HSL-2/RIO-2 cables 2.5m or longer and can only attach to SPCN cables 3m or longer. Shorter cable lengths do not allow the system unit to be pulled out from the rack far enough for concurrent maintenance.

► iSeries Models 825, 870, 890 with OS/400 V5R2 or i5/OS V5R3 do not support HSL-2/RIO-2 even with RIO-G nodes attached. A link between two RIO-G nodes runs at HSL-2/RIO-2 speed only.

► The speed allowed by the two nodes of a link with @server i5 servers attached are:
   – 1 GB/s for RIO-G to RIO-G
   – 500 MB/s for RIO to RIO-G

Due to the high bandwidth of HSL, you should see comparable performance, whether using copper or optical HSL, even though optical runs at a slower speed. However, if you have intensive I/O bandwidth requirements (for example, large system data mining), you may experience some performance degradation with optical HSL. The recommendation is to use less than the allowed maximum number of I/O towers on an optical fiber HSL loop to optimize performance.

HSL was initially implemented at OS/400 V5R1 using copper interconnect cables. These cables allow for high-speed and high-quality parallel data transfer. In August 2001, technology was introduced using optical fibres and optical adapters to interconnect the Central Electronic Complex (CEC) and the towers of the iSeries server.

Copper HSL cables have a higher bandwidth compared to the optical HSL cables. The optical cables are available in longer lengths (up to 250m compared to 15m for copper). Optical HSL cables are smaller and easier to work with, particularly during installation.

The longer optical cable lengths extend the distance between I/O units and the Model 550, 570, 595, 825, 830, 840, 870, and 890 servers from the current 15m to 250m. Expanded I/O location alternatives can help improve data reliability and protection.

The HSL bus structure provides:

► Performance improvements and future system growth
   – Up to 1 GB/s technology with HSL or HSL-2 (copper HSL or HSL-2 cables)
   – Up to 2 GB/s technology with HSL-2/RIO-2 (copper HSL-2 cables) on Models 520, 550, 570, and 595 up to the 10m cable length: Use of the 15m cables on these loops results in reduced speeds.

- ► Simplified implementation

  - – Loop technology for redundancy
  - – Multiple towers per loop
  - – 1.75m, 3m, 6m, 15m copper HSL cables
  - – 6m, 30m, 100m 250m optical HSL cables
  - – 4m,10m, 15m copper HSL-2 cables
  - – 6m, 10m HSL to HSL-2 cables
  - – Migration tower attachment supports SPD I/O towers and #5065/#5066 Storage/PCI Expansion Towers

- ► Homogeneous HSL network with HSL adapters

  - – Simple HSL clusters (two iSeries)
  - – Complex HSL clusters (three iSeries with OS/400 V5R2 or later)
  - – xSeries for iSeries HSL connectivity
  - – Switchable HSL connected tower with IASP

Note: Servers and I/O towers can be on the same copper loop, whether the connection is HSL or HSL-2. The appropriate HSL cabling must be used.

For more information about HSL configuration per model, see the product sections within this book. You can find the base rules for tower placement in the *IBM @server iSeries and AS/400e System Builder*, SG24-2155. For HSL rules and migration considerations, see *IBM @server iSeries Migration: System Migration and Upgrades at V5R1 and V5R2*, SG24-6055.

The following figure shows the HSL connectivity of loops.

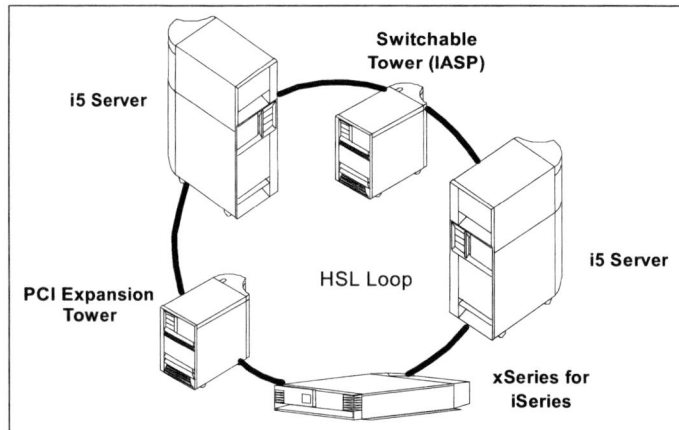

HSL OptiConnect

In system complexes that contain only V5R1 HSL hardware, the HSL OptiConnect loop implementation consists of loops that may contain up to four PCI/PCI-X I/O towers and units or external xSeries servers between two iSeries servers. The same is also true for OS/400 V5R2 scenarios. However, V5R2 allows for three iSeries servers to be connected on an HSL OptiConnect loop. When there are three iSeries servers on a loop, there cannot be any I/O towers or external xSeries servers on that loop.

In an HSL OptiConnect loop, external xSeries servers count against the per loop tower limits. Depending on the number of towers and I/O operations performed in these towers, overall system performance may be impacted.

HSL copper

@server i5 models have HSL-2/RIO-2 ports to serve loops at a maximum speed of 2 GB per second. Only a limited number of towers can be enabled for this higher speed.

See "Summary of the iSeries expansion units and towers" on page 119 for the maximum number of features supported in each iSeries expansion tower.

The #5094, #5294, #0595 and #5095 towers can be converted to HSL-2/RIO-G. The #5088/#0588 have an HSL-2 interface, but cannot be upgraded to the new HSL-2/RIO-2 interface. The #5075 and #0578/#5078 have an HSL adapter. They are not supported on @server i5 models.

New #5094, #5294, #5095 and #0595 towers ship with a #9517 Base HSL-2/RIO-G Bus Adapter for attachment to the @server i5 models. Existing #5094, #0595, #5095 and #5294 towers that attach to an @server i5 model using copper HSL cabling must have the HSL-2 adapters exchanged for a #6417 HSL-2/RIO-G Bus Adapter.

Connecting supported HSL, HSL-2 and HSL-2/RIO-2 is possible with the correct combination of cables. However, one adapter or cable in the loop can slow down the complete loop. If this is necessary, we recommend that you keep these items on one loop so that you do not slow down the HSL-2/RIO-2 loop if applicable.

> **Note:** HSL-2 also supports HSL towers (such as #5074 or #5079) in the loop. However, mixing these towers with HSL-2 in the same loop slows down faster devices.

The following table identifies the HSL cables, which can be attached directly to each iSeries server. See "Summary of today's iSeries" on page 79 for the maximum number of HSL features supported by each iSeries server.

Cable feature	270	520	550	570	595	800 810	820	825	830 840	870 890
Copper										
#1307 -1.75m Copper HSL-2 Cable		X^5	X	X	X			X		X
#1308 -2.5m Copper HSL-2 Cable		X	X	X	X			X		X
#1460 - 3m Copper HSL Cable	X					X	X		X	
#1461 - 6m Copper HSL Cable	X					X	X		X	
#1462 - 15m Copper HSL Cable	Note 2						Note 2		X	
#1474 - 6m HSL to HSL-2 Cable	X	X	X	X	X	X	X	X	X	X
#1475 - 10m HSL to HSL-2 Cable		X	X	X	X			X	X	X
#1481 - 1m HSL-2 Cable		X^5	X^5	X	X					
#1482 - 3.5m HSL-2 Cable		X	X	X	X			X		X
#1483 - 10m HSL-2 Cable		X	X	X	X			X		X
#1485 - 15m HSL-2 Cable[6]		X	X	X	X			X		X
Fiber optic[1]										
#1470 - 6m Optical HSL Cable			X	X	X			X	X	X
#1471 - 30m Optical HSL Cable			X	X	X			X	X	X
#1472 - 100m Optical HSL Cable			X	X	X			X	X	X
#1473 - 250m Optical HSL Cable			X	X	X			X	X	X
SPCN[3]										
#1463 - 2m SPCN Cable	X	X	X	X	X	X	X	X	X	X
#1464 - 6m SPCN Cable	X	X	X	X	X	X	X	X	X	X
#1465 - 15m SPCN Cable	X	X	X	X	X	X	X	X	X	X
#1466 - 30m SPCN Cable	X	X	X	X	X	X	X	X	X	X
#1468 - 250m Optical SPCN Cable	X		X	X	X		X	X	X	X
#0369 100m Optical SPCN Cable	X		X	X	X		X	X	X	X
#6001 Power Control Cable - 2M				X^4						

Cable feature	270	520	550	570	595	800 810	820	825	830 840	870 890
#6006 Power Control Cable - 3M		X	X	X	X					
#6007 Power Control Cable - 15M		X	X	X	X					
#6008 Power Control Cable - 6M		X	X	X	X					
#6029 Power Control Cable - 30M		X	X	X	X					

[1] A fiber optic cable requires a base or feature optical HSL port card in the system.
[2] Not supported on the A1 port of the Model 270 or 820. Is supported on the A0 port.
[3] Fiber optic SPCN cables include two copper to fiber adapter, p/n 90H6827.
4 Cannot be plugged into a rack mounted model 520.

The following table identifies the HSL cables, which can be attached directly to each iSeries supported expansion tower. See "Summary of the iSeries expansion units and towers" on page 119 for the maximum number of HSL features supported in each iSeries expansion tower.

Cable feature	#5074	#5075	#5078 #0578	#5079 #8079	IXA card	#5094 #9094	#5095 #0595	#5088 #0588	#5294 #8094	#5790
Copper										
#1307 -1.75m Copper HSL-2 Cable						X	X[3]	X[3]	X	X
#1308 -2.5m Copper HSL-2 Cable						X	X	X	X	X
#1460 - 3m Copper HSL Cable	X	X	X	X	X					X
#1461 - 6m Copper HSL Cable	X	X	X	X	X					
#1462 - 15m Copper HSL Cable	X	X	X	X	X					
#1474 - 6m HSL to HSL-2 Cable	X	X	X	X	X	X	X	X	X	X
#1475 - 10m HSL to HSL-2 Cable	X	X	X	X	X	X	X	X	X	X
#1482 - 3.5m HSL-2 Cable						X	X	X	X	X
#1483 - 10m HSL-2 Cable						X	X	X	X	X
#1485 - 15m HSL-2 Cable						X	X	X	X	X
Fiber optic[1]										
#1470 - 6m Optical HSL Cable	X		X	X		X	X	X	X	
#1471 - 30m Optical HSL Cable	X		X	X		X	X	X	X	

Cable feature	#5074	#5075	#5078 #0578	#5079 #8079	IXA card	#5094 #9094	#5095 #0595	#5088 #0588	#5294 #8094	#5790
#1472 - 100m Optical HSL Cable	X		X	X		X	X	X	X	
#1473 - 250m Optical HSL Cable	X		X	X		X	X	X	X	
SPCN [2,4]										
#1463 - 2m SPCN Cable	X	X	X	X	X	X	X	X	X	X
#1464 - 6m SPCN Cable	X	X	X	X	X	X	X	X	X	X
#1465 - 15m SPCN Cable	X	X	X	X	X	X	X	X	X	X
#1466 - 30m SPCN Cable	X	X	X	X	X	X	X	X	X	X
#1468 - 250m Optical SPCN Cable	X		X	X		X	X	X	X	
#0369 100m Optical SPCN Cable	X		X	X		X	X	X	X	
#6001 Power Control Cable - 2M	X	X	X	X	X	X[3]	X[3]	X[3]	X	
#6006 Power Control Cable - 3M	X	X	X	X	X	X	X	X	X	X
#6007 Power Control Cable - 15M	X	X	X	X	X	X	X	X	X	X
#6008 Power Control Cable - 6M	X	X	X	X	X	X	X	X	X	X
#6029 Power Control Cable - 30M	X	X	X	X	X	X	X	X	X	X

1 Optical cable requires a base or feature optical HSL port card in the tower.
2 Fiber optic SPCN cables include two copper to fiber adapter, p/n 90H6827.
3 Cannot be used on rack mounted towers.
4 On Models 520,550,570, and 595, SPCN cabling must be a single closed loop across all I/O towers/drawers.
5 Cannot be plugged into rack mounted Model 520 system unit.
6 Use when greater distance is required. Performance can be degraded.

The following table identifies the HSL loop maximums.

System maximums	270	520 550	570	595	800	810	820	825	830	840	870	890
HSL loops	1	2	8	24	1	1	1	3	4	8	8	14
HSL loops supporting fiber optic cables	0	0	1		0	0	0	2	1	2	6	12
I/O units	1	6	30	60	1	4	5	18	13	23	47	47
Integrated xSeries Adapter cards in xSeries towers	2	8	60		3	7	8	18	16	60	60	60
I/O units and Integrated xSeries Adapter cards	3	9	48		4	8	9	27	21	60	60	60
HSL OptiConnect loops	1	1	8		1	1	1	2	2	4	8	12
HSL migration tower	0	0	0	0	0	0	1	0	1	1	0	0
HSL loop maximums												
I/O units	1	6	6	6	1	4	5	6	6	6	6	6
Integrated xSeries Adapter cards in xSeries towers	2	8	8		3	7	8	8 [1]	8 [2]	8 [2]	8	8
I/O units and Integrated xSeries Adapter cards	3	9	9		4	8	9	9	9	9	9	9
HSL OptiConnect loop: Two systems												
I/O units and Integrated xSeries Adapter cards	4				4	4	4	4	4	4	4	4
HSL OptiConnect loop: Three systems												
I/O units and Integrated xSeries Adapter cards	N/A				N/A	N/A	N/A	0	0	0	0	0

Notes: I/O unit maximums do not include the base I/O tower attached to Models 840, 870, and 890. An I/O unit contains two HSL ports (0 and 1). The #5079 and #5294 I/O towers have two I/O units.
[1] Model 825: Maximum of five Integrated xSeries Adapters on loops A and C. Maximum on loop B is eight.
[2] Models 830 and 840: Maximum of eight Integrated xSeries Adapters. Limit on first loop is one, 0 if with migration tower.

Due to the high bandwidth of HSL, you should see comparable performance, whether using copper or optical HSL, even though optical runs at a slower speed. However, for intensive I/O bandwidth requirements (for example, large system data mining), you may experience some performance degradation with optical HSL. Use less than the allowed maximum number of I/O towers on an optical HSL loop to optimize performance.

OS/400 V5R1 and supporting PTFs are required. Refer to Informational APAR II12949 at:

`http://www-912.ibm.com/n_dir/nas4apar.nsf/nas4aparhome`

eServer i5 Models 520, 550, 570, and 595 tower and drawer support

This section identifies the towers and drawers supported on @server i5 Models 520, 550, 570, and 595. The following table assumes the maximum number of processor features to support the maximum number of loops. The maximum number of towers may be less on other processor features supporting a lower maximum number of loops.

A base I/O tower, where applicable to a model is not included in these maximum values.

Tower/drawer	520	550	570				595		
Number of loops	1	2	2	4	6	8	6	12	24
Towers	6	12	12	18	24	30	36^1	60^1	60^1
IXA (1519-100)	8	16	16	32	48	57	48	57	57
IXA (1519-200)	8	16	16	32	48	57	48	57	57
7040-61D*	0	0	0	0	0	0	4	4	4
7311-D10*	0		8	8	8	8			
7311-D11*	6		12	18	24	30			
7311-D20*	6		12	18	24	30			
Combined totals	9	18	18	36	54	60	36^1	60^1	60^1

* AIX and Linux partition only. Available for the purpose of consolidating existing @server p5 servers. The @server i5 and iSeries Marketing Configurator does not support the configuration of these towers.

- Includes the primary I/O tower

IBM i5/OS on eServer p5

@server p5 enables clients to run relatively large AIX 5L workloads along side a small amount of i5/OS workload. Many @server p5 I/O components are different from @server i5 I/O components. For example, i5/OS uses an IOP, and disk drives on @server i5 models are formatted differently and have additional function than disk drives on @server p5 servers. The i5/OS V5R3 operating system, for @server i5, runs on @server p5 servers to support @server i5 I/O. Each @server p5 partition acts as a separate i5/OS server.

i5/OS support on @server p5 servers is facilitated through the use of a 9411-100 @server p5 I/O subsystem for i5/OS. The 9411-100 allows clients who use the @server p5 model to consolidate i5/OS workloads onto their server. The 9411-100 is ordered for each @server p5 server running i5/OS to facilitate hardware feature orders for the I5/OS partitions.

The i5/OS operating system that runs on @server p5 servers is the same as i5/OS that runs on @server i5 servers. Since the @server i5 and @server p5 are built with the same POWER5 processors and server technology, i5/OS applications that run on @server i5 can run on @server p5 unchanged.

For a list of ISV applications that are available on i5/OS see:

http://www-1.ibm.com/servers/eserver/iseries/solutions/v5r3ready/

9411-100 eServer p5 I/O Subsystem for i5/OS

The 9411-100 @server p5 I/O Subsystem for i5/OS provides a machine type and model with prices, warranty, and service identical to that provided for the same I/O features on a @server i5 model. The 9411-100 i5/OS I/O is basically an administrative holder of @server i5 I/O that is attached to @server p5.

> **Note:** From an IBM marketing configurator view, i5/OS support on the @server p5 is like having a machine type for a subsystem. Each tower, drawer, adapter, and DASD is a feature of the subsystem machine type.

The 9411-100 is the structure under which the 5250 OTLP capability is ordered. Like the iSeries, each Enterprise Enablement feature provides one processor authorization of 5250 Online Transaction Processing (OLTP) capacity.

There is a maximum of one 9411-100 for each @server p5 server. A unique 9411-100 serial number is associated with a specific @server p5 server and stays with that server. It cannot be transferred to a different @server p5 serial number. All the I/O features associated with the 9411-100, with the exception of

the Enterprise Enablement feature, may be transferred to another 9411-100 associated with a different @server p5 server.

The 9411-100 uses the same hardware feature codes as used for the 9406 @server i5 machine type. If a @server p5 client has all the iSeries I/O they need, the 9411-100 starts as an empty model. The IBM administrative system transfers the existing @server i5 I/O features into this 9411-100. New @server i5 I/O features are ordered against the 9411.

The 9411-100 provides the I/O for any i5/OS partitions running on a 1.65 GHz @server p5 570, 590, or 595 server. Specifically, the 9411-100 is supported on the following @server p5 models:

► The 1.65 GHz 9117 570 supports one processor worth of i5/OS workload.
► The 1.65 GHz 9119 590 and 595 supports up to two processors worth of i5/OS workload.

The I/O maximums for a 9411 are consistent with an @server i5 Model 570:

► 270 disk drives
► 19 TB disk storage
► 18 Integrated xSeries Servers
► Eight Integrated xSeries Adapters
► 84 PCI slots

    – 192 communication lines
    – 36 LAN ports
    – 48 twinax controllers

► 12 internal DVD/CD/tape drives

The minimum configuration for a 94100 is:

► One IOP in an iSeries I/O tower or drawer
► One disk controller for a load source drive

For more information, see iSeries planning in the Information Center at:

http://www.ibm.com/eserver/iseries/infocenter

When you reach this site, select **Language** →**V5R3** →**Planning**.

1519-100, 1519-200 Integrated xSeries Adapter for iSeries (direct attach)

The IBM Integrated xSeries Adapter for iSeries provides a direct high-speed attachment (HSL) of an xSeries server to an iSeries server and installs in select xSeries servers. The Integrated xSeries Adapter extends iSeries integration with Windows 2000, Windows Server 2003, Linux RedHat Enterprise 3 (AS or ES)

and SUSE LINUX Enterprise Server 8 to xSeries high performance n-way Intel architecture servers. With the Integrated xSeries Adapter, more Windows users and more complex Windows and Linux applications can be integrated with iSeries servers.

There are two models of the Integrated xSeries Adapter, 1519-100 and 1519-200. These two Integrated xSeries Adapter models provide the same function, but they are designed to work with different xSeries models. The 1519-100 plugs into selected 3U, 4U, 5U n-way xSeries servers. The 1519-200 plugs into rack-optimized (2U) xSeries x236 and x346 servers. Make sure you use the Integrated xSeries Adapter model that is designed to work with your choice of xSeries server.

The direct attach server consists of an xSeries server tower that contains a 1519 Model 100 or 200 Integrated xSeries Adapter for iSeries. The 1519 reports to the iSeries Hardware Service Manager as CCIN 2689.

The external xSeries server has SPCN control. SPCN cabling for the external xSeries server follows the same rules as SPCN cabling for existing HSL-attached towers.

The iSeries and @server i5 servers and features require OS/400 V5R2 or i5/OS V5R3. The iSeries Integration for Windows Server licensed program 5722-WSV provides the necessary software and device drivers that enable Windows Server to run on the Integrated xSeries Adapter server. 5722-WSV is included with all i5/OS shipments. Refer to page 547 for iSeries Windows integration and Microsoft Cluster Support.

The external xSeries server attaches to Models 270, 520, 550, 570, 595, 800, 810, 820, 825, 830, 840, 870, and 890 servers via a copper HSL. Optical HSL is not supported.

The number of Integrated xSeries Servers and Integrated xSeries Adapters that can be attached varies by model, HSL loops, and number of I/O towers. For example, the Model 810 supports up to 13 Integrated xSeries Servers and seven Integrated xSeries Adapters. The Model 890 supports up to 48 Integrated xSeries Servers and 60 Integrated xSeries Adapters.

Refer to the xSeries servers maximums table on page 304 for the maximum external xSeries servers by model.

Refer to the HSL system maximums table on page 304 for the maximum external xSeries servers per HSL loop on each iSeries model.

For performance and stability reasons, place the external xSeries servers on their own loop, if possible, or in the middle of an HSL loop. That is, place the

external xSeries server between the end of the HSL strings (redundant part of the loop) that attach to each HSL port.

We recommend that no I/O tower should communicate with the system by having its data flow through an external xSeries server.

Do not surround any I/O tower with Integrated xSeries Adapters. Switched towers are required to be adjacent to the alternate system or a tower owned by the alternate system. If an external xSeries server must be on a loop with a switched tower, place the external xSeries server so it does not communicate with the system through a private tower.

Each external xSeries server is independent of the number of internal Integrated xSeries Servers and Integrated Netfinity Servers.

The PTF prerequisites for the 1519-200 Integrated xSeries Adapter are:

► i5/OS V5R3 requires cumulative PTF package C4209530 and MF33542 or supersede.

► OS/400 V5R2 requires cumulative PTF package C4077520 and MF33655 or supersede.

You can find additional information about PTF requirements for the Integrated xSeries Adapter on the Web at:

`http://www-912.ibm.com/e_dir/eServerPrereq.nsf`

For xSeries server requirements, supported models, and Windows integration, go to:

`http://www-1.ibm.com/servers/eserver/iseries/integratedxseries/windows/`

For Linux enablement on the Integrated xSeries Adapter, see:

`http://www-1.ibm.com/servers/eserver/iseries/integratedxseries/linux/`

Ordering information

The HSL adapter for the xSeries is ordered as machine type 1519 Models 100 or 200. It is supported as a *peripheral* in the marketing configurator. The marketing configurator uses the #0092 External xSeries Attach to ensure that the correct type and number of cables are on the order.

16

Upgrades to eServer i5 and i5/OS

Use the IBM @server i5 Prerequisite tool to find compatibility information for hardware and software features for @server i5 520, 550, 570, and 595 processors. Find this tool at:

`http://www-912.ibm.com/e_dir/eServerPrereq.nsf`

The term *upgrade* in this chapter refers to a change or enhancement to an existing server, which can result in a more powerful server, but has the same machine type and serial number. An extensive set of upgrades to iSeries servers is supported both to a different model and within an existing model.

The following table shows an overview of the supported upgrades between and within IBM @server i5 and iSeries models. The information is current as of 1 October 2004.

From Model	To Model								
	520	550	570	595	800	810	825	870	890
Model 270						Y			
Model 520	Y								
Model 550		Y							
Model 570			Y	Y					
Model 595				Y					
Model 800					Y				
Model 810	Y*	Y	Y*			Y			
Model 820	Y*	Y	Y*			Y	Y	Y	
Model 825		Y	Y*	Y			Y	Y	
Model 830	Y	Y	Y*	Y			Y	Y	Y
Model 840			Y*	Y				Y	Y
Model 870			Y*	Y				Y	Y
Model 890			Y*	Y					Y
* Restrictions apply									

Model upgrades into the 520, 550, 570, and 595 consist of a processor-to-server upgrade and either an edition-to-edition or an interactive-to-edition conversion. Model upgrades within Models 800, 810, 825, 870, and 890 consist of a processor-to-processor upgrade and a package-to-package upgrade as appropriate.

Upgrade considerations

Because there are differences in the physical packaging and underlying technologies of the newer iSeries models, upgrades within or into these iSeries models can involve a change to the system unit and input/output (I/O). Newer hardware and applications can require newer levels of software. Careful planning can minimize time, effort, change impact, and business cost.

Upgrades into the Model 520, 550, 570, and 595 use a *9406* machine designator to allow IBM to better support the server. There is no physical difference between the machine types for these models. Planning and configuration tools can be

used for configuration analysis by bypassing the difference in the 9402, 9404, or 9406 machine type designation. Refer to "Product Previews: Closed" on page 66 for planning information about upgrades using a 9402 or 9404 machine type designation.

> **Note:** IBM plans to use the same serial number in a *9402/9404 upgrade* even though the machine type designation changes to a *9406*. Clients should anticipate the change to a combined machine type/serial number as an identifier and make appropriate arrangements in the client asset tracking system. A special process will apply in the unlikely event that a 9406 already has the same serial number. You can find additional ordering process information in RPQ 847192.

Supported model upgrades for @server i5 and iSeries models are identified in the *Upgrade* topic of the Find and Compare Tool (FACT) at:

`http://www-919.ibm.com/servers/eserver/fact/`

Refer to "Planning information" on page 71 and "Withdrawn products" on page 75 to understand upgrade considerations. Refer to *IBM @server iSeries Migration: System Migration and Upgrades at V5R1 and V5R2*, SG24-6055, for guidance about upgrading to iSeries server models.

For software upgrade considerations, see "Supported software upgrade paths" on page 320, and "Current release to previous release support" on page 321. For considerations when upgrading to i5/OS V5R3, see:

`http://www-1.ibm.com/servers/eserver/iseries/support/planning/v5r3software.html`

For considerations when upgrading to OS/400 V5R2, see:

`http://www-1.ibm.com/servers/eserver/iseries/support/planning/v5r2software.html`

5250 OLTP considerations

iSeries 5250 online transaction processing (OLTP) is a powerful, efficient, and reliable transaction processor that is used by many clients. If upgrading to the Model 520, 550, 570, 595, 810, 825, 870, or 890 with an Enterprise Edition, a maximum 5250 CPW is offered. The server's entire resources are available for 5250 OLTP applications if desired. The High Availability and Capacity BackUp Editions also provide maximum 5250 CPW.

A Model 520, 550, 570, 595, 810, 825, 870, or 890 with a Standard Edition has zero 5250 commercial processing workload (CPW). The maximum 5250 CPW is available with an upgrade from a Standard to Enterprise Edition. Many additional

software, hardware, services, and education components are included in the Enterprise Edition. However, the additional components are not included during a Standard Edition upgrade to an Enterprise Edition.

The iSeries 820, 830, 840, and 890 processors that were announced in 2002 without an Enterprise Edition, as well as earlier AS/400e models, use a set of specific 5250 CPW points designated by a 5250 interactive feature code. Clients are encouraged to review current 5250 CPW utilization with PM eServer™ iSeries, Management Central, PATROL for iSeries – Predict, or Performance Tools for iSeries.

You can find further information about 5250 CPW in Chapter 3, "Workload, capacity, and performance" on page 39.

Hardware migration considerations

When migrating to iSeries models from earlier models, keep the following considerations in mind:

► Model 520, 550, 570, and 595 processor features require IBM i5/OS V5R3.

► Some upgrades require a two-step approach to reach the requested model. An upgrade is performed via an intervening processor model or edition.

► Main storage features of one model typically cannot be used in a different model. However, some Model 810 and 825 main storage features can be used in the Model 520, 550, or 570 if quad rules for these systems are fulfilled.

► Memory in the #2469 2-way Model 810 processor is not compatible and does not migrate to the Model 550 or 570. See the diagram at right for the memory that can be reused when upgrading to @server i5 servers.

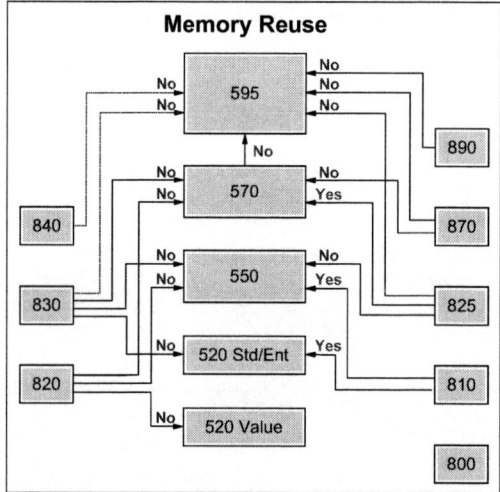

Memory Reuse

► Some features supported on earlier models cannot be ordered on new Models 520, 550, 570, 595, 800, 810, 825, 870, or 890.

► When upgrading existing I/O towers (see the following figure):

– Integrated xSeries Adapters in #5074, #5079, #5078, #0588 remain *as is.*

– Integrated xSeries Adapters and SPD I/O are not supported in #5078, #0578, and #5075.

– The #5094, #5294, #5095, and #0595 must be enhanced with higher speed high-speed link electronics (#6417 HSL-2/RIO-G Bus Adapter).

Switched I/O tower support is a third quarter 2004 exception.

I/O Tower/Drawer Migration

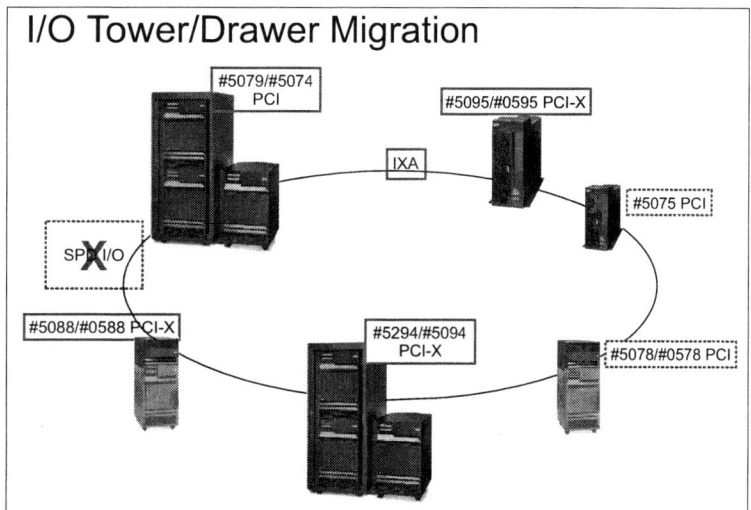

► With the exception of System Products Division (SPD) I/O and migration towers, most I/O supported on OS/400 V5R1 or later on Models 270, 820, 830, or 840 is also supported on Models 520, 550, 570, 595, 800, 810, 825, 870, or 890. Some of the features supported on earlier models cannot be ordered on new servers, but are supported if they are present.

► SPD I/O is not supported by the @server i5 models. Clients running on the 720, 730, 740, 820, 830, and 840 can continue to use their existing SPD I/O when upgrading to i5/OS V5R3. Exceptions are noted in "Products and features no longer marketed by IBM" on page 755, and on the iSeries Upgrade Planning Web site at:

http://www-1.ibm.com/servers/eserver/iseries/support/planning/
v5r3hardware.html

- Most I/O supported on OS/400 V4R1 or later is also supported on Models 820, 830, or 840. SPD I/O is supported when using a migration tower with Models 820, 830, or 840. Refer to "Migration towers" on page 262 for information about migration towers.

- A hardware upgrade to a Model 810, 825, or 870, or to a Model 890 #2497 or #2498 processor, requires the following code as a minimum:
  - February 2003 level of Licensed Internal Code (LIC)
  - OS/400 V5R2 Operating System (5722-SS1)
  - Cumulative PTF package C3021520 or later
  - Model 810 #2465 requires the May 2003 level of LIC or February level of LIC and Cumulative PTF package C3161520 or later

  For the latest information, refer to Informational APAR II13365 at:

  http://www-912.ibm.com/n_dir/nas4apar.nsf/nas4aparhome

- Models 825, 870, and 890 with On/Off Capacity on Demand features require Cumulative PTF package C3077520 or later.

- When upgrading a IBM @server Capacity Upgrade on Demand (CUoD) model to or within a newer Model 825, 870, or 890 CoD model, all interactive (standby) processors must be activated first.

- When upgrading a CUoD model to or within a newer Model 825, 870, or 890 CoD, additional OS/400 licenses must be activated. Additional i5/OS licenses are not required when upgrading to a larger Model 570 processor feature.

- When upgrading from a CoD Model 825, 830, or 870 to a CoD Model 520 or 570, CoD activation is not needed.

- Some features have software requirements. Refer to Informational APAR II13440 on the Web at:

  http://www-912.ibm.com/n_dir/nas4apar.nsf/nas4aparhome

Supported model upgrades are identified in *IBM @server iSeries Supported Upgrades*, REDP-0322. Refer to *IBM @server iSeries Migration: System Migration and Upgrades at V5R1 and V5R2*, SG24-6055, and *IBM @server iSeries Migration: A Guide to Upgrades and Migrations to POWER Technology*, SG24-7200, for a full explanation of migration considerations.

Capacity on Demand upgrades

Considerations when Capacity on Demand configurations are involved in an upgrade include:

► When upgrading from a Model 830 4/8-way to a Model 870 or 890, all eight processors must be active when upgrading.

► When upgrading from a Model 830 4/8-way, 8/12-way, 12/18-way or 18/24-way to a Model 550, 570, or 595:

  – All processor activations are not required.
  – Discounts apply to the purchase of i5 /OS licenses.

► When upgrading from a Model 825 3/6-way or 870 5/8-way to a Model 870 or 890, all processors must be active and OS/400 processor licenses in place for all processors before upgrading.

► When upgrading from a Model 825 3/6-way, 870 5/8-way, 870 5/16-way, 890 16/24-way or 890 24/32-way to a Model 550, 570, or 595:

  – Neither processor activation nor optional OS/400 licenses are required.
  – Model 825 OS/400 processor licenses can be used on the Model 550.
  – Model 825 or 870 OS/400 processor licenses can be used on the Model 570.

► When upgrading within Models, 550, 570 and 595 Capacity on Demand models:

  – All processors must be active.
  – i5/OS licenses are not required.
  – Purchase of an i5/OS license is required when upgrading from a Model 570 1/2-way or 5/8-way into the Model 570 5/8-way, 9/12-way or 13/16-way.

Edition upgrades

Considerations when Edition configurations are involved in an upgrade include:

► Upgrades from non-edition servers to edition servers are eligible for the content of the full edition.

► Upgrades from edition servers are eligible only for i5/OS or OS/400 content and 5250 capacity.

► The High Availability edition must be converted to the Enterprise Edition prior to an upgrade. No additional content is offered for the conversion.

► The Model 800 Value to Standard and Standard to Advanced Edition allow only for 5250 capacity for the upgrade.

- Upgrades from the 520 Value Edition to any other Edition are not supported.

- The iSeries for Domino (iSeries Models 810 and 825) leverage the Standard Edition and, therefore, can be upgraded to any of the supported Standard or Enterprise Edition offerings.

- Model upgrades into the Model 550 Domino or Solution Editions are not available.

- Upgrades from the Model 550 Domino Edition to the Enterprise Edition are not available.

RISC-to-RISC Data Migration (#0205)

The #0205 RISC-to-RISC Data Migration specify code is used when a client orders a new iSeries server to replace an existing RISC-based AS/400e or iSeries server. The #0205 is used when the new server has a different serial number, but is not an upgrade.

The #0205 specify code is orderable on the initial order of an iSeries Model 520, 550, 570, 595, 800, 810, 820, 825, 830, 840, 870, or 890. IBM manufacturing loads the System Licensed Internal Code (SLIC) through QSYS of OS/400 when the #0205 specify code is ordered. This limited code load allows data, profiles, user interface customizing, and so on to be moved from the existing server to the new server with less effort.

Using the #0205 specify code means that any new and additional software that might preloaded by IBM is now loaded by the client after the information from the original server is moved over.

Upgrade options for expansion towers

Converting the #5065, #5066, and #5075 PCI Expansion Tower allows you to upgrade to newer, faster, and higher function HSL-attached I/O towers. Conversions are available for:

- #5065 Storage/PCI Expansion Tower to #5074 PCI Expansion Tower
- #5066 1.8 M I/O Tower to #5079 1.8 M I/O Tower
- #5075 PCI Expansion Tower to #5074 PCI Expansion Tower

While most features from the expansion towers are supported in the new towers, many require no-charge feature conversions because the feature number is different in the new tower. Those features not supported in the new towers must be re-installed in the system unit or replaced with a new feature.

The no-charge feature conversions in the following table are available to move features from the #5065/#5066 towers to PCI or PCI-X towers and expansion units in iSeries Models 520, 550, 570, 595, 810, 820, 825, 830, 840, 870, and 890.

From feature	To feature	From feature	To feature
#2723	#4723	#9723	#4723
#2745	#4745	#2746	#4746
#2748	#4748	#2750	#4750
#2751	#4751	#2761	#4761
#4748	#4778	#2815	#4815
#2816	#4816	#2818	#4818
#2838	#4838	#4802	#4801

The converted features are physically and functionally identical.

Note: The feature numbers and some names change to designate installation information.

The #5065/#5066 features listed in the following table are not supported in the #5074/#5079 towers. They must be replaced.

From feature	Suggested replacement feature
#2718 PCI Magnetic Media Controller	#2768 PCI Magnetic Media Controller
#2721 PCI Two-line WAN IOA	#4745 PCI 2-line WAN IOA
#2722 Twinaxial Workstation IOA	#4746 PCI Twinaxial IOA
#2724 PCI 16/4 Mbps Token Ring IOA	#2744 PCI 100 Mbps Token Ring IOA
#2729 PCI Magnetic Media Controller	#2749 PCI Ultra Magnetic Media Controller
#2824 PCI Feature Controller	#2843 PCI IOP

The #5075 features listed in the following table are not supported in the #5074 tower. They must be re-installed in the system unit or replaced.

From feature	Suggested replacement feature
#2763 PCI RAID Disk Unit Controller	#4778 PCI RAID Disk Unit Controller
#2842 PCI IOP	#2843 PCI IOP
#9767 Base PCI Disk Unit Controller	#4778 PCI RAID Disk Unit Controller

Supported software upgrade paths

The following table identifies software upgrade paths supported for i5/OS and OS/400.

From OS/400:	To: OS/400 V5R1	OS/400 V5R2	i5/OS V5R3
V3R2			
V4R1			
V4R2			
V4R3			
V4R4	X		
V4R5	X	X	
V5R1		X	X
V5R2			X

Note: OS/400 V4R5 is the last release to offer single step CISC-to-RISC upgrade capabilities from V3R2. For single step CISC-to-RISC upgrades from V3R2, the Enhanced Upgrade Assistant (5798-TBU) was *withdrawn from marketing* as of 8 January 2003. Refer to *AS/400 Road Map for Changing to PowerPC Technology*, SA41-5150.

OS/400 single step upgrades

Single step RISC-to-RISC upgrades are supported as normal upgrade procedures. You can find instructions in the software installation publication that corresponds to the release.

If a new RISC iSeries server replaces an existing RISC iSeries server, order #0205 RISC-to-RISC Data Migration against the hardware to restrict the preload of all software except SLIC and the basic functions of OS/400. This allows the remaining libraries to be migrated from the existing system to the new system.

Current release to previous release support

The following table indicates which target release can be specified when compiling or saving objects on a given i5/OS and OS/400 system.

Values for the TGTRLS parameter			
Current OS/400 release	*Current	*PRV	Other valid values
V5R3	V5R3	V5R2	V5R1
V5R2	V5R2	V5R1	V4R5
V5R1	V5R1	V4R5	V4R4
V4R5	V4R5	V4R4	V4R3, V4R2, V3R2
V4R4	V4R4	V4R3	V4R2, V3R2
V4R3	V4R3	V4R2	V4R1, V3R7, V3R2
V3R7	V3R7	V3R6	V3R2, V3R1, V3R0M5

Software end-of-support dates

With the high quality and reliability of the current i5/OS and OS/400 software releases, users may not recognize the importance of periodic upgrading to stay on a supported operating system release. Each release of OS/400 has a finite support period. After the end of that support period, IBM no longer accepts problems for defect analysis.

The following table lists the dates that OS/400 and associated licensed programs were withdrawn from IBM marketing and program support.

Version/release/ modification	General availability	End of marketing	End of program support	Fee-based support extension
R7.5 SSP	8 March 1996	9 February 1999	31 May 2000	N/A
V3R0.5	3 June 1994	11 February 1997	31 May 1997	N/A
V3R1	30 June 1995	11 February 1997	31 October 1998	N/A
V3R2	21 June 1996	10 February 1998	31 May 2000	N/A
V3R6	29 September 1995	19 August 1997	31 October 1998	N/A
V3R7	8 November 1996	1 September 1998	30 June 1999	N/A
V4R1	29 August 1997	9 February 1999	31 May 2000	N/A
V4R2	27 February 1998	9 February 1999	31 May 2000	31 January 2001
V4R3	11 September 1998	15 February 2000	31 January 2001	N/A
V4R4	21 May 1999	31 May 2001	31 May 2000	30 November 2001
V4R5	28 July 2000	2 July 2002	31 December 2002	N/A
V5R1	25 May 2001	21 November 2003	30 September 2005	N/A
V5R2	30 August 2002	1 October 2005	*	N/A
V5R3	2004	---	*	N/A

* Actual termination date is declared with a minimum of 12-months advanced notice.

17

iSeries PCI I/O processors

@server i5 servers and iSeries servers are designed for business computing. One of the fundamental characteristics of that environment is that it is input/output (I/O)-intensive, rather than compute-intensive. This chapter discusses Peripheral Component Interconnect (PCI) system unit I/O processors (IOP) available from IBM for @server i5 and iSeries servers and associated towers.

Refer to "Migration towers" on page 262 for a discussion of IOPs supported in Migration Towers. Refer to Chapter 18, "iSeries I/O adapters and controllers" on page 337, for I/O adapter (IOA) information. Refer to Chapter 22, "Customer Install Features" on page 453, to identify the CIF status for each supported feature.

This chapter describes the PCI IOPs that are supported by current @server i5 and iSeries models.

Embedded 32 MB PCI IOP (CCIN 286x)

On the Model 800, a 32 MB PCI IOP (CCIN 286C) is embedded on the backplane.

For the Model 810 #2465 processor, the embedded IOP is CCIN 286D. For the Model 810 #2466 processor, the embedded IOP is CCIN 286D. For the Model 810 #2467 and #2469 processors, the embedded IOP is CCIN 286E.

#2842 PCI IOP

The #2842 PCI IOP is an I/O processor with 32 MB of memory that drives PCI IOA adapters on the Model 810. The #2842 is supported on the Model 810 and the #5095 PCI-X Expansion Tower.

The #5075 PCI Expansion Tower has a 32 MB PCI IOP (CCIN 284B) embedded on the backplane.

These IOAs are supported by the embedded PCI IOP on Models 800 and 810, the #5075, and the #2842 PCI IOP:

- ▶ #2742 Two-Line WAN IOA
- ▶ #2743 1 Gbps PCI Ethernet IOA
- ▶ #2744 PCI 100 Mbps Token Ring IOA
- ▶ #2749 PCI Ultra Magnetic Media Controller
- ▶ #2757 PCI-X Ultra RAID Disk Controller
- ▶ #2760 PCI 1 Gbps Ethernet UTP Adapter
- ▶ #2763 PCI RAID Disk Unit Controller (*withdrawn from marketing* on 21 November 2003)
- ▶ #2765 PCI Fibre Channel Tape Controller
- ▶ #2766 PCI Fibre Channel Disk Controller
- ▶ #2768 PCI Magnetic Media Controller
- ▶ #2772/#2773 PCI Dual WAN/Modem IOA
- ▶ #2793/#9793 Two-Line WAN IOA with Modem
- ▶ #2794/#9794 Two-Line IOA with Modem
- ▶ #2782 PCI-X RAID Disk Unit Controller (*withdrawn from marketing* on 01 January 2004)
- ▶ #2787 PCI-X Fibre Channel Disk Controller
- ▶ #2805/#2806 Quad Modem Adapter
- ▶ #2817 PCI 155 Mbps MMF ATM IOA
- ▶ #2849 10/100 Mbps Ethernet Adapter
- ▶ #4723 PCI 10 Mbps Ethernet Adapter
- ▶ #4745 PCI 2-line WAN IOA
- ▶ #4746 PCI Twinaxial IOA

- ▶ #4748 PCI RAID Disk Unit Controller (*withdrawn from marketing* on 21 November 2003)
- ▶ #4750 PCI ISDN BRI U IOA
- ▶ #4751 PCI ISDN BRI S/T IOA
- ▶ #4761 PCI Integrated Analog Modem (up to OS/400 V5R2, pre 2003 systems only)
- ▶ #4778/#9778 PCI RAID Disk Unit Controller
- ▶ #4801 PCI Cryptographic Coprocessor (not supported by embedded IOP)
- ▶ #4805 PCI Cryptographic Accelerator (not supported by embedded IOP)
- ▶ #4838 PCI 100/10 Mbps Ethernet IOA
- ▶ #5700 PCI 1 Gbps Ethernet IOA
- ▶ #5701 PCI 1 Gbps Ethernet UTP IOA
- ▶ #5702 PCI-X Ultra Tape Controller
- ▶ #5703 PCI-X RAID Disk Unit Controller
- ▶ #5704 PCI-X Fibre Channel Tape Controller
- ▶ #5705 PCI-X Tape/DASD Controller
- ▶ #9767 Base PCI Disk Unit Controller
- ▶ #9771 Base PCI Two-Line WAN with integrated modem

The #2842 can drive a maximum of four IOAs. Further restrictions apply, as stated in the IOP descriptions in this chapter and in the "PCI card placement rules for the iSeries server" chapter of the *IBM @server i5, iSeries, and AS/400e System Builder*, SG24-2155.

The #2842 was *withdrawn from marketing* on 21 November 2003.

#2843/#9943 PCI IOP

The #2843/#9943 is a PCI I/O processor with 64 MB of memory that drives PCI IOA adapters on the Model 890 and on the #5074 PCI Expansion Tower, the #5079 1.8 M I/O Tower, and the #5078 PCI Expansion Unit. The #2843 is supported on the Models 810, 825, 870, and 890, and the #5088, #5094, #5095 and #5294.

On the #5074 PCI Expansion Tower, a PCI IOP is not embedded, but a #9943 Base PCI IOP is included. Up to five #2843 PCI IOPs may be added to a #5074. Up to six #2843 PCI IOPs may be added to a #5078.

On the #5079 1.8 M I/O Tower, a PCI IOP is not embedded, but two #9943 Base PCI IOP are included. Up to 10 #2843 PCI IOPs may be added to the #5079.

Note: The #9943 may only be on initial system orders or on Miscellaneous Equipment Specification (MES) orders that add #5074, #5078, or #5079 towers to an installed system. The maximum number of #9943s installed on a system is one in the system unit, one in each #5074, and two in each #5079.

These IOAs are supported by the #2843/#9943 Base PCI IOP:

- #2742 Two-Line WAN IOA
- #2743 1 Gbps PCI Ethernet IOA
- #2744 PCI 100 Mbps Token Ring IOA
- #2749 PCI Ultra Magnetic Media Controller
- #2757 PCI-X Ultra RAID Disk Controller
- #2760 PCI 1 Gbps Ethernet UTP Adapter
- #2763 PCI RAID Disk Unit Controller (*withdrawn from marketing* on 21 November 2003)
- #2765 PCI Fibre Channel Tape Controller
- #2766 PCI Fibre Channel Disk Controller
- #2768 PCI Magnetic Media Controller
- #2772/#2773 PCI Dual WAN/Modem IOA
- #2780 PCI-X Ultra RAID Disk Controller
- #2787 PCI-X Fibre Channel Disk Controller
- #2793/#9793 Two-Line WAN IOA with Modem
- #2794/#9794 Two-Line IOA with Modem
- #2805/#2806 Quad Modem Adapter
- #2817 PCI 155 Mbps MMF ATM IOA
- #2849 10/100 Mbps Ethernet Adapter
- #4723 PCI 10 Mbps Ethernet Adapter
- #4745 PCI 2-line WAN IOA
- #4746 PCI Twinaxial IOA
- #4748 PCI RAID Disk Unit Controller (*withdrawn from marketing* on 21 November 2003)
- #4750 PCI ISDN BRI U IOA
- #4751 PCI ISDN BRI S/T IOA
- #4761 PCI Integrated Analog Modem (up to OS/400 V5R2, pre-2003 systems only)
- #4778 PCI RAID Disk Unit Controller
- #4801 PCI Cryptographic Coprocessor (not supported by embedded IOP)
- #4805 PCI Cryptographic Accelerator (not supported by embedded IOP)
- #4838 PCI 100/10 Mbps Ethernet IOA
- #5700 PCI 1 Gbps Ethernet IOA
- #5701 PCI 1 Gbps Ethernet UTP IOA
- #5702 PCI-X Ultra Tape Controller
- #5703 PCI-X RAID Disk Unit Controller
- #5704 PCI-X Fibre Channel Tape Controller

- #5705 PCI-X Tape/DASD Controller
- #9767 Base PCI Disk Unit Controller
- #9771 Base PCI Two-Line WAN with integrated modem
- #9778 Base PCI RAID Disk Unit Controller

The #2843/#9943 can drive a maximum of four IOAs. Further restrictions apply, as stated in the IOP descriptions in this chapter and the "PCI card placement rules for the iSeries server" chapter of the *IBM @server i5, iSeries, and AS/400e System Builder*, SG24-2155.

#2844/#9744/#9844 PCI IOP

The #2844 PCI IOP is an I/O processor which drives PCI IOA adapters on the Model 520, 550, 570, 595, 800, 810, 825, 870, and 890 system units, and on the following expansion towers and units:

- #0578 PCI Expansion Unit in Rack
- #0588 PCI-X Expansion Unit in Rack
- #0595 PCI-X Expansion Unit in Rack
- #5074 PCI Expansion Tower
- #5075 PCI Expansion Tower
- #5078 PCI Expansion Unit
- #5079 1.8 M I/O Tower
- #5088 PCI-X Expansion Unit
- #5094 PCI-X Expansion Tower
- #5095 PCI-X Expansion Tower
- #5294 1.8m I/O Tower
- #5790 PCI Expansion Drawer
- #8079 Optional Base 1.8 M I/O Rack
- #8093 Optional 1.8 M I/O Rack
- #8094 Optional 1.8 M I/O Rack
- #9079 Base I/O Tower (PCI)
- #9094 Base PCI I/O Enclosure
- #9194 Base PCI-x Expansion Tower
- #8294 Optional Base 1.8m rack

The #9844 Base PCI IOP is included with Models 520, 550, 570, 595, 825, 870, and 890, and PCI-X I/O towers #0595, #5094, #5095, #5294, #8094, and #9094.

Placement considerations include:

- Up to two #2844 PCI IOPs may be placed in Model 800 and 810 system units.

- Up to three #2844 PCI IOPs may be placed in the Model 825 system unit.

- Up to three #2844 PCI IOPs may be placed in a #5075.

- ► Up to two #2844 PCI IOPs may be placed in a #5095.

- ► Up to four #2844 PCI IOPs may be placed in the Model 890 system unit.

- ► On the #0595/#5095 PCI-X Expansion Tower, a #9844 PCI IOP is included as base. Up to two #2844 PCI IOPs may be added.

- ► On the #5094 PCI-X Expansion Tower, a #9844 PCI IOP is included as base. Up to five #2844 PCI IOPs may be added to a #5074/#5094.

- ► On the #5078#5088/#0578/#0588 PCI Expansion Unit, a #9844 PCI IOP is not included in the base. Up to six #2844 PCI IOPs may be added.

- ► On the #5294 1.8M I/O Tower, two #9844 PCI IOPs are included as base. Up to 10 #2844 PCI IOPs may be added to a #5079/#5294.

- ► On the #5790 PCI Expansion Drawer, two #2844 PCI IOP with blindswap cards are supported. Two #5790s can be placed side by side in a rack with #7311 Dual I/O Unit Enclosure.

The following IOAs are supported (driven) by the #2844/#9844 PCI IOP:

- ► CCIN 288E - Embedded 10/100 Mbps Ethernet IOA (Model 825 only)
- ► #2742 Two-Line WAN IOA
- ► #2743 1 Gbps PCI Ethernet IOA
- ► #2744 PCI 100 Mbps Token Ring IOA
- ► #2749 PCI Ultra Magnetic Media Controller
- ► #2757 PCI-X Ultra RAID Disk Controller
- ► #2760 PCI 1 Gbps Ethernet UTP Adapter
- ► #2763 PCI RAID Disk Unit Controller (*withdrawn from marketing* on 21 November 2003)
- ► #2765 PCI Fibre Channel Tape Controller
- ► #2766 PCI Fibre Channel Disk Controller
- ► #2768 PCI Magnetic Media Controller
- ► #2772/#2773 PCI Dual WAN/Modem IOA
- ► #2780 PCI-X Ultra RAID Disk Controller
- ► #2782 PCI-X RAID Disk Unit Controller (*withdrawn from marketing* on 01 January 2004)
- ► #2787 PCI-X Fibre Channel Disk Controller
- ► #2793/#9793 Two-Line WAN IOA with Modem
- ► #2794/#9794 Two-Line IOA with Modem
- ► #2805/#2806 Quad Modem Adapter
- ► #2817 PCI 155 Mbps MMF ATM IOA
- ► #2849 10/100 Mbps Ethernet Adapter
- ► #4723 PCI 10 Mbps Ethernet Adapter
- ► #4745 PCI 2-line WAN IOA
- ► #4746 PCI Twinaxial IOA
- ► #4748 PCI RAID Disk Unit Controller (*withdrawn from marketing* on 21 November 2003)

- ▶ #4750 PCI ISDN BRI U IOA
- ▶ #4751 PCI ISDN BRI S/T IOA
- ▶ #4761 PCI Integrated Analog Modem (up to OS/400 V5R2, pre-2003 systems only)
- ▶ #4778/#9778 PCI RAID Disk Unit Controller
- ▶ #4801 PCI Cryptographic Coprocessor (not supported by embedded IOP)
- ▶ #4805 PCI Cryptographic Accelerator (not supported by embedded IOP)
- ▶ #4811 PCI Integrated xSeries Server
- ▶ #4812/#9812 PCI Integrated xSeries Server
- ▶ #4813/#9813 PCI Integrated xSeries Server
- ▶ #4838 PCI 100/10 Mbps Ethernet IOA
- ▶ #5700 PCI 1 Gbps Ethernet IOA
- ▶ #5701 PCI 1 Gbps Ethernet UTP IOA
- ▶ #5702 PCI-X Ultra Tape Controller
- ▶ #5703 PCI-X RAID Disk Unit Controller
- ▶ #5704 PCI-X Fibre Channel Tape Controller
- ▶ #5705 PCI-X Tape/DASD Controller
- ▶ #5712 PCI-X Tape Controller (i5/OS V5R3 and POWER5 systems only)
- ▶ #5715 PCI-X Disk/Tape Controller (i5/OS V5R3 and POWER5 systems only)
- ▶ #9767 Base PCI Disk Unit Controller
- ▶ #9771 Base PCI Two-Line WAN with integrated modem

#2791/#2891 Integrated xSeries Server

The #2791/#2891 PCI Integrated xSeries Server contains an 850 MHz processor and four memory slots in the xSeries IOP. The #2791 is supported on the CEC of Model 890 and on the #5074 PCI Expansion Tower, on the #5078 PCI Expansion Unit, on the #5079 1.8 M I/O Tower.

Each memory slot can contain either a 128 MB, a 256 MB, or a 1024 MB xSeries IOP memory card. This provides a total memory capacity ranging from 128 MB to 4 GB.

Note: When the maximum memory is installed, only 3712 MB is addressable.

At least one memory card on the Netfinity or xSeries IOP is required. The feature numbers of the server IOP memory cards are:

- ▶ #2795 - 128 MB server memory (*withdrawn from marketing* on 19 November 2004)
- ▶ #2796 - 256 MB Server IOP Memory (*withdrawn from marketing* on 19 November 2004)
- ▶ #2797 - 1 GB Server IOP Memory

Allowable main storage increments (MB)							
128	256	384	512	640	768	896	1024
1152	1280	1408	1536	1664	1792		2048
2176	2304	2432	2560				3072
3200	3328						4096

At least one LAN IOA is required. Refer to the "PCI card placement rules for the iSeries server" chapter of the *IBM @server i5, iSeries, and AS/400e System Builder*, SG24-2155, for details and limitations.

The #2791 and #2891 support up to three, in any combination, of these LAN IOA features:

► #2743 1 Gbps PCI Ethernet IOA
► #2760 PCI 1 Gbps Ethernet UTP Adapter
► #4838 PCI 100/10 Mbps Ethernet IOA
► #2744 PCI 100 Mbps Token Ring IOA

One #0225 (1 Gbps Ethernet on the Integrated xSeries Server) is required for each 1 Gbps Ethernet adapter selected to run on the #2791/#2891.

One #0224 (100/10 Mbps Ethernet on the Integrated xSeries Server) is required for each #4838 selected to run on the #2791/#2891.

One #0223 (100 Mbps Token-Ring on the Integrated xSeries Server) is required for each #2744 selected to run on the #2791/#2891.

Native iSeries functions are not supported, and the #2791/#2891 servers do not support external host LAN.

The #2791/#2891 requires three PCI card slots on the system or expansion tower backplane. Two slots are consumed by the #2791. The third slot is reduced to a short card slot, which is then used by the first LAN IOA card.

The #2791/#2891 ships with a keyboard or mouse splitter cable.

The #2791/#2891 supports only the Windows NT and Windows 2000 operating systems. These points apply:

► The #0325 IPCS Extension Cable for Windows is the default (but may be removed).

► A minimum of 128 MB xSeries IOP memory is required.

- The #1700 IPCS Keyboard or Mouse for Windows is the default (in those countries (regions) that offer it).
- A display must be connected to the Integrated xSeries Server to support Windows.

For a non-U.S.A. keyboard or mouse and display, see:

http://www.iseries.ibm.com/windowsintegration

#2792/#2892/#9792 PCI Integrated xSeries Server

The #2792 and #2892 PCI Integrated xSeries Server contain a 1.6 GHz processor and four memory slots in the xSeries IOP.

The #2792 is supported on the CEC of Models 825, 870, and 890. It is also supported on the #0578/#5078 PCI Expansion Unit, #0588/#5088 PCI-X Expansion Unit, #0595/#5095 PCI-X Expansion Tower, #5094 PCI-X Expansion Tower, #5294 1.8m I/O Tower, #8093/#8094 Optional 1.8 M I/O Rack, and the #5075 PCI Expansion Tower when attached to these models.

The #9792 is a base feature used on Models 825, 870, and 890 when ordered with the iSeries Enterprise Edition. The #9792 includes two #9726 server memory features (must be ordered as a pair).

The feature numbers of the #2792 PCI Integrated xSeries Server memory cards are:

- #0426/#9726 - 512 MB server memory
- #0427 - 1 GB server memory

The #2892 is supported on the Model 800 and 810 system units and on all towers attached to the Models 800 and 810.

The feature numbers of the #2892 PCI Integrated xSeries Server memory cards are:

- #0446 - 512 MB server memory
- #0447 - 1 GB server memory

At least two memory cards in the xSeries IOP are required. Allowable main storage increments in MB are:

- 1024
- 2048
- 3072
- 4096

The #2792 and #2892 include one embedded 100/10 Mbps Ethernet LAN controller. The #2792 and #2892 support up to three, in any combination, of these LAN IOA features:

► #2744 PCI 100 Mbps Token Ring IOA (one #0223 required for each #2744)
► #5700 PCI 1 Gbps Ethernet IOA (one #0226 required for each #5700)
► #5701 PCI 1 Gbps Ethernet UTP IOA (one #0226 required for each #5701)

Native iSeries functions are not supported. The #2792/#2892 servers do not support an external host LAN.

The #2792/#2892 requires two PCI card slots on the system or expansion tower backplane. The card does not reduce a third slot to a short slot.

The #2792/#2892 ships with a keyboard or mouse splitter cable.

The #2792/#2892 supports only the Windows 2000 and Windows .NET Server operating systems. These points apply:

► The #0325 IPCS Extension Cable for Windows is the default (but may be removed).
► A minimum of 1 GB xSeries IOP memory is required.
► The #1700 IPCS Keyboard or Mouse for Windows is the default (in those countries (regions) that offer it).
► A display must be connected to the Integrated xSeries Server to support Windows.

For a non-U.S.A. keyboard or mouse and display, see:

http://www.iseries.ibm.com/windowsintegration

The #2792, #2892, and #9792 were *withdrawn from marketing* on 01 January 2004.

#2799 PCI Integrated xSeries Server

The #2799 PCI Integrated xSeries Server contains a 1.0 GHz Intel Pentium III processor and four memory slots in the xSeries IOP. Each memory slot can contain either a 128 MB, a 256 MB, or a 1024 MB server memory card. This provides a total memory capacity ranging from 128 MB to 4 GB.

Note: When the maximum memory is installed, only 3712 MB is addressable.

At least one server memory card is required.

The feature numbers of the xSeries IOP memory cards are:

- #2795/#2895 - 128 MB server memory (*withdrawn from marketing* on 19 November 2004, but the #2895 is *still available* for conversions)
- #2796/#2896 - 256 MB server memory (*withdrawn from marketing* on 19 November 2004, but the #2895 is *still available* for conversions)
- #2797/#2897 - 1 GB server memory

Allowable main storage increments (MB)							
128	256	384	512	640	768	896	1024
1152	1280	1408	1536	1664	1792		2048
2176	2304	2432	2560				3072
3200	3328						4096

At least one LAN IOA is required. Refer to the "PCI card placement rules for the iSeries server" chapter of the *IBM @server i5, iSeries, and AS/400e System Builder*, SG24-2155, for complete rules for placing these PCI cards in configurations.

The #2799 or #2899 supports up to three, in any combination, of these LAN IOA features:

- #2743 1 Gbps PCI Ethernet IOA
- #2760 PCI 1 Gbps Ethernet UTP Adapter
- #4838 PCI 100/10 Mbps Ethernet IOA
- #2744 PCI 100 Mbps Token Ring IOA

One #0225 (1 Gbps Ethernet on the Integrated xSeries Server) is required for each 1 Gbps Ethernet adapter selected to run on the #2799 or #2899.

One #0224 (100/10 Mbps Ethernet on the Integrated xSeries Server) is required for each #4838 selected to run on the #2799 or #2899.

One #0223 (100 Mbps Token-Ring on the Integrated xSeries Server) is required for each #2744 selected to run on the #2799 or #2899.

Native iSeries functions are not supported. The #2799 or #2899 servers do not support external host LAN.

The #2899 requires two PCI card slots on the Model 270 system unit. One slot is consumed. The second slot is reduced to a short card slot, which is then used by the first attached LAN IOA card.

The #2799 or #2899 requires three PCI card slots on the expansion tower backplane. Two slots are consumed by the #2799 or #2899. The third slot is reduced to a short card slot, which is then used by the first LAN IOA card.

The #2799 or #2899 ships with a keyboard or mouse splitter cable. The #2799 or #2899 supports only the Windows NT and Windows 2000 operating systems. These points apply:

► A #0325 IPCS Extension Cable for Windows is the default (but may be removed).

► A minimum of 128 MB server memory is required.

► The #1700 IPCS Keyboard or Mouse for Windows is the default (in those countries (regions) that offer it).

► A display must be connected to the Integrated xSeries Server to support Windows.

For a non-U.S.A. keyboard or mouse and display, see:

http://www.iseries.ibm.com/windowsintegration

The #2799 and #2899 PCI Integrated xSeries Server require OS/400 V5R1 (with program temporary fixes (PTFs)) or later. For required PTF information, see Informational APAR II13105 at:

http://www-912.ibm.com/n_dir/nas4apar.nsf/nas4aparhome

The #2799 was *withdrawn from marketing* on 21 November 2003.

#4710/#4810/#9710 PCI Integrated xSeries Server

The #4710, #4810, or #9710 has a 2 GHz processor and four memory slots. Each server memory slot can contain one of the following features, providing a total main storage capacity from 1 024 MB to 4 096 MB:

► 512 MB server memory (#0426/#9726)
► 1 GB server memory (#0427)

A minimum of two server memory cards are required and must be installed in identical capacity pairs. On model upgrades or MES orders, you may order a #4710/#4810 without memory features if usable supported memory features already exist on the installed system.

The #4710, #4810, or #9710 includes one embedded 100/10 Mbps Ethernet LAN controller. It can support the following LAN IOAs in combination:

▶ #2744 PCI 100 Mbps Token Ring IOA
▶ #5700 PCI 1 Gbps Ethernet IOA
▶ #5701 PCI 1 Gbps Ethernet UTP IOA

You can order the #4710/#4810 without any LAN IOA features.

When a LAN feature is used in conjunction with a #4710, the following ordering rules apply:

▶ If #2744 is driven, then one #0223 100 Mbps Token-Ring Specify is required for each #2744 driven.

▶ If #5700/#5701 is driven, then one #0226 1 Gbps Ethernet Specify is required for each #5700/#5701 driven.

Up to three IOA LAN features can be supported by the #4710/#4810, depending on the system unit or tower position into which the #4710/#4810 is placed.

Native AS/400 functions are *not* supported.

The #4710, #4810, or #9710 does not support an external host LAN.

The #4710/#9710 is supported in the system unit of Models 820, 825, 870, and 890. It is also supported in the following expansion towers when attached to these models and the Model 520, 550, 570, and 595: #0578, #0588, #0595, #5074, #5075, #5078, #5079, #5088, #5094, #5095, and #5294, #8079, #8094, #9079, and #9094.

The #4810 is supported in the system unit of Models 800 and 810. It is also supported in the #5075 #0578/#5078, #0588/#5088, and #0595/#5095 when these towers are attached to a Model 800 or 810. For Models 800 and 810, if the #4810 is placed in a #5094 or #5294, the installation instructions for the client indicate that a CE must be called for card installation.

The #9710 is supported in the system unit of Models 825, 870, and 890. It is also supported in the following expansion towers when attached to these Models: #0578, #0588, #0595, #5074, #5075, #5078, #5079, #5088, #5094, #5095, and #5294.

The #4710, #4810, or #9710 does not require a #2843, #2844, #9943 or #9844, but placement is limited to specific slots within the various system units and expansion towers. The #4710, #4810, or #9710 requires two PCI card slots and does not hang over a third slot.

The #4710, #4810, or #9710 ships with a standard keyboard or mouse splitter cable and can sup port either standard or USB 1.1 keyboard, mouse, or both. Windows 2000 Server and Windows 2003 Server operating systems are supported. The following conditions apply:

- The #0325 (IPCS Extension Cable for Windows) is the default but may be removed.

- A minimum of 1 GB server memory is required.

- The #1700 (IPCS Keyboard or Mouse for Windows) is the default in countries (regions) that offer it.

- A display must be connected to the Integrated Server to support Windows.

For a non-U.S.A. keyboard or mouse and display, see:

http://www.iseries.ibm.com/windowsintegration

OS/400 V5R2 plus PTFs, or later, is required. For required PTF information, refer to Informational APAR II13609 at:

http://www-912.ibm.com/n_dir/nas4apar.nsf/nas4aparhome

18

iSeries I/O adapters and controllers

This chapter discusses input/output adapters (IOA) that are available from IBM for iSeries Peripheral Component Interconnect (PCI) system units and associated PCI towers. Refer to "Migration towers" on page 262 for information about IOAs supported in System Products Division (SPD) and migration towers. Refer to Chapter 17, "iSeries PCI I/O processors" on page 323, for input/output processor (IOP) information.

Communication restrictions for Peripheral Component Interconnect (PCI) systems are defined in the "LAN/WAN adapters" section of the model chapters in the *IBM @server iSeries and AS/400e System Builder*, SG24-2155. You can find rules for individual communication cards (adapters or IOPs) and sizing rules in the specific adapter or IOP feature description within each model chapter of the System Builder. For general communications performance considerations, refer to the online document *iSeries Performance Capabilities Reference*, SC41-0607.

You can also find placement information in the IBM @server Hardware Information Center to install an adapter. Go to:

```
http://publib.boulder.ibm.com/infocenter/eserver/v1r2s/en_US/index.htm?info/
iphak/howtodecide.htm
```

When you reach this site, from the navigation panel on the left, select **Installing Hardware** →**Installing features and replacing parts**.

PCI card technology

The original AS/400 systems used SPD cards to input/output (I/O) services to the system. SPD cards integrate the IOP and IOA function on a single card. PCI I/O architecture separates IOP and IOA functions so that you can add one IOP and have several different IOAs controlled by the one IOP.

PCI architecture provides more flexibility in the placement of IOPs and IOA cards. This results in more efficient use of card slots, potentially resulting in a lower cost of implementation. PCI I/O structure enables client setup of the server and select features on all models.

The fundamental bus architecture remains unchanged in iSeries servers with the implementation of PCI adapters. PCI architecture offers advantages over other non-iSeries (or non-AS/400e) system structures. The system IOP is architected to offload the main processor, isolate the host from adapter and network errors, and to manage, configure, and service the adapters. On all current models, adding or removing PCI cards can be performed without taking the server down. This allows you to power down a PCI slot and remove the PCI card from the system without powering down the system. This improves the availability of the system and allows you to perform upgrades, maintenance, or repair without impacting the users of the system.

> **Note:** Refer to the individual PCI card descriptions and the system descriptions to see if *hot swapping* of a specific PCI card is supported.

Increased flexibility of configuration, however, adds a degree of complexity to the configuration process. With the implementation of PCI technologies, a full understanding of configuration rules associated with the various I/O features of the iSeries server is required.

Due to the possibility of having to reset an IOP occasionally as a result of tape problems, we recommend that you do not combine any other critical IOAs (particularly disk IOAs) with a tape IOA on the same IOP. Resetting an IOP causes all IOAs downstream of it to be deactivated during the reset.

> **Note:** If a system or expansion tower has the capability of concurrent maintenance, it is possible to reset only the IOA. However, there are instances that require resetting an IOP.

Refer to "PCI-X" on page 20 for a description of PCI-X, the newest generation of PCI technology used on iSeries servers.

PCI card placement rules

There are two sets of rules that govern the placement of PCI cards in the iSeries servers:

- ► **Hard rules**: Impose restrictions on the type of card, size, and valid slot placement. Hard rules are taken into account by the IBM marketing configurator.

- ► **Soft rules**: Impose restrictions based on possible performance bottlenecks associated with certain configuration and use. Soft rules depend on the use of the cards and required performance and, therefore, are not supported by the marketing configurator and must be taken into account separately.

The placement of PCI cards follows special rules. For a complete explanation of both *hard* and *soft* rules, as well the types of cards and slots supported on each system, refer to *PCI Card Placement Rules for the IBM @server iSeries Server Version 5 Release 2*, REDP-3638, before you propose any configuration. Rules and placement information are also explained in the IBM @server Hardware Information Center in the *How to install an Adapter* topic at:

```
http://publib.boulder.ibm.com/infocenter/eserver/v1r2s/en_US/index.htm?info/
iphak/howtodecide.htm
```

PCI IOP

There are several types of I/O processor controller cards:

- ► **Integrated IOPs**: These are integrated on the backplane of a system or tower.

- ► **PCI IOP controller cards**: These cards support a number of low-speed PCI card slots and a number of high-speed PCI card slots depending on how the backplane is wired. They require a controller position on the backplane. The new #481x Integrated xSeries Server also require an IOP.

- ► **Integrated xSeries Server IOP**: This is a special case of a PCI IOP controller card. It drives a select subset of supported PCI IOA cards.

In the Model 250, the Integrated xSeries Server IOP requires two specialized slots (a processor slot and bridge slot) and a PCI IOP. In Models 270, 800, 810, 820, 825, 830, 840, 870, and 890, the Integrated xSeries Server IOP occupies a valid IOP slot in the system. An additional IOP card is not required on older feature cards, but the new #481x Integrated xSeries Server does require an IOP.

It is supported in Model 520, 550, 570, and 595 expansion towers only. The 520, 550, 570 system units support the newer #481x Integrated xSeries Server, which is small and fits in the CEC. However, it requires a dedicated IOP to drive the card.

PCI IOA

When installed and configured in an OS/400 (i5/OS) partition, PCI IOAs have to be driven by a PCI IOP.

Several types of PCI adapter cards, each of which can require a specialized slot on the system backplane, exist:

► **Low-speed PCI adapter cards**: These cards require a PCI card slot and a PCI controller to drive them. The PCI controller can either be included on the backplane or as a separate PCI card that attaches to the backplane.

► **High-speed PCI adapter cards**: These cards require a higher bandwidth connection to the PCI controllers than low-speed PCI cards require. The PCI controller can be included on the backplane or as a separate PCI card that attaches to the backplane.

► **Low-speed/high-speed PCI adapter cards**: These cards can be installed in either a low-speed slot or high-speed slot.

► **PCI controller cards**: PCI controller cards support a number of low-speed PCI card slots and a number of high-speed PCI card slots depending on how the backplane is wired. They require a controller position on the backplane.

► **Integrated xSeries Server for iSeries controller cards**: The latest manufacturing variance of the PCI controller cards, the Integrated xSeries Server for iSeries, supports PCI card slots and requires a PCI controller to drive it. The Integrated xSeries Server occupies a reserved two-slot controller position on the backplane. One slot is for the Integrated xSeries Server processor card, and one is for the Integrated iSeries Server Bridge card.

Refer to the system diagrams to identify which slots are supported.

> **Note:** If the card is configured as a dedicated IOA in a Linux partition, then it does not require an IOP nor support the enhanced functions stated previously.

PCI adapters are Customer Install Features. Refer to Chapter 22, "Customer Install Features" on page 453, for a list of CIF features for current iSeries models.

AIX and Linux Direct Attach features overview

The IBM marketing configurator supports ordering IOAs without IOPs when an AIX or Linux partition is defined using the feature codes listed in the following table.

Feature code	AIX[4]	RedHat[5]	SLES 9[6]	iSeries equivalent
#0601 - Direct Attach - #2743 PCI 1 Gbps Ethernet IOA		X	X	#2743
#0602 - Direct Attach - #2760 PCI 1 Gbps Ethernet UTP IOA		X	X	#2760
#0603 - Direct Attach - #2744 PCI 100 Mbps Token-Ring IOA		X	X	#2744
#0607 - Direct Attach - #4838 PCI 100/10 Mbps Ethernet IOA		X	X	#4838
#0608 - Direct Attach - #4745 PCI WAN IOA		X	X	#4745
#0609 - Direct Attach - #2772 PCI Dual WAN/Modem IOA		X	X	#2772
#0610 - Direct Attach - #2773 PCI Dual WAN/ModemIOA		X	X	#2773
#0611 - Direct Attach - #2765 PCI Fibre Channel Tape Controller	X	X	X	#2765
#0612 - Direct Attach - #2766 PCI Fibre Channel Disk Controller		X	X	#2766
#0613 - Direct Attach - #2742 PCI 2-Line WAN IOA		X	X	#2742
#0614 - Direct Attach - #2793 PCI 2-Line WAN w/Modem		X	X	#2793
#0615 - Direct Attach - #2794 PCI 2-Line WAN w/Modem		X	X	#2794
#0616 - Direct Attach - #2805 PCI Quad Modem IOA		X	X	#2805
#0617 - Direct Attach - #2806 PCI Quad Modem (CIM)		X	X	#2806
#0620 - Direct Attach - #5700 PCI 1 Gbps Ethernet IOA	X	X	X	#5700
#0621 - Direct Attach - #5701 PCI 1 Gbps Ethernet UTP IOA	X	X	X	#5701
#0623 - Direct Attach - #2849 PCI 100/10 Mbps Ethernet IOA		X	X	#2849
#0624 - Direct Attach - #5702 PCI-X Ultra Tape Controller		X	X	#5702
#0625 - Direct Attach - #5704 PCI-X Fibre Channel Tape Controller	X	X	X	#5704
#0626 - Direct Attach - #2787 PCI-X Fibre Channel Disk Controller		X	X	#2728
#0627 - Direct Attach - #2780 PCI-X Ultra4 RAID Disk Controller	X	X	X	#2780
#0628 - Direct Attach - #5703 PCI-X RAID Disk Unit Controller	X	X	X	#5703
#0632 - PCI USB 2.0 Adapter	X	X	X	None
#0633 - Graphics Adapter	X	X	X	None

Feature code	AIX[4]	RedHat[5]	SLES 9[6]	iSeries equivalent
#0634 128-port ASYNC Adapter	X			None
#0635 - SDLC/X.25 - 2-port Adapter	X			None
#0637 - 100/10 Mbps 4-port Ethernet Adapter	X	X	X	None
#0638 - SSA (40 MB/s) Adapter	X			None
#0639 - 128MB SSA Adapter Memory	X			None
#0640 - Fast Write Cache Option	X			None
#0642 PCI Ultra-3 RAID Adapter	X(1)			None
#0645 - Direct Attach - #5712 PCI-X Tape/DASD Controller	X	X	X	#5712
#0646 #0646 - Direct Attach-5716	X	X	X	#5716
#2848 #2848 - PCI 2D Entry Graphics Adapter	X	X	X	None
#2732 - PCI Serial HIPPI Adapter	X(2)			None
#2737 - PCI USB 1.1 Adapter	X(2)	X(2)	X(2)	None
#2943 - 8-Port ASYNC Adapter	X			None
#2947 - PCI Multiprotocol Adapter	X			None
#4953 - 155 Mbps ATM UTP Adapter	X(3)			None
#4957 - 155 Mbps ATM Fiber Adapter	X(2)			None
#4959 - PCI 16/4 Mbps Token-Ring IOA	X			None
#4960 - Cryptographic Accelerator-	X(2)			None
#4962 - PCI 100/10 Mbps Ethernet IOA	X	X	X	None
#4963 PCI Crypto Coprocessor	X(2)			None
#5718 10 Gbps Ethernet IOA (Short)	X			None
#6203 PCI Ultra3 SCSI Adapter	X(2)	X(2)	X(2)	None
#6204 Differential SCSI Adapter	X(2)	X(2)	X(2)	None

[1] Model 520 and 570 only
[2] Model 570 and 595 only
[3] Model 595 only
[4] AIX 5L for POWER V5.2 for IBM @server or later
[5] Red Hat Enterprise Linux AS for POWER Version 3 or later
[6] SUSE LINUX Enterprise Server 9 for POWER or later

Not all features are supported on all models. Some features may be withdrawn but are in the table for reference. AIX-specific adapters are not described in this book.

> **Note:** The IBM marketing configurator does not add IOPs to #06xx direct attach features because they are not needed. The #06xx features can be moved to OS/400 or i5/OS partitions if there is sufficient IOP to support them. The equivalent @server i5 or iSeries features can be moved to a Linux or AIX partition (if supported) without the IOP.

System unit hardware (PCI)

iSeries PCI IOAs available from IBM are described in this section. IOAs that are supported but are now *withdrawn from marketing* are described in the *IBM @server i5, iSeries, and AS/400e System Builder*, SG24-2155. Withdrawn features are identified in "Products and features no longer marketed by IBM" on page 755.

Refer to Chapter 22, "Customer Install Features" on page 453, to identify the CIF status for each supported feature.

#2742 Two-Line WAN IOA

The #2742 Two-Line WAN IOA supports up to two multiple protocol communications ports when one or two (in any combination) of the following cables are attached:

- ► #0348 V.24/EIA232 20-ft. (6m) PCI cable
- ► #0349 V.24/EIA232 50-ft. (15m) PCI cable (*withdrawn from marketing* on 03 December 2002)
- ► #0353 V.35 20-ft. PCI cable
- ► #0354 V.35 50-ft./15m PCI cable (*withdrawn from marketing* on 03 December 2002)
- ► #0355 V.35 80-ft. PCI cable (*withdrawn from marketing* in July 2000)
- ► #0356 V.36 20-ft. PCI cable
- ► #0358 V.36 150-ft. PCI cable (*withdrawn from marketing* in July 2000)
- ► #0359 X.21 20-ft. PCI cable
- ► #0360 X.21 50-ft./15m PCI cable (*withdrawn from marketing* on 03 December 2002)

- ▶ #0365 V.24/EIA232 80-ft. PCI cable (*withdrawn from marketing* in December 2002)

- ▶ #0367 Operations Console PCI Cable

Multiple #0367 cables may be ordered (but only one per #2742) to serve as consoles for secondary partitions when logical partitioning (#0140) is specified.

When #2742 is selected to support ECS, one #0348, #0349 or #0365 cable must be specified. The #2742 does not support Remote Power On.

When used as a direct attach adapter for Linux, order the #0613 in place of the #2742.

#2743 1 Gbps PCI Ethernet IOA

The #2743 1 Gbps PCI Ethernet IOA allows iSeries servers to attach to IEEE standard 802.3Z high-speed Ethernet local area networks (LANs) (1 Gbps). The adapter supports multi-mode fibre media attachment from the adapter to a Gb-capable switch with at least one port that supports a 1000 BASE-SX interface with IEEE 802.3z and 802.3u compliance. The #2743 supports a multi-mode fibre interface with a 62.5 micron or 50.0 micron cable for attachment to client-supplied cabling.

The #2743 1 Gbps PCI Ethernet IOA supports a 1000 Mbps (1 Gbps) full duplex interface only and TCP/IP only. It cannot negotiate down to a lower speed. Stations on 10 Mb, 100 Mb, and 1000 Mb (1 Gb) switched LANs can interface with the #2743 through a switch that is capable of handling the lower speed. The #2743 can run under a #2791 or #2799 or #2891/#2899 PCI Integrated xSeries Server in V5R1. A #0225 1 Gbps Ethernet Specify is needed for each #2743 running under one of these integrated servers.

The #2743 adapter only supports TCP/IP. SNA and IPX protocols are not supported.

When used as a direct attach adapter for Linux, order the #0601 in place of the #2743.

#2744 PCI 100 Mbps Token Ring IOA

The #2744 PCI 100 Mbps Token Ring IOA provides a single attachment to a 100 Mbps, 16 Mbps, or 4 Mbps IBM Token Ring network. The feature consists of an IOA card, internal code, which supplies IEEE 802.5 Media Access Control (MAC), and IEEE 802.2 Logical Link Control (LCC) functions. The 100/16/4 Token Ring IOA is capable of operating in half or full duplex mode.

The #2744/#9744 comes standard with an 8-ft./2.44m Token-Ring cable. Alternately, a separately purchased twisted-pair cable to the RJ-45 connection on the IOA may be attached.

If the #2744 is selected to run on a #2791 or #2799 or #2891/#4810/#2899 PCI Integrated xSeries Server, one #0223 (100 Mbps Token-Ring on Integrated Netfinity Server) is required for each #2744 ordered.

When used as a direct attach adapter for Linux, order the #0603 in place of the #2744.

#2749 PCI Ultra Magnetic Media Controller

The #2749 PCI Ultra Magnetic Media Controller is an Ultra SCSI high voltage differential (HVD) controller for attachment of an external HVD tape device or an external HVD optical device. When attaching Ultra SCSI to a #2749, the instantaneous data transfer rate is 40 MB per second, and the sustained rate is 38 MB per second. The #2749 feature is hot pluggable.

The #2749 PCI Ultra Magnetic Media Controller is announced to be *withdrawn from marketing* in March 2005.

Note: If a #3995 Optical Library Dataserver is attached to a #2749, the #2749 should not be placed under the same IOP that drives the Load Source direct access storage device (DASD).

The devices that are supported by the #2749 include:

► 3490E

  − C11/C22/C1A/C2A ½-inch Cartridge Tape Subsystem with the #5040
  − E01/E11 ½-inch Cartridge Tape Subsystem
  − F00/F01/F11/F1A ½-inch Cartridge Tape Subsystem

► 3494

  − L10 ½-inch Cartridge Tape Library Control Unit Frame (one 3490E-C1A/C2A with the #5040 or one or two 3490E-F1A)

  − L12 ½-inch Cartridge Tape Library Control Unit Frame (one or two 3590-B1A)

  − D10 ½-inch Cartridge Tape Library Device Frame (one 3490E-C1A/C2A with the #5040 or one or two 3490E-F1A)

  − D12 ½-inch Cartridge Tape Library Device Frame (one to six 3590-B1A)

- ▶ 3570

  - – B00/B01/B02/B11/B12/B1A Cassette Tape Subsystem
  - – C00/C01/C02/C11/C12/C1A Cassette Tape Subsystem

- ▶ 3575-L06/L12/L18/L24/L32 ½-inch Cartridge Tape Subsystem
- ▶ 3580-H11/H13/H23 Ultrium Tape Drive
- ▶ 3581-H17 Ultrium Tape Autoloader
- ▶ 3583-Lxx Ultrium Scalable Tape Library
- ▶ 3584-L32 or D32 UltraScalable Tape Library
- ▶ 3590-B11/B1A/E11/H11/E1A/H1A ½-inch Cartridge Tape Subsystem
- ▶ 3995-C40/C42/C44/C46/C48 Optical Library Dataserver
- ▶ 7208-012/222/232/234/342 8mm Cartridge Tape Device
- ▶ 9348-001 ½-inch Reel Tape Device–Rack Mount
- ▶ 9348-002 ½-inch Reel Tape Device–Table Top
- ▶ 9427-21x 8mm Tape Library

> **Tip:** Use the #5702 PCI-X Ultra Tape Controller to attach tape devices with low voltage differential (LVD) connections.

#2757 PCI-X Ultra RAID Disk Controller

The #2757 PCI-X Ultra RAID Disk Controller is an Ultra SCSI disk unit controller with a 757 MB compressed maximum cache that provides RAID-5 protection for internal disk units. It also supports internal tape devices, CD-ROM, and DVD units. The #2757 has four Ultra SCSI buses.

The #2757 is designed to work as a high performance controller for disks protected by system mirroring or disks with no protection. In a RAID-5 configuration, disk unit protection is provided at less cost than mirroring and with greater performance than system checksums. DASD compression is not supported.

The #2757 controls up to two removable media devices (internal tape, CD-ROM, and DVD).

The #2757 is not supported in the system unit of Models 520, 550, 570, or 595.

The number of disk units per #2757 varies by configuration:

- ▶ Up to 20 disk units per #2757 are supported in a #5094 PCI-X Expansion Tower attached to a Model 520, 550, 570,or 595.

- ▶ Up to 18 disk units per #2757 are supported in the system unit or external tower disk cage of the Model 270, 800, and 810.

- ▶ Up to 15 disk units per #2757 are supported in a #9094 Base PCI I/O Enclosure attached to a Model 870 or 890.

For all other configurations, contact your IBM marketing representative.

A minimum of three disk units of the same capacity is needed for a valid RAID-5 configuration. A maximum of six arrays is allowed per controller, with a maximum of 18 disk units allowed per array.

Parity is spread across either two, four, eight, or 16 disk units in an array, dependent upon the number of disk units started in the array, as represented in the following table.

Number of units in the array	Number of units parity is spread across
3	2
4 - 7	4
8 - 15	8
16 - 18	16

#2763 PCI RAID Disk Unit Controller

The #2763 PCI RAID Disk Unit Controller is an Ultra2 SCSI disk unit controller with a 10 MB write-cache that provides RAID-5 protection for internal disk units and supports internal tape and CD-ROM units.

The #2763 is designed to work as a high-performance controller for disks protected by system mirroring or disks with no protection. In the RAID-5 configuration, disk unit protection is provided at a lower cost than mirroring and with greater performance than system checksums.

The #2763 controller supports a maximum of 12 disk units and up to two removable media devices including a DVD. The #2763 is available on the Model 270, the Model 820, and the #5075 PCI Expansion Tower.

A minimum of four drives of the same capacity is needed for a valid RAID-5 configuration. A maximum of three arrays is allowed, with a maximum of 10 drives allowed per array. All drives in an array must be of the same capacity.

The #2763 PCI RAID Disk Unit Controller is hot pluggable. When used as a direct attach adapter for Linux, order the #0604 in place of the #2763.

The #2763 was *withdrawn from marketing* on 21 November 2003. The #5703 PCI-X RAID Disk Unit Controller is the recommended replacement.

#2768 PCI Magnetic Media Controller

The #2768 PCI Magnetic Media Controller is an Ultra SCSI HVD controller for attachment of an external tape device or an external CD-ROM device that has a single-ended SCSC interface.

The #2768 PCI Magnetic Media Controller supports one, or a combination, of these devices:

- ► 7207 Model 122 QIC-SLR Tape Bridge Box
- ► 7207 Model 330 External SLR60 Tape Drive
- ► 7210 Model 330
- ► 7210 Model 020 CD-ROM Bridge Box
- ► 7210 Model 025 DVD-RAM drive
- ► 7329 Model 308 SLR100 ¼-inch Tape Autoloader
- ► 7208 Model 345 60 GB External 8mm Tape Drive

- ► One 7210 Model 025 and one 7210 Model 025: The two devices are daisy-chained.

- ► One 7210 Model 025 and one 7210 Model 020: The two devices are daisy chained with the 7210-025 physically connected first. No #0120 attachment specify code is required for the 7210-020.

- ► One 7207 Model 122 and one 7210 Model 020: The two devices are daisy chained with the 7207-122 physically connected first. No #0120 attachment specify code is required for the 7210-020.

- ► One 7207 Model 122 and one 7210 Model 025: The two devices are daisy chained with the 7207-122 physically connected first.

- ► One 7208-345 and one 7210-020: The two devices are daisy chained with the 7208-345 physically connected first. No #0120 attachment specify code is required for the 7210-020.

- ► One 7208-345 and one 7210-025: The two devices are daisy chained with the 7208-345 physically connected first.

- ► The #0120 7210-020 Attachment Specify: This is required for each 7210 Model 020 CD-ROM Bridge Box.

The 7210-020 External CD-ROM Drive is to be connected directly (not daisy chained) to the system through a #2768 PCI Magnetic Media Controller.

> **Note:** If the 7210-020 is to be daisy chained with another external device, the #0120 specify code must not be present.

The #0162 Extended Single Ended Attach Specify is required when these devices are directly attached (not second on a daisy-chained string) to an iSeries server via a #2768 PCI Magnetic Media Controller:

- ► 7329 Model 308 SLR100 ¼-inch Tape Autoloader
- ► 7210-025 External DVD- RAM Drive

Note: If either of the previous devices is daisy chained from another device, the #0162 specify code must not be present.

The #2768 PCI Magnetic Media Controller is hot pluggable.

#2772 and #2773 PCI Dual WAN/Modem IOA

The #2772 PCI Dual WAN/Modem IOA and #2773 PCI Dual WAN/Modem IOA are basically the same interface. The #2772 is the non-Complex Impedance Matching (CIM) version of this card. Both are 2-line WAN adapters, with two ports (RJ11) supporting V.90 56K Async PPP and FAX applications at data rates up to 14.4K via internal modems. Connection to the V.90 ports is via a telephone cable. Both of these features do not support remote power on. The new cards can be used for the purpose of multilink. These cards need country (region)-specific telephone cables (a minimum of one and a maximum of two per card).

Feature #2773, the Complex Impedance Matching version, is intended for Australia and New Zealand only. All cable features must be the same on the same iSeries server.

Cable features supported with the #2772 are:

- ► #1010 Modem Cable-Austria
- ► #1011 Modem Cable-Belgium
- ► #1012 Modem Cable-Africa
- ► #1013 Modem Cable-Israel
- ► #1014 Modem Cable-Italy
- ► #1015 Modem Cable-France
- ► #1016 Modem Cable-Germany
- ► #1017 Modem Cable-U.K.
- ► #1018 Modem Cable-Iceland/Sweden
- ► #1020 Modem Cable-China (Hong Kong S.A.R. of China)/New Zealand
- ► #1021 Modem Cable-Finland/Norway
- ► #1022 Modem Cable-Netherlands
- ► #1023 Modem Cable-Swiss
- ► #1024 Modem Cable-Denmark
- ► #1025 Modem Cable-U.S.A./Canada

Cable features supported with the #2773 are:

- ► #1019 Modem Cable-Australia
- ► #1020 Modem Cable-China (Hong Kong S.A.R. of China)/New Zealand

When used as a direct attach adapter for Linux, order the #0609 in place of the #2772, and the #0610 ordered in place of the #2773.

#2780 PCI-X Ultra RAID Disk Controller

The #2780 PCI-X Ultra RAID Disk Controller is an Ultra4 (u320) SCSI disk unit controller with a maximum compressed write cache of 757 MB and a maximum compressed read cache of 1GB that provides RAID-5 protection for internal disk units. It also supports internal tape devices, CD-ROM, and DVD units. The #2780 has four Ultra4 SCSI buses.

The #2780 is designed to work as a high performance controller for disks protected by system mirroring or disks with no protection. In a RAID-5 configuration, disk unit protection is provided at less cost than mirroring, and with greater performance than system checksums. DASD compression is not supported. When used in an AIX or Linux environment, the #2780 can help provide significant speed and throughput improvements.

The #2780 controls up to two removable media devices (internal tape, CD-ROM, and DVD). The #2780 is not supported in the system unit of the Model 520, 550, 570, or 595.

The number of disk units per #2780 varies by configuration:

- ► Up to 20 disk units per #2780 are supported in a #5094 PCI-X Expansion Tower attached to a Model 520, 550, 570, or 595.
- ► Up to 18 disk units per #2780 are supported in the system unit or external tower disk cage of the Model 270, 800, and 810.
- ► Up to 15 disk units per #2780 are supported in a #9094 Base PCI I/O Enclosure attached to a Model 595, 870, or 890.

For all other configurations, contact your IBM marketing representative.

A minimum of three disk units of the same capacity is needed for a valid RAID-5 configuration. A maximum of six arrays is allowed per controller, with a maximum of 18 disk units allowed per array.

Parity is spread across either two, four, eight, or 16 disk units in an array, dependent upon the number of disk units started in the array, as represented in the following table.

Number of units in the array	Number of units parity is spread across
3	2
4 - 7	4
8 - 15	8
16 - 18	16

Note: The battery for cache in the #2780 can be replaced without removing the #2780 adapter from the system.

#2787 PCI-X Fibre Channel Disk Controller

The #2787 PCI-X Fibre Channel Disk Controller provides Fibre Channel attachment capability for external disk devices. The #2787 supports point-to-point and arbitrated loop topologies and has an LC-type cable connector. Each #2787 is shipped with a wrap connector (part number 05N6767). The #2787 supports 64-bit, 133MHz PCI-X bus speeds.

The following adapter kits are required when connecting SC-type cables to the #2787:

► #0371 - LC-SC Adapter Kit (50 um) can be ordered, both on initial, model upgrades, and simple MES orders. This optional kit is used to attach SC-type fibre (50 micron) cables to a #2787. The #0371 kit contains a 2m LC-ST cable and ST-SC adapter for 50 micron fiber cable.

► #0372 - LC-SC Adapter Kit (62.5 um) can be ordered, both on initial, model upgrades, and simple MES orders. This optional kit is used to attach SC-type fiber (62.5 micron) cables to a #2787. The #0372 kit contains a 2m LC-ST cable and ST-SC adapter for 62.5 micron fiber cable.

An optics cleaning kit (part number 46G6844) and instruction sheet (part number 21P6238, form number SY27-2604) is supplied, one per system, when a #2787 is present or ordered.

Note: Clients are to supply all Fibre Channel cables for the #2787 PCI-X Fibre Channel Disk Controller.

The #2787 PCI-X Fibre Channel Disk Controller is the recommended replacement card for the #2766 PCI Fibre Channel Disk Controller. When used as the direct attach adapter for Linux, order the #0626 in place of the #2787.

#2793/#2794/#9793/#9794 PCI Dual WAN/Modem IOA

The #2793/#2794/#9793/#9794 PCI Dual WAN/Modem IOA cards all provide the same interface. The #2793/#9793 are offered in all countries (regions) except Australia and New Zealand, where the #9793/#9794 is offered instead. The #9793/#9794 are base models.

The #2793/#9793 is a two-line WAN with Modem adapter and is the non-CIM version. The #2794/#9794 is the CIM version.

Port 0 is the modem port and supports V.92 56K Async PPP, V.92 data modem, V.44 data compression, V.34 FAX modem and FAX functions such as ECM and 2D/1D conversion. Port 0 does not provide Sync modem capabilities (SDLC and Sync PPP). Port 1 is the RVX port and supports multiple communications protocols.

Select one of the following cables to attach to port 0 (the modem port):

- ► #1010 Modem Cable-Austria
- ► #1011 Modem Cable-Belgium
- ► #1012 Modem Cable-Africa
- ► #1013 Modem Cable-Israel
- ► #1014 Modem Cable-Italy
- ► #1015 Modem Cable-France
- ► #1016 Modem Cable-Germany
- ► #1017 Modem Cable-U.K.
- ► #1018 Modem Cable-Iceland/Sweden
- ► #1020 Modem Cable-China (Hong Kong S.A.R. of China)/New Zealand
- ► #1021 Modem Cable-Finland/Norway
- ► #1022 Modem Cable-Netherlands
- ► #1023 Modem Cable-Swiss
- ► #1024 Modem Cable-Denmark
- ► #1025 Modem Cable-U.S.A./Canada

Cable features supported with the #2794 are:

- ► #1019 Modem Cable-Australia
- ► #1020 Modem Cable-China (Hong Kong S.A.R. of China)/New Zealand

Select one of the following cables to attach to port 1 (the RVX port):

- ► #0348 V.24/EIA232 20-ft. (6m) PCI cable
- ► #0349 V.24/EIA232 50-ft. (15m) PCI cable (*withdrawn from marketing* on 03 December 2002)
- ► #0353 V.35 20-ft. PCI cable

- ▶ #0354 V.35 50-ft./15m PCI cable (*withdrawn from marketing* on 3 December 2002)

- ▶ #0356 V.36 20-ft. PCI cable

- ▶ #0359 X.21 20-ft. PCI cable

- ▶ #0360 X.21 50-ft./15m PCI cable (*withdrawn from marketing* on 03 December 2002)

- ▶ #0365 V.24/EIA232 80-ft. PCI cable

- ▶ #0367 Operations Console PCI Cable

Multiple #0367 cables can be ordered (but only one per #2793) to serve as consoles for secondary partitions when logical partitioning (#0140) is specified.

ECS is supported from the RVX port. A #0348, #0349, or #0365 cable is required to support ECS. ECS is also supported from the modem port.

The #2793/#2794/#9793/#9794 PCI Dual WAN/Modem IOA does not support the remote ring indicate function. When used as a direct attach adapter for Linux, order the #0614 in place of the #2793, and order the #0615 in place of the #2794.

#2805 and #2806 PCI Quad Modem IOA

The #2805 PCI Quad Modem IOA and #2806 PCI Quad Modem (CIM) are basically the same interface. The #2805 is the non-CIM version of the card. Both are 4-line WAN modem adapters, with four RJ-11 ports that support V.92 56K Async SLIP/PPP and V.34 Fax applications at data rates up to 33.6K via internal modems. Connection to the V.92 ports is via a telephone cable.

The V.92 functions offer increased throughput for upload operations, improved V.44 data compression, and shortened modem synchronization periods. The call waiting and modem-on-hold functions associated with V.92 are not supported. Remote Power-On via ring-indicator, SDLC, and synchronous PPP are not supported.

The #2805 and #2806 cards need country (region)-specific telephone cables (a minimum of one and a maximum of four per card). Feature #2806, the CIM version, is intended for Australia and New Zealand only. The #2805/#2806 require country (region) certification/homologation.

A minimum of one modem cable must be ordered for each #2805/#2806. All modem cables installed on a system must be the same feature number.

The cable features that are supported with the #2805 are:

- ▶ #1010 Modem Cable-Austria
- ▶ #1011 Modem Cable-Belgium
- ▶ #1012 Modem Cable-Africa
- ▶ #1013 Modem Cable-Israel
- ▶ #1014 Modem Cable-Italy
- ▶ #1015 Modem Cable-France
- ▶ #1016 Modem Cable-Germany
- ▶ #1017 Modem Cable-U.K.
- ▶ #1018 Modem Cable-Iceland/Sweden
- ▶ #1020 Modem Cable-China (Hong Kong S.A.R. of China)/New Zealand
- ▶ #1021 Modem Cable-Finland/Norway
- ▶ #1022 Modem Cable-Netherlands
- ▶ #1023 Modem Cable-Swiss
- ▶ #1024 Modem Cable-Denmark
- ▶ #1025 Modem Cable-U.S.A./Canada

Cable features supported with the #2806 are:

- ▶ #1019 Modem Cable-Australia
- ▶ #1020 Modem Cable-China (Hong Kong S.A.R. of China)/New Zealand

When used as a direct attach adapter for Linux, order the #0616 in place of the #2805, and order the #0617 in place of the #2806.

OS/400 V5R1 (with PTFs) or later is required. For required PTF information, availability, and ordering information, refer to Informational APAR II13079 at:

http://www-912.ibm.com/n_dir/nas4apar.nsf/nas4aparhome

#2849/#9749 10/100 Mbps Ethernet Adapter

The #2849 10/100 Mbps Ethernet Adapter and #9749 card allows an iSeries server to attach to standardized 100 Mbps high speed Ethernet LANs and allows attachment to existing 10 Mbps Ethernet LANs. The adapter comes standard with an RJ45 connector for attachment to UTP-5 media.

The #2849 is not supported on any Integrated Netfinity or Integrated xSeries Server. When used as a direct attach adapter for Linux, order the #0623 in place of the #2849.

#4745 PCI 2-line WAN IOA

The #4745 PCI 2-line WAN IOA supports up to two multiple protocol communications ports when one of two (in any combination) of these cables are attached:

- ► #0348 V.24/EIA232 20-ft./6m PCI cable
- ► #0349 V.24/EIA232 50-ft./15m PCI cable (*withdrawn from marketing* on 03 December 2002)
- ► #0353 V.35 20-ft./6m PCI cable
- ► #0354 V.35 50-ft./15m PCI cable (*withdrawn from marketing* on 03 December 2002)
- ► #0355 V.35 80-ft./24m PCI cable
- ► #0356 V.36 20-ft./6m PCI cable
- ► #0358 V.36 150-ft./45m PCI cable
- ► #0359 X.21 20-ft./6m PCI cable
- ► #0360 X.21 50-ft./15m PCI cable (*withdrawn from marketing* on 03 December 2002)
- ► #0365 V.24/EIA232 80-ft./24m PCI cable
- ► #0367 Operations Console PCI Cable

Only one #0367 Operations Console PCI Cable is allowed per #4745. Multiple #0367s can be ordered (but only one allowed per #4745) to serve as consoles for secondary partitions when logical partitioning (#0140) is specified. When used as a direct attach adapter for Linux, order the #0608 in place of the #4745.

#4746 PCI Twinaxial IOA

The #4746 PCI Twinaxial IOA is an 8-port twinaxial workstation IOA with a 20-foot attachment cable for attaching up to 40 5250-type displays and printers. Each port supports seven attached devices and allows up to 56 attached addresses of which only 40 can be active. When the attached display supports address sharing, a maximum of 120 shared sessions is supported.

#4778/#9778 Base PCI RAID Disk Unit Controller

The #4778/#9778 Base PCI RAID Disk Unit Controller is an Ultra2 SCSI adapter with a maximum compressed write cache size of 104 MB that provides RAID-5 protection and compression for internal disk units, as well as support for internal tape devices, CD-ROM, and DVD units. The #4778/#9778 has three Ultra2 SCSI buses.

The #4778/#9778 supports both disk compression and enhanced modes. The mode of operation is determined by a hardware jumper. The #4778/#9778 Ultra2 SCSI adapter is shipped in enhanced mode, which enables compression of the

write cache. Extended Adaptive Cache (requires a Read Cache Device) or RAID-protection is also supported.

Note: Data compression is not supported on 70 GB or larger disk units.

In addition to providing RAID-5 protection for disks, the #4778/#9778 is designed to work as a high performance controller for disks protected by system mirroring or disks with no protection.

The #4778/#9778 controller supports a maximum of 18 disk units. Hardware data compression is supported for 35 GB or smaller disk units.

Note: Due to system CEC and external tower disk unit cage SCSI bus designs, only the Models 270, 800, and 810 have a suitable system configuration to allow 18 disk units to attach to a single #4778. All other CEC or tower disk unit configurations restrict the number of attaching disk units to 15 or less.

The #4778/#9778 requires OS/400 V5R1 or later. When used as a direct attach adapter for Linux, order the #0606 in place of the #4778.

The #4778/#9778 Base PCI RAID Disk Unit Controller was withdrawn from marketing on November 2004.

#4801 PCI Cryptographic Coprocessor

The #4801 PCI Cryptographic Coprocessor is a hardware cryptography solution based on the IBM 4758-023 card. The #4801 is a half-length PCI card that offers rich cryptography function, secure storage of cryptographic keys, and triple DES capability. The Cryptographic Access Provider licensed program (no-charge 5722-AC3) must be installed to set the key length prior to using the adapter.

The #4801 is available worldwide.

Note: On new systems from the plant, the #4801 is shipped with the system. Due to temperature requirements (card temperature must not drop below 5 degrees Fahrenheit (-15 degrees Celsius)), it is not installed.

#4802 PCI Cryptographic Processor

The #4802 PCI Cryptographic Processor is a hardware cryptography solution based on the IBM 4758-023 card. The #4802 is a half-length PCI card that offers rich cryptography function, secure storage of cryptographic keys, and triple DES

capability. The #4802 provides greater security by use of 112-bit keys (compared to a 56-bit key of the #4800). The Cryptographic Access Provider licensed program (no-charge 5722-AC3) must be installed to set the key length prior to using the adapter.

The #4802 is only supported in the #5065 Storage/PCI Expansion Tower and the #5066 1.8 M I/O Tower.

The #4800 is not supported on iSeries Models 820, 830, 840, and 890 nor in #503x/#5077 Migration Tower II and their attached expansion towers. Convert each #4800 PCI Cryptographic Processor installed in a Model 720, 730, or 740 or attached expansion towers to a #4802 PCI Cryptographic Processor.

Note: On new shipments from the plant, the #4802 is shipped with the system. Due to temperature requirements (card temperature must not drop below 5 degrees Fahrenheit (-15 degrees Celsius)), it is not installed.

The #4802 is available worldwide.

#4805 PCI Cryptographic Accelerator

The #4805 PCI Cryptographic Accelerator feature provides improved performance for high transaction rate secure Web applications, which use the Secure Sockets Layer (SSL) or Transport Layer Security (TLS) protocols. Establishing SSL/TLS secure Web connections requires very compute intensive cryptographic processing.

You can use the Cryptographic Accelerator to offload cryptographic processing. SSL/TLS secure Web connections typically protect information (for example, credit card number) as it is transferred over the Internet, for example between a Web browser and a server.

There is a maximum of two #4805 PCI Cryptographic Accelerators per IOP. They are restricted to a maximum of one per IOP if the IOP also drives a 1 Gbps #2743, #2760, #5700, or #5701 Ethernet LAN card.

FIPS: Applications that require a FIPS 140 certified, tamper-resistant module for storing cryptographic keys or require financial PIN processing should continue to use the IBM 4758-023 Cryptographic Coprocessor PCI card (#4801 or #4802).

FIPS 140-1 is a U.S. Government National Institute of Standards & Technology (NIST) administered standard and certification program for cryptographic modules.

#4811/#4812/#4813/#9812/#9813 PCI-X Integrated xSeries Server

The #4811, #4812, #4813, #9812, or #9813 PCI-X Integrated xSeries Server contains an Intel Pentium 2.0 GHz processor with 2 MB integrated L2 cache. Features #4811, #4812, #4813 are functionally identical but have some physical differences depending on the model in which they are used.

The #4811 is supported in the 520 system tower. The #4812 is supported in the 550, 595, 800, 810, 825, 870 and 890 system towers and in the #0588, #0595, #5088, #5095, #5074, #5079, #5094 and #5294 expansion towers. The #4813 is supported in the 570 system tower and in the #5790 expansion unit.

The #9812 and #9813 are functionally identical to the #4812 and #4813 but are included in the base with orders for Enterprise Editions on system models 550, 595 and 570

The #4811, #4812, #4813, #9812, or #9813 PCI-X Integrated xSeries Server has two memory slots and supports up to 2 GB of memory. Both slots must always contain a pair of identical memory features. When the #4811, #4812, #4813, #9812, or #9813 is ordered, the IBM @server Marketing Configurator adds two #9726 base 512 MB server memory features to the order. The two #9726 features may be replaced with two #8546 optional base 1 GB server memory features.

The following main storage cards provide memory for the #4811, #4812, #4813, #9812, or #9813 PCI-X Integrated xSeries Server:

- ▶ #0446 - 512MB DDR Server Memory (upgrade only)
- ▶ #0447 - 1GB DDR Server Memory (upgrade only)
- ▶ #9726 - Base 512MB Server Memory (initial order only)
- ▶ #8546 - Opt Base 1GB Server Memory (initial order only)

The #4811, #4812, #4813, #9812, or #9813 PCI-X Integrated xSeries Server occupies two PCI slots and requires an IOP #9744, #9844 or #2844 to drive it. The IBM @server Marketing Configurator adds #9744 Base PCI IOP to the order. The #9744 can be removed from the order to conserve PCI slots. The IOP may be shared, but only one #4811, #4812, #4813, #9812, or #9813 is permitted per IOP.

Placement of the PCI-X Integrated xSeries Server is limited to specific slots:

- ▶ Placement of the #4811 is limited to slot P1-C4 in the Model 520 system unit. The #4811 hangs over slot P1-C5 and occupies two PCI slots. If a #6594 4-Disk Slot Expansion is in the 520 system unit, it repositions the SCSI cable connector so that a long card can be placed in card slot 4 and forces card slot 5 to be a short card. Therefore, a #4811 Integrated xSeries Server cannot be in the 520 system unit when a #6594 is also installed.

► Placement of the #4812/#9812 is limited to specific PCI slots within the Model 550, 595, 800, 810, 825, 870 and 890 system towers and the various expansion towers.

► Placement of the #4813/#9813 is limited to specific PCI slots within the 570 system unit and #5790 expansion unit.

The #4811, #4812, #4813, #9812, or #9813 PCI-X Integrated xSeries Server includes two embedded 1000/100/10 Mbps UTP Ethernet LAN ports for attachment to IEEE standard 802.3Z high-speed (1 Gbps) Ethernet LANs. The Ethernet LAN ports may also be used to connect to existing 10 and 100 Mbps Ethernet LANs by using switches with 10/100/1000 Mbps ports. The adapter supports UTP CAT 5 or higher media interface and TCP/IP.

i5/OS V5R3 is required to support the Integrated xSeries Server.

The #4811, #4812, #4813, #9812, or #9813 PCI-X Integrated xSeries Server ships with a standard keyboard/mouse splitter cable and supports either a standard or USB 1.1 keyboard or mouse. An SVGA video port is included for connecting a display.

The #4811, #4812, #4813, #9812, or #9813 PCI-X Integrated xSeries Server runs Windows or Linux. The supported versions of Windows are:

► Windows Server 2003 Standard, Enterprise and Web Editions
► Windows 2000 Server and Windows 2000 Advanced Server Windows 2000

The supported versions of Linux are:

► Red Hat Enterprise Linux ES 3
► Red Hat Enterprise Linux AS 3

The following rules apply when ordering the PCI-X Integrated xSeries

► The #0325 IPCS Extension Cable for Windows is the default but may be removed.

► The #1700 IPCS Keyboard and Mouse for Windows is the default in those countries or regions offering it.

► A display is required and must be connected to the #4811/#4812/#4813/9812/#9813 to support Windows 2000.

► A display is not required for Windows 3000. If no display is connected the Virtual system Console is used.

For a non-U.S. keyboard, mouse and display, see:

`http://www.ibm.com/eserver/iseries/windowsintegration/`

For the latest information about Windows on @server i5 and iSeries, see:

http://www.ibm.com/eserver/iseries/windowsintegration/xseriesmodels

For the latest information about Linux on @server i5 and iSeries, see:

http://www.ibm.com/eserver/iseries/integratedxseries/linux

#5700 PCI 1 Gbps Ethernet IOA

The #5700 PCI 1 Gbps Ethernet IOA allows attachment to IEEE standard 802.3Z high-speed (1 Gbps) Ethernet LANs. It can also be used to connect to existing 100 Mbps Ethernet LANs via switches capable of handling multiple speeds with 10 Mbps, 100 Mbps, or 1000 Mbps ports. It cannot be directly attached (crossover cables are not supported) to 10 Mbps or 100 Mbps networks.

The #5700 supports a multimode fiber interface with a 62.5 micron or 50.0 micron cable requirement. The adapter has a duplex LC fiber optic connector for attachment to client supplied cabling.

The #5700 adapter supports TCP/IP only. TCP/IP Checksum Offload and TCP Segmentation Offload are not supported. SNA and IPX protocols are not supported.

There is a maximum of one #5700 per Multi-Adapter Bridge Boundary (MABB), except where the second #5700 is controlled by an Integrated xSeries Server. Combinations of Integrated xSeries Server controlled and PCI IOP controlled #5700s within a MABB are permitted. If a #5700 is controlled by a #2792/#4810/#2892 PCI Integrated xSeries Server, then the #0226 1 Gbps Ethernet Specify is ordered for each #5700 controlled by an Integrated xSeries Server.

When used as a direct attach adapter for Linux or AIX, order the #0620 in place of the #5700.

#5701 PCI 1 Gbps Ethernet UTP IOA

The #5701 PCI 1 Gbps Ethernet UTP IOA allows attachment to IEEE standard 802.3Z high-speed (1 Gbps) Ethernet LANs. The #5701 PCI 1 Gbps Ethernet UTP IOA can negotiate to a lower speed and can directly attach to 10 Mbps or 100 Mbps networks with appropriate switches and hubs. Direct attachment via crossover cables is not supported. The #5701 adapter supports a UTP CAT 5 media interface.

The #5701 adapter supports TCP/IP only. TCP/IP Checksum Offload and TCP Segmentation Offload are not supported. SNA and IPX protocols are not supported.

There is a maximum of one #5701 per MABB, except where the second #5701 is controlled by an Integrated xSeries Server. Combinations of Integrated xSeries Server controlled and PCI IOP controlled #5701s within a MABB are permitted. If a #5701 is controlled by a #2792 or #4810 or #2892 Integrated xSeries Server, then specify code #0226 - 1 Gbps Ethernet Specify is specified for each #5701 controlled by an Integrated xSeries Server.

When used as a direct attach adapter for Linux or AIX, order the #0621 in place of the #5701.

The #2760 PCI 1 Gbps Ethernet UTP Adapter and the #5701 PCI 1 Gbps Ethernet UTP IOA are functionally equivalent.

#5702 PCI-X Ultra Tape Controller

The #5702 PCI-X Ultra Tape Controller is an Ultra SCSI LVD controller for attachment of two external tape devices or an external CD-ROM device that has a single-ended SCSI interface.

Each port of the #5702 PCI-X Ultra Tape Controller supports one, or a combination, of these devices:

- ► 3580-L23 IBM TotalStorage Ultrium 2 Tape Drive
- ► 3582-L23 IBM Ultrium Tape Library, LVD Ultrium 2 drive feature
- ► 3583-Lxx IBM Ultrium Scalable Tape Library, LVD Ultrium 2 drive feature
- ► 3584 UltraScalable Tape Library, LVD Ultrium 2 drive feature
- ► 7206-VX2 80 GB VXA-2 External Tape Drive
- ► 7207-122 QIC-SLR Tape Bridge Box (4 GB External ¼-inch Cartridge Tape Drive)
- ► 7208-345 60 GB External 8mm Tape Drive
- ► 7210-020 External CD-ROM
- ► 7210-025 External DVD-RAM
- ► 7329-308 SLR100 ¼-inch Tape Autoloader
- ► One 7210 Model 025 and one 7210 Model 025: The two devices are daisy chained.
- ► One 7210 Model 025 and one 7210 Model 020: The two devices are daisy chained with the 7210-025 physically connected first. No #0120 attachment specify code is required for the 7210-020.
- ► One 7207 Model 122 and one 7210 Model 020: The two devices are daisy chained with the 7207-122 physically connected first. No #0120 attachment specify code is required for the 7210-020.

- One 7207 Model 122 and one 7210 Model 025: The two devices are daisy chained with the 7207-122 physically connected first.

- One 7208 Model 345 and one 7210 Model 020: The two devices are daisy chained with the 7208-345 physically connected first. No #0120 attachment specify code is required for the 7210-020.

- One 7208 Model 345 and one 7210 Model 025: The two devices are daisy chained with the 7208-345 physically connected first.

The #0120 7210-020 Attachment Specify is required for each 7210-020 External CD-ROM Drive to be connected directly (not daisy chained) to the system through a #5702.

> **Note:** If the 7210-020 is daisy chained with another external device, the #0120 specify code must not be present.

The #0162 Extended Single Ended Attach Specify is required when these devices are directly attached (not second on a daisy chained string) to an iSeries server, via a #5702 PCI-X Ultra Tape Controller:

- 7329-308 SLR100 ¼-inch Tape Autoloader
- 7210-025 External DVD-RAM

> **Note:** If either of these devices is daisy chained with another device, the #0162 specify code must not be present.

The #5702 PCI-X Ultra Tape Controller is hot pluggable. When used as a direct attach adapter, order the #0624 in place of the #5702.

> **Note:** The #5702 has both internal and external SCSI ports. Devices cannot be attached both internally and externally on the same bus.

#5703 PCI-X RAID Disk Unit Controller

The #5703 PCI-X RAID Disk Unit Controller is an Ultra3 SCSI controller with a cache size of 40 MB that provides RAID-5 protection for internal disks and internal tape units, CD-ROM, DVD-RAM, and DVD-ROM units. The #5703 has two Ultra3 SCSI buses and runs on a U320 (320 MB/s) data rate.

In addition to providing RAID-5 protection for disks, the #5703 is designed to work as a high performance controller for disks protected by system mirroring or disks with no protection. In the RAID-5 configuration, disk unit protection is provided at less cost than mirroring, and with greater performance than system checksums.

The #5703 controller supports a maximum of 12 disk units. DASD compression is not supported.

Restriction: Due to a system CEC and external tower disk unit cage SCSI bus designs, only Models 270, 800, and 810, and the #0595/#5095 PCI-X Expansion Tower have a suitable system configuration to allow 12 disk units to attach to a single #5703. All other CEC and tower disk configurations restrict the number of attaching disk units to 10 or less.

A minimum of three disk units of the same capacity are needed for a valid RAID-5 configuration. A maximum of four arrays are allowed per controller, with a maximum of 12 disk units allowed per array. All disk units in an array must be of the same capacity. Parity is spread across either two, four, or eight disk units in an array. If an array of three disk units is started, parity is spread across two disk units. If an array of four to seven disk units is started, parity is spread across four disk units. If an array of 8 to 12 disk units is started, parity is spread across eight disk units.

The number of arrays and size of each array can be influenced by specifying an optimization of either Balance, Performance, or Capacity in Operations Navigator when starting arrays. An optimization of *Balance* is used by default when starting arrays from the green screens. If disk units are included into an existing array, parity may be spread across less than the preferred number of disk units. In this case, you must stop and then start the RAID function to redistribute the parity.

The #5703 can control up to two removable media devices (internal tape, CD-ROM, DVD-RAM, DVD-ROM).

The #5703 PCI-X RAID Disk Unit Controller is the recommended replacement for the #2782 PCI-X RAID Disk Unit Controller.

When used as a direct attach adapter, order the #0628 in place of the #5703. The #0143 Disk Controller Placement Exception is a prerequisite for the #5703.

#5704 PCI-X Fibre Channel Tape Controller

The #5704 PCI-X Fibre Channel Tape Controller provides Fibre Channel attachment capability for external tape devices. The #5704 supports point-to-point and arbitrated loop topologies and has an LC-type cable connector. Each #5704 is shipped with a wrap connector (part number 05N6767). The #5704 supports 64-bit, 133 MHz PCI-X bus speeds.

The following adapter kits are required when connecting SC-type cables to the #5704:

► #0371 - LC-SC Adapter Kit (50 micron)

The #0371 can be ordered on initial, model upgrades, and simple MES orders. This optional kit is used to attach SC-type fibre (50 micron) cables to a #5704. The #0371 kit contains a 2m LC-ST cable and ST-SC adapter for 50 micron fiber cable.

► #0372 - LC-SC Adapter Kit (62.5 micron)

The #0372 can be ordered on initial, model upgrades, and simple MES orders. This optional kit is used to attach SC-type fibre (62.5 micron) cables to a #5704. The #0372 kit contains a 2m LC-ST cable and ST-SC adapter for 62.5 micron fiber cable.

An optics cleaning kit (part number 46G6844) and instruction sheet (part number 21P6238, form number SY27-2604) are supplied, one per system, when you order a #5704.

Note: Clients are to supply all Fibre Channel cables for the #5704 PCI-X Fibre Channel Tape Controller.

The #5704 PCI-X Fibre Channel Tape Controller is the PCI-X card replacement for the #2765 PCI Fibre Channel Tape Controller. When used as a direct attach adapter for Linux or AIX, order the #0625 in place of the #5704.

#5705 PCI-X Tape/DASD Controller

The #5705 PCI-X Tape/DASD Controller provides SCSI Ultra PCI attachment capability for external tape devices, up to two removable media devices (internal tape, CD-ROM or DVD), and internal disk devices. The #5705 has two SCSI buses, with each bus providing an internal and an external device port (four ports total: two internal and two external). Each bus can only support one connection, either an internal DASD connection or internal tape on the internal port, or an external tape or removable media connection on the external port.

The internal SCSI DASD port supports up to six disk units. RAID is not supported.

The internal tape port supports one #4585 80 GB VXA-2 Tape Device. The external tape port supports one, or a combination, of these devices:

► 3580-L23 IBM TotalStorage Ultrium 2 Tape Drive

► 3582-L23 IBM Ultrium Tape Library, LVD Ultrium 2 drive feature

- 3583-Lxx IBM Ultrium Scalable Tape Library, LVD Ultrium 2 drive feature
- 3584 UltraScalable Tape Library, LVD Ultrium 2 drive feature
- 7206-VX2 80 GB VXA-2 External Tape Drive
- 7207-122 QIC-SLR Tape Bridge Box (4 GB External ¼-inch Cartridge Tape Drive)
- 7208-345 60 GB External 8mm Tape Drive
- 7210-020 External CD-ROM
- 7210-025 External DVD-RAM
- 7329-308 SLR100 ¼-inch Tape Autoloader
- One 7210-025 External DVD-RAM and one 7210-025 External DVD-RAM: The two devices are daisy chained.
- One 7210-025 External DVD-RAM and one 7210-020 External CD-ROM: The two devices are daisy chained with the 7210-025 physically connected first. No #0120 attachment specify code is required for the 7210-020.
- One 7207-122 QIC-SLR Tape Bridge Box (4 GB External ¼-inch Cartridge Tape Drive) and one 7210-020 External CD-ROM: The two devices are daisy chained with the 7207-122 physically connected first. No #0120 attachment specify code is required for the 7210-020.
- One 7207-122 QIC-SLR Tape Bridge Box (4 GB External ¼-inch Cartridge Tape Drive) and one 7210-025 External DVD-RAM: The two devices are daisy chained with the 7207-122 physically connected first.
- One 7208-345 60 GB External 8mm Tape Drive and one 7210-020 External CD-ROM: The two devices are daisy chained with the 7208-345 physically connected first. No #0120 attachment specify code is required for the 7210-020.
- One 7208-345 60 GB External 8mm Tape Drive and one 7210-025 External DVD-RAM: The two devices are daisy chained with the 7208-345 physically connected first.

The #0120 7210-020 Attachment Specify is required for each 7210-020 External CD-ROM to be connected directly (not daisy chained) to the system through a #5705.

Note: If the 7210-020 is daisy chained with another external device, the #0120 specify code must not be present.

The #0162 Extended Single Ended Attach Specify is required when these devices are directly attached (not second on a daisy-chained string) to an iSeries server via a #5705 PCI-X Tape/DASD Controller:

- ► 7329-308 SLR100 ¼-inch Tape Autoloader
- ► 7210-025 External DVD-RAM

Note: If either of these devices is daisy chained with another device, the #0162 specify code must not be present.

If two external SCSI ports are required, order a #5702.

#5706 PCI-X 1Gbps Ethernet-TX IOA

The #5706 PCI-X 1Gbps Ethernet-TX IOA is a 2-port 1000/100/10 Mbps Base-TX Ethernet PCI-X Adapter. The #5706 is a full duplex, dual ported, Gigabit Ethernet adapter designed with highly integrated components. This adapter can be configured to run each port at 1000, 100, or 10 Mbps data rates. This adapter interfaces to the system via a PCI or PCI-X bus and connects to a network using a 4-pair CAT-5 Unshielded Twisted Pair (UTP) cable for distances of up to 100m. The adapter conforms to the IEEE 802.3ab 1000Base-T standard. The #5706 also supports jumbo frames when running at the 1000 Mbps speed.

i5/OS V5R3 for adapter #5706 does not supports a function called *Large Send* or sometimes known as *TCP Segmentation*. This function offloads the TCP segmentation operation from the IP layer to the adapter for outgoing (transmit side) TCP segments. AIX 5L for POWER V5.2 or later supports this function

i5/OS V5R3 for adapter #5706 does not support a function known as *Checksum Offload*, which offloads the TCP/UDP Checksum Operation or workload from the CPU to the adapter. AIX 5L for POWER V5.2 or later, SUSE LINUX Enterprise Server 9 for POWER with 2.6 kernel can support these functions.

The #5706 IOA does not require a PCI IOP. The IOP functions are already integrated into the IOA.

There are no additional restrictions of where the #5706 can be placed. The system recognizes IOP-less cards and handles them appropriately, regardless of where they are placed (in front of or behind IOPs).

Note: For optimum performance, place the adapter in a 64-bit PCI-X card slot whenever possible.

Note the following restrictions:

- ► The 1000 Mbps speed is not supported in half duplex (HDX) mode.
- ► Systems Network Architecture (SNA) is not supported.
- ► A cross-over cable is not supported.

It is supported in Models 520, 550, 570, or 595 with i5/OS V5R3.

When used as a direct attach adapter for Linux or AIX, order the #0643 in place of the #5706. The #5706 is a Customer Install Feature.

#5707 PCI-X 1 Gbps Ethernet-SX IOA

The #5707 PCI-X 1 Gbps Ethernet-SX IOA is a 2-Port Gigabit Ethernet-SX PCI-X Adapter that provides two 1 Gbps (1000 Base-SX) full-duplex Ethernet LAN connections with throughput on a standard shortwave multimode optical cable that conforms to the IEEE 802.3z standard. The adapter supports distances of 260m for 62.5 micron Multi Mode Fiber (MMF) and 550m for 50.0 micron MMF.

i5/OS V5R3 for adapter #5707 does not supports a function called *Large Send* or sometimes known as *TCP Segmentation*. This function offloads the TCP segmentation operation from the IP layer to the adapter for outgoing (transmit side) TCP segments. AIX 5L for POWER V5.2 or later supports this function

i5/OS V5R3 for adapter #5707 does not supports a function known as *Checksum Offload*, which offloads the TCP/UDP Checksum Operation or workload from the CPU to the adapter. AIX 5L for POWER V5.2 or later, SUSE LINUX Enterprise Server 9 for POWER with 2.6 kernel can support these functions.

The #5707 IOA does not require a PCI IOP. The IOP functions are already integrated into the IOA.

There are no additional restrictions of where the #5707 can be placed. The system recognizes IOP-less cards and handles them appropriately, regardless of where they are placed (in front of or behind IOPs).

Note: For optimum performance, place the adapter in a 64-bit PCI-X card slot whenever possible.

The 2-Port IBM Gigabit Ethernet-SX PCI-X Adapter incorporates an LC type connector on the card.

Note the following restrictions:

- ► Half duplex (HDX) mode is not supported.
- ► Systems Network Architecture (SNA) is not supported.
- ► A cross-over cable is not supported.

It is supported in Models 520, 550, 570, and 595 with i5/OS V5R3.

When used as a direct attach adapter for Linux or AIX, order the #0644 in place of the #5707. The #5707 is a Customer Install Feature.

#5709 RAID Enabler Card

The #5709 RAID Enabler Card has 16 MB write cache. It supports up to eight disk unit positions in the Model 520 and 550 system unit and up to six disk unit positions in the Model 570 system unit. The #5709 is not supported on the Model 595. The #5709 provides RAID capability to the embedded SCSI controller. It plugs into its own specific internal slot and does not require or use a PCI card slot. Hardware disk compression is not supported.

> **Note:** The i5/OS operating system does not have the capability to interface directly to the embedded SCSI controller. The #5709 communicates solely with the embedded controller. An IOP must be present for the #5709 to communicate with the i5/OS operating system.

In the Model 520, you can use the #5709 with or without a #6574 4-Disk Slot Exp - Base Controller. When installed without a #6574, the #5709 supports four disk units. When installed with a #6574, the #5709 supports a maximum of eight disk units.

In the Model 550, you can use the #5709 with a #6592 4-Disk Slot Expansion. When installed without a #6592 the #5709 supports four disk units. When installed with a #6592, the #5709 supports a maximum of eight disk units.

The #5709 is an optional feature for the Model 520 and 550. It is required for the Model 570. It is supported in Models 520, 550, and 570 with i5/OS V5R3. It is not supported on the Model 595.

The #5709 is a Customer Install Feature.

#5712 PCI-X Tape/DASD Controller

The #5712 is an Ultra SCSI controller for attachment of two external tape devices or an external CD-ROM device that has a single-ended SCSI interface.

Note: The #5712/5702 is the best choice when the client is using i5/OS V5R3 or OS/400 V5R2 and the tape drive being attached uses an Low Voltage Differential (LVD) SCSI interface such as the 358x LTO-2, 7207-330 (30 GB QIC) and 7206-VX2 (80 GB VXA-2).Note the #5712/5702 is rated at up to 160 MBps. This is a good match for 358x LTO-2 tape drives.

Each port of the #5712 PCI-X Tape/DASD Controller supports one, or a combination, of these devices:

- 3580-L23 IBM TotalStorage Ultrium 2 Tape Drive
- 3581-Lxx IBM Ultrium Tape Autoloader
- 3582-L23 IBM Ultrium Tape Library, LVD Ultrium 2 drive feature
- 3583-Lxx IBM Ultrium Scalable Tape Library, LVD Ultrium 2 drive feature
- 3584 UltraScalable Tape Library, LVD Ultrium 2 drive feature
- 7206-VX2 80 GB VXA-2 External Tape Drive
- 7207-122 QIC-SLR Tape Bridge Box (4 GB External ¼-inch Cartridge Tape Drive)
- 7208-345 60 GB External 8mm Tape Drive
- 7210-020 External CD-ROM
- 7210-025 External DVD-RAM
- 7329-308 SLR100 ¼-inch Tape Autoloader
- Two 7210 Model 025 External DVD-RAMs. The two devices are daisy chained.
- One 7210 Model 025 and one 7210 Model 020: The two devices are daisy chained with the 7210-025 physically connected first. No #0120 attachment specify code is required for the 7210-020.
- One 7207 Model 122 and one 7210 Model 020: The two devices are daisy chained with the 7207-122 physically connected first. No #0120 attachment specify code is required for the 7210-020.
- One 7207 Model 122 and one 7210 Model 025: The two devices are daisy chained with the 7207-122 physically connected first.
- One 7208 Model 345 and one 7210 Model 020: The two devices are daisy chained with the 7208-345 physically connected first. No #0120 attachment specify code is required for the 7210-020.
- One 7208 Model 345 and one 7210 Model 025: The two devices are daisy chained with the 7208-345 physically connected first.

The #0120 7210-020 Attachment Specify is required for each 7210-020 External CD-ROM Drive to be connected directly (not daisy chained) to the system through a #5702.

Note: If the 7210-020 is daisy chained with another external device, the #0120 specify code must not be present.

The #0162 Extended Single Ended Attach Specify is required when these devices are directly attached (not second on a daisy chained string) to an iSeries server, via a #5702 PCI-X Ultra Tape Controller:

► 7329-308 SLR100 ¼-inch Tape Autoloader
► 7210-025 External DVD-RAM

Note: If either of these devices is daisy chained with another device, the #0162 specify code must not be present.

The #5712 can be placed in any expansion tower. It cannot be used to drive the internal removable media bays in #5074/#5094 towers.

The #5712 is hot pluggable.

When used as a direct attach adapter, order the #0645 in place of the #5712.

Note: The #5712 has both internal and external SCSI ports. Devices cannot be attached both internally and externally on the same bus.

#5715 PCI-X Tape/DASD Controller

The #5715 PCI-X Tape/DASD Controller provides Ultra SCSI attachment is the follow on to #5705. The #5715 has two SCSI buses, one bus provides one internal and the one external SCSI port. Each bus can only support one connection, an internal DASD connection or an external tape or removable media connection on the external port. The #5715 does not supports RAID-5. It does not support hardware data compression.

The external tape port supports one, or a combination, of these devices:

► 3580-L23 IBM TotalStorage Ultrium 2 Tape Drive

► 3582-L23 IBM Ultrium Tape Library, LVD Ultrium 2 drive feature

► 3583-Lxx IBM Ultrium Scalable Tape Library, LVD Ultrium 2 drive feature

► 3584 UltraScalable Tape Library, LVD Ultrium 2 drive feature

► 7206-VX2 80 GB VXA-2 External Tape Drive

- ▶ 7207-122 QIC-SLR Tape Bridge Box (4 GB External ¼-inch Cartridge Tape Drive)
- ▶ 7208-345 60 GB External 8mm Tape Drive
- ▶ 7210-020 External CD-ROM
- ▶ 7210-025 External DVD-RAM
- ▶ 7329-308 SLR100 ¼-inch Tape Autoloader
- ▶ Two 7210-025 External DVD-RAMs. The two devices are daisy chained.
- ▶ One 7210-025 External DVD-RAM and one 7210-020 External CD-ROM: The two devices are daisy chained with the 7210-025 physically connected first. No #0120 attachment specify code is required for the 7210-020.
- ▶ One 7207-122 QIC-SLR Tape Bridge Box (4 GB External ¼-inch Cartridge Tape Drive) and one 7210-020 External CD-ROM: The two devices are daisy chained with the 7207-122 physically connected first. No #0120 attachment specify code is required for the 7210-020.
- ▶ One 7207-122 QIC-SLR Tape Bridge Box (4 GB External ¼-inch Cartridge Tape Drive) and one 7210-025 External DVD-RAM: The two devices are daisy chained with the 7207-122 physically connected first.
- ▶ One 7208-345 60 GB External 8mm Tape Drive and one 7210-020 External CD-ROM: The two devices are daisy chained with the 7208-345 physically connected first. No #0120 attachment specify code is required for the 7210-020.
- ▶ One 7208-345 60 GB External 8mm Tape Drive and one 7210-025 External DVD-RAM: The two devices are daisy chained with the 7208-345 physically connected first.

The #0120 7210-020 Attachment Specify is required for each 7210-020 External CD-ROM to connect directly (not daisy chained) to the system through a #5705.

Note: If the 7210-020 is daisy chained with another external device, the #0120 specify code must not be present.

The #0162 Extended Single Ended Attach Specify is required when these devices are directly attached (not second on a daisy-chained string) to an iSeries server via a #5705 PCI-X Tape/DASD Controller:

- ▶ 7329-308 SLR100 ¼-inch Tape Autoloader
- ▶ 7210-025 External DVD-RAM

Note: If either of these devices is daisy chained with another device, the #0162 specify code must not be present.

If two external SCSI ports are required, order a #5712.

Homologation

Homologation is the process to obtain a country's (region's) government approval to ship a device and connect it to the country's (region's) telecommunications network. The action is similar to Federal Communications Commission (FCC) approval in the United States.

There are features on the system that require homologation by a country's (region's) government organizations, usually Post Telephone and Telegram (PTTs) departments. The following table summarizes the PCI features that may require homologation in certain countries (regions).

Feature code	Description
#0032	High-speed modem
#2750	PCI ISDN Bri U IOA - 2-wire
#2751	PCI ISDN Bri S/T IOA - 4-wire
#2761	PCI Integrated Analog Modem
#2772	PCI Two-Line WAN with integrated modems
#2773	PCI Two-Line WAN with integrated modems
#2793	PCI Two-Line WAN with integrated modem
#2794	PCI Two-Line WAN with integrated modem
#2805	PCI Quad Modem IOA
#2806	PCI Quad Modem IOA
#4750	PCI ISDN Bri U IOA - 2-wire
#4751	PCI ISDN Bri S/T IOA 4-wire
#4761	PCI Integrated Analog Modem
#9771	Base PCI Two-Line WAN with Modem
#9793	Base PCI Two-Line WAN with modem
#9794	Base PCI Two-Line WAN with modem

#2760 PCI 1 Gbps Ethernet UTP Adapter

The #2760 PCI 1 Gbps Ethernet UTP Adapter allows attachment to IEEE standard 802.3Z high-speed Ethernet LANs (1 Gbps) to provide a significant performance improvement over other LAN solutions. The adapter supports a UTP CAT 5 media interface. The #2760 supports half and full duplex mode, and TCP/IP only. IPX and SNA protocol is not supported.

The #2760 can negotiate to a lower speed and can directly attach to 10 Mbps or 100 Mbps networks with appropriate switches and hubs. Direct attachment via crossover cables is not supported. A #2760 is supported under a #2791 or #2799 or #2891/#2899 PCI Integrated xSeries Server in V5R1. A #0225 1 Gbps Ethernet Specify is needed for each #2760 running under one of these Integrated Netfinity Servers or Integrated xSeries Servers. Use the Enhanced Category 5 cable for the best results.

The #2760 adapter only supports TCP/IP. SNA and IPX protocols are not supported. When used as a direct attach adapter for Linux, order the #0602 in place of the #2760.

The #2760 PCI 1 Gbps Ethernet UTP Adapter and the #5701 PCI 1 Gbps Ethernet UTP IOA are functionally equivalent.

The #2760 was withdrawn from marketing in October 2004.

#2765 PCI Fibre Channel Tape Controller

The #2765 PCI Fibre Channel Tape Controller provides Fibre Channel attachment capability for external tape devices. The #2765 supports point-to-point and arbitrated loop topologies. The #2765 is auto-sensing and is fully enabled for 1 Gbps and 2 Gbps. OS/400 V5R2 is required for 2 Gbps. Each #2765 is shipped with a wrap connector (PN #05N6767).

The following options are available to attach SC-type fibre cables:

► A #0371 two meter LC-SC Adapter kit is used to connect the #2765 to a 50 micron cable.

► A #0372 two meter LC-SC Adapter kit is used to connect the #2765 to a 62.5 micron cable.

Fibre Channel attachment for tape devices offer tremendous performance capabilities and long distance options. It is also easier to share these valuable resources with multiple systems.

The tape subsystems that are supported by the #2765 PCI Fibre Channel Tape Controller are:

► 3590 Models E11/H11 or E1A/H1A with feature #9510 (on new orders)
► 3590 Models E11/H11 or E1A/H1A with feature #3510 (upgrade of installed SCSI tape devices to Fibre Channel)
► 3583 with drive feature #8005
► 3584 with drive feature #1456
► 3584 LTO 2 with drive feature #1476

Only one tape device can be connected per IOA.

The #2765 was *withdrawn from marketing* in October 2004. The #5704 PCI-X Fibre Channel Tape Controller is the recommended replacement.

#2766 PCI Fibre Channel Disk Controller

The #2766 PCI Fibre Channel Disk Controller provides Fibre Channel attachment capability for external disk devices. The #2766 supports point-to-point and arbitrated loop topologies. The #2766 is auto-sensing and is fully enabled for 1 Gbps and 2 Gbps. OS/400 V5R2 is required for 2 Gbps. Each #2766 is shipped with a wrap connector (PN #05N6767).

The following options are available to attach SC-type fibre cables:

► A #0371 two meter LC-SC Adapter kit is used to connect the #2765 to a 50 micron cable.

► A #0372 two meter LC-SC Adapter kit is used to connect the #2765 to a 62.5 micron cable.

The #2766 requires a dedicated IOP. No other IOA is allowed on an IOP with the #2766.

Some iSeries clients may find storage area network (SAN)-attached DASD devices to be appealing for their environment. If consolidating large amounts of DASD from different platforms is important, consider SAN. However, a complex commercial business environment usually requires good, predictable response time to maintain user productivity and satisfaction. Carefully consider the performance implications of sharing resources in this environment, because the sharing may introduce more variable performance. For critical workloads, dedicated direct attach DASD resources can ensure more predictable performance.

When used as a direct attach adapter for Linux, order the #0612 in place of the #2766.

Important: A #2766 PCI Fibre Channel Disk Controller, supported on the iSeries with OS/400 V5R1, can be used to attach the IBM TotalStorage Enterprise Storage Server (ESS). The #2766 is not supported as a load source IOP in secondary (system is unable to IPL via a #2766), but remote load source mirroring is supported through the #2766.

The #2782 was *withdrawn from marketing* in October 2004. The #2787 PCI-X Fibre Channel Disk Controller is the recommended replacement.

#2782 PCI-X RAID Disk Unit Controller

The #2782 PCI-X RAID Disk Unit Controller is an Ultra SCSI disk unit controller with a 40 MB cache that provides RAID-5 protection for internal disk units. It also supports internal tape devices, CD-ROM, and DVD units. The #2782 has two Ultra SCSI buses.

The #2782 is designed to work as a high performance controller for disks protected by system mirroring or disks with no protection. In the RAID-5 configuration, disk unit protection is provided at less cost than mirroring, and with greater performance than system checksums.

The #2782 controller supports a maximum of 12 disk units. DASD compression is not supported. The #2782 controls up to two removable media devices (internal tape, CD-ROM and DVD).

Note: Due to a system unit and external tower disk cage designs, only the Models 270 and 810, and the #0595/#5095 PCI-X Expansion Tower have a suitable system configuration to allow 12 disk units to attach to a single #2782. All other system unit and tower disk configurations restrict the number of attaching disk units to 10 or less.

A minimum of three disk units of the same capacity are needed for a valid RAID-5 configuration. A maximum of four arrays are allowed per controller, with a maximum of 12 disk units allowed per array.

Parity is spread across either two, four, eight, or 16 disk units in an array, as represented in the following table.

Number of units in the array	Number of units parity is spread across
3	2
4 - 7	4
8 - 12	8

The #2782 and #0619 Linux Direct Attach - #2782 PCI-X RAID Disk Unit Controller were *withdrawn from marketing* on 01 January 2004. The #5703 PCI-X RAID Disk Unit Controller is the recommended replacement for the #2782. The #0628 is the recommended replacement for the #0619.

The #2782 was *withdrawn from marketing* in October 2004.

#4748/#9748 Base PCI RAID Disk Unit Controller

The #4748/#9748 Base PCI RAID Disk Unit Controller is an Ultra2 SCSI disk unit controller with a 26 MB write-cache that provides RAID-5 protection for internal disk units and supports internal tape, CD-ROM, and DVD devices. The #4748/#9748 supports both compression and non-compression modes. The mode of operation is determined by a hardware jumper, which is in the non-compression mode position when shipped. By moving the hardware jumper, the controller functions in compression mode.

In addition to providing RAID-5 protection for disks, the #4748/#9748 is also designed to work as a high-performance controller for disks protected by system mirroring or disks with no protection. In the RAID-5 configuration, disk unit protection is provided at a lower cost than mirroring and with greater performance than system checksums.

Note: Data compression is not supported on 35 GB or larger disk units.

The #4748/#9748 controller supports a maximum of 18 drives. A minimum of four drives of the same capacity is needed for a valid RAID-5 configuration. A maximum of four arrays is allowed, with a maximum of 10 drives allowed per array. All drives in an array must be of the same capacity.

The #4748/#9748 also supports two removable media devices.

The #4748 feature is hot pluggable. When used as a direct attach adapter for Linux, order the #0605 in place of the #4748.

The #4748 was *withdrawn from marketing* on 21 November 2003. The recommended replacement is a #2757 PCI-X Ultra RAID Disk Controller.

#4838 PCI 100/10 Mbps Ethernet IOA

The #4838 PCI 100/10 Mbps Ethernet IOA allows iSeries servers to attach to a standardized 100 Mbps high-speed Ethernet LAN. It also allows the attachment to existing 10 Mbps Ethernet LANs. The adapter comes with an RJ-45 connector for attachment to UTP-5 media. Cabling for 10 Mbps must be CAT-3 or CAT-5. Cabling for 100 Mbps must be CAT 5 that meets or exceeds Industry Standard EIA/TIA T568A or T568B. The maximum cable length is 100 meters. The Ethernet/IEEE 802.3 IOA is capable of operating in half or full duplex mode.

If the #4838 is selected to run on a #2791/#2799 PCI Integrated xSeries Server or #2891/#2899 PCI Integrated xSeries Server, one #0224 (100/10 Mbps Ethernet on Integrated Netfinity Server) is required for each #4838 ordered.

When used as a direct attach adapter for Linux, order the #0607 in place of the #4838.

The #4838 was *withdrawn from marketing* in October 2004. The #2849 is the recommended replacement.

19

Internal disk, tape, CD-ROM, DVD-RAM, DVD-ROM storage

This chapter discusses disk storage, tape, CD-ROM, and DVD-RAM internal to the system unit or tower complex. It also presents information about speeds, specifications, and feature descriptions, including disk protection, hardware disk compression, and alternate initial program load (IPL) options.

PCI disk units

This section summarizes information for Peripheral Component Interconnect (PCI) disk features supported by iSeries servers. The following table identifies the system and expansion units, which support each PCI disk feature, and specifications such as RAID and mirror support, number of bytes, and the minimum operating system level required.

PCI internal disks		System and expansion units supported					
Feature description	Bytes	520 550 570 595	800 810 825 870 890	#5074 #5075 #5079	#5094 #5095 #5294	RAID/Mirror[1]	Minimum operating system level (OS/400)[2]
#4317 8.58 GB 10k RPM Disk Unit[3]	2	S	S	S	S	G/7	V4R5
#4318 17.54 GB 10k RPM Disk Unit[4]	2	S	S	S	S	H/8	V4R5
#4319 35.16 GB 10k RPM Disk Unit	2	N	N	N	N	J/9	V5R1
#4326 35.16 GB 15k RPM Disk Unit	2	N	N		N	J/9	OS/400 V5R2
#4327 70.56 GB 15k RPM Disk Unit	2	N	N		N	K/10	OS/400 V5R2
#6817 8.58 GB 10k RPM Disk Unit	2	R	R	R	R	D/7	V4R5
#6818 17.54 GB 10k RPM Disk Unit	2	R	R	R	R	E/8	V4R5
#8817 8.58 GB Optional Base Two-byte Disk Unit 10k RPM	2	R	R	R	R	D/7	V4R5
#8818 17.54 GB Optional Base Two-byte Disk Unit 10k RPM	2	R	R	R	R	E/8	V4R5
#8917 8.58 GB Optional Base 10 k RPM Disk Unit	2	R	R	R	R	D/7	V4R5
#8918 17.54 GB Optional Base 10 k RPM Disk Unit	2	R	R	R	R	E/8	V4R5

Notes:

1. Like lettered disks can be part of the same RAID array, and like numbered disks can mirror each other.
2. Minimum operating system support level on iSeries.
3. This feature is supported for conversion only on Model 595. This feature is withdrawn effective December 2002.
4. This feature is supported for conversion only on Model 595. This feature is withdrawn effective September 2004.

N Available as a new disk.

M Available via Miscellaneous Equipment Specification (MES) only.

R Feature conversion to #4317 or #4318 during an MES upgrade is required to allow mounting of disk units in #5074, #5075, #5079, #5094, #5095 and #5294 towers or @server i5 or iSeries System Units. Feature conversion is not available when the NEWSYS function of the IBM marketing configurator is used to replace a system. RPQ 847102 may be used in place of feature conversion to obtain mounting hardware and instructions.

S Supported but not orderable.

Disk storage specifications comparison

This section outlines a comparison of disk storage specifications and provides descriptions for disk units that are supported on the IBM @server i5 and iSeries servers. The following table shows the specifications of the current IBM internal disk technologies supported on the IBM @server i5 servers.

Disk type	Disk diameter	Capacity	SCSI type	Average seek time	Average latency	RPM	Data-rate (burst)	Areal density Mb/inch	Read ahead cache
#4317	3.5 inches	8.58 GB	Ultra 2	R 5.3 ms W 6.3 ms	2.99 ms	10 K	80 MB/s	1353 to 2024	4 MB
#4318	3.5 inches	17.54 GB	Ultra 2	R 4.9 ms W 5.9 ms	2.99 ms	10 K	80 MB/s	3197 to 3535	2 MB
#4319	3.5 inches	35.16 GB	Ultra 2	R 4.9 ms W 5.9 ms	3.00 ms	10 K	80 MB/s	7040	3.58 MB
#4326	3.5 inches	35.16 GB	Ultra3	R: 3.6 ms W: 4 ms	2 ms	15 K	160 MB/s	34000	8 MB
#4327	3.5 inches	70.56 GB	Ultra3	R: 3.6 ms W: 4 ms	2 ms	15 K	160 MB/s	34000	8 MB

Disk unit conversion

The direct access storage device (DASD) units that can be migrated to the 810, 825, 870, 890, 520, 550, 570, or 595 servers, or their supporting towers, include those features that support 80-pin connections and are of 10K RPM or faster.

10k RPM Disk Unit Conversion

Conversion of 10k RPM Disk Unit features is available to support upgrades to 810, 820, 825, 830, 840, 870, 890, 520, 550, 570, and 595 servers. Feature conversion facilitates moving existing disk units to newer HSL expansion towers.

The feature conversions that are supported are:

- #6817 and #8817 to #4317
- #6818 and #8818 to #4318

RPQ 847102 10K RPM DASD to PCI tower mounting

Note: On 12 February 2002, this RPQ was replaced with direct support in the marketing configurator to convert #6817 and #8817 Disk Units to #4317 Disk Units and #6818 and #8818 Disk Units to #4318 Disk Units during MES upgrades. RPQ 847102 remains available for those instances when a MES upgrade path is not available to facilitate the feature conversion.

RPQ 847102 ships the disk mounting hardware and instructions to convert one #6817/#8817 disk unit (8.58 GB) to a #4317 or one #6818/#8818 disk unit to a #4318. This conversion allows the client to move their 8.5 GB 10K RPM and 17 GB 10K rpm files from current towers to the PCI Storage Tower Feature #5065, #5066, #5074, #5075, #5079, the Model 270, and the 8xx models, the Model 520, and the Model 570. This conversion also allows the client to move their 8.5 GB 10K RPM and 17 GB 10K RPM files from current towers to the PCI-X Storage Tower Features #5094, #5095, #5294, and the new 8xx models (800, 810, 825, 870, 890), the Model 520, and the Model 570.

After the conversion, process an RPO change to add a #4317 or #4318 feature for each #6817/#6818/#8817/#8818 feature converted, and remove the appropriate number of #6817/#6818/#8817/#8818 features.

Load source specify features

One of the following load source specify codes is required on all initial orders of an iSeries server:

- ► #0826 - #4314 Load Source specify
- ► #0827 - #4324 Load Source specify
- ► #0828 - #4317 Load Source specify
- ► #0829 - #4318 Load Source specify
- ► #0830 - #4319 Load Source specify
- ► #0834 - #4326 Load Source specify
- ► #0835 - #4327 Load Source specify

Manufacturing uses this specify to place the corresponding disk unit feature in the load source position. These specify codes can be changed on server upgrades or on simple MES orders.

Effective 01 September 2004, feature #4318 is withdrawn for new orders. Coversions to feature remain available.

Disk protection and hardware compression

This section discusses the functions that can be used to protect iSeries disk drives.

Device parity protection

Device parity protection is a hardware function that protects data from being lost because of a disk unit failure or damage to a disk. Calculating and saving a parity value for each bit of data protects data. Conceptually, the parity value is computed from the data at the same location on each of the other disk units in the device parity set. When a disk failure occurs, the data on the failing unit can be reconstructed by using the saved parity value and the values of the bits in the same locations on the other disk.

Device parity protection is a high-availability function. It allows the @server i5 or iSeries server to continue to operate when a single disk failure has occurred. The system runs in an exposed mode until the repair operation is complete and the data is rebuilt. If a failure occurs, correct the problem quickly. Otherwise, in the unlikely event that another disk fails, you can lose data.

The base disk unit controller in the 9406 Server 520, 550, 570, and 820 does not support device parity protection. The #5709 RAID Enabler Card supports device parity protection. In the Model 595, a #2780 PCI-X Ultra RAID Disk Controller is required to support the base drives in the #9194 Base PCI-X Expansion Tower.

The disk array subsystems supplied by IBM enhance the selection of recovery options available on @server i5 and iSeries servers. This method of protection is based on the RAID specifications that were published by the University of California in 1987. The high-availability servers with device parity protection use a technique similar to RAID-5 data-redundancy technology to protect data. Throughout this documentation, RAID and RAID-5 are often referenced, and are, for the most part, synonymous with device parity protection.

RAID-5

With the #2757 PCI-X Ultra RAID Disk Controller and #2782 PCI-X RAID Disk Unit Controller available with OS/400 V5R2 and #2780 PCI-X Ultra RAID Disk Controller available with i5/OS V5R3, a minimum of three disk units of the same capacity are required for a valid RAID-5 configuration. Previous disk controllers have a minimum requirement of four disks.

Parity information can be spread across two, four, eight, or 16 of the disk units in an array, and is automatically maintained as part of the RAID-5 protection

feature. Internal disk units of different technology (that is, different feature numbers), but of the same capacity, can be either mirrored or RAID-5 protected.

Number of units in the array	Number of units parity is spread across
3	2
4 - 7	4
8 - 15	8
16 - 18	16

Having parity spread across 16 disk units gives better performance in the event of a disk unit failure, since the data required to dynamically rebuild the data on the failed disk is accessed from one sixteenth of the disk units as opposed to an eighth, quarter, or half of the disk units.

If one disk unit fails, it cannot be used to read or write data. The disk unit controller then reads the parity and data from the same data areas as the other disk units to dynamically rebuild the original data from the failed disk unit to satisfy ongoing read requests. When data needs to be written, the controller generates the parity information for the failed disk unit as though it were still operating. As far as the @server i5 and iSeries servers are concerned, the disk units continue to respond to I/O even though a single disk unit has failed.

RAID-5 protection is supported for all internal disks, provided that it is supported by the disk controller. A RAID controller is required to support concurrent maintenance.

Mirroring

Mirrored protection is a function that increases the availability of @server i5 and iSeries servers in the event of a failure of a disk-related hardware component. It can be used on all iSeries servers. Software support is a part of the Licensed Internal Code (LIC).

Different levels of mirrored protection are possible, depending on the hardware that is duplicated. Mirroring involves duplicating disk-related hardware (bus, IOP, disk device). When a disk-related mirrored component fails, the system remains available.

Cross-site mirroring

Cross-site mirroring (XSM), combined with the geographic mirroring function, enables you to mirror data on disks at sites that can be separated by a significant geographic distance. This technology can be used to extend the functionality of a device cluster resource group (CRG) beyond the limits of physical component connection.

Geographic mirroring provides the ability to replicate changes made to the production copy of an independent auxiliary storage pool (IASP) to a mirror copy of that IASP. As data is written to the production copy of an IASP, the operating system mirrors that data to a second copy of the IASP through another system. This process keeps multiple identical copies of the data.

Integrated hardware disk compression

Data is dynamically compressed or uncompressed by the DASD controller as data is written to and read from disk. Disk compression has no effect on the main CPU utilization since compression is performed by the DASD controller input/output processor (IOP).

Support for Integrated Hardware Disk Compression is provided by the #4748 PCI RAID Disk Unit Controller or #4778/#9778 PCI RAID Disk Unit Controller (*withdrawn from marketing* on 19 November 2004).

The #4748 does not support data compression on 35 GB or larger disk units. The #4778 does not support data compression on 70 GB or larger disk units.

The compression ratio results of DASD varies. The compression ratio achieved and the impact on DASD performance depends on the data and how it is accessed. Compression is limited to user auxiliary storage pools (ASPs).

Internal tape, CD-ROM, DVD-RAM, and DVD-ROM

The following table shows which internal storage devices are supported in the iSeries 800, 810, 820, 825, 830, 840, 870, 890 and @server i5 520, 550, 570 and 595 system units. It also shows the internal storage devices that are supported in the #5074/#5079 PCI and #5094/#5294 PCI-X expansion towers.

Internal storage media	System units supported								
Feature	520	550	570	595	800	810	825 870 890	#5074 #5079	#5094 #5294
CD									
#4425 CD-ROM							S	X	S
#4525 CD-ROM					S	S			
#4625 CD-ROM						S	S	X	S
DVD									
#2640 DVD-ROM	X	X	X						
#4430 DVD-RAM							X	X	S
#4530 DVD-RAM					X	X			
#4531 DVD-ROM					X	X			
#4533 DVD-RAM					X	X			
#4630 DVD-RAM							X	X	X
#4631 DVD-ROM				X			X	X	X
#4633 DVD-RAM				X			X	X	X
#5751 DVD-RAM	X	X	X						
¼-inch Cartridge Tape Devices									
#4482 4 GB ¼-inch Cartridge Tape Device							X	X	S
#4483 16 GB ¼-inch Cartridge Tape Device							S	S	S
#4486 25 GB ¼-inch Cartridge Tape Device							S	S	S
#4487 50 GB ¼-inch Cartridge Tape Device							X	X	X
#4582 4 GB ¼-inch Cartridge Tape Device					X	X			
#4583 16 GB ¼-inch Cartridge Tape Device						S			
#4584 30 GB ¼-inch Cartridge Tape Device					X	X			
#4682 4 GB ¼ inch							X	X	X

Internal storage media	System units supported								
Feature	520	550	570	595	800	810	825 870 890	#5074 #5079	#5094 #5294
#4684 30 GB ¼ inch				X			X	X	X
#4686 25 GB ¼-inch Cartridge Tape Device						S		S	S
#4687 50 GB ¼-inch Cartridge Tape Device				X	X		X		X
#5753/#9653 30 GB ¼ inch Cartridge Tape Unit	X	X							
#5754/#8754 Optional Base 50 GB ¼-inch Cartridge Tape Device	X	X							
#8287 50 GB ¼ inch Cartridge Tape Unit				X					
#9284 30 GB ¼ inch Cartridge Tape Unit				X					
#9285 80 GB ¼ inch Cartridge Tape Unit				X					
VXA-2 Tape Devices									
#1889/#9689 80 GB VXA-2 Tape Device	X	X							
#4685 80 GB VXA-2 Tape Device				X			X	X	X
8mm Tape Devices									
#6134 60 GB 8mm Tape Device	X	X							

Notes:
▸ All tape features #44xx and #45xx are CIF. Orders for these devices are installed by the client. The IBM Service Representative can install the CIF as a billable service.
X Available as a new device.
S Supported but not orderable. May only be supported as part of a conversion.

Internal tape device specifications

The following table identifies the read/write capability, operating system requirements, capacity, media part numbers, performance and compression specifications of internal tape devices available for the @server i5 and iSeries.

Through optional tape compaction or compression, the tape devices identified in the following table can double their storage capacities (except the #6380 2.5 GB ¼-inch Cartridge Tape Unit). The following table shows the internal tape read/write compatibilities.

IBM Tape Drive					QIC-2GB	QIC-2GB DC	4/8GB SLR5 QIC-4G DC	MLR1 QIC 5010 DC	MLR1 QIC 5010 DC	MLR3	SLR 60	SLR 100	VXA-2
Drive storage capability					2.5 GB[4]	2.5 GB[4]	4 GB	13 GB[4]	16 GB	25 GB	30 GB	50 GB	80 GB
Compaction algorithm						LZ1	LZ1	LZ1	LZ1	LZ1	LZ1	LZ1	ALDC
Minimum OS level (OS/400)					V4R1	V4R1	V4R1	V3R7	V4R1	V4R1	V4R5	V5R1	V5R1
Format	Capacity	Native date transfer rate	Media	Media part number	#6380	#6381 #6481	#4482 #4582 #6382 #6482	#6385[7] #6485[7]	#4483 #4583 #6383 #6483	#4486 #4586 #6386 #6486	#4584 #4684 #5753[6] #6384 #6484 #9284 #9653[6]	#4487 #4587 #5754[6] #8287 #8754[6]	#1889[6] #4585 #4685 #9285 #9689[6]
MLR3 [1]	25 GB[8]	2 MB/s	MLR3-25GB	59H4128	--	--	--	--	--	R/W	R/W	R/W	
QIC5010 [1]	16 GB	1.5 MB/s	MLR1-16GB	59H4175	--	--	--	R/W	R/W	R/W	R/W	R	
	13 GB	1.5 MB/s	DC5010	16G8574	--	--	--	R/W	R/W	R/W	R/W	R	
	2 GB	1.5 MB/s	MLR1-2GB	35L0589	--	--	--	R/W	R/W	R/W	R/W	R	
QIC4DC [2]	8 GB	760 KB/s	SLR5-4GB	59H3660	--	--	R/W	--	R	R	R	R	
QIC4GB	4 GB	380 KB/s	SLR5-4GB	59H3660	--	--	R/W	--	R	R	R	R	
QIC2DC [2]	5 GB	600 KB/s	DC9250	16G8436	--	R/W	R/W	--	R	R	R		
QIC2GB	2.5 GB	300 KB/s	DC9250	16G8436	R/W	R/W	R/W	R/W	R	R	R		
QIC1000	1.2 GB	300 KB/s	DC9120	21F8730	R/W	R/W	R/W	R/W	--	--			
QIC525	525 MB	200 KB/s	DC6525	21F8597	R/W	R/W	R/W	R/W[5]	--	--			
QIC525	320 MB	200 KB/s	DC6320	21F8583	R/W	R/W	R/W	R/W	--	--			
QIC120	120 MB	120 KB/s	DC6150	21F8578	R/W	R/W	R/W	R/W[5]	--	--			
QIC24 [3]	60 MB		DC6150		R	R	--	--	--	--			
SLR100	50 GB	5 MB/s	SLR100-50GB	35L0968	--	--	--	--	--	--	--	R/W	
	5 GB	5 MB/s	SLR100-5GB	35L0961	--	--	--	--	--	--	R/W	R/W	
SLR60	30 GB	4 MB/s	SLR60-30GB	19P4209	--	--	--	--	--	--	R/W	R/W	
VXA 2 [1]	80 GB	6 MB/s	V23-80GB	19P4876	--	--	--	-	-	-	-	-	R/W
	59 GB	6 MB/s	V17-59GB	19P4877	--	--	--	-	-	-	-	-	R/W
	20 GB	6 MB/s	V6-20GB	19P4878	--	--	--	-	-	-	-	-	R/W

IBM Tape Drive					QIC-2GB	QIC-2GB DC	4/8GB SLR5 QIC-4G DC	MLR1 QIC 5010 DC	MLR1 QIC 5010 DC	MLR3	SLR 60	SLR 100	VXA-2
Drive storage capability					2.5 GB[4]	2.5 GB[4]	4 GB	13 GB[4]	16 GB	25 GB	30 GB	50 GB	80 GB
Compaction algorithm						LZ1	LZ1	LZ1	LZ1	LZ1	LZ1	LZ1	ALDC
Minimum OS level (OS/400)					V4R1	V4R1	V4R1	V3R7	V4R1	V4R1	V4R5	V5R1	V5R1
Format	Capacity	Native date transfer rate	Media	Media part number	#6380	#6381 #6481	#4482 #4582 #6382 #6482	#6385[7] #6485[7]	#4483 #4583 #6383 #6483	#4486 #4586 #6386 #6486	#4584 #4684 #5753[6] #6384 #6484 #9284 #9653[6]	#4487 #4587 #5754[6] #8287 #8754[6]	#1889[6] #4585 #4685 #9285 #9689[6]

Notes:

1. Indicates that the capacity can double typically when the compression option is selected.
2. QIC-2DC and QIC-4DC are compression formats. Cartridge capacity is data dependent. Capacities shown are typical.
3. QIC24 format is written by S/36.
4. Available as a migration feature only during an upgrade.
5. Use of DC6150 and DC6525 media may shorten the life of the tape device and require more frequent maintenance.
6. Requires i5/OS V5R3
7. The internal 13 GB tape drives with feature code #6385 or #6485 also supports the 16 MB IBM MLR1 tape media. For the correct operation of the #6385 and #6485 tape drives with the MLR1 tape media, these PTFs are required:
   - MF19447 for V3R7
   - MF19448 for V4R1
   - MF19449 for V4R2
   - MF19450 for V4R3
   - With V4R4, support is built in.
8. Minimum operating system to support the 25Gb capacity cartridge drive: OS/400 V4R1

Tape device technology

This section describes the functions that are supported by the tape technologies supported on iSeries servers.

4 GB ¼-inch Internal Cartridge Tape Device Technology

The 4 GB tape technology may be used for save/restore, alternate IPL, program distribution, migration, and ¼-inch cartridge tape exchange. Backward read/write capability to previous generations of QIC drives protects the client's investment in QIC technology.

This tape is not compatible with System/36 tape devices. For read and write compatibility, refer to the internal tape read/write compatibilities table on page 388.

16 GB ¼-inch Internal Cartridge Tape Device Technology

The 16 GB tape technology can be used for save/restore, alternate IPL, program distribution, migration, and ¼-inch cartridge tape exchange. Backward read/write capability to the previous MLR1-S format and backward read capability to the last three QIC formats protects the client's investment in QIC technology.

It provides 16 GB capacity native and 32 GB capacity compressed with a data transfer rate of 1.5 MB per second (native) and 3 MB per second (with compression) using a 1500-foot cartridge tape.

It also is capable of 13 GB capacity native and 26 GB capacity compressed with a data transfer rate of 1.5 MB per second (native) and 3 MB per second (with compression) using a 1200-foot cartridge tape.

However, the tape compression used by the #6381/#6481 2.5 GB and #4482, #4582, #6382, and #6482 4 GB tape devices is not compatible with the compaction on the #4483, #4583, #6383, and #6483 16 GB. The #6385/#6485 uncompacted or uncompressed tapes are compatible within each device's format limitations.

This tape is not compatible with System/36 tape devices. For read and write compatibility, refer to the internal tape specifications table on page 387.

25 GB ¼-inch Internal Cartridge Tape Device Technology

The 25 GB tape technology can be used for save/restore, alternate IPL, program distribution, migration, and ¼-inch cartridge tape exchange.

Tape tensioning control improvements in the tape device eliminate the need for an auto-retension pass during the data cartridge load sequence. This is a major time saving since the auto-retension pass on earlier QIC tape devices can take up to five minutes. The tape device retensions the data cartridge only when a loss of tension is detected. For typical operating conditions, this is expected to happen infrequently.

However, the tape compression used by the #6381/#6481 2.5 GB and #4482, #4582, #6382, and #6482 4 GB tape devices is not compatible with the compaction on the #4486, #4586, #6386, and #6486 25 GB tape devices. Uncompacted or uncompressed tapes are compatible within each device's format limitations.

This tape is not compatible with System/36 tape devices. For read and write compatibility, refer to the internal tape read/write compatibilities table on page 388.

30 GB ¼-inch Cartridge Tape Device Technology

The 30 GB ¼-inch Cartridge Tape Device technology may be used for save/restore, alternate IPL, program distribution, migration, and ¼-inch cartridge tape exchange. The 30 GB tape technology provides 30 GB of storage capacity. With data compression, up to 60 GB can be stored per cartridge, providing unattended backup capability for a broad range of medium sized iSeries servers.

The unit can store data at a rate of 4 MB per second (8 Mb per second with two to one (2:1) compression). It writes 30 GB with IBM SLR60-30 GB Data Cartridge (up to 60 GB with compression in SLR60 format), 25 GB with IBM MLR3-25GB Data Cartridge (up to 50 GB with compression in MLR3 format), 16 GB with IBM MLR1-16GB Data Cartridge (up to 32 GB with compression in QIC5010 format), and 2 GB with IBM MLR1-2GB Data Cartridge (up to 4 GB with compression in QIC5010 format). The unit reads 4 GB with SLR5-4GB Data Cartridge (QIC4GB format) and 2.5 GB with IBM DC9250 Data Cartridge (QIC2GB format).

This tape is not compatible with System/36 tape devices. For read and write compatibility, refer to the internal tape read/write compatibilities table on page 387.

50 GB ¼-inch Cartridge Tape Device Technology

The 50 GB ¼-inch Cartridge Tape Device technology may be used for save/restore, alternate IPL, program distribution, migration, and ¼-inch cartridge tape exchange. The 50 GB tape technology provides 50 GB of storage capacity. With data compression, up to 100 GB can be stored per cartridge, providing unattended backup capability for a broad range of medium sized iSeries servers.

These tape features are an iSeries specific implementation of Scalable Linear Recording (SLR) technology, identified as SLR100. The unit can store data at a rate of 5 MB per second (10 MB per second with a 2:1 compression). This data rate is twice the rate of previous ¼-inch tape backup used on the iSeries. In addition to reading and writing on new SLR100 50 GB or 5 GB data cartridges, there is backward write and read compatibility with MLR3 (SLR50) and backward read compatibility with MLR1 (DC 5010) tape formats.

This tape is not compatible with System/36 tape devices. For read and write compatibility, refer to the internal tape read/write compatibilities table on page 388.

80 GB VXA-2 Tape Device Technology

The VXA technology tape device offerings can store 80 GB of data on a 230 meter cartridge at 6 MB per second data transfer rate (160 GB capacity and 12 MB per second data rate with software data compression). These tape devices

can provide an unattended backup solution for a large number of low-end iSeries servers.

The 80 GB VXA-2 Tape Devices (#1889, #4585, #4685, #9285, #9689) are integrated features. The IBM 7206-VX2 Tape Device is a stand-alone external device.

The VXA-2 devices use a new media format that is not compatible with any of the tape devices that are currently offered on the iSeries server.

Internal tape features

This section describes the internal tape devices supported in the iSeries server.

#1889 80 GB VXA-2 Tape Device
The #1889/#9689 80/160 GB Internal Tape Device with VXA Technology is a 5.25-inch, half-high, Ultra2 LVD 16-bit tape device. It provides a high capacity for save/restore and archive functions. It uses VXA tape data cartridges and is compression capable, providing a capacity of up to 160 GB. The #1889 is a CIF.

#4483 16 GB ¼-inch Cartridge Tape Device
The #4483 can be mounted in the system unit of iSeries 830 and 840, and in the #5074/#5079 PCI Expansion Towers. The #4483 is a CIF.

#4486 25 GB ¼-inch Cartridge Tape Device
The #4486 can be mounted in the system unit of iSeries 830 and 840, and in the #5074/#5079 PCI Expansion Towers. The #4486 is a CIF.

#4582 4 GB ¼-inch Cartridge Tape Device
The #4582 can be mounted in the system unit of the iSeries 270 or 820. The #4582 is a CIF.

#4583 16 GB ¼-inch Cartridge Tape Device
The #4583 can be mounted in the system unit of the iSeries 270 or 820. The #4583 is a CIF.

#4584 30 GB ¼-inch Cartridge Tape Device
The #4584 can be mounted in the system unit of the iSeries 270, 800, 810, or 820. The #4584 is a CIF.

#4585 80 GB VXA-2 Tape Device

The #4585 can be mounted in a removable media device slot of a 270, 800, 810, or 820 system unit. The #4585 is a CIF.

#4586 25 GB ¼-inch Cartridge Tape Device

The #4586 can be mounted in the system unit of the iSeries 270, 810, or 820. The #4586 is a CIF.

#4587 50 GB ¼-inch Cartridge Tape Device

The #4587 can be mounted in the system unit of the iSeries 270, 800, 810, or 820. The #4587 is a CIF.

#4684 30 GB ¼-inch Cartridge Tape Device

The #4684 can be mounted in the system unit of iSeries 830, 840, and 890 and in the #5074/#5079 PCI and #5094/#5294 PCI-X Expansion Towers. The #4684 is a CIF.

#4685 80 GB VXA-2 Tape Device

The #4685 can be mounted in a removable media device slot of a Server 825, 830, 840, 870, or 890 system unit, or a #5065, #5066, #5074, #5079, #5094, #5294 Expansion Tower on any 800, 810, 825, 870, or 890 server. The #4685 is a CIF.

#5753 30 GB ¼-inch Cartridge Tape Device

The #5753/#9653 is a 30 GB ¼-inch Cartridge Tape Unit that can be mounted in a removable media device slot of a 520 and 550 system unit. The #5753 may be used for save/restore, alternate IPL, program distribution, migration and ¼-inch cartridge tape exchange. It is supported in the Model 520 and 550 system unit with i5/OS V5R3. The #5753 is a CIF. The CCIN is 63A0.

#5754 50 GB ¼-inch Cartridge Tape Device

The #5754 is a 50 GB ¼-Inch Cartridge Tape Unit that can be mounted in a removable media device slot of a 520 and 550 system unit. The #5754 may be used for save/restore, alternate IPL, program distribution, migration and ¼-inch cartridge tape exchange. It is supported in the Model 520 and 550 system unit with i5/OS V5R3. The #5754 is a CIF.

#6134 60 GB 8mm Tape Device

The #6134 is a 8mm, 5.25-inch half-high, 16-bit, internal Auto-docking tape drive, usable with AIX 5L V5R2, Red Hat Enterprise Linux AS for POWER Version 3, or SUSE LINUX Enterprise Server 9 for POWER. This drive provides a high capacity tape drive for save/restore and archiving functions. This tape drive uses

IBM 8mm data cartridges and is compression capable, providing a capacity of up to 150 GB. It is supported in Model 520 and 550 Linux and AIX partitions only. The #6134 is a CIF.

#8754 Optional Base 50 GB ¼-inch Cartridge Tape Device
The #8754 is the optional base #5754 50 GB ¼-inch Cartridge Tape Device.

#8287 50 GB ¼-inch Cartridge Tape Device
The #8287 can be used for save/restore, alternate IPL, migration, and ¼-inch cartridge tape exchange using appropriate media and density.

#9284 30 GB ¼-inch Cartridge Tape Device
The #9284 can be used for save/restore, alternate IPL, migration, and ¼-inch cartridge tape exchange using appropriate media and density.

#9285 80 GB VXA-2 8mm Tape Device
The #9285 can be used for save/restore, alternate IPL, migration, and 8mm cartridge tape exchange using appropriate media and density.

#9653 30 GB ¼-inch Cartridge Tape Device
The #9653 is the base #5753 30 GB ¼-inch Cartridge Tape Device.

#9689 80/160 GB Internal Tape Device
The #9689 is the base #1889 80 GB VXA-2 Tape Device.

Internal CD-ROM, DVD-RAM, and DVD-ROM drives

A prerequisite disk controller is required in the system unit or tower where the CD-ROM, DVD-RAM, or DVD-ROM is mounted.

Valid PCI controllers are:

- ► #2757 PCI-X Ultra RAID Disk Controller
- ► #2768 PCI Magnetic Media Controller
- ► #2780 PCI-X Ultra RAID Disk Controller
- ► #4778 PCI RAID Disk Unit Controller (*withdrawn from marketing* on 19 November 2004)
- ► #5702 PCI-X Ultra Tape Controller
- ► #5705 PCI-X Tape/DASD Controller

- ► #5709 RAID Enabler Card
- ► #5715 PCI-X Tape/DASD Controller
- ► #9778 Base PCI RAID Disk Unit Controller (*withdrawn from marketing* on 19 November 2004)

The following table identifies the CD-ROM, DVD-ROM, and DVD-RAM devices supported in @server i5 and iSeries servers. Also listed is the supported format, maximum capacity, minimum operating system level, write supported media and the required IOA. All DVD drives support ISO 9660 and UDF formats.

Feature	Description	Minimum operating system	Adapter	Supported formats	Write Supported Media	Maximum capacity (compressed)[1]
#2640[2]	DVD-ROM	i5/OS V5R3	System Unit of Model 520, 550 and 570	CD ROM	N/A	650 MB
				DVD-ROM Single-sided		9.4 GB
				DVD-ROM Double-sided		17GB
#4525 #4625	CD-ROM	OS/400 V4R4	#2757 #4778 #5705 #9778	CD-ROM Read Only	N/A	650 MB
#4530 #4630	DVD-RAM	OS/400 V5R1	#2757 #4778 #5705 #9778	CD-ROM Read Only	N/A	650 MB
			#2768, #5702	DVD-RAM Single-sided	4.7 GB - Bare[5] 2.6 GB & 4.7 GB Cartridge	2.6 GB[4] 4.7 GB
				DVD-RAM Double-sided		9.4 GB
#4533[2, 3]	DVD-RAM	i5/OS V5R3	System unit of Model 800 and 810	CD-ROM Read Only	N/A	650 MB
		OS/400 V5R2 with resave		DVD-RAM Single-sided	4.7 GB Bare	4.7 GB
				DVD-RAM Double-sided		9.4 GB
#4633[2, 3]	DVD-RAM	i5/OS V5R3	Expansion towers of 520,550, 570, 800, 810, 825, 870, 890, 595	CD-ROM Read Only	N/A	650 MB
		OS/400 V5R2 with resave	#2768, #5702	DVD-RAM Single-sided	4.7 GB Bare	4.7 GB
				DVD-RAM Double-sided		9.4 GB

Feature	Description	Minimum operating system	Adapter	Supported formats	Write Supported Media	Maximum capacity (compressed)[1]
#5751[2]	DVD-RAM	i5/OS V5R3	System unit of Model 520, 550 and 570	CD-ROM Read Only	N/A	650 MB
				DVD-RAM Single-sided	4.7 GB Bare	4.7 GB
				DVD-RAM Double-sided		9.4 GB
#4531[2] #4631[2]	DVD-ROM	OS/400 V5R2	#2757, #4778 #5705 #9778 #2768, #5702	CD-ROM (Read only)	N/A	650 MB
				DVD-RAM Single-sided (read only)	N/A	4.7 GB
				DVD-RAM Double-sided (read only)	N/A	9.4 GB

Notes:
1. Compressed values assume a 2:1 compression. Actual results may vary depending on the type and volume of data.
2. Use of a cleaning kit could damage the drive.
3. See Information APAR II13797 for software requirements of #4533 and #4633 when run with OS/400 V5R2.
4. Only the #4530 and #4630 drives support writing of 2.6GB media
5. Base i5/OS V5R3 supports writing bare 4.7Gb and 9.4GB media. OS/400 V5R2 requires PTF MF32271 to support the writing of 4.7GB and 9.4GB bare media.

#2640 DVD-ROM

The #2640 slimline DVD-ROM Drive is an internal tray loading DVD-ROM. It is supported in Model 520, 550, and 570 with i5/OS V5R3. The #2640 is a CIF.

#4525 CD-ROM

The #4525 is a feature CD-ROM that can be mounted in the system unit of Servers 810 (migration only), 270, and 820. The #4525 can be used for alternate IPL (IBM distributed CD-ROM media only) and program distribution.

#4530 DVD-RAM

The #4530 is an half high internal DVD-RAM feature that mounts in the system unit of Servers 270, 800, 810, and 820.

DVD-RAM may be selected in place of a CD-ROM drive in the minimum server configuration of a 270 or 820.

The #4530 is capable of writing and reading 4.7 GB on a single disk. The #4530 is also capable of reading 650 MB CD-ROM disks.

The #4530 can be used for alternate IPL, program distribution, and data interchange. The #4530 is not supported as an alternate installation device (by Boot Manager in DST) with OS/400 V5R1.

#4531 DVD-ROM

The #4531 is a half high DVD-ROM device which can be selected as the base optical device for iSeries servers. The #4531 is mounted in a removable media device slot in the system unit of the Servers 270, 800, 810, or 820. The #4531 is capable of reading 640 MB CD-ROM, CD-R, CD-RW media, DVD-ROM, and 4.7 GB DVD-RAM (non-cartridge) media.

The #4531 can be used for Alternate IPL (IBM distributed CD-ROM media only) and program distribution.

#4533 DVD-RAM

The #4533 is a half high DVD-RAM optical media device. The #4533 uses cartridgeless media only. This is different from the #4630, which can use cartridge media. The media can be removed from the cartridge to be used in the #4533 drive. Media support is limited to writing DVD-RAM only and reading of CD-ROM, CD-R, DVD-ROM and DVD-RAM.

It is supported in the Model 270, 800, and 810 system unit. The minimum operating system level is OS/400 V5R2. The #4533 is a CIF.

#4625 CD-ROM

The #4625 is a CD-ROM device that can be mounted in the system unit of a Model 825, 830, 840, 870 or 890, and in a #5074, #5079, #5094, #5294, #8093, #8094, #9079, or #9094 tower. It replaces the #4425 CD-ROM and differs from the #4425 in its mounting hardware. A #4625 can be placed in every removable media position in which a #4425 can be placed, but unlike its predecessor, #4625 can also be placed in a Model 825 system unit.

The #4625 can be used for Alternate IPL (IBM distributed CD-ROM media only) and program distribution.

#4630 DVD-RAM

The #4630 is a half high DVD-RAM device which is supported in a removable media device slot of a Server 825, 830, 840, 870 or 890, or a #5074, #5079, #5094, #5294, #8093, #8094, or #9094 tower. It is capable of writing and reading 4.7 GB on a single disk (single side). For double-sided media, the media must be manually flipped. The #4630 is also capable of reading 640 MB CD-ROM media.

The #4630 may be used for Alternate IPL, program distribution, and data interchange.

The #4630 is not supported as an alternate installation device (by Boot Manager in DST) with OS/400 V5R1.

#4631 DVD-ROM
The #4631 is a half high DVD-ROM device which is supported in a removable media device slot of a Server 825, 830, 840, 870 or 890, 595 or a #5074, #5079, #5094, #5294, #8093, #8094, or #9094 tower. The #4631 is capable of reading 640 MB CD-ROM media and 4.7 GB DVD-RAM media.

The #4631 can be used for Alternate IPL (IBM distributed CD-ROM media only) and program distribution.

#4633 DVD-RAM
The #4633 is a half high DVD-RAM optical media device. The #4633 uses cartridgeless media only. This is different from the #4630 which can use cartridge media. The media can be removed from the cartridge to be used in the #4633 drive. Media support is limited to writing DVD-RAM only and reading of CD-ROM, CD-R, DVD-ROM, and DVD-RAM.

The #4633 is supported in Model 820, 825, 830 and 840, 595 system units and in #5074, #5079, #5094, #5294 and #9094 towers. The minimum operating system level is OS/400 V5R2. The #4633 is a CIF.

#5751 DVD-RAM
The #5751 is an slimline DVD-RAM device with read/write capability. It is supported in Models 520, 550 and 570 with i5/OS V5R3. The #5751 is a CIF.

Internal optical device media positioning and use

For @server i5 and iSeries DVD-RAM media is the only media supported for writing. For reading CD-ROM, CD-R, CD-RW, DVD-ROM and DVD-RAM are supported. DVD-RAM media comes in different capacities. It comes in 2.6 GB, 4.7 Gb, 5.2 GB and 9.4 GB capacities. Each of these types of media are available in cartridges. Bare media is available in 4.7 GB and 9.4 GB capacities.

Using DVD-RAM for system backup is supported but not recommended for business environments where performance is required. The recommended solution for such environments is to use tape backup.

Using bare double side media (9.4 B) is not recommended because it is easily marked with finger prints and so on, which can cause read and write problems. Double-sided media requires the media to be flipped in the drive.

DVD-ROM is available in 4.7 GB (single-side, single layer), 8. 5GB (single-side, double layer), 9.4 GB (double-side, single layer), 17 GB (double-side, double layer) media types. DVD-ROM media can only be used for reading.

iSeries server code distribution

@server i5 and iSeries server code is distributed on CD-ROM media. One CD-ROM, DVD-RAM, or DVD-ROM drive is required on all 520, 550, 570, 595, 800, 810, 825, 870, and 890 servers, and must be ordered as a separate feature on the system unit. The CD-ROM and DVD-ROM can also be used for alternate IPL but not as a save/restore device for the system. The DVD-RAM can be an alternate IPL and save/restore device but is not recommended as a save/restore device for performance reasons.

LPAR support and CD-ROM, DVD-RAM, and DVD-ROM

Logical partition (LPAR) requirements may cause a need for external devices. In this case, the 7210-025 External DVD-RAM, 7210-030 External DVD-RAM or 7212-102 IBM TotalStorage Device Enclosure may be used. For a full description of these devices, see "IBM 7210 Model 025 External DVD-RAM Drive" on page 418,"IBM 7210 Model 030 External DVD-RAM Drive" on page 419, or "IBM 7212 Model 102 TotalStorage Storage Device Enclosure" on page 412

For information about LPAR and the CD-ROM, DVD-RAM, and DVD-ROM feature requirements, see:

http://www.ibm.com/eserver/iseries/lpar/

RPQ 847184 Convert #64xx to #45xx/46xx

RPQ 837184 provides the mounting hardware to convert selected iSeries #64xx features into the #45xx/#46xx equivalents for installation in iSeries servers or expansion towers. System records should be updated via RPO to reflect removal of the #64xx device from the prior server and installation of the #45xx/46xx device on the iSeries.

Installation is not included in the price of this RPQ.

Alternate IPL

Throughout this book and in the *IBM @server i5, iSeries, and AS/400e System Builder*, SG24-2155, the term *alternate IPL* (ALT-IPL) is used to describe both alternate IPL devices and alternate installation devices. It is important to understand the differences between the two concepts.

An alternate IPL device must be attached to an IOA adapter card that is controlled by the base IOP in the system. Any other tape device can be an alternate installation device.

Alternate installation device support allows you to perform installation and recovery procedures using a combination of devices. Prior to V4R1, these types of activities could only be performed using devices attached to the first system bus. The first system bus connects to the service processor IOP. Typically this is where the optical device or tape devices used for installations are attached. On OS/400 V4 and later systems, you can use a combination of devices that are attached on the first system bus and on additional buses. The alternate installation device is not attached to the first system bus.

On the 520, 550, 570, 595, 800, 810, 825, 870, and 890 servers, the alternate IPL device is attached to an I/O adapter that is controlled by a base IOP in the system.

> **Note:** The #2765 PCI Fibre Channel Tape Controller and #5704 PCI-X Fibre Channel Tape Controller do not support the alternate IPL device function. A D-mode IPL is required using CD-ROM, DVD-ROM, or another alternate IPL tape device. Then select a #2765 or #5704 to complete the installation or recovery process.

If you use the alternate installation function, the system uses existing support (a device on the first system bus) to install or recover enough of the Licensed Internal Code required to perform an IPL with an IPL-type D. When using the alternate installation device support, the system continues the operation using media in the alternate installation device. This function supports installation and recovery from tape media, such as SAVSYS tapes or distribution tapes that you created, which contain Licensed Internal Code and may contain the operating system, licensed programs, and data.

See *Backup and Recovery V5R3*, SC41-5304, for more information.

20

External tape, DVD-RAM, optical, disk storage, and SAN components

This chapter describes the latest external storage media devices that are marketed today for @server i5 and iSeries servers. Specification charts are provided for the supported attachment methods and external devices. It also covers storage area network (SAN) components that are marketed and supported by the @server i5 and iSeries server.

You can find more information about iSeries storage on the Web at:

http://www.storage.ibm.com/

External storage tape

This section describes select external storage tape devices supported by the current iSeries product line.

IBM TotalStorage 358x Ultrium Solutions with LTO Technology

The 358x Ultrium tape family of devices supports the latest industry standard Linear Tape-Open (LTO) technology. LTO technology enhances data compression capacity, performance, and reliability. A powerful open tape architecture, Ultrium sets the stage for a new generation of tape storage products expected to surpass current tape capacity and performance benchmarks while maintaining the highest data integrity.

Ultrium 1 technology offers:

- ► Cartridge capacity (using Ultrium 1 media)

    - 100 GB native capacity
    - 200 GB with two to one (2:1) compression

- ► Data transfer rate

    - 15 MB/s native
    - 30 MB/s with 2:1 compression

Ultrium 2 technology offers:

- ► Cartridge capacity (using Ultrium 2 media)

    - 200 GB native capacity
    - 400 GB with 2:1 compression

- ► Data transfer rate

    - 35 MB/s native
    - 70 MB/s with 2:1 compression

> **Note:** Compressed data rates are estimates and are data, application, and processor dependent. User results may vary.

The 3580, 3581, 3582, 3583, and 3584 are connected to @server i5 and iSeries servers by Fibre Channel, low-voltage differential (LVD) Ultra 160 SCSI, or high-voltage differential (HVD) Ultra Small Computer System Interface (SCSI) adapters. IBM i5/OS, OS/400, Windows 2000, Windows NT, and other open systems operating systems are supported.

Some advantages of the Ultrium family include:

► Latest Open Standard technology and a strategic IBM platform

► Cost effective solution for high capacity and fast tape storage

► The 3583 and 3584 are modular and expandable

► Enables larger-capacity or higher-performance tape backup

► Better alternative product to other externally attached Digital Linear Tape, ¼-inch, 4 mm, or 8 mm tape

► Supports random and auto modes on library models

Five models of the 358x are supported on the @server i5 and iSeries servers as shown in the following table.

Models	Device description	Number of drives	Maximum number of cartridges	Interface
3580 L23, H23	Ultrium 2 Tape Drive	1	1	LVD HVD
3581 H17, H13 (withdrawn from marketing on 1 October 2004)	Ultrium 1 Tape Autoloader	1	7	HVD
3581 L23, H23 (withdrawn from marketing on 1 October 2004)	Ultrium 2 Tape Autoloader	1	7	LVD HVD
3581 L28, F28	Ultrium 2U Tape Autoloader	1	8	LVD, HVD[1] FC
3582 L23	Ultrium Tape Library	1 - 2	24	LVD, HVD, FC
3583 L18 - 18 Carts L36 - 16 Carts L72 - 72 Carts	Ultrium Scalable Tape Library	1 - 6	72	LVD, HVD FC
3584 L22 - Base Frame D22 - Expansion Frame (up to 16 frames)	Ultrascalable Tape Library For 3592-J1A drives	1- 192	6260 (maximum number of cartridges decreases as tape drives are added)	FC
3584 L32 / L52[2] - Base Frame D32 / D522 - Expansion Frame (up to 16 frames)	Ultrascalable Tape Library For Ultrium 1 or Ultrium 2 LTO drives	1- 192	6881 (maximum number of cartridges decreases as tape drives are added)	LVD, HVD, FC[2]

[1] The 3581-L28 can only have an HVD interface when the #3104 HVD Converter Kit is included in the configuration.
[2] Only Fibre Channel drives are supported in L52 and D52 frames.

The adapter speed is also a factor in tape performance. Note that the LTO Ultrium 2 HVD drives may not see a performance increase over LTO Ultrium 1 HVD drives when attached to #2749 PCI Ultra Magnetic Media Controller.

Installing more than one Ultrium drive on a SCSI bus can impact the save rate of the device.

The IBM TotalStorage 358x tape devices that are supported on @server i5 and iSeries servers include:

▶ **IBM TotalStorage Ultrium External Tape Drive 3580**

The IBM LTO 3580 tape drive is one building block of a family of scalable, flexible tape solutions. By leveraging advanced LTO technology, the IBM Tape Drive is suited for handling the backup, save and restore, and archival data storage needs of a wide range of small systems.

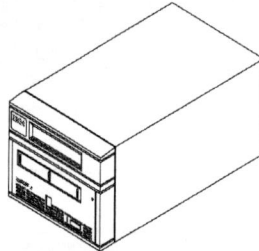

The IBM LTO Ultrium 2 models of the IBM TotalStorage Ultrium External Tape Drive have a capacity of up to 400 GB with compression (2:1) with the use of the new IBM TotalStorage LTO Ultrium 200 GB Data Cartridge. IBM Ultrium 2 Tape Drives can read and write first generation LTO Ultrium Data Cartridges at original capacities and with improved performance (20 MB/s).

The IBM LTO 3580 Ultrium 2 drive more than doubles tape drive performance over LTO Ultrium 1 drives with a 35 MB/s native data transfer rate (70 MB/s with 2:1 compression). The IBM Ultrium External Tape Drive 3580 is an excellent alternative to S-DLT, DLT, ¼-inch, 4 mm, or 8 mm tapes drives.

▶ **IBM TotalStorage Ultrium Tape Autoloader 3581**

The IBM LTO 3581 Autoloader is an external stand-alone rack-mountable unit and contains a LTO Ultrium tape drive designed for the heavy demands of backup tape storage. The Ultrium Tape Autoloader 3581 capacity is seven to eight tape cartridges depending on the model.

The new Ultrium 2 models of the IBM TotalStorage Ultrium Tape Autoloader 3581 (L28/F28) incorporate the IBM TotalStorage Ultrium 2 Tape Drives. This more than doubles tape drive performance over the first generation LTO Ultrium Tape Drive. It is designed to support up to 35 MB/s native data transfer rates (70 MB/s with 2:1

compression). In addition, with the use of the IBM TotalStorage LTO Ultrium 200 GB Data Cartridge, the IBM TotalStorage Ultrium 2 Tape Drive doubles the tape cartridge capacity up to 200 GB native capacity (400 GB with 2:1 compression). The IBM TotalStorage Ultrium 2 Tape Drives can read and write first generation LTO Ultrium Data Cartridges at original capacities and with improved performance.

It is an ideal automation solution for handling the storage needs of small- to medium-sized environments.

▶ **IBM TotalStorage Ultrium Tape Library 3582**

The IBM LTO 3582 Tape Library is an external stand-alone unit that my be optionally rack-mounted. It supports up to two IBM TotalStorage Ultrium 2 Tape Drives with up to 35 MB/s native data transfer rates (70 MB/s with 2:1 compression) per drive.

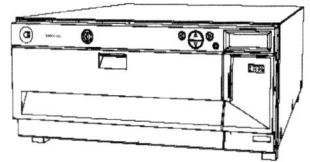

The 3582 provides tape cartridge capacity up to 200 GB native capacity (400 GB with 2:1 compression) when using the new IBM TotalStorage LTO Ultrium 200 GB Data Cartridge. The IBM TotalStorage Ultrium 2 Tape Drives can read and write original LTO Ultrium data cartridges at first generation Ultrium 1 capacities with improved performance.

The 3582 is an ideal automation solution for handling the storage needs of small to medium sized environments. The Ultrium Tape Library is designed to leverage the LTO technology to cost-effectively handle growing storage requirements. Using IBM patented multipath technology, the library can be partitioned so that different tape drives and cartridge slots can be used by multiple heterogeneous servers.

▶ **IBM TotalStorage Ultrium ScalableTape Library 3583**

The IBM LTO 3583 Tape Library supports the IBM TotalStorage Ultrium 2 Tape Drive. It more than doubles tape drive performance over the first generation LTO Ultrium Tape Drive.

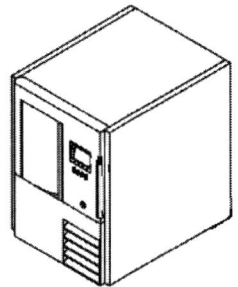

The 3583 is designed to support up to 35 MB/s native data transfer rates (70 MB/s with 2:1 compression). In addition, with the use of the IBM TotalStorage LTO Ultrium 200 GB Data Cartridge, the IBM TotalStorage Ultrium 2 Tape Drive doubles the tape cartridge capacity up to 200 GB native capacity (400 GB with 2:1 compression).

The IBM TotalStorage Ultrium 2 Tape Drives can read and write original LTO Ultrium data cartridges at first generation Ultrium 1 capacities with improved

performance. The Ultrium 2 tape drives and cartridges can be resident in the same 3583 library with first generation Ultrium tape drives and cartridges. Using IBM patented multipath technology, the library can be partitioned so that different tape drives and cartridge slots can be used by multiple heterogeneous servers.

► **IBM TotalStorage UltraScalable Tape Library 3584**

The IBM LTO 3584 Tape library provides a highly scalable mid-range, open systems, and network server tape storage solution. It combines reliable, automated tape handling, and storage with reliable, high-performance IBM LTO Ultrium tape drives and IBM TotalStorage 3592 tape drives.

The 3584 supports up to 16 frames housing a maximum of 6,881 LTO Ultrium tape cartridges and 192 LTO Ultrium tape drives. Support for the IBM TotalStorage Ultrium 2 Tape Drive more than doubles tape drive performance over the first generation LTO Ultrium Tape Drive. It is designed to support up to 35 MB/s native data transfer rates (70 MB/s with 2:1 compression).

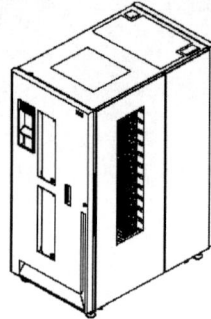

With the use of the IBM TotalStorage LTO Ultrium 200 GB Data Cartridge, the IBM TotalStorage Ultrium 2 Tape Drive doubles the tape cartridge capacity up to 200 GB native capacity (400 GB with 2:1 compression). The IBM TotalStorage Ultrium 2 Tape Drives can read and write original LTO Ultrium data cartridges at first generation Ultrium 1 capacities with improved performance. The Ultrium 2 tape drives and cartridges can reside in the same 3584 Library frame with first generation Ultrium tape drives and Cartridges.

The UltraScalable Tape Library is designed with a variety of advanced features. The IBM Multi-path Architecture and Advance Library Management System (ALMS) are designed to simultaneously attach heterogeneous servers and applications to LTO logical library partitions, including mixed Ultrium drives and media.

In addition, the IBM TotalStorage UltraScalable Tape Library 3584 supports IBM TotalStorage Enterprise Tape System 3592-J1A. When 3592 tape drives are installed, the maximum number of library cartridge slots is 6260 and the maximum number of drives is 192. The 3584 is designed to support up to 40 MB/s native data transfer rates (120 MB/s with 3:1 compression) and offers a cartridge capacity of 300 GB native (900 GB with compression).

For additional information about the 3592-J1A Enterprise Tape System on the 3584 UltraScalable Tape Library, see the following Web site:

`http://www.storage.ibm.com/tape/lto/3584/index.html`

For additional information about the 3580, 3581, 3582, 3583, 3584, and all LTO products, see the following Web site:

`http://www-1.ibm.com/servers/storage/tape/lto/index.html`

IBM TotalStorage Enterprise Tape System 3590

The IBM TotalStorage Enterprise Tape System 3590 is designed to provide high levels of performance and data reliability for both stand-alone and automated systems.

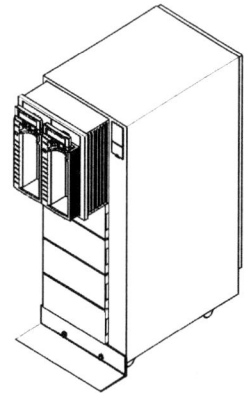

The Enterprise Tape System 3590 offers:

▶ Native drive data rate

   – Up to 14 MB/s

   – 3590 Models E and H with Ultra SCSI attachment are capable of reaching sustained data rates of up to 34 MB/s (with 3:1 compression). With native Fibre Channel attachment, the maximum sustained data rate is 42 MB/s (with three to one (3:1) compression).

▶ Standard LZ1 compression

▶ Support for extended-length cartridges (60 GB native capacity, H models)

▶ Fast and wide SCSI-2 interface, Ultra SCSI interface, or native Fibre Channel attachment

▶ Two ports

   Each port can be connected to a different iSeries server and the 3590 can be shared between two systems.

The 3590 Models B11, E11, and H11 incorporate a standard 10-slot ACF for high-capacity stand-alone unattended operation. The 3590 Models B1A, E1A, and H1A come without the ACF. They are designed to go into the IBM 3494 Enterprise Automated Tape Library.

For additional information about all 3590 products, see the following Web site:

`http://www.storage.ibm.com/tape/drives/3590/index.html`

IBM TotalStorage 3592 Tape Drive Model J1A

The IBM TotalStorage 3592 Tape Drive Model J1A surpasses the capabilities of its predecessors by providing up to five times the capacity and two and a half times the data transfer rates of the Enterprise Tape System 3590 E or H Model. The IBM TotalStorage 3592 Tape Drive offers:

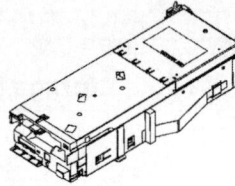

► Up to 300 GB native cartridge capacity; up to 900 GB with compression using rewritable cartridges

► 60 GB short length rewritable native capacity

► Average locate time using rewritable cartridges is 30% of the locate time of using 300 GB cartridges

> **Note:** Write-Once-Read-Many (WORM) and Cartridge Scaling is not supported when the 3592 is attached to @server i5 or iSeries servers

► Up to 40 MB/s native data rate

► Throughput capability of up to 20% more than LTO (type2); can restore up to 390 GB per hour from a single drive

► Dual Fibre Channel ports

► Attachment via the #2765 PCI Fibre Channel Tape Controller or #5704 PCI-X Fibre Channel Tape Controller adapters

► Supported in the IBM TotalStorage UltraScalable Tape Library 3584

► Small form factor which allows double the drives in a single 3494 frame, as compared to the Enterprise Tape System 3590

► Stand-alone rack option available

Stand-alone rack option does not include an autoloader function.

The 3592 also has additional enhancements that may help improve performance, capacity and availability including N+1 power supplies, channel calibration, a large internal data calibration, large internal data buffer, digital speed matching and more.

For more information about the Enterprise Tape System 3592, go to:

http://www-1.ibm.com/servers/storage/tape/3592/index.html

IBM TotalStorage 3494 Enterprise Tape Library

The IBM TotalStorage 3494 Enterprise Tape Library is a stand-alone automated tape storage subsystem for 3590 and 3592 ½-inch cartridges available for attachment to the @server i5 and iSeries servers. It provides an automated tape solution for automating tape operations such as save and restore, migration of data between disk and tape, and other mass data applications.

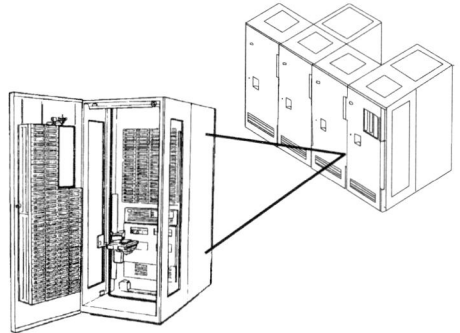

Flexible configuration choices start at a single frame configuration with up to two tape drives and up to 240 tape cartridges. Optional drives and cartridge storage can be added as needed to create an automated tape library multiple frame or tape drives, and up to 6,240 tape cartridges. Choices in tape drives for the 3494 include:

- ▶ IBM TotalStorage Enterprise Tape Drive 3592
- ▶ IBM TotalStorage Enterprise Tape Drive 3590
- ▶ IBM 3490E

Different tape drives can be installed in different frames in the same 3494 library.

The IBM TotalStorage 3494 Automated Tape Library supports up to 64 TCP/IP open system hosts and the attachment of up to 128 3592 or 92 3590 open systems tape drives. The 3494 supports heterogeneous attachment of multiple IBM and non-IBM hosts including zSeries, S/390®, pSeries, RS/6000, @server i5, iSeries, Sun, HP, and Intel-compatible servers running Microsoft Windows. Also available is the IBM TotalStorage Enterprise High Availability Tape Frames (HA1 Models). The HA1 Frames provide a second tape cartridge accessory and library manager for high library availability and performance.

All this, in addition to remote console support, Simple Network Management Protocol (SNMP) reporting capabilities, multi-host attachment, and modular design, assist in making the 3494 flexible, easy to use, and well-suited for automated tape library solutions.

For additional information about the 3494 Enterprise Tape Library, see:

`http://www-1.ibm.com/servers/storage/tape/3494/index.html`

IBM 7206 Model VX2 80 GB External VXA-2 Tape Device

The IBM 7206 Model VX2 External Tape Drive is a VXA-2 Packet Drive that features capacity of 80 and 160 GB (native and compressed) and six and 12 MB/s transfer rates (native and compressed). The VXA Packet Technology provides a digital solution to the long-standing mechanical problem of head-to-tape alignment. This is a common problem that causes conventional tape storage products to trade off costly mechanical complexity with data restore integrity.

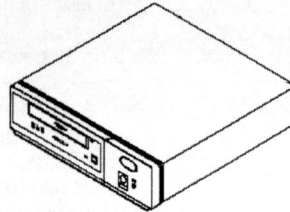

VXA Packet Tape Drives write and read data in individually addressed *packets*, accomplished by the heads sweeping the entire face of the tape rather than the conventional method of sequentially tracing every track embedded on the tape. During a read operation, discrete data packets are dynamically gathered and reassembled in the VXA buffer, resulting in dramatically higher data restore integrity with reduced cost. VXA Packet Technology eliminates the need for expensive, complex mechanisms to maintain the tight tolerances required for tracking resulting in greater capacity, speed and data reliability at a lower cost.

The IBM 7206 Model VX2 is an excellent solution for midrange tape requirements with an entry level price.

For additional information about the 7206-VX2 and other 7206 products, see:

http://www.storage.ibm.com/tape/drives/7206/models/model_vx2.html

IBM 7207 Model 122 4 GB External SLR5 QIC Tape Drive

The IBM 7207 Model 122 4 GB External SLR5 QIC Tape Drive is a stand-alone streaming linear tape drive in a raven black enclosure incorporating the most recent Single Channel Linear Recording (SLR5) QIC technology.

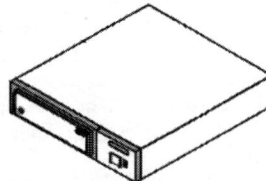

It provides up to 4 GB (8 GB with 2:1 compression) data storage per cartridge. It has a sustained data transfer rate of 380 KB per second (760 KB /sec with 2:1 compression). The 7207 Model 122 uses the QIC-4GB format, but is read and write backward compatible with QIC-120/150, QIC-525, QIC-1000, and QIC-2GB formats. It has two dual-ported wide connectors and attaches to a wide SCSI bus.

The Model 122 is an excellent solution if you use QIC tape or require a low-cost entry solution for tape backup.

For additional information about the 7207-122 and other 7207 products, see:

`http://www-1.ibm.com/servers/storage/tape/7207/index.html`

IBM 7207 Model 330 30 GB External SLR60 Tape Drive

The IBM 7207 Model 330 30 GB External SLR60 Tape Drive is a stand-alone streaming tape drive in a single, externally attached enclosure. It incorporates new 4-Channel Scalable Linear Recording (SLR) technology.

The Model 330 provides up to 30 GB (60 GB with 2:1 compression) of data storage per cartridge and a sustained data transfer rate of 4 MB per second (8 MB per second with 2:1 compression). It has two SCSI-wide input and output connectors. It uses the SLR60 30 GB format and is designed to be backward read and write compatible with SLR100, MLR3, and MLR1 for all members of the quarter-inch cartridge (QIC) family of products. The Model 330 is also designed to be read-only compatible with SLR5 and DC9250 QIC tape formats.

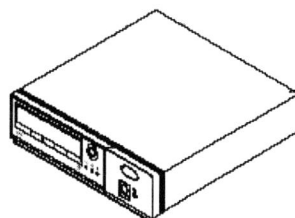

The 7207 Model 330 tape drive is an enhancement to the IBM 7207 Model 122 tape drive. It can be used to replace other tape technologies (such as Mammoth and DLT tape drives) that attach externally to the iSeries families of workstations and servers. It offers flexible read and write compatibility with SLR, MLR, and QIC tape formats for data exchange and software distribution.

For additional information about the 7207-330 and other 7207 products, go to:

`http://www-1.ibm.com/servers/storage/tape/7207/index.html`

IBM 7208 Model 345 60 GB External 8mm Tape Drive

The 7208 Model 345 is a stand-alone SCSI 8mm streaming tape device with the capacity of a 60 GB per cartridge. It uses the IBM Mammoth-2 AME media data cartridge with SmartClean technology. The Model 345 also provides backward read compatibility with previous 20.0 GB 8mm AME tape cartridges.

The 7208 Model 345 can provide a media capacity of up to 150 GB of data storage per cartridge using the ALDC algorithm for compression. It has a sustained data rate of 12 M per second (20 M per second with

a 2.5:1 compression ratio). This gives three times the capacity and four times the date rate of the 7208 Model 342.

The 7208 Model 345 is an excellent migration and interchange path from other 8mm tape drives and is a cost-effective solution for save-and-restore and archiving functions.

For additional information about the 7208-345 and other 7208 products, see:

http://www.storage.ibm.com/tape/drives/7208/index.html

IBM 7212 Model 102 TotalStorage Storage Device Enclosure

The 7212 Model 102 is designed to mount in one EIA unit of standard 19-inch rack using an optional rack-mount hardware feature kit. The 7212 Model 102 can also be configured for desktop installation.

The 7212 Model 102 is an excellent choice for applications where:

▶ Availability of server bays for storage devices is limited or not available (depending on model).

▶ It is important to consolidate storage devices in a single, convenient location to minimize space and cabling impacts.

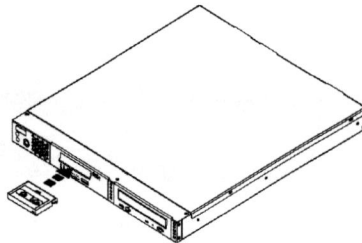

The two bays of the 7212 Model 102 can accommodate any two of the following features codes on the 7212 to support iSeries servers:

▶ #1103 DVD-RAM 2 Drive
▶ #1104 VXA-2 Tape Drive
▶ #1106 DVD ROM Drive
▶ #1107 SLR60 Tape Drive
▶ #1108 SLR100 Tape Drive

The 7212 Model 102 can be attached to an @server i5 or iSeries server with one of the following @server i5 and iSeries controllers:

▶ #2768 PCI Magnetic Media Controller
▶ #5702 PCI-X Ultra Tape Controller
▶ #5705 PCI-X Tape/DASD Controller
▶ #5712 PCI-X Tape/DASD Controller

The 7212 Model 102 requires OS/400 V5R2 or later.

For additional information about the 7212-102, see the following Web site:

`http://www-1.ibm.com/servers/storage/tape/7212/index.html`

VXA, QIC, 8mm tape and DVD-RAM specifications summary

The following table helps to distinguish the technical characteristics of the IBM 7206, 7207, 7208, 7212 tape, and 7210 DVD devices.

Machine model	7206-VX2	7207-122 7207-330	7208-345	7210-025	7210-030	7212-102
Description	VXA-2	QIC ¼ inch	8mm Mammoth-2	DVD-RAM	DVD-RAM	Storage Device Enclosure
Native / Compressed[1]	80 GB / 160 GB	**122**: 4 GB/8 GB **330**: 30 GB/60 GB	60 GB / 150 GB	2.6 GB / 4.7 GB	2.6 GB / 4.7 GB	DDS-4: 20/40 GB DAT72: 36/72GB VXA-2: 80/160 B
Maximum Data Rate/sec[2]	6 MB/s 12 MB/s	**122**: 380 KB/s 760 KB/s **330**: 4 MB/s 8 MB/s	12 MB/s 20 MB/s	CD: 3.6 MB/s DVD-RAM: 1.35 MB/s[3] 2.7 MB/s[4]	CD: 3.6 MB/s DVD-RAM: 2.7 MB/s[3] 2.7 MB/s[4]	DDS/DAT72: 3/6 MB/s VXA: 6/12 MB/s
Interface	Ultra2 SCSI LVD	**122**: Wide SCSI **330**: Ultra2 SCSI LVD	LVD/SE Ultra wide SCSI-2	SCSI-2	SCSI-2 SE Fast/Wide Fast/Narrow	SCSI-2 F/W SE, LVS/SE
Supported Controllers	#2768 #5702[5] #5705[5]	#2768 #5702[5] #5705[5]	#2768 #5702[5] #5705[5]	#2768 #5702[5] #5705[5]	#2768 #5702[5] #5705[5] #5712[6]	#2768 #5702[5] #5705[5] #5712[6]
Minimum operating system level	OS/400 V5R1	**122**: OS/400 V4R2 with PTFs **330**: OS/400 V5R1 with PTFs	OS/400 V4R5	OS/400 V5R1	**7xx and 8xx**: OS/400 V5R2 **@server i5**: i5/OS V5R3	OS/400 V5R2

Notes:
1. The degree of compression that is achieved is highly sensitive to the characteristics of the data being compressed.
2. Compressed data rates are estimates and are data, application, and processor dependent. User results may vary.
3. Write rate of DVD
4. Read rate of DVD
5. Minimum operating system to support the #5702 and #5705: OS/400 V5R2
6. Minimum operating system to support the #5712: i5/OS V5R3

External tape storage automated library specifications

The following table helps to distinguish the technical characteristics of the external storage automated tape library devices supported by the @server i5 and iSeries servers marketed today.

Note: The last models of the 3490E, 3570, and 3575 range were *withdrawn from marketing* in 2002. They are included in the table for comparison purposes.

Machine model	Desktop 3490E-F10 Rack 3490E-F11 Library 3490-F1A [9]	3494-L12 3494-L22 3494-L10 3494-D12 3494-D22 3494-D10 3494-HA1	Desktop 3570-C01 3570-C02 Rack 3570-C11 3570-C12	3575-L06 3575-L12 3575-L18 3575-L24 3575-L32	Desktop/Rack 3581-L28, F28 3582-L23 Library, Floor/Rack 3583-L18 3583-L36 3583-L72 Library 3584-L52, L22, L32 [9] 3584-D52, D22, D32	3590-B1A 3590-B11 3590-E1A 3590-E11 3590-H1A 3590-H11 3592-J1A
Description	½-inch tape	Library for 3490-x1A 3590-x1A 3592-J1A	C-XL format 0.31 inch	C-XL format 0.31 inch	LTO Ultrium 1 or 2 3592-J1A (3584 L22 and D22)	½-inch tape
Recording technology	Longitudinal Serpentine	Longitudinal Serpentine or Linear Serpentine (J)	Longitudinal Serpentine	Longitudinal Serpentine	Longitudinal Serpentine	Longitudinal Serpentine J: Linear Serpentine
Native/compressed[1]	800 MB /2.4 GB	Depends on installed drives; See columns **3590-X1A** and **3592-J1A**.	7 GB/21 GB	7 GB/21 GB	**Ultrium 1** 100/200 GB **Ultrium 2** 200/400 GB **3592-J1A** 300GB/900GB	**B:** 10/30 GB or 20/60 GB[7] **E:** 20/60 GB or 40/120 GB[7] **H:** 30/90 GB[7] **J1A** 300GB/900GB
Maximum number of cartridges/ library	10	6240	20	**L06:** 60 **L12:** 120 **L18:** 180 **L24:** 240 **L32:** 324	**L28/F28:** 8 **L23:** 24 **L18:** 18 **L36:** 32 **L72:** 72 **L52, D52:** 64-6887[12] **L22, D22:** 58 - 6260[12] **L32, D32:** 281-6881[12]	**B1A:** 1 **B11:** 10 **E1A:** 1 **E11:** 10 **H1A:** 1 **H11:** 10 **J1A:** 1

Machine model	Desktop 3490E-F10 Rack 3490E-F11 Library 3490-F1A [9]	3494-L12 3494-L22 3494-L10 3494-D12 3494-D22 3494-D10 3494-HA1	Desktop 3570-C01 3570-C02 Rack 3570-C11 3570-C12	3575-L06 3575-L12 3575-L18 3575-L24 3575-L32	Desktop/Rack 3581-L28, F28 3582-L23 Library, Floor/Rack 3583-L18 3583-L36 3583-L72 Library 3584-L52, L22, L32 [9] 3584-D52, D22, D32	3590-B1A 3590-B11 3590-E1A 3590-E11 3590-H1A 3590-H11 3592-J1A
Maximum total capacity	24 GB	1.12 PB (3590H) 5.62PB 3592J (3:1 comp)	420 GB	**L06:** 1.2 TB **L12:** 2.5 TB **L18:** 3.78 TB **L24:** 5.04 TB **L32:** 6.8 TB	**L28:** 3.2 TB **L23:** 9.6 TB **L18:** 7.2TB **L36:** 14.4 TB **L72:** 28.8 TB L32 + D32: 56.2 to 2752 TB **L52, D52:** 25.6 TB to 2.76PB (2:1 comp) **L22, D22:** 52TB to 5.63PB (3:1 comp) **L32, D32:** 112TB to 2.75PB (2:1 comp)	B1A: 60 GB B11: 0.6 TB E1A: 120 GB E11: 1.2 TB H1A: 180 GB H11: 1.8 TB J1A: 900GB (3:1 comp)
Maximum data rate/sec (native) [2]	3 MB/s	Depends on installed drives; see columns **3590-X1A** and **3592-J1A**.	7MB/s	7MB/s	35 MB/s	B11: 9 MB/s E11: 14 MB/s H11 14 MB/s J1A:40 MB/s
Time to load and thread a cartridge	81 sec	See columns **3590-X1A** and **3592-J1A**.	19 sec	20 sec	15 sec, LTO Ultrium 2	40 sec (3590 J media) 60 sec (3590 K media) 19 sec (3592 J1A)
Interface	SCSI-2 Fast/wide differential	RS232 Async or LAN for Library Manager/ robotics	SCSI-2 Fast/wide differential	SCSI-2 Fast/wide differential	Ultra160 SCSI LVD Fibre Channel SCSI-2 HVD (with #3104 Converter Kit)	3590 SCSI-2 Fibre Channel 3592 Fibre Channel only
Compression/ compaction method[6]	HDC IDRC	Depends on installed drives; see columns **3590-X1A** and **3592-J1A**.	LZ1	LZ1	LTO-DC (LZ1)	I3590 - ALDC (LZ1) 3592 - SLDC (LZ1)

Machine model	Desktop 3490E-F10 Rack 3490E-F11 Library 3490-F1A [9]	3494-L12 3494-L22 3494-L10 3494-D12 3494-D22 3494-D10 3494-HA1	Desktop 3570-C01 3570-C02 Rack 3570-C11 3570-C12	3575-L06 3575-L12 3575-L18 3575-L24 3575-L32	Desktop/Rack 3581-L28, F28 3582-L23 Library, Floor/Rack 3583-L18 3583-L36 3583-L72 Library 3584-L52, L22, L32 [9] 3584-D52, D22, D32	3590-B1A 3590-B11 3590-E1A 3590-E11 3590-H1A 3590-H11 3592-J1A
Controllers supported	#2749[3]	Depends on installed drives; see columns **3590-X1A** and **3592-J1A**	#2749[3]	#2749[3]	#2749[3] #2765[4, 5] #5702[8] #5704[8] #5705[8] #5712[10]	3590 #2749[3] #2765[4, 6] #5704[11] 3592 #2765, #5704[11]
Minimum operating system level	OS/400 V4R1	OS/400 V2R3	OS/400 V3R1	OS/400 V4R1	OS/400 V5R1	**B1x:** OS/400 V3R1 **E1x:** OS/400 V4R1 **H1x:** OS/400 V4R5 **J1A:** OS/400 V5R1
Alternate IPL device specify	#5504	Depends on tape devices installed; see columns **3590-X1A** and **3592-J1A**	#5515	#5515	#5537	#5519 for 3590

Notes:

1. The actual degree of compression achieved is highly sensitive to the characteristics of the data compressed.

2. This entry illustrates the best possible performance. Other components of the system may limit the actual performance achieved. The best source of information about performance is the *iSeries Performance Capabilities Reference*, SC41-0607.

3. The #2749 PCI Ultra Magnetic Media Controller attachment requires a minimum of OS/400 V4R5.

4. The #2765 PCI Fibre Channel Tape Controller attachment requires a minimum of OS/400 V5R1.

5. The #2765 PCI Fibre Channel Tape Controller supports attachment to the 3582, 3583, and 3584 only.

6. The #2765 PCI Fibre Channel Tape Controller supports attachment to the 3590-Exx and 3590-Hxx only.

7. The 3590 capacities depend on cartridge type. The Extended High Performance Cartridge has twice the capacity of the original High Performance Cartridge. The compressed capacities assume 3:1 compression.

8. Minimum operating system to support the #5702 PCI-X Ultra Tape Controller, #5704 PCI-X Fibre Channel Tape Controller and #5705 PCI-X Tape/DASD Controller attachment is OS/400 V5R2.

9. The maximum number of drives depends on the adapter used to attach to the iSeries server:
   - #2765, #5702: 16 drives, media changers, or both per adapter with a maximum of 96 devices in the library partition.
   - OS/400 is limited to 32 drives pooled per library, regardless of how the drives are attached (one versus multiple).

10. Minimum operating system to support #5712 PCI-X Tape/DASD Controller attachment: i5/OS V5R3.

11. Minimum operating system to support #2765 attachment: OS/400 V5R1.
    Minimum operating system to support #5704 attachment: OS/400 V5R2

12. Multiple frame combinations are possible.

Refer to *IBM TotalStorage Tape Selection and Differentiation Guide*, SG24-6946 to assist you in finding the best tape product solution for the designated backup environment. The 2004 edition of this Redbook covers the 3494, 3580, 3581, 3582, 3583, 3584, 3590, 3592, and other tape products.

Tape device terminology

To help you understand the meaning of some of the functional characteristics of each tape device, refer to these descriptions:

- **Random mode**: A mode where the library can retrieve and load cartridges at random from cartridge inventory based on user demand.

- **Auto mode**: A mode where the library sequentially loads cartridges to save or retrieve data and automatically advances to the next cartridge after a cartridge is filled or restored sequentially.

- **Base mode**: All drives see all tapes. Must be attached to one system.

- **Split mode**: The tape device is split into two groups. The library can be shared between systems, but the cartridges can be used only by the tape device dedicated to them.

- **Multi-control path architecture**: Each drive in the library has a control path to the SCSI media changer. This allows each tape device in a library access to the robot arm as though it was the only drive in the library.

- **Multiple partitions**: The tape library can be split into partitions. Each drive has assigned cartridge slots it can use.

- **Tape pooling**: Tape drives are manage as a set (pool of drives). Tape devices can be attached to separate controllers, but the system software recognizes resources with equal capabilities in a common library device. At vary on, all equal resources are displayed under the common library device description. This allows Backup Recovery and Media Services (BRMS) to assign jobs for a specific resource to a pool of tapes that are available under this resource. It is available on OS/400 V4R5 or later.

- **Performance**: The actual throughput that you may achieve is a function of many components, such as system processor, disk data rate, data block size, data compressibility, input/output (I/O) attachments, and the system or application software used. The numbers stated here are the maximum throughput attainable by the tape device. The best source of information about performance is the *iSeries Performance Capabilities Reference*, SC41-0607.

Magnetic media controller transfer rates

The following table identifies the theoretical transfer rates of @server i5 and iSeries media controllers. Refer to appropriate benchmarks for an accurate representation of performance capabilities. Refer to the following two guides for benchmark information:

- ► *iSeries Performance Capabilities Reference*, SC41-0607
- ► *iSeries in Storage Area Networks*, SG24-6220

IOP or IOA	Transfer rate
#2749 PCI Ultra Magnetic Media Controller IOA OS/400 V4R5	Up to 38 MB/s Aggregate sustained data rates up to 108 GB/hour
#2765 PCI Fibre Channel Tape Controller OS/400 V5R1	Up to 100 MB/s
#2766 PCI Fibre Channel Disk Controller OS/400 V5R1	Up to 100 MB/s
#2787 PCI-X Fibre Channel Disk Controller OS/400 V5R2	Up to 200 MB/s
#5702 PCI-X Ultra Tape Controller OS/400 V5R2	80 MB/s Up to 160 MB/s with MF30636 applied
#5704 PCI-X Fibre Channel Tape Controller i5/OS V5R3	Up to 200 MB/s
#5705 PCI-X Tape/DASD Controller OS/400 V5R2	80 MB/s Up to 160 MB/s with MF30636 applied
#5712 PCI-X Tape/DASD Controller i5/OS V5R3	Up to 160 MB/s

External storage DVD-RAM

This section describes select external storage DVD-RAM devices supported by the current iSeries product line.

IBM 7210 Model 025 External DVD-RAM Drive

The IBM 7210 External DVD-RAM drive provides data interchange capability in support of LPAR configurations for iSeries. DVD-RAM is an optical technology that advances the capabilities that CD-ROM brings to the iSeries. You can use DVD-RAM on iSeries servers to help lower costs associated with:

- Software distribution
- Data and software backup
- System backup
- Data interchange (ISO 9660 and UDF formats)

The 7210 Model 25 is flexible, supporting synchronous and asynchronous data transfer and accommodates both 12 cm and 8 cm disks. The Model 025 reads multi-session disks, CD-recordable disks, and CD-RW disks. DVD disk capacities of 2.6 GB, 4.7 GB, 5.2 GB, and 9.4 GB are supported. The IBM 7210 External DVD-RAM Drive enhances the function and capabilities of the iSeries.

The capacity of the DVD media is over seven times larger than CD-ROM. Software that may have been distributed on multiple CDs may now need only one DVD-RAM cartridge, reducing the cost of media. The 7210-025 can be used as an alternate IPL device. The 7210 Model 025 is not supported by BRMS (5722-BR1).

For additional information about the 7210-025, see the following Web site:

http://www-1.ibm.com/servers/storage/tape/7210/index.html

IBM 7210 Model 030 External DVD-RAM Drive

The high-performance IBM 7210 External DVD-RAM drive provides data interchange capability in support of LPAR configurations for @server i5 and iSeries servers. DVD-RAM is an optical technology that advances the capabilities that CD-ROM brings to @server i5 and iSeries servers. You can use DVD-RAM on @server i5 and iSeries servers to help lower costs associated with:

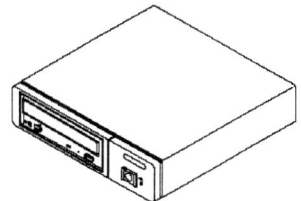

- Software distribution
- Data and software backup
- System backup
- Data interchange (ISO 9660 and UDF formats)

The 7210 Model 30 is flexible, supporting synchronous and asynchronous data transfer and accommodates both 12 cm and 8 cm disks. The Model 030 reads multi-session disks, CD-recordable disks, and CD-RW disks. The Model 030 writes to DVD-RAM, but only reads CD-RW and other CD-recordable media. DVD disk capacities of 2.6 GB, 4.7 GB, 5.2 GB, and 9.4 GB are supported. The high performance IBM 7210 External DVD-RAM Drive enhances the function and capabilities of the @server i5 and iSeries servers.

The capacity of the DVD media is over seven times larger than CD-ROM. Software that is distributed on multiple CDs may now need only one DVD-RAM cartridge, reducing the cost of media. The 7210-030 can be used as an alternate IPL device.

The 7210-030 supports Ultra-3 SCSI LVD attachment to @server i5 and iSeries servers.

For additional information about the 7210-030, see the following Web site:

http://www-1.ibm.com/servers/storage/tape/7210/index.html

External optical storage

This section describes select external storage optical devices supported by the current @server i5 and iSeries product line.

IBM 3995 Optical Library Cxx models

The IBM 3995 Optical Library C-Models feature high capacity 5.2G or Extended Multifunction optical drives, known as *8X technology*. It is eight times the capacity of the first generation optical technology.

The following table summarizes the 3995 C-Models supported on the @server i5 and iSeries servers.

3995 Optical Library Models C40, C42, C46, and C48

3995 model	Capacity		Number of drives	Attachment	Number of auto changer grippers	Supported controllers
	GB	Disks				
C40	104	20	1-2	Direct	1	#2749
C42	270	52	2	Direct	2	
C44	540	104	2 or 4	Direct	2	
C46	811	156	4 or 6	Direct	2	
C48	1341	258	4 or 6	Direct	2	

The only supported model upgrade is the 3995 Model C44 to the Model C46.

All 3995 Optical Libraries were *withdrawn from marketing* on 30 July 2004. For additional support information about the 3995 Optical Library, go to:

http://www-1.ibm.com/servers/storage/support/tape/3995/

The @server i5 and iSeries with i5/OS V5R3 support the Plasmon's Ultra Density Optical (UDO) drives in the Plasmon G-series libraries. For more information about Plasmon Optical Library support, see the following Web sites:

http://www-1.ibm.com/servers/eserver/iseries/optical/
http://www.plasmon.com/professional/os400.html

Also, refer to "Product Previews: Closed" on page 66 for future optical library direction.

External disk storage devices

This section describes select external storage disk storage devices that are supported by the current @server i5 and iSeries product line.

IBM TotalStorage DS6000

The IBM TotalStorage DS6000 series is designed to deliver enterprise-class storage capabilities in a space-efficient, modular design at a low price. This functionality, as well as the high performance and advanced functions found in enterprise disk storage devices, is available in 19-inch rack mountable packages with the base storage server enclosure 5.25-inch (3U) high, and modular expansion enclosures of the same size to add capacity as your needs grow.

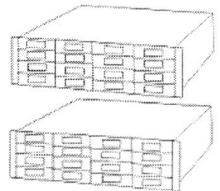

The IBM TotalStorage DS6800 (Model 511) and Expansion Enclosure (Model EX1) provide an intelligent disk system that delivers enterprise-class storage capabilities in a space-efficient 2 Gbps fibre architecture.

The IBM TotalStorage DS6800 consists of redundant, hot-swappable power supplies and cooling fan assemblies, redundant RAID controllers, supporting RAID 5, RAID 10 and optional IBM TotalStorage Resiliency Family functions, IBM TotalStorage FlashCopy®, Metro Mirror, Global Mirror, and Metro/Global Copy.

The DS6800 with Expansion Enclosures supports up to 224 disk drives for a total of up to 67.2 TB of storage. IBM TotalStorage DS6000 Expansion Enclosure

attaches to the DS6800. The 2 Gbps Fibre Channel disk drive sets are available in 73 GB 15,000 rpm, 146 GB 10,000 rpm, and 300 GB 10,000 rpm capacities.

The IBM TotalStorage DS6800 supports the attachment of 13 DS6000 Expansion Enclosures. Storage capacity is among the attached servers using the Browser-based Management GUI, the IBM TotalStorage DS Storage Manager.

The DS6000 is designed to support a broad range of operating environments including zSeries, @server i5 or iSeries, and pSeries servers, as well as servers from Sun, HP, and other Intel-based providers. SCSI attachment is not supported on the DS6000. For the @server i5 or iSeries, attachment via 2 Gbps Fibre Channel controllers is supported.

For additional information about DS6000, see the following Web site:

http://www-1.ibm.com/servers/storage/disk/ds6000/index.html

IBM TotalStorage DS8000

The IBM TotalStorage DS8000 series is designed to provide unmatched functionality, flexibility, and performance for enterprise disk storage systems. It incorporates a high bandwidth internal fabric designed to support fault tolerance, highly expandable and flexible processor memory, and Fibre Channel attached disks. It has a dual processor complex implementation base on IBM POWER5 technology that supports concurrent microcode loads, transparent I/O failover and failback support, and redundant, hot-swappable components for 24 x 7 business environments. The maximum host I/O operations per second of a DS8300 is up to six times the maximum of a IBM TotalStorage Enterprise Storage Server (ESS) Model 800. The DS8000 series also offers all new power and packaging which takes 20% less floor space than a base IBM TotalStorage ESS Model 800.

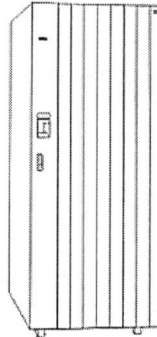

The DS8000 series offers support for IBM TotalStorage Resiliency Family technologies. The IBM TotalStorage Resiliency Family includes FlashCopy, Global Mirror, and Metro Mirror. The DS8000 supports RAID-5 and RAID-10 disk protection. Both RAID-5 and RAID-10 protection are intermixable within a single system. The DS8000 models come standard with the IBM TotalStorage DS Storage Manager. The IBM TotalStorage DS Storage Manager is an all new, easy to use, high-function GUI-based manager for performing and managing logical configuration and copy services functions. A single command line interface is also available which can help automate these functions.

The DS8000 is designed to support a broad range of operating environments including zSeries, @server i5 or iSeries, and pSeries servers, as well as servers from Sun, HP, and other Intel-based providers. SCSI attachment is not supported on the DS8000. For the @server i5 or iSeries, attachment via 2 Gbps Fibre Channel controllers is supported.

The IBM TotalStorage DS8000 Family is comprised of two series of models, the DS8100 and DS8300. The model DS8300 is offered as non-partitionable (model 922) and partitionable (model 92A) configurations. These models are described in the following sections.

Model DS8100

The DS8100 offers scalability of physical capacity from 1.1 to 115.2 TB. Fibre Channel disks are available in 73 GB, 146 GB, and 300 GB capacities, and these are intermixable within a single system. The DS8100 incorporates IBM POWER5 processor technology in a dual two-way processor-complex offering, the Model 921.

Model DS8300

The DS8300 offers scalability of physical capacity up to 192TB. Fibre Channel disks are available in 73 GB, 146 GB, and 300 GB capacities, intermixable within a single system. The DS8300 incorporates IBM POWER5 processor technology in two dual four-way processor complex offerings, the DS8300 Models 922 and 9A2. The DS8300 Model 9A2 enables the creation of multiple IBM TotalStorage Storage System logical partitions (LPARs).

For additional information about DS8000, see the following Web site:

http://www-1.ibm.com/servers/storage/disk/ds8000/index.html

IBM TotalStorage Enterprise Storage Server Model 750

The IBM TotalStorage ESS Model 750 is designed to help meet the needs of clients who do not require the full range of capacity and performance scalability offered by the IBM TotalStorage ESS Model 800, but need enterprise level functionality intended to support reliable, continuous access to data at an affordable price.

The ESS Model 750 provides an entry point into the IBM TotalStorage ESS product family comprised of ESS Model 750 and ESS Model 800. The ESS Model 750 offers many of the features of ESS Model 800, but is based on a two-way processor with 8 GB cache and 2 GB of Non Volatile Storage (NVS). This is in contrast to the 4-way or 6-way processors available with the ESS Model 800.

With support for up to 4.6 TB of physical capacity and six 2 Gb Fibre Channel/FICON® or ESCON® host adapters, the ESS Model 750 is designed to provide an attractive price/performance balance for clients requiring smaller configurations. The ESS Model 750 is well-suited for environments where the workload access densities average two operations per second per GB.

With i5/OS V5R3 release Multipath function provides an alternative path support for host attachment. With Multipath should there be a FC adapter failure, input/outputs are routed through another Fibre Channel IOA in the same multipath group. This is a low cost availability option that would typically cost an FC adapter for any currently installed. This does not alter the requirement for a load source disk that must be mounted in the iSeries. Multipath support for ESS is provided in i5/OS V5R3.

For additional information about ESS, see the following Web site:

http://www-1.ibm.com/servers/storage/disk/ess/

IBM TotalStorage Enterprise Storage Server Model 800

The IBM TotalStorage Enterprise Storage Server Model 800, the third generation of IBM intelligent storage, sets yet another milestone in ESS functionality, flexibility, performance, and overall value available to meet today's storage requirements. The Model 800 is designed to provide performance, scalability, and flexibility. Meanwhile, it supports 24 x 7 operations to help provide the access and protection demanded by today's business environment and delivers the flexibility and centralized management needed to lower long-term costs.

The Model 800 integrates a new generation of hardware, including faster symmetrical multiprocessors (SMP) with an optional Turbo feature, 64 GB cache, double internal bandwidth, and 2 Gb Fibre Channel/FICON Host Adapters. This hardware, in addition to RAID-10 support and 15,000 rpm drives, enables the Model 800 to deliver excellent levels of performance throughput.

With i5/OS V5R3 release Multipath function provides an alternative path support for host attachment. With Multipath should there be a FC adapter failure. I/Os are routed through another FC IOA in the same multipath group. This is a low cost availability option that would typically cost an FC adapter for any currently installed. This does not alter the requirement for a load source disk that must be mounted in the iSeries. Multipath support for ESS is provided in i5/OS V5R3.

For additional information about ESS, see the following Web site:

http://www-1.ibm.com/servers/storage/disk/ess/

Storage area network components

SAN can be defined as a combination of technologies (including hardware, software, and networking components) that provide any-to-any interconnection of server and storage elements.

SANs connect SAN storage (usually tape, disk) together with servers into a network called a *fabric*. Today's industry standard for interconnecting components of a SAN is Fibre Channel. The IBM @server i5 and iSeries support connection of disk and tape using Fibre Channel. The advantage of SAN are greater distances to devices and the ability to share resources on a SAN. Both 1 Gbps and 2 Gbps Fibre Channel are common each supporting different connectivity distances depending on the cables and "light" used. There are three basic fiber cable types primarily in use in Fibre Channel today. They are typically:

- 50 micron fiber: A multimode cable which is thinner and can go longer distances (1 Gb 500m, 2 Gb 300m)

- 62.5 micron fiber: A multimode fiber and can go the least distance (1Gb 175m, 2 Gb 90m)

- 9 micron fiber: A singlemode fiber that can go much longer distances (1Gb and 10KM)

Two types of connectors are common with Fibre Channel devices and controllers:

- **Lucent Connector (LC)**: This connector type is the most prevalent today. It is much smaller allowing higher port densities and is found almost everywhere 2 Gb speeds are supported.

- **Subscriber Connector (SC)**: This is an older connector type found with the majority of devices supporting 1 Gb Fibre Channel.

The components that are supported by the #2765 and #5704 Fibre Channel Tape Controllers, and the #2766 and #2787 PCI-X Fibre Channel Disk Controller Fibre Channel Disk Controllers, include:

- IBM TotalStorage DS6000 and DS8000 Family
- IBM TotalStorage Enterprise Storage Server
- IBM TotalStorage 3592 Tape Drive Model J1A
- IBM TotalStorage Enterprise Tape Drive 3590
- IBM LTO Ultrium 3581 2U
- IBM Ultrium Tape Library 3582
- IBM Ultrium Scalable Tape Library 3583
- IBM UltraScalable Tape Library 3584

Fibre attachment is either directly from the @server i5 or iSeries adapter to an storage server or tape drive, or via a Fibre Channel switch or fabric. For

additional information about @server i5 and iSeries with SAN, refer to *IBM @server iSeries in Storage Area Networks: Implementing Fibre Channel Disk and Tape with iSeries*, SG24-6220.

IBM SAN switches and directors for eServer i5 and iSeries

SAN switches are supported on @server i5 and iSeries servers for connecting multiple host servers with storage servers and devices, creating a SAN. There are a variety of SAN switches supported by the @server i5 and iSeries servers. For more information, see the following Web site:

`http://www-1.ibm.com/servers/storage/san/`

SAN components can be categorized into Entry-Midrange Fibre Channel switches and Enterprise Fibre Channel switches and directors. These switches and directors are summarized in the following sections.

Entry and Midrange Fibre Channel Switches

Several entry level and midrange Fibre Channel switches are offered by IBM. These switches provide affordable, easy to manage SAN solutions for clients who are new to a SAN environment and for midrange clients. This section describes the highlights and specifications of the various models currently marketed by IBM. For information about all SAN models supported with @server i5 and iSeries servers, see the *IBM @server i5, iSeries, and AS/400e System Builder*, SG24-2155.

IBM TotalStorage SAN Switches 2005-H08/-H16, 3534-F08 and 2109-F16/-F32

These switches offer next generation fabric switch providing 4-32 ports, 2 Gbps fabric switching for heterogeneous platforms, infrastructure simplification and business continuity solutions. The switches offer zoning, Fabric Watch, and WEBTOOLS. Highlights of this family of switches include:

► 2 Gbps switching with 4-8/8-16; 4-8 and 8-16/16-32 ports

► High-availability design with hot swappable, redundant power supplies (F16 and F32), optics and concurrent firmware activation (H08, H16 and F32)

► Switched Fabric and FC-AL support

► Up to 8 Gbps aggregate speed with Inter-Switch Link (ISL) trunking

► Advanced fabric services such as end-to-end performance monitoring

► WEBTOOLS and Fabric Manager V4 management software

► Secure Fabric OS

IBM TotalStorage SAN Switches SAN12M-1 2026-E12 and SAN24M-1 2026-224

IBM TotalStorage SAN12M-1 and SAN24M-1 are 2 Gbps fabric switches with FlexPort scalability from 4 to 24 ports for affordable, easy to manage midrange SMB infrastructure simplification and business continuity solutions.

The SAN12M-1 switch is designed to provide high availability advanced technology with a minimum number of components and concurrent firmware activation. High-density packaging and small form factor pluggable (SFP) transceivers provide 12-ports in 1U high rack space.

The SAN24M-1 switch is designed to provide high availability with redundant, hot-swappable fans, power supplies, optics and concurrent firmware activation. High-density packaging and SFP transceivers provide 24-ports in 1U high rack space. Highlights of this family of switches include:

- ► 4, 8, 12-ports, 2 Gbps fabric switching (SAN12M-1 2026-E12)
- ► 8, 16, 24-ports, 2 Gbps fabric switching (SAN24M-1 2026-224)
- ► Designed to support high availability with minimum number of components
- ► Switched Fabric and FC-AL support
- ► HotCAT™ online code activation
- ► Integrated browser-based SANpilot management for first-time storage area network (SAN) users
- ► Offers zoning and SANpilot

Cisco MDS 9216 Multilayer Fabric Switch 2062-D01 and 9120/9140 2061-020/-040

Cisco MDS 9216 Multilayer Fabric Switch provides 16 to 48 ports, with 2 Gbps performance and a modular design with improved availability capabilities.

Cisco MDS 9120 and 9140 Multilayer Fabric Switches provide 20 and 40 ports, with 2 Gbps performance, space saving design and improved reliability capabilities. Host-optimized and target-optimized Fibre Channel ports help to reduce TCO. Highlights of this family of switches include:

- ► 2 Gbps switching with 16 to 48 ports and 20/40 ports
- ► High-availability design with redundant, hotswappable fans, power supplies, optics and concurrent firmware activation
- ► Switched Fabric and FC-AL support
- ► Up to 32 Gbps aggregate speed with PortChannel

- Virtual SAN (VSAN) for SAN consolidation on a single physical fabric
- Cisco Fabric Manager management software
- FICON, FCP and FICON/FCP intermix (D01)

Enterprise Fibre Channel Switches and Directors

A number of enterprise level switches and directors are offered by IBM. These switches and directors provide highly scalable, high available SAN solutions for clients with business critical environments. This section describes the highlights and specifications of the various models currently marketed by IBM. For information about all SAN models supported with @server i5 and iSeries servers, see *IBM @server i5, iSeries, and AS/400e System Builder*, SG24-2155.

IBM TotalStorage SAN Switch SAN32M-1 2027-232 and Director SAN140M 2027-140

IBM TotalStorage SAN32M-1 (2027-232) is a 2 Gbps FICON and Fibre Channel switch with scalability from 8 to 32 ports for easy to manage midrange infrastructure simplification and business continuity solutions. The SAN32M-1 can be used as an edge switch for highly scalable m-type enterprise-to-edge SAN solutions.

IBM TotalStorage SAN140M (2026-140) is a 2 Gbps FICON and Fibre Channel director with scalability from 16 to 140 ports for highest availability enterprise infrastructure simplification and business continuity solutions. Highlights of this family of switches include:

- SAN140M director (2027-140): From 16 to 140 non-blocking Fibre Channels ports, in 12 U rack space, and support for FCP and FICON environments
- SAN32M-1 switch (2027-232): From 8 to 32-port non-blocking Fibre Channel ports, in 1.5 U rack space, and support for FCP and FICON environments
- LC connections
- Enterprise Fabric Connectivity (EFC) Management that includes "call-home" and simple network management protocol (SNMP) alerts, e-mail notification, and support for up to 48 SAN m-type directors and switches across a private LAN
- In-band management with Open Systems Management Server features

CNT UltraNet Multi-service Director (UMD) 2042-N16, CNT FC/9000 Fibre Channel Director 2042-256/128/001

IBM offers the CNT FC/9000Fibre Channel Director to support the ultrascalability and upgradability required by rapidly growing On Demand Business and other important applications. The CNT FC/9000Fibre Channel Director Designed to provide ultra-scalability, upgradability and data center-level high availability with N+1 redundancy for all active components.

To help enable infrastructure simplification and business continuity solutions for on demand enterprises, IBM offers the CNT UltraNet® Multi-service Director (UMD), designed to provide ultra-scalability, high availability and extensible architecture. Highlights of this family of directors include:

► 2 Gbps switching: 2042-N16 and 2042-256 with 32 to 256 ports; 2042-128 with 24 to 128 ports; 2042-001 with 16 to 64 ports with 8-port increments

► High-availability design with redundant power supplies and cooling fans, automatic failover, call-home and concurrent firmware activation

► FC/9000-64 upgradable to FC/9000-128; FC/9000-128 upgradable to FC/9000-256

► Logical domains; virtual ISLs and extensibility to 512-ports (UMD)

► FICON, FCP and FICON/FCP intermix

► IN-VSN management software

Cisco MDS Multilayer Director 9509 2062-D07 and 9506 2062-D04

The Cisco MDS 9509 and 9506 Multilayer Directors support 1 Gbps and 2 Gbps Fibre Channel switch connectivity and intelligent network services to help improve the security, performance and manageability required to consolidate geographically dispersed storage devices into a large enterprise SAN.

The Cisco MDS 9509 Multilayer Director offers dual Supervisor Modules with up to 128 Fibre Channel ports in a 7U enclosure.

The Cisco MDS 9509 Multilayer Director offers dual Supervisor Modules with up to 224 Fibre Channel ports in a 14U enclosure. Highlights of this family of directors include:

► 2 Gbps switching: 9509 with 16 to 224 ports; 9506 with 16 to 128 ports

► High-availability design with redundant, hot-swappable fans, power supplies, automatic failover, concurrent firmware activation and call-home capability

► Up to 32 Gbps aggregate speed with PortChannel

► VSAN for SAN consolidation on a single physical fabric

► FICON, FCP and FICON/FCP intermix

IBM TotalStorage SAN Director 2109-M14/M12 and Cabinet 2109-C36

IBM TotalStorage SAN Switch M14 is a next generation enterprise director which provides high availability, scalability to 128 ports and an expandable architecture for higher speeds and additional functions. It provides advanced features that enable enterprise infrastructure simplification and business continuity solutions. It also has compatibility with prior generation IBM SAN Switches and the Brocade Silkworm family of switches.

IBM TotalStorage SAN Switch M12 provides one or two 64-port, 2 Gigabit per second director with high availability features including non-disruptive CP failover and firmware activation. It provides Fibre Channel switching for high availability, scalable large enterprise SANs with a common management system. Advanced Security can help create a secure storage network infrastructure. Compatibility with the Brocade Silkworm family of switches can enable interoperability with a wide range of non-IBM server and storage devices. Highlights of this family of directors include:

► 2 Gbps switching with 32 to 128 ports (M12 with two 64-port fabrics), with 16-port increments

► High-availability design with redundant power supplies and cooling fans, automatic failover, concurrent firmware activation and call-home with Fabric Manager V4

► Up to 8 Gbps aggregate speed ISL trunking

► Advanced fabric services such as end-to-end performance monitoring

► WEBTOOLS and Fabric Manager V3, V4 management software

► FICON, FCP and FICON/FCP intermix

► Secure Fabric OS

21

I/O devices and other components

This chapter describes the printers that are offered and supported today for iSeries servers.

iSeries printers

iSeries printers are designed, built, tested, and supported as an integrated component of the system. Printer options are scalable from desktop to production, impact to laser, with 375 characters per second up to 2200 impressions per minute.

This section describes the current line of printers for the iSeries. The descriptions are divided into three sections depending on typical usage:

► Workgroup printers
► Departmental and production printers
► Industrial printers

You can find information about iSeries print applications on the iSeries printing Web site at:

`http://www.printers.ibm.com/R5PSC.NSF/Web/as400overview`

The following table summarizes the characteristics of each of these printers, including the duty cycle ratings.

Category	Printer	Machine number	Printer form	Speed (IPM)	Maximum monthly usage (pages)*	IPDS™
Workgroup monochrome	Infoprint® 1412	4547	Cutsheet laser	27 IPM	15K	N
	Infoprint 1422	4523		32 IPM	65K	N
	Infoprint 1226	4526		26 IPM	65K	Y
	Infoprint 1332	4527		35 IPM	175K	Y
	Infoprint 1352	4528		40 IPM	200K	Y
	Infoprint 1372	4529		45 IPM	225K	Y
	Infoprint 1145	4545		45 IPM	250K	Y
	Infoprint 1410	4541		(22 ppm)	50K	
Workgroup color	Infoprint Color 1357	4928	Cutsheet laser	28 IPM	100K	Y
	Infoprint Color 1454	4924		25 IPM	85K	Y
	Infoprint Color 1464	4924		24 IPM	85K	Y

Category	Printer	Machine number	Printer form	Speed (IPM)	Maximum monthly usage (pages)*	IPDS™
Midrange	Infoprint 2060ES	2761	Cutsheet laser	60 IPM	300K	Y
	Infoprint 2075ES	2775		75 IPM	300K	Y
	Infoprint 2085	2785		85 IPM	800K	Y
	Infoprint 2090ES	2790		90 IPM	800K	Y
	Infoprint 2105	2705		105 IPM	1M	Y
	Infoprint 2105ES	2706		105 IPM	1M	Y
	Infoprint 2000	2710		110 IPM	2M	Y
Production	Infoprint 3000	3300	Continuous form laser	344 IPM	4.4M - 8.8M	Y
	Infoprint 4000	4000		1002 IPM	11.6M	Y
	Infoprint 4100	4100		2200 IPM	23.2M	Y
Thermal	IBM 4400	4400	Thermal	10 IPS	---	Y
Impact	IBM 4230	4230	Continuous form matrix	600 CPS	---	Y
	IBM 4232	4232		600 CPS	---	N
	IBM 4247	4247		1100 CPS	---	Y
	IBM 6400-i05	6400	Continuous form line matrix	500 LPM	---	Y
	IBM 6400-i5p	6400		500 LPM	---	Y
	IBM 6400-i10	6400		1000 LPM	---	Y
	IBM 6400-i1P	6400		1000 LPM	---	Y
	IBM 6400-i15	6400		1500 LPM	---	Y
	IBM 6400-i2S	6400		2000 LPM	---	Y

IPM Impressions per minute
IPS Inches per second
CPS Characters per second
LPM Lines per minute
K 1,000
M 1,000,000
* IBM does not recommend printing at the maximum monthly usage rate on a continuous basis.

iSeries workgroup printers

IBM Infoprint workgroup printers are a family of high-performance laser printers designed for iSeries and network printing environments. iSeries workgroup printers provide high fidelity (600 dots-per-inch (dpi) or 1200 dpi) and multiple concurrent connections. They support multiple print data streams (Advanced Function Printing™ (AFP™)/Intelligent Printer Data Stream™ (IPDS), PostScript, Printer Control Language (PCL), Portable Document Format (PDF), a wide range of paper handling options, high-performance color, and a complete line of multifunction printer (MFP) options.

Key features shared by IBM Infoprint workgroup printers include:

► Connections to multiple client and server systems

  – iSeries and local area network (LAN) connectivity, including token-ring, Ethernet, twinaxial, and parallel

  – Concurrent handling of iSeries, network, and client print applications

► Complete integrated IPDS printer featuring:

  – Native, system-managed printing with page-level error recovery

  – Current AFP document features such as 2D barcodes and finishing

  – Full range of AFP fonts: iSeries and printer-resident, raster, and outline formats

  – IPDS connection over TCP/IP provides the same level of application and print management support as twinaxial-connected iSeries printers

> **Note:** The IPDS is not available on Infoprint 1412.

► One-stop support from IBM, the experts in iSeries printing

IBM Infoprint 1412 Workgroup Laser Printer

With a small footprint and a low acquisition price, the IBM Infoprint 1412 delivers the function needed to support small businesses and small workgroups. With a fast print speed, 32 MB of memory, a first page out time as fast as eight seconds, and a 200 MHz processor, the Infoprint 1412 allows you to keep up with the pace of On Demand Business. The highlights of this printer include:

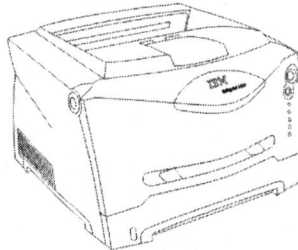

- ▶ Print up to 27 impressions per minute
- ▶ Adjustable print resolution settings to optimize print quality and performance
- ▶ Intuitive operating panel and easy paper loading
- ▶ Fast Ethernet, token-ring, and Wireless Ethernet networking
- ▶ Support for PCL 6 and Postscript Level 3 standard
- ▶ Supported by OS/400 Host Print Transform (PCL)

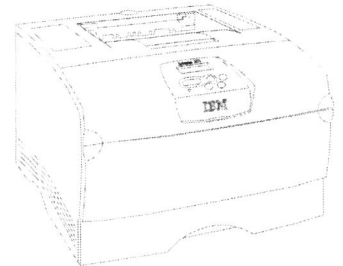

IBM Infoprint 1145 Workgroup Laser Printer

This is the fastest workgroup printer from IBM. It offers robust finishing and connectivity functions, including:

- ▶ Up to 45 pages per minute throughput with fast time to first page

- ▶ Optional finisher provides stacking, stapling, and hole punching

- ▶ iSeries integration and support

- ▶ Rich print data stream support includes IBM AFP/IPDS (option), PCL, and PostScript

- ▶ Supports a variety of media up to ledger size paper

- ▶ IBM MFP option adds copy, fax, and scan capabilities

- ▶ Onsite support from IBM Service, the experts in iSeries printing

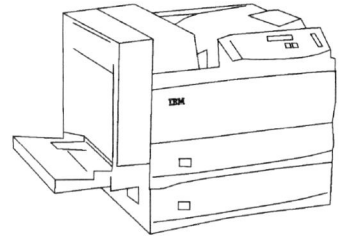

IBM Infoprint 1422 Workgroup Laser Printer

The Infoprint 1422 is a low-cost, high-performance, black-and-white laser printer with enclosed paper drawers and a very small footprint. A 366 MHz processor enables fast processing of complex jobs and a first-page-out-time of eight seconds for quick turnaround and increased productivity.

- ▶ Prints up to 32 impressions per minute

- ▶ Optional duplex capability to save paper costs and enable a lower total cost of printing

- ▶ Fast Ethernet, token-ring, and Wireless Ethernet networking

- ▶ Support for PCL 6 and Postscript Level 3 standard

- ▶ Supported by OS/400 Host Print Transform (PCL)

IBM Infoprint 1226 Workgroup Laser Printer

The IBM Infoprint 1226 provides fast printing and large-format support at an attractive price. It offers:

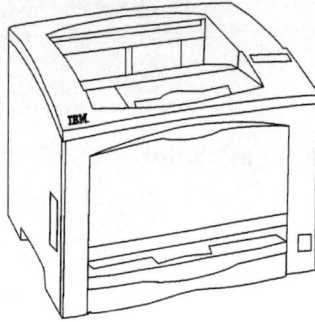

- ► Up to 26 pages per minute throughput with fast time to first page
- ► iSeries integration
- ► IPDS option for robust iSeries printing, full management, and complete error recovery
- ► High-speed processor for faster handling of complex applications

IBM Infoprint 1332 Workgroup Laser Printer

The IBM Infoprint 1332 is a mid-speed laser printer designed for both iSeries and workgroup applications. The highlights of this printer include:

- ► Up to 35 impressions per minute, with fast first-page-out time
- ► True 1200 x 1200 dpi image quality
- ► Memory and hard-drive options to boost performance with large jobs
- ► Print and hold function facilitates secure printing of confidential documents
- ► Available MFP to add scan, fax, and copy functions to the hardware
- ► IPDS and PDF data stream support

IBM Infoprint 1352 Workgroup Laser Printer

The IBM Infoprint 1352 is a high-speed workgroup laser printer at a low cost-per-page and with a wide array of options. The highlights of this printer include:

- Up to 40 impressions per minute with fast first-page-out time

- Versatile and extensive finishing options including staple, hole punch, and job offset

- True 1200 x 1200 dpi image quality

- Available MFP to add scan, fax, and copy functions

- Integrated IPDS for reliable business printing

- PCL 6, Postscript Level 3, and PDF data stream support

IBM Infoprint 1372 Workgroup Laser Printer

The IBM Infoprint 1372 provides high-performance monochrome workgroup laser printing with the memory and speed to handle complex documents at a high throughput rate. The key features include:

- Up to 45 impressions per minute with fast first-page-out time

- Versatile and extensive finishing options including staple, hole punch, and job offset

- True 1200 x 1200 dpi

- Available MFP to add scan, fax, and copy functions

- IPDS for reliable business printing includes latest document features such as 2D barcode support

- PCL 6, Postscript Level 3, and PDF data stream support

- Minimize operator intervention with high yield supplies and MarkVision printing management software

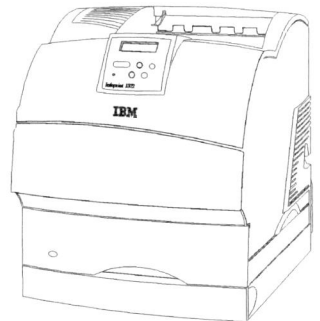

IBM Infoprint Color 1454 and 1464 Laser Printer

The IBM Infoprint Color 1454 and 1464 are high-value workgroup color printers that provide high-speed printing for both color and black-and-white jobs. The outstanding performance, reliability and fast page delivery of the 1454 and 1464 laser printers can help workgroups become more efficient.

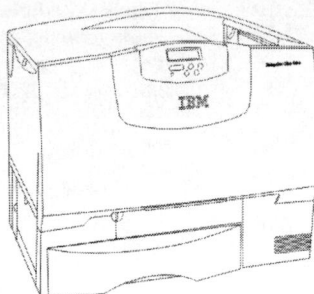

- ► Prints color and black-and-white at 25 impressions per minute

- ► Supports full-color printing with optional color IPDS card

- ► Monochrome lock-down capability to control access to color printing

- ► Fast Ethernet, token-ring, and Wireless Ethernet networking

- ► Support for PCL 6 with color extension and Postscript Level 3 standard

- ► Available MFP to add scan, fax, and copy functions

IBM Infoprint Color 1357 Laser Printer

The IBM Infoprint Color 1357 provides high-performance color and monochrome laser printing at a low cost-per-page and with a wide array of options. The key features include:

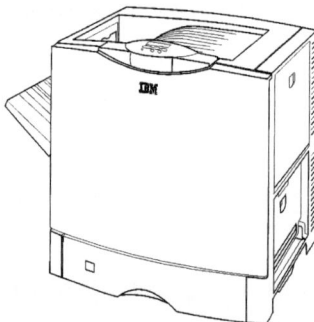

- ► Up to 28 impressions per minute color and black-and-white, with fast first-page-out time

- ► Supports A3/ledger paper and banner printing up to three feet

- ► Helps manage supply costs with authorization control

- ► True 1200 x 1200 dpi and 2400 image quality with automatic color correction

- ► Available MFP to add scan, fax, and copy functions

- ► IPDS integrated option for reliable business printing

- ► Direct PDF data stream support available

IBM Infoprint 1410 MFP Printer

The IBM Infoprint 1410 MFP is a low-cost,
high-performance machine that is ideal for
small workgroups and businesses, especially
those with limited space. The operational
advantages include:

- ► Obtain advanced functionality by replacing
  aging output equipment with a new
  multifunction device

- ► Up to 22 ppm with a first-page-out-time as
  fast as 10 seconds

- ► Resolution settings of up to 600 dpi and
  1200 image quality

- ► One supply item, a single toner cartridge

- ► Range of network access capabilities, including wireless Ethernet

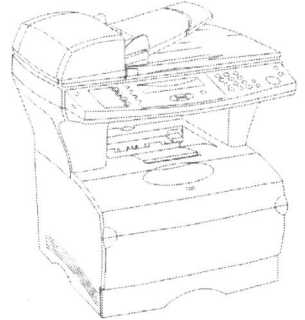

Multifunction printing options

MFP options enable you to protect and expand your printer investment by adding
scan, fax, and copy functions to IBM Infoprint 1000 series workgroup printers.
MFP options can be included with the printer or purchased later. The following
table summarizes current Infoprint MFP options.

MFP option	Mono scan (IPM)	Color scan (IPM)	Duplex	Printers supported
M22	15	14	N	Infoprint 1332, 1352, 1372
M26	23	14	Y	Infoprint 1332, 1352, 1372
M30	23	14	Y	Infoprint 1332, 1352, 1372, 1464
M32	34	19	Y	Infoprint 1357
M35	40	N/A	N	Infoprint 1145

iSeries departmental and production printers

In the same manner that the iSeries server scales up in performance, IBM system printers provide a wide range of choices at midrange and production printing speeds (generally 60 impressions per minute and up). These include both cutsheet and continuous form printers, currently achieving up to 2200 impressions per minute (with the IBM Infoprint 4100). All of the departmental and production printers feature the Advanced Function Common Control Unit (AFCCU™), a high-performance controller using the same processor technology as the iSeries servers.

IBM Infoprint 2060ES

The IBM Infoprint 2060ES is the 60 impression per minute member of the ES midrange production printing family. This cutsheet printer effectively combines high-speed iSeries production printing with full reproduction capabilities. The highlights of this printer include:

► Print speeds up to 60 impressions per minute at 1200 dpi resolution

► Duplication facilities are standard with 60 impressions per minute scanning

► Cutsheet production printing at an affordable price

► Finishing includes 50-staple finisher, 100-staple finisher, booklet finisher, and hole-punch options

► Web and Extensible Markup Language (XML)-based job ticketing

► Integrated IPDS for reliable, high-speed iSeries business printing

► The latest AFP enhancements include 2D barcodes and color grayscale printing

► A standard 40 GB hard-drive improves print caching and performance (for example, AFP fonts are preloaded for fast IPDS throughput)

► Full support for PostScript, PCL and PDF data streams is available

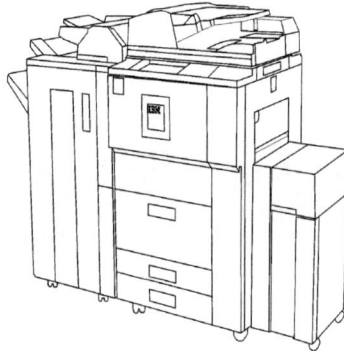

IBM Infoprint 2075ES

The IBM Infoprint 2075ES is the 675 impression per minute member of the ES midrange production printing family. This cutsheet digital multi-function system effectively combines high-speed iSeries production printing with full reproduction capabilities. The highlights of this printer include:

- ► Print speeds up to 75 impressions per minute at 1200 dpi resolution
- ► Duplication (copier) facilities are standard
- ► Cutsheet production printing at an affordable price
- ► Finishing includes a 50-staple finisher, 100-staple finisher, booklet finisher, and hole-punch options
- ► Web and XML-based job ticketing
- ► IPDS for reliable, high-speed iSeries business printing
- ► A standard 40 GB hard drive improves print caching and performance (for example, AFP fonts are preloaded for fast IPDS throughput)
- ► The latest AFP enhancements include 2D barcodes and color grayscale printing
- ► PostScript, PCL, and PDF data streams are available

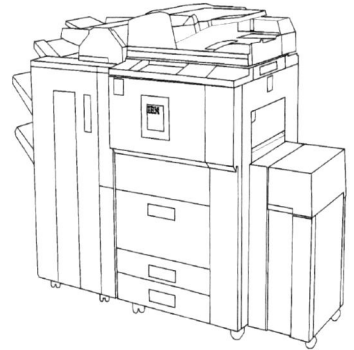

IBM Infoprint 2085

The IBM Infoprint 2085 cutsheet laser printer is a midrange production printer that effectively combines high-speed iSeries production printing with full reproduction capabilities. The highlights of this printer include:

- Print speeds up to 85 impressions per minute
- Duplication facilities are standard
- Cutsheet production printing at an affordable price
- 600 dots-per-inch resolution with automatic conversion of lower-resolution applications
- Fully integrated with IPDS for reliable, high-speed iSeries printing
- PostScript, PCL, and PDF data streams are available

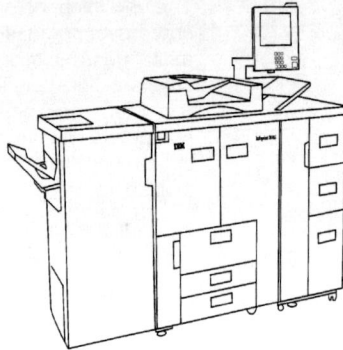

IBM Infoprint 2090ES

The IBM Infoprint 2090ES is the 90 impression per minute member of the ES midrange production printing family. This cutsheet digital multifunction system effectively combines high-speed iSeries production printing with full reproduction capabilities. The highlights of this printer include:

- Print speeds up to 90 impressions per minute at 1200 dpi resolution
- Duplication (copier) facilities are standard
- Cutsheet production printing at an affordable price
- Finishing options include a 50-staple finisher, 100-staple finisher, booklet finisher, and hole-punch
- Web and XML-based job ticketing
- IPDS for reliable, high-speed iSeries business printing

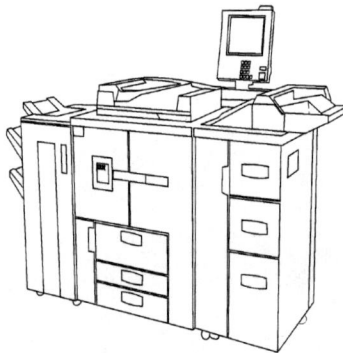

- A standard 40 GB hard drive improves print caching and performance (for example, AFP fonts are preloaded for fast IPDS throughput)
- The latest AFP enhancements include 2D barcodes and color grayscale printing
- PostScript, PCL, and PDF data streams are available

IBM Infoprint 2105

The IBM Infoprint 2105 cutsheet laser printer is a midrange production printer that effectively combines high-speed iSeries production printing with full reproduction capabilities. The highlights of this printer include:

- Print speeds up to 105 impressions per minute
- Duplication facilities are standard
- Cutsheet production printing at an affordable price
- 600 dots-per-inch resolution with automatic conversion of lower-resolution applications
- Fully integrated with IPDS for reliable, high-speed iSeries printing
- Full support available for ASCII (PostScript, PCL, and PDF) data streams

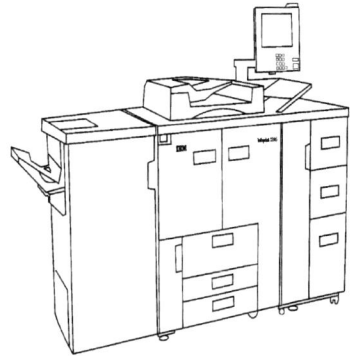

IBM Infoprint 2105ES

The IBM Infoprint 2105ES is the 105 impression per minute member of the ES midrange production printing family. This cutsheet digital multi-function system effectively combines high-speed iSeries production printing with full reproduction capabilities. The highlights of this printer include:

- Print speeds up to 105 impressions per minute at 1200 dpi resolution
- Duplication (copier) facilities are standard

- Cutsheet production printing at an affordable price
- Finishing options include a 50-staple finisher, 100-staple finisher, booklet finisher, and hole-punch
- Web and XML-based job ticketing
- IPDS for reliable, high-speed iSeries business printing
- A standard 40 GB hard drive improves print caching and performance (for example, AFP fonts are preloaded for fast IPDS throughput)
- The latest AFP enhancements include 2D barcodes and color grayscale printing
- Full support available for ASCII (PostScript, PCL, and PDF) data streams

IBM Infoprint 2000

Infoprint 2000 printers bring cutsheet printer capabilities to address the output needs of an On Demand Business. This high-speed cutsheet printer combines advanced hardware and software technologies to provide exceptional performance, flexibility, and control. The integration with Infoprint Manager brings Infoprint 2000 into heterogeneous environments, converting PostScript and PCL jobs to AFP/IPDS. The software creates a central point for managing all print jobs through the enterprise and provides workload balancing to help ensure printers are always printing.

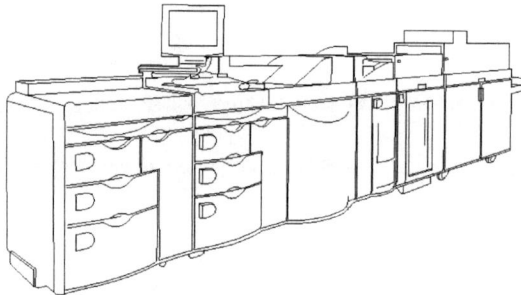

Inherent with this solution, Infoprint 2000 supports Internet Printing Protocol (IPP) and is ready for On Demand Business. IPP provides mobile users the means to address a printer from anywhere, allows companies to provide their clients with direct access to their printer, and provides notifications to communicate printer status.

Powered by an advanced imaging technology, Infoprint 2000 is designed to monitor and self-adjust print quality as needed. Establishing new AFP/IPDS benchmark print quality, Infoprint 2000 produces fine lines and offset-like halftones. To ensure user-friendly paper support and reliability, the system has a straight paper path, as well as three standard and three optional vacuum fed

paper drawers for preventing paper mis-feeds. In addition, IBM Infoprint 2000 with AFCCU offers:

▶ Up to 110 impressions per minute at 600 dpi

▶ Up to 2,000,000 impressions per month

▶ Superb image quality with Grayscale Resolution Enhancement Technology (GRET) producing crisper, clearer halftones, and more accurate reproduction of finer fonts

▶ Automatic enhancement of existing 240 dpi and 300 dpi applications

▶ Simple, direct attachment with Ethernet or token-ring

▶ Supports paper sizes ranging from 8-by-10.5 to 11-by-17 and paper weights in the range of 16 pound bond to 110 pound index

▶ Input and output paper capabilities of up to 8,000 sheets (4,000 sheets are standard)

▶ Trayless duplexing and a shorter, straighter paper path means benchmark levels of reliability

▶ Software support provided by PSF/400

▶ IBM world class service and support

IBM Infoprint 3000 Advanced Function Printing System

IBM Infoprint 3000 is a high-speed, high-resolution, continuous-form production printing system designed and integrated for high-volume iSeries printing. IBM Infoprint 3000 printers deliver print speeds from 112 to 344 impressions per minute, with the ability to perform two-up printing (8.5-by-11-inch pages) using the new 17-inch print-head technology. Monthly print volumes can go up to 4.4 million impressions.

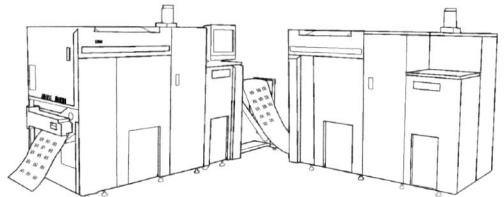

This new printing system prints at high speeds and with high quality. Print fidelity is at 480 dpi or 600 dpi, and the print resolution is switchable. Existing iSeries applications developed at 240 dpi or 300 dpi are automatically enhanced to either 480 dpi or 600 dpi.

The IBM Infoprint 3000 is directly attached to the iSeries (using Ethernet or token-ring) and is fully supported by Print Services Facility/400, the full-function print management subsystem of OS/400. Full application enablement includes

system printer file function, DDS, Infoprint Designer for iSeries, AFP Utilities, Advanced Print Utility (APU), Page Printer Formatting Aid (PPFA/400), AFP Toolbox, and many other IBM and third-party document composition products.

With high-volume applications such as reports, statements, documents, and direct mail, continuous-forms printing ensures high reliability. They also ensure the attachment of a wide variety of pre- and post-processing devices (paper roll input, cutters, inserters, and so on) for a smooth end-to-end process. This is an intelligent process that starts with blank paper and can end up a complete package ready for mailing.

Additional features include:

► Simplex and duplex configurations. Duplex configurations (two Infoprint 3000 printers in tandem) can also be run in dual simplex mode when required.

► The RISC-based Advanced Function Controller provides comprehensive print and document functionality, as well as high performance for even the most complex jobs.

► It has the smallest footprint (up to 25% smaller) in its class.

IBM Infoprint 4000 Advanced Function Printing Systems

Infoprint 4000 is a high-speed, continuous-form production printer family for iSeries servers. Speeds range up to 1002 impressions (on 8.5-by-11-inch sheets) per minute. Models include simplex, wide, and duplex with resolutions of 240, 480, and 600 dpi.

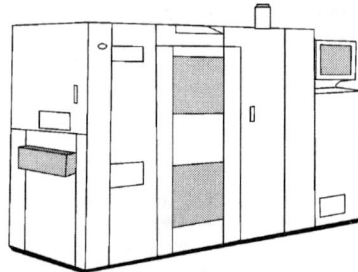

Infoprint architecture provides higher resolutions and support for PostScript data streams to meet far more wide-ranging organizational document requirements, including the replacement of applications that traditionally went to offset printing. Infoprint 4000 attaches to iSeries servers over a token-ring or Ethernet network.

The key features include:

► Maximum usage of up to 17.4 million impressions per month

► Driven by IBM AFCCU, which provides high-speed processing of complex documents, full IPDS function, and comprehensive connectivity

► Wide models provide 17-inch wide platen for two-up printing of 8.5-by-11-inch output

- Designed for production print environments with appropriate intelligent preprocessing (such as roll paper input) and postprocessing (for example, cutters and collators) equipment
- Optional pinless drive replaces traditional tractor-fed paper
- Optional Infoprint Hi-lite Color post processor enables variable data in color, up to three colors per page

IBM Infoprint 4100 Advanced Function Printing Systems

The Infoprint 4100 offers continuous forms printing with 19-inch wide print line for digital publishing and statements printing. Speeds up to 762 two-up, duplex letter or 718 two-up, duplex A4 impressions per minute with 480/600 dpi resolution. Simplex and duplex models are available in this printer family.

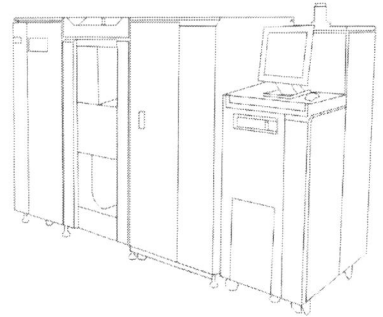

Infoprint architecture provides higher resolutions and support for PostScript data streams. This helps to meet far more wide-ranging organizational document requirements, including replacement of applications that traditionally went to offset printing. The Infoprint 4100 attaches to the iSeries server over an Ethernet or token-ring network.

The key features include:

- Industry leading 600 dpi image quality
- Prints true 3-up 6-by-9-inch pages at up to 2200 impressions per minute
- Extra-wide format (19-inch print width)
- Reduced total cost of printing

iSeries industrial printers

Central to today's supply chain environments, iSeries industrial printers are designed for harsh environments and multi-part form applications. The printer technology is either dot matrix or line matrix. IPDS is supported throughout, both for complete print management and graphics function (for example, barcodes). This category includes the IBM 4230, IBM 4232, IBM 4247, and IBM 6400 printer families.

IBM 4230 Impact Matrix Printer

The 4230 range of printers provides heavy-duty, impact matrix printing. The six models of 4230, the 101, 1S2, 4S3, 1I1, 102, and 4I3, can all be twinaxial attached to an iSeries server using the twinaxial workstation controller. The Model 4S3 and 4I3 also offer serial and parallel attach.

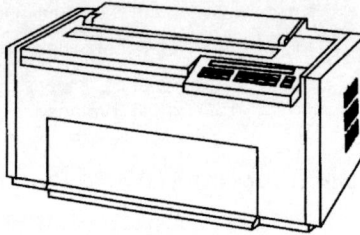

All 4230s have an LCD display that provides prompts and menu selections in a choice of eight languages. They also have forms handling modules for continuous forms and document insertion. One of these forms modules is supplied with the initial order, as selected by the client. The others are available as options.

Models 101 and 1S2 have 32K memory as standard and support the IBM 4214 data stream SNA Character String (SCS). Models 1I1 and 102 have 128K memory as standard and support the IBM IPDS. Memory on the 1I1 and 102 can be increased to 512K as an option. Models 4S3 and 4I3 have 128K memory as standard. Model 4S3 supports the SCS data stream, while Model 4I3 supports IPDS. The following table shows each model's print speeds.

Model	Mode			
	Fast draft	DP	DP text	NLQ
101, 1I1	375 cps	300 cps	150 cps	75 cps
1S2, 102	480 cps	400 cps	200 cps	100 cps
4S3, 4I3	600 cps	400 cps	200 cps	100 cps

IBM 4232 Impact Dot Matrix Printer

The 4232 is a heavy-duty, unattended impact dot matrix printer, capable of printing 600 cps. It is designed for workstation printing or shared printer applications using an ASCII data stream.

The 4232 Model 302 can be used for printing data processing, office, and business documents, as well as barcode labels and multipart forms.

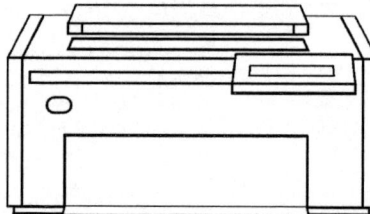

The 4232 has an LCD display that provides prompts and menu selections in a choice of eight languages. It also has forms handling modules for continuous forms and document insertion.

IBM 4247 MultiForm Matrix Printer

The 4247 printers are desktop model impact printers. They are capable of printing up to 1100 cps in its fastest data processing (DP) mode. They include two continuous paper paths and a standard manual cutsheet input.

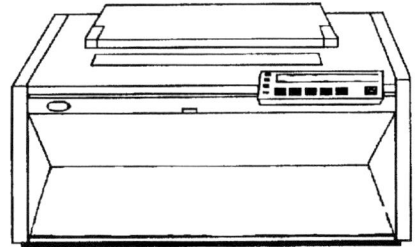

The 4727 can be used as a directly attached workstation printer, as a system printer, remote or distributed, or for departmental printing. Supported applications include word processing and spreadsheets, business graphics such as pie charts, barcode printing, line drawings from CAD/CAM applications, and special forms for checks, labels, and mailers.

The 4247 models have a duty cycle of up to 20 million characters-per-month and print qualities include DP, DP Text, and Near Letter Quality (NLQ).

▶ Attachment to the system can be Twinaxial, Serial/Parallel, Ethernet, and token-ring; coax and attachment to LAN using ASCII interface are also available

▶ IPDS support for the full range of electronic printing capabilities (barcode, electronic forms, image, graphics, and variable fonts), and full printing error recovery

IBM 4400 Thermal Label Printers

The IBM 4400 Thermal Label printers provide high-performance, high-quality thermal printing geared to the iSeries, network, and Supply Chain industrial environments in which they must operate. This is an environment where iSeries application integration, reliable output management, and network deployment and administration are essential.

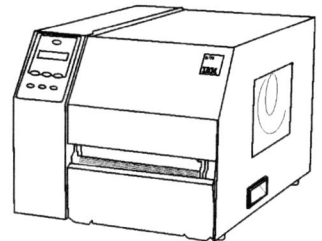

The key design elements of the system, which are integration, reliability, scalability, ease of use, and designed for On Demand

Business, are reflected in the IBM 4400 Thermal Laser printers. Support for Intelligent Printer Data Stream means that any Advanced Function Presentation™ application interface can be used. IPDS also means industrial-strength printing management, even when the printer is deployed in a TCP/IP network. Support for additional thermal data streams ensures compatibility with existing applications.

Features of the IBM 4400 series include:

- ▸ Print resolution up to 300 dots per inch, print speeds up to 10 inches per second, and media widths of 6.8 inches or 8.75 inches

- ▸ Ideal for barcode and graphics applications, supporting IPDS barcodes (including new 2D symbologies), and existing Code V and Intelligent Graphics Processor (IGP) barcode applications

- ▸ Supported by IBM Printer Management Utility for remote administration

- ▸ Rugged footprint and construction designed for tough industrial environments

- ▸ IPDS support for iSeries application integration and robust print management

IBM 6400 Line Matrix Printers

The dependable IBM 6400 line matrix printer family is designed for heavy-duty, continuous use in both system and network environments. Extensive data stream support (SCS, IPDS, ASCII, Code V, IGP) ensures application compatibility. Speeds range from a low-cost 500 line-per-minute pedestal model to models supporting print speeds up to 2000 lines per minute. The new, integrated Ethernet IPDS enables the IBM 6400 to be placed in an IP network, yet retains all the application function and print management control of a direct-attached iSeries printer.

The 6400 family of line matrix printers provides heavy-duty, continuous-form impact line printing with low total cost of operation. A variety of emulations, options, and speeds address just about any print requirements.

Six models of the 6400 family are shown in the following table.

Model	Speed (lines per minute)	Package
6400-i05	500	Cabinet
6400-i5P	500	Pedestal
6400-i10	1000	Cabinet
6400-i1P	1000	Pedestal
6400-i15	1500	Cabinet
6400-i20	2000	Cabinet

An optional feature for Intelligent Printer Data Stream support enables full graphical applications with electronic forms, barcodes, graphics, scalable fonts, and optical character recognition.

Web access to operator panel enables remote control of network-connected 6400 models.

22

Customer Install Features

Many iSeries models are designated as Customer Setup (CSU). Several of the features for the current product line are Customer Install Features (CIF). CIF and CSU designations provide the client with flexibility in installing new iSeries servers and adding new features to installed systems. Clients can schedule installations to minimize the disturbance to their business operations.

Miscellaneous Equipment Specification (MES) is an IBM term for IBM-supplied changes to an installed or on-order system. On MES orders that include a mixture of IBM install and CIF features, the client may choose to have the IBM service representative install all of the features, including those designated as CIF. On MES orders where all features are CIF, the client can install all of the features.

The client is responsible for the installation of external cables, displays, printers, and modems. IBM service personnel can perform these activities for a charge. IBM installation for CSU and CIF units is available for a charge under normal service contracts.

OS/400 features supported on iSeries servers

The tables in this chapter list the commonly ordered feature codes for the latest iSeries models marketed by IBM. They identify which features are CIF features, in which iSeries model and expansion unit the feature is supported, and the minimum release of OS/400 required to support the feature.

For a comprehensive list of features, as a cross reference of feature codes and CCIN number, see the "Feature Code" and "CCIN" chapters of the *IBM @server i5, iSeries, and AS/400e System Builder*, SG24-2155. These chapters include most power cord and cable features, as well as the load source specify features. Refer to "Editions" on page 55 for a list of the features codes for iSeries Editions. Cable information, including feature and part numbers, is also available at the Information Center Web site:

http://www.ibm.com/eserver/iseries/infocenter

When you reach this site, select the **Planning** →**Cables**.

The columns in the following tables contain:

- ▶ The feature code (FC)
- ▶ The feature description as used in the IBM marketing configurator
- ▶ A Y if the feature is a CIF, or an N if it is an "installed by IBM" feature
- ▶ How the features are installed in each of the iSeries models currently marketed by IBM

  The installation options are defined as follows:

  - **B**: Plant or MES installation
  - **M**: MES install only (available for field installation only)
  - **P**: Plant install only (available on new system orders only)
  - **PU**: Plant install only; for model upgrades, an MES install
  - **S**: Supported in the specified iSeries model configuration

    The feature may be migrated to the specified iSeries model as part of a model upgrade, but individual orders are not available.

  - **SC**: Supported for conversion
- ▶ Minimum operating system level

  The operating system version and release that supports the feature, either natively or with program temporary fixes (PTFs)

Model 520, 550, 570, 595 system unit and tower features

The following table shows the features supported in Models 520, 550 and 570, the associated expansion units, the CIF designation, and minimum operating system level of each feature.

Note: Only the Linux for Power versions of Linux are supported on the @server i5 Model 520, 550, 570, and 595 servers.

FC and description	CIF	Model or tower								Min. OS/400 or i5/OS	Min. AIX 5L
		520 (9405/9406)	550	570	595	#5095/#0595	#5074/#5094/#5294	#5088/#0588	#5790		
#0040 Mirrored System Disk Level	Y	B	B	B	B	-	-	-	-	V5R3	V5.2
#0041 Device Parity Protection-All	Y	B	B	B	B	-	-	-	-	V5R3	V5.2
#0042 Mirrored System IOP Level	Y	B	B	B	B	-	-	-	-	V5R3	V5.2
#0043 Mirrored System Bus Level	Y	B	B	B	B	-	-	-	-	V5R3	V5.2
#0092 External xSeries Attach	Y	B	B	B	B	-	-	-	-	V5R3	-
#0123 #5074 Lower Unit in Rack	Y	S	-	S		-	-	-	-	V5R3	-
#0126 CEC Reduction Specify	N				B					V5R2	
#0140 Logical Partitioning Specify	Y	B	B	B	B	-	-	-	-	V5R3	V5.2
#0141 HSL OptiConnect Specify	Y				B					V5R3	
#0142 Linux Partition Specify	Y	B	B	B	B	-	-	-	-	V5R3	V5.2
#0145 AIX Partition Specify	Y	B	B	B	B	-	-	-	-	V5R3	V5.2
#0325 IPCS Extension Cables for NT	Y	B	B	B	B	B	B	B	B	V5R3	-
#0367 Operations Console PCI Cable	Y	B	B	B	B	B	B	B	B	V5R3	-
#0369 100m Optical SPCN Cable	Y	-	-	B		B	B	B	B	V5R3	-
#0371 LC-SC Adapter Kit (50 um)	Y	B	B	B	B	B	B	B	B	V5R3	V5.2
#0372 LC-SC Adapter Kit (62.5 um)	Y	B	B	B	B	B	B	B	B	V5R3	V5.2

| FC and description | CIF | Model or tower | | | | | | | | Min. OS/400 or i5/OS | Min. AIX 5L |
		520 (9405/9406)	550	570	595	#5095/#0595	#5074/#5094/#5294	#5088/#0588	#5790		
#0446 512 MB DDR Server Memory	Y	B	B	B	B	B	B	B		V5R3	-
#0447 1 GB DDR Server Memory	Y	B	B	B	B	B	B	B		V5R3	-
#0551 iSeries Rack	Y	B	B	B	B	-	-	-	-	V5R3	V5.2
#0553 2M iSeries Rack		B	B	B	B					V5R3	
#0588 PCI-X Expansion Unit in Rack	Y	B	B	B	B	-	-	-	-	V5R3	-
#0595 PCI-X Expansion Unit in Rack	Y	B	B	B	B	-	-	-	-	V5R3	V5.2
#0601 - Direct Attach - #2743 PCI 1 Gbps Ethernet IOA	Y	SC	SC	SC	SC	S	S	S	S	V5R3	-
#0602 - Direct Attach - #2760 PCI 1 Gbps Ethernet UTP IOA	Y	SC	SC	SC	SC	S	S	S	S	V5R3	-
#0603 - Direct Attach - #2744 PCI 100 Mbps Token-Ring IOA	Y	B	B	B	B	B	B	B	B	V5R3	-
#0607 - Direct Attach - #4838 PCI 100/10 Mbps Ethernet IOA	Y	SC	SC	SC	SC	S	S	S	S	V5R3	-
#0608 - Direct Attach - #4745 PCI WAN IOA	Y	SC	SC	SC	SC	S	S	S	S	V5R3	-
#0609 - Direct Attach - #2772 PCI Dual WAN/Modem IOA	Y	B	B	B		B	B	B	B	V5R3	-
#0610 - Direct Attach - #2773 PCI Dual WAN/ModemIOA	Y	B	B	B	B	B	B	B	B	V5R3	-
#0611 - Direct Attach - #2765 PCI Fibre Channel Tape Controller	Y	B	B	B	B	B	B	B	B	V5R3	V5.2
#0612 - Direct Attach - #2766 PCI Fibre Channel Disk Controller	Y	M	M	M	M	B	B	B	B	V5R3	-
#0613 - Direct Attach - #2742 PCI 2-Line WAN IOA	Y	B	B	B	B	B	B	B	B	V5R3	-
#0614 - Direct Attach - #2793 PCI 2-Line WAN w/Modem	Y	B	B	B	B	B	B	B	B	V5R3	-

FC and description	CIF	520 (9405/9406)	550	570	595	#5095/#0595	#5074/#5094/#5294	#5088/#0588	#5790	Min. OS/400 or i5/OS	Min. AIX 5L
#0615 - Direct Attach - #2794 PCI 2-Line WAN w/Modem	Y	B	B	B	B	B	B	B	B	V5R3	-
#0616 - Direct Attach - #2805 PCI Quad Modem IOA	Y	B	B	B	B	B	B	B	B	V5R3	-
#0617 - Linux Direct Attach #2806	Y	B	B	B	B	B	B	B	B	V5R3	-
#0620 - Direct Attach - #5700 PCI 1 Gbps Ethernet IOA	Y	B	B	B	B	B	B	B	B	V5R3	V5.2
#0621 - Linux/AIX Direct Attach #5701	Y	B	B	B	B	B	B	B	B	V5R3	V5.2
#0623 - Direct Attach - #2849 PCI 100/10 Mbps Ethernet IOA	Y	B	B	B	B	B	B	B	B	V5R3	-
#0624 - Linux Direct Attach #5702	Y	M	M	M	M	B	B	B	B	V5R3	V5.2
#0625 - Linux/AIX Direct Attach #5704	Y	B	B	B	B	B	B	B	B	V5R3	V5.2
#0626 - Linux Direct Attach #2787	Y	B	B	B	B	B	B	B	B	V5R3	-
#0627 - Linux Direct Attach #2780	Y	B	B	B	B	B	B	-		V5R3	V5.2
#0628 - Linux/AIX Direct Attach #5703	Y	B	B	B	B	B-	B	-		V5R3	V5.2
#0632 PCI USB 2.0 Adapter	Y	B	B	B	B	B	B	B	B	-	V5.2
#0633 Graphics Adapter	Y	B	B	B	B	B	B	B	B	-	V5.2
#0634 128-Port Async Adapter	Y	B	B	B	B	B	B	B	B	-	V5.2
#0635 SDLC/X.25 - 2-Port Adapter	Y	B	B	B	B	B	B	B	B	-	V5.2
#0642 PCI Ultra-3 RAID Adapter	Y	B	B	B		B	B	-	B	-	V5.2
#0643 Linux/AIX Direct Attach #5706	Y	B	B	B		B	B	B	B	V5R3	V5.2
#0644 Linux/AIX Direct Attach #5707	Y	B	B	B		B	B	B	B	V5R3	V5.2
#0645 - Direct Attach - #5712 PCI-X Tape/DASD Controller	Y	B	B	B	B	B	B	B	B	-	V5.2
#0694 #5094 Equivalent	Y	B	B	B	B	-	B	-	-	V5R3	V5.2
#1307 - 1.75m HSL-2/RIO-2 Cable	Y	B	B	B	B	B	B	B	B	V5R3	V5.2

FC and description	CIF	Model or tower								Min. OS/400 or i5/OS	Min. AIX 5L
		520 (9405/9406)	550	570	595	#5095/#0595	#5074/#5094/#5294	#5088/#0588	#5790		
#1308 - 2.5m HSL-2/RIO-2 Cable	Y	B	B	B	B	B	B	B	B	V5R3	V5.2
#1460 - 3m Copper HSL Cable	Y	B	B	B	B	-	-	-		V5R3	-
#1461 - 6m Copper HSL Cable	Y	-	-	-	B	-	-	-		V5R3	-
#1462 - 15m Copper HSL Cable	Y	-	-	-	B	-	-	-		V5R3	-
#1463 - 2m SPCN Cable	Y	S	S	S	S	B	B	B		V5R3	V5.2
#1464 - 6m SPCN Cable	Y	S	S	S	S	B	B	B		V5R3	V5.2
#1465 - 15m SPCN Cable	Y	S	S	S	S	B	B	B		V5R3	V5.2
#1466 - 30m SPCN Cable	Y	S	S	S	S	B	B	B		V5R3	V5.2
#1468 - 250m Optical SPCN Cable	Y	-	-	B	B	B	B	B	B	V5R3	V5.2
#1470 - 6m Optical HSL Cable	Y	-		B	B	B	B	B		V5R3	V5.2
#1471 - 30m Optical HSL Cable	Y	-	-	S	S	B	B	B		V5R3	V5.2
#1472 - 100m Optical HSL Cable	Y	-	-	B	B	B	B	B		V5R3	V5.2
#1473 - 250m Optical HSL Cable	Y	-	-	B	B	B	B	B		V5R3	V5.2
#1474 - 6m HSL to HSL-2 Cable	Y	B	B	B	B	B	B	B	B	V5R3	V5.2
#1475 - 10m HSL to HSL-2 Cable	Y	B	B	B	B	B	B	B	B	V5R3	V5.2
#1476 - 4.3m 200V/12A Power Cord U.K.	Y	B	B	B	B	-	B	-		V5R3	V5.2
#1481 - 1.2m HSL-2/RIO-2 Cable	Y	B	B	B	B	-	-	-	B	V5R3	V5.2
#1482 - 3.5m HSL-2 Cable	Y	B	B	B	B	-	B	B	B	V5R3	V5.2
#1483 - 10m HSL-2 Cable	Y	B	B	B	B	-	B	B	B	V5R3	V5.2
#1485 - 15m HSL-2 Cable	Y	B	B	B	B	-	B	B	-	V5R3	V5.2
#1700 IPCS Keyboard/Mouse for NT	Y	B	B	B	B	B	B	B	B	V5R3	V5.2
#1800 HSL-2 Ports - 2 Copper	Y	-	-	B		-	-	-		V5R3	V5.2
#1801 Optical Bus Expansion Card - 2 port	Y	-	-	B		-	-	-		V5R3	V5.2

FC and description	CIF	520 (9405/9406)	550	570	595	#5095/#0595	#5074/#5094/#5294	#5088/#0588	#5790	Min. OS/400 or i5/OS	Min. AIX 5L
#1893 36.4 GB 10K RPM Disk Unit	Y	B	B	B	S	-	-	-		-	V5.2
#1894 73.4 GB 10K RPM Disk Unit	Y	B	B	B	S	-	-	-		-	V5.2
#1895 146.8 GB 10K RPM Disk Unit	Y	B	B	B	S	-	-	-		-	V5.2
#1896 36.4 GB 15K RPM Disk Unit	Y	B	B	B	B	-	-	-		-	V5.2
#1897 #1897 73.4 GB 15K RPM Disk Unit	Y	B	B	B	B	-	-	-		-	V5.2
#2591 External 1.44 GB Disk Drive	Y	B	B	B	B	-	-	-		-	V5.2
#2640 IDE DVD-ROM (slim-line)	Y	B	B	B		-	-	-		V5R3	V5.2
#2737 PCI HIPPI SW	Y	-		S	S	-	-	-		-	V5.2
#2739 Optical Bus Adapter	N	-	-	B	B	-	-	-		V5R3	-
#2742 Two-Line WAN IOA	Y	B	B	B	B	B	B	B	B	V5R3	-
#2743 1 Gbps PCI Ethernet IOA	Y	SC	SC	SC	SC	S	S	S	S	V5R3	-
#2744 PCI 100 Mbps Token Ring IOA	Y	B	B	B	B	B	B	B	B	V5R3	-
#2749 PCI Ultra Magnetic Media Controller	Y	S	S	S	B	B	B	B	B	V5R3	-
#2757 PCI-X Ultra RAID Disk Controller	Y	B	B	B	B	B	B	-	-	V5R3	-
#2760 PCI 1 Gbps Ethernet UTP Adapter	Y	SC	SC	SC	SC	S	S	S	S	V5R3	-
#2763 PCI RAID Disk Unit Controller	Y	S		S	S	SC	-	-	-	V5R3	-
#2765 PCI Fibre Channel Tape Controller	Y	S		S	S	S	S	S	S	V5R3	V5.2
#2766 PCI Fibre Channel Disk Controller	Y	SC		SC	SC	S	S	S	S	V5R3	-
#2768 PCI Magnetic Media Controller	Y	-	-	-		-	-	-	-	V5R2	-
#2772 PCI Dual WAN/Modem IOA	Y	B	B	B	B	B	B	B	B	V5R3	-
#2773 PCI Dual WAN/Modem IOA	Y	B	B	B	B	B	B	B	B	V5R3	-
#2780 PCI-X Ultra RAID Disk Controller	Y	B	B	B	B	B	B	-	-	V5R3	V5.2

| FC and description | CIF | Model or tower | | | | | | | | Min. OS/400 or i5/OS | Min. AIX 5L |
		520 (9405/9406)	550	570	595	#5095/#0595	#5074/#5094/#5294	#5088/#0588	#5790		
#2782 PCI-X RAID Disk Unit Controller	Y	S	S	S	S	B	B	-	-	V5R3	-
#2787 PCI-X Fibre Channel Disk Controller	Y	B	B	B	B	B	B	B	B	V5R3	-
#2793 Two-Line WAN IOA with Modem	Y	B	B	B	B	B	B	B	B	V5R3	-
#2794 Two-Line WAN IOA with Modem	Y	B	B	B	B	B	B	B	B	V5R3	-
#2805 PCI Quad Modem IOA	Y	B	B	B	B	B	B	B	B	V5R3	-
#2806 PCI Quad Modem (CIM)	Y	B	B	B	B	B	B	B	B	V5R3	-
#2843 PCI IOP	Y	SC	SC	SC	SC	S	S	S	S	V5R3	-
#2844 PCI IOP	Y	B	B	B	B	B	B	B	B	V5R3	-
#2849 10/100 Mbps Ethernet Adapter	Y	B	B	B	B	B	B	B	B	V5R3	-
#2886 Optical Bus Adapter	Y	-	M	M	M	M	M	M	-	V5R3	V5.2
#2887 HSL-2 Bus Adapter	Y	-	M	M	M	M	M	M	-	V5R3	-
#2890 PCI Integrated Netfinity Server	Y	-				S	S	S	-	V5R3	-
#2891 PCI Integrated xSeries Server	Y	-				S	S	S	-	V5R3	-
#2892 PCI Integrated xSeries Server	Y	-	-	-		S	S	S	-	V5R3	-
#2895 128 MB Server Memory	Y	SC	SC	SC	SC	S	S	S	-	V5R3	-
#2896 256 MB Server Memory	Y	M	M	M	M	M	M	M	-	V5R3	-
#2897 1 GB Server Memory	Y	M	M	M	M	M	M	M	-	V5R3	-
#2899 PCI Integrated xSeries Server	Y	-	-	-	-	S	S	S	-	V5R3	-
#2943 8-Port Async Adapter	Y	B	B	B	B	B	B	B	B	-	V5.2
#2947 PCI Multiprotocol Adapter	Y	B	B	B	B	B	B	-	-	-	V5.2
#3043 - 512 MB Main Storage	N	-	-	S		-	-	-		V5R3	V5.2
#3044 1024 MB Main Storage	Y	-	-	S		-	-	-		V5R3	V5.2
#3046 2048 MB Main Storage	Y	-	-	S		-	-	-		V5R3	V5.2

FC and description	CIF	520 (9405/9406)	550	570	595	#5095/#0595	#5074/#5094/#5294	#5088/#0588	#5790	Min. OS/400 or i5/OS	Min. AIX 5L
#3093 512 MB Main Storage	Y	S	S	-		-	-	-		V5R3	V5.2
#3094 1024 MB Main Storage	Y	S	S	-		-	-	-		V5R3	V5.2
#3095			S								
#3096 2048 MB Main Storage	Y	S	-	-		-	-	-		V5R3	V5.2
#3757 Service Shelf Toolkit					B					V5R3	
#4263 Direct Attach Tape Cable	Y	B	B	-		-	-	-		-	V5.2
#4317 8.58 GB 10k RPM Disk Unit	Y	SC	SC	SC	SC	S	S	-		V5R3	-
#4318 17.54 GB 10k RPM Disk Unit	Y	SC	SC	SC	SC	SC	SC	-		V5R3	-
#4319 35.16 GB 10k RPM Disk Unit	Y	B	B	B	B	B	B	-		V5R3	-
#4326 35.16 GB 15k RPM Disk Unit	Y	B	B	B	B	B	B	-		V5R3	-
#4327 70.56 GB 15k RPM Disk Unit	Y	B	B	B	B	B	B	-		V5R3	-
#4425 CD-ROM	Y	-	-	-		-	S	-		V5R3	-
#4430 DVD-RAM	Y	-	-	-		-	B	-		V5R3	V5.2
#4443 - 512 MB Main Storage	Y	B	B	-		-	-	-		V5R3	V5.2
#4444 - 1 GB Main Storage	Y	B	B	-		-	-	-		V5R3	V5.2
#4445 - 4 GB Main Storage	Y	B	B	-		-	-	-		V5R3	V5.2
#4447 - 2 GB Main Storage	Y	B	B	-		-	-	-		V5R3	V5.2
#4449 - 8 GB Main Storage	Y	B	B	-		-	-	-		V5R3	V5.2
#4450 - 16 GB Main Storage	Y	B	B	-		-	-	-		V5R3	V5.2
#4452 - 2 GB Main Storage	N	-	-	B		-	-	-		V5R3	V5.2
#4454 - 8 GB Main Storage	Y	-	-	B		-	-	-		V5R3	V5.2
#4482 4 GB ¼-inch Cartridge Tape Device	Y	SC	SC	SC		-	S	-		V5R3	-
#4483 16 GB ¼-inch Cartridge Tape Device	Y	SC	SC	SC		-	S	-		V5R3	-

FC and description	CIF	520 (9405/9406)	550	570	595	#5095/#0595	#5074/#5094/#5294	#5088/#0588	#5790	Min. OS/400 or i5/OS	Min. AIX 5L
#4486 25 GB ¼-inch Cartridge Tape Device	Y	SC	SC	SC		-	S	-		V5R3	-
#4487 50 GB ¼-inch Cartridge Tape Device	Y	SC	SC	SC		-	S	-		V5R3	-
#4490 - 4 GB Main Storage	Y	-	-	B		-	-	-		V5R3	V5.2
#4491 - 16 GB Main Storage	Y	-	-	B		-	-	-		V5R3	V5.2
#4625 CD-ROM	Y	-	-	-	M	-	SC	-		V5R3	-
#4630 DVD-RAM	Y	-	-	-	M	-	SC	-		V5R3	-
#4631 DVD-ROM	Y	-	-	-	B	-	B	-		V5R3	-
#4633 DVD-RAMB	Y	-	-	-	B	-	B	-		V5R3	-
#4643 - 7040-61D I/O Drawer attached	Y	-	-	-	S	-	-	-	-	-	V5.2
#4682 4 GB ¼-inch Cartridge Tape Device	Y	SC	SC	SC	SC	-	S	-		V5R3	-
#4683 - 16 GB QIC Cartridge Tape Device	Y	SC	SC	SC	SC		S			V5R3	-
#4684 30 GB ¼-inch Cartridge Tape Device	Y	-	-	-	B	-	B	-		V5R3	-
#4685 80 GB VXA-2 Tape Device	Y	-	-	-		-	B	-		V5R3	-
#4686 25 GB ¼-inch Cartridge Tape Device	Y	SC	SC	SC	SC	-	SC	-		V5R3	-
#4687 50 GB ¼-inch Cartridge Tape Device	Y	B	B	B	B	-	B	-		V5R3	-
#4690 Rack Status Beacon Assembly	Y	B	B	B	B	-	-	-		-	V5.2
#4710 PCI Integrated xSeries Server	Y	-	-	-		B	B	B	-	V5R3	-
#4723 PCI 10 Mbps Ethernet Adapter	Y	SC		SC	SC	S	S	S	S	V5R3	-
#4745 PCI 2-line WAN IOA	Y	S	S	S	S	S	S	S	S	V5R3	-
#4746 PCI Twinaxial IOA	Y	B	B	B	B	B	B	B	B	V5R3	-

FC and description	CIF	Model or tower								Min. OS/400 or i5/OS	Min. AIX 5L
		520 (9405/9406)	550	570	595	#5095/#0595	#5074/#5094/#5294	#5088/#0588	#5790		
#4748 PCI RAID Disk Unit Controller	Y	S	S	S	S	S	S	-		V5R3	-
#4778 PCI RAID Disk Unit Controller	Y	S	S	S	S	S	S	-		V5R3	-
#4801 PCI Cryptographic Coprocessor	Y	B	B	B	B	B	B	B	B	V5R3	-
#4805 PCI Cryptographic Accelerator	Y	B	B	B	B	B	B	B	B	V5R3	-
#4810 PCI Integrated xSeries Server	Y	-	-	-	B	B	B	B	-	V5R3	-
#4811 PCI-X Integrated xSeries Server	Y	B							-	V5R3	-
#4812 PCI-X Integrated xSeries Server	Y				B	B	B	B	-	V5R3	-
#4813 PCI-X Integrated xSeries Server	Y								B	V5R3	-
#4838 PCI 100/10 Mbps Ethernet IOA	Y	S	S	S	S	S	S	S	S	V5R3	-
#4959 PCI 16/4 Mbps Token Ring Adapter	Y	B	B	B	B	B	B	-	B	-	V5.2
#4962 PCI 100/10 Mbps Ethernet IOA	Y	B	B	B	B	B	B	-	B	-	V5.2
#5074 PCI Expansion Tower	Y	S	S	S	S	-	-	-		V5R3	-
#5079 1.8 M I/O Tower	Y	S	S	S	S	-	-	-		V5R3	-
#5088 PCI-X Expansion Unit	N	B	B	B	B	-	B	-		V5R3	-
#5094 PCI-X Expansion Tower	Y	B	B	B	B	-	-	-		V5R3	V5.2
#5095 PCI-X Expansion Tower	Y	B	B	B	B	-	-	-		V5R3	V5.2
#5108 30-Disk Expansion Feature	N	-	-	-		-	B	-		V5R3	V5.2
#5115 Dual Line Cords - Tower	Y	-	-	-		-	B	-		V5R3	V5.2
#5116 Dual Line Cords - 5294 Tower	Y	-	-	-		-	B	-		V5R3	V5.2
#5138 Redundant Power and Cooling	Y	-	B	-		B	-	-		V5R3	V5.2
#5158 AC Power Supply, 850W	Y	B	-			-	-	-		V5R3	V5.2
#5160 Power Dist Unit 1 Phase NEMA	N					-	-	-		V5R3	V5.2
#5161 Power Distribution Unit	N					-	-	-		V5R3	V5.2

FC and description	CIF	Model or tower								Min. OS/400 or i5/OS	Min. AIX 5L
		520 (9405/9406)	550	570	595	#5095/#0595	#5074/#5094/#5294	#5088/#0588	#5790		
#5162 Power Distribution Unit	N					-	-	-		V5R3	V5.2
#5163 Power Distribution Unit	Y					-	-	-		V5R3	V5.2
#5294 1.8m I/O Tower	Y	B	B	B	B	-	-	-		V5R3	V5.2
#5540 System Console on Twinaxial Workstation IOA	Y	B	B	B	B	-	-	-	-	V5R3	-
#5544 System Console on Operations Console	Y	B	B	B	B	-	-	-	-	V5R3	-
#5546 System Console on 100 Mbps Token Ring	Y	B	B	B	B	-	-	-	-	V5R3	-
#5548 System Console on 100 Mbps Ethernet	Y	B	B	B	B	-	-	-	-	V5R3	-
#5550 System Console on HMC	Y	B	B	B	B	-	-	-	-	V5R3	-
#5700 PCI 1 Gbps Ethernet IOA	Y	B	B	B	B	B	B	B	B	V5R3	V5.2
#5701 PCI 1 Gbps Ethernet UTP IOA	Y	B	B	B	B	B	B	B	B	V5R3	V5.2
#5702 PCI-X Ultra Tape Controller	Y	S	S	S	S	S	S	S	S	V5R3	-
#5703 PCI-X Tape/DASD Controller	Y	B	B	B	B	B	B			V5R3	V5.2
#5704 PCI-X Fibre Channel Tape Controller	Y	B	B	B	B	B	B	B	B	V5R3	V5.2
#5706 - 2 Port PCI-X 1000/100/10 Mbps Ethernet Adapter	Y	B	B	B	B	B	B	-	B	V5R3	V5.2
#5707 PCI-X 1 Gbps Ethernet-SX IOA	Y	B	B	B	B	B	B	-	B	V5R3	V5.2
#5709 RAID Enabler Card	Y	B	B	B		-	-	-	-	V5R3	V5.2
#5712 PCI-X Tape/DASD Controller	Y	B	B	B	B	B	B	B	B	V5R3	V5.2
#5715 PCI-X Tape/DASD Controller	Y	B	B	B	B	B	B			V5R3	-
#5718 10 Gbps Ethernet Adapter	Y	B	B	B	B	B	B	-	-	-	V5.2
#5751 IDE DVD-RAMBO (slim-line)	Y	B	B	B		-	-	-	-	V5R3	V5.2

FC and description	CIF	520 (9405/9406)	550	570	595	#5095/#0595	#5074/#5094/#5294	#5088/#0588	#5790	Min. OS/400 or i5/OS	Min. AIX 5L
#5753 30 GB ¼-inch Cartridge Tape Device	Y	B	B			-	-	-	-	V5R3	-
#5754 50 GB ¼-inch Cartridge Tape Device	Y	B	B	-		-	-	-	-	V5R3	-
#5790 PCI-X Expansion Drawer	Y	B	B	B	-					V5R3	-
#6068 Optional Front Door for 1.8m Rack	Y	B	B	B	B	-	-	-	-	V5R3	V5.2
#6134 60 GB 8mm Tape Device	Y	B	B	-		-	-	-	-	V5R3	V5.2
#6204 Differential SCSI Adapter	Y	B	B	B		-	-	-	-	-	V5.2
#6246 1.8m Rack Trim Kit	Y	B	B	B	B	-	-	-	-	V5R3	V5.2
#6258 36 GB 4mm Tape Unit	Y	B	B	-		-	B	-	-	-	V5.2
#6312 Quad Digital Trunk Adapter	Y	B	B	-		B	B	-	-	-	V5.2
#6417 HSL-2/RIO-2 Bus Adapter	Y	-	-	-	-	M	M		-	V5R3	V5.2
#6574 - 520 Ultra320 SCSI 4-pack	N	B	-	-		-	-	-	-	V5R3	V5.2
#6580 Optional Rack Security Kit	Y	B	B	B	B	-	-	-	-	V5R3	V5.2
#6587 Model 520 Rear Cover	Y	B	-	-		-	-	-	-	V5R3	V5.2
#6592 550 4-Disk Slot Expansion - Base Ctrl	Y	-	B	-		-	-	-	-	V5R3	V5.2
#6593 550 4-Disk Slot Expansion - PCI-X Ctrl	Y	-	B	-		-	-	-	-	V5R3	V5.2
#6594 - 520 4-Disk Slot Expansion - Base Ctrl	Y	B	-	-		-	-	-	-	V5R3	V5.2
#7188 Power Distribution Unit - Side Mount	Y	B	B	B	B	-	-	-	-	V5R3	V5.2
#7798 550 non-IBM Rack Mount	Y	-	PU	-		-	-	-	-	V5R3	V5.2
#7801 - 6m HMC Attachment Cable	Y	B	B	B	B	-	-	-	-	V5R3	V5.2
#7802 - 15m HMC Attachment Cable	Y	B	B	B	B	-	-	-	-	V5R3	V5.2
#7840 Side-by-side Attach Kit 1.8m Rack	Y	B	B	B	B	-	-	-	-	V5R3	V5.2

FC and description	CIF	Model or tower								Min. OS/400 or i5/OS	Min. AIX 5L
		520 (9405/9406)	550	570	595	#5095/#0595	#5074/#5094/#5294	#5088/#0588	#5790		
#7841 Ruggedize Rack Kit	Y	B	B	B	B	-	-	-	-	V5R3	V5.2
#7861 Single Wide Short Blindswap Cassette	Y	N	N	Y	N	N	N	N	N	V5R3	V5R3
#7862 Single Wide Long Blindswap Cassette	Y	Y	Y	Y	N	N	N	N	Y	V5R3	V5R3
#7863 Double Wide Long Blindswap Cassette	Y	Y	Y	Y	N	N	N	N	Y		
#7875 CPU Power Regulator	Y	-	-	B		-	-	-	-	V5R3	V5.2
#7884 520 Rack Mount	Y	PU	-	-		-	-	-	-	V5R3	V5.2
#7885 520 Deskside	Y	PU	-	-		-	-	-	-	V5R3	V5.2
#7886 550 IBM Rack Mount	Y	-	PU	-		-	-	-	-	V5R3	V5.2
#7887 550 Deskside	N	-	PU	-		-	-	-	-	V5R3	V5.2
#7889 550 Redundant Power Supply	Y	-	B	-		-	-	-	-	V5R3	V5.2
#8754 Optional Base 50 GB ¼-inch Cartridge Tape Device	Y	B	-			-	-	-	-	V5R3	
#8950 Model 520 Processor	N	P	-	-		-	-	-	-	V5R3	V5.2
#8951 Model 520 Processor	N	B	-	-		-	-	-	-	V5R3	V5.2
#8952 Model 520 Processor	N	B	-	-		-	-	-	-	V5R3	V5.2
#8953 Model 520 Processor	N	B	-	-		-	-	-	-	V5R3	V5.2
#8954 Model 520 Processor	N	B	-	-		-	-	-	-	V5R3	V5.2
#8955 Model 520 2-way Processor	N	P	-	-		-	-	-	-	V5R3	V5.2
#8961 Model 570 CoD 0/2-way Processor	Y	-	-	B		-	-	-	-	V5R3	V5.2
#9517 Base HSL-2/RIO-2 Bus Adapter	Y	-	-	-		B	B	-	-	V5R3	V5.2
#9531 Base HSL-2/RIO-2 Bus Adapter	Y	-	-	-	-	-	-	-	Y	V5R3	V5.2
#9570 Reserved Rack Space	Y	-	-	P		-	-	-	-	V5R3	V5.2

FC and description	CIF	Model or tower								Min. OS/400 or i5/OS	Min. AIX 5L
		520 (9405/9406)	550	570	595	#5095/#0595	#5074/#5094/#5294	#5088/#0588	#5790		
#9691 Base Bus Adapter		M	M	M	M		Y			V4R5	
#9710 Base PCI Integrated xSeries Server	Y	-	B	B		B	B	B	-	V5R3	-
#9726 Base 512 MB Server Memory	Y	-	-	-	B	B	B	B	-	V5R3	-
#9771 Base PCI Two-Line WAN with integrated modem	Y	S	S	S	S	-	-	-	-	V5R3	-
#9793 Two-Line WAN IOA with Modem	Y	B	B	B	B	-	-	-	-	V5R3	-
#9794 Two-Line IOA with Modem	Y	B	B	B	B	-	-	-	-	V5R3	-
#9844 Base PCI IOP	Y	B	B	B	B	B	B	-	-	V5R3	-
#9876 Base Optical Bus Adapter	N	-	B	B	B	-	P	P	-	V5R3	V5.2
#9877 Base HSL-2 Bus Adapter	N	B	B	B	B	B	B	B	-	V5R3	V5.2

Model 800, 810, 825, 870, #2497/#2498 890 system unit, tower features

The following table shows the features supported in Models 800, 810, 825, 870, and 890 (#2497 and #2498 processors), associated expansion units, the CIF designation, and minimum operating system level of each feature.

Feature code and description	CIF	Model or tower								Min. OS/400
		800	810	825	870	890	#5095/#0595	#5094/#5294	#5088 #0588	
#0041 Device Parity Protection-All	Y		B	B	B	B				V5R2
#0092 External xSeries Attach	Y	B	B	B	B	B				V5R2
#0123 #5074 Lower Unit in Rack	Y		S	S	S	S				V5R2
#0126 CEC EIA Reduction Option	N				B	B				V5R2
#0133 Plant Install in Rack	Y	B	B	-	-	-	-	-	-	V5R2
#0134 Field Install in Rack (HD)	Y	-	-	B	-	-	-	-	-	V5R2
#0197 Model 890 24-way Processor	N	-	-	-	-	B	-	-	-	V5R2
#0198 Model 890 32-way Processor	N	-	-	-	-	B	-	-	-	V5R2
#0325 IPCS Extension Cables for NT	Y	B	B	B	B	B	B	B	B	V5R2
#0367 Operations Console PCI Cable	Y	B	B	B	B	B	B	B	B	V5R2
#0369 100m Optical SPCN Cable	Y	-	-	B	B	B	B	B	B	V5R2
#0371 LC-SC Adapter Kit (50 um)	Y	B	B	B	B	B	B	B	B	V5R2
#0372 LC-SC Adapter Kit (62.5 um)	Y	B	B	B	B	B	B	B	B	V5R2
#0381 Remote Control Panel Cable										
#0383 Remote Control Panel Cable	Y	B	B	B	B	B				V5R2
#0426 512 MB Server Memory	N	-	-	B	B	B	B	B	B	V5R2
#0427 1 GB Server Memory	N	-	-	B	B	B	B	B	B	V5R2
#0446 512 MB DDR Server Memory	Y	B	B	-	-	-	B	B	B	V5R2
#0447 1 GB DDR Server Memory	Y	B	B	-	-	-	B	B	B	V5R2
#0551 iSeries Rack	Y	B	B	B	B	B	-	-	-	V5R2

Feature code and description	CIF	\multicolumn{8}{c}{Model or tower}	Min. OS/400
		800	810	825	870	890	#5095/#0595	#5094/#5294	#5088 #0588	
#0578 PCI Expansion Unit in Rack	N	-	S	S	S	B	-	-	-	V5R2
#0588 PCI-X Expansion Unit in Rack	N	B	B	B	B	B	-	-	-	V5R2
#0595 PCI-X Expansion Unit in Rack	Y	B	B	B	B	B	-	-	-	V5R2
#0601 - Direct Attach - #2743 PCI 1 Gbps Ethernet IOA	Y	-	SC	SC	SC	B	S	S	S	V5R2
#0602 - Direct Attach - #2760 PCI 1 Gbps Ethernet UTP IOA	Y	-	SC	SC	SC	B	S	S	S	V5R2
#0603 - Direct Attach - #2744 PCI 100 Mbps Token-Ring IOA	Y	B	B	B	B	B	B	B	B	V5R2
#0604 - Direct Attach - #2763 PCI RAID Disk Unit Controller	Y	SC	SC	SC	SC	SC	SC	-	-	V5R2
#0605 - Direct Attach - #4748 PCI RAID Disk Unit Controller	Y	-	-	SC	SC	SC	S	S	-	V5R2
#0606 - Direct Attach - #4778 PCI RAID Disk Unit Controller	Y	-	-	B	B	B	B	B	-	V5R2
#0607 - Direct Attach - #4838 PCI 100/10 Mbps Ethernet IOA	Y	-	SC	SC	SC	B	S	S	S	V5R2
#0608 - Direct Attach - #4745 PCI WAN IOA	Y	-	SC	SC	SC	SC	S	S	S	V5R2
#0609 - Direct Attach - #2772 PCI Dual WAN/Modem IOA	Y	B	B	B	B	B	B	B	B	V5R2
#0610 - Direct Attach - #2773 PCI Dual WAN/ModemIOA	Y	B	B	B	B	B	B	B	B	V5R2
#0612 - Direct Attach - #2766 PCI Fibre Channel Disk Controller	Y	B	B	B	B	B	B	B	B	V5R2
#0613 - Direct Attach - #2742 PCI 2-Line WAN IOA	Y	B	B	B	B	B	B	B	B	V5R2
#0614 - Direct Attach - #2793 PCI 2-Line WAN w/Modem	Y	B	B	B	B	B	B	B	B	V5R2
#0615 - Direct Attach - #2794 PCI 2-Line WAN w/Modem	Y	B	B	B	B	B	B	B	B	V5R2

Feature code and description	CIF	Model or tower								Min. OS/400
		800	810	825	870	890	#5095/#0595	#5094/#5294	#5088 #0588	
#0616 - Direct Attach - #2805 PCI Quad Modem IOA	Y	B	B	B	B	B	B	B	B	V5R2
#0617 - Direct Attach - #2806 PCI Quad Modem (CIM)	Y	B	B	B	B	B	B	B	B	V5R2
#0618 - Direct Attach - #2757 PCI-X Ultra RAID Disk Controller	Y	B	B	B	B	B	B	B	-	V5R2
#0619 - Direct Attach - #2782 PCI-X RAID Disk Unit Controller	Y	B	B	B	-	-	B	-	-	V5R2
#0620 - Direct Attach - #5700 PCI 1 Gbps Ethernet IOA	Y	B	B	B	B	B	B	B	B	V5R2
#0621 - Direct Attach - #5701 PCI 1 Gbps Ethernet UTP IOA	Y	B	B	B	B	B	B	B	B	V5R2
#0623 - Direct Attach - #2849 PCI 100/10 Mbps Ethernet IOA	Y	B	B	B	B	B	B	B	B	V5R2
#0624 Linux Direct Attach-5702	Y	B	B	B	B	B	B	B	B	V5R2
#0626 Linux Direct Attach-2787	Y	B	B	B	B	B	B	B	B	V5R2
#0628 Linux Direct Attach-5703	Y	B	B	B	B	B	B	B	B	V5R2
#0694 #5094 Equivalent	Y	-	-	-	-	-	-	B	-	V5R2
#1460 - 3m Copper HSL Cable	Y	B	B	B	-	-	-	-	-	V5R2
#1461 - 6m Copper HSL Cable	Y	B	B	B	-	-	-	-	-	V5R2
#1462 - 15m Copper HSL Cable	Y	B	B	B	-	-	-	-	-	V5R2
#1463 - 2m SPCN Cable	Y	B	B	B	B	B	B	B	B	V5R2
#1464 - 6m SPCN Cable	Y	B	B	B	B	B	B	B	B	V5R2
#1465 - 15m SPCN Cable	Y	B	B	B	B	B	B	B	B	V5R2
#1466 - 30m SPCN Cable	Y	B	B	B	B	B	B	B	B	V5R2
#1468 - 250m Optical SPCN Cable	Y	-	-	B	B	B	B	B	B	V5R2
#1470 - 6m Optical HSL Cable	Y	-	-	B	B	B	B	B	B	V5R2
#1471 - 30m Optical HSL Cable	Y	-	-	B	B	B	B	B	B	V5R2

Feature code and description	CIF	Model or tower								Min. OS/400
		800	810	825	870	890	#5095/#0595	#5094/#5294	#5088 #0588	
#1472 - 100m Optical HSL Cable	Y	-	-	B	B	B	B	B	B	V5R2
#1473 - 250m Optical HSL Cable	Y	-	-	B	B	B	B	B	B	V5R2
#1474 - 6m HSL to HSL-2 Cable	Y	B	B	B	B	B	B	B	B	V5R2
#1475 - 10m HSL to HSL-2 Cable	Y	B	B	B	B	B	B	B	B	V5R2
#1476 4.3m 200V/12A Power Cd U.K.	Y	-	-	-	-	-	-	B	-	V5R2
#1482 - 3.5m HSL-2 Cable	Y	-	-	B	B	B	-	B	B	V5R2
#1483 - 10m HSL-2 Cable	Y	-	-	B	B	B	-	B	B	V5R2
#1485 - 15m HSL-2 Cable	Y	-	-	B	B	B	-	B	B	V5R2
#1576 5250 CPW Capacity Card	N	-	-	-	-	PU	-	-	-	V5R2
#1577 5250 CPW Capacity Card	N	-	-	-	-	B	-	-	-	V5R2
#1578 5250 CPW Capacity Card	N	-	-	-	-	B	-	-	-	V5R2
#1579 5250 CPW Capacity Card	N	-	-	-	-	B	-	-	-	V5R2
#1581 5250 CPW Capacity Card	N	-	-	-	-	B	-	-	-	V5R2
#1583 5250 CPW Capacity Card	N	-	-	-	-	B	-	-	-	V5R2
#1585 5250 CPW Capacity Card	N	-	-	-	-	B	-	-	-	V5R2
#1587 5250 CPW Capacity Card	N	-	-	-	-	B	-	-	-	V5R2
#1588 5250 CPW Capacity Card	N	-	-	-	-	B	-	-	-	V5R2
#1591 5250 CPW Capacity Card	N	-	-	-	-	B	-	-	-	V5R2
#1609 825 CUoD Activation	Y	-	-	B	-	-	-	-	-	V5R2
#1610 890 CUoD Activation	Y	-	-	-	-	B	-	-	-	V5R2
#1611 870 CUoD Activation	Y	-	-	-	B	-	-	-	-	V5R2
#1612 890 CUoD Activation	Y	-	-	-	-	B	-	-	-	V5R2
#1613 890 CUoD Activation	Y	-	-	-	-	B	-	-	-	V5R2
#1700 IPCS Keyboard or Mouse for NT	Y	B	B	B	B	B	B	B	B	V5R2
#1773 TCoD Enablement for Mod 825	Y	-	-	M	-	-	-	-	-	V5R2

Feature code and description	CIF	800	810	825	870	890	#5095/#0595	#5094/#5294	#5088 #0588	Min. OS/400
#1776 TCoD Enablement for Mod 870	Y	-	-	-	M	-				V5R2
#1777 TCoD Enablement for Mod 890	Y	-	-	-	-	M	-	-	-	V5R2
#1778 TCoD Enablement for Mod 890	Y	-	-	-	-	M	-	-	-	V5R2
#2463 Model 800 Processor	N	P	-	-	-	-	-	-	-	V5R2
#2464 Model 800 Processor	N	B	-	-	-	-	-	-	-	V5R2
#2465 Model 810 Processor	N	-	B	-	-	-	-	-	-	V5R2
#2466 Model 810 Processor	N	-	B	-	-	-	-	-	-	V5R2
#2467 Model 810 Processor	N	-	B	-	-	-	-	-	-	V5R2
#2469 Model 810 2-way Processor	N	-	B	-	-	-	-	-	-	V5R2
#2473 Model 825 3/6-Way POD Processor	N	-	-	B	-	-	-	-	-	V5R2
#2486 Model 870 8/16-way Processor	N	-	-	-	B	-	-	-	-	V5R2
#2487 Model 890 16/24-way Processor	N	-	-	-	-	B	-	-	-	V5R2
#2488 Model 890 24/32-way Processor	N	-	-	-	-	B	-	-	-	V5R2
#2497 Model 890 16/24-way Processor	N	-	-	-	-	B	-	-	-	V5R2
#2498 Model 890 24/32-way Processor	N	-	-	-	-	B	-	-	-	V5R2
#2738 HSL Ports - 8 Copper	N	-	-	M	M	M	-	-	-	V5R2
#2739 Optical Bus Adapter	N	-	-	-	-	-	-	-	-	V5R2
#2742 Two-Line WAN IOA	Y	B	B	B	B	B	B	B	B	V5R2
#2743 1 Gbps PCI Ethernet IOA	Y	-	S	S	S	B	S	S	S	V5R2
#2744 PCI 100 Mbps Token Ring IOA	Y	B	B	B	B	B	B	B	B	V5R2
#2749 PCI Ultra Magnetic Media Controller	Y	B	B	B	B	B	B	B	B	V5R2
#2757 PCI-X Ultra RAID Disk Controller	Y	B	B	B	B	B	B	B	-	V5R2
#2760 PCI 1 Gbps Ethernet UTP Adapter	Y	-	S	S	S	S	S	S	S	V5R2
#2763 PCI RAID Disk Unit Controller	Y	-	SC	SC	SC	SC	SC	-	-	V5R2
#2765 PCI Fibre Channel Tape Controller	Y	B	B	B	B	B	B	B	B	V5R2

Feature code and description	CIF	800	810	825	870	890	#5095/#0595	#5094/#5294	#5088 #0588	Min. OS/400
#2766 PCI Fibre Channel Disk Controller	Y	B	B	B	B	B	B	B	B	V5R2
#2768 PCI Magnetic Media Controller	Y	-	S	S	S	B	S	S	S	V5R2
#2772 PCI Dual WAN/Modem IOA	Y	B	B	B	B	B	B	B	B	V5R2
#2773 PCI Dual WAN/Modem IOA	Y	B	B	B	B	B	B	B	B	V5R2
#2776 HSL-2 Ports - 8 Copper	N	-	-	-	B	B	-	-	-	V5R2
#2780 PCI-X Ultra4 RAID Disk Ctrl		B	B	B	B	B	B	B		V5R2
#2782 PCI-X RAID Disk Unit Controller	Y	B	B	B	-	-	B	-	-	V5R2
#2785 HSL-2 Ports - 2 Copper	Y	-	-	B	-	-	-	-	-	V5R2
#2786 HSL Ports - 2 Optical	Y	-	-	B	-	-	-	-	-	V5R2
#2787 PCI-X Fibre Channel Disk Controller	Y	B	B	B	B	B	B	B	B	V5R2
#2788 HSL Ports - 8 Optical	N	-	-	-	B	B	-	-	-	V5R2
#2790 PCI Integrated Netfinity Server	N	-	-	S	S	S	S	S	S	V5R2
#2791 PCI Integrated xSeries Server	N	-	-	S	S	S	S	S	S	V5R2
#2792 PCI Integrated xSeries Server	N	-	-	B	B	B	B	B	B	V5R2
#2793 Two-Line WAN IOA with Modem	Y	B	B	B	B	B	B	B	B	V5R2
#2794 Two-Line WAN IOA with Modem	Y	B	B	B	B	B	B	B	B	V5R2
#2795 128 MB Server Memory	N	-	-	M	M	B	M	M	M	V5R2
#2796 256 MB Server Memory	N	-	-	M	M	B	M	M	M	V5R2
#2797 1 GB Server Memory	N	-	-	M	M	B	M	M	M	V5R2
#2799 PCI Integrated xSeries Server	N	-	-	S	S	B	S	S	S	V5R2
#2805 PCI Quad Modem IOA	Y	B	B	B	B	B	B	B	B	V5R2
#2806 PCI Quad Modem (CIM)	Y	B	B	B	B	B	B	B	B	V5R2
#2817 PCI 155 Mbps MMF ATM IOA	Y	-	S	S	S	S	S	S	S	V5R2
#2842 PCI IOP	Y	-	S	-	-	-	S	-	-	V5R2
#2843 PCI IOP	Y	-	S	S	S	B	S	S	S	V5R2

Feature code and description	CIF	Model or tower								Min. OS/400
		800	810	825	870	890	#5095/#0595	#5094/#5294	#5088 #0588	
#2844 PCI IOP	Y	B	B	B	B	B	B	B	B	V5R2
#2849 10/100 Mbps Ethernet Adapter	Y	B	B	B	B	B	B	B	B	V5R2
#2886 Optical Bus Adapter	Y	-	-	-	-	-	M	M	M	V5R2
#2887 HSL-2 Bus Adapter	Y	-	-	-	-	-	M	M	M	V5R2
#2890 PCI Integrated Netfinity Server	Y	-	SC	-	-	-	S	S	S	V5R2
#2891 PCI Integrated xSeries Server	Y	-	SC	-	-	-	S	S	S	V5R2
#2892 PCI Integrated xSeries Server	Y	B	B	-	-	-	B	B	B	V5R2
#2895 128 MB Server Memory	Y	-	M	-	-	-	M	M	M	V5R2
#2896 256 MB Server Memory	Y	-	M	-	-	-	M	M	M	V5R2
#2897 1 GB Server Memory	Y	-	M	-	-	-	M	M	M	V5R2
#2899 PCI Integrated xSeries Server	Y	-	SC	-	-	-	S	S	S	V5R2
#3015 8 GB Main Storage	N	-	-	-	B	B	-	-	-	V5R2
#3016 8 GB Main Storage	N	-	-	-	-	B	-	-	-	V5R2
#3017 32 GB Main Storage	N	-	-	-	B	B	-	-	-	V5R2
#3018 32 GB Main Storage	N	-	-	-	-	B	-	-	-	V5R2
#3020 4 GB Main Storage	N	-	-	-	B	B	-	-	-	V5R2
#3021 4 GB Main Storage	N	-	-	-	-	B	-	-	-	V5R2
#3022 128 MB Main Storage	Y	-	M	-	-	-	-	-	-	V5R2
#3024 256 MB Main Storage	Y	-	B	-	-	-	-	-	-	V5R2
#3025 512 MB Main Storage	Y	-	S	-	-	-	-	-	-	V5R2
#3026 512 MB Main Storage	Y	-	B	-	-	-	-	-	-	V5R2
#3027 1 GB Main Storage	Y	-	B	-	-	-	-	-	-	V5R2
#3029 128 MB Main Storage	Y	-	B	-	-	-	-	-	-	V5R2
#3035 16 GB Main Storage	N	-	-	-	B	B	-	-	-	V5R2
#3036 16 GB Main Storage	N	-	-	-	-	B	-	-	-	V5R2

Feature code and description	CIF	800	810	825	870	890	#5095/#0595	#5094/#5294	#5088 #0588	Min. OS/400
#3042 256 MB Main Storage	Y	-	-	B	-	-	-	-	-	V5R2
#3043 512 MB Main Storage	Y	-	-	B	-	-	-	-	-	V5R2
#3044 1024 MB Main Storage	Y	-	-	B	-	-	-	-	-	V5R2
#3045 1024 MB Main Storage	Y	-	-	B	-	-	-	-	-	V5R2
#3046 2048 MB Main Storage	Y	-	-	B	-	-	-	-	-	V5R2
#3092 256 MB Main Storage	Y	B	B	-	-	-	-	-	-	V5R2
#3093 512 MB Main Storage	Y	B	B	-	-	-	-	-	-	V5R2
#3094 1024 MB Main Storage	Y	B	B	-	-	-	-	-	-	V5R2
#3095 1024 MB Main Storage	Y	B	B	-	-	-	-	-	-	V5R2
#3096 2048 MB Main Storage	Y	B	B	-	-	-	-	-	-	V5R2
#4308 4.19 GB Disk Unit	Y	-	-	-	-	-	-	S	-	V5R2
#4314 8.58 GB Disk Unit	Y	-	S	S	S	S	S	S	-	V5R2
#4317 8.58 GB 10k RPM Disk Unit	Y	-	SC	SC	SC	SC	S	S	-	V5R2
#4318 17.54 GB 10k RPM Disk Unit	Y	B	B	B	B	B	B	B	-	V5R2
#4319 35.16 GB 10k RPM Disk Unit	Y	B	B	B	B	B	B	B	-	V5R2
#4324 17.54 GB Disk Unit	Y	-	S	S	S	S	S	S	-	V5R2
#4326 35.16 GB 15k RPM Disk Unit	Y	B	B	B	B	B	B	B	-	V5R2
#4327 70.56 GB 15k RPM Disk Unit	Y	B	B	B	B	B	B	B	-	V5R2
#4425 CD-ROM	Y	-	-	-	S	S	-	S	-	V5R2
#4430 DVD-RAM	Y	-	-	-	S	B	-	S	-	V5R2
#4482 4 GB ¼-inch Cartridge Tape Device	Y	-	-	-	S	B	-	S	-	V5R2
#4483 16 GB ¼-inch Cartridge Tape Device	Y	-	-	-	S	S	-	S	-	V5R2
#4486 25 GB ¼-inch Cartridge Tape Device	Y	-	-	-	S	S	-	S	-	V5R2
#4487 50 GB ¼-inch Cartridge Tape Device	Y	-	-	-	S	B	-	S	-	V5R2
#4525 CD-ROM	Y	-	SC	-	-	-	-	-	-	V5R2

Feature code and description	CIF	800	810	825	870	890	#5095/#0595	#5094/#5294	#5088 #0588	Min. OS/400
#4530 DVD-RAM	Y	B	B	-	-	-	-	-	-	V5R2
#4531 DVD-ROM	Y	B	B	-	-	-	-	-	-	V5R2
#4533 DVD-RAM	Y	B	B	-	-	-	-	-	-	V5R2
#4582 4 GB ¼-inch Cartridge Tape Device	Y	B	B	-	-	-	-	-	-	V5R2
#4583 16 GB ¼-inch Cartridge Tape Device	Y	-	SC	-	-	-	-	-	-	V5R2
#4584 30 GB ¼-inch Cartridge Tape Device	Y	B	B	-	-	-	-	-	-	V5R2
#4585 80 GB VXA-2 Tape Device	Y	B	B	-	-	-	-	-	-	V5R2
#4586 25 GB ¼-inch Cartridge Tape Device	Y	-	SC	-	-	-	-	-	-	V5R2
#4587 50 GB ¼-inch Cartridge Tape Device	Y	B	B	-	-	-	-	-	-	V5R2
#4625 CD-ROM	Y	-	-	SC	SC	SC	-	SC	-	V5R2
#4630 DVD-RAM	Y	-	-	B	B	B	-	B	-	V5R2
#4631 DVD-ROM	Y	-	-	B	B	B	-	B	-	V5R2
#4633 DVD-RAM	Y	-	-	B	B	B	-	B	-	V5R2
#4682 4 GB ¼-inch Cartridge Tape Device	Y	-	-	B	B	B	-	B	-	V5R2
#4684 30 GB ¼-inch Cartridge Tape Device	Y	-	-	B	B	B	-	B	-	V5R2
#4685 80 GB VXA-2 Tape Device	Y	-	-	B	B	B	-	B	-	V5R2
#4686 25 GB ¼-inch Cartridge Tape Device	Y	-	-	SC	SC	SC	-	SC	-	V5R2
#4687 50 GB ¼-inch Cartridge Tape Device	Y	-	-	B	B	B	-	B	-	V5R2
#4723 PCI 10 Mbps Ethernet Adapter	Y	-	SC	SC	SC	SC	S	S	S	V5R2
#4745 PCI 2-line WAN IOA	Y	-	S	S	S	B	S	S	S	V5R2
#4746 PCI Twinaxial IOA	Y	B	B	B	B	B	B	B	B	V5R2
#4748 PCI RAID Disk Unit Controller	Y	-	SC	SC	SC	SC	SC	SC	-	V5R2
#4778 PCI RAID Disk Unit Controller	Y	B	B	B	B	B	B	B	-	V5R2
#4801 PCI Cryptographic Coprocessor	Y	B	B	B	B	B	B	B	B	V5R2
#4810 PCI Integrated xSeries Server	Y	B	B							V5R2

| Feature code and description | CIF | Model or tower | | | | | | | | Min. OS/400 |
		800	810	825	870	890	#5095/#0595	#5094/#5294	#5088 #0588	
#4805 PCI Cryptographic Accelerator	Y	B	B	B	B	B	B	B	B	V5R2
#4815 PCI ATM 155 Mbps UTP OC3	Y	-	SC	SC	SC	SC	S	S	S	V5R2
#4816 PCI ATM 155 Mbps MMF	Y	-	SC	SC	SC	SC	S	S	S	V5R2
#4818 PCI ATM 155 Mbps SMF OC3	Y	-	SC	SC	SC	SC	S	S	S	V5R2
#4838 PCI 100/10 Mbps Ethernet IOA	Y	-	SC	SC	SC	B	SC	SC	SC	V5R2
#5074 PCI Expansion Tower	Y	-	SC	SC	SC	B	-	-	-	V5R2
#5075 PCI Expansion Tower	Y	-	S	S	-	-	-	-	-	V5R2
#5078 PCI Expansion Unit	N	-	-	-	-	-	-	S	-	V5R2
#5079 1.8 M I/O Tower	Y	-	SC	SC	SC	B	-	-	-	V5R2
#5088 PCI-X Expansion Unit	N	-	-	-	B	B	-	B	-	V5R2
#5094 PCI-X Expansion Tower	Y	B	B	B	B	B	-	-	-	V5R2
#5095 PCI-X Expansion Tower	Y	B	B	B	B	B	-	-	-	V5R2
#5107 30 Disk Expansion	N	-	-	-	B	B	-	-	-	V5R2
#5108 30-Disk Expansion Feature	N	-	-	-	-	-	-	B	-	V5R2
#5111 30 Disk Expansion with Dual Line Cord	N	-	-	-	-	-	-	-	-	V5R2
#5114 Dual Line Cords - Tower	N	-	-	-	B	B	-	-	-	V5R2
#5115 Dual Line Cords - Tower	Y	-	-	-	B	B	-	B	-	V5R2
#5116 Dual Line Cords - 5294 Tower	Y	-	-	-	-	-	-	B	-	V5R2
#5138 Redundant Power and Cooling	Y	-	-	-	-	-	B	-	-	V5R2
#5160 Power Dist Unit 1 Phase NEMA	N	B	B	B	B	B	-	-	-	V5R2
#5161 Power Distribution Unit	N	B	B	B	B	B	-	-	-	V5R2
#5162 Power Distribution Unit	N	B	B	B	B	B	-	-	-	V5R2
#5294 1.8m I/O Tower	Y	-	B	B	B	B	-	-	-	V5R2
#5540 System Console on Twinaxial Workstation IOA	Y	B	B	B	B	B	-	-	-	V5R2
#5544 System Console on Operations Console	Y	B	B	B	B	B	-	-	-	V5R2

Feature code and description	CIF	800	810	825	870	890	#5095/#0595	#5094/#5294	#5088 #0588	Min. OS/400
#5546 System Console on 100 Mbps Token Ring	Y	B	B	-	B	B	-	-	-	V5R2
#5548 System Console on 100 Mbps Ethernet	Y	B	B	B	B	B	-	-	-	V5R2
#5700 PCI 1 Gbps Ethernet IOA	Y	B	B	B	B	B	B	B	B	V5R2
#5701 PCI 1 Gbps Ethernet UTP IOA	Y	B	B	B	B	B	B	B	B	V5R2
#5702 PCI-X Ultra Tape Controller	Y	B	B	B	B	B	B	B	B	V5R2
#5703 PCI-X Tape/DASD Controller	Y	B	B	B	B	B	B	B		V5R2
#5705 PCI-X Tape/DASD Controller	Y	P	B	-	-	-	-	-	-	V5R2
#7002 HSL Enabler	Y	B	-	-	-	-	-	-	-	V5R2
#7116 System Unit Expansion	Y	B	B	-	-	-	-	-	-	V5R2
#7124 DASD Expansion Unit - 5 slot	Y	-	-	B	-	-	-	-	-	V5R2
#7136 DASD Expansion Unit - 6 slot	Y	B	B	-	-	-	-	-	-	V5R2
#7137 DASD Concurrent Maintenance Cage	Y	B	-	-	-	-	-	-	-	V5R2
#7188 Power Dist Unit - Side Mount	Y	B	B	B	B	B	-	-	-	V5R2
#8093 Optional 1.8 M I/O Rack	N	-	-	-	-	PU	-	-	-	V5R2
#8094 Optional 1.8 M I/O Rack	N	-	-	-	PU	PU	-	-	-	V5R2
#9079 Base I/O Tower	N	-	-	-	SC	SC	-	-	-	V5R2
#9094 Base PCI I/O Enclosure	N	-	-	-	PU	PU	-	-	-	V5R2
#9603 POD Activation	N	-	-	-	P	P	-	-	-	V5R2
#9691 Base Bus Adapter										V4R5
#9726 Base 512 MB Server Memory	Y	-	-	PU	PU	PU	PU	PU	PU	V5R2
#9730 Base HSL-2 Ports - 4 Copper	Y				PU	PU				V5R2
#9746 Base PCI Twinax Wrkstn IOA	Y	P	-	-	-	-	P	P	P	V5R2
#9749 Base PCI 100/10 Ethernet IOA	Y	P	-	-	-	-	P	P	P	V5R2
#9771 Base PCI Two-Line WAN with integrated modem	Y	P	PU	PU	PU	PU	-	-	-	V5R2
#9785 Base HSL-2 Ports - 2 Copper	Y	-	-	PU	-	-	-	-	-	V5R2

Feature code and description	CIF	800	810	825	870	890	#5095/#0595	#5094/#5294	#5088 #0588	Min. OS/400
#9786 Base HSL Ports - 2 Optical	Y	-	-	PU	-	-	-	-	-	V5R2
#9787 Base HSL-2 Ports - 2 Copper	N	-	-	B	-	-	-	-	-	V5R2
#9789 Base HSL Ports - 4 Optical	Y				-	PU				V5R2
#9792 Base PCI Integrated xSeries Server	Y	-	-	PU	PU	PU	PU	PU	PU	V5R2
#9793 Two-Line WAN IOA with Modem	Y	P	PU	PU	PU	PU	-	-	-	V5R2
#9794 Two-Line IOA with Modem	Y	P	PU	PU	PU	PU	-	-	-	V5R2
#9844 Base PCI IOP	Y	-	-	PU	PU	PU	B	B	-	V5R2
#9886 Base Optical Bus Adapter	Y	-	-	-	-	-	B	B	B	V5R2
#9887 Base HSL-2 Bus Adapter	Y	-	-	-	B	B	B	B	B	V5R2
#9943 Base PCI IOP	Y	-	-	-	-	B	-	-	-	V5R2

Model 250, 270, 820, 830, 840, #2487/#2488 890 system unit and tower

The following table shows the features supported in the Model 250, 270, 820, 830, 840, and 890 (#2487, #2488, #0197, and #0198 processors), associated expansion units, the CIF designation, and minimum operating system level of each feature.

Feature code and description	CIF	Model or tower																Min. OS/400
		250	270	820	830	840	890	#503X	#5065	#5074	#5075	#5078	#5079	#8079	#8093	#9074	#9079	
0041 Device Parity Protection-All	Y	-	B	B	B	B	B	-	-	-	-	-	-	-	-	-	-	V4R5
0087 7207-122 Attachment	Y	-	B	B	B	B	-	-	-	-	-	-	-	-	-	-	-	V4R4
0089 External Tape Attach	Y	-	B	B	B	B	-	-	-	-	-	-	-	-	-	-	-	V4R5
0092 External xSeries Attach	Y	-	B	B	B	B	B	-	-	-	-	-	-	-	-	-	-	V5R1
0120 7210-020 Attachment	Y	-	B	B	B	B	-	-	-	-	-	-	-	-	-	-	-	V4R5
0121 270 Lower Unit in Rack	Y	-	P	-	-	-	-	-	-	-	-	-	-	-	-	-	-	V4R5
0122 270 Upper Unit in Rack	Y	-	P	-	-	-	-	-	-	-	-	-	-	-	-	-	-	V4R5
0123 #5074 Lower Unit in Rack	Y	-	-	B	B	B	S	-	-	-	-	-	-	-	-	-	-	V4R5
0125 #9079 Lower Unit in Rack	Y	-	-	-	-	P	S	-	-	-	-	-	-	-	-	-	-	V4R5
0126 CEC Reduction Option	N	-	-	-	-	-	P	-	-	-	-	-	-	-	-	-	-	V5R2
0127 Field Install in Rack	N	-	B	-	-	-	-	-	-	-	-	-	-	-	-	-	-	V4R5
0133 Field Install in Rack	Y	-	B	-	-	-	-	-	-	-	-	-	-	-	-	-	-	V5R2
0140 Logical Partitioning Specify	Y	-	B	B	B	B	B	-	-	-	-	-	-	-	-	-	-	V4R4
0141 HSL OptiConnect Specify	Y	-	B	B	B	B	B	-	-	-	-	-	-	-	-	-	-	V5R1
0142 Linux Partition Specify	Y	-	B	B	B	B	B	-	-	-	-	-	-	-	-	-	-	V5R1
0150 Model 820 Base Processor	N	-	-	B	-	-	-	-	-	-	-	-	-	-	-	-	-	V5R1
0151 Model 820 Base Processor	N	-	-	B	-	-	-	-	-	-	-	-	-	-	-	-	-	V5R1
0152 Model 820 Base Processor	N	-	-	B	-	-	-	-	-	-	-	-	-	-	-	-	-	V5R1
0153 Model 830 8-way Processor	N	-	-	-	B	-	-	-	-	-	-	-	-	-	-	-	-	V5R2
0158 Model 840 12-way Processor	N	-	-	-	-	B	-	-	-	-	-	-	-	-	-	-	-	V5R2
0159 Model 840 24-way Processor	N	-	-	-	-	B	-	-	-	-	-	-	-	-	-	-	-	V5R2

Feature code and description	CIF	250	270	820	830	840	890	#503X	#5065	#5074	#5075	#5078	#5079	#8079	#8093	#9074	#9079	Min. OS/400
0162 Extended Single Ended Attach	Y	-	B	B	B	B	B	-	-	-	-	-	-	-	-	-	-	V5R1
0163 Fibre Channel Attach	Y	-	B	B	B	B	B	-	-	-	-	-	-	-	-	-	-	V5R1
0164 Differential Attach	Y	-	-	-	-	-	B	-	-	-	-	-	-	-	-	-	-	V5R1
0197 Model 890 24-way Processor	N	-	-	-	-	-	B	-	-	-	-	-	-	-	-	-	-	V5R2
0198 Model 890 32-way Processor	N	-	-	-	-	-	B	-	-	-	-	-	-	-	-	-	-	V5R2
0208 No Alt Install Device Use	Y	-	P	P	P	P	-	-	-	-	-	-	-	-	-	-	-	V4R5
0223 100 Mbps Token-Ring Specify	Y	-	B	B	B	B	B	-	-	-	-	-	-	-	-	-	-	V4R5
0224 100/10 Mbps Ethernet Specify	Y	-	B	B	B	B	B	-	-	-	-	-	-	-	-	-	-	V4R5
0225 1 Gbps Ethernet Specify	Y	-	B	B	B	B	B	-	-	B	B	B	B	B	B	B	B	V5R1
0226 1 Gbps Ethernet Specify	Y	-	B	B	B	B	B	-	-	-	-	-	-	-	-	-	-	V5R2
0297 Model 250 Package	Y	S	-	-	-	-	-	-	-	-	-	-	-	-	-	-	-	V5R1
0298 Model 250 package	Y	S	-	-	-	-	-	-	-	-	-	-	-	-	-	-	-	V5R1
#0369 100m Optical SPCN Cable	Y	-	-	-	B	B	B	-	-	B	-	B	B	B	B	B	B	V5R1
0371 LC-SC Adapter Kit (50 um)	Y	-	B	B	B	B	B	-	-	B	B	B	B	B	B	B	B	V5R1
0372 LC-SC Adapter Kit (62.5 um)	Y	-	B	B	B	B	B	-	-	B	B	B	B	B	B	B	B	V5R1
#0381 Remote Control Panel Cable																		
#0382 Remote Control Panel Cable	Y	-	S	S	S	S	S	-	-	-	-	-	-	-	-	-	-	V4R5
#0383 Remote Control Panel Cable	Y	-	B	B	B	B	B	-	-	-	-	-	-	-	-	-	-	V5R2
0426 512 MB Server Memory	N	-	-	B	B	B	B	-	-	B	B	B	B	B	B	B	B	V5R2
0427 1 GB Server Memory	N	-	-	B	B	B	B	-	-	B	B	B	B	B	B	B	B	V5R2
0446 512 MB DDR Server Memory	Y	-	B	-	-	-	-	-	-	B	-	-	-	-	-	-	-	V5R2
0447 1 GB DDR Server Memory	Y	-	B	-	-	-	-	-	-	B	-	-	-	-	-	-	-	V5R2
0550 830 Rack	N	-	-	-	P	-	-	-	-	-	-	-	-	-	-	-	-	V4R5
0551 #0551 iSeries Rack	Y	-	B	B	B	B	B	-	-	-	-	-	-	-	-	-	-	V4R5
0565 #5065 Equivalent	Y	-	-	-	-	-	-	S	-	-	-	-	-	-	-	-	-	V4R4
0574 #5074 Equivalent	Y	-	-	B	B	B	B	-	-	-	-	-	-	-	-	-	-	V4R5
0578 PCI Expansion Unit in Rack	N	-	-	B	B	B	B	-	-	-	-	-	-	-	-	-	-	V5R1

Feature code and description	CIF	250	270	820	830	840	890	#503X	#5065	#5074	#5075	#5078	#5079	#8079	#8093	#9074	#9079	Min. OS/400
0588 PCI Expansion Unit in Rack	N	-	-	B	B	B	B	-	-	-	-	-	-	-	-	-	-	V5R2
#0595 PCI-X Expansion Unit in Rack	Y	-	B	B	B	B	B	-	-	-	-	-	-	-	-	-	-	V5R2
#0601 - Direct Attach - #2743 PCI 1 Gbps Ethernet IOA	Y	-	B	B	B	B	B	-	-	B	B	B	B	B	B	B	B	V5R1
#0602 - Direct Attach - #2760 PCI 1 Gbps Ethernet UTP IOA	Y	-	B	B	B	B	B	-	-	B	B	B	B	B	B	B	B	V5R1
#0603 - Direct Attach - #2744 PCI 100 Mbps Token-Ring IOA	Y	-	B	B	B	B	B	-	-	B	B	B	B	B	B	B	B	V5R1
#0604 - Direct Attach - #2763 PCI RAID Disk Unit Controller	Y	-	B	B	-	-	-	-	-	-	B	-	-	-	-	-	-	V5R1
#0605 - Direct Attach - #4748 PCI RAID Disk Unit Controller	Y	-	B	S	S	S	S	-	-	S	S	-	S	S	S	S	S	V5R1
#0606 - Direct Attach - #4778 PCI RAID Disk Unit Controller	Y	-	B	B	B	B	B	-	-	B	B	-	B	B	B	B	B	V5R1
#0607 - Direct Attach - #4838 PCI 100/10 Mbps Ethernet IOA	Y	-	B	B	B	B	B	-	-	B	B	B	B	B	B	B	B	V5R1
#0608 - Direct Attach - #4745 PCI WAN IOA	Y	-	B	B	B	B	M	-	-	B	B	B	B	B	B	B	B	V5R1
#0609 - Direct Attach - #2772 PCI Dual WAN/Modem IOA	Y	-	B	B	B	B	B	-	-	B	B	B	B	B	B	B	B	V5R1
#0610 - Direct Attach - #2773 PCI Dual WAN/ModemIOA	Y	-	B	B	B	B	B	-	-	B	B	B	B	B	B	B	B	V5R1
#0611 - Direct Attach - #2765 PCI Fibre Channel Tape Controller	Y	-	B	B	B	B	B	-	-	B	B	B	B	B	B	B	B	V5R1
#0612 - Direct Attach - #2766 PCI Fibre Channel Disk Controller	Y	-	B	B	B	B	B	-	-	B	B	B	B	B	B	B	B	V5R1
#0613 - Direct Attach - #2742 PCI 2-Line WAN IOA	Y	-	B	B	B	B	B	-	-	B	B	B	B	B	B	B	B	V5R2
#0614 - Direct Attach - #2793 PCI 2-Line WAN w/Modem	Y	-	B	B	B	B	B	-	-	B	B	B	B	B	B	B	B	V5R2
#0615 - Direct Attach - #2794 PCI 2-Line WAN w/Modem	Y	-	B	B	B	B	B	-	-	B	B	B	B	B	B	B	B	V5R2
#0616 - Direct Attach - #2805 PCI Quad Modem IOA	Y	-	B	B	B	B	B	-	-	B	B	B	B	B	B	B	B	V5R1

Feature code and description	CIF	250	270	820	830	840	890	#503X	#5065	#5074	#5075	#5078	#5079	#8079	#8093	#9074	#9079	Min. OS/400
#0617 - Direct Attach - #2806 PCI Quad Modem (CIM)	Y	-	B	B	B	B	B	-	-	B	B	B	B	B	B	B	B	V5R1
#0618 - Direct Attach - #2757 PCI-X Ultra RAID Disk Controller	Y	-	B	B	B	B	B	-	-	B	B	B	B	B	B	B	B	V5R2
#0619 - Direct Attach - #2782 PCI-X RAID Disk Unit Controller	Y	-	-	B	-	-	-	-	-	-	-	-	-	-	-	-	-	V5R2
#0620 - Direct Attach - #5700 PCI 1 Gbps Ethernet IOA	Y	-	B	B	B	B	B	-	-	B	B	B	B	B	B	B	B	V5R2
#0621 - Direct Attach - #5701 PCI 1 Gbps Ethernet UTP IOA	Y	-	B	B	B	B	B	-	-	B	B	B	B	B	B	B	B	V5R2
#0623 - Direct Attach - #2849 PCI 100/10 Mbps Ethernet IOA	Y	-	B	B	B	B	B	-	-	B	B	B	B	B	B	B	B	V5R2
#0624 - Direct Attach - #5702 PCI-X Ultra Tape Controller	Y	-	B	B	B	B	B	-	-	B	B	B	B	B	B	B	B	V5R2
0705 Forced #2749 Placement	Y	-	-	-	-	-	B	-	-	-	-	-	-	-	-	-	-	V5R1
0707 Forced #2768 Placement	Y	-	-	-	-	-	B	-	-	-	-	-	-	-	-	-	-	V5R1
0826 #4314 Load Source Specify	Y	-	M	M	M	M	M	-	-	-	-	-	-	-	-	-	-	V4R5
0827 #4324 Load Source Specify	Y	-	M	M	M	M	M	-	-	-	-	-	-	-	-	-	-	V4R5
0828 #4317 Load Source Specify	Y	-	B	B	B	B	M	-	-	-	-	-	-	-	-	-	-	V4R5
0829 #4318 Load Source Specify	Y	-	B	B	B	B	B	-	-	-	-	-	-	-	-	-	-	V4R5
0830 #4319 Load Source Specify	Y	-	B	B	B	B	B	-	-	-	-	-	-	-	-	-	-	V5R1
#1460 - 3m Copper HSL Cable	Y	-	B	B	B	B	-	B	-	B	B	B	B	B	B	B	B	V4R5
#1461 - 6m Copper HSL Cable	Y	-	B	B	B	B	-	B	-	B	B	B	B	B	B	B	B	V4R5
#1462 - 15m Copper HSL Cable	Y	-	B	B	B	B	-	B	-	B	B	B	B	B	B	B	B	V4R5
#1463 - 2m SPCN Cable	Y	-	B	B	B	B	B	B	-	B	B	B	B	B	B	B	B	V4R5
#1464 - 6m SPCN Cable	Y	-	B	B	B	B	B	B	-	B	B	B	B	B	B	B	B	V4R5
#1465 - 15m SPCN Cable	Y	-	B	B	B	B	B	B	-	B	B	B	B	B	B	B	B	V4R5
#1466 - 30m SPCN Cable	Y	-	B	B	B	B	B	B	-	B	B	B	B	B	B	B	B	V4R5
#1468 - 250m Optical SPCN Cable	Y	-	-	-	B	B	B	-	-	B	-	B	B	B	B	B	B	V5R1
#1470 - 6m Optical HSL Cable	Y	-	-	-	B	B	B	-	-	B	-	B	B	B	B	B	B	V5R1

Feature code and description	CIF	250	270	820	830	840	890	#503X	#5065	#5074	#5075	#5078	#5079	#8079	#8093	#9074	#9079	Min. OS/400
#1471 - 30m Optical HSL Cable	Y	-	-	-	B	B	B	-	-	B	-	B	B	B	B	B	B	V5R1
#1472 - 100m Optical HSL Cable	Y	-	-	-	B	B	B	-	-	B	-	B	B	B	B	B	B	V5R1
#1473 - 250m Optical HSL Cable	Y	-	-	-	B	B	B	-	-	B	-	B	B	B	B	B	B	V5R1
#1474 - 6m HSL to HSL-2 Cable	Y	-	B	B	B	B	B	-	-	B	B	B	B	B	B	B	B	V5R2
#1475 - 10m HSL to HSL-2 Cable	Y	-	B	B	B	B	B	-	-	B	B	B	B	B	B	B	B	V5R2
#1482 - 3.5m HSL-2 Cable	Y	-	-	-	-	-	B	-	-	-	-	-	-	-	-	-	-	V5R2
#1483 - 10m HSL-2 Cable	Y	-	-	-	-	-	B	-	-	-	-	-	-	-	-	-	-	V5R2
#1485 - 15m HSL-2 Cable	Y	-	-	-	-	-	B	-	-	-	-	-	-	-	-	-	-	V5R2
1516 5250 CPW Capacity Card	N	-	P	-	-	-	-	-	-	-	-	-	-	-	-	-	-	V4R5
1517 5250 CPW Capacity Card	N	-	B	-	-	-	-	-	-	-	-	-	-	-	-	-	-	V4R5
1518 5250 CPW Capacity Card	N	-	B	-	-	-	-	-	-	-	-	-	-	-	-	-	-	V4R5
1519 5250 CPW Capacity Card	N	-	B	-	-	-	-	-	-	-	-	-	-	-	-	-	-	V4R5
1520 5250 CPW Capacity Card	N	-	B	-	-	-	-	-	-	-	-	-	-	-	-	-	-	V4R5
1521 5250 CPW Capacity Card	N	-	-	B	-	-	-	-	-	-	-	-	-	-	-	-	-	V4R5
1522 5250 CPW Capacity Card	N	-	-	B	-	-	-	-	-	-	-	-	-	-	-	-	-	V4R5
1523 5250 CPW Capacity Card	N	-	-	B	-	-	-	-	-	-	-	-	-	-	-	-	-	V4R5
1524 5250 CPW Capacity Card	N	-	-	B	-	-	-	-	-	-	-	-	-	-	-	-	-	V4R5
1525 5250 CPW Capacity Card	N	-	-	B	-	-	-	-	-	-	-	-	-	-	-	-	-	V4R5
1526 5250 CPW Capacity Card	N	-	-	B	-	-	-	-	-	-	-	-	-	-	-	-	-	V4R5
1527 5250 CPW Capacity Card	N	-	-	B	-	-	-	-	-	-	-	-	-	-	-	-	-	V4R5
1531 5250 CPW Capacity Card	N	-	-	-	B	-	-	-	-	-	-	-	-	-	-	-	-	V4R5
1532 5250 CPW Capacity Card	N	-	-	-	B	-	-	-	-	-	-	-	-	-	-	-	-	V4R5
1533 5250 CPW Capacity Card	N	-	-	-	B	-	-	-	-	-	-	-	-	-	-	-	-	V4R5
1534 5250 CPW Capacity Card	N	-	-	-	B	-	-	-	-	-	-	-	-	-	-	-	-	V4R5
1535 5250 CPW Capacity Card	N	-	-	-	B	-	-	-	-	-	-	-	-	-	-	-	-	V4R5
1536 5250 CPW Capacity Card	N	-	-	-	B	-	-	-	-	-	-	-	-	-	-	-	-	V4R5
1537 5250 CPW Capacity Card	N	-	-	-	B	-	-	-	-	-	-	-	-	-	-	-	-	V4R5

Feature code and description	CIF	250	270	820	830	840	890	#503X	#5065	#5074	#5075	#5078	#5079	#8079	#8093	#9074	#9079	Min. OS/400
1540 5250 CPW Capacity Card	N	-	-	-	-	B	-	-	-	-	-	-	-	-	-	-	-	V4R5
1541 5250 CPW Capacity Card	N	-	-	-	-	B	-	-	-	-	-	-	-	-	-	-	-	V4R5
1542 5250 CPW Capacity Card	N	-	-	-	-	B	-	-	-	-	-	-	-	-	-	-	-	V4R5
1543 5250 CPW Capacity Card	N	-	-	-	-	B	-	-	-	-	-	-	-	-	-	-	-	V4R5
1544 5250 CPW Capacity Card	N	-	-	-	-	B	-	-	-	-	-	-	-	-	-	-	-	V4R5
1545 5250 CPW Capacity Card	N	-	-	-	-	B	-	-	-	-	-	-	-	-	-	-	-	V4R5
1546 5250 CPW Capacity Card	N	-	-	-	-	B	-	-	-	-	-	-	-	-	-	-	-	V4R5
1547 5250 CPW Capacity Card	N	-	-	-	-	B	-	-	-	-	-	-	-	-	-	-	-	V4R5
1548 5250 CPW Capacity Card	N	-	-	-	-	B	-	-	-	-	-	-	-	-	-	-	-	V5R1
1576 5250 CPW Capacity Card	N	-	-	-	-	-	P	-	-	-	-	-	-	-	-	-	-	V5R2
1577 5250 CPW Capacity Card	N	-	-	-	-	-	B	-	-	-	-	-	-	-	-	-	-	V5R2
1578 5250 CPW Capacity Card	N	-	-	-	-	-	B	-	-	-	-	-	-	-	-	-	-	V5R2
1579 5250 CPW Capacity Card	N	-	-	-	-	-	B	-	-	-	-	-	-	-	-	-	-	V5R2
1581 5250 CPW Capacity Card	N	-	-	-	-	-	B	-	-	-	-	-	-	-	-	-	-	V5R2
1583 5250 CPW Capacity Card	N	-	-	-	-	-	B	-	-	-	-	-	-	-	-	-	-	V5R2
1585 5250 CPW Capacity Card	N	-	-	-	-	-	B	-	-	-	-	-	-	-	-	-	-	V5R2
1587 5250 CPW Capacity Card	N	-	-	-	-	-	B	-	-	-	-	-	-	-	-	-	-	V5R2
1588 5250 CPW Capacity Card	N	-	-	-	-	-	B	-	-	-	-	-	-	-	-	-	-	V5R2
1591 5250 CPW Capacity Card	N	-	-	-	-	-	B	-	-	-	-	-	-	-	-	-	-	V5R2
#1604 CUoD Activation	Y	-	-	-	-	B	-	-	-	-	-	-	-	-	-	-	-	V4R5
#1605 CUoD Activation	Y	-	-	-	B	-	-	-	-	-	-	-	-	-	-	-	-	V5R1
#1610 890 CUoD Activation	Y	-	-	-	-	-	B	-	-	-	-	-	-	-	-	-	-	V5R2
2248 Model 270 Processor	N	-	P	-	-	-	-	-	-	-	-	-	-	-	-	-	-	V4R5
2250 Model 270 Processor	N	-	B	-	-	-	-	-	-	-	-	-	-	-	-	-	-	V4R5
2252 Model 270 Processor	N	-	B	-	-	-	-	-	-	-	-	-	-	-	-	-	-	V4R5
2253 Model 270 2-way Processor	N	-	B	-	-	-	-	-	-	-	-	-	-	-	-	-	-	V4R5
2301 Model 270 Processor	N	-	B	-	-	-	-	-	-	-	-	-	-	-	-	-	-	V5R1

Feature code and description	CIF	250	270	820	830	840	890	#503X	#5065	#5074	#5075	#5078	#5079	#8079	#8093	#9074	#9079	Min. OS/400
2302 Model 270 Processor	N	-	B	-	-	-	-	-	-	-	-	-	-	-	-	-	-	V5R1
2303 Model 820 Processor	N	-	-	B	-	-	-	-	-	-	-	-	-	-	-	-	-	V5R1
2315 Model SB2 8-way Processor	N	-	-	-	-	-	-	-	-	-	-	-	-	-	-	-	-	V4R5
2316 Model SB3 12-way Processor	N	-	-	-	-	-	-	-	-	-	-	-	-	-	-	-	-	V4R5
2318 Model SB3 24-way Processor	N	-	-	-	-	-	-	-	-	-	-	-	-	-	-	-	-	V4R5
2349 Model 830 4/8-way Proc	N	-	-	-	P	-	-	-	-	-	-	-	-	-	-	-	-	V5R1
2351 Model 830 1/8-way POD	N	-	-	-	P	-	-	-	-	-	-	-	-	-	-	-	-	V5R1
2352 Model 840 8/12-way POD	N	-	-	-	-	B	-	-	-	-	-	-	-	-	-	-	-	V5R1
2353 Model 840 12/18-way POD	N	-	-	-	-	B	-	-	-	-	-	-	-	-	-	-	-	V5R1
2354 Model 840 18/24-way POD	N	-	-	-	-	B	-	-	-	-	-	-	-	-	-	-	-	V5R1
2395 Model 820 Processor	N	-	-	B	-	-	-	-	-	-	-	-	-	-	-	-	-	V4R5
2396 Model 820 Processor	N	-	-	B	-	-	-	-	-	-	-	-	-	-	-	-	-	V4R5
2397 Model 820 2-way Processor	N	-	-	B	-	-	-	-	-	-	-	-	-	-	-	-	-	V4R5
2398 Model 820 4-way Processor	N	-	-	B	-	-	-	-	-	-	-	-	-	-	-	-	-	V4R5
2400 Model 830 2-way Processor	N	-	-	-	B	-	-	-	-	-	-	-	-	-	-	-	-	V4R5
2402 Model 830 4-way Processor	N	-	-	-	B	-	-	-	-	-	-	-	-	-	-	-	-	V4R5
2403 Model 830 8-way Processor	N	-	-	-	B	-	-	-	-	-	-	-	-	-	-	-	-	V4R5
2416 Model 840 8/12-way POD	N	-	-	-	-	B	-	-	-	-	-	-	-	-	-	-	-	V4R5
2417 Model 840 12/18-way POD	N	-	-	-	-	B	-	-	-	-	-	-	-	-	-	-	-	V4R5
2418 Model 840 12-way Processor	N	-	-	-	-	B	-	-	-	-	-	-	-	-	-	-	-	V4R5
2419 Model 840 18/24-way POD	N	-	-	-	-	B	-	-	-	-	-	-	-	-	-	-	-	V4R5
2420 Model 840 24-way Processor	N	-	-	-	-	B	-	-	-	-	-	-	-	-	-	-	-	V4R5
2422 Dedicated Domino Processor	N	-	P	-	-	-	-	-	-	-	-	-	-	-	-	-	-	V4R5
2423 Dedicated Domino Processor	N	-	B	-	-	-	-	-	-	-	-	-	-	-	-	-	-	V4R5
2424 Dedicated Domino 2-way Proc	N	-	B	-	-	-	-	-	-	-	-	-	-	-	-	-	-	V4R5
2425 Dedicated Domino Processor	N	-	-	P	-	-	-	-	-	-	-	-	-	-	-	-	-	V4R5
2426 Dedicated Domino 2-way Proc	N	-	-	B	-	-	-	-	-	-	-	-	-	-	-	-	-	V4R5

Feature code and description	CIF	250	270	820	830	840	890	#503X	#5065	#5074	#5075	#5078	#5079	#8079	#8093	#9074	#9079	Min. OS/400
2427 Dedicated Domino 4-way Proc	N	-	-	B	-	-	-	-	-	-	-	-	-	-	-	-	-	V4R5
2431 Model 270 Processor	N	-	B	-	-	-	-	-	-	-	-	-	-	-	-	-	-	V5R1
2432 Model 270 Processor	N	-	B	-	-	-	-	-	-	-	-	-	-	-	-	-	-	V5R1
2434 Model 270 2-way Processor	N	-	B	-	-	-	-	-	-	-	-	-	-	-	-	-	-	V5R1
2435 Model 820 Processor	N	-	-	B	-	-	-	-	-	-	-	-	-	-	-	-	-	V5R1
2436 Model 820 Processor	N	-	-	B	-	-	-	-	-	-	-	-	-	-	-	-	-	V5R1
2437 Model 820 2-way Processor	N	-	-	B	-	-	-	-	-	-	-	-	-	-	-	-	-	V5R1
2438 Model 820 4-way Processor	N	-	-	B	-	-	-	-	-	-	-	-	-	-	-	-	-	V5R1
2452 Dedicated Domino Processor	N	-	B	-	-	-	-	-	-	-	-	-	-	-	-	-	-	V5R1
2454 Dedicated Domino 2-way Proc	N	-	B	-	-	-	-	-	-	-	-	-	-	-	-	-	-	V5R1
2456 Dedicated Domino Processor	N	-	-	P	-	-	-	-	-	-	-	-	-	-	-	-	-	V5R1
2457 Dedicated Domino 2-way Proc	N	-	-	B	-	-	-	-	-	-	-	-	-	-	-	-	-	V5R1
2458 Dedicated Domino 4-way Proc	N	-	-	B	-	-	-	-	-	-	-	-	-	-	-	-	-	V5R1
2460 Model 840 12-way Processor	N	-	-	-	-	B	-	-	-	-	-	-	-	-	-	-	-	V5R1
2461 Model 840 24-way Processor	N	-	-	-	-	B	-	-	-	-	-	-	-	-	-	-	-	V5R1
2487 Model 890 16/24-way Proc	N	-	-	-	-	-	B	-	-	-	-	-	-	-	-	-	-	V5R2
2488 Model 890 24/32-way Proc	N	-	-	-	-	-	B	-	-	-	-	-	-	-	-	-	-	V5R2
#2723 PCI Ethernet IOA (CIF=Y in #5033 and 250)	N	S	-	-	-	-	-	S	S	-	-	-	-	-	-	-	-	V4R1
#2724 PCI 16/4 Mbps Token Ring IOA (CIF=Y in #5033 and 250)	N	S	-	-	-	-	-	S	S	-	-	-	-	-	-	-	-	V4R1
#2729 PCI Magnetic Media Controller (CIF=Y in #5033, 250)	N	S	-	-	-	-	-	S	S	-	-	-	-	-	-	-	-	V4R1
2738 HSL Ports - 8 Copper	N	-	-	-	-	-	B	-	-	-	-	-	-	-	-	-	-	V5R2
#2739 Optical Bus Adapter	N	-	-	-	-	-	-	-	-	M	-	M	M	M	M	M	M	V5R1
#2742 Two-Line WAN IOA	Y	-	B	B	B	B	B	-	-	B	B	B	B	B	B	B	B	V5R2
#2743 1 Gbps PCI Ethernet IOA	Y	-	B	B	B	B	B	-	-	B	B	B	B	B	B	B	B	V4R5
#2744 PCI 100 Mbps Token Ring IOA	Y	-	B	B	B	B	B	-	-	B	B	B	B	B	B	B	B	V4R5

Feature code and description	CIF	250	270	820	830	840	890	#503X	#5065	#5074	#5075	#5078	#5079	#8079	#8093	#9074	#9079	Min. OS/400
#2745 PCI Two-Line WAN IOA (CIF=Y in 5033 and 250)	N	M	-	-	-	-	-	M	M	-	-	-	-	-	-	-	-	V4R4
#2746 PCI Twinaxial Workstation IOA (CIF=Y in 5033 and 250)	N	M	-	-	-	-	-	M	M	-	-	-	-	-	-	-	-	V4R4
#2748 PCI RAID Disk Unit Controller (CIF=Y in 5033 and 250)	N	S	-	-	-	-	-	S	S	-	-	-	-	-	-	-	-	V4R4
#2749 PCI Ultra Magnetic Media Controller	Y	-	B	B	B	B	B	-	-	B	B	B	B	B	B	B	B	V4R5
#2750 PCI ISDN BRI U Adapter (CIF=Y in #5033 and 250)	N	S	-	-	-	-	-	S	S	-	-	-	-	-	-	-	-	V4R4
#2751 PCI ISDN BRI S/T IOA (CIF=Y in #5033 and 250)	N	S	-	-	-	-	-	S	S	-	-	-	-	-	-	-	-	V4R4
#2754 HSL Ports - 8 Copper	N	-	-	-	M	-	-	-	-	-	-	-	-	-	-	-	-	V5R1
#2755 HSL Ports - 16 Copper	N	-	-	-	-	M	-	-	-	-	-	-	-	-	-	-	-	V5R1
#2757 PCI-X Ultra RAID Disk Controller	Y	-	B	B	B	B	B	-	-	B	B	-	B	B	B	B	B	V5R2
#2758 HSL Ports - 2 Optical/6 Copper	N	-	-	-	M	-	-	-	-	-	-	-	-	-	-	-	-	V5R1
#2759 HSL Ports - 4 Optical/12 Copper	N	-	-	-	-	M	-	-	-	-	-	-	-	-	-	-	-	V5R1
#2760 PCI 1 Gbps Ethernet UTP Adapter	Y	-	B	B	B	B	B	-	-	B	B	B	B	B	B	B	B	V5R1
#2761 Integrated Analog Modem (CIF=Y in #5033)	N	S	-	-	-	-	-	S	S	-	-	-	-	-	-	-	-	V4R4
#2763 PCI RAID Disk Unit Controller (CIF=N in 250)	Y	M	B	B	-	-	-	-	-	-	B	-	-	-	-	-	-	V4R5
#2765 PCI Fibre Channel Tape Controller	Y	-	B	B	B	B	B	-	-	B	B	B	B	B	B	B	B	V5R1
#2766 PCI Fibre Channel Disk Controller	Y	-	B	B	B	B	B	-	-	B	B	B	B	B	B	B	B	V5R1
#2768 PCI Magnetic Media Controller	Y	-	B	B	B	B	B	-	-	B	B	B	B	B	B	B	B	V4R5
#2772 PCI Dual WAN/Modem IOA	Y	-	B	B	B	B	B	-	-	B	B	B	B	B	B	B	B	V5R1
#2773 PCI Dual WAN/Modem IOA	Y	-	B	B	B	B	B	-	-	B	B	B	B	B	B	B	B	V5R1
#2774 HSL Ports - 2 Optical/6 Copper	N	-	-	-	M	-	-	-	-	-	-	-	-	-	-	-	-	V5R1
#2776 HSL-2 Ports - 8 Copper	N	-	-	-	-	-	B	-	-	-	-	-	-	-	-	-	-	V5R2
#2777 HSL Ports - 8 Copper	N	-	-	-	M	-	-	-	-	-	-	-	-	-	-	-	-	V5R1
#2778 PCI RAID Disk Unit Controller	N	-	-	-	-	-	-	-	M	-	-	-	-	-	-	-	-	V5R1

Feature code and description	CIF	250	270	820	830	840	890	#503X	#5065	#5074	#5075	#5078	#5079	#8079	#8093	#9074	#9079	Min. OS/400
#2782 PCI-X RAID Disk Unit Controller	Y	-	B	B	-	-	-	-	-	-	-	-	-	-	-	-	-	V5R2
#2788 HSL Ports - 8 Optical	N	-	-	-	-	-	B	-	-	-	-	-	-	-	-	-	-	V5R2
#2790 PCI Integrated Netfinity Server	N	-	-	S	S	S	S	-	-	S	S	S	S	S	S	S	S	V4R5
#2791 PCI Integrated xSeries Server	N	-	-	S	S	S	S	-	-	S	S	S	S	S	S	S	S	V4R5
#2792 PCI Integrated xSeries Server	N	-	-	B	B	B	B	-	-	B	B	B	B	B	B	B	B	V5R2
#2793 Two-Line WAN IOA with Modem	Y	-	B	B	B	B	B	-	-	B	B	B	B	B	B	B	B	V5R2
#2794 Two-Line WAN IOA with Modem (CIM)	Y	-	B	B	B	B	B	-	-	B	B	B	B	B	B	B	B	V5R2
2795 128 MB Server Memory	N	-	-	B	B	B	B	-	-	B	B	B	B	B	B	B	B	V4R5
2796 256 MB Server Memory	N	-	-	B	B	B	B	-	-	B	B	B	B	B	B	B	B	V4R5
2797 1 GB Server Memory	N	-	-	B	B	B	B	-	-	B	B	B	B	B	B	B	B	V4R5
#2799 PCI Integrated xSeries Server	N	-	-	B	B	B	B	-	-	B	B	B	B	B	B	B	B	V5R1
#2805 PCI Quad Modem IOA	Y	-	B	B	B	B	B	-	-	B	B	B	B	B	B	B	B	V5R1
#2806 PCI Quad Modem (CIM) (CIM)	Y	-	B	B	B	B	B	-	-	B	B	B	B	B	B	B	B	V5R1
#2817 PCI 155 Mbps MMF ATM IOA	Y	-	B	B	B	B	B	-	-	B	B	B	B	B	B	B	B	V5R1
#2824 PCI Feature Controller (CIF=Y in #5033 and 250)	N	M	-	-	-	-	-	M	M	-	-	-	-	-	-	-	-	V4R4
#2838 PCI 100/10 Mbps Ethernet IOA (CIF=Y in #5033 and 250)	N	M	-	-	-	-	-	M	M	-	-	-	-	-	-	-	-	V4R1
#2842 PCI IOP	Y	-	B	-	-	-	-	-	-	-	-	B	-	-	-	-	-	V4R5
#2843 PCI IOP	Y	-	-	B	B	B	B	-	-	B	B	B	B	B	B	B	B	V4R5
#2844 PCI IOP	Y	-	B	B	B	B	B	-	-	B	B	B	B	B	B	B	B	V4R5
#2849 10/100 Mbps Ethernet Adapter	Y	-	B	B	B	B	B	-	-	B	B	B	B	B	B	B	B	V5R2
2881 Main Storage Expansion	N	-	-	-	B	-	-	-	-	-	-	-	-	-	-	-	-	V4R5
2884 Main Storage Expansion	Y	-	B	B	-	-	-	-	-	-	-	-	-	-	-	-	-	V4R5
#2890 PCI Integrated Netfinity Server	Y	-	S	-	-	-	-	-	-	-	-	S	-	-	-	-	-	V4R5
#2891 PCI Integrated xSeries Server	Y	-	S	-	-	-	-	-	-	-	-	S	-	-	-	-	-	V4R5
#2892 PCI Integrated xSeries Server	Y	-	B	-	-	-	-	-	-	-	-	B	-	-	-	-	-	V5R2

Feature code and description	CIF	250	270	820	830	840	890	#503X	#5065	#5074	#5075	#5078	#5079	#8079	#8093	#9074	#9079	Min. OS/400
2895 128 MB Server Memory	Y	-	B	-	-	-	-	-	-	-	B	-	-	-	-	-	-	V4R5
2896 256 MB Server Memory	Y	-	B	-	-	-	-	-	-	-	B	-	-	-	-	-	-	V4R5
2897 1 GB Server Memory	Y	-	B	-	-	-	-	-	-	-	B	-	-	-	-	-	-	V4R5
#2899 PCI Integrated xSeries Server	Y	-	B	-	-	-	-	-	-	-	B	-	-	-	-	-	-	V5R1
3000 Migrated 128 MB Main Storage	N	-	-	M	M	-	-	-	-	-	-	-	-	-	-	-	-	V4R5
3005 512 MB Main Store	Y	-	-	B	-	-	-	-	-	-	-	-	-	-	-	-	-	V4R5
3006 512 MB Main Storage	Y	-	-	B	-	-	-	-	-	-	-	-	-	-	-	-	-	V4R5
3007 1 GB Main Storage	Y	-	-	B	-	-	-	-	-	-	-	-	-	-	-	-	-	V5R1
3009 128 MB Main Storage	Y	-	-	B	-	-	-	-	-	-	-	-	-	-	-	-	-	V5R1
3015 8 GB Main Storage	N	-	-	-	-	-	B	-	-	-	-	-	-	-	-	-	-	V5R2
3016 8 GB Main Storage	N	-	-	-	-	-	B	-	-	-	-	-	-	-	-	-	-	V5R2
3017 32 GB Main Storage	N	-	-	-	-	-	B	-	-	-	-	-	-	-	-	-	-	V5R2
3018 32 GB Main Storage	N	-	-	-	-	-	B	-	-	-	-	-	-	-	-	-	-	V5R2
3020 4 GB Main Storage	N	-	-	-	-	-	B	-	-	-	-	-	-	-	-	-	-	V5R2
3021 4 GB Main Storage	N	-	-	-	-	-	B	-	-	-	-	-	-	-	-	-	-	V5R2
3022 128 MB Main Storage	Y	M	B	-	-	-	-	-	-	-	-	-	-	-	-	-	-	V4R5
3024 256 MB Main Storage	Y	M	B	-	-	-	-	-	-	-	-	-	-	-	-	-	-	V4R5
3025 512 MB Main Storage	Y	-	B	-	-	-	-	-	-	-	-	-	-	-	-	-	-	V4R5
3026 512 MB Main Storage	Y	-	B	-	-	-	-	-	-	-	-	-	-	-	-	-	-	V4R5
3027 1 GB Main Storage	Y	-	B	-	-	-	-	-	-	-	-	-	-	-	-	-	-	V5R1
3029 128 MB Main Storage	Y	-	B	-	-	-	-	-	-	-	-	-	-	-	-	-	-	V5R1
3032 256 MB Main Storage	Y	-	B	-	-	-	-	-	-	-	-	-	-	-	-	-	-	V5R1
3033 512 MB Main Storage	Y	-	B	-	-	-	-	-	-	-	-	-	-	-	-	-	-	V5R1
3034 1 GB Main Storage	Y	-	B	-	-	-	-	-	-	-	-	-	-	-	-	-	-	V5R1
3035 16 GB Main Storage	N	-	-	-	-	-	B	-	-	-	-	-	-	-	-	-	-	V5R2
3036 16 GB Main Storage	N	-	-	-	-	-	B	-	-	-	-	-	-	-	-	-	-	V5R2
3062 128 MB Main Storage	N	-	-	-	B	-	-	-	-	-	-	-	-	-	-	-	-	V4R5

Feature code and description	CIF	Model or tower																Min. OS/400
		250	270	820	830	840	890	#503X	#5065	#5074	#5075	#5078	#5079	#8079	#8093	#9074	#9079	
3064 256 MB Main Storage	N	-	-	-	B	-	-	-	-	-	-	-	-	-	-	-	-	V4R5
3065 512 MB Main Storage	N	-	-	-	B	-	-	-	-	-	-	-	-	-	-	-	-	V4R5
3066 512 MB Main Storage	N	-	-	-	B	-	-	-	-	-	-	-	-	-	-	-	-	V4R5
3067 1 GB Main Storage	Y	-	-	-	B	-	-	-	-	-	-	-	-	-	-	-	-	V5R1
3195 4096 MB Main Storage	N	-	-	-	-	S	-	-	-	-	-	-	-	-	-	-	-	V4R5
3196 8192 MB Main Storage	N	-	-	-	-	B	-	-	-	-	-	-	-	-	-	-	-	V4R5
3197 1024 MB Main Storage	N	-	-	-	-	S	-	-	-	-	-	-	-	-	-	-	-	V4R5
3198 2048 MB Main Storage	N	-	-	-	-	S	-	-	-	-	-	-	-	-	-	-	-	V4R5
3612 1024 MB Main Storage	N	-	-	-	-	B	-	-	-	-	-	-	-	-	-	-	-	V4R5
3613 2048 MB Main Storage	N	-	-	-	-	B	-	-	-	-	-	-	-	-	-	-	-	V4R5
3614 4096 MB Main Storage	N	-	-	-	-	B	-	-	-	-	-	-	-	-	-	-	-	V4R5
4308 4.19 GB Disk Unit	Y	-	-	-	-	-	-	-	S	S	-	-	S	S	S	S	S	V4R4
4314 8.58 GB Disk Unit	Y	-	S	S	S	S	S	-	S	S	S	-	S	S	S	S	S	V4R4
#4317 8.58 GB 10k RPM Disk Unit	Y	-	B	B	B	B	S	-	M	B	B	-	B	B	B	B	B	V4R4
#4318 17.54 GB 10k RPM Disk Unit	Y	-	B	B	B	B	B	-	M	B	B	-	B	B	B	B	B	V4R4
4319 35.16 GB 10k rpm Disk Unit	Y	-	B	B	B	B	B	-	-	B	B	-	B	B	B	B	B	V5R1
#4324 17.54 GB Disk Unit	Y	-	S	S	S	S	S	-	S	S	S	-	S	S	S	S	S	V4R4
#4326 35.16 GB 15k RPM Disk Unit	Y	-	-	-	-	-	B	-	-	-	-	-	-	-	-	-	-	V5R2
#4327 70.56 GB 15k RPM Disk Unit	Y	-	-	-	-	-	B	-	-	-	-	-	-	-	-	-	-	V5R2
#4331 1.6 GB Read Cache Device	Y	-	S	S	S	S	-	-	S	S	S	-	S	S	S	S	S	V4R4
#4425 CD-ROM	Y	-	-	-	B	B	S	-	M	B	-	-	B	B	B	B	B	V4R4
#4430 DVD-RAM	Y	-	-	-	B	B	B	-	-	B	-	-	B	B	B	B	B	V4R5
#4482 4 GB ¼-inch Cartridge Tape Device	Y	-	-	-	B	B	B	-	M	B	-	-	B	B	B	B	B	V4R4
#4483 16 GB ¼-inch Cartridge Tape Device	Y	-	-	-	B	B	S	-	M	B	-	-	B	B	B	B	B	V4R4
#4486 25 GB ¼-inch Cartridge Tape Device	Y	-	-	-	B	B	S	-	M	B	-	-	B	B	B	B	B	V4R4

Feature code and description	CIF	250	270	820	830	840	890	#503X	#5065	#5074	#5075	#5078	#5079	#8079	#8093	#9074	#9079	Min. OS/400
#4487 50 GB ¼-inch Cartridge Tape Device	Y	-	-	-	B	B	B	-	M	B	-	-	B	B	B	B	B	V5R1
#4525 CD-ROM	Y	-	B	B	-	-	-	-	-	-	-	-	-	-	-	-	-	V4R5
#4530 DVD-RAM	Y	-	B	B	-	-	-	-	-	-	-	-	-	-	-	-	-	V4R5
#4582 4 GB ¼-inch Cartridge Tape Device	Y	-	B	B	-	-	-	-	-	-	-	-	-	-	-	-	-	V4R5
#4583 16 GB ¼-inch Cartridge Tape Device	Y	-	B	B	-	-	-	-	-	-	-	-	-	-	-	-	-	V4R5
#4584 30 GB ¼-inch Cartridge Tape Device	Y	-	B	B	-	-	-	-	-	-	-	-	-	-	-	-	-	V4R5
#4585 80 GB VXA-2 Tape Device	Y	-	B	B	-	-	-	-	-	-	-	-	-	-	-	-	-	V5R1
#4586 25 GB ¼-inch Cartridge Tape Device	Y	-	B	B	-	-	-	-	-	-	-	-	-	-	-	-	-	V4R5
#4587 50 GB ¼-inch Cartridge Tape Device	Y	-	B	B	-	-	-	-	-	-	-	-	-	-	-	-	-	V5R1
#4684 30 GB ¼-inch Cartridge Tape Device	Y	-	-	-	B	B	B	-	M	B	-	-	B	B	B	B	B	V4R5
#4685 80 GB VXA-2 Tape Device	Y	-	-	-	B	B	B	-	B	B	-	B	-	-	-	-	-	V5R1
#4687 50 GB ¼-inch Cartridge Tape Device	Y	-	-	-	B	B	B	-	-	B	-	-	B	B	-	B	B	V5R1
#4723 PCI 10 Mbps Ethernet Adapter	Y	-	S	S	S	S	S	-	-	S	S	S	S	S	S	S	S	V4R5
#4745 PCI 2-line WAN IOA	Y	-	B	B	B	B	B	-	-	B	B	B	B	B	B	B	B	V4R5
#4746 PCI Twinaxial IOA	Y	-	B	B	B	B	B	-	-	B	B	B	B	B	B	B	B	V4R5
#4748 PCI RAID Disk Unit Controller	Y	-	S	S	S	S	S	-	-	S	S	-	S	S	S	S	S	V4R5
#4750 PCI ISDN BRI U IOA	Y	-	S	S	S	S	-	-	-	S	S	S	S	S	S	S	S	V4R5
#4751 PCI ISDN BRI S/T IOA	Y	-	S	S	S	S	-	-	-	S	S	S	S	S	S	S	S	V4R5
#4761 PCI Integrated Analog Modem	Y	-	S	S	S	S	-	-	-	S	S	S	S	S	S	S	S	V4R5
#4778 PCI RAID Disk Unit Controller	Y	-	B	B	B	B	B	-	-	B	B	-	B	B	B	B	B	V5R1
#4801 PCI Cryptographic Coprocessor	Y	M	B	B	B	B	B	-	-	B	B	B	B	B	B	B	B	V4R5
#4802 PCI Cryptographic Processor (CIF=Y in 5033)	N	-	-	-	-	-	-	S	S	-	-	-	-	-	-	-	-	V4R5

Feature code and description	CIF	250	270	820	830	840	890	#503X	#5065	#5074	#5075	#5078	#5079	#8079	#8093	#9074	#9079	Min. OS/400
#4805 PCI Cryptographic Accelerator	Y	-	B	B	B	B	B	-	-	B	B	B	B	B	B	B	B	V5R2
#4815 PCI ATM 155 Mbps UTP OC3	Y	-	S	S	S	S	S	-	-	S	S	S	S	S	S	S	S	V4R5
#4816 PCI ATM 155 Mbps MMF	Y	-	S	S	S	S	S	-	-	S	S	S	S	S	S	S	S	V4R5
#4818 PCI ATM 155 Mbps SMF OC3	Y	-	S	S	S	S	S	-	-	S	S	S	S	S	S	S	S	V4R5
#4838 PCI 100/10 Mbps Ethernet IOA	Y	-	B	B	B	B	B	-	-	B	B	B	B	B	B	B	B	V4R5
5029 Software Version V5R2	Y	M	B	B	B	B	B	-	-	-	-	-	-	-	-	-	-	V5R2
#5033 Migration Tower I	N	-	-	M	S	-	-	-	-	-	-	-	-	-	-	-	-	V4R5
#5034 Migration Tower I	N	-	-	M	M	-	-	-	-	-	-	-	-	-	-	-	-	V4R5
#5035 Migration Tower I	N	-	-	M	M	-	-	-	-	-	-	-	-	-	-	-	-	V4R5
#5065 Storage/PCI Expansion Tower	Y	-	-	-	-	-	-	S	-	-	-	-	-	-	-	-	-	V4R4
#5066 1.8 M I/O Tower	Y	-	-	-	-	-	-	S	-	-	-	-	-	-	-	-	-	V4R4
#5074 PCI Expansion Tower	Y	-	-	B	B	B	B	-	-	-	-	-	-	-	-	-	-	V4R5
#5075 PCI Expansion Tower	Y	-	B	B	-	-	-	-	-	-	-	-	-	-	-	-	-	V4R5
#5077 Migration Tower II	N	-	-	-	B	B	-	-	-	-	-	-	-	-	-	-	-	V4R5
#5078 PCI Expansion Unit	N	-	-	-	-	B	-	-	-	B	-	-	B	B	B	B	B	V5R1
#5079 1.8 M I/O Tower	Y	-	-	B	B	B	B	-	-	-	-	-	-	-	-	-	-	V4R5
#5088 PCI-X Expansion Unit	N	-	-	-	-	B	B	-	-	B	-	-	-	-	-	-	B	V5R2
#5094 PCI-X Expansion Tower	Y	-	B	B	B	B	B	-	-	-	-	-	-	-	-	-	-	V5R2
#5095 PCI-X Expansion Tower	Y	-	B	B	B	B	B	-	-	-	-	-	-	-	-	-	-	V5R2
#5101 30 Disk Unit Expansion	N	-	-	-	B	B	-	-	M	B	-	-	B	B	B	B	B	V4R4
5102 Dual Line Cords - 820 CEC	N	-	-	B	-	-	-	-	-	-	-	-	-	-	-	-	-	V5R1
5103 Dual Line Cords - 830 CEC	N	-	-	-	B	-	-	-	-	-	-	-	-	-	-	-	-	V5R1
5104 Dual Line Cords - 840 CEC	N	-	-	-	-	B	-	-	-	-	-	-	-	-	-	-	-	V5R1
5105 Dual Line Cords - I/O Tower	N	-	-	-	-	-	-	-	-	B	-	-	B	B	B	B	B	V5R1
5106 Dual Line Cords - 5079 Tower	N	-	-	-	-	-	-	-	-	B	-	-	B	B	B	B	B	V5R1
5107 30-Disk Expansion Feature	N	-	-	-	-	-	B	-	-	-	-	-	-	-	-	-	-	V5R2
5111 30-Disk Exp w/Dual Line Cord	N	-	-	-	B	B	B	-	-	B	-	-	B	B	B	B	B	V5R1

Feature code and description	CIF	250	270	820	830	840	890	#503X	#5065	#5074	#5075	#5078	#5079	#8079	#8093	#9074	#9079	Min. OS/400
5114 Dual Line Cords - Tower	Y	-	-	-	-	-	B	-	-	-	-	-	-	-	-	-	-	V5R2
5117 30-Disk Exp w/Dual Line Cord	N	-	-	-	-	-	B	-	-	-	-	-	-	-	-	-	-	V5R2
5155 Redundant Power and Cooling	Y	-	-	B	-	-	-	-	-	-	-	-	-	-	-	-	-	V4R5
5156 Redundant Power and Cooling	Y	-	-	-	-	-	-	-	-	-	-	B	-	-	-	-	-	V4R5
5157 Feature Power Supply	Y	-	-	B	-	-	-	-	-	-	-	-	-	-	-	-	-	V4R5
5160 Power Dist Unit 1 Phase NEMA	N	-	B	B	B	B	B	-	-	-	-	-	-	-	-	-	-	V5R1
5161 Power Dist Unit 1 Phase IEC	N	-	B	B	B	B	B	-	-	-	-	-	-	-	-	-	-	V5R1
5162 Power Dist Unit 2 of 3 Phase	N	-	B	B	B	B	B	-	-	-	-	-	-	-	-	-	-	V5R1
#5294 1.8m I/O Tower	Y	-	-	B	B	B	B	-	-	-	-	-	-	-	-	-	-	V5R2
5537 Alt IPL spec for 3580	Y	-	B	B	B	B	-	-	-	-	-	-	-	-	-	-	-	V4R5
5538 Alt IPL spec for DVD-RAM	Y	-	B	B	B	B	-	-	-	-	-	-	-	-	-	-	-	V4R5
5546 Sys Console 100 Mbps Token-Rng	Y	-	B	B	B	B	B	-	-	-	-	-	-	-	-	-	-	V5R1
#5548 System Console on 100 Mbps Ethernet	Y	-	B	B	B	B	B	-	-	-	-	-	-	-	-	-	-	V5R1
5599 No Save/Restore Device	-	-	B	B	B	B	-	-	-	-	-	-	-	-	-	-	-	V4R5
#5700 PCI 1 Gbps Ethernet IOA	Y	-	B	B	B	B	B	-	-	B	B	B	B	B	B	B	B	V5R2
#5701 PCI 1 Gbps Ethernet UTP IOA	Y	-	B	B	B	B	B	-	-	B	B	B	B	B	B	B	B	V5R2
#5702 PCI-X Ultra Tape Controller	Y	-	B	B	B	B	B	-	-	B	B	B	B	B	B	B	B	V5R2
6384 30 GB ¼-inch Cartridge Tape	Y	M	-	-	-	-	-	-	-	-	-	-	-	-	-	-	-	V4R5
6425 CD-ROM (CIF=Y in 5033)	N	-	-	-	-	-	-	S	-	-	-	-	-	-	-	-	-	V4R4
6484 30 GB ¼-inch Cartridge Tape (CIF=Y in 5033)	N	-	-	-	-	-	-	M	-	-	-	-	-	-	-	-	-	V4R5
#6818 17.54 GB 10k RPM Disk Unit (CIF=Y in 5033 and 250)	N	M	-	-	-	-	-	M	-	-	-	-	-	-	-	-	-	V4R4
#6831 1.6 GB Read Cache Device (CIF=Y in 5033 and 250)	N	S	-	-	-	-	-	S	-	-	-	-	-	-	-	-	-	V4R4
#7002 HSL Enabler	Y	-	B	-	-	-	-	-	-	-	-	-	-	-	-	-	-	V4R5
#7104 System Unit Expansion	Y	-	B	-	-	-	-	-	-	-	-	-	-	-	-	-	-	V4R5

Feature code and description	CIF	250	270	820	830	840	890	#503X	#5065	#5074	#5075	#5078	#5079	#8079	#8093	#9074	#9079	Min. OS/400
#7123 DASD Expansion Unit	Y	-	B	-	-	-	-	-	-	-	-	-	-	-	-	-	-	V4R5
#7127 DASD Expansion Unit	Y	-	-	B	-	-	-	-	-	-	-	-	-	-	-	-	-	V4R5
#7133 DASD Concurrent Maintenance Cage	N	-	B	-	-	-	-	-	-	-	-	-	-	-	-	-	-	V4R5
7500 Quantity 150 of #4314	Y	-	-	S	S	S	S	-	S	S	-	-	S	S	S	S	S	V4R5
7501 Quantity 150 of #4317	Y	-	-	B	B	B	S	-	M	B	-	-	B	B	B	B	B	V4R5
7502 Quantity 150 of #4318	Y	-	-	B	B	B	B	-	M	B	-	-	B	B	B	B	B	V4R5
7503 Quantity 150 of #4324	Y	-	-	S	S	S	S	-	S	S	-	-	S	S	S	S	S	V4R5
7504 Quantity 150 of #4319	Y	-	-	B	B	B	B	-	-	B	-	-	B	B	B	B	B	V5R1
8079 Opt Base 1.8 M I/O Rack	Y	-	-	-	-	P	-	-	-	-	-	-	-	-	-	-	-	V4R5
8093 Opt Base 1.8 M I/O Rack	Y	-	-	-	-	-	P	-	-	-	-	-	-	-	-	-	-	V5R2
9002 Dual Line Cord Enabler	N	-	-	P	-	-	-	-	-	-	-	-	-	-	-	-	-	V5R1
9057 Storage Exp Unit	N	-	-	-	B	B	-	-	-	-	-	-	-	-	-	-	-	V4R5
9074 Base I/O Enclosure	Y	-	-	-	B	-	-	-	-	-	-	-	-	-	-	-	-	V4R5
#9079 Base I/O Tower	Y	-	-	-	-	B	-	-	-	-	-	-	-	-	-	-	-	V4R5
#9094 Base PCI I/O Enclosure	Y	-	-	-	-	-	P	-	-	-	-	-	-	-	-	-	-	V5R2
9301 Upgraded 30-Disk Expansion	N	-	-	-	-	M	-	-	-	-	-	-	-	-	-	-	-	V4R5
#9330 PCI Integrated Expansion Unit	N	-	-	-	-	-	-	S	-	-	-	-	-	-	-	-	-	V4R4
#9691 Base Bus Adapter	Y	-	-	-	-	-	-	-	-	M	-	M	M	B	B	B	B	V4R5
#9730 Base HSL-2 Ports - 4 Copper	Y	-	-	-	-	-	P	-	-	-	-	-	-	-	-	-	-	V5R2
#9732 Base HSL Ports - 8 Copper	Y	-	-	-	B	-	-	-	-	-	-	-	-	-	-	-	-	V4R5
#9733 Base HSL Ports - 8 Copper	Y	-	-	-	B	-	-	-	-	-	-	-	-	-	-	-	-	V4R5
#9737 Base HSL Ports - 16 Copper	Y	-	-	-	-	B	-	-	-	-	-	-	-	-	-	-	-	V4R5
#9739 Base Optical Bus Adapter	Y	-	-	-	-	-	-	-	-	B	-	B	B	B	B	B	B	V5R1
#9748 Base PCI RAID Disk Unit Controller	Y	-	-	-	S	S	-	-	-	-	-	-	-	-	-	-	-	V4R5
#9752 Base HSL Ports - 8 Copper	Y	-	-	-	P	-	-	-	-	-	-	-	-	-	-	-	-	V5R1
#9755 Base HSL Ports - 16 Copper	Y	-	-	-	-	P	-	-	-	-	-	-	-	-	-	-	-	V5R1

Feature code and description	CIF	Model or tower																Min. OS/400
		250	270	820	830	840	890	#503X	#5065	#5074	#5075	#5078	#5079	#8079	#8093	#9074	#9079	
9758 Base HSL Ports - 2 Opt/6 Copper	-	-	-	-	B	-	-	-	-	-	-	-	-	-	-	-	-	V5R1
#9759 Base HSL Ports - 4 Optical/12 Copper	-	-	-	-	-	B	-	-	-	-	-	-	-	-	-	-	-	V5R1
#9767 Base PCI Disk Unit Controller	Y	-	P	P	-	-	-	-	-	-	-	S	-	-	-	-	-	V4R5
#9771 Base PCI Two-Line WAN with integrated modem	Y	S	P	P	P	P	P	-	-	-	-	-	-	-	-	-	-	V4R5
#9774 Base HSL Ports - 2 Optical/6 Copper	-	-	-	-	B	-	-	-	-	-	-	-	-	-	-	-	-	V5R1
#9777 Base HSL Ports - 8 Copper	N	-	-	-	P	-	-	-	-	-	-	-	-	-	-	-	-	V5R1
#9778 Base PCI RAID Disk Unit Controller	Y	-	-	-	B	B	-	-	-	-	-	-	-	-	-	-	-	V5R1
#9789 Base HSL Ports - 4 Optical	Y	-	-	-	-	-	P	-	-	-	-	-	-	-	-	-	-	V5R2
#9793 Two-Line WAN IOA with Modem	Y	-	P	P	P	P	P	-	-	-	-	-	-	-	-	-	-	V5R2
#9794 Two-Line IOA with Modem	Y	-	P	P	P	P	P	-	-	-	-	-	-	-	-	-	-	V5R2
#9887 Base HSL-2 Bus Adapter	Y	-	-	-	-	-	B	-	-	-	-	-	-	-	-	-	-	V5R2
#9943 Base PCI IOP	Y	-	-	-	B	B	B	-	-	B	-	B	B	B	B	B	B	V4R5

Software

23

i5/OS: Architecture

The iSeries operating system is architected as a single entity. This means that such facilities as relational database, communication and networking capabilities, online help, Web enablement technologies, easy enterprise management, and much more are fully integrated into the operating system and the machine. The user communicates with all components of i5/OS using a single command language Control Language (CL) or administers and manages the system using a graphical user interface (GUI).

i5/OS provides the industry's foremost application flexibility with support for iSeries, Linux, Windows 2000, Java, and UNIX applications. It combines high availability with superior workload management and logical partitioning. The next generation of applications can be quickly deployed and managed in a single, partitioned server alongside current business applications.

With i5/OS, a business can simply and rapidly deploy applications for On Demand Business with seamless integration of existing applications and data. With extensions to its robust security and networking options, i5/OS enables business-to-business (B2B) connectivity through the supply chain and to clients.

499

This chapter describes the capabilities and enhancements integrated into the iSeries operating system which enable iSeries as servers in a network-centric design. Features of the operating system product itself are described in "i5/OS (5722-SS1): Operating system licensed products" on page 547.

i5/OS base functions

> **Note:** i5/OS V5R3 is the required operating system release level for all @server i5 servers. i5/OS V5R3, OS/400 V5R2 and earlier releases are supported on earlier iSeries servers. See "i5/OS overview" on page 549 and "Summary of today's iSeries" on page 79 for further information.

i5/OS is a 64-bit operating system. With its base function, i5/OS provides ease of implementation, management, and operation in one totally integrated object-oriented operating system. The integrated features are:

▶ Advanced GUI support to provide for:

– Easy setup and management of the system, including TCP/IP functions
– Database functions
– User and printer job administration
– System management
– Software distribution
– Performance monitoring
– Centralized management of multiple systems
– Plug-in support for Domino, Backup Recovery and Media Services (BRMS), and others

▶ Network computing

▶ IFS with industry standards

▶ Multiple operating environments and logical partitions (LPARs)

– Different versions and releases of i5/OS and OS/400
– Linux
– AIX 5L
– OS/400 Portable Application Solutions Environment (PASE)
– Resource sharing

▶ Clustering and shared resources
▶ High system availability
▶ Client/server connectivity
▶ DB2 Universal Database (UDB) for iSeries
▶ Transaction processing
▶ Batch processing

- Extensive run-time applications
- Openness standards
- PM eServer iSeries
- Electronic Customer Support (ECS)
- Comprehensive security for system resources
- Interfaces to system functions
- Connectivity to remote devices, systems, and networks
- Office services
- National language versions and multilingual support

Each function of i5/OS follows a consistent design philosophy. This consistency is one of the cornerstones of iSeries ease of use. Ease-of-use translates into higher productivity for its users and easier systems management.

The cornerstone functions are highlighted next.

iSeries Navigator

i5/OS has an extensive GUI that provides visualization, wizards, and integration for simplicity of advanced operations from both PCs and pervasive or mobile devices. Operating your server has never been this simple.

> **Note:** Prior to V5R2 of OS/400, iSeries Navigator was known as *Operations Navigator.*

Management Central-Pervasive

Management Central-Pervasive offers a leading-edge capability to manage multiple systems via an Internet-capable phone, personal digital assistant (PDA), or Web browser.

DB2 Universal Database

For iSeries servers with OS/400 Version 4 or later, the system price includes OS/400 at no additional charge. The full function robust commercial database, DB2 UDB for iSeries, is also included at no additional cost. The operating system and the database do not have user-based charges. This provides for an effective return on investment with no surprise fees for additional users.

Logical partitioning and server consolidation

With dynamic and granular logical partitioning, i5/OS makes it easy to manage multiple applications in a single server. Logical partitioning supports multiple i5/OS and OS/400 releases, Linux, and AIX 5L. A server consolidation focus allows multiple copies of i5/OS, OS/400, Linux, and AIX 5L on a single system. This reduces or eliminates initial program load (IPL) requirements when changing LPAR configurations and resources.

The iSeries can now provide a storage area network for directly attached Windows 2000 and Windows 2003 servers.

Clustering and high availability

High availability options include faster, less expensive system-to-system clustering options and the ability to switch applications, data, and resources between multiple iSeries servers. Cross-site mirroring (XSM), new with i5/OS V5R3, extends mirrored support for independent auxiliary storage pools (IASPs) to geographically distant servers.

High-speed link (HSL) OptiConnect is much faster and lower cost than System Products Division (SPD) OptiConnect. Switchable disk with switchable IASPs offers a way to switch applications and data to a backup system to keep the data constantly available.

i5/OS Version 5 Release 3 (V5R3) supports output queues, some operating system objects, and integrated file systems (IFS) in the IASPs.

TCP/IP

On Demand Business runs on Transmission Control Protocol/Internet Protocol (TCP/IP). iSeries TCP/IP is rich in function and is designed for high performance and ease of use. Dynamic Domain Name System and Network Quality of Service are among the features supported.

Wireless capabilities

This built-in feature enables B2B solutions and connects mobile devices to core business solutions with Extensible Markup Language (XML) enablers built into i5/OS.

OS/400 PASE

OS/400 PASE offers improved enablement for porting UNIX applications to the iSeries server. OS/400 PASE now provides 64-bit support for AIX 5L Version 5.2.

OS/400 Directory Services

OS/400 Directory Services supports IBM SecureWay® Directory Version 3.2. It provides distributed functions support for products such as WebSphere, Policy Director, MQSeries, Meta-Directory, and HTTP Server.

Internet Printing Protocol

Internet Printing Protocol (IPP) provides Web-enabled worldwide print support.

Linux for iSeries

Linux enables a stream of applications for On Demand Business to complement the strengths of the iSeries as an integrated core business solution. Linux inherits important strengths and reliability features of the iSeries architecture.

i5/OS is enhanced to support Linux running in a secondary LPAR. The primary partition must run OS/400 V5R1 or later. Up to 31 Linux partitions are supported, depending on the iSeries model. The @server i5 Models 520, 550, 570 and 595 running i5/OS support from 2 to 254 partitions based on the model.

Processor features for iSeries Model 270, 800, 810, 820, and 840 servers using SSTAR technology, Models 825, 870, and 890 using POWER4 technology, and @server i5 Models 520, 550, 570, and 595 POWER5 technology-based processors, allow Linux to run in a shared processor pool, where one processor can be shared between four IBM i5/OS, OS/400, and Linux partitions. On n-way processor features for iSeries Models 820, 830, and 840 servers with ISTAR technology, Linux requires a minimum of one processor per Linux partition.

The iSeries extends support for Linux on the Integrated xSeries Server, feature #4811/#4812/#4813/#9812/#9813.

RedHat 3 supports the #2792, #2892, #4710, #4810, #9710, and #9792 Integrated xSeries Server features, as well as the 1519 Integrated xSeries Adapter models 100 and 200.

SUSE LINUX Enterprise Server (SLES) 8 is not supported on the #4710, #9710, #4810, #2792, #9792, #2892 Integrated xSeries Server features. SLES 8 does support the 1519 Integrated xSeries Adapter models 100 and 200.

The 2 GHz Intel Pentium Integrated xSeries Server is offered as a uniprocessor Intel Server to support Linux applications within the packaging of an @server i5 server.

For details about supported operating systems and xSeries models, refer to the Web site:

`http://www.ibm.com/servers/eserver/iseries/integratedxseries`

Models x346, x236, x445, x440, x365, x360 and x235 are supported on OS/400 V5R2 or later when using the following Linux operating system versions:

► Red Hat Enterprise Linux 3.0 ES Edition
► Red Hat Enterprise Linux 3.0 AS Edition
► SLES 8

New with i5/OS V5R3 Linux for iSeries

Linux for iSeries is enhanced with i5/OS V5R3 with such features as the following:

► Linux partition management with iSeries Navigator support for:
  – Starting and shutting down a server
  – Creating and deleting a disk
  – Linking and unlinking disk drives to the server

► Enhanced grid participation via IBM Grid Toolbox V3 for Linux on iSeries (5733-GD1)

Linux on the iSeries can be implemented as either hosted or non-hosted. In a hosted environment, Linux uses virtual resources (such as disk, tape, CD-ROM, and LAN), which are owned by an i5/OS partition and shared with the i5/OS partition. Linux is started from the hosting i5/OS partition by varying on a network server description (NWSD).

The NWSD is used to control the LPAR functions. LPAR can only be active when the server is active and not in a restricted state. When i5/OS is in a restricted state, all NWSDs are automatically varied off.

An i5/OS partition can host multiple LPARs subject to appropriate capacity planning.

In a non-hosted environment, the Linux partition does not depend on a hosting i5/OS partition for any input/output (I/O) resources. The LPAR has its own disk units or the partition uses networking support to perform a network start.

You can start a non-hosted LPAR can be started even if the primary partition is not fully active. You can start it from the Work with Partitions Status display. The non-hosted LPAR has its own resources defined to it.

> **Note:** Linux is not part of i5/OS or OS/400. Therefore, it must have its own partition of the system processor resources segregated from i5/OS and OS/400.

Virtual I/O in a Linux partition

Virtual I/O resources are devices owned by the hosting i5/OS partition that provides I/O function to the LPAR. The @server i5 or iSeries Linux kernel and i5/OS supports several different kinds of virtual I/O resources:

- ► Virtual console

  Virtual console provides console function for the LPAR through an i5/OS partition. Using virtual console allows the installation program to communicate with the user prior to networking resources being configured.

- ► Virtual disk unit

  A virtual disk unit provides access to virtual disks for Linux. The Create Network Server Storage Space (CRTNWSSTG) command creates a storage space to be used by a network server, in this case the Linux partition. The Linux installation program reformats the disk for Linux or you can use Linux commands, such as `fdisk` and `mke2fs`, to format the disk for Linux.

- ► Virtual CD

  A virtual CD is needed to support the installation of Linux. By default, a Linux partition can see all CD drives on the host LPAR. You can restrict Linux from accessing some or all of those drives.

- ► Virtual tape

  Virtual tape provides access to the i5/OS tape drive from an LPAR. By default, an LPAR can see all tape drives on the host partition. You can restrict Linux from accessing some or all of those drives.

- ► Virtual Ethernet

  Virtual Ethernet provides the same function as using a 1 Gbps Ethernet adapter. An LPAR can use virtual Ethernet to establish multiple high speed inter-partition connections. i5/OS or OS/400 and Linux partitions can communicate with each other using TCP/IP over the virtual Ethernet communication ports.

Directly attached I/O in a Linux partition

With directly attached I/O, Linux manages the hardware resources directly. All I/O resources are under the control of the Linux operating system.

Disk units, tape devices, optical devices, and LAN adapters can all be allocated to an LPAR that is running Linux. A NWSD is necessary to install Linux in an partition. After Linux is installed, the partition can be configured to start independently. For directly attached hardware, all failure and diagnostic messages are displayed within the LPAR.

With direct I/O, devices are owned by Linux. i5/OS or OS/400 does not see the devices and cannot directly use them. Since Linux does not support input/output processors (IOPs), they are not used with direct I/O. Refer to "AIX and Linux Direct Attach features overview" on page 340 for a list of Linux Direct Attach features.

The Linux console is a PC connected to the iSeries primary or hosting partition via a TCP/IP LAN. Operations Console with LAN Connectivity (a function of iSeries Access) is required to establish a secure connection to i5/OS. A Telnet environment is then used to connect into the Linux environment through the Virtual Ethernet. The console is used for installation and problem determination operations. There is no console adapter in the Linux partition.

The @server i5 servers, based on IBM POWER5 technology, are capable of running POWER Linux distributions.Linux for iSeries is available directly from Linux distributors, as well as product upgrades, support, and maintenance. Red Hat and Novell offer the following Linux distributions for the @server i5.

► Red Hat

   Red Hat Enterprise Linux AS 3, based on the 2.4 version of the 64-bit kernel supports the @server i5 and the earlier iSeries servers.

► SUSE

   – SUSE LINUX Enterprise Server 9 (based on the 2.6 version of the 64-bit Linux kernel) supports the eServer i5 and the earlier iSeries servers.

   – SUSE LINUX Enterprise Server 8, uses the 2.4 kernel, and supports the earlier iSeries servers and Integrated xSeries Adapter attach.

> **Note:** When an iSeries server or processor upgrade is ordered, Red Hat Enterprise Linux AS 3 (5639-RDH) can be ordered through IBM.

Linux integration with i5/OS

The following products help to integrate Linux and the iSeries:

► iSeries Open Database Connection (ODBC) driver for Linux

   Linux programs written to the ODBC interface can access DB2 UDB for iSeries databases via an ODBC driver for Linux. The ODBC driver is called to carry out database requests. These requests are sent to the iSeries for processing via the database host server over an IP connection.

   For further information and to download the product, go to:

   `http://www-1.ibm.com/servers/eserver/iseries/linux/odbc/`

► iSeries Access for Linux

   iSeries Access for Linux offers Linux-based access to iSeries servers. It allows you to access the DB2 UDB for iSeries using its ODBC driver and to establish a 5250 session to an iSeries server from a Linux client.

   For more information and to download the product, see:

   `http://www-1.ibm.com/servers/eserver/iseries/access/linux/`

- Grid Toolbox V3 for Linux on iSeries (5733-GD1)

  Grid Toolbox V3 for Linux on iSeries assists enterprises that deploy, manage, and control grid computing. It also assists developers who create products that assist in managing and deploying grids.

  For further information, see:

  http://www.alphaworks.ibm.com/tech/gridtoolbox

- DB2 UDB Workgroup Server Edition for Linux (5733-LD1)

  DB2 UDB Workgroup Server Edition for Linux is a database designed for the small business or department involving a small number of internal users. It is available only on the 520, 570, 810, 825, 870 and 890 Enterprise Editions (otherwise orderable via Passport Advantage®).

  For more information, see:

  http://www-306.ibm.com/software/data/db2/udb/edition-wse.html

- WebSphere Application Server Express for Linux (5733-WL1)

  WebSphere Application Server Express for Linux is a tightly integrated development tool and application server that provides an easily affordable entry point to On Demand Business for companies creating dynamic Web sites. It is available on the 570, 810, 825, 870, and 890 Enterprise Editions (otherwise orderable via Passport Advantage).

Suggested reading

For additional information about Linux, see the following Web site:

http://www.ibm.com/eserver/iseries/linux

XML enablers

IBM has committed the iSeries server to support XML. This support is demonstrated by the suite of XML application enablers delivered with i5/OS, providing a core of XML services for applications to build on.

XML is a key technology for B2B solutions that links together trading partners and pervasive computing applications, which connect mobile devices such as cell phones to core business solutions.

The XML application enablers provided in i5/OS include:

- XML parsers for use with Java and C++ applications

  XML parsers are a common building block that XML-based solutions use to work with data in XML format.

- XML parsing interfaces for procedural languages such as RPG, COBOL, and C

  These interfaces open the realm of XML to existing solutions, providing an easy path to extend these solutions with XML support.
- An XSL processor used to apply XSL stylesheets to transform an XML document into another markup language format

  XSL stylesheets are the standard way to convert data between two XML document types. They are commonly used to convert XML data to HTML for presentation in a Web browser environment.

iSeries system support for XML is delivered through IBM XML Toolkit for iSeries (5733-XT1). See "XML Toolkit for iSeries (5733-XT1)" on page 656 for more information.

IBM Java for iSeries

Java is a key application development environment for the iSeries server. The Java virtual machine (JVM), which resides below the iSeries Layer, enables fast interpretation and execution of Java code on the iSeries servers. A *class transformer* enables the direct execution of Java on the system without the overhead of interpretation.

Java is a complete computing environment, reaching new standards for program portability and programmer productivity. Java provides an object-oriented programming environment that is dramatically simpler than C++. iSeries Java implementation provides improved scalability compared to other Java platforms and synergy with the iSeries object-based architecture.

Because of its portability, Java is the programming language for On Demand Businesses. And the iSeries system support for Java is the best of breed.

Components

Java support on the iSeries is delivered in the following components:

- IBM Developer Kit for Java (5722-JV1)
- IBM Toolbox for Java (5722-JC1)

Both are included with every i5/OS V5R3 and OS/400 order of V5R2. See "IBM Toolbox for Java (5722-JC1)" on page 638 and "IBM Developer Kit for Java (5722-JV1)" on page 639 for product information.

Solutions and benefits

A Java-compatible JVM is integrated under the iSeries machine interface (MI) to optimize Java software performance. Java programs are compiled into

platform-independent object code interpreted by the run-time support (JVM) on each platform.

Remote method invocation (RMI) is built into the iSeries Java software. IBM Toolbox for Java can run on any platform to access iSeries data. Data in XML format is a key requirement for developing mobile, heterogeneous solutions for On Demand Business.

Features

Java support includes these primary functions and capabilities:

▶ An Object-Oriented Programming Language, developed at Sun Microsystems

▶ A JVM that is integrated in the i5/OS operating system

▶ A Java "static compilation" option, designed for improved performance, that compiles Java into iSeries-dependent object code

Java's primary benefit is its ability to develop portable applications using the Internet and intranets, whose "objects" can run on many different platforms in the same network.

▶ A Java Secure Sockets Layer (SSL) package that is included with i5/OS to leverage the integrated SSL function built into the iSeries server

You can easily build more secure distributed applications using Java. All data exchanged between the tiers on the multiple platforms can be encrypted using the SSL protocol.

▶ SQL embedded in the Java programming language at V5R1 and later

Supported SQL statements include SQL data-manipulation statements to operate on data stored in tables in relational databases.

i5/OS integrated functions

The following sections explain the functions that are integrated into the i5/OS operating system.

NetServer: File and print serving

iSeries NetServer is an operating system function that is used to satisfy file and print serving needs for end users. NetServer unites the IFS and iSeries output queues into the Microsoft Network Neighborhood. User benefits include better control of user visibility to resources, for example. The only directories or printers that can be seen by end users are those set up as "shared" by an administrator or resource owner.

Desktop users can fully satisfy their file and print serving needs through the iSeries NetServer function. Therefore, the file and print serving functions facilitated with other iSeries Client Access clients are removed from the Express client. To use the iSeries NetServer, only the client for Microsoft Networks (shipped with Microsoft 32-bit operating systems) is required. Current supported clients are Windows NT, Windows 2000, Windows XP and Windows Server 2003, and a Linux/Samba client.

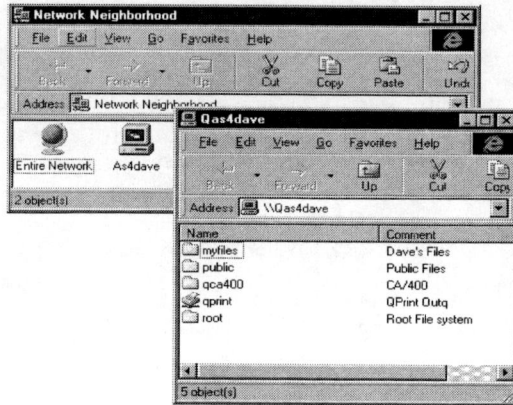

iSeries NetServer file and printer "shares" are easy to create, locate, and manage by using the iSeries Navigator printer list and IFS list. The current file shares can be listed separately to make it easy to explore the contents of a file share or map a drive to it. File shares support CCSID-to-CCSID conversion.

Features

▶ iSeries NetServer can operate as the *Logon Server* for Windows clients. i5/OS can authenticate logging onto Windows, provide the home directory, and log on scripts to the Windows user. In addition, you can store and retrieve Windows user profiles, including Desktop, Start Menu, Favorites, and policies, from an iSeries server. A separate networked Windows 2000 or Windows 2003 server is no longer needed.

▶ The iSeries Navigator provides an enhanced management of users, including managing disabled user profiles with menus. Application programming interfaces (APIs) are also available.

▶ A Windows-compatible 128-character password and NTLMV2 password hash are now supported.

▶ User IDs longer than 10 characters are truncated (to 10 characters) instead of being rejected when checking for an iSeries user ID.

▶ An iSeries NetServer Setup wizard within iSeries Navigator helps you set up your iSeries NetServer. This wizard can also help to configure logon support.

▶ You can access of files larger than 2 GB in the IFS.

- Using iSeries Navigator and APIs, a new session identifier allows better management and tracking of iSeries NetServer sessions. This is extremely important in a Windows Terminal Serving environment where many users have sessions through a single Windows system. You can end sessions or observe properties on single sessions rather than all the sessions coming from a single system.

- Windows NT Background services can access the iSeries NetServer without user intervention.

- Printer Shares can be published in Directory Services (Lightweight Directory Access Protocol (LDAP)) for use by Windows 2000 systems using *Active Directory* to find printers.

- iSeries support for the Windows Network Neighborhood program complies with the Common Internet File System (CIFS) standard currently proposed by Microsoft.

For additional information, refer to:

`http://www.ibm.com/servers/eserver/iseries/netserver`

Network printing support

Distributed print support provides a connection to local area network (LAN)-attached ASCII printers and support for Advanced Function printers. The iSeries server provides a seamless path for clients to direct printed output through an iSeries network and to other print servers. You can use Systems Network Architecture (SNA) or TCP/IP protocols (line printer requester/line printer daemon (LPR/LPD)) to transport the spooled file and its attributes to the remote system.

This integrated i5/OS function supports the printing of text, images, graphics, barcodes, electronic forms, multiple fonts, logos, signatures, and more. These formats provide the basis for business solutions such as business reports, preprinted forms, customer statements and invoices, and letters. Double byte character set (DBCS) documents that enable printing of Chinese, Korean, Japanese, or Thai characters are also supported.

i5/OS supports IBM and non-IBM printers, which vary in price, function, speed, and use.

Host print transform

Most printers are designed to work with a specific data stream. i5/OS includes a function to automatically transform the program-generated data stream to that required by the printer to which it is sent. It is not necessary for the application to generate the correct data stream. The system automatically transforms it as necessary at print time.

Customization objects are provided for over 125 popular IBM and non-IBM ASCII printers, such as Hewlett Packard PCL, Lexmark PPDS, and HP LaserJet TIFF Packbit. An API brings the capabilities of Host Print Transform to the iSeries application developer.

Printer load balancing

Local and remote output queues permit more than one active writer, allowing spooled output on one output queue to be printed on multiple printers. In addition, you can place a limit on the size of spooled files printed during a specified time period. With these features, large print jobs can be deferred to print during non-peak hours.

Communication and networking

This section discusses the communications and networking features.

Connectivity to remote devices, systems, and networks

i5/OS offers many integrated capabilities and functions that enable communications with a variety of IBM and non-IBM systems, either in batch or interactive modes. This integrated connectivity function provides client solutions by enhancing the integration of business systems. Worldwide standard TCP/IP or the traditional SNA hierarchy, as well as SNA peer networks and Systems Application Architecture® (SAA®) standards, are supported and offer the greatest flexibility possible in network design.

For a list of supported networks, communication facilities, and protocols, see Appendix A, "Referenced lists" on page 749.

Other communication facilities are available as licensed programs, such as IBM Communications Utilities for iSeries (5722-CM1). See Chapter 30, "IBM licensed programs: Networking and communications products" on page 657, for further information.

TCP/IP Utilities (5722-TC1) is included with i5/OS (although not part of i5/OS) from OS/400 V3R1 onward and automatically ships with each order of i5/OS. TCP/IP Utilities include applications such as Telnet, File Transfer Protocol (FTP), support for Domain Name system, and many others. For more information about TCP, see "IBM TCP/IP Connectivity Utilities for iSeries (5722-TC1)" on page 560.

Network management facilities

Several communications and systems management functions are available to manage iSeries servers. Some are integrated into i5/OS, and some are separately-priced features. These functions help manage and control local

systems and distributed systems that operate within a network controlled by a host system or by another iSeries server.

Network management functions available for the iSeries server include:

► Systems management in TCP/IP networks
► Alerts support to NetView®, System/36, System/38, iSeries
► Distributed System Node Executive (DSNX)

Security

The many levels of security available with i5/OS eases the job of system security management. The five levels of security range from minimal to an enhanced level that enables the iSeries servers to operate at the C2 level of trust as defined by the United States Government. Security foundation offered with i5/OS includes system integrity with digital signature and object signing, a Digital Certificate Manager (DCM), and password protection.

The base level of security is set simply by using a system value, as shown in the following table.

Security level	Description	Use of this level	Considerations
10	Minimal security	No passwords are used.	Any user can perform any function.
20	Password security	Passwords are used to provide access to the system.	Any user can perform any function once they are signed on.
30	Resource security	Passwords are required and object usage can be controlled.	Users can be restricted to specific functions.
40	Resource security and operating system integrity	Passwords are required and object usage can be controlled. Users can be restricted to specific functions.	Using unsupported interfaces is restricted.
50	Enhanced resource security and operating system integrity*	Passwords are required and object usage can be controlled. Users can be restricted to specific functions. Using unsupported interfaces is restricted.	Parameter validation into the operating system and restrictions on use of user domain objects. A security journal is provided that logs all security violations.

* Enables iSeries servers to operate at the C2 level of trust as defined by the U.S. Government. Refer to publication DOD 5200.28-STD, "Department of Defense Trusted Computer System Evaluation Criteria" (Orange Book), for details about the U.S. Government definition of C2 trust level.

i5/OS is distributed with the security level set to 40.

See *Tips and Tools for Securing Your iSeries*, SC41-5300, for information about iSeries security implementation.

Network security

i5/OS includes many ways to secure network connections and transactions between other servers and clients. The strategic methods include:

▶ Secure Sockets Layer

SSL has become the industry standard for enabling applications for secure communication sessions over an unprotected network such as the Internet. SSL involves two protocols:

– *Record protocol*: This protocol controls the flow of the data between the two endpoints of an SSL session.

– *Handshake protocol*: This protocol authenticates one or both endpoints of the SSL session and establishes a unique symmetric key, which is used to generate keys to encrypt and decrypt data for that SSL session.

▶ Digital Certificate Management

A digital certificate is an electronic credential to establish proof of identity in an electronic transaction. Digital certificates are increasingly used to provide enhanced network security measures. They are essential to configure and use the SSL to secure connections between users and server applications across an untrusted network, such as the Internet, by protecting such key data as user names and passwords. Many iSeries services and applications (including FTP, Telnet, and HTTP Server for iSeries) provide SSL support to ensure data privacy.

i5/OS provides extensive digital certificate support to use digital certificates as credentials with SSL or for client authentication in both SSL and virtual private network (VPN) transactions. Digital certificates can also sign objects, making it possible to detect changes or possible tampering to object contents.

The Digital Certificate Manager allows the creation and management of certificates on the iSeries and those obtained from another Certificate Authority (CA).

▶ Enterprise Identity Mapping (EIM)

EIM for iSeries is the i5/OS implementation of an IBM infrastructure intended to solve the problem of managing multiple user registries across an enterprise. The need for multiple user registries evolves into a large administrative problem that affects users, administrators, and application developers. EIM enables inexpensive solutions for easier management of multiple user registries and user identities in your enterprise.

EIM allows the creation of a system of identity mappings called associations, between the various user identities in various user registries for a person in

your enterprise. It also provides a common set of APIs. They can be used to develop applications that use these identity mappings to look up the relationships between user identities across platforms.

In conjunction with network authentication service, the i5/OS implementation of Kerberos, EIM provides an SSO environment that is managed and configured though iSeries Navigator.

► Network Authentication Service

Network Authentication Service allows the iSeries server and several iSeries services, such as iSeries Access for Windows, to use a Kerberos ticket as an optional replacement for a user name and password for authentication. The Kerberos protocol, developed by Massachusetts Institute of Technology (MIT), allows a principal (a user or service) to prove its identity to another service within an unsecure network. Authentication of principals is completed through a centralized server called a Kerberos server or key distribution center (KDC).

► Virtual private networking

VPN allows a company to extend its private intranet securely over the existing framework of a public network, such as the Internet. It controls network traffic while providing important security features such as authentication and data privacy.

i5/OS VPN is an optionally-installable component of iSeries Navigator. It allows the creation of a secure end-to-end path between any combination of host and gateway. i5/OS VPN uses authentication methods, encryption algorithms, and other precautions to ensure that data sent between the two endpoints of its connection remains secure.

► IP filtering and Network Address Translation (NAT)

IP filtering and NAT act as a firewall to protect internal network from intruders. With IP filtering, IP traffic is controlled by filtering packets according to rules that are user-defined. NAT allows the hiding of unregistered private IP addresses behind a set of registered IP addresses. This serves to protect internal networks from outside networks. NAT also alleviates the IP address depletion problem, since many private addresses can be represented by a small set of registered addresses.

DB2 Universal Database for iSeries

DB2 UDB for iSeries offers state-of-the-art database functions and open systems, standards-based technology, while providing the maturity, stability, and ease of use that is the trademark of the iSeries server. It is not a separate product. DB2 UDB for iSeries is fully integrated into i5/OS software.

DB2 UDB for iSeries can be used for both transaction processing and *complex* decision support applications. Advanced parallel processing and advanced query optimization techniques support queries of large decision support databases for applications such as business-to-business, business-intelligence, customer relationship management (CRM), and other applications for On Demand Business.

In an on demand world, standards and globalization are important for integration and openness. Application portability through standards and the flexibility to access the database via numerous client interfaces from Linux partitions and Windows systems allows the application provider and the client the most flexibility possible.

DB2 UDB for iSeries embodies that flexibility through the support of its traditional database interface along with enhancing the Structured Query Language (SQL)-based database required by today's enterprise application systems. Enhancements to the RPQ SQL pre-compiler help clients and independent software vendors (ISVs) to more easily make use of both interfaces.

Features

► Object-relational technology

Object-relational technology with Large Object (LOB) and Data Link Support enables you to store and manage non-traditional data elements as a normal part of the database. DB2 UDB for iSeries can store and manipulate LOB data fields. An iSeries record with LOB fields can hold up to 2 GB of data. This improves the ability of DB2 UDB for iSeries to support applications that hold data such as very large text, image, and audio.

► DATALINK data type

For the DATALINK data type, actual data stored in the column is only a pointer to the object such as an image file, a voice recording, or a text file. You can store a Uniform Resource Locator (URL) to resolve to the object.

- DB2 UDB Extenders for iSeries

  DB2 UDB Extenders provide enablers to link and exchange data in XML and Text Extender documents with DB2 UDB. They also provide sophisticated text search capabilities.

  DB2 XML Extender allows you to convert your existing relational data into an XML document and vice-versa. DB2 Text Extender enables high-speed rich text and multimedia search and manipulation capabilities such as fuzzy searches and synonym searches.

- Advanced query optimization technologies

  Query optimization, including the IBM patented encoded vector indexing technology, enhances the performance of query and SQL processes.

- DB2 UDB family compatibility

  There is compatibility across the DB2 UDB family with such cross-family utilities as Data Propagator, DB2 OLAP, QMF™, and more.

- Database SQL portability

  DB2 UDB for iSeries adds Java to the list of languages in which stored procedures can be written. Additional languages supported are C, C++, Cobol, Rexx, Fortran, and PL1.

- National language support (NLS)

  Data in multiple national languages can reside in the same table. You can access it across distributed database platforms.

  NLS allows clients to interact with DB2 UDB for iSeries and store data in their preferred language, character set, and sort sequence. You can also store double-byte graphic characters and compare data in different character sets.

- User-defined types

  User-defined types are derived from existing predefined types such as integer and character. You can create your own data types for strong typing and for creating functions for different types. You can call a function for each row of a result set and return a value based on the user-defined data type.

- User-defined functions (UDF)

  SQL lets you define your own functions to use within SQL itself. This saves you time by reusing common building blocks that you develop yourself. UDFs are necessary building blocks to support the database extenders.

- Declarative referential integrity

  Declarative referential integrity provides SQL database integrity support intrinsic to the database, eliminating the need to code integrity constraints into each application program. This support ensures database consistency by preventing conflicting data from being entered into the database.

- ► Column-level security

    You can control access to individual table columns for each user. Row-level locking individual records (such as, records) are locked from simultaneous, conflicting access as appropriate to the type of processing being done. Using commitment control, the user can define a group of records all of whose locks are held until the user application declares a multiple-change transaction complete.

- ► Two-phase commit transaction management

- ► Data replication

- ► Open Database Connectivity (ODBC) driver for DB2 UDB for iSeries enhanced with ODBC 3.5 support and support for Microsoft Transaction Server (MTS)

    MTS support enables DB2 UDB for iSeries to participate in transactions involving two-phase commit coordinated through MTS. ODBC 3.5 support also delivers support for Unicode.

- ► System-wide database catalog

- ► Multiple-level concurrency control

    Multiple-level concurrency control provides read stability, cursor stability, uncommitted read, repeatable read, and no-commit isolation levels with row-level locking to support large numbers of users in complex application scenarios.

- ► Server consolidation

    Multiple DB2 UDB database images within a single instance of the operating system allows for application flexibility and server consolidation. It provides the ability for a single application to access multiple database instances with common database names.

- ► SQL enhancements

    - A major SQL enhancement is *Identity columns*. You can use them to generate artificial or surrogate key values by telling DB2 to auto-increment the column value as new rows are inserted into the table.

    - Support for unions in a view allows the user to shift some programming effort into DB2. Instead of forcing the user to remember to combine (union) all of the required tables, you can create a single SQL view to simplify this process.

    - The SQL procedural language used in the creation of SQL user-defined table functions (UDTF), UDFs, triggers and stored procedures is also enhanced in OS/400 V5R2 to improve DB2 UDB compatibility. Most significant is support for nested compound statements. They enable the

user to bundle related statements together into their own execution block within an SQL procedure, trigger, or function.

- Removal of the *Order By* restriction that required any column used to order/sort query results to be included in the results. Statement 3 is supported with OS/400 V5R2.

- SQL procedures, functions, and triggers no longer require licensed program product 5722-ST1 to be installed on the iSeries. Interactive SQL and embedded SQL require 5722-ST1 to function on the iSeries server.

► SQL Repeatable Read

A standard compliant isolation level, Repeatable Read support, is included in MQSeries for iSeries, a separately-licensed program, 5722-MQ1.

► Journaling and SQL DDL operation journaling (V5R1)

Open standards-based interoperability

Support for client/server environments is greatly enhanced in DB2 UDB for iSeries by incorporating popular database standards and transmission protocols, such as support for:

► ANSI X3.135.1999, ISO 9075-1999, and FIPS 127-2 SQL

► The Open Group's Distributed Relational Database Architecture™ (DRDA®) Distributed Unit of Work - Application Directed

► Microsoft's ODBC

► Apple's Data Access Language (DAL)

► XML

► JDBC

► Object Link Embedded (OLE) DB and ADO

► U.S. Government C2 security

► UCS-2 (Unicode or ISO 10646)

► Euro character support

► Stored procedures

► Triggers

► Join operators

► Enhanced SQL query support

X/Open's Call Level Interface (CLI) supported transmission protocols for the iSeries include:

- TCP/IP
- Advanced Program-to-Program Communication (APPC)
- Advanced Peer-to-Peer Networking® (APPN)
- X/Open Call Level Interface to SQL

The integrated database is a full-function database with features competitive to other widely used databases, reducing the need for a dedicated Database Administrator. The fact that the database is integrated allows the operating system to control some of its management functions and makes it easier to maintain than a competitive database. With security built-into i5/OS, DB2 UDB allows a better security model than other database where additional tools are purchased to provide the security functions.

The SQL Client Integration API allows providers of gateways and client/server solutions to integrate their products with DB2 UDB for iSeries. Many iSeries clients need applications that both access DB2 UDB for iSeries data, and access data on other databases platforms such as Oracle or Sybase.

Distributed database support

i5/OS supports distributed relational databases using SQL. Distributed database support allows read and write access from an iSeries server to another iSeries server or to any other database supporting the Open Group DRDA architecture, including DB2 UDB for OS/390® and z/OS®, DB2 UDB for Windows, and DB2 UDB for AIX.

DB2 Relational Connect, a feature of DB2 UDB for Windows and UNIX servers, allows access to additional databases such as Oracle, Microsoft SQL Server, and others. An iSeries server can connect to a system running DB2 Relational Connect to access data in the databases accessible by DB2 Relational Connect.

The CPI for database is SQL. The client's investment in data is protected by distributed support with data connectivity across platforms. Interactive access to distributed database is possible using the prompted facilities of interactive SQL (ISQL). This is available in DB2 Query Manager and SQL Development Kit for iSeries (5722-ST1), which is a separately licensed program.

High performance database server (centralized and distributed server)

The high performance iSeries server and improvements in communication performance combine to strengthen the position of the iSeries server as a high performance database server. In addition, DB2 UDB for iSeries offers enhanced

performance for both centralized and distributed client/server database access, making the iSeries the database server of choice for many computing needs.

The following DB2 UDB for iSeries functions are available to enhance application performance:

- Advanced SQL optimizer

  This optimizer converts SQL requests into optimally efficient database access methods, using proven mathematical rules and to query specific cost estimates. Optimal performance is maintained over time by the automatic rebind feature, which redetermines access methods based on changes to the database objects and statistics. The optimizer detects changes in the number of processors on each query. When processors are moved to an LPAR or when IBM @server Capacity Upgrade on Demand (CUoD) adds additional processors, the query plan is automatically re-optimized if necessary.

- SQL encoded vector indexes (EVIs)

  An EVI can be created through SQL and improve query performance, especially for long-running queries that run against large files using many selection criteria. An EVI has several advantages over a traditional index with the same keys, for example:

  - Precise statistics about the distribution of key values are automatically maintained and can be accessed quicker by the query optimizer than traditional indexes.

  - EVIs can be built much faster and take significantly less storage than traditional indexes. Less storage means less main storage is necessary to run the query.

  - The query optimizer can scan EVIs and dynamically build bitmaps quicker than from traditional indexes.

- Explain function

  The Explain function examines and reports the access method used by individual SQL queries. The output can be examined to determine whether the access method generated for the query can be improved by query or database changes.

- Block INSERT and FETCH

  Block Insert and Fetch provides applications with the ability to store and retrieve arrays of data directly, instead of one row at a time.

- Automatic record blocking

  An automatic recording blocking function improves client/server performance by returning rows to the client in blocks rather than individually. Subsequent

record access of the current block can then be performed locally at the client without accessing the server. This ability is provided for all isolation levels.

- ▶ Parallel data access

  Queries returning or requiring DB2 UDB for iSeries to process large amounts of data require significant I/O activity. Due to the iSeries' single-level store architecture, this data is often spread across many physical devices. The parallel data access feature allows multiple internal DB2 UDB for iSeries tasks to be activated for each physical device, allowing DB2 UDB for iSeries to transfer data from disk to memory faster than with the previous single task I/O architecture.

- ▶ Query Governor

  Long-running queries can have negative performance effects for other users of a database, so that a single query can consume an unusually large amount of resources, which negatively affects the performance of other users.

  The governor facility allows a time limit to be set for a query. Before the query is started, its run time is estimated. If the estimate exceeds the specified time limit, the query is not started. This is advantageous over similar functions on other databases that let the query run for a portion of time and then stop it since no unnecessary processing of the query occurs.

- ▶ Query tuning

  DB2 UDB for iSeries provides both iSeries Navigator graphical and programmatical CL command interfaces to help tune SQL queries. Users can dynamically control how DB2 UDB for iSeries is to optimize queries by changing a set of query attributes (such as the parallel degree characteristic). Both summary and detailed database performance monitors can be used to track and analyze SQL statement performance. A Visual Explain capability can be used to graphically show how a specific query has been optimized and can suggest indexes that may help performance.

- ▶ Scalability

  DB2 UDB for iSeries supports very large database environments. A single table can be up to one TB and 4.2 billion rows. Distributed tables can be up to 32 TB.

  DB2 Symmetric Multiprocessing (SMP) for iSeries and DB2 Multisystem support enable both horizontal and vertical growth.

Database ease of use and management

The iSeries' reputation for usability and maintainability is unsurpassed in the industry. This is due in part to the tight integration of i5/OS and DB2 UDB for iSeries. Users do not have to learn separate operating system and database functions, nor are they burdened with maintaining the complex interfaces

between multiple layers of software. In addition to seamless integration, a rich set of utilities continue to be provided for easy management of DB2 UDB for iSeries databases.

New with i5/OS V5R3 DB2 Universal Database for iSeries

► Enhancements that promote globalization and portability through adherence to standards:

 – UTF-8 and UTF-16 support within the database

 – SEQUENCE Object support enabled DB2 to handle key value (for example, order ID) generation on behalf of your application

 – EXCEPT/INTERSECT SQL set operators

 – New BINARY/VARBINARY data type support

 – More robust error handling with GET DIAGNOSTICS SQL statement

 – Encryption capabilities enhanced with DB2 Family Column Encryption functions

 – NATIVE Microsoft .NET provider

 – CLI column-wise binding

 – Availability of Materialized Query Tables (MQTs) as a technology preview with the ability to create and refresh MTQs

 – Additional SQL enhancements that satisfy ISO and ANSI standards

► Performance improvements to DB2 UDB for iSeries including:

 – Parallel Concurrent table reorganize

 – SQL Query Engine enhancements that have performance improvements on a variety of client queries

 – Star Join enhancements

 – Faster SQL deletes

 – Faster stored procedure call processing

 – On demand statistics generation

► Improved server consolidation and enterprise growth by increasing limits on the system and providing additional Migration Toolkits for moving data and queries from other databases; example of limits that increased are:

 – 1.7 TB tables
 – Partitioned table support
 – Larger decimal presision
 – 256 tables (members) in a view

Refer to "Summary of today's iSeries" on page 79 to see a source of documentation identifying these and other software limits for i5/OS.

Integrated file system

A file system provides the support to access specific segments of storage that are organized as logical units. These logical units on the iSeries server are files, directories, libraries, and objects.

Each file system has a set of logical structures and rules for interacting with information in storage. These structures and rules can be different from one file system to another. In fact, from the perspective of structures and rules, the i5/OS support for accessing database files and various other object types through libraries can be thought of as a file system. Similarly, the i5/OS support for accessing documents (which are really stream files) through the folders structure can be thought of as a separate file system.

The IFS is a part of i5/OS that lets you support stream input, output, and storage management similar to personal computer and UNIX operating systems. The IFS treats the library and folders support as separate file systems. Other types of file management support that have differing capabilities are also treated as separate file systems.

Supported file systems within the IFS are:

- **Network File System (NFS)**: This file system provides the user with access to data and objects that are stored on a remote NFS server. An NFS server can export an NFS that NFS clients then mount dynamically.

- **QDLS**: The document library services file system. This file system provides access to documents and folders.

- **QFileSvr.400**: The QFileSvr.400 file system provides access to other file systems that reside on remote iSeries servers.

- **QNetWare**: The QNetWare file system provides access to local or remote data and objects that are stored on a server that runs stand-alone PC servers running Novell NetWare. A user can dynamically mount NetWare file systems over existing local file systems.

- **QNTC**: QNTC is the Windows NT Server file system. This file system provides access to data and objects that are stored on a server running Windows NT 4.0 or later. It allows iSeries applications to use the same data as Windows NT clients. This includes access to the data on a Windows NT Server that is running on an Integrated PC Server (IPCS).

The QNTC file system lets you share data with servers that can communicate using the Windows NT LM 0.12 dialect.

The QNTC file system can communicate with Windows NT servers. This includes a stand-alone server and any Windows NT Application Processors (NTAP) servers running in the domain. See *IBM AS/400 Integration for Windows Server - Setup*, SC41-5439, for details.

> **Note**: The QNTC file system lets you share data with servers that can communicate using the Windows NT LM 0.12 dialect. The SMB server (iSeries support for Windows Network Neighborhood) does not use the Windows NT LM 0.12 dialect.

▶ **QOpenSys**: QOpenSys is the open systems file system. QOpenSys is compatible with UNIX-based open system standards, such as Portable Operating System Interface (POSIX) and XPG. Like the root file system, QOpenSys takes advantage of the stream file and directory support that is provided by the IFS. It also supports case-sensitive object names.

▶ **QOPT**: QOPT is the optical file system. QOPT provides access to stream data that is stored on optical media.

▶ **QSYS.LIB**: QSYS.LIB is the library file system. QSYS.LIB supports the iSeries library structure and provides access to database files and all of the iSeries object types that the library support manages.

▶ **root (/)**: "root" is the / file system. The root file system takes full advantage of the stream file support and hierarchical directory structure of the IFS. The root file system has the characteristics of a Disk Operating System (DOS) and OS/2® file systems.

▶ **UDFS**: User-defined file system (UDFS). The UDFS file system resides on an auxiliary storage pool (ASP). The user creates and manages the UDFS file system. Independent ASPs in V5R1 use the UDFS structure.

You can interact with any of the file systems through a common interface that includes commands, menus, displays, and APIs. The interface is optimized for the I/O of stream data, in contrast to the record I/O provided through the data management interfaces.

Features

▶ Is a hierarchical directory structure

▶ Provides support for storing information in stream files that can contain long continuous strings of data

- Is a common interface that allows users and applications to access not only the stream files, but also database files, documents, and other objects that are stored in the iSeries server
- Provides a common view of stream files that are stored locally on the iSeries server, an Integrated Netfinity Server for iSeries, or a remote Windows NT server
- User applications can store and manipulate stream file sizes up to 256 GB in the root (/), QOpenSys, and user-defined file systems
- Includes a set of 64-bit UNIX-type APIs and easy mapping of existing 32-bit UNIX-type APIs to 64-bit APIs
- Supports threadsafe IFS API interfaces to access objects in a multithreaded job
- Ability for text file I/O to convert between CCSIDs with characters of differing lengths
- Management of PC-created files (even read only files) through a command and API interfaces
- Ability to copy whole subtrees on the iSeries without using an interactive interface or user-written programming
- Program-to-program communication through file system objects via Pipes and First In First Out (FIFO) objects

  A *dev/null* character is useful for applications to discard output from sub-applications without changing the subapplication. The dev/null character special file can be written to forever, but is always empty when read.
- Stream I/O supports save files. This allows you to extract the contents of a save file, transport the save file through the network using stream file protocols, and place the contents back into another save file.
- File system APIs support parameters and buffers in teraspace for large I/O operations.
- Deadlock detection helps diagnose applications with a conflict in locking order.

Benefits

The IFS offers the following benefits:

- Fast access to i5/OS data
- Efficient handling of stream data, including images, audio, and video
- A file system and directory base to support UNIX-based open system standards, such is POSIX and XPG

- ► File management through a common interface
- ► Consistent use of object names and associated object information across national languages

New with i5/OS V5R3 IFS

A new security page sets scanning settings for objects created in files and folders. It also specifies auditing value, change options, user ID, and primary group ID.

- ► Ability to make objects savable
- ► Ability to set objects created in a folder to be scanned
- ► Restrict rename and unlink
- ► UDFS enhancements
  - – Ability to set objects to be scanned
  - – Can restrict rename and unlink
  - – Ability to specify a default file format for UDFS
  - – Unable to change user and group ID settings on a mounted UDFS

Ease of installation, use, and maintenance with i5/OS

i5/OS is renowned for its ease-of-use and management. Some of these utilities contributing to this notoriety include:

- ► iSeries Navigator database (Database Navigator)

The iSeries Navigator database is a graphical interface that you can use to perform many common administrative database options. From iSeries Navigator you can create, change, delete, move, and copy database objects. You can enter data into tables, view table contents, run SQL scripts, graphically display the relationships of your database objects, graphically display your query optimization with Visual Explain, monitor database performance, and perform other database management tasks.

The iSeries Navigator is enhanced with a Database Navigator interface that displays the relationship among relational objects such as tables, views, and indexes. Another enhancement to the iSeries Navigator interface is the ability to generate the SQL statements used to create a database object regardless of whether it was created with SQL.

- ► Online backup and restore

Online database maintenance can be performed, including the ability to backup and restore, while users are accessing and changing the database. This provides for around-the-clock operation.

- Object-level recovery

  Recovery can be at an object level. This allows you to restore a single file when necessary. It is not necessary to restore the entire database to "fix" a single file.

- Roll forward and backward recovery

  The ability to roll forward and backward to recover records allows database changes made after the last backup to be reapplied after a restore, or for recent changes to be backed out if the database needs to be returned to a specific state. This can be done for a specific user, time, or job.

- Audit trail

  An audit trail maintains a record of database changes such as the user, program, and job making the change.

- Performance tuning and trace

  The performance tuning and trace function analyzes processor and disk workloads for improved performance. The integrated nature of the database allows the entire system to be tuned, not just the database.

Operations Console

iSeries 800, 810, 825, 870, and 890 servers support a directly-attached or LAN-attached full-function 5250 PC console that includes a graphical control panel application. The user interface of the control panel application resembles its hardware counterpart.

The console emulator application (PC5250) serves as the console "device" of the iSeries server. The graphical control panel application permits remote entry of most of the functions supported by the hardware control panel mounted on the front of iSeries server units.

Control panel functions, such as power up/down, re-IPL, and mode changes, are supported. The console and control panel applications can be used together or separately, but each requires its own direct cable attachment to an iSeries server. Each cable must be purchased separately from IBM for the iSeries model being used. Both cables are available only in a single length of six meters.

Functions provided by Operations Console and Remote Operator and Control Panel, are managed via the Hardware Management Console (HMC) for the Model 520, 550, 570 and 595. To understand equivalent functions to operations console for the Models 520, 550, 570 and 595, refer to "Hardware Management Console" on page 679.

For further information about Operations Console, refer to "eServer i5 and iSeries Operations Console: Direct attach, LAN, remote, Hardware Management Console" on page 672.

Remote capabilities

The direct-attach Operations Console can serve as a gateway for a remote, dial-in Operations Console. The remote Operations Console can be configured to run the 5250 emulator application and the graphical control panel application. In general, both applications make it possible to perform the majority of system operations tasks, for example backup and recovery, with the iSeries servers and managing staff in physically separate locations.

The connection between the remote and direct-attach Operations Consoles uses Windows dial-up networking (Point-to-Point Protocol (PPP). Direct-attach Operations Console uses Windows NT Remote Access Service (RAS) for access.

See "eServer i5 and iSeries Operations Console: Direct attach, LAN, remote, Hardware Management Console" on page 672 for details about Operations Console and cabling requirements.

Software requisites

Operations Console is a component of iSeries Access for Windows (known as *Client Access Express for iSeries* in releases prior to OS/400 V5R2). The PC must be running the Windows NT 4.0, 2000, or XP Professional operating system to be supported. The LAN-attached Operations Console is supported on servers with i5/OS V5R3 and OS/400 V5R2 or V5R1.

EZ-Setup

EZ-Setup is part of the iSeries Access code, and is delivered on the Setup and Operations CD-ROM which is shipped with all orders. The code runs on a PC on Microsoft Windows 98, Windows Me, Windows NT 4.0, Windows 2000, and Windows XP. An Operations Console connection is required to set up TCP/IP if you are using a PC console. EZ-Setup then uses a TCP/IP connection to communicate with the server.

EZ-Setup consists of two parts:

▶ An interview process
▶ The task list

Clients can complete the interview either on the Internet or on the PC where they have installed iSeries Access. The output of this interview includes a setup definition file that is used to customize the EZ-Setup task list. EZ-Setup also

requires a connection to the iSeries Information Center, either on the Internet or locally installed.

EZ-Setup wizard

EZ-Setup wizard reduces both the number of decisions you need to make during setup and the amount of installation information you need to enter. The interface is all graphical as shown in the image on the right. *Guided Setup* is a collection of HTML pages for the same tasks as those in the EZ-Setup wizard.

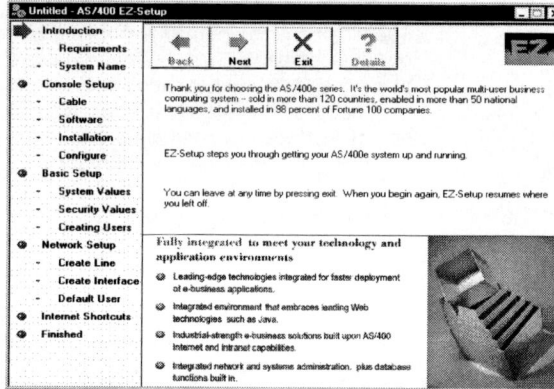

The EZ-Setup wizard is designed to provide the following functions through wizards:

- ▶ Begin PM eServer iSeries Data Collection
- ▶ Install Information Center
- ▶ Set server date, time, and name
- ▶ Configure NetServer
- ▶ Configure Operations Console
- ▶ Create administrative user profiles
- ▶ Configure Directory Services
- ▶ Configure security settings
- ▶ Create a TCP/IP interface
- ▶ Set up iSeries servers for the Internet
- ▶ Change TCP/IP attributes
- ▶ Register the server
- ▶ Configure Universal Connection for Information Center and software updates
- ▶ Set up Extreme Support
- ▶ Install and configure Domino

EZ-Setup also provides convenient links to the iSeries Information Center for information to help complete other tasks such as installing licensed programs and preparing a backup and recovery plan.

iSeries Navigator

i5/OS provides iSeries Navigator, the premier iSeries user interface for managing and administering your iSeries servers from your Windows desktop. The iSeries Navigator interface is packaged as a component of iSeries Access for Windows. No license is required. The installation image for iSeries Access for Windows comes pre-loaded on i5/OS V5R3 and OS/400 V5R2 iSeries systems. You can install the image over a TCP/IP network using iSeries NetServer, from a CD-ROM, or from a peer server.

iSeries Navigator provides wizards that help simplify iSeries management for a wide variety of functions including security, TCP/IP services, applications, and more. You can customize the powerful iSeries Navigator displays to optimize your productivity.

iSeries Navigator includes Management Central, a technology for doing systems management tasks across one or more servers simultaneously. This includes task scheduling, real-time performance monitoring, managing fixes, distributing objects, and running commands from a central system. Systems management tasks can be requested on multiple servers with just one request.

The Setup and Operations CD provided with every system can be used to install iSeries Navigator and EZ-Setup. If you do not install everything, you can add iSeries Navigator components at any time by selecting **File** →**Install Options** → **Selective Setup** from the iSeries Navigator window.

Availability and recovery

Many functions are available to help maintain the availability of an iSeries server. They include:

► System Managed Access Path Protection (SMAPP)

SMAPP supports and automates the process of selecting which access paths should be protected. This can improve IPL performance.

► Uninterruptable power supply

Uninterruptable power supply maintains power to the iSeries server during a site power loss.

► Redundant Array of Independent Disks (RAID)

The iSeries provides disk protection and availability. RAID-0, RAID-1 (disk, controller, and bus level protection), and RAID-5 are supported. Concurrent maintenance of disks is also supported.

- Journaling

  Journaling provides the ability to record all changes to records in a file as they occur. These journaled changes are applied to the file if the system is lost. With the implementation of remote journals, faster transport to a second iSeries server on behalf of high availability can be achieved. Faster IPL recovery can be achieved for critical access paths within the database by either explicitly journaling these objects, or by establishing an appropriate Systems Management Access Path protection target value. Byte stream files and directories can also be journaled.

- Commitment control

  Commitment control ensures that if a transaction requires multiple database changes, all of them (or none of them) are made.

- Batch journal caching

  The caching of journals in batch provides a significant performance improvement for batch environments which use journaling. Applications that perform large numbers of database add, update, or delete operations typically see the greatest improvement. Although directed primarily toward batch jobs, some interactive applications may also benefit from this feature.

- Save-while-active (SWA)

  Save-while-active allows one or more libraries to be saved while operations, including changes, continue against the libraries. SWA can be used with a short period of acquiesced operation where a checkpoint is taken of all libraries being saved before the first save operation begins, so that all libraries are synchronized.

  In i5/OS V5R3, the new *partial transaction save* (ragged SWA) feature allows for a save with open committed transactions or open commit cycles.

- Save/restore to multiple tapes concurrently

  Otherwise known as *parallel save and restore*, V5R1 supports the capability to use multiple tape devices (from 2 to 32), or multiple resources in a tape library, in parallel. In particular, parallel tape support reduces the amount of time required to save and restore very large objects.

- ASPs

  ASPs are individual disks reserved for particular objects, such as individual libraries. ASPs can be used to isolate those objects to assist in their recovery. Up to 31 user ASPs and 223 independent ASPs are supported offered with OS/400 V5R2. All systems ship with one system ASP configured.

- IASP

  IASPs can be defined as stand-alone or switched. UDFSs or database and program, journals, or operating system objects can be created in these

IASPs. When the IASP is moved from one system to another, the IASP can then be mounted on the new system and made available to applications and users. This protects clients from hardware failures other than hard disk failures of the IASP.

> **Note:** All I/O, not just the disk in the I/O tower, are switched. Any LAN, wide area network (WAN), workstation controllers, and so on in the I/O tower are switched at the same time.

▶ Large capacity disk load balancing

The ability to balance data across disk arms in an ASP, based on performance, capacity, average utilization, and hot and cold data is provided. i5/OS V5R3 supports an optimization of "Availability" (in addition to Balance, Performance, and Capacity).

A parity set optimized for availability offers a greater level of protection because it allows a parity set to remain functional in the event of a SCSI bus failure. The availability optimization value ensures that a parity set is formed from at least three disk units of equal capacity each attached to a separate bus on the input/output adapter (IOA). For example, if an I/O adapter had 15 disk units and was optimized for availability, the result may be five parity sets with three disk units each attached to separate SCSI buses on the adapter. i5/OS V5R3 is required to optimize for availability.

These functions are controlled with CL commands.

▶ Teraspace storage

Each iSeries job has up to 1 TB of contiguous, process-local, temporary storage. Applications can allocate dynamic storage in excess of 16 MB using C dynamic storage functions (malloc, calloc, realloc, and free) and POSIX shared memory APIs.

▶ Expert Cache

Expert Cache provides a disk cache tuner option, which allows the iSeries server to take advantage of available main storage capacity. It dynamically responds to system jobs to cache pages of data in main storage to reduce the time to process disk I/O.

▶ Integrated hardware disk compression

The compression of data on disk is supported by i5/OS. Data is dynamically compressed and uncompressed by the direct access storage device (DASD) controller as data is written to and read from disk. Disk compression does not affect the main CPU utilization since this function is performed by the DASD controller IOP. Integrated Hardware Disk Compression is supported by select DASD controllers.

Compression is limited to user ASPs only. Most data compresses at a 20% to 40% reduction. The compression reduction and subsequent impact on DASD performance depends on the attributes of the data.

► Hierarchical Storage Management (HSM)

i5/OS includes HSM APIs used by BRMS for iSeries (5722-BR1) to provide HSM functions. Use these APIs to develop custom HSM applications.

► Concurrent maintenance

Concurrent maintenance can be done for I/O cards, power, and other components contained in expansion towers. With concurrence maintenance, you can power off an expansion tower and add, remove, replace, upgrade, move, or swap a card or other component without stopping or powering off your system. Concurrent maintenance of some components are feature or configuration dependent.

Select models of 270, 250, 520, 550, 570, 595, 800, 810, 820, 825, 830, 840, 870, and 890 hardware also support concurrent maintenance. This allows the operator to identify and power off IOPs and associated IOA card slots so concurrent maintenance of the PCI cards can be performed.

Logical partitions

Logical partitioning enhances the role of the iSeries as a consolidated server. With LPAR, companies have both the power and flexibility to address multiple system requirements in a single machine to achieve server consolidation, business unit consolidation, a mix of production and test environments, and integrated clusters.

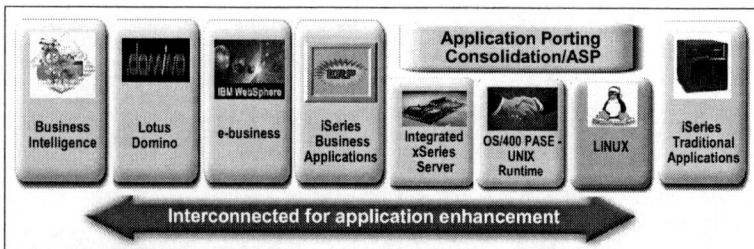

LPARs are ideal for companies that want to run varied workloads in a single iSeries system. They allow the CPW performance of an iSeries system to be flexibly allocated between partitions. Licenses can be managed across partitions.

Each partition's system name is distinct and the system values can be set independently. Each partition can have a different primary and secondary

national language and can be operated using different time zones. This flexibility is ideal for multinational companies to centralize operations in a single location, yet retain the national characteristics of each system.

LPAR allows for the simultaneous running of multiple independent servers, each with its own system processor or (with V5R1 onward) with parts of shared processors. Memory can be shared within a single iSeries server.

The iSeries LPAR capabilities have been improved with every new release since V4R4. Enhancements with i5/OS V5R3 include:

► Hardware Management Console

This is required for POWER5 processors implementing LPAR. It features a specific NetVista workstation running Linux with preloaded HMC software to perform multi-partition LPAR management function (and CoD) as well as console functions. A single HMC supports up to 160 partitions and up to 32 servers (Model 520, 550, 570 and 595 only).

Refer to "Product Previews" on page 66 to understand the future direction of HMC.

► Dynamic creation and deletion of partitions

► Partition shared processor resource specified as *uncapped* (Model 520, 550, 570 and 595 only)

Idle processing resources may be used by that partition up to the number of virtual processor specified.

► Unallocated, powered off dedicated or newly added processor resources (via CoD) can make part of a shared pool that is used by uncapped partitions (Model 520 and 570 only)

► Software Licensed Management (SLM) APIs

These APIs allow clients and business partners to monitor usage counts across the system rather than for each partition.

► A dynamic movement of processor, memory, and 5250 CPW performance between partitions spreads the system workload to where resources are needed, and potentially reduces the total amount of resource required on a system. The granularity of this processor movement can be one tenth of each processor.

► The capability to support partial (fractional) processors was introduced with V5R1. The number of partitions allowed per physical processor depends on the processor type. With i5/OS and @server i5 servers, the maximum number of partitions per system has increased to 254.

- ▶ Multiple operating system support
  - – i5/OS and OS/400
  - – Linux
  - – AIX 5L
  - – Windows (via Integrated xSeries Server or Integrated xSeries Adapter)
- ▶ Multiple i5/OS and OS/400 versions within a partitioned environment on appropriate systems

  See the LPAR table on page 536 to understand what operating system release is supported in the primary and secondary partitions of each iSeries server.
- ▶ Virtual OptiConnect emulates external OptiConnect hardware by providing a virtual bus between LPARs. To use Virtual OptiConnect, you only need to purchase OptiConnect for OS/400. Additional hardware is not required. If multiple paths between partitions are available, OptiConnect software selects the Virtual OptiConnect path over either a HSL or SPD OptiConnect external path. An IPL of the affected partitions is not required.
- ▶ Up to 4064 virtual networks using IEEE 802.1Q VLAN are supported between partitions on the Models 520, 550, 570 and 595. Virtual Ethernet provides 16 independent high-speed virtual 1 Gb Ethernet internal bus-to-bus communication paths between LPARs on Models 270, 800, 810, 825, 870, and 890.

  Virtual Ethernet supports TCP/IP. Additional communication hardware is not required. The enablement and setup of Virtual Ethernet is easy and does not require an IPL.
- ▶ iSeries Navigator support creates and manages partitions including a scheduled movement of resources where HMC is not available including:
  - – Configuration support of Linux with the Create Partition wizard
  - – The ability to save partition configuration data
  - – The ability to export configuration data to HTML format for hardcopy prints
  - – Partition numbers are visible with names
  - – The ability to change virtual processors when moving processing units
  - – Updates to partition profiles for shared and dedicated processors
  - – The ability to select views by selecting columns to display

Note: Some LPAR capabilities have hardware or software dependencies.

LPAR partition support

The following table shows the operating system releases that are supported in secondary and primary LPARs on iSeries Model 270, 800, 820, 820, 825, 830, 840, 870, and 890 servers.

Supported processors	Primary partition (i5/OS or OS/400)	Shared processor	Partitions per processor	Secondary partition					
				OS/400 V4R5[3]	OS/400 V5R1	OS/400 V5R2	i5/OS V5R3	Linux	AIX 5L
Model 270 (SSTAR Uni) #2431, #2432, #2452	V5R1	Yes	4	Yes	Yes	Yes		Yes	No
	V5R2	Yes	4	No	Yes	Yes	Yes	Yes	No
	V5R3	Yes	4	No		Yes	Yes	Yes	No
Model 270 (SSTAR 2-way) #2434 and #2454	V5R1	Yes	4	Yes	Yes	Yes		Yes	No
	V5R2	Yes	4	No	Yes	Yes	Yes	Yes	No
	V5R3	Yes	4	No		Yes	Yes	Yes	No
Model 800 (SSTAR Uni) #2463 and #2464	V5R2	Yes	4	No	Yes	Yes	Yes	Yes	No
	V5R3	Yes	4	No		Yes	Yes	Yes	No
Model 810 (SSTAR Uni & 2-way) #2465, #2466, #2467, #2469 (2-way)	V5R2	Yes	4	No	Yes	Yes	Yes	Yes	No
	V5R3	Yes	4	No		Yes	Yes	Yes	No
Model 820 (Pulsar Uni) #2395, #2396, #2425	V5R1	Yes	4	Yes	Yes	Yes		No	No
	V5R2	Yes	4	No	Yes	Yes	Yes	No	No
	V5R3	Yes	4	No		Yes	Yes	No	No
Model 820 #2397, #2398, #2426, #2427	V5R1	Yes[2]	4	Yes	Yes	Yes		Ded	No
	V5R2	Yes[2]	4	No	Yes	Yes	Yes	Ded	No
	V5R3	Yes	4	No		Yes	Yes	Ded	No
Model 820 (SSTAR Uni) #0150, #2435, #2436, #2456	V5R1	Yes	4	Yes	Yes	Yes		Yes	No
	V5R2	Yes	4	No	Yes	Yes	Yes	Yes	No
	V5R3	Yes	4	No		Yes	Yes	Yes	No
Model 820 (SSTAR n-way) #0151, #0152, #2437, #2438, #2457, #2458	V5R1	Yes	4	Yes	Yes	Yes		Yes	No
	V5R2	Yes	4	No	Yes	Yes	Yes	Yes	No
	V5R3	Yes	4	No		Yes	Yes	Yes	No
Model 825 (POWER4 n-way) #2473	V5R2	Yes	10	No	Yes	Yes	Yes	Yes	No
	V5R3	Yes	10	No		Yes	Yes	Yes	No
Model 830 (ISTAR n-way) #0153 and #2349	V5R1	Yes	4	Yes	Yes	Yes		Ded	No
	V5R2	Yes	4	No	Yes	Yes	Yes	Ded	No
	V5R3	Yes	4	No		Yes	Yes	Ded	No

Supported processors	Primary partition (i5/OS or OS/400)	Shared processor	Partitions per processor	Secondary partition					
				OS/400 V4R5[3]	OS/400 V5R1	OS/400 V5R2	i5/OS V5R3	Linux	AIX 5L
Model 830 (ISTAR n-way) #2400, #2402, #2403	V5R1	Yes[2]	4	Yes	Yes	Yes		Ded	No
	V5R2	Yes[2]	4	No	Yes	Yes	Yes	Ded	No
	V5R3	Yes[2]	4	No		Yes	Yes	Ded	No
Model 840 (ISTAR n-way) #2416, #2417,#2418, #2419, #2420	V5R1	Yes[2]	4	Yes	Yes	Yes		Ded	No
	V5R2	Yes[2]	4	No	Yes	Yes	Yes	Ded	No
	V5R3	Yes[2]	4	No		Yes	Yes	Ded	No
Model 840 (SSTAR n-way) #0158 and #0159	V5R1	Yes	4	Yes	Yes	Yes		Yes	No
	V5R2	Yes	4	No	Yes	Yes	Yes	Yes	No
	V5R3	Yes	4	No		Yes	Yes	Yes	No
Model 840 (SSTAR n-way) #2461, #2460,#2352, #2353, #2354	V5R1	Yes	4	Yes	Yes	Yes		Yes	No
	V5R2	Yes	4	No	Yes	Yes	Yes	Yes	No
	V5R3	Yes	4	No		Yes	Yes	Yes	No
Model 870 (POWER4 n-way) #2486	V5R2	Yes	10	No	Yes	Yes	Yes	Yes	No
	V5R3	Yes	10	No		Yes	Yes	Yes	No
Model 890 (POWER4 n-way) #0197, #0198, #2487, #2488, #2497, #2498	V5R2	Yes	10	No	Yes	Yes	Yes	Yes	No
	V5R3	Yes	10	No		Yes	Yes	Yes	No

Notes:
1. All partitions must be at V5R1 or later to support processor sharing and dynamic movement of processor resources.
2. Linux is supported on Dedicated Processors only; other partitions support processor sharing.
3. Dedicated processors only.

The following table shows the operating system releases that are supported in partitions of the @server i5 Models 520, 550, 570, and 595.

Supported processors	Shared processor	Partitions per processor	Release of partition					
			OS/400 V4R5[3]	OS/400 V5R1	OS/400 V5R2	i5/OS V5R3	Linux	AIX 5L
Model 520 (POWER5) #8950[4]	Yes	2	No	No	No	Yes	Yes	Yes
Model 520 (POWER5) #8951, #8952	Yes	4	No	No	No	Yes	Yes	Yes
Model 520 (POWER5) #8953, #8954,#8955	Yes	10	No	No	No	Yes	Yes	Yes
Model 550 (POWER5)	Yes	10	No	No	No	Yes	Yes	Yes
Model 570 (POWER5) #8961, #8971	Yes	10	No	No	No	Yes	Yes	Yes
Model 595 (POWER5)	Yes	10	No	No	No	Yes	Yes	Yes

Notes:
1. All partitions must be at V5R1 or later to support processor sharing and dynamic movement of processor resources.
2. Linux is supported on Dedicated Processors only; other partitions support processor sharing.
3. Dedicated processors only.
4. Refer to the following table.

The following table lists the partitioning limitations with shared processor and uncapped capacity of the #8950, #8951, and #8952 Model 520 processors.

Model 520 processor	Maximum partitions with full processor activation	Dedicated processors	Shared processor/ uncapped capacity
#8950	2	No	Yes / No
#8951	4	No	Yes / No
#8952	4	No	Yes / No

Suggested reading

For additional information about logical partitioning, see:

http://www.ibm.com/servers/eserver/iseries/lpar
http://www-1.ibm.com/servers/eserver/iseries/service/itc

iSeries clustering

A cluster is a group of independent servers that appears on a network as a single machine. It is a collection of complete systems that work together to provide a single unified computing resource.

> **Note:** On systems prior to V5R1, the iSeries server offered multisystem coupling that provides peer or tiered node clusters, constructed by Solution Developers using distributed data management and journaling. Systems in the cluster are managed separately by the client. Database replication is provided by high-availability business partner solutions. However, this is not clustering.

Today, iSeries clusters enable you to set up an environment to provide availability beyond 99.94% for critical applications and critical data. iSeries server high availability business partners and Solution Developers complete the solution with easy-to-use cluster management, robust data resiliency, and resilient applications that take advantage of the new technology.

IASPs offer significant functions that allow even more flexibility and improved availability. Data residing in IASPs can be switched between servers using HSL OptiConnect loop. IASPs allow you to take data offline and bring data online independent of the system ASP and other user ASPs. IASPs also support:

- ► Journaling of IFS objects, data areas and data queues, and options to reduce the amount of data journaled
- ► System services support of HA Switchable Resources, which allows use of resilient device cluster resource groups that contain IASPs
- ► HSL OptiConnect support as a cluster communications fabric
- ► Options to adjust the tuning and configuration parameters of your cluster to match better your communications environment
- ► IBM Cluster Management Utility, which allows you to create and manage a simple four-node, switched disk cluster

See *IBM @server iSeries Independent ASPs: A Guide to Moving Applications to IASPs*, SG24-6802, and *Independent ASP Performance Study on the IBM @server iSeries Server*, REDP-3771, for more information about IASPs.

Cluster Resource Services consists of an open set of APIs that provide cluster facilities. iSeries application providers and clients use the APIs to enhance their application availability and to create, configure, and administer the cluster. Systems are defined into the cluster as *cluster nodes*. Communication interface addresses are defined to form the cluster node-to-node interconnection links. Resilient resources (objects replicated to one or more nodes) are associated with a Cluster Resource Group (CRG) so they can be managed as a single unit.

Two types of CRGs are supported: one for data resilience and one for application resilience. Data CRGs provide the control to switch the point of access for a set of data to a backup node that maintains an exact replica of that data. Application CRGs control switching an IP address that represents the application server to a backup node and restart the application in the event of a primary node failure.

Cluster Resource Services includes integrated facilities such as heartbeat monitoring, reliable message delivery, switch-over administration, and distributed activities. The services are built on a robust cluster topology and messaging functions that keep track of each node in the cluster and ensure that all nodes have consistent information about the state of cluster resources.

Heartbeat monitoring ensures that each node is active. When the heartbeat for a node fails, the condition is reported so that the cluster can automatically failover to the resilient resources on the backup node. System services for high availability solutions are enhanced with real-time recording of IFS stream file changes into journals. Data resiliency applications can use this function to provide enhanced support for this class of objects.

IBM works closely with the cluster middleware business partners to provide easy-to-use cluster management applications, including Lakeview Technology and Vision Solutions.

iSeries clusters support up to 128 nodes. Any OptiConnect, WAN, and LAN connectivity options can be used to build a cluster, as follows:

► HSL copper and fiber bus connections are fully supported system features. When used with OptiConnect software, they are attractive connectivity methods for high-end and mid-range models existing in the same location. IASPs and switched disk work in this environment as of V5R1.

► ATM provides a high-performance connection to remote systems in the cluster.

► Ethernet and token-ring LANs are ideal for connecting low-end iSeries models into the cluster.

All systems are managed from a single workstation that contains the high-availability business partner cluster management application. The required minimum release of OS/400 to support each node in the cluster is V4R4.

High Availability Switchable Resources installs as Option 41 of i5/OS. A chargeable option of i5/OS, HA Switchable Resources provides the capability to achieve a highly available environment using switchable resources (IASPs). The resources are physically switched between systems so that only one copy of the resource is required.

New with i5/OS V5R3 iSeries clustering

i5/OS V5R3 enhances iSeries clustering with additional capabilities, including:

- ► IASPs containing i5/OS DB2 library-based objects and output queues

- ► Groups of IASPs that can be linked together

- ► Thread relative naming for controlling job attributes

- ► Multiple library namespaces that allow multiple databases and duplicate library names across different namespaces

- ► Clustered Hash Table Server for sharing and replicating of non-persistent data between cluster nodes

- ► Clustered Hash Table APIs for connection control, storage, and retrieval table of entries, and generate keys and information about stored entries

- ► Cluster GUI enhancements

- ► On rejoin, cluster node ability to self start

- ► Fully supported cluster commands

- ► User control of automatic failover

- ► Fully supported cluster commands

Suggested reading

For additional information about clustering, refer to the following Web sites:

```
http://www-1.ibm.com/servers/eserver/iseries/ha
http://www-1.ibm.com/servers/eserver/iseries/service/itc
```

iSeries Windows integration and Microsoft cluster support

iSeries Integrated xSeries Server and Integrated xSeries Adapter offerings support Virtual Ethernet LAN, Microsoft Cluster Services, and Automatic Cartridge Loader support. With OS/400 V5R2, new xSeries models are now supported using the Integrated xSeries Adapter.

Virtual Ethernet LAN

The Virtual Ethernet introduced in V5R1 to enable high-speed communications between i5/OS and OS/400 and Linux partitions within the iSeries server is extended to support Integrated xSeries Servers and xSeries servers attached with Integrated xSeries Adapters. With this support, Windows servers can communicate with each other and with i5/OS and OS/400 and Linux partitions over the fast, more secure, and reliable Virtual Ethernet LANs.

Microsoft Cluster Services

With the clustering support provided in Windows 2000 Advanced Server, two Integrated xSeries Servers or two xSeries servers attached with Integrated xSeries Adapters can form a cluster and use the 16 new shared storage spaces available with OS/400 V5R2. In the cluster environment, if there is an outage on one of the Windows servers, the storage spaces can be switched to the second Windows server. The applications can be restarted automatically to reduce the length of the system outage.

Auto Cartridge Loader

Clients who have systems with large amounts of data often have Auto Cartridge Loader (ACL) tape devices (3570, 3580, and 3590) with the ability to automatically load another tape cartridge. Support is now added in the Windows integration support to handle commands for ACLs. Multiple tape cartridges can be accessed during backup/restore operations initiated from the Windows server.

Suggested reading

For additional information about Windows integration, see the following Web site:

`http://www-1.ibm.com/servers/eserver/iseries/windowsintegration`

Integration with Windows servers

The iSeries servers offer integration with Windows to support larger and more complex Windows applications and additional tools to help reduce the cost of managing a Windows server environment.

Attachment of n-way xSeries servers

The iSeries server supports the attachment of n-way xSeries servers via the high-speed link. With the Integrated xSeries Adapter, select xSeries servers running:

▶ Microsoft Windows Server 2003 Standard Edition
▶ Microsoft Windows Server 2003 Enterprise Edition
▶ Microsoft Windows Server 2003 Web Edition
▶ Microsoft Windows 2000 Server
▶ Microsoft Windows 2000 Advanced server

They help to extend Windows application scalability, while retaining the storage consolidation and systems management advantages of the Integrated xSeries Server.

Enhanced hardware support

Enhancements for the Integrated xSeries Server includes support for:

▶ Up to 32 servers on select iSeries models
▶ 1 Gb Ethernet LAN adapter
▶ iSeries DVD device

iSeries Navigator support for Windows disk and user management

Additional facilities are added to iSeries Navigator to manage Integrated xSeries Servers and xSeries servers that are directly attached to iSeries via the Integrated xSeries Adapter. In addition to server management, iSeries Navigator now supports disk and user management for these Windows servers. Enhancements include the ability to create, delete, copy, link, unlink, and show status for Windows server disks. Administrators can manage i5/OS user profiles that are enrolled into a Windows server environment.

GUI management and administration

This section discusses the i5/OS GUI management and administration functions.

Work Management

The Work Management function of i5/OS eases the job of systems management by giving the operator control of the activities of a job and of its performance characteristics. Work Management supports concurrent execution of batch jobs, 5250 CPW jobs, and non-conversational transactions on the system. Each job is protected from other jobs on the system. However, job-to-job communication is allowed.

The system can be setup to dynamically adjust the execution priority of jobs that are forced to wait for an opportunity to use the CPU. This configuration is designed to prevent high priority jobs from monopolizing the CPU at the expense of all other jobs in the system.

Save/restore

Save is the capability of making a backup copy of objects or members on tape or online save file. Restore is the capability to copy saved objects back to the original or a different system.

Save-while-active enables objects to be saved while they are being used by applications. The system ensures the object saved to save media is consistent with the status of the object when the save operation is initiated.

For more information, see the High Availability and Clusters Web site at:

`http://www-1.ibm.com/servers/eserver/iseries/ha`

Graphical (GUI) management of a system

iSeries Navigator and Management Central run on a Windows NT 4.0, XP, or Windows 2000 client. It provides a GUI for most administrative and configuration tasks on the iSeries, and a central management point to manage distributed iSeries servers. Performance is monitored graphically.

Performance collection and evaluation

Users can manually collect system performance data for a single time period or automatically collect data on a weekly schedule using a set of commands and menus. This systems management function provides data to assist the user in workload scheduling, system tuning, performance reporting, performance problem analysis, and capacity planning. The user can also work with this data using the Performance Tools/400 licensed program (5722-PT1).

Network system management

i5/OS system management functions include Simple Network Management Protocol (SNMP) APIs and access to additional management information. The SNMP APIs for managing applications have the ability to manipulate management data via local or remote SNMP agents. Information can be retrieved from systems on SNA or TCP/IP networks. This makes it easier to discover and manage potential problems anywhere within the network.

Application programming interfaces

Hundreds of i5/OS APIs can provide access to functions and data not available through any other interface or levels of performance not available through other interfaces. These CLIs are intended for use by Solution Developers and IBM Business Partners whose applications require these functions and data. You can find a complete list in *System API Reference*, SC41-5801.

Extensive run-time application function

OS/400 is a functionally-rich platform for applications. Because it is enabled to run a wide range of applications, clients can easily grow their application base as their business needs grow. The extensive run-time function integrated into the i5/OS licensed programs enables application programs created with these languages, utilities, and support:

- ► ILE RPG for iSeries
- ► RPG/400®
- ► IBM System/36-Compatible RPG II
- ► IBM System/38-Compatible RPG III
- ► ILE COBOL for iSeries
- ► COBOL/400®
- ► IBM System/36-Compatible COBOL
- ► IBM System/38-Compatible COBOL
- ► ILE C for iSeries
- ► SAA AD/Cycle® C/400®
- ► System C/400
- ► VisualAge® C++ for iSeries
- ► AS/400 BASIC
- ► AS/400 Pascal
- ► AS/400 PL/I
- ► RM/COBOL-85 for the AS/400

The corresponding licensed programs are not required for systems that execute the code.

24

i5/OS (5722-SS1): Operating system licensed products

The computing industry is moving rapidly toward a network-centric world made up of global networks. The newest release of IBM i5/OS builds on this to make the iSeries servers key players in this vibrant and vital area.

This chapter describes the features and enhancements of the iSeries operating system product. The functionality and integrated capabilities of the operating system are described in "i5/OS: Architecture" on page 499. Associated licensed programs and enhancements are described in the following chapters of this Handbook.

IBM i5/OS (5722-SS1)		
Version and release	i5/OS V5R3	
HIPO	1000	
Availability	11 June 2004	
Software type	Usage Processor based Software Subscription - Yes IPLA - Yes Keyed - Yes	
Installation prerequisites	None	
Related products	All	
Client code	Delivered as 5722-XE1, which is stored in an integrated file system (IFS) directory and is downloaded to the PC	
Replaces product	5722-JC1 (functions included in OS/400) 5769-SS1, 5716-SS1, 5763-SS1, 5763-VP1	
Further information	http://www.iseries.ibm.com/infocenter	

New with i5/OS V5R3

i5/OS is necessary for the new POWER5 technology-based hardware. Consider it as an upgrade from previous versions of OS/400 to take advantage of new and enhanced functions such as:

► Capacity on Demand to include memory, trial processor, and reserve processor

Refer to "Product Previews" on page 66 to understand the future direction for iSeries clients.

► Automatic processor balancing with uncapped processor partitioning

► Hardware Management Console (HMC) that is used to manage multiple logical partitions (LPARs) without needing a primary partition

► AIX 5L to be run in an LPAR on Models 520, 550, 570, and 595

► POWER5 Linux kernel and distributions in common with pSeries servers

Extended storage area network (SAN) and storage connectivity options for the Linux environment

- Extending Windows integration options with support for Windows 2003 server
- Increased storage space size up to 1 TB for Windows and Linux storage spaces
- Storage allocation for Linux and AIX 5L in iSeries Navigator
- DB2 scalability enhanced with partition tables and materialized query tables
- Configuration of Management Central as a highly available application
- Independent auxiliary storage pool (IASP) support extended to include output queues
- Cross-site mirroring (XSM) extends mirroring support for geographic mirroring, a part of High Availability Switchable resources
- New time zone architecture that includes Simple Network Time Protocol (SNTP) client and server support and is positioned for future benefits
- Enhanced OS/400 Portable Application Solutions Environment (PASE) and now based on AIX 5.2
- New and enhanced functions for single signon (SSO) including enhancements and a Synchronize Functions wizard for Enterprise Identity Mapping (EIM) and network authentification service
- Partial transaction saves (ragged save) of save-while-active when the commit cycle has not completed

Support is another reason to upgrade to i5/OS V5R3. The intended policy is that there is a 12-month notice to announce end-of-service for i5/OS V5R3 when *release +2* is announced. The date of support will be extended further to the last day of September or March, whichever comes first.

i5/OS overview

i5/OS contains the base operating system, additional optional feature components, and separate licensed programs bundled with the operating system at no extra charge. The client can purchase advanced features and functions that are not included in the base group of products shipped with the operating system.

V5R3 of i5/OS provides system support for the following RISC models:

- 170
- 250
- 270
- 520, 550, 570, 595
- 720, 730, 740

- 800, 810, 820, 825, 830, 840, 870, 890
- SB1, SB2, SB3

> **Important:** Some functions of the operating system are available *only* on newer hardware.

V5R2 of OS/400 is the last release to support the following RISC models:

- 150
- 600, 620, 640, 650
- S10, S20, S30, S40

> **Note:** V5R2 of OS/400 does not run on models of the AS/400 system based on internal microprogram instruction (IMPI) processors (CISC models) and some earlier RISC models, namely, the Bxx, Cxx, Dxx, Exx, Fxx, 100, 135, 140, 2xx, 3xx, 4xx, 500, 510, and 530.

Refer to "Planning information" on page 71 for information about OS/400 and processor compatibility.

Version 5 of OS/400 is offered for no additional charge. See "New with i5/OS V5R3" on page 586.

The following sections briefly describe the components of i5/OS. Programs within i5/OS are described in "Programs within i5/OS" on page 553. Refer to "i5/OS V5R3 options" on page 565 and "Options included in OS/400 V5R2" on page 750 for a list of all OS/400 options available at i5/OS V5R3 and OS/400 V5R2.

Version 5 of OS/400 is delivered on CD-ROM to speed loading of software and to reduce the risk of media errors. All manuals are delivered in softcopy on CD-ROM.

National language and multilingual support

The iSeries server with i5/OS is a worldwide product that addresses many country (region)-unique requirements. For different countries (regions) and languages, specific support is provided, either with translated machine-readable information (MRI), such as screens and messages, or with keyboards and displays on the local or remote workstation twinaxial controller.

Multilingual support allows multiple users on the same system to operate in different languages. This means that system messages, displays, and help information, as well as user applications, can be presented to the end user in their national language.

Note: 5722-SS1 can be ordered in Farsi, Albanian, Bulgarian, Estonian, Macedonian, Latvian, Lithuanian and Serbian, Laotian, Vietnamese, Belgium, and English.

Translations are available in Albanian, Arabic, Brazilian-Portuguese, Bulgarian, Chinese (Simplified and Traditional), Croatian, Czech, Danish, Dutch, Dutch-Belgium, English, English-Belgium, English DBCS, English Uppercase, English Uppercase DBCS, Estonian, Farsi, Finnish, French, French-Belgium, French Canadian, French-MNCS, German, German-MNCS, Greek, Hebrew, Hungarian, Icelandic, Italian, Italian MNCS, Japanese, Korean, Lao, Latvian, Lithuanian, Macedonian, Norwegian, Polish, Portuguese, Portuguese-MNCS, Romanian, Russian, Serbian, Slovakian, Slovene, Spanish, Swedish, Thai, Turkish, and Vietnamese.

Not all licensed programs are translated into all languages, nor are all national language versions available from all program release support centers. All MRIs are in English.

Primary and secondary national languages

The national language in which licensed programs are ordered is considered the primary national language. New in i5/OS V5R3 is the ability to order additional primary languages for use in LPAR situations where some partitions support a different country (region) to other partitions.

Second languages in a single partition are known as *secondary languages*. Users can switch among the languages as necessary. Multiple national language versions can be installed on a single iSeries server. Regardless of the national language version, all system commands are in U.S.A. English. Therefore, a single set of system commands works in all national language environments.

Universal Coded Character Set support

Many clients do business in a worldwide environment. It is too costly and time consuming to redesign and rewrite an application to support users in another national language or culture. These applications require the ability to store and process character data from more than one national language.

For example, a database file may need to contain customer names in English, German, Greek, Arabic, Japanese, and Thai characters. This capability must be available in a client/server environment and in a network of heterogeneous systems that exchanges character data via client applications.

The Universal Coded Character Set (UCS) is an emerging global character encoding, developed jointly by the industry (UNICODE 1.1) and the International

Organization for Standardization (ISO). ISO/IEC 10646-1 defines a code page (UCS-2) encompassing the characters used by all currently significant languages, a rich set of scientific and publishing symbols, and a variety of script languages. This common code page spans the character sets of many languages. It can ease application development and management issues historically found in multiple code page system environments and networks. This capability is provided in i5/OS with the UCS2 Level 1 support for database to permit characters of any national language to "coexist" in database files.

Locale support of cultural values

Cultural values change from one national language to another. Examples of cultural values are:

- ▶ Date and time format
- ▶ Currency symbol
- ▶ Sort (collating) sequence

Locale support allows for the creation, deletion, and access of locale-based information. C-applications can access locale information via C-runtime functions. Non-C applications can retrieve locale information via application programming interfaces (APIs). i5/OS simplifies the tasks that an application must perform to provide local cultural values. This support can be used whether a national language version (primary or secondary) is installed for that language on the iSeries server.

Bidirectional language support

Bidirectional language support (BIDI) is a series of routines to transform the physical order of characters to a logical order. Culturally correct BIDI language support requires that the flow of text, left to right or right to left, be determined by the character entered or displayed at the workstation or printer device. However, the data must be stored in DB2 Universal Database (UDB) for iSeries (or any file system) in the sequence the characters are entered, and not how they are displayed.

Euro currency support

Euro currency sign support is offered to those countries (regions) that are currently supported in the iSeries national language structure, that are inside and outside the European Monetary Units (EMU), and whose national standards authorities have approved the appropriate standards. This support has been available in OS/400 since V4R5.

Options and licensed programs offered with i5/OS

The following sections describe the options that can be ordered or ship with the i5/OS operating system.

Note: A table is shown in each option description. It summarizes whether the product is included with the operating system automatically or if it must be ordered separately. The status states whether the product is a chargeable or a no-charge feature.

Programs within i5/OS

The licensed programs in the following table appear within the iSeries Software Resources and Licensed Program menus as a separate product. Each is part of the base i5/OS (product 5722-SS1). Each program ships with i5/OS automatically with no additional charge and does not need to be ordered separately.

The following programs are included with all i5/OS shipments:

- 5722-DG1 HTTP Server*
- 5722-IA1 Software Integration Assistant
- 5722-JC1 Toolbox for Java*
- 5722-JV1 Developer Kit for Java*

  - Option 5 Java Developer Kit 1.3*
  - Option 6 Java Developer Kit 1.4

- 1TME-LCF Tivoli Management Agent*
- 5722-TC1 TCP/IP Utilities*
- 5722-WSV Integration for Windows 2000 and 2003*
- 5722-XE1 iSeries Access for Windows*
- 5722-XP1 iSeries Access for Wireless
- Business Solutions V1.0

Note: All of the previously listed software is included in the software order. Those product and product options identified with an asterisk (*) are preloaded on all new system orders.

Product name	Product number	For further information, see:
DB2 UDB for iSeries	N/A	Chapter 26, "IBM licensed programs: Database accessories" on page 597
HTTP Server for iSeries	5722-DG1	"IBM TCP/IP Connectivity Utilities for iSeries (5722-TC1)" on page 560
IBM Software Integration Assistant for iSeries	5722-IA1	"IBM Software Integration Assistant for iSeries (5733-IA1)" on page 689
IBM Toolbox for Java	5722-JC1	Chapter 29, "IBM LPP Application Development Products" on page 635
Integration for Windows Server	5722-WSV	"iSeries Windows integration and Microsoft cluster support" on page 542
IBM Developer Kit for Java	5722-JV1	Chapter 29, "IBM LPP Application Development Products" on page 635
TCP/IP Connectivity Utilities for iSeries	5722-TC1	"IBM TCP/IP Connectivity Utilities for iSeries (5722-TC1)" on page 560
iSeries Access for Windows iSeries Navigator*	5722-XE1	Chapter 31, "IBM eServer iSeries Access products" on page 663
Tivoli Management Agent	1TMELCF	"IBM Tivoli Storage Manager Extended Edition (5698-A11)" on page 685
* Formerly known as Client Access Express and Operations Navigator		

HTTP Server for iSeries (5722-DG1)

HTTP servers are the core foundation of technology at the heart of all applications for On Demand Business. They handle the communication with the client (typically browsers or Extensible Markup Language (XML)-rendering devices such as personal digital assistant (PDAs)) and provide the entry point into server resources. These resources can range from simple Hypertext Markup Language (HTML) and GIF files, to On Demand Business and e-commerce applications, all the way to complete business-to-business, collaborative enterprises.

For @server i5 and iSeries servers, network computing is supported with HTTP Server for iSeries. An iSeries server can access a vast network of computers as though they were a single entity. Everyone and everything can access and distribute information, applications, and services provided by the network.

Based on the popular Apache 2.0 open-source software, the HTTP Server (powered by Apache) is the IBM strategic HTTP server. Multiple HTTP servers can be active simultaneously on a single iSeries.

The HTTP Server for iSeries product also contains several Internet-enablement tools to aid in Web/Internet application development:

► Apache Software Foundation (ASF) Jakarta Tomcat
► Net.Data®
► Search and Web Crawler

These tools are described further in this section.

HTTP Server for iSeries (5722-DG1)	
Included in base	Yes
Status	Shipped with OS/400 as no charge feature
Further information	http://www.ibm.com/eserver/iseries/software/http http://www.webdav.org/ http://www.apache.org/

Refer to the following Web site for information about preventive service planning (PSP) for the iSeries HTTP Server:

http://www.ibm.com/eserver/iseries/software/http

Apache, a freeware HTTP server, is open-source software that implements the industry standard HTTP/1.1 protocol. The focus is on being highly configurable and easily extendable. It is built and distributed under the Apache Software License by the ASF. You can find it on the Web at:

http://www.apache.org

Features
► Support for the latest Apache 2.0 level

   Apache 2.0 offers multiple benefits including multithreaded mode, filtering, input/output (I/O) buffering, and new Apache APIs.

► Apache Portable Run-Time and multiprocessing modules

► Support and documentation of the Apache Portable Runtime (APR) APIs

   APR APIs allow user-written modules to be platform-independent. They allow Web developers to write modules and applications independent of the platform. This makes it easier to bring applications to the iSeries product line. Operating system specific functionality is encapsulated into the APIs.

- Header files are provided for all supported APIs.

- The sample user module mod_example is provided. This module demonstrates a use of the Apache APIs.

► Easy to use IBM Web Administration GUI

The IBM Web Administration for iSeries interface combines forms, tools, and wizards to create a simplified environment to set up and manage many different servers and server types on your iSeries server.

► Support for Server Side Includes (SSI)

SSI tags are comments within HTML that direct the Web server to dynamically generate information for the page. SSI tags allow a Web developer to easily include common HTML statements such as headers and footers, so that they are easily managed and consistent across an entire Web site. SSI can be used to include static HTML, to call and execute programs (such as through Common Gateway Interface (CGI) programs) to allow the insertion of results.

Added SSI support includes two varieties of SSI and CGI combinations:

- Parse an HTML document and include the output of a CGI program as dynamic content on an HTML page.

- Parse the output of a CGI program to resolve SSI tags before returning the output to the client browser.

► Support for WebDAV (MOD_DAV)

World Wide Web distributed authoring and versioning is a set of extensions to the HTTP protocol that allows users to collaborate to edit and manage files on remote Web servers. WebDAV provides a network protocol to create interoperable, collaborative applications. Features of the protocol include:

- *Locking (Concurrency Control)*: Long-duration exclusive and shared-write locks prevent the overwrite problem, where two or more collaborators write to the same resource without first merging changes.

- *Properties*: XML properties provide storage for arbitrary metadata, such as a list of authors on Web resources. These properties can effectively be set, deleted, and retrieved using the DAV protocol.

- *Namespace manipulation*: Since resources may need to be copied or moved as a Web site evolves, DAV supports copy and move operations. Collections, similar to file system directories, can be created and listed.

► Support for Apache Module MOD_REWRITE

This module provides a rule-based rewriting engine to rewrite requested Uniform Resource Locators (URLs) on the fly.

- Lightweight Directory Access Protocol (LDAP) used to store configuration information and user authentication information
- A Domino plug-in to allow the HTTP server to access documents stored in Notes
- Integrated with OS/400 security, enabling exploitation of the Internet for marketing and merchandising

  Multiple HTTP servers are supported to balance content and workload. A Web browser can be used to administer and configure these servers.
- Tracking world-wide Web (WWW) activity through the server to identify the audiences accessing the client's server
- Client Authentication supports Secure Sockets Layer (SSL) V3 and Transport Layer Security (TLS) V1, including client and server authentication

  You can associate client certificates with iSeries user profiles or validation lists, allowing users seamless access to your Web server's resources without having to sign on.
- Expanded CGI support, which includes RPG, REXX, C, C++, Cobol, Perl, and Control Language

  You can bypass the server on output using no-parsed header CGIs. You can also fully configure any codepage conversions the server performs on your Web application's input or output. Multithreaded CGI programs are supported.
- Automatic Browser Detection for different documents for different clients, allowing your Web site to seamlessly exploit the unique capabilities of whatever browser your customers use
- Support for SSL provided by the cryptographic product IBM Cryptographic Access Provider 128-bit for iSeries (5722-AC3)
- Digital ID authentication requires SSL client authentication for HTTP server client certificates. This offers resource protection with:
  - Valid client certificates
  - Client certificates with certain distinguished names values
  - Client certificates associated with iSeries user profiles
  - Client certificates associated with iSeries validation lists
- The administration of certificates centralized in the DCM product

  The HTTP server is a certificate "customer".
- Authentication using LDAP, iSeries user profiles, validation lists, and Kerberos
- Caching of Web pages in server's local memory cache for better static page serving performance
- Socks and SSL tunneling

- Support for named protection setups

  Named protection setup allows the same set of authentication directives to be defined in multiple containers by the use of include files

- Support for group files

  Group files provide the ability to grant access to resources based on a defined group of users.

- Logging of World Wide Web server access for tracking activity

  This allows iSeries owners to obtain feedback on who accesses their servers and what parts are accessed.

- National Language Support (NLS) enablement

- Denial of Service detection and prevention

- Support for all iSeries file system types

- With the highly available HTTP Server, the possibility to build a highly available Web site, improving the availability of business-critical Web applications

  - Highly available HTTP servers provide function that monitors a URL that is part of your Web site and takes recovery action if the Web server is no longer serving your Web content. For example, the monitor function attempts to end and start your Web server or initiates a switch-over to move your HTTP server function to the backup node in the cluster.

  - You can write your CGI programs using highly available CGI APIs to save CGI state into the iSeries cluster. In the event of a failed node in the cluster, a CGI program can maintain its state, even after the application switches to a new node in the cluster.

- Log rollover providing the ability to automatically close the current log file and open a new one based on a set of user-defined parameters

- Log maintenance providing the ability to automatically delete log files based on age, aggregate size, or both

- Improved navigation, usability, and accessibility enhancements for the HTTP Server administration interface

- Fast Response Cache Accelerator (FRCA), which is a caching technology that can more than double capacity for serving static content compared to conventional server architectures

  FRCA has allowed IBM to establish a leadership position in Web server performance. It is a general purpose architecture that enables the iSeries to move performance-critical TCP/IP application functions, such as the HTTP server, into lower levels of the operating system, greatly improving Web serving performance.

- HTTP data collection category to contain HTTP performance data for Collection Services

  The HTTP performance data can then be queried to analyze HTTP server activity and better understand the types of HTTP transactions that are being processed by the iSeries (for example, static files, CGI, or Java Servlets).

- Support for Apache Module MOD-DEFLATE

  This module does compression on the data that is sent to the browser. This decreases the amount of data that the server needs to send over the network thus improving network performance and response times.

New with i5/OS V5R3

The IBM HTTP Server for iSeries adds support for:

- CGI enhancements for running an initialization URL at startup and ability to set CGI jobs' library list
- Kerberos authentication

  This enhancement offers Windows clients that are using Active Directory and Kerberos login a single signon between a Windows desktop and Microsoft Internet Explorer accessing HTTP Server on iSeries. EIM can be used in this environment.

The Web Administration GUI included in the IBM HTTP Server for iSeries adds support for:

- WebSphere Application Server Base Edition

  This same level of function is provided for WebSphere Application Server - Express via browser-based administration. It offers easy-to-use wizards for creating HTTP and application server instances, deploying Java 2 Platform, Enterprise Edition (J2EE) applications, and managing HTTP and application servers and their applications.

- WebSphere Portal - Express

  An easy-to-use interface helps you to set up a WebSphere Portal via a wizard that walks the user through the necessary steps to create and configure all the necessary servers. You can also perform other setup necessary to get Portal up and running.

- Retrieval and display of HTTP statistical information via a Web browser

  Statistics used to track cached and non-cached data sent and received to a particular HTTP server. Statistical subsets indicate whether the data has been handled by the IBM HTTP server (powered by Apache), a CGI program, an application server, or a user module.

Apache Software Foundation Jakarta Tomcat (5722-DG1)

The HTTP Server includes the popular ASF Tomcat Servlet Engine. With ASF Tomcat, you can serve both servlets and JavaServer Pages (JSPs) using an "In Process" or "Out of Process" servlet engine. Tomcat, which is based on open source software, is compatible with the IBM HTTP Server (powered by Apache).

Features

- ► Lightweight and easy-to-use software provided as an extension to the IBM HTTP Web server

- ► ASF Jakarta Tomcat support, which can be used as a simple starting point for IBM Business Partners and Clients who are interested in learning about or piloting Java Servlet applications

- ► ASF Jakarta Tomcat 3.2.4
- ► Compliance with JSP 1.1
- ► Compliance with Java Servlet 2.2 specification
- ► In-process ASF Jakarta Tomcat
- ► Out-of-process ASF Jakarta Tomcat using mod_jk ajp12 protocol support
- ► Out-of-process ASF Jakarta Tomcat using mod_jk ajp13 protocol support
- ► Support of JDK 1.2 and 1.3

Net.Data

The IBM HTTP Server product includes Net.Data. IBM Net.Data is an application that allows Web developers to easily build dynamic Internet applications using "Web Macros". Net.Data Web Macros combine the simplicity of HTML with the power of dynamic SQL. Net.Data provides connectivity to a variety of relational data sources as well as flat files.

Features

- ► High performance connectivity to dynamic data
- ► Enables the use of existing business logic to Web-enable client/server applications
- ► Rapid development of Internet and intranet applications
- ► Helps to power your IBM DB2 UDB applications

For more information, see the following Web site:

http://www.iseries.ibm.com/netdata

IBM TCP/IP Connectivity Utilities for iSeries (5722-TC1)

iSeries servers come with a complete and robust suite of TCP/IP protocols, servers, and services. It is easy to implement full-featured intranets by simply cabling iSeries servers and workstations together and starting the desired services. In most cases, no additional software or hardware is required.

TCP/IP networking on iSeries is administered and managed directly from iSeries Navigator running on a PC client. You can define Dynamic Host Configuration Protocol (DHCP), Domain Name System (DNS), and Dynamic Domain Name System (DDNS) servers from a single graphical interface.

iSeries TCP/IP configuration can be managed through graphical user interfaces integrated with iSeries Navigator. Included is a graphical wizard that provides simplified step-by-step guidance for configuring TCP/IP. The administration service based on the DHCP is built into OS/400 to centrally administer all workstation configuration data for IP networks. iSeries server network administration has never been easier.

The TCP/IP protocol stack on the iSeries is tuned for robust, secure, and scalable TCP/IP services and servers. This results in significant improvements in capacity for TCP/IP users.

The base protocols are implemented within OS/400 and OS/400 microcode for excellent performance, security, and stability. A wide range of physical interfaces is supported.

IBM TCP/IP Connectivity Utilities	
Product number	5722-TC1
Ordering	Included free of charge with OS/400
Minimum operating system level	V5R1
Program size	56 MB
HIPO	-
Availability	25 May 2001
Software type	Software Subscription
Replaces product	5769-TC1
Further information	http://www-1.ibm.com/servers/eserver/iseries/tcpip
	IBM @server *iSeries IP Networks: Dynamic!*, SG24-6718

New with i5/OS V5R3

For i5/OS V5R3, many TCP/IP enhancements are implemented with additional security features. TCP/IP is updated to include:

► Enhancements to iSeries Kerberos support
► Adding a Kerberos Server in OS/400 PASE
► Implementation of new Java security standards

Features

TCP/IP Connectivity Utilities for iSeries (5722-TC1) has a rich suite of servers and services including:

► Graphical user interface (GUI) configuration support
► File Transfer Protocol (FTP) client and server
► Simple Mail Transfer Protocol (SMTP)
► Post Office Protocol (POP) Version 3 server
► Line printer requester (LPR)/line printer daemon (LPD)
► TELNET client and server
► REXEC client and server

TCP/IP is an extremely popular protocol that is regarded as the de facto standard for computer networking. TCP/IP is fundamental to the network computing paradigm and helps make the iSeries an even more powerful On Demand Business server. Much of the iSeries On Demand Business infrastructure runs exclusively on TCP/IP, including Lotus Domino, Java, WebSphere, Web serving, and IBM Network Stations. The TCP/IP communication protocol function, along with related administration and configuration support, are packaged with OS/400.

TCP/IP Connectivity Utilities (5722-TC1) is automatically shipped to all clients who order OS/400. TCP/IP applications shipped as part of the TCP/IP Utilities include TELNET, SMTP, FTP, Remote Execution (REXEC) Server, and LPR/LPD (remote print support).

For a full description of TCP functions and features, refer to the Networking - TCP/IP section of the iSeries Information Center, and *IBM @server iSeries IP Networks: Dynamic!*, SG24-6718.

Internet Printing Server for iSeries

The Internet Printing Protocol (IPP) defines an industry-standard method of delivering print jobs using Internet technologies providing for Web-enabled print around the world. The IPP was developed by the Printer Working Group, a consortium of all major companies involved in network printing. IPP is fast becoming the single standard interface for printing on the Internet, with broad vendor implementation and client acceptance.

The IPP Server for iSeries, included in OS/400, provides an IPP Version 1.0 compatible print server for the iSeries. The IPP Server for iSeries allows anyone working remotely, to submit and manage print jobs on a distant iSeries. IPP is built on top of HTTP, which in turn, runs over TCP/IP. Clients can now use the same print solution on local area networks, intranets, and the Internet. The same process used to send a print document to the department printer down the hall can be used to send the document to the corporate printer across the country (region).

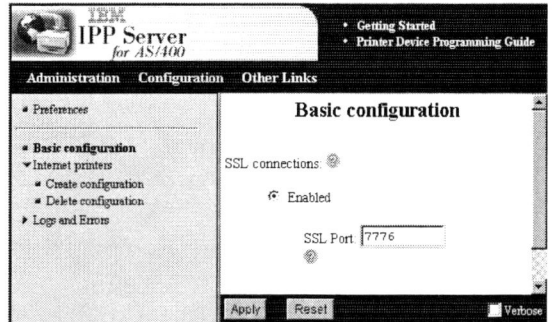

The IPP Server for iSeries provides security features for user authentication and encryption of print jobs using SSL 3.

iSeries Webserver Search Engine

The iSeries Webserver Search Engine allows you to perform full text searches on HTML and text files from any Web browser. The Webserver Search Engine also includes a Web crawler.

Features

► Indexes documents for fast searching

Indexes HTML or text files into a format that allows a large number of documents to be searched quickly. Multiple indexes can be created and documents from multiple directories can be placed in a single index.

► Advanced search functions

Supports advanced search capabilities such as exact search, fuzzy search, wild card search, proximity search, English word stemming, case sensitive search, boolean search, and document ranking.

► Search with thesaurus

Search results can be improved by automatically accessing a thesaurus during search. The thesaurus is user defined so that terms that are relevant to the indexed documents can be included in the thesaurus.

► Customizable search forms

The search form and the search result form are completely customizable by the end user using the Net.Data scripting language. This gives the user the ability to specify the type of search to be done and how the results are to be displayed.

The information that can optionally be displayed on the results page includes:

- The number of documents satisfying the search
- The number of occurrences of the search term
- The number of documents returned on this page
- The URL associated with each document
- The document's ranking, last modified date, and size

Any and all of this information can be displayed however the user chooses.

► Web-based administration

Administration of the search indexes is handled as part of the IBM Web Administration GUI pages. The search administration forms allow you to create and delete search indexes, update search indexes when documents are modified, and view the status of an index.

Administration using CL commands. All the functions supported on the Search Setup form can also be performed using the CL commands.

► Multiple language support

The Webserver Search Engine supports indexing and searching documents in multiple national languages including the double byte languages Chinese, Japanese, and Korean.

► Web crawler

Crawl remote Web sites and download the files to your system. The Web crawler is another way to build a document list for creating a search index.

You can set up the Web crawler to crawl one URL or use a URL object with a list of URLs to crawl. Crawling attributes such as the HTTP proxy server and port can be stored in an options object for re-use. The Web crawler also supports basic and server authentication.

For more information, see:

```
http://www-1.ibm.com/servers/eserver/iseries/software/http/services/
searchinfo.htm
```

```
http://www-1.ibm.com/servers/eserver/iseries/software/http/services/
webcrawler.htm
```

i5/OS V5R3 options

The programs in the following list appear within the iSeries Software Resources and Licensed Program menus as a separate product. Each is part of the base i5/OS (product 5722-SS1). Some programs ship with i5/OS automatically with no additional charge. Others are ordered separately or are a chargeable option.

▶ Option 1 OS/400 - Extended Base Support*
▶ Option 2 OS/400 - Online Information*
▶ Option 3 OS/400 - Extended Base Directory Support*
▶ Option 5 OS/400 - System/36 Environment
▶ Option 6 OS/400 - System/38 Environment
▶ Option 7 OS/400 - Example Tools Library
▶ Option 8 OS/400 - AFP Compatibility Fonts
▶ Option 9 OS/400 - PRV CL Compiler Support*
▶ Option 12 OS/400 - Host Servers*
▶ Option 13 OS/400 - System Openness Includes
▶ Option 14 OS/400 - GDDM®
▶ Option 21 OS/400 - Extended NLS Support
▶ Option 22 OS/400 - ObjectConnect
▶ Option 25 OS/400 - NetWare Enhanced Integration
▶ Option 30 OS/400 - Qshell*
▶ Option 31 OS/400 - Domain Name System*
▶ Option 33 OS/400 - Portable Application Solutions Environment*
▶ Option 34 OS/400 - Digital Certificate Manager*
▶ Option 35 OS/400 - CCA Crypto Service Provider
▶ Option 39 OS/400 - International Components for Unicode
▶ Option 43 OS/400 - Additional Fonts

For a list of options included in OS/400 V5R2, refer to "Options included in OS/400 V5R2" on page 750.

System/36 environment (5722-SS1 Option 5)

Most System/36 applications can run on the iSeries server using the System/36 environment. When running in the System/36 environment, OS/400 supports a set of commands designed to migrate data between the System/36 and the iSeries server or the iSeries server and the System/36. These commands save and restore library source, procedure members, and data files between the two systems.

System/36 environment (5722-SS1 Option 5)	
Included in base	Yes
Status	No charge

System/38 environment (5722-SS1 Option 6)

The System/38 environment provides:

► Migration from System/38 systems
► Intermixing System/38 and iSeries functions
► Maintenance of System/38 applications on the iSeries server

System/38 environment (5722-SS1 Option 6)	
Included in base	Yes
Status	No charge

The System/38 environment allows the execution of most programs written for a System/38 system. The same job can execute any combination of iSeries or System/38 programs. The programmer menu on the iSeries supports source types to enable the identification of System/38 syntax. The programmer can maintain either iSeries or System/38 programs during the same job.

System Openness Includes (5722-SS1 Option 13)

System Openness Includes provides developers with header files for the many callable APIs and exits found in OS/400. The header files are provided in a high-level language source for application development in languages such as C, C++, OPM RPG, ILE RPG, OPM COBOL, and ILE COBOL. They provide for easier access to many of the functions found in OS/400.

The Pthread APIs are based on open APIs described in the ANSI/IEEE Standard 1003.1, 1996 edition (also known as ISO/IEC 9945-1: 1996) and the Single UNIX Specification, Version 2, 1997 standards.

System Openness Includes (5722-SS1 Option 13)	
Included in base	Yes
Status	No charge

Some of the header files provided are based on industry standards from the POSIX and the single UNIX specification. These standards enable source code portability of applications over platforms such as OS/400, AIX, MVS™, and other non-IBM operating systems. Industry standard interfaces include the IFS, Interprocess Communications, Pthreads, Remote Procedure Call (RPC), Signal, SNMP, Sockets, Secure Sockets, LDAP, NLS, and network authentication.

Header files are also provided for callable APIs and exits unique to the iSeries, allowing platform unique customization of the system. System-unique interfaces include clustering, Dynamic Screen Manager, object management, OS/400 PASE, NLS, software and PTF management, and work management.

Media and Storage Extensions (5722-SS1 Option 18)

For software developers who want to customize their own storage management applications, Media and Storage Extensions provides an API to enable application monitoring and control of media usage, including volumes to be selected and volume expiration dates. The API also enables fast search for IBM 3480, 3490, 3490E, and 3575 tape devices.

Media and Storage Extensions (5722-SS1 Option 18)	
Included in base	No
Status	Charged feature
Related products	Backup Recovery and Media Services (BRMS) (5722-BR1) Tivoli Storage Manager (5697-TSM)
Further information	

An API is provided to handle the interruption that occurs when an application tries to open a database file that has been migrated to offline media. The API enables an on demand recall of a database file from offline media to direct access storage device (DASD) and resumption of the application. Application changes are not required.

These APIs provide support to use or build applications to manage tape usage and the recall of data from offline media to DASD. This feature is a prerequisite

feature to BRMS. It is also required when developing HSM dynamic retrieval functions.

Object Connect for iSeries (5722-SS1 Option 22)

Object Connect for iSeries provides support to simply and efficiently move individual objects, entire libraries, or entire IFS directories from one iSeries server to another over a standard communications connection. Systems can be connected via standard APPC (using APPN), TCP/IP communications lines (using AnyNet), local area network (LAN), or an high-speed link (HSL) OptiConnect loop (fiber or copper). The economy of not requiring intermediate save file procedures and copies to distribution queues saves DASD and improves performance in a manner that is nondisruptive to system operations.

Object Connect for iSeries (5722-SS1 Option 22)	
Included in base	Yes
Status	No Charge

OptiConnect for iSeries (5722-SS1 Option 23)

OptiConnect for iSeries provides high-speed transparent access to data through SPD fiber optic bus connections or HSL fiber optic and copper bus connections. It also includes performance enhancements to iSeries Distributed Data Management (DDM).

OptiConnect for iSeries (5722-SS1 Option 23)	
Included in base	No
Status	Charged feature
Further information	`http://www-1.ibm.com/servers/eserver/iseries/ha/opticonnect`

The mechanism used by OptiConnect for iSeries to access database files on connected systems is modeled after DDM. Just as DDM uses a DDM file and APPC communications to redirect file access operations, OptiConnect for iSeries uses DDM files and a specialized transport service to redirect file access operations to a target system.

Using OptiConnect for iSeries among systems sharing the same bus (connected with SPD fiber or HSL fiber/copper cables only) can achieve transport efficiencies not possible with more general purpose, wide-area communications protocols.

With HSL OptiConnect for iSeries, clients can offload the database application CPU cycles of up to 28 iSeries servers given three CECs per loop. However when three CECs are on a loop, no I/O towers can exist on that loop.

The major advantages of OptiConnect for iSeries are realized by clients who are rapidly approaching system capacity limits, and who intend to implement distributed database application servers within a data center or short-distance campus environment. OptiConnect for iSeries is also an integral part of high availability configurations.

When used with the Object Connect for iSeries facility, OptiConnect for iSeries provides a high-efficiency migration aid for the iSeries Advanced Series.

OS/400 - NetWare Enhanced Integration (5722-SS1 Option 25)

OS/400 - NetWare Enhanced Integration provides NetWare client and integration services for iSeries users, operators, and applications. This is achieved using a Network Loadable Module (NLM) that runs on NetWare 6.0.

Note: Novell no longer supports NetWare 4.2 and NetWare 5.0, and therefore, nor does IBM. A license is required for each NetWare server.

TCP/IP support in OS/400 is used to connect the iSeries using a token-ring adapter, an Ethernet adapter, IPCS, X.25, or frame relay adapters. OS/400 Enhanced Integration for Novell NetWare provides user profile and password integration from the iSeries to NetWare. iSeries user or group profiles can be propagated to multiple NetWare Directory Services (NDS) trees. When iSeries users change their passwords, the change is propagated to NetWare.

OS/400 - NetWare Enhanced Integration (5722-SS1 Option 25)	
Included in base	Yes
Status	No charge
Further information	http://www-1.ibm.com/servers/eserver/iseries/netware/as4nwhm.htm

OS/400 - NetWare Enhanced Integration provides iSeries-to-NetWare printing support. An iSeries user's printed output is sent from an iSeries output queue to a printer queue managed by the NetWare server. OS/400 host print transform services are used to translate the output to print on common PC printers.

IFS support is provided, allowing iSeries users, including iSeries Access users, and applications access to files and directories in multiple NDS trees throughout

the network. Full integration with NetWare security ensures that each iSeries user of these services is fully authenticated in NetWare Directory Services. Another use of the file system is to access files on NetWare servers to be served by OS/400 Internet connection support:

- Internet Connection Server for AS/400 (V4R1 and V4R2 only)
- HTTP Server for iSeries (V4R3 or later release)

Server configuration and management tasks can operate from iSeries interfaces. This is not intended to provide full management and operations of a NetWare server. However, iSeries operators can manage user connections and disk resources. Facilities are provided for creating, extending, and mounting or dismounting volumes on NetWare servers.

OS/400 - DB2 Symmetric Multiprocessing (5722-SS1 Option 26)

OS/400 - DB2 Symmetric Multiprocessing (SMP) expands on the parallel capabilities of DB2 UDB for iSeries. This separately priced feature of OS/400 improves the performance of the database for the iSeries server. This improved performance is critical, especially in a data warehouse or decision-support environment. The performance gains provided by this feature allow for better and more effective business decisions to be made in a timely manner.

OS/400 - DB2 Symmetric Multiprocessing further enables DB2 UDB for iSeries with SMP on any n-way iSeries server. SMP capabilities have existed since the introduction of the iSeries n-way systems. This form of SMP allows multiple database operations to take place simultaneously on multiple processors. Each database operation runs on a single processor, therefore, optimizing DB2 UDB for iSeries for online transaction processing.

OS/400 - DB2 Symmetric Multiprocessing (5722-SS1 Option 26)	
Included in base	No
Status	Charged feature
Related products	DB2 Multisystem for iSeries
Further information	http://www-1.ibm.com/servers/eserver/iseries/db2/db2sym.htm

With the DB2 Symmetric Multiprocessing, a single database operation can run on multiple processors at the same time or in parallel. These database operations are typically queries. However, parallel processing is also supported for import and export between DB2 UDB for iSeries and other databases.

This parallel index build, splitting an individual query into many smaller subtasks, can then be run independently on separate processors before the subtask results

are combined again. This allows for significant performance increases. These performance increases become more pronounced with the addition of more processors. For example, if a query is running in 20 seconds on an iSeries with a dedicated processor, adding a second dedicated processor along with the DB2 Symmetric Multiprocessing feature may allow this query to run in approximately 10 seconds. Adding two additional processors may allow this query to run in approximately 5 seconds.

This example illustrates how scalable the technology is, which is important with database parallelism. Scalability governs how much benefit is gained from adding additional processors. Perfect scalability allows for four processors to run a query in one-fourth of the time that a single processor could, as explained in the previous example. The advanced architecture of the iSeries and of OS/400 have enabled DB2 Symmetric Multiprocessing to show industry-leading scalability across all iSeries n-way systems.

OS/400 - DB2 Symmetric Multiprocessing can be configured differently for each user of the system. This allows a system administrator to have the greatest control over how parallelism is used on a system, and therefore, greater control over how system resources are used. Part of this enablement process allows the selection of how much parallelism is used, or how many subtasks are used for each query. Using fewer subtasks than processors available allows a greater amount of the total system resources to be used by other users. Using more subtasks than available processors allows an individual user to use more of the total system resources. This flexibility allows administrators to balance the needs of all system users with the available resources.

OS/400 - DB2 Multisystem (5722-SS1 Option 27)

The iSeries server and OS/400 - DB2 Multisystem provide a scalable solution for data warehousing that spans from the smallest datamart to the largest enterprise data warehouse. DB2 Multisystem allows multiple iSeries servers to be connected to allow the processing power and storage capacity of all the servers to be used. From a database perspective, these interconnected iSeries servers appear as a single large system. It is intended for use when iSeries servers are used for large data warehouse installations.

OS/400 - DB2 Multisystem (5722-SS1 Option 27)	
Included in base	No
Status	Charged feature
Related products	DB2 Symmetric Multiprocessing

OS/400 - Domain Name System (5722-SS1 Option 31)

OS/400 includes a full-function Domain Name System server. It can be configured for primary, secondary, and caching roles. DNS configuration data from other platforms can easily be migrated to the iSeries DNS server. In addition, a migration utility that moves existing iSeries host table information into the DNS configuration databases is provided.

OS/400 - Domain Name System (5722-SS1 Option 31)	
Included in base	Yes
Status	No charge feature
Related products	Requires 5722-SS1 Option 33 (OS/400 PASE) to run with full functionality

Dynamic DNS

OS/400 DNS services are based on the widely used industry-standard DNS reference implementation. A dynamic update capability is offered that transforms the DNS into a DDNS.

The Version 8.2 BIND option of the DNS services requires the installation of OS/400 Option 33 (OS/400 PASE).

Combined with iSeries DHCP server, dynamic DNS update transactions can be sent to enable an integrated Dynamic IP solution that automatically manages TCP/IP addresses and their associated DNS host names on your networks.

OS/400 Portable Application Solutions Environment (5722-SS1 Option 33)

OS/400 PASE is an integrated runtime that provides simplified porting of selected solution provider UNIX applications. OS/400 PASE complements and expands the iSeries solution portfolio by focusing on rapidly porting UNIX applications to the iSeries platform.

OS/400 PASE is a library of APIs and system services that enable AIX programs to run in OS/400. It provides a subset of AIX functionality to support running 32-bit and 64-bit UNIX applications directly on iSeries hardware. OS/400 PASE includes full support for X-Windows.

OS/400 PASE applications are created on an AIX workstation and execute on iSeries hardware. As of OS/400 V5R2, OS/400 PASE applications written in C or

C++ can be compiled within OS/400 PASE. The environment provides libraries containing hundreds of basic system APIs that are compatible with:

► 32-bit applications for AIX 4.2.1 or later
► 64-bit application for AIX 5.1

OS/400 PASE (5722-SS1 Option 33)	
Included in base	Header and export file extensions are packaged with OS/400 Option 33
Status	No charge feature
Further information	http://www-1.ibm.com/servers/enable/site/porting/iseries/pase

OS/400 PASE exploits the iSeries processor's ability to switch between OS/400 and AIX runtime modes within an OS/400 job. This allows applications deployed using OS/400 PASE to run directly on iSeries hardware and take full advantage of OS/400 services such as file systems, security, and DB2 UDB for iSeries.

OS/400 PASE is not an operating system. It does not provide support for developing UNIX applications. Any changes or additions required to port UNIX applications to OS/400 PASE are compiled and linked on an RS/6000 workstation running a level of AIX supported by OS/400 PASE. Applications deployed using OS/400 PASE run in a normal OS/400 job and are managed using standard OS/400 operations. Serviceability, backup and restore, and other administrative tasks are performed using standard OS/400 operations and system management facilities.

OS/400 PASE contains the same command line interface (CLI) set of APIs for DB2 UDB iSeries that is supported for Integrated Language Environment (ILE). Data returned from DB2 UDB iSeries can be presented in ASCII format, which is expected by the majority of UNIX applications.

OS/400 PASE applications can be fully integrated with other iSeries server applications, for example, an Enterprise Resource Planning (ERP) application implemented in ILE, a WebSphere application written in Java, or Lotus Domino. A suite of applications can run together in a job mix or be separated into their own LPARs, depending on the performance and scheduling requirements of the client.

New with OS/400 V5R2
► AIX 5L support
► Linux library support through AIX 5L
► Compile C, C++ programs *within* OS/400 PASE
► PTY, TTY support
► Support for launching JVM from OS/400 PASE

OS/400 PASE supports an expanded application development environment. It has additional installation support and use of the IBM VisualAge C++ Professional for AIX V6 (5765-F56) and IBM C for AIX V6 (5765-F57) compiler programs. These compilers can be installed and used in OS/400 PASE, eliminating the need to compile OS/400 PASE applications on a separate AIX system.

OS/400 PASE programs can now also launch the iSeries integrated JVM. Conversely, the iSeries integrated JVM supports native methods implemented as procedures in an OS/400 PASE executable. It is easier to port AIX applications that use a combination of Java and C/C++ code to OS/400 PASE.

IBM Print Services Facility (5722-SS1 Options 36, 37, 38)

IBM Print Services Facility™ for OS/400 (PSF/400) provides support for high-function Advanced Function Presentation (AFP) electronic printing and print management of Intelligent Printer Data Stream (IPDS) printers. With AFP, application output can be transformed into fully graphical documents with electronic forms, image, graphics, barcoding, lines, boxes, and text in a wide variety of fonts. This flexibility enables the production of electronic documents that are more effective, and enables the re-engineering of business processes.

Documents and reports can be produced using a variety of enabling tools, including Infoprint Designer for iSeries (5733-ID1). Other enabling tools include OS/400 printer file keywords (for front and back overlays, N-up, and duplex), DDS printer files, iSeries page and form definitions, Advanced Print Utility (APU), and AFP Toolbox. Output created by network and client applications can be transformed to AFP, and, therefore, managed by PSF/400 to IPDS printers. OS/400 Version 5 includes capabilities (via Infoprint Server for iSeries) to handle PCL, PostScript, and PDF output with PSF/400 print management.

PSF/400 is the OS/400 subsystem driving the interactive management of IPDS printers. IPDS is a bidirectional print architecture that ensures that the printing process can be managed every step of the way. When an OS/400 writer is started to an IPDS printer, PSF/400 provides these services:

► Establishes communication and query printer capabilities and status

► Manages overlay, image, and font resources required in the printer

► Transforms the iSeries spooled file (from AFP, IPDS, or SCS) into a printer-specific IPDS data stream

► Manages the print process, including handling error conditions and managing error recovery down to the page level

The net effect of this level of print management is to ensure each page of each spooled file is printed completely and accurately. PSF/400 enables all parameters of the printer file and all DDS print keywords (subject to printer limitations). IPDS printing takes on added significance across the network. TCP/IP print support is more limited than traditional iSeries print management. The Send Network Spooled Files (SNDNETSPLF) command (LPR in TCP/IP terminology) simply sends a spooled file with limited instructions and no feedback as to whether it was received and printed correctly.

Applying IPDS to a TCP/IP network restores the same level of print support (as described above) as twinaxial-connected printers. This includes sending standard SCS spooled files across the network.

To create an IPDS printer on the system, after specifying the device type as IPDS, you must specify AFP(*YES) in the printer device description. Any printer defined as Type(*IPDS) and AFP(*YES) needs PSF/400. Twinaxial connected IPDS printers can be defined as AFP(*NO) and, therefore, do not require PSF/400. Regardless of connection type, AFP (*NO) means that there is no AFP resource management for fonts, images, or overlays. All IP-connected IPDS printers must be configured with AFP(*YES) and, therefore, require PSF/400.

The PSF feature of OS/400 required is based on the speed of the fastest printer measured in impressions per minute (IPM), not by your CPU size. The number of printers is not important, although the speed of the fastest printer is important.

The following table lists the OS/400 option number associated with each tier.

Option number	Feature description
36	1 to 45 IPM
37	1 to 100 IPM
38	Any speed printer support

An unlimited number of printers within each tier is supported.

IBM Print Services Facility (5722-SS1 Options 36, 37, 38)	
Included in base	No
Status	Charged feature/keyed stamped media
Related products	Advanced Function Printing Utilities (5722-AF1) Infoprint Designer for iSeries (5733-ID1) iSeries Facsimile Support (5722-FAX) Infoprint Server for iSeries (5722-IP1) IBM AFP Font Collection (5648-B45) IBM Infoprint Fonts for Multiplatforms (5648-E77)
Further information	`http://www.printers.ibm.com/internet/wwsites.nsf/vwwebpublished/` `psfhome_i_ww`

New with V5R3

Print Services Facility for OS/400 (PSF/400) is the integrated AFP system manager and Intelligent Printer Data Stream (IPDS) printer driver for the iSeries servers. V5R3 brings significant fundamental enhancements to the iSeries output architecture. These changes include:

► Continued Unicode implementation

► Support for TrueType and OpenType fonts

► Capabilities to import network standard image and graphic formats directly into iSeries documents

► Enhanced support for full color

Both OS/400 and PSF/400 are enhanced to add these functions. The net result is an output architecture supporting a much broader range of document content and function.

► PSF/400 V5R3 also provides support for new iSeries printers.

► Print Services Facility implements phase II of Unicode. Unicode is the emerging text encoding standard that uses an expanded 16-bit data address to represent nearly all of the characters in the all the world's languages in one interface. Phase II of the Unicode comprises most of the world's languages except those that require complex text support. With Unicode, applications that require multiple languages are greatly simplified.

► Prior to V5R3, iSeries documents used EBCDIC-encoded AFP fonts. TrueType and OpenType fonts are ASCII-encoded and represent the standard in many personal, network, and UNIX environments. With V5R3, TrueType and OpenType fonts can be specified directly in iSeries output. These fonts can be cataloged in the IFS and referenced with the FONTNAME keyword.

The Infoprint Fonts for Multiplatforms product (5648-E77) has a font installer program that enables simple installation of TrueType and OpenType fonts. AFP, TrueType, and OpenType fonts can be intermixed on the same page. The ability to use TrueType and OpenType fonts greatly expands the universe of fonts available for iSeries applications while providing for flexibility and consistency among various organization documents.

► Full color and image capabilities are significantly extended with V5R3. Full process color debuted in OS/400 V5R2 with the implementation of high-resolution, highly-compressed AFP color (called IOCA Function Set 45, or FS45, of the AFP image object architecture). With V5R3, PSF/400 supports the new OS/400 capabilities to import network or Web standard graphics objects directly into iSeries documents. These graphic or image object types reside on the IFS and are referenced with the AFPRSC keyword. The ASCII formats supported are:

  − JFIF (JPEG File Image Format, commonly referred to as JPEG)
  − TIFF (Tag Image File Format)
  − EPS (Encapsulated Postscript)
  − EPSTR (EPS with transparency)
  − PDFSPL (PDF single page)
  − PDFSPOTR (PDF single page with transparency)
  − PCLPO (PCL page object)

The AFP objects types that can be imported directly from the IFS are:

  − BCOCA™ (AFP barcode object)
  − GOCA (AFP graphics object)
  − IOCA (AFP image object)

These object types are stored in a new structure within the AFP data stream called an object container. Object containers support a mixture of EBCDIC and ASCII-encoded data within the same document or report.

► Document content within object containers also integrates with the PDF services support in Infoprint Server for iSeries (5722-IP1). For example, a full color logo can be pulled from an IFS directory into an iSeries document and then passed to Infoprint Server and converted into PDF for distribution.

► Support for the following iSeries printers (as IPDS printers) is added with PSF/400 V5R3:

  − IBM Infoprint 1312 Printer
  − IBM Infoprint 1332L Printer
  − IBM Infoprint 1354 Printer
  − IBM Infoprint 1354L Printer
  − IBM Infoprint 1372 Printer
  − IBM Infoprint Color 1354L Printer
  − IBM Infoprint 2060ES Printer

- IBM Infoprint 2075ES Printer
- IBM Infoprint 2090ES Printer
- IBM Infoprint 2105ES Printer
- IBM 4247 IPDS

OS/400 High Availability Switchable Resources (5722-SS1 Option 41)

OS/400 High Availability (HA) Switchable Resources provides the capability to achieve a highly available environment using switchable resources. The resources are physically switched between systems so that only one copy of the resource is required.

High Availability Switchable Resources (5722-SS1 Option 41)	
Included in base	No
Status	Charged feature Keyed - Yes
Further information	http://www-1.ibm.com/servers/eserver/iseries/ha/ clustertech.htm

Option 41 includes support for:

- ► **Switchable IASPs**: Allow you to move the data to a backup system to keep the data constantly available. The data is contained in a collection of switchable disk units such as an I/O tower.

- ► **IBM Simple Cluster Management GUI**: Allows you to create and manage a simple four-node, switched disk cluster. The utility includes wizards and help text that simplify the tasks involved in and managing the cluster.

To define switchable IASPs or to use the IBM Cluster Management Utility, OS/400 Option 41, HA Switchable Resources is required.

OS/400 High Availability Journal Performance (5722-SS1 Option 42)

For OS/400 V5R2, there are several improvements and additions to journal management. For the most demanding high-availability clustering environments supported by our high availability Business Partners, Journal Standby Mode and Asynchronous Journaling capabilities enable faster failover and reduce performance bottlenecks. Both the Journal Caching feature and the Journal Standby feature are provided by installing OS/400 option 42.

OS/400 High Availability Journal Performance (5722-SS1 Option 42)	
Included in base	No
Status	Charged feature Keyed - Yes

Journal Caching feature

The Journal Caching feature was available as PRPQ 84486 before OS/400 V5R2 and is now a standard orderable feature in V5R2. This feature allows batch applications to substantially reduce the number of synchronous disk write operations performed, thereby reducing overall elapsed batch execution time.

Journal Caching provides significant performance improvement for batch applications that perform large numbers of add, update, or delete operations against journaled objects. Applications using commitment control see less improvement (commitment control already performs some Journal Caching). Journal Caching is especially useful for situations where journaling is being used to enable replication to a second system.

Important: We recommend that you do *not* use Journal Caching if it is unacceptable to lose any recent change in the event of a system failure where the contents of main memory are not preserved. This type of journaling is directed toward batch jobs. It may not be suitable for interactive applications where single system recovery is the primary reason for using journaling.

Journal Standby feature

You may want to place a journal in standby state if the journal is on a backup system. By having the journal in standby state, a switchover to the target system can be accomplished more quickly because all objects on the backup system can be journaled, therefore allowing the switchover processing to skip the costly step of starting journaling for all objects. At the same time, the backup system does not incur the overhead of journaling because most journal entries are not deposited when the journal is in standby state.

Using commitment control is not allowed while in *STANDBY state.

Suggested reading

You can find more information about backup and recovery and learn which journal entries are allowed to be deposited in these states in the iSeries Information Center at:

http://www.iseries.ibm.com/infocenter

25

Software terms

This chapter discusses software migration, upgrade paths, previous release support, software maintenance, terms and conditions, and software upgrades.

Software on iSeries servers is priced in one of three ways:

► Processor based by the grouping of processors into one of seven tiers
► By the number of processors on which the software is running
► By the number of users

Processor-based software is grouped into seven groups: P05, P10, P20, P30, P40, P50, and P60. Each server is placed into a group based on its processor and, for older models, its 5250 commercial processing workload (CPW) feature. Software pricing is then based on this group for that server. Each server in the hardware section has a software group indicated.

Some software products are chargeable by the number of processors on which the software is running, rounded up to the nearest processor. If the number of processors is increased, by IBM @server Capacity Upgrade on Demand (CUoD) for example, an additional charge becomes payable.

User-based pricing depends on the number of actual active users using that software on a system. Keyed software where user pricing is required needs a software key for the "base" license and for the allowed number of users. In some cases, after purchasing a certain amount of licenses in a particular software group, the user is then entitled to unlimited use of that software on that system.

Where user pricing is applicable, the terms of use are stated in the respective chapters.

Software Maintenance for iSeries

Software Maintenance for iSeries (SWMA) is a processor group priced offering that provides entitlement to new versions and releases of Operating System/400 (OS/400) and selected iSeries Licensed Program Products (LPP) and provides access to IBM world class iSeries software support services for assistance with routine, short duration installation and usage (how-to) questions, and code-related problems. The eligible Software Maintenance products are listed on the Web at:

http://www-1.ibm.com/servers/eserver/iseries/sftsol/subscript3.htm

In addition to being able to acquire support during normal business hours, SWMA clients can receive severity-1 assistance 24 hours a day, every day.

Each newly configured iSeries system includes one year of SWMA with an associated charge. This may be upgraded to a three-year coverage period. For an additional fee, active U.S. Software Maintenance for iSeries clients can add a 24 x 7 all-severity support option.

This option consists of:

► Access to IBM remote technical software support, regardless of severity, 24 hours per day, seven days per week

► Processor-based pricing at a single price per system

Software license and upgrades

With the one- or three-year Software Maintenance option included for a price with every new @server i5 and iSeries purchase, clients are entitled to order future versions and releases for eligible software products during the period they are covered by Software Maintenance. At renewal time, the client is required to purchase Software Maintenance for iSeries to maintain their entitlement to future versions and releases of eligible products they are licensed for.

Failure to renew makes a client ineligible to receive new versions, releases, or updates. The client becomes liable for an After License fee in addition to the applicable Software Maintenance for iSeries offering charge when renewal of Software Maintenance eventually takes place. The client *must* ensure that renewals are on a timely basis to avoid this After License Fee.

The pricing structure for Software Maintenance for iSeries is based on the software group within which the covered system is contained.

The Software Subscription for iSeries offerings were *withdrawn from marketing* on 31 July 2003. They are replaced by this new Software Maintenance for iSeries offering. Existing Software Subscription for iSeries contracts are honored through to their renewal date. Software Subscription for iSeries clients who let their contract lapse, and later want to re-establish their coverage, are subject to a Software Maintenance After License Fee in addition to Software Maintenance for iSeries offering charges.

> **Note:** On 13 July 2004, IBM announced one program number (5733-UX1 and UX3) to replace the existing two program numbers (5733-SX1 and 5733-SU1 or 5733-SX3 and 5733-SU3) for the one- and three- year coverage options.

Products that are not listed within the eligible Software Maintenance for iSeries products table have software upgrade entitlement and support available via Passport Advantage. This is an IBM program that covers software license acquisition and maintenance options under a single common set of agreements, processes, and tools. Using Passport Advantage Online, IBM Clients can submit contact updates, view purchase history, and more.

When you have moved to one of the Passport Advantage offerings for the affected products, you receive an e-mail notification of the availability of refreshes of software products that you can then download from a Passport Advantage Web site. Or you can elect to have media refreshes shipped directly to you.

> **Note:** If you have a current Passport Advantage Agreement, the contact for media refreshes can be different than the contact currently receiving media refreshes under your current terms.

If you have subscription agreements in effect, but have not enrolled in Passport Advantage and have not been registered in Passport Advantage Express as of 15 August 2003 in the United States, Canada, Latin America, and Asia Pacific or by 16 January 2004 in Europe or the Middle East and Africa, you can continue to order media for the duration of your coverage.

The following table lists the iSeries software product number and correlating Passport Advantage number.

> **Note:** The following table is a work in process to provide a starting point for product identifier to Passport Advantage part number cross reference.

Product identifier	Passport Advantage part number*	Description
5698-AMM	- - -, E009CLL	Tivoli Access Manager for Business Integration
5698-APD	D510GLL, E008ZLL	Tivoli Storage Manager for Databases
5698-APE	D5104LL, E008VLL	Tivoli Storage Manager for Mail
5698-APH	D510LLL, E0090LL	Tivoli Storage Manager for Hardware
5698-APR	D512SLL, E009NLL	Tivoli Storage Manager for Enterprise Resource Planning
5698-APW	D51MHLL, E00I9LL	Tivoli Storage Manager for Application Servers
5724-A18	D5B9GLL, E1B9FLL	WebSphere Commerce Pro
5724-A85	- - -, E1CDULL	WebSphere Partner Agreement Manager
5724-A86	- - -, E1CEZLL	WebSphere Partner Agreement View
5724-A87	- - -, E1CEILL	WebSphere Partner Agreement Connect
5724-A98	D51LKLL, E00HZLL	DB2 Life Sciences Data
5630-A36	D5ALWLL, E1ALVLL	WebSphere Application Server
5630-A37	D5ALELL, E1ALDLL	WebSphere Application Server Enterprise V5.0
5733-A38	D5241LL, E00N5LL	WebSphere MQ for iSeries V5.3
5733-A78	D50HYLL, E0049LL	Host Access Client Package for iSeries, V3
5733-A80	D51RALL, E00JDLL	WebSphere Portal for iSeries
5724-B20	D5AMTLL, E1AMSLL	WebSphere Collaborative Profiles, Personalizations Edition V2.0
5648-D38	- - -, E00HZLL	DB2 Relational Connect V7
5769-DL1	N/A, N/A	Dictionaries and Linguistic Tools for AS/400(R) Tivoli Storage Manager
5765-E51	D5BCXLL, E1BCWLL	Communications Server for AIX, V6.1
5648-E63	D50XFLL, E0083LL	WebSphere Channel Protocol for cXML
5648-E81	D5BGFLL, E1BGELL	Host Access Client Package for Multiplatforms V3
5698-FRA	- - -, E00ESLL	Tivoli Management Framework (Distributed only)
5765-F06	D5BHZLL, E1BHYLL	WebSphere Transcoding Publisher 4.0 (Multilingual)

Product identifier	Passport Advantage part number*	Description
5765-F30	D5AW3LL, E1AW2LL	DB2 Connect™ Enterprise Edition
5765-F31	D5AR1LL, E1ARHLL	DB2 Datalinks Manager V8.1
5765-F32	- - - , E00BHLL	DB2 Intelligent Miner™ Modeling, V8.1
5765-F33	- - - , E00BGLL	DB2 Intelligent Miner Visualization, V8.1
5765-F34	D5B52LL, E1B51LL	DB2 UDB Univ Developer's Edition, V8.1
5765-F35	- - - , E1B7HLL	DB2 Workgroup Server Edition V8.1
5765-F36	- - - , E1CVFLL	DB2 Intelligent Miner Scoring
5765-F38	D5ASNLL, E1ASMLL	DB2 Net Search Extender V8.1
5765-F40	D5ATTLL, E1ATSLL	DB2 Spatial Extended
5765-F41	D518ILL, E00BILL	DB2 Enterprise Server DB2 UDB ESE DB Partitioning V8.1
5765-F42	D5AU1LL, E1AU0LL	DB2 Warehouse Manager V8.1
5765-F43	D51NFLL, E00IHLL	DB2 Workgroup Server Unlimited Edition V8.1
5697-F48	D5C0ALL, E1C09LL	SecureWay Firewall AIX
5697-H08	D50XPLL, E0086LL	WebSphere Channel Protocol WebSphere Channel for RosettaNet
5733-IM3	D5AWKLL, E1AWJLL	Intelligent Miner for Data for iSeries
5698-GS2	- - - , E00FHLL	Tivoli SecureWay Global Sign-On
5697-H10	D50Y1LL, E008ALL	WebSphere Channel Protocol for XML
5698-HSM	- - - , E00IFLL	Tivoli Storage Manager for Space Management
5698-ISX	D51MMLL, E00IALL	Tivoli Storage Manager Extended Edition (Continued)
5698-KID	D56G7LL, E16G6LL	Tivoli SecureWay Public Key Infrastructure
5639-M68	- - - , E1AD2LL	Object REXX Development Edition (Windows)
5698-NTV	- - - , E00EULL	Tivoli NetView
5698-PDO	- - - , E00ELLL	Tivoli Access Manager for Operating Systems
5722-RD1	D5C8TLL, E1C8SLL	Content Manager On-Demand for iSeries
5698-SAN	- - - , E00IDLL	Tivoli Storage Manager for Storage Area Networks
5698-SFS	D57FBLL, E17F3LL	Tivoli SANergy® File Sharing

Product identifier	Passport Advantage part number*	Description
5698-SRC	- - -, E00JVLL	Tivoli Storage Resource Manager for Chargeback
5698-SRD	- - -, E00JTLL	Tivoli Storage Resource Manager for Databases
5698-SRE	D51TDLL, E00K0LL	Tivoli Bonus Pack for SAN Management
5698-SRM	D51TALL, E00JZLL	Tivoli Storage Resource Manager
5698-SRS	D51M2LL, E00I4LL	Tivoli SAN Manager
5698-SYS	- - -, E00MHLL	Tivoli Storage Manager for System Backup and Recovery
5722-VI1	D5D1JLL, E1D1ILL	Content Manager for iSeries
5733-WA4	D5ALWLL, E1ALVLL	WebSphere Application Server Advanced Edition for iSeries
5733-WS4	D5CBCLL, E1CBBLL	WebSphere Application Server Advanced Single Server Edition
5698-WSE	- - -, E00FLLL	Tivoli Workload Scheduler for Applications
5698-WSH	- - -, E00FTLL	Tivoli Workload Scheduler

* Passport Advantage part numbers starting with a D represent a new license with maintenance or re-instatement of an expired license. Part numbers starting with an E represent renewals.

You can find full details about Passport Advantage on the Passport Advantage Home page at:

`http://www.lotus.com/services/passport.nsf/WebDocs/Passport_Advantage_Home`

A tutorial on Passport Advantage is available at:

`http://www.lotus.com/services/passport.nsf/startpa.htm`

New with i5/OS V5R3

OS/400 is included with iSeries systems and licensed under the International Program License Agreement (IPLA). OS/400 Version 5 is software keyed to the designated serial number of the machine where it is initially installed. Version 5 of OS/400 is licensed to operate on only that serial number machine. It may not be moved or transferred from one machine to another except in an emergency backup situation.

A per-processor charge applies when running OS/400 on iSeries Models 520, 550, 570, 595, 800, 810, 825, 870, and 890 (processors #2497 and #2498 only).

These terms do not apply to Model 890 systems with #0197, #0198, #2487, or #2488 feature processor cards.

Terms are not changed for OS/400 running on other models of iSeries or AS/400e servers.

For Models 520, 550, 570, 595, 800, 810, 825, 870, and 890 (processors #2497 and #2498 only), OS/400 is priced based on the number of processors using OS/400 on the system. If Linux or AIX 5L is run on a n-way system, an OS/400 license may not be required for the standby processors in the secondary partition.

The number of processors that need an OS/400 license entitlement are the aggregation of all processors, including partial shares of a processor, across all partitions of a single system where OS/400 is used, rounded up to the next highest whole number. Clients must license based on what the iSeries is configured to use, the dedicated and capped partitions, and the virtual processor quantity for uncapped partitions. If large Virtual Processor quantities are configured for uncapped partitions, IBM does not require OS/400 licensing for processors larger than the number of processors in a system.

Each iSeries Edition feature includes the quantity of OS/400 processor licenses for the startup processors of the hardware model, for example:

► A uni-processor Model 520 or 550 with the iSeries Standard or Enterprise Edition includes one OS/400 processor license entitlement.

► A Model 570 2/4-way system with the Standard or Enterprise Edition includes two OS/400 processor license entitlements.

When upgrading from a previous AS/400e or iSeries model to Models 520,550, 570, 810, 825, 870, or 890 (processors #2497 and #2498 only), one of either the Standard or Enterprise Edition feature must be selected. If a software version or release upgrade of OS/400 is needed to support the hardware upgrade, a current Software Subscription or Software Maintenance contract for the system is required, or an After License Fee paid and the Software Maintenance contract acquired for the system.

When upgrading Models 520, 550, 570, 595, 800, 810, 825, 870, or 890 (processors #2497 and #2498 only), the hardware upgrade includes a quantity of OS/400 processor license entitlements. For example, clients with the server package on a 3/6-way system upgrading to an 8/16-way system receive an additional five OS/400 processor license entitlements (startup to startup) for no additional charge as a part of the hardware upgrade. In this example, the startup quantity of the "from" system is three and the startup quantity of the "to" system is eight. The hardware upgrade includes five OS/400 processor license

entitlements, so that after the upgrade, there are license entitlements for all of the startup processors.

Activating standby processors requires that a processor license entitlement for OS/400 be acquired, if OS/400 is run on any fraction of the standby processor. If a standby processor that only uses the Linux operating system is activated, an OS/400 license entitlement is not necessary. A model-to-model per processor upgrade charge applies to OS/400 license entitlements for standby processors.

Software License Manager/400 (SLM/400) assists in license compliance by counting the number of processors using OS/400 and comparing this level of use to the usage limit in the Work License Information (WRKLICINF) interface. If the license entitlement is exceeded, additional OS/400 processor licenses must be acquired, or the configuration of the system must be changed to run OS/400 only on the quantity of processors licensed. A software license key for OS/400 must be entered for continued use past 70 days. This software license key is preloaded by IBM on new iSeries hardware purchases.

A Proof of Entitlement (POE) document may not be shipped with software as proof of a valid license. Otherwise an Electronic Proof of Entitlement (ePoE) is available from the Web. See "OS/400 terms and conditions changes" on page 589 for a full description of this.

In the event that the designated system is transferred (or sold), OS/400 must transfer with it. Notify the receiving party of the program's terms, and provide the POE, LID, IPLA, and Software License Key Sheet documents for OS/400 to the purchaser. IBM licenses the receiving party when that party accepts the program's license terms by initial use of the program. Your OS/400 license is then terminated. When OS/400 is transferred with the system, the bonus programs are also transferred.

When ordering upgrades to software licensed under the IPLA, such as OS/400, provide a copy of the POE to your IBM Representative or IBM Business Partner to validate the license to the software.

To operate on the system with the designated serial number, OS/400 Version 4 or later requires a unique software key supplied by IBM. This is an 18-character alphanumeric code that allows a software product or feature to be used on a specific iSeries server. The OS/400 software key is preloaded by IBM on new iSeries server purchases.

In the case of a hardware upgrade to a Version 5 server or a software-only upgrade to an OS/400 Version 5 release, the OS/400 software key provided by IBM should be entered at the time of installation. However, the system and software operate for 70 days without the software key. During those 70 days, the system generates daily warning messages requesting that the client obtain and

enter an OS/400 software key from IBM. The first IPL requested after 70 days requires a valid OS/400 software key to complete the successfully.

For software-only OS/400 Version 5 orders, the OS/400 License Authorization Code is ordered from IBM. Contact your IBM Representative or IBM Business Partner for ordering information.

Many of the program products and optional features also require a software key to function. These are all included in the Keyed Stamped Media distribution.

OS/400 terms and conditions changes

Note the following changes to the terms and conditions for OS/400:

► Online software agreements

In i5/OS V5R3, it is a system requirement that online software agreements are accepted for the Licensed Internal Code (LIC) and OS/400 operating system. On software upgrades, this is through the Prepare for Install menu. If these software agreements are not accepted, the upgrade of LIC cannot continue. Any other programs that have software agreements must also be accepted before they are upgraded to i5/OS V5R3.

Software agreements can be accessed from the WRKSFWAGR command.

► Electronic Proof of Entitlement

With i5/OS V5R3, the following products have an ePoE, which replaces the printed POE that shipped in the past.

Product	OS/400 option
Operating System	5722-SS1
Media and Storage Extensions	5722-SS1 Opt.18
OptiConnect	5722-SS1 Opt. 23
DB2 Symmetric Multiprocessing	5722-SS1 Opt. 26
DB2 Multisystem	5722-SS1 Opt. 27
PSF/400 1-45 IPM Printer Support	5722-SS1 Opt. 36
PSF/400 1-100 IPM Printer Support	5722-SS1 Opt. 37
PSF/400 Any Speed Printer Support1	5722-SS1 Opt. 38
High Availability (HA) Switchable Resources	5722-SS1 Opt. 41
HA Journal Performance	5722-SS1 Opt.42

Product	OS/400 option
Cryptographic Access Provider 128-bit for iSeries	5722-AC3
Advanced Function Printing Utility	5722-AF1
Advanced DBCS Printer Support for AS/400	5722-AP1
Backup, Recovery, and Media Services (BRMS) for iSeries	5722-BR1
Cryptographic Access Provider 128-bit	5722-CE3
Communications Utilities for iSeries	5722-CM1
Connect for iSeries V2.0	5733-CO2
Cryptographic Support for AS/400	5722-CR1
System/38 Utilities	5722-DB1
DB2 Universal Database (UDB) Extenders for iSeries V8	5722-DE1
CICS® for iSeries	5722-DFH
Business Graphics Utility for AS/400	5722-DS1
DB2 DataPropagator 7.2	5722-DP4
Facsimile Support for iSeries	5798-FAX
Domino Fax for iSeries	5733-FXD
Infoprint Designer for iSeries	5733-ID1
Grid Toolbox for iSeries	5733-GT1
Infoprint Server for iSeries	5722-IP1
Advanced Job Scheduler for iSeries	5722-JS1
DB2 Universal Database (UDB) Express Server Edition for Linux as available with iSeries Enterprise Editions	5722-LD1
Managed System Services for iSeries	5722-MG1
Application Program Driver for AS/400	5722-PD1
WebSphere Portal - Express Plus V5.0.2 for iSeries as available with iSeries Enterprise Editions (5733-ED1)	5733-PE1
Performance Tools	5722-PT1
Query for iSeries	5722-QU1
System Manager for iSeries	5722-SM1
DB2 Query Management and SQL Developers Kit for iSeries	5722-ST1

Product	OS/400 option
Tivoli Monitoring for Web Infrastructure as available with iSeries Enterprise Editions	5733-TMW
WebSphere Development Studio for iSeries as available with iSeries Enterprise Editions	5722-WDS
Web Enablement	5722-WE1
XML Toolkit for iSeries	5733-XT1
iSeries Access Family	5722-XW1

An ePoE is created for new software orders for which entitlement is purchased at Version 5 Release 1, 2, or 3. To access an ePoE, you must register first at this site to receive a Web ID:

http://www.ibm.com/account/registration/selfreg

After you receive the Web ID, you can access the ePoE and software key from the following Web site:

http://www.ibm.com/software/lms

You access ePoE and software key data to view and print, transfer to another system, or update customer information about which the product is installed.

For OS/400 V5R1 and V5R2 products purchased prior to 11 June 2004, the capability to transfer those products outside the enterprise will continue to require a hardcopy POE. For those purchased after 11 June 2004, an ePoE is available. When a product is upgraded, destroy the original IBM-printed POE.

For the i5/OS V5R3 products mentioned, these programs are not transferable to another party outside of the enterprise and its subsidiaries (where a subsidiary is more than 50% owned by the enterprise).

Keyed Stamped Media Distribution

Many OS/400 product features are available on Keyed Stamped Media shipped with OS/400. This provides on demand delivery of these products and features and allows a 70-day evaluation period for any of the provided products or features. To use the software distributed on the Keyed Stamped Media after the 70-day evaluation period, the software license must be ordered and a software key is created. Contact your IBM Representative or IBM Business Partner for ordering information.

New software license keys are required when the version, release, or modification level of the software changes, or the software is transferred to a different system. Some software is keyed based on the software group. A new software key must be obtained when the software group changes.

> **Note**: When ordering software license keys for the iSeries 720, 730, 740, and newer models, the Processor Feature code that is used is displayed in the QPRCFEAT system value or in the Hardware Service Manager report.

If a keyed product or feature is to be upgraded, the current Proof of Entitlement or the invoice must be provided to your IBM Representative or IBM Business Partner as proof of license.

Keyed Stamped Media Distribution for i5/OS V5R3

The following products are included with the standard set for every software or upgrade order.

- **5722-SS1** IBM i5/OS
    - Option 18 Media and Storage Extensions
    - Option 36 Print Services Facility 1-45 IPM Printer Support
    - Option 37 Print Services Facility 1-100 IPM Printer Support
    - Option 38 Print Services Facility Any speed Printer Support
    - Option 41 High Availability Switchable Resources
    - Option 42 High Availability Journal Performance

- **5722-AF1** AFP Utilities for iSeries

- **5722-AP1** Advanced DBCS Printer Support for iSeries
    - Option 1 Advanced DBCS Printer Support - IPDS

- **5722-BR1** Backup Recovery and Media Services for iSeries
    - Option 1 - Network
    - Option 2 - Advance

- **5722-CM1** Communication Utilities for iSeries

- **5722-DE1** DB2 Universal Databases Extenders for iSeries V7.2

- **5722-DP4** DB2 DataPropagator for iSeries V8.1

- **5722-IP1** Infoprint Server for iSeries

- **5722-JS1** Advanced Job Scheduler for iSeries

- **5722-PT1** Performance Tools for iSeries
    - Option 1 - Manager
    - Option 2 - Agent

- **5722-QU1** Query for iSeries
- **5722-ST1** DB2 Query Manager and SQL Development Kit for iSeries
- **5722-WDS** WebSphere Development Studio
- **5722-XH2** iSeries Access for Web
- **5722-XW1** iSeries Access Family
  - Option 1 - iSeries Access Enablement Support

Software keys and guidance for LPAR system upgrades

Clients running logical partitioning may have more than one version or release of a software product on the same iSeries server. Version and release upgrades are acquired via Software Maintenance for clients running in a logical partition (LPAR) just as they are for clients without a LPAR.

It is now possible at OS/400 V5R2 and V5R3 to order additional primary languages for use in a partitioned iSeries which has multiple languages. This is supported by the feature codes listed in the following table.

Language	OS/400 V5R2	i5/OS V5R3
Dutch	8023	8123
English U/L SBCS	8024	8124
Danish	8026	8126
French	8028	8128
German	8029	8129
Spanish	8031	8131
Italian	8032	8132
Swedish	8037	8137
English U/C DBCS	8038	8138
German	8039	8139
Japanese	8062	8162
English U/L DBCS	8084	8184
Korean	8086	8186
Traditional Chinese	8087	8187

Clients who perform both a software group upgrade and a release upgrade at the same time must also perform the software group upgrade for the current product version and release, and then upgrade the release to the desired level. The necessary keys are sent automatically with this method.

Clients who perform a software group upgrade following a software release upgrade must contact the software key center to request necessary back level keys at the higher software group level. Ensure that the software key center is informed that it is an LPAR system. Clients with an LPAR system are entitled to keys for the latest version and release they own and for any earlier version and release.

When calling the software key center, the client should have their:

► IBM customer number
► Specific product and feature information for requested software keys
► If available, incomplete Software Key Sheet shipped with their software order
► The POE document (or IBM invoice for the software product)
► Hardware serial number for the system about which they are calling

Temporary software keys (40-day usage) are provided if a permanent software key cannot be provided due to entitlement or other problems requiring an IBM Business Partner or IBM Representative support to correct.

Key center contact information			
Site	Hours	Telephone number	e-mail address
U.S.A	Monday to Friday 06:00 to 17:00 MST	1-800-446-8989 1-303-924-4671 Fax: 1-303-924-9644	uskeys@dk.ibm.com®
Canada	Monday to Thursday 09:00 to 18:00 Eastern Time Friday 09:00 to 17:00 Eastern Time	1-800-426-2255 1-905-316-0323 Fax: 1-905-316-5267	swkeys@ca.ibm.com
Asia Pacific South	08:30 to 17:00	61-2-9951-9629 1-800-812-894 (Australia only) Fax: 61- 2-9951-9791 and 1-800-650-434 (Aus. only)	keys@au1.ibm.com
Japan	09:00 to 17:30 Japan Time	81-46-215-6808 Fax:81-462-74-4714	E20721@jp.ibm.com
Austria	08:00 to 23:00 Central European Time	0800-291461 Fax: +45 48 14 03 91	dekeys@dk.ibm.com

Key center contact information			
Site	**Hours**	**Telephone number**	**e-mail address**
Belgium	08:00 to 23:00 Central European Time	0800-738-21 0800-716-04 Fax: +45 48 14 03 91	bnlkeys@dk.ibm.com
Denmark	08:00 to 23:00 Central European Time	80-32-16-19 Fax: +45 48 14 03 91	nordkeys@dk.ibm.com
Finland	08:00 to 23:00 Central European Time	0800-1-145 66 Fax: +45 48 14 03 91	nordkeys@dk.ibm.com
France	08:00 to 23:00 Central European Time	0800-910-212 Fax: +45 48 14 03 91	frkeys@dk.ibm.com
Germany	08:00 to 23:00 Central European Time	0800-1817683 Fax: +45 48 14 03 91	dekeys@dk.ibm.com
Ireland	08:00 to 23:00 Central European Time	1-800-554-507 Fax: +45 48 14 03 91	ukkeys@dk.ibm.com
Italy	08:00 to 23:00 Central European Time	800-876319 Fax: +45 48 14 03 91	itkeys@dk.ibm.com
Luxembourg	08:00 to 23:00 Central European Time	0800-2250 (French) Fax: +45 48 14 03 91	bnlkeys@dk.ibm.com
Netherlands	08:00 to 23:00 Central European Time	0800-022-3305 Fax: +45 48 14 03 91	bnlkeys@dk.ibm.com
Norway	08:00 to 23:00 Central European Time	80-01-00-62 Fax: +45 48 14 03 91	nordkeys@dk.ibm.com
Poland	08:00 to 23:00 Central European Time	00800-4511308 Fax: +45 48 14 03 91	eastkeys@dk.ibm.com
Portugal	08:00 to 23:00 Central European Time	080-084-5770 Fax: +45 48 14 03 91	ibekeys@dk.ibm.com
South Africa	08:00 to 23:00 Central European Time	0800-994-407 Fax: +45 48 14 03 91	ukkeys@dk.ibm.com
Spain	08:00 to 23:00 Central European Time	900-994-547 Fax: +45 48 14 03 91	ibekeys@dk.ibm.com
Sweden	08:00 to 23:00 Central European Time	020-798-456 Fax: +45 48 14 03 91	nordkeys@dk.ibm.com
Switzerland	8:00 to 23:00 Central European Time	0800-787371 Fax: +55 11 885 2263	dekeys@dk.ibm.com
United Kingdom	08:00 to 23:00 Central European Time	0800-965-441 Fax: +45 48 14 03 91	ukkeys@dk.ibm.com

Key center contact information			
Site	**Hours**	**Telephone number**	**e-mail address**
Other countries (regions) including Europe, Middle East, Africa, Latin America	08:00 to 23:00 Central European Time	+45-48-14-03-91 Fax: +45 48 14 03 91	eastkeys@dk.ibm.com

For more information about key centers, see:

http://www.ibm.com/servers/eserver/iseries/wwkms

26

IBM licensed programs: Database accessories

DB2 Universal Database (UDB) for iSeries is the relational database manager that is fully integrated on your iSeries server. Because it is integrated, DB2 UDB for iSeries is easy to use and manage. DB2 UDB for iSeries embodies flexibility through the support of its traditional database interface along with enhancing the Structured Query Language (SQL)-based database required by today's Enterprise Application Systems.

Multiple databases are now supported on an iSeries server through the use of independent disk pools. You can manage all of the databases on the server using iSeries Navigator. DB2 UBD provides databases access from client interfaces such as Linux partitions and Windows systems.

This chapter describes the accessories available from IBM to complement the IBM i5/OS integrated database.

Product name	Product number	Refer to page
DB2 OLAP Server™ for iSeries, V8.1	5724-B78	599
IBM System/38 Utilities for AS/400	5722-DB1	603
IBM DB2 Universal Database Extenders for iSeries V7.2	5722-DE1	607
IBM DB2 DataPropagator for iSeries, V8.1	5722-DP4	600
IBM DB2 Warehouse Manager V8	5724-E66	603
DB2 QMF Distributed Edition V8.1 for Multiplatforms	5724-E86	602
DB2 Spatial Extender Version 8	5765-F40	604
DB2 Table Editor for iSeries V4.3	5697-G84	605
IBM DB2 Web Query Tool for iSeries V1.3	5697-G85	606
IBM DB2 UDB Workgroup Server Edition	5733-LD1	608
IBM Query for iSeries	5722-QU1	601
IBM DB2 Query Manager and SQL Development Kit for iSeries	5722-ST1	601

The following database accessory products are part of the iSeries Access Family (5722-XW1):

► iSeries Access for Windows (5722-XE1) delivers an iSeries Open Database Connectivity (ODBC) driver and OLE DB provider for accessing DB2 for iSeries. It also provides an end-user graphical user interface (GUI) and ActiveX Automation Objects, for uploading PC data to DB2 for iSeries or downloading DB2 for iSeries data to the PC.

► iSeries Access for Web (5722-XH2) delivers an end-user GUI for uploading or downloading DB2 UDB for iSeries data. It also provides the capability to download database information to a PC browser or spreadsheet, and to convert it to Portable Document Format (PDF) or Extensible Markup Language (XML) format.

Refer to Chapter 31, "IBM eServer iSeries Access products" on page 663, for a description of these products.

DB2 OLAP Server for iSeries V8.1 (5724-B78)

DB2 OLAP Server for iSeries V8.1 (5724-B78)	
With DB2 OLAP Server for iSeries, V8.1, parallelism is extended to help exploit the modern hardware and to improve system performance and throughput. DB2 OLAP Server for iSeries can access lower-level data in a relational database in a seamless way. It improves scalability of the cube and relational drill-through.	
DB2 OLAP Server can be used for management, reporting, analysis, modeling, planning and data warehousing applications. Typical applications include Sales Profitability, Market share, Supplier Analysis, Executive Information System (EIS) Financial consolidations, Budgeting, Forecasting, and Enterprise performance measurement. The DB2 OLAP Server for iSeries V8.1 program is based on Hyperion Essbase 6.5.	
Relational Storage Manager is included with DB2 OLAP Server. The optional features include Currency Conversion, API, Extended Spreadsheet Toolkit, DB2 OLAP Server for iSeries Partitioning Option V8.1, DB2 OLAP Server for iSeries Builder V8.1, and Data distribution.	
The Hybrid Analysis function in DB2 OLAP Server V8.1 extends the online analytical processing (OLAP) Server. It has moved from a multidimensional OLAP (MOLAP) to a hybrid OLAP (HOLAP), which combines MOLAP with relational OLAP (ROLAP). This allows the OLAP application designed to create cubes based on optimized query performance and data scalability.	
DB2 OLAP Integration Server is required for data description tasks of Hybrid Analysis. DB2 OLAP Integration Server is based on Essbase Integration Services 6.5.	
The included OLAP Miner feature combines the powerful IBM data mining technologies with OLAP technologies.	
Minimum operating system level	OS/400 V5R2
Availability	15 November 2002
Software type	Passport Advantage and Software Maintenance
Installation prerequisites	Refer to the announcement letter for prerequisites required for the client.
Related products	ESSBASE-Ready ISV Products DB2 Data Warehouse Center and DB2 Warehouse Manager DB2 Intelligent Miner for Data
Client code	Packaged and delivered with server code separate from OS/400
Replaces product	DB2 OLAP Server for AS/400, Version 7.1 (5686-OLP)
Further information	http://www.ibm.com/software/data/db2/db2olap/ http://publib.boulder.ibm.com/html/as400/infocenter.html http://www.redbooks.ibm.com http://www-1.ibm.com/servers/solutions/bi/iseries/

IBM DB2 DataPropagator for iSeries V8.1 (5722-DP4)

IBM DB2 DataPropagator for iSeries V8.1 (5722-DP4)		
IBM DB2 DataPropagator for iSeries V8.1 provides read-only, update anywhere, and on demand replication between relational sources and targets. It consists of the Administration, Capture, and Apply autonomous components and programs.		
DataPropagator for iSeries provides capabilities to view and analyze multiple aspects of business information. Replication provides the ability to share the same data among multiple locations, or multiple business functions. Data replication can consistently deliver he right data, to the right people, at he right time, allowing them to improve decision making, increase online throughput, improve data availability, and reduce application costs		
Data replication has proven value in application areas with a need to share access to data in a distributed computer environment. In addition to one-for-one copying of data from source to target, replication allowed clients to combine data from multiple sources into a single target location for easy access and analysis.		
Ordering	OS/400 software group-based	
Minimum operating system level	OS/400 V5R2	
Program size	15 MB	
HIPO	1035	
Availability	30 August 2002	
Software type	Software Subscription	
Prerequisites	OS/400 V5R2 The Replication Center requires Windows	
Replaces products	IBM DB2 DataPropagator Version 7.1 for AS/400 (5769-DP3) IBM DB2 DataPropagator Relational for AS/400 V5.1 (5769-DP2) IBM DB2 DataPropagator Relational Capture and Apply OS/400 (5769-DP1)	

Further information	`http://www.ibm.com/software/data/dpropr/`
	`http://publib.boulder.ibm.com/html/as400/infocenter.html`
	`http://www.redbooks.ibm.com`
	`http://www.ibm.com/software/data/dpropr/cmd/as400cmd.html`	

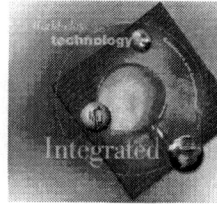

IBM Query for iSeries (5722-QU1)

IBM Query for iSeries (5722-QU1)	
We recommend Query for iSeries for non-programming users of 5250-family workstations or remotely attached 3270-family Web links who must extract, display, and format reports containing data from the iSeries database, and merge resulting data into documents.	
Further information	`http://www.ibm.com/eserver/iseries/software/query/`

IBM DB2 Query Manager and SQL Development Kit for iSeries (5722-ST1)

IBM DB2 Query Manager and SQL Development Kit for iSeries (5722-ST1)	
The DB2 Query Manager and SQL Development Kit for iSeries provides an interactive query and report writing interface. It also provides precompilers and tools to assist in writing SQL application programs in high-level programming languages. Most SQL functions can be performed interactively or in application programs.	
The DB2 Query Manager and SQL Development Kit for iSeries provides an SQL Development Kit for relational database access using programming languages such as C, RPG, COBOL, PL/I, and REXX. The interactive query interfaces, *Query Manager* and *Interactive SQL*, are provided for users to generate queries and reports, and for programmers to test complex SQL statements.	
Ordering	▶ Shipped as a chargeable LPO ▶ OS/400 software group-based ▶ A software key is required. ▶ Included on the Distribution Keyed Media CD
Minimum operating system level	i5/OS V5R3
Program size	24.6 MB
HIPO	1101
Availability	11 June 2004

IBM DB2 Query Manager and SQL Development Kit for iSeries (5722-ST1)	
Software type	Software Subscription (Keyed Media) 5733-SW1 or 5733-SW3 5733-SU1 or 5733-SU3 Software Support 5733-SX1 or 5733-SX3
Prerequisites	Any RISC model of the iSeries or AS/400 except the Model 236
Related product	IBM Query for AS/400 (5722-QU1)
Replaces product	IBM DB2 Query Manager and SQL Development Kit for AS/400 (5769-ST1)
Further information	http://www-1.ibm.com/servers/eserver/iseries/db2/db2sql.htm http://www.ibm.com/eserver/iseries/infocenter http://www.ibm.com/servers/eserver/iseries/db2/

IBM DB2 QMF Distributed Edition for Multiplatforms V8.1 (5724-E86)

IBM DB2 QMF Distributed Edition for Multiplatforms V8.1 (5724-E86)		
Minimum client and OS/400 level	Microsoft Windows (on the Integrated xSeries Server) or client based Server capable of running OS/400 V5R1	
Availability	26 March 2004 Electronic software delivery, media, and documentation	
Software type	Passport Advantage	
Replaces	QMF for Windows for iSeries 5697-G24	
Further information	http://www-3.ibm.com/software/data/qmf/ ftp://ftp.software.ibm.com/software/data/qmf/pdfs/r202046.pdf http://www.ibm.com/servers/eserver/iseries/db2/db2udbprod.htm http://www.ibm.com/software/data/qmf/library.html	

IBM DB2 UDB Data Warehouse Enterprise and Standard Edition V8.1 (5724-E66)

IBM DB2 UDB Data Warehouse Enterprise Edition and Standard Edition V8.1 (5724-E66)	
IBM is a leader in Business Intelligence. The technology built into the DB2 UDB Data Warehouse Editions enables real-time information integration, insight, and decision making. The new editions combine the strength of DB2 UDB with the essential IBM BI infrastructure.	
Ordering	**5724-E66** Part number BB0HENA for DB2 UDB Data Warehouse Enterprise Edition V8.1 Media Pack Part number BB0HFNA for DB2 UDB Data Warehouse Standard Edition V8.1
Prerequisites	`http://www-3.ibm.com/software/data/db2/` `datawarehouse/`
Availability	27 June 2003 (electronic software delivery) 25 July 2003 (media and documentation)
Software type	Passport Advantage
Replaces product	DB2 Warehouse Manager V8 (5765-F42)
Further information	`http://www-3.ibm.com/software/data/db2/datawarehouse/`

IBM System/38 Utilities for AS/400 (5722-DB1)

IBM System/38 Utilities for AS/400 (5722-DB1)	
System/38 Utilities is used to run applications that were written using System/38 Data File Utility or System/38 Query and that were migrated from the System/38. The alternative is to rewrite all these existing System/38 applications. The Text Management/38 component of System/38 Utilities for AS/400 is for use by migrators whose word processing and data processing personnel use the Text Management/38 component of System/38 Personal Services.	
Further information	`http://www.ibm.com/eserver/iseries/software/s38utilities/`

DB2 Spatial Extender Version 8 (5765-F40)

DB2 Spatial Extender Version 8 (5765-F40)	
DB2 Spatial Extender allows you to store, manage, and analyze spatial data (information about the location of geographic features) in DB2 UDB along with traditional data for text and numbers. With this capability, you can generate, analyze, and exploit spatial information about geographic features, such as the locations of office buildings or the size of a flood zone. DB2 Spatial Extender extends the function of DB2 UDB with a set of advanced spatial data types that represent geometries such as points, lines, and polygons and many functions and features that interoperate with those new data types. These capabilities allow you to integrate spatial information with your business data, adding another element of intelligence to your database.	
Further information	`http://www.ibm.com/eserver/iseries/db2/extender/`

DB2 Table Editor for iSeries V4.3 (5697-G84)

DB2 Table Editor for iSeries V4.3 (5697-G84)		
DB2 Table Editor lets you easily support your business processes and empower novice end users, with customized task-specific table editing forms. Database experts gain a robust set of tools to perform ad hoc table editing tasks across multiple databases and platforms. Since end users only need a browser, the solutions you choose to create with DB2 Table Editor have maximum reach. DB2 Table Editor makes it possible to provide direct DB2 database access to anyone, for creating, reviewing, or updating data. Task-specific forms restricted to specific data and actions can be quickly built and rolled out to novice end users An expert interface can be used for browsing existing databases and ad hoc actions. A Java-enabled browser is all you need on the client machine for using DB2 Table Editor solutions.		
Ordering	Shipped as a chargeable LPO OS/400 software group-based	
Minimum operating system level	OS/400 V5R1	
Availability	26 July 2002	
Software type	Software Subscription 5733-SW1 or 5733-SW3	
Replaces product	IBM DB2 Forms for iSeries V2 (5697-G14)	
Further information	http://www-3.ibm.com/software/data/db2imstools/ http://www-306.ibm.com/software/data/db2imstools/db2tools/db2te/	

IBM DB2 Web Query Tool for iSeries V1.3 (5697-G85)

IBM DB2 Web Query Tool for iSeries V1.3 (5697-G85)		
IBM DB2 Web Query Tool connects all your users to multiple enterprise databases, securely and simultaneously, regardless of database size, hardware, operating system, or location.		
Ordering	Shipped as a chargeable LPO OS/400 software group-based	
Minimum operating system level	OS/400 V5R1	
Availability	26 July 2002	
Software type	Software Subscription 5733-SW1 or 5733-SW3	
Prerequisites	DB2 UDB for iSeries Version 4 or later	
Replaces product	DB2 Web Query Tool for iSeries, Version 1.2	
Further information	http://www-3.ibm.com/software/data/db2imstools/	

IBM DB2 UDB Extenders for iSeries V8 (5722-DE1)

IBM DB2 Universal Database Extenders for iSeries V8 (5722-DE1)	
Web-enabled On Demand Business is driving most companies to redefine their IT strategy. Moving away from proprietary data formats toward an open, interchangeable format, such as XML, to transact business on the Web is a key part of the strategy.	
In this electronic age, the bulk of a company's managed data (90%), including e-mail, technical and business documents, contracts, problem reports, and customer complaints, is still in textual form. Companies continue to look for efficient ways to leverage such massive textual data to provide valuable information. IBM DB2 Universal Database Extenders for iSeries V8 can help.	
Ordering	Shipped as a chargeable LPO OS/400 software group-based
Minimum operating system level	i5/OS V5R3
Program size	73 to 300 MB + indexes
HIPO	1004
Availability	11 June 2004
Software type	Software Subscription (Keyed Stamped Media) 5733-SW1 or 5733-SW3 5733-SU1 or 5733-SU3 Software Support 5733-SX1 or 5733-SX3 SUx and SXx must be combined
Further information	http://www.ibm.com/software/data/db2/extenders/ http://www-1.ibm.com/servers/eserver/iseries/db2/

IBM DB2 UDB Workgroup Server Edition for Linux (5733-LD1)

IBM DB2 Universal Database Workgroup Server Edition for Linux (5733-LD1)	
IBM DB2 V8 for Linux, UNIX, and Windows marks the next stage in the evolution of the relational database. DB2 is the database of choice for the development and deployment of such critical solutions as: ▶ On Demand Business ▶ Business Intelligence ▶ Content management ▶ Enterprise Resource Planning ▶ Customer Relationship Management DB2 for Linux supports and embraces open standards including Java and XML. It integrates with many open source products such as Apache, PHP, Perl, and Python. DB2 UDB is the most scalable database in production today that can manage important data on a single PC, symmetric multiprocessors (SMPs), clusters, and the mainframe for Linux. Also, with IBM DB2 Everyplace®, clients can manage important data on linux and embedded Linux devices.	
Minimum operating system level	OS/400 V5R2
Software type	When the Enterprise Edition for iSeries is ordered on Models 825, 870, and 890 IBM IPLA
Maintenance	Includes Software Maintenance for one year from the Hardware Edition purchase. Clients need to register for this Software Maintenance coverage, along with the Software Maintenance for other Passport Advantage products in the Hardware Editions at: http://www.ibm.com/servers/eservers/iseries/hardware/editions/index.html
Availability	12 September 2003
System requirements	The validation status for new Linux kernels and distributions is frequently updated. To obtain the current information for supported Linux software levels, see: http://www.ibm.com/software/data/db2/linux/validate/
Further information	http://www.ibm.com/software/data/db2/udb/edition-wse.html http://www.ibm.com/software/data/db2/udb/opsys-linux.html

27

WebSphere and On Demand Business for iSeries

IBM i5/OS contains everything you need to quickly create a Web presence. As the integrated platform, it provides the infrastructure and components necessary to "Start Simple" with On Demand Business adoption. For example, WebSphere Application Server - Express is now included in i5/OS V5R3.

In addition to these base features, a set of On Demand Business products is available to help you "Grow Fast", allowing you to build a complete On Demand Business Web site that is secure and easy to develop, maintain, and scale based on your needs. These products (listed in the following table) belong to the WebSphere family of products offered by IBM for the iSeries server.

Each of these products addresses specific client requirements to build applications for On Demand Business quickly and easily. They often include graphical user interface (GUI)-based PC development and management tools.

The base of these WebSphere products is the WebSphere Application Server technology. An application server "serves" applications written in Java, which in turn can leverage your existing iSeries programs and data.

Product name	Product number	Refer to page
IBM Business Solutions	5722-BZ1	615
IBM Connect for iSeries Version 2.0	5733-CO2	619
IBM WebSphere Application Server Version 5.1, Developer Edition	5724-D18	617
IBM WebSphere Application Server - Express Version 5.1 for iSeries	5722-E51	613
IBM WebSphere Host Access Transformation Services (HATS)		621
IBM WebSphere Portal Express and Express Plus	5724-E77	620
IBM Grid Toolbox V3 for OS/400	5733-GT1	622
IBM WebSphere Commerce for iSeries, Version 5.6 Express Edition IBM WebSphere Commerce for iSeries, Version 5.6 Business Edition, IBM WebSphere Commerce for iSeries, Version 5.6 Professional Edition	5724-I36 5724-I38 5724-I40	618
IBM WebSphere Application Server Version 4.0, Advanced Edition for iSeries	5733-WA4	611
IBM Web Enablement for iSeries	5722-WE1	614
IBM WebSphere Application Server Version 4.0, Advanced Single Server Edition for iSeries	5733-WS4	611
IBM WebSphere Application Server Version 5.1 for iSeries	5733-W51	616
IBM WebSphere Application Server Version 5.1, Network Deployment for iSeries	5733-W51	616

WebSphere Application Server offerings

iSeries clients have the following WebSphere Application Server offerings from which they can choose:

► **IBM WebSphere Application Server - Express for iSeries**: This is a Java application server based on a servlet-based engine that turns your existing Web server (IBM HTTP Server for iSeries) into a Java Web application server. This offers small and mid-sized companies with an integrated package with:

- IBM WebSphere Application Server - Express, Version 5 for iSeries, an application server with JavaServer Pages (JSPs) and Java Servlets
- WebSphere Development Studio Client for iSeries, the latest in tool integration for iSeries application development
- IBM Telephone Directory V 5.1 for iSeries, a business application that can be used for a company's directory of white pages
- Web Services Object Runtime Framework (WORF), a Web service for accessing DB2 Universal Database (UDB)

► **IBM WebSphere Application Server V5.1 for iSeries**: WebSphere Application Server Network Deployment Version 5.1 extends WebSphere Application Server Version 5.1, for iSeries with clustering, edge services, and high availability for distributed configurations. As the foundation of the WebSphere software platform, WebSphere Application Server V5.1 reinforces its reputation as the premier Java and Web Services technology-based application platform, integrating enterprise data and transactions with the dynamic On Demand Business world. It offers a rich On Demand Business application deployment environment with a set of application services that includes transaction management, security, clustering, performance availability, connectivity, and scalability.

WebSphere Application Server is designed for full Java 2 Platform, Enterprise Edition (J2EE) V1.3 compatibility. It supports SDK 1.4 to meet the changing requirements of On Demand Business.

► **WebSphere Application Server Version 4.0, Advanced Single Server Edition (5733-WS4)**: This is a Java application server based on a servlet-based engine that turns your existing Web server (IBM HTTP Server for iSeries) into a Java Web application server. As the core element of the Application Framework for e-business, Advanced Edition, single server option is the foundation of the WebSphere application server family.

► **WebSphere Application Server Version 4.0, Advanced Edition (5733-WA4):** This is a powerful Java-based development and deployment environment for applications for On Demand Business. WebSphere Advanced Edition provides support for scaling Web sites into security-enhanced, transactional-based On Demand Business application sites.

WebSphere Advanced Edition provides Enterprise JavaBean (EJB) support for host-based transactions, and offers sophisticated tools to simplify distributed, component-based application development. The EJB architecture is component-based for the development and deployment of server-based business applications. It greatly simplifies the separation of business applications from underlying system services.

To understand the IBM On Demand Business strategy for the iSeries server, and the positioning of strategic WebSphere products, refer to *WebSphere for IBM @server iSeries Server Buying and Selling Guide*, REDP-3646.

> **Note:** The commercial processing workload (CPW) and memory configuration references for the WebSphere products in this chapter represent the recommended minimum requirements. Deployments that must support many users, or require shorter response times, may require additional resources. Use the IBM @server Workload Estimator to help size all system configurations:
>
> http://www-912.ibm.com/wle/EstimatorServlet

Product positioning: WebSphere Application Server and Jakarta Tomcat

The strategic Web application server from IBM is WebSphere Application Server. The latest version of WebSphere Application Server is Version 5.1. All WebSphere Application Server offerings support Servlets, JSPs, EJBs, and more.

Some iSeries clients want a basic, no-cost Web application server that supports servlets and JavaServer Pages. Relying on the IBM HTTP Server (powered by Apache) as its Web server, the Apache Software Foundation's Jakarta Tomcat provides a basic Web application server for iSeries clients. Jakarta Tomcat is available with OS/400 and at no additional cost to clients.

Jakarta Tomcat is offered as a way for iSeries clients to "get started" with Java server-side components and Web application serving. Clients should select WebSphere Application Server when they need to deploy solutions for On Demand Business that are J2EE compliant, provide the most function, and deliver the highest levels of reliability, scalability, and security.

If an IBM or Solution Developer application requires WebSphere Application Server as the base Web application server, do not consider Jakarta Tomcat as an alternative Web application server. Examples of IBM products that require WebSphere Application Server as the base Web application server include

WebSphere Commerce, WebSphere Payment Manager, and WebSphere Host Publisher.

Clients who require a robust and scalable Web application server can select WebSphere Application Server. Jakarta Tomcat provides fewer functions and capabilities compared to the IBM WebSphere Application Server. For example, Jakarta Tomcat does not support Enterprise JavaBeans, is not J2EE compliant, and does not provide Domino integration.

For more information, see *iSeries e-business Handbook: A Technology and Product Reference*, SG24-5694.

IBM WebSphere Application Server - Express Version 5.1 for iSeries (5722-E51)

IBM WebSphere Application Server - Express Version 5.1 for iSeries (5722-E51)		
IBM WebSphere Application Server - Express for iSeries is for fast, productive development, deployment, and management of dynamic Web sites. With smaller budgets and limited IT resources, you face special challenges getting started in On Demand Business. IBM WebSphere Application Server - Express for iSeries, delivers broad server functionality with a smaller, up-front investment. Think of it as your low-risk, affordable entry to On Demand Business.		
Ordering	5724-D06 Also see http://publib-b.boulder.ibm.com/Red books.nsf/portals/iseriesRedbooks	**IBM WebSphere Software**
Minimum operating system level	OS/400 V5R1	
HIPO	N/A	
Availability	20 February 2004	
Software type	Passport Advantage	
Installation prerequisites	http://www-1.ibm.com/servers/eserver/iseries/software/ websphere/wsappserver/	
Program size	796 MB	
Related products	IBM WebSphere Application Server, Version 5 for iSeries (5733-WS5) WebSphere Application Server Version 4.0, Advanced Single Server Edition (5733-WA4) WebSphere Application Server Version 4.0, Advanced Edition (5733-WS4) IBM Web Enablement (5722-WE1 IBM WebSphere Application Server - Express Version 5.0 for iSeries	
Replaces product	WebSphere Application Server Standard Edition V3.5 (5733-AS3)	

IBM WebSphere Application Server - Express Version 5.1 for iSeries (5722-E51)	

Further information	`http://www-3.ibm.com/software/webservers/appserv/`
	`http://www-1.ibm.com/servers/eserver/iseries/software/`
	`websphere/wsappserver/`
	`http://publib-b.boulder.ibm.com/Redbooks.nsf/portals/`
	`iseriesRedbooks`

IBM Web Enablement for iSeries (5722-WE1)

IBM Web Enablement for iSeries (5722-WE1)	
IBM Web Enablement for iSeries is a license only product that delivers WebSphere Application Server - Express Version 5.0 and Version 5.1 (5722-IWE and 5722-E51). Web Enablement is included on every i5/OS order. It can be removed from the order if desired. This makes an application server available with i5/OS at no additional cost to the client.	
Ordering	5722-WE1
Minimum operating system level	i5/OS V5R3
HIPO	No
Availability	11 June 2004
Software type	LP specific
Installation prerequisites	See 5722-E51
Program size	N/A
Related products	IBM WebSphere Application Server - Express, Version 5.1 for iSeries (5722-E51) IBM WebSphere Application Server - Express, Version 5.0 for iSeries (5722-IWE)
Replaces product	N/A
Further information	`http://www.ibm.com/servers/eserver/iseries/software/websphere/` `products.html`

IBM Business Solutions Version 1.0 (5722-BZ1)

IBM Business Solutions Version 1.0 (5722-BZ1)

IBM Business Solutions Version 1.0 (5722-BZ1) provides a set of enterprise Web applications available for iSeries servers. Each application is an integrated solution to a common business need that works in conjunction with your existing applications, server components, and enterprise data. The applications demonstrate the value of integrated solutions for On Demand Business, increase worker productivity, provide services that virtually any business may find useful, and are easy to understand and use.

Ordering	5722-BZ1	*IBM WebSphere Software*
Minimum operating system level	OS/400 V5R1	
HIPO	No	
Availability	December 2003	
Software type	LP specific	
Installation prerequisites	`http://www-1.ibm.com/servers/eserver/iseries/software/websphere/ wsappserver/bizapps/product/about.html`	
Program size	N/A	
Related products	IBM WebSphere Application Server - Express, Version 5.1 for iSeries (5722-E51) IBM WebSphere Application Server - Express, Version 5.0 for iSeries (5722-IWE) WebSphere Application Server for iSeries and WebSphere Application Server - Network Deployment for iSeries (5733-WS5 or 5733-WS5)	
Replaces product	N/A	
Further information	`http://www-1.ibm.com/servers/eserver/iseries/software/websphere/ wsappserver/bizapps/product/about.html`	

IBM WebSphere Application Server Version 5.1 for iSeries and Network Deployment for iSeries (5733-W51)

IBM WebSphere Application Server Version 5.1 for iSeries and IBM WebSphere Application Server Version 5.1, Network Deployment for iSeries (5733-W51)	
As the foundation of the WebSphere software platform, IBM WebSphere Application Server Version 5.1 for iSeries and the Network Deployment option reinforce their reputation as premier Java and Web Services technology-based application platforms, integrating enterprise data and transactions with the dynamic On Demand Business world. WebSphere Application Server offers a rich On Demand Business application deployment environment with a set of application services that includes transaction management, security, clustering, performance availability, connectivity, and scalability.	
Ordering product number	Passport Advantage BA0BWML BA0BVML - Network Deployment
HIPO	N/A
Minimum operating system level	OS/400 V5R1
Program size	830 MB ► Plus 635 MB for Network Deployment ► Plus 102 MB for WebSphere MQ
Availability	16 January 2004
Software type	Passport Advantage
Installation prerequisites	http://www.ibm.com/servers/eserver/iseries/software/websphere/wsappserver/
Related products	IBM WebSphere Application Server - Express, Version 5.1 for iSeries (5722-E51) IBM WebSphere Application Server - Express, Version 5.0 for iSeries (5722-IWE) IBM WebSphere Application Server Version 5.0 for iSeries (5733-WS5) IBM WebSphere Application Server Version 5.0, Network Deployment for iSeries (5733-WS5) WebSphere Application Server Version 4.0, Advanced Single Server Edition (5733-WA4) WebSphere Application Server Version 4.0, Advanced Edition (5733-WS4)
Replaces products	IBM WebSphere Application Server Version 5.0 for iSeries (5733-WS5) IBM WebSphere Application Server Version 5.0, Network Deployment for iSeries (5733-WS5) WebSphere Application Server Version 4.0, Advanced Single Server Edition (5733-WA4) WebSphere Application Server Version 4.0, Advanced Edition (5733-WS4) WebSphere Applications Server Advanced Edition V3.5 (5733-WA3)

IBM WebSphere Application Server Version 5.1 for iSeries and IBM WebSphere Application Server Version 5.1, Network Deployment for iSeries (5733-W51)	
Further information	`http://www.ibm.com/servers/eserver/iseries/software/` `websphere/wsappserver/` `http://publib-b.boulder.ibm.com/Redbooks.nsf/portals/` `iseriesRedbooks` `http://www-1.ibm.com/servers/eserver/iseries/software/` `websphere/wsappserver/product/announceb51.html`

IBM WebSphere Application Server Version 5.1 for iSeries, Developer Edition (5724-D18)

IBM WebSphere Application Server Version 5.1 for iSeries, Developer Edition (5724-D18)		
The IBM WebSphere Application Server V5.1 for iSeries Developer Edition is shipped as a licensed program option (LPO). It is the same product as WebSphere Application Server V5.1 for iSeries (Base edition) with different licensing.		
Ordering product number	BA0BUML	
HIPO	N/A	
Minimum operating system level	OS/400 V5R1	
Program size	830 MB	
Availability	16 January 2004	
Software type	Passport Advantage	
Installation prerequisites	`http://www.ibm.com/servers/eserver/iseries/software/websphere` `/wsappserver/`	
Related products	IBM WebSphere Application Server Version 5.1 for iSeries (5733-W51) IBM WebSphere Application Server Version 5.1, Network Deployment for iSeries (5733-W51)	
Replaces product	N/A	
Further information	`http://www.ibm.com/servers/eserver/iseries/software/websphere` `/wsappserver/` `http://www-1.ibm.com/servers/eserver/iseries/software/` `websphere/wsappserver/product/announceb51.html`	

IBM WebSphere Commerce for iSeries, Version 5.6 Business Edition (5724-I38), Professional Edition (5724-I40), and Express Edition (5724-I36)

IBM WebSphere Commerce for iSeries, Version 5.6 Business Edition (5724-I38), Professional Edition (5724-I40), and Express Edition (5724-I36)	
IBM WebSphere Commerce for iSeries, Version 5.6 is a complete e-commerce solution for your business-to-consumer (B2C) or business-to-business (B2B) Web sites.	
WebSphere Commerce Express is an easily installed, yet complete solution to help growing mid-market companies do business on the Web. It is ready to go out-of-the-box to affordably build and maintain an e-commerce site for B2B or B2C.	
WebSphere Commerce Professional Edition increases site functionality for B2B and B2C retailers. By enhancing client buying experiences and improving operational efficiencies, Professional Edition can increase customer satisfaction and loyalty.	
WebSphere Commerce Business Edition provides a powerful solution for running large high-volume B2B and advanced B2C e-commerce Web sites for global On Demand Businesses. It is a flexible infrastructure based on a unified platform for running complex and high volume sites.	
WebSphere Commerce V5.6 is a comprehensive set of integrated software components that help to build, maintain, and manage stores to sell goods and services on the Web. V5.6 builds on the reputation for dependability, scalability, and performance by adding new capabilities to interact with complete context, leverage best practices and to integrate across and beyond the enterprise. Marketing and sales teams can attract and retain customers, and store developers can create and maintain their stores using an improved set of tools.	
Ordering	5724-I38, 5724-I40, 5724-I36 Ordered via Passport Advantage
Minimum operating system level	OS/400 V5R2
HIPO	No
Availability	30 April 2004
Software type	Passport Advantage
Installation prerequisites	http://www.ibm.com/software/webservers/commerce/
Program size	1.25 GB
Related products	IBM WebSphere Payment Manager V5.6 (5733-PYS)
Replaces products	IBM WebSphere Commerce for iSeries Version 5.5 (5724-A18) IBM WebSphere Payment Manager for iSeries Version 5.5 (5722-PY3) WebSphere Commerce Suite Version 5.1 (5798-WC5) WebSphere Commerce V5.4 (5733-WC5

IBM WebSphere Commerce for iSeries, Version 5.6 Business Edition (5724-I38), Professional Edition (5724-I40), and Express Edition (5724-I36)	
Further information	http://www.ibm.com/software/webservers/commerce/ http://www7b.software.ibm.com/wsdd/zones/commerce/

IBM Connect for iSeries Version 2.0 (5733-CO2)

IBM Connect for iSeries Version 2.0 (5733-CO2)	
The Internet market continues to evolve. B2B commerce and collaboration are major growth areas. Increased efficiencies and access to broader markets can improve your competitive advantage.	
Connect for iSeries, a software enablement framework for On Demand Business, enables you to integrate your existing core business applications with applications of other companies, more securely, more quickly, and more easily. With Connect for iSeries, you can:	
► Implement flexible, integrated solutions that work seamlessly with existing business processes	
► Reduce the complexity of implementing new solutions for On Demand Business	
Connect for iSeries Version 2.0 builds on the B2B supplier-enablement function provided in V1 (5733-B2B) by adding the ability to handle many XML protocols. In addition, a broad range of transactions beyond e-commerce transactions is supported.	
The objective of business-to-business operations is to reduce costs, increase responsiveness, and increase communications between businesses. With Connect for iSeries, you extend your processes and products to other businesses.	
Connect for iSeries Version 2.0 enables seamless and secure integration of your existing core business applications with the business applications of your trading partners. Connect for iSeries helps you achieve low-cost, high-function business integration previously only available with EDI solutions.	
Ordering product number	5733-CO2
HIPO	No
Minimum operating system level	OS/400 V5R1
Availability	18 October 2002
Software type	Software Subscription
Installation prerequisites	Advanced Edition (5733-WA3) Cryptographic Access Provider for AS/400 (5769-AC3 or 5722-AC3) http://www-1.ibm.com/servers/eserver/iseries/btob/connect/library.htm
Related products	WebSphere Application Server, WebSphere Commerce Suite, Lotus Domino

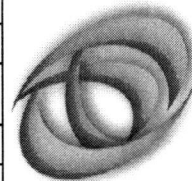

IBM Connect for iSeries Version 2.0 (5733-CO2)	
Replaces product	Connect for iSeries V1(5733-B2B)
Further information	http://www-1.ibm.com/servers/eserver/iseries/btob/connect/ http://www.software.ibm.com http://www.redbooks.ibm.com

IBM WebSphere Portal - Express and Express Plus for Multiplatforms Version 5 (5724-E77)

IBM WebSphere Portal - Express, IBM WebSphere Portal - Express Plus for Multiplatforms, Version 5 (5724-E77)	
IBM WebSphere Portal - Express for Multiplatforms (5724-E77) is one of the industry's most comprehensive portal offerings. It contains a wide range of portal technologies that can help develop and maintain first-class B2C, B2B, and business-to-employee (B2E) portals. Portals serve as a simple, unified access point to Web applications and do much more. They provide valuable functions such as security, search, collaboration, and workflow. A portal delivers integrated content and applications, plus a unified, collaborative workplace. Indeed, portals are the next-generation desktop, delivering applications for On Demand Business over the Web to all kinds of client devices.	
Ordering product number	Express BAOBYML, Express Plus BAOCOML 5724-E77 via Passport Advantage
Minimum operating system level	OS/400 V5R2
HIPO	No
Availability	19 December 2003
Software type	Passport Advantage
Installation prerequisites	http://www.ibm.com/developerworks/websphere/zones/portal/proddoc.html http://www.ibm.com/software/genservers/portalexpress/requirements/index.html
Program size	1.5 GB
Related products	WebSphere Application Server Version 5 for iSeries (5733-WS5) Enterprise Enablement for WebSphere Application Server and Enterprise Enablement for WebSphere Application Server Network Deployment (limited availability offering; bundled with WebSphere Portal)
Replaces product	N/A A WebSphere Portal Enable V4.1 upgrade to WebSphere Portal Express V5 is not supported

IBM WebSphere Portal - Express, IBM WebSphere Portal - Express Plus for Multiplatforms, Version 5 (5724-E77)	
Further information	`http://www.ibm.com/servers/eserver/iseries/software/websphere/portal` `http://www-106.ibm.com/developerworks/websphere/zones/portal/proddoc.html`

IBM WebSphere Host Access Transformation Services

IBM WebSphere Host Access Transformation Services (HATS)		
IBM WebSphere Host Access Transformation Services (HATS) is a Web-to-host HTML emulator with a rules-based transformation engine that converts 5250 green screens to GUIs in real time. This significantly improves the navigation and productivity of host applications. HATS has all the features of WebSphere Portal - Express and adds collaboration features such as instant messaging and virtual team rooms. This allows you to: ▶ Increase employee productivity through easy access to critical business applications and information. ▶ Improve customer and business partner satisfaction and loyalty resulting from portals that are customized to each user's unique needs and interests. ▶ Reduce costs for building and maintaining first class portals. ▶ Quickly build portals to simplify and accelerate access to personalized information and applications. Instant messaging for real-time collaboration with customers, trading partners, or members of your team. ▶ Create discussion areas, group calendars, and assign tasks to team members.		
Product number		*IBM WebSphere Software*
Ordering product number		
Minimum operating system level	i5/OS V5R3	
Availability		
Installation prerequisites	`http://www.ibm.com/developerworks/websphere`	
Related products		
Software type	Passport Advantage	
Replaces product		
Further information	`http://www.ibm.com/servers/eserver/iseries/software/websphere`	

IBM Grid Toolbox V3 for OS/400 (5733-GT1)

IBM Grid Toolbox V3 for OS/400 (5733-GT1)		
The IBM Grid Toolbox V3 for OS/400 is designed to provide building blocks for the emerging grid computing environment that can enable rapid deployment and integration of business applications and processes in a grid. This grid-enabling toolkit contains accepted, standardized development code approved by the Global Grid Forum as part of the Global Toolkit, plus an added database and run-time environment.		
Ordering product number	5733-GT1	*IBM WebSphere Software*
HIPO	No	
Minimum operating system level	i5/OS V5R3	
Program size	650 MB	
Availability	Download - 25 June 2004 CD - 30 July 2004	
Software type	LP specific	
Installation prerequisites	i5/OS V5R3, IBM Developer Kit for Java V1.3, Qshell, Host Servers, PASE, Digital Certificate Manager, IBM HTTP Server, IBM WebSphere Application Server - Express V5.0 and Cryptographic Access Provider (5722-AC3) `http://publib.boulder.ibm.com/eserver/v1r1/en_US/index.html`	
Related product	IBM Web Enablement for iSeries (5722-WE1)	
Replaces product	N/A	
Further information	`http://publib.boulder.ibm.com/eserver/v1r1/en_US/index.html` `http://www.ibm.com/common/ssi`	

28

Lotus products for iSeries

IBM Lotus Domino is the brand name for the server component in a family of integrated messaging, collaboration, and Web application software from IBM. Domino is a software, a framework, and an infrastructure that connects your business to anyone, anywhere, anytime.

Domino is designed for growing organizations that need to improve customer responsiveness and streamline business processes. As we begin the new millennium, electronic business-to-business communication, which was once a luxury, is now a necessity. Electronic mail has become an important application. Web-enabling your business (On Demand Business) is a requirement to remain competitive in the marketplace.

IBM and Lotus work in partnership to offer solutions for today's business environment by combining the strengths of Lotus Domino collaborative software and iSeries™ hardware. The combination of Lotus Domino and the iSeries server delivers a highly scalable and reliable infrastructure for e-collaboration. Lotus Domino for iSeries enables existing iSeries clients to build and deploy messaging, mail, and collaborative applications on the same system as their enterprise applications and data.

For clients who are looking to reduce their service delivery cost by eliminating server farms and consolidating to a single platform, iSeries delivers the scalability and reliability to support thousands of users and applications.

This chapter describes the following IBM products that are offered by Lotus Software.

Product name	Product number	Refer to page
Lotus Domino 6 Message Server	Licensing option	626
Lotus Domino 6 Enterprise Server	Licensing option	626
Lotus Domino 6 Utility Server	Licensing option	626
IBM Lotus Domino Collaboration Express offering	Licensing option	624
IBM Lotus Domino Utility Server Express offering	Licensing option	624
IBM Lotus Domino 6.5 for iSeries	5733-L65	627
Lotus Domino client	Varies	628
IBM Lotus Enterprise Integrator® for iSeries	5733-LEI	630
IBM Lotus Instant Messaging and Web Conferencing for iSeries	5733-LST	631
IBM Lotus Team Workplace for iSeries	5733-LQP	632
IBM Lotus Domino Document Manager	5769-LDD	633
IBM Integrated Domino Fax for iSeries	5733-FXD	634

Refer to *Lotus Domino for the IBM @server iSeries Server Buying and Selling Guide*, REDP-3845, to further understand Domino solutions for the iSeries server.

Domino on iSeries

A Domino on iSeries solution uses the same iSeries values that are discussed in "Reliable, managed availability" on page 23 to provide a compelling case for using the iSeries as the Domino server of choice. Of particular interest to Domino users are:

► Reliability

The stability of the iSeries hardware and software coupled with the iSeries architecture, which logically insulates applications from one another, promotes uninterrupted performance.

- ► Availability

  Centralized backup and recovery for applications and data and the ability to run multiple partitioned Domino servers (DPARs) on one physical iSeries server leads to increased system availabilty.

- ► Scalability

  The iSeries server product line allows for nondisruptive growth from a uni-processor to a 32-way system on the same operating system, using the same skill sets.

- ► Server efficiency

  iSeries servers feature system management capabilities that allow processor resources to be highly used. Servers that lack these capabilities lead to server farms of poorly used systems.

- ► Server consolidation

  Multiple physical Domino servers can be consolidated into one iSeries server, and additional users can be catered for without additional servers. This saves cost and eases the management environment. Local area network (LAN) traffic declines as Domino servers communicate over the virtual Ethernet within the iSeries hardware.

- ► Integration

  Domino for iSeries is designed to integrate with many of the built-in Operating System/400 (OS/400) services including security, backup and recovery, systems management, iSeries Navigator, Java virtual machine (JVM), and IBM DB2 Universal Database (UDB) for iSeries. Furthermore, the iSeries is the only server that allows deployment of Linux, Java, UNIX, Windows, AIX 5L and Domino-based applications on a single server.

Domino server options

Lotus Domino for iSeries is a powerful, popular, versatile, and integrated groupware product from Lotus Software. It provides functions that include e-mail, workflow-based computing, and the integration and management of both structured and unstructured data. Domino is a *server* product that runs on a variety of platforms, providing easy-to-manage interpretability in a heterogeneous network.

Versions of IBM Lotus Domino prior to Version 6 are not supported at i5/OS V5R3. Lotus Domino 6 for iSeries includes five separately orderable components, as represented in the following table.

Domino Server Options	Description
IBM Lotus Domino Messaging Server	IBM Lotus Domino Messaging Server combines full support for the latest Internet mail standards with Domino's state of the art messaging and calendaring capabilities, all in one manageable and reliable package.
IBM Lotus Domino Enterprise Server	IBM Lotus Domino Enterprise Server includes all functions of the messaging server, plus support for custom intranet and Internet applications, and partitioning and clustering technology for high availability.
IBM Lotus Domino Utility Server	IBM Lotus Domino Utility Server is an application server license option that includes unlimited access to non-mail applications. Entitlement to messaging capability is *not* available with this option.
IBM Lotus Domino Collaboration Express offering	The IBM Lotus Domino Collaboration Express offering is powered by the Domino Enterprise Server and allows clients to use both the messaging and collaborative capabilities of Domino. Clients can choose to access Domino via Lotus Notes® or Lotus Domino Web Access (iNotes™) clients for both e-mail and collaborative applications.
IBM Lotus Domino Utility Server Express offering	The IBM Lotus Domino Utility Server Express offering is powered by the Domino Enterprise Server. It provides unlimited access to collaborative applications, but does not allow the use of individual mail files. Clients can choose to access their Domino applications through a Web browser or via a separately purchased Lotus Notes client. IBM Lotus Domino Utility Server Express makes applications available to users who are internal to that organization and to external users. Access is allowed for individually authenticated and anonymous users.

IBM Lotus Domino 6.5 for iSeries (5733-L65)

IBM Lotus Domino 6.5 for iSeries (5733-L65)

With the delivery of Domino 6.5 Lotus continues to play a major role in the On Demand Business revolution. To meet the challenges of business globalization, frequent mergers and acquisitions, and the increasing demand for Web-based business tools, Lotus has combined both evolution and innovation in its latest upgrade of Domino server technology. The features in Domino 6.5 build on the features in previous releases to address rapidly changing industry trends and meet their challenges directly.

Ordering product number	5724-E70
Minimum operating system level	OS/400 V5R1
HIPO	N/A
Availability	September 2003 (6.5) March 2004 (6.5.1)
Software type	Software Maintenance
Installation prerequisites	http://www.lotus.com/products/product4.nsf/wdocs/ 65dominosysrequirements http://www-10.lotus.com/ldd/notesua.nsf/RN?OpenView
Related products	IBM Integrated Domino Fax for iSeries (5733-FXD) Lotus Enterprise Integrator (LEI) (5733-LE1)
Replaces product	Lotus Domino Server for iSeries R5
Ordering	Domino 6 is orderable through standard Lotus channels only. http://www.ibm.com/software/howtobuy
Further information	http://www.ibm.com/servers/eserver/iseries/domino/ http://www.lotus.com/products/r5web.nsf/webpi/ Domino+for+iSeries/ http://www.lotus.com/ldd/domino6

Domino Notes client choices

The choice of clients supported by Domino for iSeries are represented in the following table.

Lotus Notes clients	Description
IBM Lotus Domino Access for Microsoft Outlook	IBM Lotus Domino Access for Microsoft Outlook allows Microsoft Outlook users to access e-mail and calendar features based on Lotus Domino.
IBM Lotus Domino Web Access (iNotes)	IBM Lotus Domino Web Access extends Domino messaging and collaboration, personal information management (PIM), and offline services to Web browsers clients.
IBM Lotus Notes for Messaging	IBM Lotus Notes for Messaging is a license-only Lotus Notes client option with capability limited to messaging, calendar, and discussions. The degree of function available to the user is controlled by the administrator via a parameter in the Domino Directory.
IBM Lotus Notes for Collaboration	IBM Lotus Notes for Collaboration is a full-function integrated client for messaging, calendar, and discussions, plus the capability to use custom Domino applications.
Domino Administrator	Domino Administrator is the Win32 graphical interface for administration and management of the Domino environment, including registration of users and servers. It is provided with the Domino server and with the Domino Designer® client. It is not available separately.
Domino Designer	Domino Designer is the interactive, Win32 graphical development environment for creation of powerful intranet and Internet applications. The Domino Designer client option also includes Lotus Notes for Collaboration and Domino Administrator.

New with Lotus Domino Client 6.5

The clients provided for Domino build upon previous clients. They include such enhancements as:

► Single access point for Lotus Notes users

Improve productivity by providing unified access to the tools, tasks, and people with whom users work. There is also an introduction to portals.

► Lotus Instant Messaging integration

Single signon gives users the ability to view and manage online status and be aware of a colleagues presence through online status indicators while users remain within the context of a e-mail or task.

► Enablement of applications to start IBM Lotus Instant Messaging via application integration

► Follow up

You have the ability the mark e-mails with a follow up flag (high, normal, or low) to indicate further action is necessary. Alarms can be set for a specific

date and time, including e-mail notifications. The inbox can be sorted via the follow-up priority flags.

► Inbox management features

Anti-spam features block e-mails from specified senders reducing junk mail. A QuickRules option on the Tools menu automates the creation of rules by populating sender, domain, and subject from selected messages.

► Further productivity features

You have the ability to drag and drop e-mails from the inbox view to the calender. You can view only unread mail in the inbox view by toggling the message on and off. A facility is included to allow Lotus Notes to be set as the default mail client, so that when users click a mailto: link on a Web page, a new message window is automatically open in Notes.

► Linux client support via a Mozilla browser in Lotus Domino Web Access (iNotes)

► Lotus Domino Web Access 6.5 integration of Lotus Instant Messaging functionality and an increased feature parity with Lotus Notes

► Changes to Lotus Domino Access for Microsoft Outlook

The new architecture uses open Internet standards (IMAP/Simple Mail Transfer Protocol (SMTP)/iCAL), with improved scalability, lower resource use, and a more solid solution. It also supports Outlook 2000 and 2002 clients.

Refer to the following Web site for information about Domino client choices:

`http://www.lotus.com/engine/jumpages.nsf/wdocs/products`

IBM Lotus Enterprise Integrator 6.5 for iSeries (5733-LEI)

IBM Lotus Enterprise Integrator 6.5 for iSeries (5733-LEI)	
The Lotus Enterprise Integrator (LEI) is a server-based product that provides data movement between DB2 UDB for iSeries and Domino with no programming required. LEI allows the exchange of data with the integrated file system (IFS) of the iSeries and Enterprise Resource Planning (ERP) applications. Domino forms-based interfaces are used to map fields in a Domino database to columns in a DB2 table. Lotus Enterprise Integrator takes care of the movement and conversion of data between the data sources.	
Ordering product number	5724-E89
Minimum operating system level	OS/400 V5R1
HIPO	N/A
Availability	September 2003 (6.5) March 2004 (6.5.1)
Software type	Software Maintenance
Installation prerequisites	None
Related product	Lotus Domino Enterprise Server for iSeries (5733-LD6)
Replaces product	IBM Lotus Enterprise Integrator for Domino R5 (5769-LNP)
Ordering	LEI is orderable through standard Lotus Channels only.

Further information	`http://www.lotus.com/products/product4.nsf/wdocs/`
	`enterpriseintegrator/`
	`http://www-1.ibm.com/servers/eserver/iseries/domino/related/`
	`lei.htm`

The following table shows the Domino and LEI release compatibility.

LEI for iSeries versions and updates	Compatible Domino releases
LEI 6.5.1 for iSeries	Domino 6.5.1
LEI 6.5.0 for iSeries	Domino 6.5.0 and Domino 6.0.3
LEI 6 for iSeries	LEI 6.0.1 for Domino 6.0.1, LEI 6.0.2 for Domino 6.0.2

IBM Lotus Instant Messaging and Web Conferencing (5733-LST)

IBM Lotus Instant Messaging and Web Conferencing (5733-LST)	
Lotus Instant Messaging and Web Conferencing is real-time collaboration software, with online awareness, instant messaging, application sharing and virtual meetings. Lotus Instant Messaging and Web Conferencing helps your organization be more responsive and more efficient by allowing your employees, customers, partners, and suppliers to easily interact with one another in real-time.	
Real-time collaboration is a natural extension to e-mail. You not only chat with colleagues, but you use the Web to improve customer service, reduce travel costs, and create communities among your employees, customers, partners, and suppliers.	
The product is also included within WebSphere Portal - Express Plus. WebSphere Portal - Express Plus is included with the Enterprise Edition of the Models 520, 550, 570, and 595 as well as the Solutions Edition of 550. For more information about WebSphere Portal Express Plus, refer to "IBM WebSphere Portal - Express, IBM WebSphere Portal - Express Plus for Multiplatforms, Version 5 (5724-E77)" on page 620.	
Minimum operating system level	OS/400 V5R1
Availability	07 October 2002
Software type	Software Maintenance Passport Advantage
Installation prerequisites	http://www.ibm.com/eserver/iseries/sametime/sysreq.html
Related products	IBM Lotus Domino 6 for iSeries (5733-LD6) IBM Lotus Domino 6.5 for iSeries (5733-L65) IBM Lotus Team Workplace (QuickPlace) (5733-LQP)
Replaces product	None
Ordering	Through standard Lotus channels or free with the Enterprise Edition of Models 825, 870, and 890
Further information	http://www.ibm.com/eserver/iseries/sametime http://www.lotus.com/sametime http://www.lotus.com/ldd

IBM Lotus Team Workplace for iSeries (5733-LQP)

IBM Lotus Team Workplace for iSeries (5733-LQP)	
IBM Lotus Team Workplace (QuickPlace) is the Web-based solution for creating team work spaces for collaboration. The product is also included within WebSphere Portal - Express Plus. WebSphere Portal - Express Plus is included with the Enterprise Edition of the Models 520, 550, 570, and 595 as well as the Solutions Edition of the 550. For more information about WebSphere Portal Express Plus, refer to "IBM WebSphere Portal - Express, IBM WebSphere Portal - Express Plus for Multiplatforms, Version 5 (5724-E77)" on page 620.	
Minimum operating system level	OS/400 V5R1
Availability	15 November 2002
Software type	Software Maintenance Passport Advantage
Installation prerequisites	http://www.ibm.com/eserver/iseries/quickplace/sysreq.htm
Related products	IBM Lotus Domino 6.5 for iSeries (5733-L65) IBM Lotus Instant Messaging and Web Conferencing (5733-LST)
Replaces product	None
Ordering	Via Lotus Reseller or included with iSeries Models 825, 870, and 890 Enterprise Edition
Further information	http://www.ibm.com/eserver/iseries/quickplace http://www.lotus.com/quickplace http://www.lotus.com/ldd

IBM Lotus Domino Document Manager (5769-LDD)

IBM Lotus Domino Document Manager (5769-LDD)	
IBM Lotus Domino Document Manager (Domino.Doc®) brings scalable, flexible document Management capabilities to Domino. It extends the concept of a shared document library via an open, Web accessible, distributed, and collaborative environment.	
Minimum operating system level	OS/400 V4R5
Availability	July 2001
Software type	Software Maintenance Passport Advantage
Installation prerequisites	`http://www-1.ibm.com/servers/eserver/iseries/domino/related/` `domdoc.htm`
Related products	IBM Lotus Workflow™ IBM Instant Messaging and Web Conferencing
Replaces product	None
Ordering	Through standard Lotus channels
Further information	`http://www.lotus.com/products/domdoc.nsf/content/` `domdochomepage`

IBM Integrated Domino Fax for iSeries (5733-FXD)

IBM Integrated Domino Fax for iSeries (5733-FXD)		
IBM Integrated Domino Fax for iSeries enables Lotus Notes users to send and receive faxes directly from their Notes client, using their current telephone system and Domino infrastructure. Domino Fax for iSeries supports more than just simple text. Notes memos containing rich text and graphics can also be faxed. Files attached to Notes memos can also be formatted and faxed. In addition with the Print-to-Fax driver (available for download at no charge), Notes users can send faxes directly from within a Microsoft Windows application, such as word processing or spreadsheet software.		
Minimum operating system level	OS/400 V5R1	
Availability	12 December 2000	
Software type	Software Subscription	
Installation prerequisites	http://www-1.ibm.com/servers/ eserver/iseries/domino/ related/fxd/	
Related product	Lotus Domino 6 for iSeries	
Replaces product	Lotus Fax for Domino V4R1	
Ordering	IBM Licensed Program Product. Not available through Passport Advantage.	
Further information	http://www-1.ibm.com/servers/eserver/iseries/domino/ related/fxd/	

29

IBM LPP Application Development Products

Business leaders who are looking to solve business problems with automation start by choosing an application to fit their business goals and needs. iSeries clients worldwide have tens of thousands of proven business applications from which to select. Application development is an undeniable strength of the iSeries server. This strength is based on the support for traditional and On Demand Business development provided in the iSeries operating system.

This chapter describes today's application development Licensed Program Offerings (LPOs). It focuses on the key tools for application development for the iSeries server.

To learn about the IBM On Demand Business strategy for the iSeries server, refer to *WebSphere for IBM @server iSeries Server Buying and Selling Guide*, REDP-3646. See Chapter 27, "WebSphere and On Demand Business for iSeries" on page 609, to understand the strength of the WebSphere family of products.

Tip: As an operating system (AIX within OS/400) and an application development suite (AIX/UNIX application development for OS/400), OS/400 Portable Application Solutions Environment (PASE) gives application providers a path to the iSeries product line. Refer to "OS/400 PASE" on page 502 for a description of OS/400 PASE.

Product name	Product number	Refer to page
IBM CICS Transaction Server for iSeries	5722-DFH	637
IBM WebSphere Application Server Version 5.1 for iSeries Developer Edition	5724-D18	617
IBM Grid Toolbox V3 for OS/400	5733-GT1	622

IBM Java for iSeries
    IBM Toolbox for Java
    IBM Developer Kit for Java
	
	5722-JC1
	5722-JV1
		
		638
		639

System/36 Migration Aid	5727-MG1	639
System/38 Migration Aid	5714-MG1	640
IBM Application Program Driver for AS/400	5722-PD1	640
IBM VisualAge Generator Server for AS/400	5769-VG1	641

IBM WebSphere Development Studio for iSeries
Server components:
    Application Development ToolSet
    ILE RPG
    ILE COBOL
    ILE C
    ILE C++
Workstation components:
    IBM WebSphere Development Studio Client for iSeries, V5.1.2
 	
    IBM WebSphere Development Studio Client Advanced Edition for iSeries V5.1.2
	5722-WDS
	
	5722-WDS (Standard client is free with entitlement)
	
	(Advanced client is offered via the Passport Advantage channel)
		642
		
		649
		643
		645
		647
		647
		649
		650
		
		652

IBM XML Toolkit for iSeries	5733-XT1	656

IBM CICS Transaction Server for iSeries (5722-DFH)

IBM CICS Transaction Server for iSeries (5722-DFH)	
The Customer Information Control System (CICS) platform is widely used as a basis for implementing business solutions. The CICS architecture defines a common programming interface and inter-system communications between various systems. Because of this architecture, CICS Transaction Server for iSeries enables many of these applications to be made available on the iSeries server without excessive costs of code conversion. CICS applications and data can coexist with iSeries applications and data.	
Ordering product number	5722-DFH
Minimum operating system level	OS/400 V5R2
HIPO	Yes
Availability	30 August 2002
Software type	Software Subscription
Installation prerequisites	IBM WebSphere Development Studio for iSeries Application Development Toolset (5722-WDS) for creating CICS application programs ILE COBOL for AS/400 (5769-CB1 or 5722-WDS) or ILE C for compiling programs on the server
Program size	92 MB
Related product	WebSphere Development Studio for iSeries (5722-WDS)
Replaces products	CICS Transaction Server for iSeries (5722-DFH) (V5R1) CICS for AS/400 (5769-DFH)
Further information	http://www-3.ibm.com/software/ts/cics/

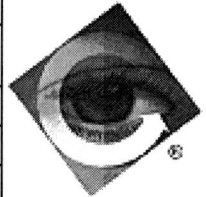

IBM Toolbox for Java (5722-JC1)

IBM Toolbox for Java (5722-JC1)		
IBM Toolbox for Java is a set of Java classes that allow you to write Java applications, applets, and servlets to access data on your iSeries server. IBM Toolbox for Java also provides a set of graphical user interface (GUI) classes. These classes use the access classes to retrieve data and then present the data to the user.		
Ordering product number	Included with 5722-SS1	
Minimum operating system level	OS/400 V5R1	
HIPO	Yes, with 5722-SS1	
Availability	11 June 2004	
Software type	Software Subscription	
Installation prerequisites	Host Server (option 12 of 5722-SS1) and TCP/IP http://publib.boulder.ibm.com/iseries/v5r2/ic2924/index.htm	
Program size	83 MB	
Related products	The IBM Developer Kit for Java, WebSphere Application Server for iSeries, Qshell	
Replaces product	N/A	
Further information	http://publib.boulder.ibm.com/iseries/v5r2/ic2924/index.htm http://www-1.ibm.com/servers/eserver/iseries/toolbox	

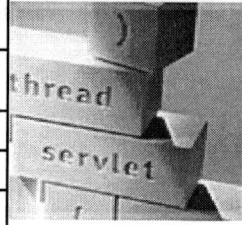

IBM Developer Kit for Java (5722-JV1)

IBM Developer Kit for Java (5722-JV1)	
IBM Developer Kit for Java facilitates the creation of Java applets and full-scale applications. It includes a collection of development tools, help files, and documentation for Java programmers. As Sun Microsystems, Inc. rolls out new Java technologies and provides updates, the Developer Kit is also updated. iSeries server support of Java is planned to be made available over several releases, and applications written using the Developer Kit are portable. The iSeries server supports multiple Java 2 Software Developer Kit (SDK) (J2SDK) Standard Editions. It also supports the use of multiple JDKs simultaneously, but only through multiple JVMs. A single JVM runs one specified JDK. Find the JDK that you are using or want to use, and select the coordinating option to install. You can install more than one JDK at one time. The java.version system property determines which JDK to run. After a JVM is up and running, changing the java.version system property has no effect.	
Further information	`http://publib.boulder.ibm.com/iseries/v5r3/ic2924/index.htm`

System/36 Migration Aid (5727-MG1, 5714-MG1)

System/36 Migration Aid (5727-MG1, 5714-MG1)
System/36 Migration Aid provides the facilities on System/36 to analyze data, libraries, files, and programs prior to saving them for migration to the iSeries server. Files and data providing system-related information, for example, security, configuration information, and document folders, can also be migrated. After they are saved using a choice of media, facilities are provided on the iSeries server to load and reformat the data as required. These facilities are part of OS/400. The System/36 Migration AID is no longer shipped as part of the operating system beginning with i5/OS V5R3.
System/38 Migration Aid provides facilities and functions to select and migrate System/38 objects to the iSeries server. System/38 programs can be transported in object format and re-encapsulated automatically on the iSeries server. The System/38 Migration Aid is no longer shipped as part of the operating system beginning with i5/OS V5R3.

IBM Application Program Driver for AS/400 (5722-PD1)

IBM Application Program Driver for AS/400 (5722-PD1)		
Application Program Driver (APD) for AS/400 is a tool that can help bring productivity to both developers and users of AS/400 applications. For developers, it provides a set of standardized functions that are needed in almost every business application. These are run-time functions, such as backup nd restore, sophisticated security controls, and more, that can be incorporated with little or no change into existing code.		
Ordering	Shipped as a chargeable, Licensed Program Offering (LPO) OS/400 software group-based	
Minimum operating system level	OS/400 V5R1	
HIPO	Yes	
Availability	25 May 2001	
Software type	Software Subscription	
Installation prerequisites	ILE COBOL for AS/400 (5769-CB1 or 5722-WDS) for compile on server	
Program size	77 MB	
Replaces products	IBM Application Program Driver/400 Version 3 (5763-PD1) IBM Application Program Driver/400 Version 4 (5769-PD1)	

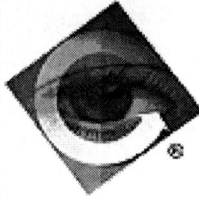

IBM VisualAge Generator Server for AS/400 (5769-VG1)

IBM VisualAge Generator Server for AS/400 (5769-VG1)	
VisualAge Generator is the IBM VisualAge offering focused on bringing productivity to organizations. It is a powerful, integrated development workbench used by programmers to fully define, test, build, and deploy traditional and Web-ready enterprise level systems on a variety of platforms in record time. With VisualAge Generator, applications are defined from a productive desktop environment, using easy-to-learn, powerful, and high-level specifications. The application definition is completely independent from the target runtime environment. The complexity of the system software infrastructure (transactional and database management system (DBMS) APIs, Web server complexity, and communications protocols) is hidden.	
Further information	http://www.ibm.com/eserver/iseries/software/visualage/

IBM WebSphere Development Studio for iSeries (5722-WDS)

IBM WebSphere Development Studio for iSeries (5722-WDS)		
WebSphere Development Studio for iSeries is an attractively-priced, integrated, comprehensive suite of application development tools for both On Demand Business and traditional iSeries development. It is the pervasive iSeries development tool set, shipping on over 80% of iSeries OS/400 V5R2 systems. This suite of tools contains both server and workstation components that are optimized for iSeries development. With WebSphere Development Studio for iSeries, you can create new iSeries server applications and new applications for On Demand Business more productively. You can also quickly and easily convert existing business applications to Web-enabled solutions.		
Ordering product number	5722-WDS	*IBM WebSphere Software*
Minimum operating system level	OS/400 V5R1	
HIPO	Yes	
Availability	Server tools: 11 June 2004 Workstation tools: 16 July 2004	
Software type	Software Subscription	
Installation prerequisites	`http://www-306.ibm.com/software/awdtools/wds400/`	
Program size	22 - 449 MB based on installed components	
Replaces products	5769-CB1 ILE COBOL for AS/400 5769-CL2 VA RPG and CODE/400 5769-CL3 WebSphere Development Tools for AS/400 5769-CX2 ILE C for AS/400 5769-CX5 VisualAge for C++ for AS/400 5799-GDW ILE C++ for AS/400 PRPQ 5769-PW1 Application Development ToolSet for AS/400 (ADTS) 5769-RG1 ILE RPG for AS/400 **Note:** Clients with Software Subscription can upgrade, at no additional charge, to 5722-WDS from any of the products listed, except 5799-GDW.	
More information	`http://www-306.ibm.com/software/awdtools/wds400/` `http://www-306.ibm.com/software/awdtools/library/` `http://www.ibm.com/servers/eserver/iseries/support/planning/nav.html`	

The following diagram shows the server (host) and workstation (client) components of WebSphere Development Studio 5.1.2. The workstation components are those included with the "base" client.

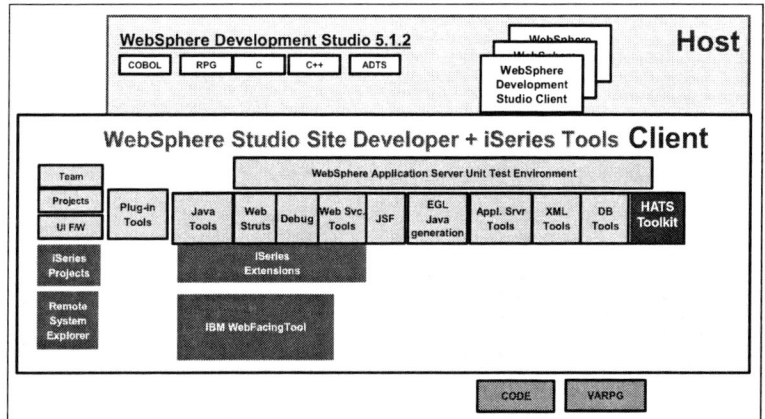

A description of the host and workstation components of WebSphere Development Studio and enhancements offered with i5/OS V5R3 are highlighted in the following sections.

Server components of 5722-WDS

The host (server-based programming tools) components of WebSphere Development Studio include:

► IBM Integrated Language Environment RPG for iSeries
► IBM Integrated Language Environment Cobol for iSeries
► IBM Integrated Language Environment C and C++ for iSeries
► Application Development ToolSet

Each component is described in the following sections.

IBM Integrated Language Environment RPG for iSeries

RPG is the most popular language for writing iSeries business logic because of its ease of use and tight integration with the server. V5R3 is the largest release of RPG IV since the introduction of ILE RPG in V3R1. V5R1 enhancements include totally free-form C-specs, improved RPG-calling-Java support, and improved data structure support, such as support for data structures, qualified names, and more built-in functions.

IBM ILE RPG/400 consists of the RPG compilers listed in the following table.

RPG compiler option	Install option in 5722-WDS
ILE RPG IV	31
IBM System/36-Compatible RPG II	32
IBM System/38-Compatible RPG III	33
RPG/400	34
ILE RPG-IV *PRV	35

ILE RPG for iSeries is designed for writing various types of application programs. This language is easy to learn, yet offers many advanced functions for experienced programmers. It delivers RPG IV, the next evolution of the programming language. The RPG IV compiler offers improved programmer productivity and application growth and quality.

Features
► Java enablement to simplify coding of calls to Java classes and methods
► More granular exception monitoring (MONITOR operation code)
► Built-in functions %ALLOC, %REALLOC, %CHECK, %CHECKR, %LOOKUPxx, %TLOOKUPxx, %OCCUR, %SHTDN, %SQRT, and %XLATE
► Date, time, and timestamp operations allowed in expressions
► Free-form calculation specifications
► Runtime control of the file to be opened
► LICOPT support to pass options directly to the translator
► Qualified names in data structures
► ELSEIF operation code
► Predefined /DEFINE names
► Compiler directive /INCLUDE

New with V5R3
The IBM tradition of adding more function to the RPG IV compiler continues with ILE RPG. These enhancements to the compiler include:

► New built-in function %SUBARR (assign to, sort, or return, a subarray)

► Direct conversion of date, time, and time stamp to numeric using %DEC

► Control specification CCSID(*CHAR: *JOBRUN) for correct conversion of character data at runtime

► Second parameter for %TRIM, %TRIMR and %TRIML indicating what characters to trim

► New prototype option OPTIONS(*TRIM) to pass a trimmed parameter

- Support for 63-digit packed and zoned decimal values
- An RPG preprocessor enabling the SQL preprocessor to handle conditional compilation and nested/COPY
- Relaxation of the rules for using a result data structure for I/O to externally-described files and record formats
- Support for new environment variables for use with RPG programs calling Java methods

For an exhaustive list of the current and previous enhancements to the RPG compiler, see:

`http://www.ibm.com/software/awdtools/wds400/about/ile_rpg.html`

IBM ILE COBOL for iSeries

COBOL is also a popular language for writing iSeries business logic because of its ease of use and integration with the system. V5R1 enhancements include COBOL-calling-Java support (along with the appropriate documentation), UCS-2 (UNICODE) support, and three new process options to enable developers port applications from the mainframe platform to the iSeries server.

IBM ILE COBOL for iSeries consists of the COBOL components listed in the following table.

COBOL compiler option	Install option in 5722-WDS
ILE COBOL	41
System/36-Compatible COBOL	42
System/38-Compatible COBOL	43
OPM COBOL	44
ILE COBOL *PRV	45

ILE COBOL for iSeries is a programming language that is used in the processing of business problems. COBOL can be used to manipulate DB2 Universal Database (UDB) for iSeries database files in a relatively simple way. COBOL uses English-like syntax to assist the programmer in generating self-documenting, structured programming constructs.

Through ANSI-85 high-level functions of ILE COBOL for iSeries, such as nested source programs, it is easier to port code to the iSeries server from other platforms. Programmer productivity is increased with ILE COBOL for iSeries, through its extensive database and workstation support, static, inter-language

calls, interactive syntax checking, debug facilities, and a full complement of compile-time error diagnostics.

Features

► UCS-2 (Unicode) support

– National data, a new type of data item, is added to provide support for the coded character set specified in ISO/IEC 10646-1 as UCS-2. The code set is the basic set defined in the Unicode standard.

– Includes the NTLPADCHAR compiler option and PROCESS statement option.

► Java interoperability support

The QCBLLESRC.JNI file provides the same definitions and prototypes that are provided in the JNI.j file, but written in COBOL rather than C.

► iSeries portability support

– PROCESS statement option NOCOMPASBIN/COMPASBIN
– PROCESS statement option NOLSPTRALIGN/LSPTRALIGN
– Complex OCCURS DEPENDING ON (ODO) support

► LICOPT parameter added to the CRTCBLMOD and CRTBNDCBL commands to allow advanced users to specify Licensed Internal Code (LIC) options

New with V5R3

The host tools of WebSphere Development Suite offer significant enhancements to ILE COBOL at V5R3:

► Large VALUE clause support

► CONSTANT data type

► XML PARSE statement that provides the interface to a high-speed XML parser, which is part of the COBOL runtime

► Alternate Record Key support

► DBCS data item names (DBCS word support)

► 63-digit support

► Seven new ANSI Intrinsic functions

► New CRTBNDCBL and CRTCBLMOD options

► New PROCESS statement options

► Program status structure

For an exhaustive list of current and previous enhancements to the COBOL compiler, see:

http://www.ibm.com/software/awdtools/wds400/about/ile_cobol.html

IBM ILE C and C++ for iSeries

The following sections describe ILC and C++ for the iSeries.

ILE C

The ILE C compiler is updated this release to the most current C compiler that IBM offers on any platform. This new compiler has added more ANSI support and significant improvement for cross-platform portability. Portability is further enhanced with the new teraspace support, which allows for pointer usage and memory management that is more consistent with other platforms. This new compiler retains all of the iSeries-specific functionality that it had in previous releases.

ILE C++

In this release, the C++ compiler has been updated to the most current C++ compiler that IBM offers. It includes support for the latest C++ language features such as namespaces, improved template support, bool data type, and so on. It also includes an improved AT&T class library, a complete ANSI Standard Template Library, and the latest version of IBM Open Class library.

Improvements to the stream classes in the ILE C++ libraries include 64-bit indexing and explicit control on CCSID-translation. The compiler now reads source from and produces listings to either the IFS or the native iSeries file system. This new compiler features excellent cross-platform portability, which is enhanced with new support for the teraspace memory management model. The compiler retains all of the iSeries-specific functionality as in previous releases. The C++ PRPQ compiler is included for previous release support and to ease migration to the latest ANSI standard. This iSeries native compiler replaces both the VisualAge C++ cross-compiler and the native C++ PRPQ compiler.

IBM ILE C and C++ for iSeries consists of the C components listed in the following table.

C and C++ compiler options	Install option in 5722-WDS
ILE C	51
ILE C++	52
ILE C *PRV	53
ILE C++ *PRV	54

ILE C features

► Completely refreshed compiler from the latest AIX compiler
► Compliant with the ANSI ISO/IEC 9899-1990 (1992) C standard
► Read source and includes from IFS or native, but still produces *MODULEs in native file system
► Produce native or IFS spooled file listings
► Teraspace Phase 2 support
► A third parameter for main() contains current set of environment variables
► Target V4R4, V4R5, and V5R1
► A wider variety of source file CCSIDs
► Preprocessor output targeting a specified file
► A Qshell command for compiling
► New LICOPT and CSOPT command keywords
► Asynchronous signals
► More in-sync with ILE C++

ILE C++ features

► Completely refreshed compiler from the latest AIX compiler
► Compliant with the latest ANSI ISO/IEC 14882-1998 C++ standard
► Template library and namespace support
► Replaces that VAC++ cross compiler and native PRPQ compiler
► Support of release V5 of IBM Open Class class libraries bool data type
► Read source and includes from IFS or native database
► Produce native database or IFS spooled file listings
► 64-bit file indexing for stream classes
► Teraspace addressing support to improve portability and performance
► Preprocessor output targeting specified file
► A Qshell command for compiling
► Functions more in-sync with ILE C

New with V5R3

► Removal of IOC runtime and headers (C++ only)
► GB18030 support (C and C++)
► Namespace support for debugging (C++ only)
► 63-digit packed decimal (C only)
► C++ 8-byte runtime (Teraspace Phase III)
► Linkage improvements (C and C++)
► Template registry support (C++ only)
► Alias option (C and C++)
► Weak definition for static template members (C++ only)
► Removal of pragma enumsize (replaced with pragma enum, C and C++)
► Removal of restriction for PRFDTA (C and C++)
► Increased parameters passed to PEP (C and C++)

For an exhaustive list of the current and previous enhancements to the C and C++ compilers, see:

`http://www.ibm.com/software/awdtools/wds400/about/ile_ccpp.html`

Application Development ToolSet

Application Development ToolSet (ADTS) is the traditional tool suite for iSeries application development programmers. These tools are included in the package so that existing iSeries programmers can more easily make the shift to the new development tools and environment.

ADTS contains these utilities:

► Programming Development Manager (PDM)
► Source Entry Utility (SEU)
► Screen Design Aid (SDA)
► Report Layout Utility (RLU)
► Data File Utility/Application Development (DFU/AD)
► File Compare and Merge Utility (FCMU)
► Interactive Source Debugger (ISDB)

New with V5R3

ADTS has made minor enhancements to support the V5R3 system changes. For details about the components of ADTS, see the following Web site:

`http://www.ibm.com/software/awdtools/wds400/about/adts.html`

ADTS no longer offers the optional server features available prior to V5R3:

► Application Dictionary Services
► Application Development Manager

Workstation components of 5722-WDS

The client (workstation-based programming tools) components of WebSphere Development Studio are delivered in IBM WebSphere Development Studio Client for iSeries, V5.1.2. The following diagram shows the workstation (client) and server (host) components of WebSphere Development Studio.

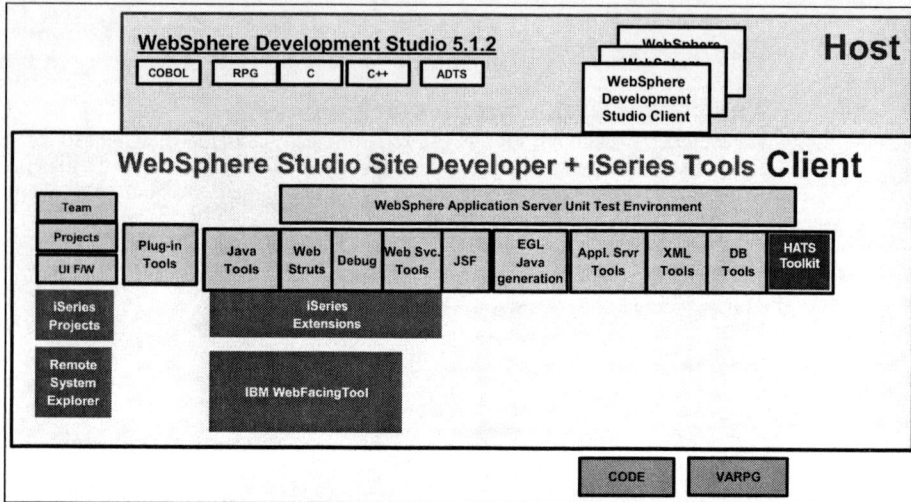

WebSphere Development Studio 5.1.2 | COBOL | RPG | C | C++ | ADTS | WebSphere Development Studio Client | Host

WebSphere Studio Site Developer + iSeries Tools **Client**

Team Projects, UI F/W | Plug-in Tools | WebSphere Application Server Unit Test Environment | Java Tools | Web Struts | Debug | Web Svc. Tools | JSF | EGL Java generation | Appl. Srvr Tools | XML Tools | DB Tools | HATS Toolkit | iSeries Projects | iSeries Extensions | Remote System Explorer | IBM WebFacingTool | CODE | VARPG

Each product is described in the following sections. The Host Access Transformation Services (HATS) Toolkit is introduced on page 651.

Note: You must have i5/OS V5R3 for the server portion of WebSphere Development Studio, but the client V5.1.2 can work with OS/400 V5R1, V5R2 or i5/OS V5R3. The C++ compiler requires a machine capable of running OS/400 PASE and Option 33 of OS/400 (5722-SS1).

IBM WebSphere Development Studio Client for iSeries, V5.1.2

WebSphere Development Studio Client for iSeries inherits and extends the robust, easy-to-use development environment of WebSphere Studio Site Developer V5.1.2. WebSphere Studio Site Developer V5.1.2 is an easy-to-use, highly productive IDE for visually constructing, testing, and deploying dynamic Web sites, Web services, and Java applications. Site developer simplifies Java development with RAD tools, templates, and wizards.

Site Developer V5.1.2 is built on the Eclipse, an open standards-based development platform for building integrated development environments (IDE). Site Developer enables you to maximize developer productivity by integrating best-of-breed plug-in tools from IBM, IBM Business Partners, and the Eclipse community and customizing your development environment to meet your needs.

For more information about Eclipse, refer to:

http://www.eclipse.org/

Site Developer V5.1.2 offers enhancements to make Web development faster and developers' productivity higher. There is support for new industry standards that simplify the development of rich Web user interfaces and business logic. Site Developer also offers high productivity tools for business-oriented developers that are new to Java. The benefits of Site Developer include the ability to:

► Build dynamic Web user interfaces with minimal coding using standards-based JSF components

► Visually design and develop rich Web user interfaces using drag-and-drop reusable components and visual Page Designer

► Build data-driven Web pages with minimal coding and point-and-click database connectivity

► Use a fourth generation language, EGL, to generate business logic and data-driven Web applications in Java

► Build rich Web user interfaces with performance and maintenance characteristics of thin clients using JSF extensions

The IBM WebFacing Tool quickly, easily, and cost effectively generates Web interfaces to 5250 applications that run in batch mode:

► Source code-based application modernization for the Web

► Support for the INVITE and DSPATR keywords is added

► Improved Web page response times when connecting to the IBM WebFacing server that has the latest service level applied

► Improved performance of iSeries job and system information retrieval

The HATS Toolkit quickly and easily generates a default dynamic runtime transformation of the 5250 data stream. The resulting Web interface can also be customized with the HATS Toolkit. The Web interface can be deployed to production with the purchase of HATS separately.

► Allow users to give Host applications a Web "look and feel"
► Improve the navigation of host applications and generate portal interfaces
► No access to source code required

For a detailed comparison of the IBM WebFacing Tool and the HATS Toolkit, see:

http://www.ibm.com/software/awdtools/wdt400/about/webfacing.html

New with V5.1.2

- ▶ Remote System Explorer continues to enhance the editor functions. The V5R3 iSeries RPG, COBOL, CL (syntax checking only), and DDS language support for syntax checking, program verifying, and help is included. There is also SQL syntax checking for ILE RPG, and expanded remote searching capabilities.

- ▶ iSeries Web Tools provides improved integration with the Web Diagram Editor and Web Site Designer, and improved message handling.

- ▶ iSeries Java Tools provides enhancements to make the import and export extensions more widely available by moving the extensions into the Eclipse base. There are improved PCML support, Program Call Wizard usability and Web service generation.

- ▶ The Eclipse debugger provides support in RSE (service entry point) for debugging Web applications.

- ▶ iSeries programs and commands can be started via run launch configurations.

- ▶ Improved access to remote Linux, UNIX, and Windows systems

The Remote System Explorer can also be used for accessing remote Linux, UNIX and Windows systems. This includes running remote commands, remote editing, compiling and searching. The 5.1.2 release adds support for working with remote archives.

WebSphere Development Studio for iSeries (5722-WDS) orders ship the workstation tools, WebSphere Development Studio Client for iSeries, V5.1.2 as free automatic entitlement.

WebSphere Development Studio Client Advanced Edition for iSeries V5.1.2

WebSphere Development Studio Client Advanced Edition for iSeries inherits and extends the capabilities of WebSphere Studio Application Developer (Application Developer) V5.1.2, which is the IBM core development environment for visually designing, constructing, testing, and deploying Web services, portal applications, and J2EE applications. Application Developer speeds J2EE development by providing a complete set of high productivity tools, templates, and wizards.

The following diagram shows the workstation (client) components of WebSphere Development Studio Client Advanced Edition for iSeries V5.1.2.

WebSphere Studio Application Developer + iSeries Tools **Client**

WebSphere Application Server Unit Test Environment

Team																
Projects	Plug-in Tools	Java Tools	Web Struts	Debug	Web Svc. Tools	JSF	Appl. Srvr Tools	EGL Java gen	XML Tools	DB Tools	EJB Tools		Profiling Tracing Tools	Performance Analysis Tools	HATS Toolkit	Portal Toolkit
UI F/W																

iSeries Projects

iSeries Extensions

Remote System Explorer

IBM WebFacingTool

EGL COBOL generation

CODE | VARPG

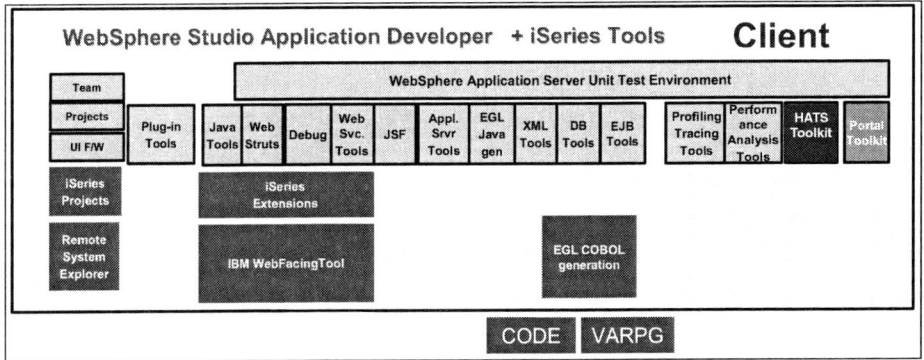

With WebSphere Studio Application Developer (Application Developer) V5.1.2, you can:

► Accelerate the development of Web services and J2EE applications with visual tools, templates, and wizards

► Detect performance issues early with graphical performance and profiling trace tools

► Visualize and graphically edit code through the Unified Modeling Language (UML) Visual Editor for Java and EJB

► Collaborate and share assets across the team using the included Rational® ClearCase® LT version control

► Create and test portlets in a visual environment along with Portal Toolkit:
  – Create JSF portlets
  – Create Struts portlets using Web Diagram Editor
  – Perform testing and debugging on WebSphere Portal Test Environment

Note: Portal Toolkit and WebSphere Portal installation are required to create a portlet development environment on top of WebSphere Studio Application Developer.

New with V5.1.2

In V5.1.2, the IBM Development Studio Client Advanced Edition delivers significant advanced capabilities including:

▶ IBM WebFacing Tool

– Support for iSeries system screens (non-DDS screens)

The 5250 data streams associated with the system screens are converted into Web GUIs which run in batch mode.

– Support for generating Struts portlets

– Single signon (SSO) support using Enterprise Identity Mapping (EIM)

– A wizard for generating a Struts-compliant interface to a 5250 application

This is an architected interface that can be easily extended with other Struts-based Web applications. Struts actions can be added to enhance the generated application.

– Ability for the developer to use command keys to invoke user-defined actions to integrate new functions delivered by a Web application into the Web-enabled interface

– Support for displaying and printing iSeries spooled files

▶ Enterprise Generation Language

– Support for the generation of 5250 COBOL applications as well as Java applications from Enterprise Generation Language

The runtime components for both types of applications are provided in the tool.

– Offers EGL, with support for generating both Java and ILE COBOL applications, as the replacement for the VisualAge Generator product

There is an upgrade option in WebSphere Development Studio Client Advanced Edition for Visual Generator clients.

▶ iSeries Web Tools

– Support for SSO using EIM

▶ iSeries Java Tools

– Allows the specification of J2EE Connection Architecture (JCA) connector using Java Naming and Directory Interface (JNDI) name in the Program Call Wizard

WebSphere Development Studio Client Advanced Edition for iSeries V5.1.2 is a workstation product delivered through the Passport Advantage channel. It is priced on a "per developer seat" basis.

Web technology choices

The following table summarizes the technology choices that can help you achieve your objectives.

Your goal	Technology	Features
Quickly Web-enable existing interactive iSeries applications	IBM WebFacing Tool	Converts a display file (DSPF) DDS to JSPs built on struts
Build Web applications with iSeries business logic	Web Tools for iSeries	Wizards and Web components for building JSP files that provide a user interface for iSeries business logic; build on Struts
Build Web applications with iSeries data	JavaServer Faces (JSF)	Rich tagging choices for user interface; strategic choice for data-driven applications that have little business logic; emerging technology (a potential follow-on to Struts)
Build Web applications with iSeries data, moving more user interface logic to the client	JSFs with client-side scripting	Provides better response times by reducing trips to the server; validation and formatting is done on the client; uses JSF extensions
Build Web applications with Java business logic	Struts and Struts tools	Rich tagging choices for model-controller; leverages JSPs for the user interface
Encapsulate your applications from future technology changes and enable them for multiple platforms	EGL	Fourth generation language (4GL); abstracts your applications at a higher level and generated the appropriate Java (standard edition) or iSeries COBOL code (Advanced Edition only); leverages JSF; learning time relatively short for COBOL or RPG programmers

XML Toolkit for iSeries

The XML Toolkit for iSeries is described in the following section.

XML Toolkit for iSeries (5733-XT1)	
XML is widely touted as a solution to the problem of information exchange between applications and within B2B environments. It is simple, extensible, and non-proprietary. XML parser APIs assist in the creation, navigation, or modification of XML document content.	
Ordering product number	5733-XT1
Minimum operating system level	OS/400 V5R1
HIPO	No
Availability	25 June 2004.
Software type	Software Subscription
Installation prerequisites	http://www.ibm.com/servers/eserver/iseries/software/xml
Program size	48 MB; varies
Related product	IBM DB2 UDB XML Extender (5722-DE1)
Replaces product	XML parsers service programs QXML4C310 and QXMLPR310
Further information	http://www.ibm.com/servers/eserver/iseries/software/xml

30

IBM licensed programs: Networking and communications products

Access to network resources is a fundamental requirement for today's business environment. This chapter describes the Licensed Program Products (LPP) that serve to connect users to the iSeries server or to link the iSeries server to a network. It also covers licensed programs that support secure network access.

Product name	Product number	Refer to page
IBM Cryptographic Access Provider 128-bit for iSeries	5722-AC3	659
IBM WebSphere MQ for iSeries, V5.3	5724-B41	661
iSeries Client Encryption (128-bit)	5722-CE3	659
IBM Communications Utilities for iSeries	5722-CM1	660
IBM Cryptographic Support for AS/400	5722-CR1	659
IBM Distributed Computing Environment DES Library Routines for AS/400	5769-DC3	660
IBM MQSeries Integrator for iSeries and DB2 Version 1.1	5697-F49	661

Product name	Product number	Refer to page
IBM WebSphere Host Integration Solution for iSeries V4.1	5724-F84 / F86	661

IBM Cryptographic Access Provider 128-bit for iSeries (5722-AC3)

IBM Cryptographic Access Provider 128-bit for iSeries (5722-AC3)	
The Cryptographic Access Provider 128-bit for iSeries product (5722-AC3) provides the support to secure On Demand Business transactions by implementing the security needed to send proprietary or confidential information over the Internet and corporate intranets. This product enables encryption in the iSeries server for use by other products such as IBM HTTP Server for iSeries. Install the Cryptographic Access Provider product on the iSeries server to enable the Secure Sockets Layer (SSL) function of the Hypertext Transfer Protocol (HTTP) server.	
The SSL protocol is widely used to enable secure communications between servers and clients on the World Wide Web. Data transferred between the server and client is encrypted to ensure the data remains private. In addition, the identity of the server is authenticated by the client, through the use of a certificate (or digital ID). Most popular Web browsers support SSL. This means that SSL-enabled Web browsers can establish a secure communications session with the iSeries server, where the browser authenticates the identity of the iSeries server and the data transferred is encrypted.	
Cryptographic Access Provider 128-bit supports 128-bit data encryption.	
Note: IBM Cryptographic Access Provider 128-bit for iSeries (5722-AC3) is not a chargeable feature. This feature usually supports applications for On Demand Business on iSeries.	
Minimum operating system level	OS/400 V5R1
Installation prerequisites	None
Related products	iSeries Client Encryption (128 bit) (5722-CE3)
Replaces product	IBM Cryptographic Access Provider 128-bit for AS/400 (5769-AC3)

IBM eServer iSeries Client Encryption (128-bit) (5722-CE3)

IBM @server iSeries Client Encryption (128-bit) (5722-CE3)	
IBM @server iSeries Client Encryption (128-bit) provides SSL for use by iSeries Access Family (5722-XW1) and the IBM Toolbox for Java (5722-JC1). The Client Encryption 128-bit product includes an SSL for Windows 95, 98, Me, 2000, XP, and NT, and an SSL for Java.	
Minimum operating system level	OS/400 V5R1
HIPO	1019
Installation prerequisites	IBM Cryptographic Access Provider 128-bit for iSeries (5722-AC3)
Related products	IBM Cryptographic Access Provider 128-bit for iSeries (5722-AC3) Part of an i5/OS V5R3 5722-XW1 refresh feature which allows OS/400 V5R2 XW1 clients to get V5R3 iSeries Access Family products.
Replaces product	IBM AS/400 Client Encryption (40-bit) (5769-CE1)
Client code	5722-CE3 is client code. The code is shipped in the LPP, stored in the IFS directory, and downloaded from the IFS directory to the PC.

IBM Cryptographic Support for AS/400 (5722-CR1)

IBM Cryptographic Support for AS/400 (5722-CR1)	
Cryptographic Support for AS/400 is a legacy product designed to be functionally equivalent to the cryptographic facilities of the IBM 4700 Finance Controller. Cryptographic Support for AS/400 supports the following functions: ▶ Data encryption/decryption using the Data Encryption Standard (DES) and 56-bit keys ▶ Message Authentication Code generation and verification using DES ▶ Key management ▶ 3624 Personal Identification Number (PIN) generation and verification	
Minimum operating system level	OS/400 V5R1
Installation prerequisites	None
Related product	None
Replaces product	None

IBM Communications Utilities for iSeries (5722-CM1)

IBM Communications Utilities for iSeries (5722-CM1)	
The Communications Utilities for iSeries comprise the MVS/VM bridge and Remote Job Entry (RJE) functions. These capabilities provide the interchange of mail and files and the submitting or receiving of jobs between connected systems.	
Minimum operating system level	OS/400 V5R1
Installation prerequisites	None
Related product	None
Replaces product	None

IBM Distributed Computing Environment DES Library Routines for AS/400 (5769-DC3)

IBM Distributed Computing Environment DES Library Routines for AS/400 (5769-DC3)	
The IBM Distributed Computing Environment (DCE) DES Library Routines for AS/400 product provides data encryption support for the DCE Base Services. It provides secure communications when using DCE services on the iSeries.	
Minimum operating system level	OS/400 V4R3
Installation prerequisites	None
Related product	None
Replaces product	None

IBM WebSphere MQ for iSeries V5.3 (5724-B41)

IBM WebSphere MQ for iSeries V5.3 (5724-B41)	
IBM WebSphere MQ for iSeries provides an open, scalable, industrial-strength messaging backbone which supports high volume throughput, time-independent communication, with assured one-time delivery. To this, WebSphere MQ V5.3 adds enhanced security via SSL support, enhanced performance especially for Java Message Service (JMS) applications and other new features that enhance system scalability and reliability.	
Minimum operating system level	OS/400 V5R1
Availability	28 June 2002
Software type	Passport Advantage One-year subscription (5733-M27) Three-year subscription (5733-M28)
Related product	None
Replaces product	MQSeries for iSeries V5.2 5733-A38
Further information	http://www.ibm.com/software/ts/mqseries/messaging/

IBM WebSphere Host Integration Solution for iSeries V4.1 (5724-F84/F86)

IBM WebSphere Host Integration Solution for iSeries V4.1 (5724-F84/F86)	
Every user in an organization should be able to access critical business applications via one of the programs in the Host Integration Solution package. What was called Host Access Client Package (HACP) has been renamed and enhanced to include: ► IBM Communications Server (Windows V6.1.1 and AIX V6.1) ► WebSphere Application Server - Express (5.0.2) ► WebSphere Host On-Demand V8.0 ► IBM Personal Communications V5.7 ► WebSphere Studio Site Developer and WebSphere Studio Client for iSeries ► IBM WebSphere Host Access Transformation Services (HATS) V5.0	
Further information	http://www.ibm.com/software/webservers/hostintegration/

31

IBM eServer iSeries Access products

IBM @server iSeries Access Family (5722-XW1) provides the middleware software to connect other systems and platforms to iSeries servers. This chapter describes the iSeries Access products.

Product name	Product number	Refer to page
IBM @server iSeries ODBC Driver for Linux	5733-L01	670
IBM @server iSeries Access for Windows	5722-XE1	665
IBM @server iSeries Access for Web	5722-XH2	666
IBM @server iSeries Access for Linux	5722-XL1	667
IBM @server iSeries Access for Wireless	5722-XP1	669
IBM @server iSeries Access Family	5722-XW1	663
IBM WebSphere Host Access Transformation Servers Limited Edition (HATS LE)	5724-F97-01	668

IBM eServer iSeries Access Family (5722-XW1)

IBM @server iSeries Access Family (5722-XW1)	
iSeries Access Family is a single product to solve all your desktop-to-iSeries connectivity needs. It provides data connectivity from other systems and platforms to iSeries servers. Increasingly, application providers are taking advantage of heterogeneous platforms to deliver solutions. iSeries Access Family provides the middleware so that applications can easily be built to run on the desktop, browsers, and wireless devices, yet work with iSeries resources simply and efficiently. This combination provides iSeries clients with more application options and helps to lower the cost of management for these solutions. Deploying PCs to your users should enhance their productivity without increasing your PC network administration costs. iSeries Access is your ideal connectivity solution because it contains a unique set of products that integrate the use of a variety of PCs and workstation desktops, browsers, and wireless devices with the iSeries server. It has the functions that end users need, yet it is built to be centrally administered.	
Minimum operating system level	i5/OS V5R3
Program size	2.7 MB
Availability	11 June 2004
Software type	Software Subscription
Related products	All
Client code	5722-XE1
Replaces products	Client Access Family (5722-XW1) Client Access Family (5769-XW1)

IBM eServer iSeries Access for Windows (5722-XE1)

IBM @server iSeries Access for Windows (5722-XE1)

IBM @server iSeries Access for Windows, previously known as iSeries Client Access Express for iSeries, is a component of the IBM @server iSeries Access Family (5722-XW1). It offers a powerful set of capabilities to connect PCs to iSeries servers. It also enables end users and application programmers to leverage business information, applications, and resources across an enterprise by extending the iSeries resources to the PC desktop.

iSeries Access for Windows provides:

▶ TCP/IP connectivity with Secure Sockets Layer (SSL) for client functions to improve TCP/IP network security

▶ iSeries NetServer for PC file serving and network print support

▶ Operations Console for both local and remote system console access

▶ All functions of iSeries Navigator for working with iSeries resources and administering and operating iSeries servers, plus graphical interfaces to work with these iSeries

Integrated graphical user interface (GUI) features deliver increased productivity for end users who access resources on iSeries servers.

iSeries Access for Windows is compatible with Windows 98, Windows Me, Windows 2000, Windows XP, and Windows NT 4.0 operating systems.

Minimum operating system level	i5/OS V5R3
Program size	188.2 MB
HIPO	1000
Availability	11 June 2004
Software type	Software Subscription
Ordering	Included with i5/OS
Installation prerequisites	*IBM @server iSeries Access for Windows – Setup*, SC41-5507 Some functions of iSeries Access for Windows require the XW1 product on the server, specifically the PC5250 display/printer emulation and Data Transfer components.
Related products	iSeries Access for Web (5722-XH2), iSeries Access for Wireless (5722-XP1), and iSeries Access for Linux (5722-XL1)
Client code	This is an iSeries Access client that runs on Windows operating systems. The code is shipped in the LPP and stored in IFS directory and is downloaded from the IFS directory to the PC and is shipped on a PC CD.
Replaces products	Client Access Express (5722-XE1) Client Access Express (5769-XE1)

IBM @server iSeries Access for Windows (5722-XE1)	
Further information	`http://publib.boulder.ibm.com/iseries/v5r2/ic2924/index.htm` `http://www.ibm.com/eserver/iseries/access`

IBM eServer iSeries Access for Web (5722-XH2)

IBM @server iSeries Access for Web (5722-XH2)	
IBM @server iSeries Access for Web is a Java application that runs in a Web application server (for example, WebSphere Application Server or Apache Software Foundation ASF Tomcat) on OS/400 V5R2 or later iSeries servers. End users access its functions by starting their browser and connecting to an iSeries server. iSeries Access for Web can now be used with the Mozilla browser as well as Internet Explorer and Netscape. This enables users on desktop operating systems such as Windows, UNIX, Linux, and MacIntosh to access iSeries resources. It provides a variety of functions, such as 5250 emulation, and access to iSeries printers, printer output, database, jobs, job queues, message queue, and so on. It also provides the ability to run OS/400 CL batch commands without using a 5250 emulation session. iSeries Access for Web also contains iSeries Access for Linux which provides an ODBC driver to access the DB2 UDB for iSeries and a 5250 emulator.	
Minimum operating system level	i5/OS V5R3
Program size	192 MB
HIPO	1012
Availability	11 June 2004
Software type	Software Subscription
Installation prerequisites	`http://www.ibm.com/eserver/iseries/access/web/guide.htm`
Related products	iSeries Access for Windows (5722-XE1) and iSeries Access for Web (5722-XP1)
Replaces product	5722-XH1

Further information	`http://www-1.ibm.com/eserver/iseries/access/web/`
	`http://www-1.ibm.com/servers/eserver/iseries/access/linux/`
	`http://www.ibm.com/eserver/iseries/access/web/5250.html`

IBM eServer iSeries Access for Linux (5722-XL1)

IBM @server iSeries Access for Linux (5722-XL1)	
IBM @server iSeries Access for Linux runs natively on Linux operating systems. Linux can be used on systems with Intel processors or Power PCs, or in an iSeries server logical partition (LPAR). iSeries access for Linux contains a 5250 emulator and an ODBC driver. It is not available as an individually orderable product. However, it is available with the iSeries Access for Web (5722-XH2) client or via download from the Web: `http://www14.software.ibm.com/webapp/download/search.jsp?go=y&rs=ilinux` The 5250 Display Emulation component requires an iSeries Access Family (5722-XW1) license before it can be used.	
Minimum operating system level	OS/400 V5R1
Program size	2.6 MB
Availability	17 December 2003 (Version1.3)
Software type	Software Subscription ordering ID (5722-XW1)
Installation prerequisites	`http://www-1.ibm.com/servers/eserver/iseries/access/linux/guide/`
Related products	iSeries Access for Web 5722-XH2
Web link	`http://www.ibm.com/eserver/iseries/access/linux/`

IBM WebSphere Host Access Transformation Server Limited Edition (5724-F97-01)

IBM WebSphere Host Access Transformation Server Limited Edition (5724-F97-01)	
WebSphere HATS LE is a new member of the iSeries Access family. HATS LE dynamically transforms all 5250 screens with a point-and-click Web interface. Screens are converted in real time and delivered as HTML to the end user's Web browser (Internet Explorer or Netscape).	
Minimum operating system level	OS/400 V5R1
Availability	30 June 2003
Software type	Software Subscription ordering ID 5733-XW1
Ordering	5722-XW1
Further information	http://www.ibm.com/eserver/iseries/access/hats http://www.ibm.com/software/webservers/hostintegration/

IBM eServer iSeries Access for Wireless (5722-XP1)

IBM eServer iSeries Access for Wireless (5722-XP1)	
IBM @server iSeries Access for Wireless provides access to iSeries administrative functions and development tools intended for wireless devices such as personal digital assistants (PDAs) and Internet-enabled phones. Using the functions of the iSeries Access for Wireless licensed program, you can use your wireless device to access and administer your servers. iSeries Access for Wireless consists of two separate services that can be used individually, or together, to provide the access you need: ▸ iSeries Navigator for Wireless ▸ IBM Toolbox for Java 2 Micro Edition	
Minimum operating system level	i5/OS V5R3
Availability	4 June 2002
Software type	Software Subscription
Ordering	Included with i5/OS for no additional charge
Related products	iSeries Access for Windows (5722-XE1) and iSeries Access for Web (5722-XH2)
Client code	This product is client code that runs on wireless devices. The code is shipped in the LPP and stored in IFS directory and is downloaded to the client device.
Further information	http://www-1.ibm.com/servers/eserver/iseries/access/wireless/

iSeries ODBC Driver for Linux (5733-L01)

iSeries ODBC Driver for Linux (5733-L01)	
The iSeries ODBC Driver for Linux is an ODBC driver that allows you to access the iSeries database from a Linux client. Linux applications written to the ODBC API can use this driver to connect to an iSeries server to access the database.	
Minimum operating system level	OS/400 V5R1
Related products	iSeries Access for Windows (5722-XE1) and iSeries Access for Web (5722-XH2)
Client code	This product is client code.
Further information	`http://www-1.ibm.com/servers/eserver/iseries/linux/odbc`

32

IBM licensed programs: System management products and services

The management of an @server i5 or iSeries is handled by built-in functions and licensed programs for specific needs, each complemented by service offerings. This chapter discusses the products and services that are listed in the following table.

Product or service name	Product number	Refer to page
iSeries Operations Console: Direct Attach, LAN, and Remote	---	672
IBM @server Technical Support Advantage	---	671
IBM Intelligent Communications Trace Analyzer for iSeries, Version 1.0	5733-AZ1	689
IBM Tivoli Storage Manager Extended Edition V5.2	5698-A11	685
IBM Backup Recovery and Media Services for iSeries	5722-BR1	686
Enterprise Edition Installation Assistant	5733-ED1	688
PATROL for iSeries – Predict	5620-FIF	690
IBM Software Integration Assistant for iSeries	5722-IA1	689

Product or service name	Product number	Refer to page
IBM Advanced Job Scheduler for iSeries	5722-JS1	687
IBM Managed System Services for iSeries	5722-MG1	687
IBM Performance Tools for iSeries	5722-PT1	689
IBM System Manager for iSeries	5722-SM1	688

System management services

This section discusses the features and services that are integrated in i5/OS.

eServer i5 and iSeries Operations Console: Direct attach, LAN, remote, Hardware Management Console

With i5/OS V5R3, the following types of consoles help to control i5/OS:

► Operations Console direct-connect
► Operations Console LAN-connect
► Hardware Management Console (HMC)
► Advanced System Management Interface (ASMI)

The chosen console solution depends on the number of slots available as well as the function supported by the console type. This section discusses the console options and more.

Important: All existing console types are supported in IBM i5/OS V5R3 partitions and on @server i5 Models 520, 550, 570, and 595.

HMC is required for managing partitions and Capacity on Demand. Although the HMC can be used as a console device, all previously available console types are still valid.

The #0367 is to be used for direct attached Operations Console and is delivered when Operations Console on the local area network (LAN) is selected. The #0367 is also orderable for each partition running i5/OS when the client chooses a console type making use of this cable.

The remote operator panel function of Operations Console is not supported on @server i5 Models 520, 550 and 570, and 595. Refer to "Hardware Management Console" on page 679 for equivalent support for Model 520, 550, and 570 and 595 operators.

The following table lists the functions that are available for each console option.

Function supported	Twinax	Operations Console	HMC: @server i5 models only
Local 5250 access	Yes	Yes	Yes
Remote 5250 access	No	Yes	Yes via passthru
Many partitions and systems managed with one console PC	No	Yes LAN-only	Yes
Manage logical partitions (LPARs) and IBM @server Capacity Upgrade on Demand (CUoD)	No	Yes pre-@server i5 models only	Yes
Graphical disk management	No	Yes via iSeries Navigator	No
Remote Control panel	No	Yes Remote power capability not available on i5 Models	Yes
Requires IOP and dedicated IOA	Yes	Yes	No
Supported via LAN	No	Yes	Yes
Software required on console	No	Yes	No
All languages supported by OS/400 and i5/OS	Yes	Yes	No Language support is limited
EZ Setup	No	Yes	No
Remote service	No	Yes	Yes with Service Focal Point

Some @server i5 and iSeries models do not have enough slots to have both an Integrated xSeries Server and a twinax or LAN console in the main tower. Placement rules are summarized as follows:

▶ Operations Console LAN

   – Uses slot C3 for #9771, #9793, and #9794
   – Can use Slots C2 and C5 if a #2849 or #2744 is installed
   – Cannot use the embedded Ethernet port
   – Cannot use dual Ethernet adapter

▶ Operations Console direct

   – Models 520 and 570 use Slot C3 for the #9771, #9793, and #9794

- ▶ Twinax console

  - – Models 520 and 570 use Slot C3 for the #9771, #9793, and #9794
  - – Model 520 uses Slots C2 and C5 if a #4746 is installed
  - – Model 570 uses Slots C4 and C6 if a #4746 is installed

iSeries Operations Console features

Operations Console is a Model 270, 800, 810, 825, 870, and 890 operator interface for systems management. These iSeries servers support integrated remote console and control panel capabilities to simplify remote systems management tasks. iSeries Operations Console support allows a personal computer (PC) to be a local or remote console of iSeries servers. This allows a system administrator to monitor the system from another location. A twinaxial connection for console functions is not required.

The remote console application is a full-function 5250 PC console session. The remote control panel application complements the remote console function and provides a graphical user interface (GUI) that resembles its hardware counterpart. Both applications, in general, make it possible to perform the majority of system operations tasks, for example backup and recovery, when the iSeries server and the operations staff are in physically separate locations.

Operations Console enables connections across a LAN and enables directly cabled connections. Multiple Operations Console LAN connections can be active per system or partition at a time. Only one interface can be the console at a time even though they all have data on the screen. A separate dedicated interface for each partition is required.

A single PC can have multiple connections to multiple iSeries servers and can be the console for multiple iSeries servers. Only one PC can have control of the iSeries server at a given time. It also allows multiple local consoles on a network connection, with only one directly cabled configuration.

You can use the remote control panel functions on the same PC for any connected iSeries server. You can use the remote control panel for logical partitions through a LAN connection to the primary partition.

There is a high level of security for the connections of Operations Console on the LAN. Enhanced authentication and data encryption provide network security for console procedures. Operations Console with LAN connectivity uses a version of Secure Sockets Layer (SSL) that supports device and user authentication, without using certificates.

These scenarios are illustrated in the following figure.

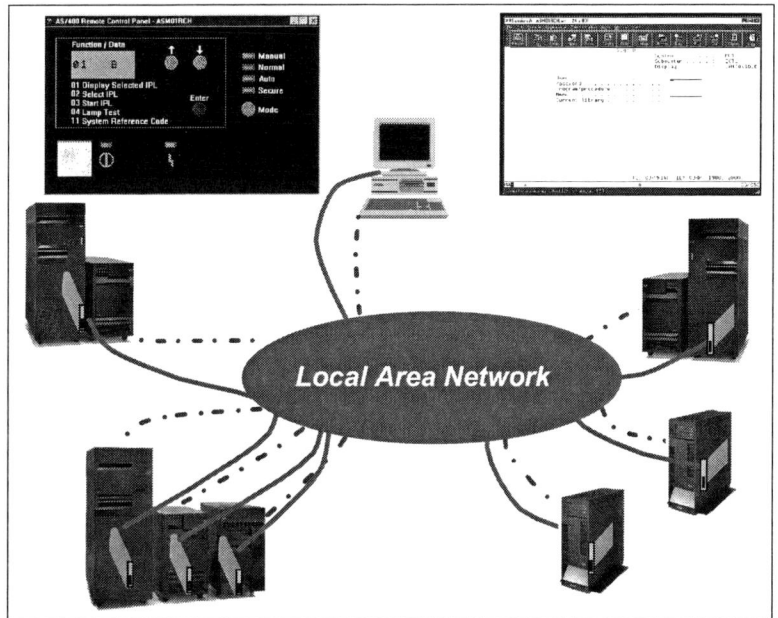

Basic knowledge of the Service Tools Security framework is necessary to understand how Operations Console on the LAN works. The main concepts are:

► **Service tools device ID**: This is a unique device description with an associated password (can be 128 characters long). Service device authentication assures which physical device is the console.

► **Service tools user ID**: Service tools user IDs are used to access the service tools functions for which the profile has been granted authorization. You can create service tools user IDs yourself and grant authority for specific service tools functions. Service tools user IDs of QSECOFR, QSRV, 11111111, and 22222222 are provided with i5/OS.

► **Service tools security log**: The service tools security log contains entries of actions performed against service tools security such as granting or revoking authority, creating or deleting profiles, or attempting to violate service tools security. A service tools user ID with the proper authority can work with the service tools security log to view, display, print, save, or restore service tools security log data.

> **Note:** You can specify a device ID for security that permits only specific PC workstations to perform Operations Console LAN connections and Control Panel functions.

The console is determined on a first in, first served basis. For example, the first LAN-connected console becomes the console. Subsequent LAN connecting PCs are presented a special Dedicated Service Tool (DST) Signon window or the Console Information Status window depending on whether the new *Allow console to be taken over by another console* option is enabled.

If concurrent standard LAN activity is desired, such as running workstation functions, configure a second LAN adapter and vary it on. Separate IP addresses are required.

Operations Console on the LAN does not need a #0383 Remote Control Panel Cable to work with the functions of the Remote Control Panel for logical partitions. This function is enabled by default during setup but can be disabled in Properties. You would use the privileges granted for the Service Tools Device ID and the Service Tools User ID to get the Remote Control Panel to work on the PC. By default the user and device ID are created with enough authority to use the remote control panel.

When you select the Operations Console on the LAN for your iSeries server, IBM delivers one #0367 Operations Console PCI Cable. It is shipped with an upgrade if that cable is not on the configuration.

Operation Console over the LAN connection is highly secured. Only one PC can use a Service Tools device ID. After a successful connection is established the associated password is changed and encrypted. You can encrypt the data flow between the console and the server by installing a Client Encryption product on the Operations Console PC (5722-CEx) and the Cryptographic Access Provider product (5722-ACx) on the iSeries server.

Operations Console and Remote Control Panel (#0383 for direct-attach) are installed and used from PCs using the Windows XP Professional PC operating system, Windows 2000 Professional PC operating system, or Windows NT Workstation 4.0. The console and control panel applications can be used together or separately. Each requires its own direct cable attachment. The cables are purchased separately and are unique to the system being used. IBM POWER5 hardware does not support a directly attached remote control panel. For remote power on capability on this platform, consider remote HMC (Remote Client) or ASMI.

The #0383 Remote Control Panel Cable replaces the #0382 Remote Control Panel Cable. The PC that connects to the #0383 cable must have OS/400 V5R2 iSeries Access for Windows with a minimum of service pack SI06631 installed.

iSeries systems use a parallel interface to connect the Remote Control Panel for Models 270, 800, 810, 820, 825, 830, 840, 870, and 890. This is valid only when the #0383 Remote Control Panel Cable is used.

iSeries Navigator can be enabled on the Operations Console PC. An advantage of this is that you can centralize system management functions through a single asynchronous connection to the iSeries server using the iSeries console, Remote Control Panel capabilities, and iSeries Navigator on one PC.

Operations Console is a follow-on to the AS/400 Client Access Communications console. It is packaged with the iSeries Access for Windows product (5722-XE1), which is part of the iSeries Access Family (5722-XW1). Operations Console is an optionally installed component of 5722-XE1, but no 5722-XW1 license is required to use this component.

Operations Console supports three types of local console configurations:

► **Local console directly attached**: A PC is locally attached to an iSeries server through the Operations Console cable.

   Remote users are unable to connect to this PC.

► **Local console directly attached with remote access allowed**: A PC is locally attached to an iSeries server through the Operations Console cable.

   Remote users can connect to this PC, with or without the intervention of an operator.

► **Local console on a network**: A PC uses the Service Tools Security framework and connects to the iSeries Server over the LAN.

   The PC can be set up to have the console function as well as the Remote Control Panel function. A dedicated LAN adapter is required. To allow the Remote Control Panel function which allows an iSeries server to be powered on, the #0383 Remote Control Panel Cable must also be installed for Models 270, 800, 810, 820, 825, 830, 840, 870, and 890.

> **Remote console through dial-up support:** Remote consoles are PCs that dial in to a local console directly attached with remote access allowed for remote access to the iSeries server. The PC dialing in remotely can then become the console. If the remote control panel is installed and configured on the local console, you can also use the remote control panel functions.

iSeries Access for Windows must be installed to use iSeries Operations Console. During the installation of iSeries Access for Windows, iSeries Operations Console support is installed. If PC5250 or IBM Personal Communications Version 5.7 with CSD 1 minimum or later is not already installed, a 5250 emulator is installed during the iSeries Access for Windows installation. The Operations Console Cable is required to use the console function for a direct attached Operations Console PC. The remote control panel cable is required to use the remote control panel function (a graphical control panel to operate as the iSeries control panel). The control panel cable part number is 53P5704 (CCIN is 0383).

iSeries Operations Console support is available for OS/400 V5R1 and later. For V5R1 and later, it is the only type of PC console supported by the iSeries Model 270, 800, 810, 820, 825, 830, 840, 870, and 890 systems.

You can find setup information in the iSeries Information Center at:

http://www.ibm.com/eserver/iseries/infocenter

Under Connecting to iSeries, select the **Operations Console** topic.

Remote control panel

iSeries 270, 800, 810, 820, 825, 830, 840, 870, and 890 servers use a parallel interface (LPT) instead of a COM port for the Remote Control Panel. The @server i5 Models 520, 550, and 570 and 595 do not support a directly cabled remote control panel.

The #0383 Remote Control Panel Cable enables use of the Remote Control Panel function on a PC supporting a Model 270, 800, 810, 820, 825, 830, 840, 870, and 890.

For cable connection details and PC requirements, see the iSeries Information Center on the Web at:

http://www.ibm.com/eserver/iseries/infocenter

When you reach this Web site, select the topics **Connecting to iSeries** → **Operations Console** for more information.

Consider these points:

► OS/400 V5R1 and later Operations Console users may want to consider Virtual Control Panel to obtain Remote Control Panel functions without needing a direct parallel cable connection.

For further information about installing Virtual Control Panel, see the How to Install the Virtual Control Panel in the Information Center at:

http://www-1.ibm.com/servers/eserver/iseries/access/console/pdf/installing_vcp_520.pdf

> ► Use of the Remote Control Panel function is independent of the System Console.

> ► The Remote Control Panel Cable is not required for a #5546 System Console on 100 Mbps Token Ring or #5548 System Console on 100 Mbps Ethernet LAN-attached console.

Remote Control Panel is installed and used from PCs that run the Windows NT 4.0, Windows 2000 Professional PC, or Windows XP Professional operating system.

Hardware Management Console

The IBM Hardware Management Console is a PC-based console that runs a Linux-based server management application. It is required for any of the new POWER5 technology-based IBM @server systems that implement partitions, Capacity on Demand, or support concurrent maintenance. It is only available for POWER5 technology-based servers and runs on a pre-installed Linux-based workstation via an Ethernet LAN connection. An Ethernet cable attaches to the HMC port.

The following figure illustrates the basic attachment of an HMC to an @server i5 Model 595.

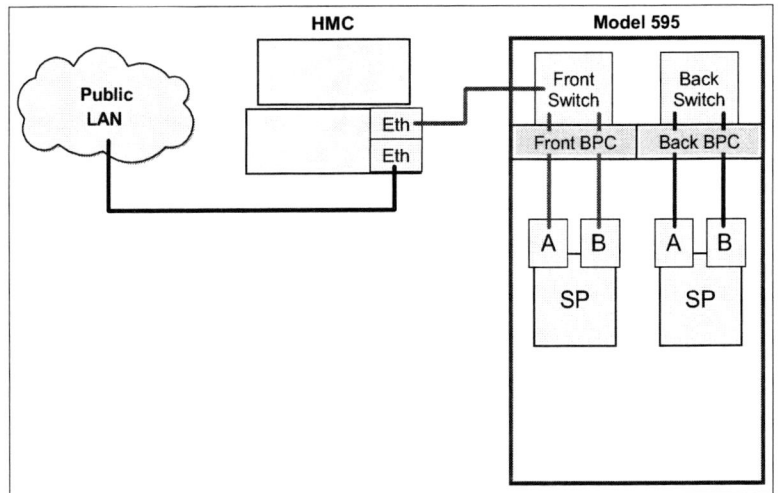

The HMC can be used to manage from one to thirty-two partitioned systems. It is not required for non-logically partitioned systems. It can connect to one or more

managed systems. A Model 520, 550, or 570 and 595 can be managed by only one HMC. A virtual console terminal can be configured to run on the HMC for each partition, reducing the need for extra hardware in each partition.

Some service functions available with System and Dedicated Service Tools can be performed by the HMC. Management functions offered through the use of HMC include the ability to:

► Create and maintain a LPAR environment

► Display a virtual console session for each i5/OS partition

► Detect, report, and store changes in hardware conditions

► Power managed systems on and off

► Act as a service focal point for IBM Service Representatives to determine an appropriate service strategy and enable Service Agent to call home to IBM

► Activate additional resources on demand

The HMC operates as a single, dedicated console for iSeries servers, providing 5250 console support to run diagnostics and monitor operations. Updates to the HMC are made via microcode (firmware). In some ways, the HMC replaces the primary partition of system.

The HMC is available in the following models:

► 7310-C03: Desktop HMC
► 7310-CR2: Rack-mounted HMC with or without a 7316-TF3: Rack-mounted HMC kit

> **Note:** The HMC can be used only for the control and service functions of the POWER5 technology-based servers it servers. It is not available for use as a general purpose computing resource.

Advanced System Management Interface

ASMI is a browser-based interface. It allows you to perform general and privileged service tasks such as reading service processor error logs and vital product data, setting up the service processor, and controlling the system power. If you already have an HMC or an ASCII console, ASMI is not required.

> **Note:** User access to HMC applications is via a GUI only.

Refer to the iSeries Information Center for setup information for the Hardware Management Console:

```
http://www.ibm.com/eserver/iseries/infocenter
http://publib.boulder.ibm.com/infocenter/eserver/v1r2s/en_US/info/ipha1/
hardwaremanagementconsolehmc.htm
```

Refer to *Logical Partitions on IBM PowerPC: A Guide to Working with LPAR on POWER5 for IBM @server i5 Servers*, SG24-8000, for a setup guide and information about working with the HMC.

To help decide which type of console to use on @server i5 servers, see the *V5R3 i5/OS Console Positioning Paper* on the Web at:

```
http://www-1.ibm.com/servers/eserver/iseries/literature/index.html
```

IBM eServer Technical Support Advantage for iSeries

An important aspect of technology is technical support that helps make that technology work for us as people. The IBM @server Technical Support Advantage is a comprehensive set of resources available to IBM Clients, each focused on one objective: the simplification and streamlining support of each IBM @server solution. It offers easier access to total iSeries solutions in this increasingly Web-based world.

The Technical Support Advantage initiative offers total server support that you need for today's On Demand Business world. You receive great support that is personalized, flexible, and in the form you need it. What counts is keeping your business running and helping you drive your business to the next level.

Technical Support Advantage is the total solutions focus of IBM for iSeries servers. It involves voice and Web-based technical support and support that is integrated into the product. Emphasis is on a collaborative approach to technical support that helps to ensure a personal touch.

As the part of Technical Support Advantage that covers the iSeries product line, IBM has enhanced its Extreme Support through Personalization initiative to include more easy-to-use, proactive and personalized tools. Extreme Support features and functions for the iSeries include:

▶ Management Central-Pervasive for remote management of servers
▶ Easier access to IBM @server Technical Support Web sites
▶ IBM Electronic Services for iSeries
▶ Universal Connection: ECS over TCP/IP
▶ PM eServer iSeries Integrated with IBM @server Workload Estimator
▶ Physical Device Placement Assistant (PDPA)
▶ Software Inventory Assistant

- ► iSeries University
- ► Web interface to manage software keys
- ► Enhanced software knowledge base
- ► Streamlined fix downloads
- ► Easy search for technical information

You can find more information about technical support and resources at:

`http://www.ibm.com/eserver/iseries/support`

Management Central-Pervasive

Management Central-Pervasive allows network administrators to monitor the performance and status of their iSeries servers while away from their workstation or office. Using a cellular phone or personal digital assistant (PDA) with a wireless modem, the administrator can check on iSeries server status and monitor performance metrics on the iSeries servers. Management Central-Pervasive also runs from a Web browser running on PCs or Network Stations.

For more information about Management Central-Pervasive, see "IBM eServer iSeries Access for Wireless (5722-XP1)" on page 669.

Menu interface

System-supplied menus to most system functions provide a task-oriented approach so that a user unfamiliar with control language can set up and use i5/OS. The menus use an object-oriented approach by providing a list of objects for the user to work with. A fast path gives quick access to system functions for the more experienced users.

Online help

The iSeries help facility provides comprehensive explanations of display functions to help users be more productive. The index search facility can be used to request help for a task that involves multiple displays. Index search includes many synonyms so that users can ask for information in their own words or in the terms used by the system.

The help information provided is determined by the current location of the cursor on the display. It can be specific to a field or line on the screen, or to extended help on the use of the display.

iSeries Information Center

The i5/OS V5R3 iSeries Information Center is available with tips, techniques, scenarios, and technical information to help you take advantage of all of the features of your iSeries server. From hardware specifications to wireless

management and Enterprise Identity Mapping (EIM) information, the iSeries Information Center is a prime technical resource for your iSeries information needs.

See the *Basics* section to find everything you need to get started if you are new to iSeries. Find what you are looking for with advanced search functions and use advisors to identify considerations for your business' network infrastructure. You can use interactive finders to search over 2000 APIs and 1600 CL commands.

The Supplemental Library on Portable Document Format (PDF) is integrated with the Information Center to provide a one-stop place to obtain technical information. You can search the PDF and Hypertext Markup Language (HTML) files in one search at the Internet site. The iSeries Information Center is available on the Internet at:

`http://www.ibm.com/eserver/iseries/infocenter`

The iSeries Information Center is also provided on CD-ROM with iSeries hardware and i5/OS orders. The CD-ROM includes a wizard to install the iSeries Information Center to an intranet server from the iSeries server. The wizard can even configure your HTTP server and setup search on the intranet.

Program temporary fixes

Program temporary fixes (PTFs) can be shipped to a central site, either on media or electronically, and then packaged and distributed to remote license sites, either on media or electronically. Clients can download PTFs over the Internet. The client hardware needed is a PC with Windows 95/NT, a TCP connection to the iSeries over a LAN, and access to the Internet. Configuration and setup information is documented on the Web at:

`http://www-912.ibm.com/supporthome.nsf/document/10000045`

Except for the medium of transport (Internet), the functionality and entitlement rules are the same as for the ECS method of transport.

PTFs (including Licensed Internal Code (LIC) changes) are loaded and applied using a command.

System detected software problems

Symptom strings are automatically created by the i5/OS licensed programs at the time an error occurs. They make the management of problems in the system easier and recovery quicker by improving the rate at which clients can find appropriate fixes for problems. Problem resolution time is decreased when failure data is collected at the time of occurrence and reduces the need to recreate failures.

Electronic Customer Support

Electronic Customer Support (ECS) is an integrated approach to help users service and support single or complex systems and networks. It is menu-driven and supported by online help text. ECS includes functions available locally, with access to remote marketing support systems and IBM service support.

Simplicity and ease-of-use characteristics mean that configuring and supporting systems requires limited data processing knowledge or experience. Electronic Customer Support enables third-party software and support organizations to support systems and networks from a central site, providing business solutions and partnerships to maintain service and support to iSeries clients.

Systems management capabilities of ECS include:

- ► Resource management and configuration management
- ► Problem management, network management, and change management
- ► Online and remote technical support
- ► Electronic hardware and software service support
- ► Remote marketing support
- ► Universal Connection

The ability to run Electronic Customer Support over TCP/IP is available using the integrated high-speed V.90 modem. This includes electronic fix retrieval and problem reporting. In addition, IBM remote support over a dial-up connection using the integrated high-speed V.90 modem is enabled. This includes making available CL commands for creating simple point- to-point configurations to aid in connecting to IBM Support for the client to use as well. In addition, you can configure a safe reliable VPN connection to run over an Internet connection.

For the PTFs required to enable these functions, see:

http://www.ibm.com/servers/eserver/iseries

If a hardware or software problem arises, you can download PTFs to the iSeries server to assist in problem determination and resolution. The ECS connection can also be used for IBM Electronic Service Agent™ for iSeries, where the iSeries server initiates a call to an IBM service center at a prearranged time for its error logs to be checked and to enable service actions to be taken. This often occurs before the client is aware of the existence of a problem.

Internet PTFs

iSeries clients can download PTFs over the Internet. The client system required is a PC with Windows NT, 2000, or XP, a TCP connection to the iSeries server over a LAN, and access to the Internet. Selected configurations and setup information are documented on the Web at:

http://www.ibm.com/eserver/iseries/support

Except for the medium of transport, the functionality and entitlement of PTF download over the Internet is the same as the Electronic Customer Support method of transport. The user selects the PTFs and options using a Web browser and submits the order. At the iSeries service Web site, the user can also search for and read PTF cover letters before the order is placed. The same entitlement rules that apply on the ECS connection are enforced. If a user can acquire PTFs electronically with ECS, they can acquire PTFs over the Internet.

System management products

This section discusses the products available to manage @server i5 and iSeries systems.

IBM Tivoli Storage Manager Extended Edition (5698-A11)

IBM Tivoli Storage Manager Extended Edition (5698-A11)	
IBM Tivoli Storage Manager Extended Edition core functions include data backup and restore, managed data archive and retrieve, planning for disaster recovery, Network Data Management Protocol (NDMP), and support for large tape libraries. It has a UNIX look and feel, but contains the necessary modification to permit it to function in the OS/400 Portable Application Solutions Environment (PASE) environment. It supports the non-storage area network (SAN) environment. The IBM Tivoli Storage Manager product provides a server that runs using OS/400 PASE. OS/400 PASE is an integrated runtime environment for AIX or other UNIX-like applications running on the iSeries server.	
Minimum operating system level	OS/400 V5R1
Related products	Backup Recovery and Media Services (5722-BR1) Tivoli Storage Manager V5.1 (5698-ISM)
Replaces product	Tivoli Storage Manager Extended Edition V5.1 (5698-ISX)
Further information	http://www.ibm.com/software/tivoli/

IBM Backup Recovery and Media Services for iSeries (5722-BR1)

IBM Backup Recovery and Media Services for iSeries (5722-BR1)	
IBM Backup Recovery and Media Services is the IBM strategic solution for planning and managing the backup of the iSeries server. It provides all of the functions that most iSeries users need to implement a fully automated, single system, backup, recovery, and media management strategy.	
BRMS facilitates centralized management of media by maintaining a consistent view of removable tape media, its contents, location, and availability across multiple iSeries servers or OS/400 partitions referred to as *networked systems*. This common media scratch pool contains shared tape volumes, which are eligible for use by any participating networked system. When a networked system uses one of the shared volumes, that usage is broadcast to all networked systems so that each system has a current view of the active media and the available expired media.	
BRMS provides the iSeries server with support for policy-oriented setup and execution of archive, backup, recovery, and other removable media-related operations. BRMS uses a consistent set of intuitive concepts and operations, which can be used to develop and implement a backup strategy tailored to your business requirements. The user interface is menu-driven, with a significant number of functions enabled through the optional BRMS iSeries Navigator client, a plug-in to iSeries Navigator.	
Minimum operating system level	i5/OS V5R3
Program size	Base - 275 MB Option 1 - 8 KB Option 2 - 8 KB
HIPO	1002
Availability	30 April 2004
Software type	Software Subscription
Installation prerequisites	5722-SS1 Option 18 Media and Storage Extensions 5733-197 IBM Tivoli Storage Manager Application Programming Interface for iSeries (Required for Tivoli Storage Manager)
Related product	Tivoli Storage Manager for OS/400 PASE (5698-A13)
Replaces products	5769-BR1, 5716-BR1
Client code	Delivered with the server. More functions on i5/OS V5R3 than OS/400 V5R2 and V5R1.
Further information	http://www-1.ibm.com/servers/eserver/iseries/service/brms/ http://www-1.ibm.com/servers/eserver/iseries/service/brms/ adsmperf.htm

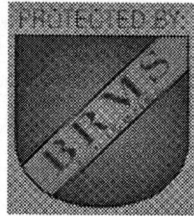

IBM Advanced Job Scheduler for iSeries (5722-JS1)

IBM Advanced Job Scheduler for iSeries (5722-JS1)	
Easily manage your job automation across multiple systems running the IBM Advanced Job Scheduler for iSeries. For example, with the Advanced Job Scheduler on multiple systems, you can condition jobs on one system to only start when a job on another system is successful or ends in error. Supported network environments for the Advanced Job Scheduler include TCP/IP.	
Further information	http://www.ibm.com/eserver/iseries/jscheduler/product.html

IBM Managed System Services for iSeries (577-MG1)

IBM Managed System Services for iSeries (5722-MG1)	
IBM Managed System Services for iSeries (MSS) licensed program is part of an integrated offering Operation Control Center/400, which includes System Manager for iSeries. MSS enables an iSeries server to be managed from a central site running either S/390 NetView Distribution Manager for MVS (Release 5 or later) for MVS-based networks or System Manager for iSeries-based networks. The central site defines, schedules, and tracks software distribution (change management) requests sent to an iSeries server with Managed System Services for iSeries installed. These change management requests include sending, receiving, and deleting iSeries system files, programs, and other objects (libraries, save files, message files, documents, folders, PTFs, and so on).	
Minimum operating system level	OS/400 V5R1
Installation prerequisites	None
Related product	System Manager for iSeries (5722-SM1)
Replaces product	5769-MG1

IBM System Manager for iSeries (5722-SM1)

IBM System Manager for iSeries (5722-SM1)	
iSeries objects can be sent directly to or received from iSeries libraries or through the local iSeries distribution repository with IBM System Manager for iSeries. Non-iSeries objects can be received into, stored, and distributed from the iSeries distribution directory. The capability for the central site iSeries to define, schedule, run these change requests one time or repetitively, and track their status significantly enhances unattended operation of the remote systems supported by System Manager.	
Minimum operating system level	OS/400 V5R1
Software type	Part of the integrated offering Operations Control Center/400, which includes Managed System Services for iSeries
Installation prerequisites	None
Related product	Managed System Services for iSeries (5722-MG1)
Replaces product	5769-SM1

IBM eServer iSeries Enterprise Edition Installation Assistant (5733-ED1)

IBM @server iSeries Enterprise Edition Installation Assistant (5733-ED1)	
The iSeries Enterprise Edition Installation Assistant consists of CD images for some of the products included with the Enterprise Editions offering. It includes an installation assistant to use in installing those products on the iSeries.	
Minimum operating system level	OS/400 V5R2
Software type	Software maintenance, yes
Ordering	Shipped with OS/400 at no charge
Replaces product	N/A
Included in base	Not orderable; included with Enterprise Editions
Further information	http://www.ibm.com/servers/eserver/iseries/hardware/editions

IBM Software Integration Assistant for iSeries (5733-IA1)

IBM Software Integration Assistant for iSeries (5733-IA1)	
Some IBM software products are created and packaged so that a single version of the software can be installed on any one of several operating system platforms, including i5/OS. The IBM Software Integration Assistant for iSeries provides mechanisms that enable standard iSeries fix (PTF) delivery and application procedures for these multiplatform products. These products are not packaged as iSeries licensed programs because the same product can be installed on platforms other than iSeries.	
Minimum i5/OS level	i5/OS V5R3
Software type	Shipped with i5/OS at no charge
Replaces product	New in i5/OS V5R3

IBM Intelligent Communications Trace Analyzer for iSeries Version 1.0 (5733-AZ1)

IBM Intelligent Communications Trace Analyzer for iSeries, Version 1.0 (5733-AZ1)	
The IBM Intelligent Communications Trace Analyzer for iSeries, Version 1.0 runs as an iSeries Navigator plug-in.	
Minimum operating system level	OS/400 V5R1
Installation prerequisites	None
Related product	Performance Tools for iSeries (5722-PT1)
Replaces product	N/A

IBM Performance Tools for iSeries (5722-PT1)

IBM Performance Tools for iSeries (5722-PT1)	
Performance Tools for iSeries is a program product that provides a set of reporting, analysis, and modeling functions to assist an iSeries administrator to manage the performance of the system. It provides printed and online reports. These can be in graphic or tabular form.	
The Performance Advisor function assists the user in analyzing system performance and provides recommendations. Performance Tools for iSeries, through its modeling facility, can be used to help predict probable system performance before changes are made.	
Minimum operating system level	OS/400 V5R1
HIPO	1008
Installation prerequisites	None
Related product	PATROL for iSeries – Predict (5620-FIF)
Client code	Client Access Express plug-in distributed with 5722-PT1
Replaces products	5769-PT1, 5716-PT1, 5763-PT1, 5769-GP1, 5769-VP1, 5798-RYP
Further information	`http://www-1.ibm.com/servers/eserver/iseries/perfmgmt/pt400.htm`

PATROL for iSeries – Predict (5620-FIF)

PATROL for iSeries – Predict (5620-FIF)	
PATROL for iSeries – Predict is a performance analysis and capacity planning product for iSeries. Using existing performance data from Collection Services or STRPFRMON, PATROL for iSeries – Predict provides comprehensive response-time analysis and predictive modeling capabilities. The "what-if" analysis capabilities reveal the impact of changes, such as load, configuration, and users across the iSeries environment. With this approach, users can prevent performance, service and response-time problems before they occur, and ensure ongoing success by provisioning the right hardware upgrades, at the right time.	
Minimum operating system level	OS/400 V4R4
Availability	02 September 2002
Related products	5722-PT1
Replaces product	BEST/1-400 function of 5722-PT1
Further information	`http://www.bmc.com/products/proddocview/0,2832,19052_19429_23137_7064,00.html`

Valupak for iSeries (5722-VP1)

Valupak for iSeries is a package of chargeable products which provides a discount rather than buy all the products separately. Valupak consists of:

- ► 5722-PT1 Performance Tool for iSeries
- ► 5722-PT1 - Option 1 Manager Feature
- ► 5722-QU1 Query for iSeries
- ► 5722-ST1 DB2 Query Manager and SQL Development Kit for iSeries
- ► 5722-XW1 iSeries Access Family (user based)

The number of iSeries Access licenses varies with the software tier of the Valupak ordered as shown in the following table.

Software tier	Client Access users
P05	10
P10	20
P20	50
P30	70
P40	125
P50	150
P60	175

When upgrading to a new version or release, the upgrade is achieved by using individual product upgrades, and not by upgrading to a new ValuPak. Similarly if an iSeries upgrade involves a processor upgrade, which requires moving to a new software tier, the software charges are calculated on an individual product basis, not as a Valupak upgrade.

33

IBM licensed programs: Printing and document handling products

Office and printing products provide the vehicle for communications both inside and outside a company. To help you understand the iSeries print solutions that are available for a particular set of business requirements, refer to this Web site:

`http://www.printers.ibm.com/internet/wwsites.nsf/vwwebpublished/main_ww`

The office and printing products that are listed in the following table are discussed in this chapter.

Product name	Product number	Refer to page
IBM Advanced Function Printing Utilities for iSeries	5722-AF1	695
IBM Advanced DBCS Printer Support for iSeries	5722-AP1	696
IBM AFP Font Collection for Workstations and OS/400	5648-B45	697
IBM Dictionary and Linguistics Tools for AS/400	5769-DL1	697
IBM Business Graphics Utility for AS/400	5722-DS1	699
IBM Infoprint Fonts for Multiplatforms	5648-E77	700
IBM Facsimile Support for iSeries	5798-FAX	700
IBM Advanced Function Printing Fonts for AS/400	5769-FNT	701
IBM Advanced Function Printing DBCS Fonts for AS/400 V4R3	5769-FN1	702
IBM Infoprint Designer for iSeries	5733-ID1	703
Infoprint Server for iSeries	5722-IP1	704
IBM Content Manager OnDemand for iSeries	5722-RD1	705
IBM Content Manager for iSeries	5722-VI1	706
IBM Print Services Facility for iSeries (PSF/400)	5722-SS1 options 36, 37, and 38	707

IBM Advanced Function Printing Utilities for iSeries (5722-AF1)

IIBM Advanced Function Printing Utilities for iSeries (5722-AF1)	
Advanced Function Printing (AFP) Utilities consists of three integrated utilities that support AFP print applications. Included are Overlay Utility for electronic forms, Resource Management Utility for managing document resources, and Print Format Utility, a "Query/AFP" tool to help you build advanced electronic output directly from iSeries database files. For most iSeries document design functions, look at Infoprint Designer (5733-ID1).	
The user can interactively design, create, and verify AFP resources such as overlays. In addition to the AFP resource creation and management, it provides the capability to print users' data contained in a database file in various formats, with various fonts and barcodes on the Intelligent printer Data Stream (IPDS) printer without developing any application programs. For example, it allows users to print barcode labels from data stored in the database file.	
Uses with various levels of experience can easily take full advantage of IPDS printer capability that is either not accessible to them now or accessible only with great difficulty.	
Components include the Overlay Utility, Print Format Utility, and the Resource Management Utility.	

Minimum operating system level	OS/400 V5R1
Program size	18.1 MB
HIPO	1001
Availability	23 April 2001
Software type	Software Subscription 5733-SW1 or 5733-SW3
Ordering	Chargeable software group-based OS/400 Licensed Program Offering (LPO).
Installation prerequisites	5722-SS1 Option 36, 37, or 38 PSF is required
Related products	Infoprint Server, Infoprint Designer, Page Printer Formatting Aid, AFP Toolbox, and iSeries Access
Replaces product	IBM Advanced Function Printing for AS/400 (5769-AF1)
Further information	http://www.printers.ibm.com/internet/wwsites.nsf/ vwwebpublished/supportoverview_ww http://www.redbooks.ibm.com http://www.printers.ibm.com/R5PSC.NSF/Web/software+overview

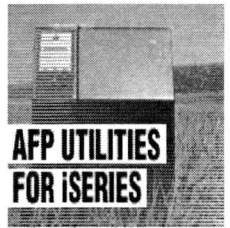

IBM Advanced DBCS Printer Support for iSeries (5722-AP1)

IBM Advanced DBCS Printer Support for iSeries (5722-AP1)		
Advanced DBCS Printer Support for iSeries is a set of the following utilities: ► Advanced Print Writer (APW) ► Advanced Page Printer Writer (APPW) ► Kanji Print Function (KPF) ► Printer Function Control (PFC) ► System/36 Resource Migration The difference in these utilities is the supported printers and the print functions.		
Minimum operating system level	OS/400 V5R1	
Program size	15.5 MB	
HIPO	1014	
Availability	25 May 2001	
Software type	Software Subscription	
Ordering	Included on the Keyed Stamped Media	
Related products	Infoprint Server, Infoprint Designer, Advanced Print Utility, Page Printer Formatting Aid, AFP Toolbox, and iSeries Access	
Replaces product	5769-AP1	

Further information	`http://www.printers.ibm.com/R5PSC.NSF/Web/software+overview`
	`http://www.redbooks.ibm.com`
	`http://www.ibm.com/eserver/iseries/infocenter`	

IBM AFP Font Collection for Workstations and OS/400 V2.1.1 (5648-B45)

IBM AFP Font Collection for Workstations and OS/400 V2.1.1 (5648-B45)	
The IBM AFP Font Collection for Workstations and OS/400 provides fonts that can be used by most Advanced Function Presentation products. Skillful use of fonts in typography can dramatically improve the readability and effectiveness of your documents. The IBM AFP Font Collection CD is bundled and shipped with all orders of PSF/400.	
The AFP Font Collection is designed to support printing on AFP/IPDS printers that accept host downloaded fonts using Print Services Facility or Infoprint Manager. The AFP Font Collection CD is shipped automatically with PSF/400.	
AFP Font Collection provides one-stop shopping for iSeries printer fonts - the fonts you need to realize the full potential of business communications. The fonts are provided in a full range of resolutions (240 dpi, 300 dpi, and outlines) and in over 48 languages. Font sizes change easily to support the latest IPDS printers, and to enable full graphical document viewing, as well as offer a performance savings over raster fonts.	
Minimum operating system level	V2
HIPO	N/A
Availability	30 June 2000
Software type	
Ordering	
Installation prerequisites	5722-SS1 Option 36, 37, or 38
Related products	Infoprint Server, Infoprint Designer, PSF/400 Advanced Print Utility, Page Printer Formatting Aid, AFP Toolbox, and iSeries Access
Replaces product	5648-B45 V2.1.0
Further information	`http://www.printers.ibm.com/internet/wwsites.nsf/` `vwwebpublished/supportoverview_ww` `http://www.redbooks.ibm.com` `http://www.printers.ibm.com/R5PSC.NSF/Web/as400overview`

IBM Dictionary and Linguistics Tools for AS/400 (5769-DL1)

IBM Dictionary and Linguistics Tools for AS/400 (5769-DL1)	
Dictionary and Linguistics Tools provides 36 dictionaries and a set of dictionary access methods (application programming interfaces (APIs)) to allow clients to write applications to access the dictionaries directly. Advanced linguistic information is built into each dictionary, such as hyphenation, synonyms, spelling aid, morphological identification, and tokenization. Dictionary and Linguistics Tools allow you to write your own APIs and support more languages than the Language Dictionary product.	
Minimum operating system level	OS/400 V5R1
Program size	69 MB
HIPO	1026
Availability	25 May 2001
Software type	Software Maintenance ► One Year 5733-M89 ► Three Year 5733-M90
Ordering	5716-DCT is shipped with the System/38 Utilities product (5722-DB1)
Installation prerequisites	None
Replaces product	Language Dictionaries (5716-DCT)

IBM Business Graphics Utility for AS/400 (5722-DS1)

IBM Business Graphics Utility for AS/400 (5722-DS1)	
The Business Graphics Utility (BGU) for AS/400 licensed program provides a very flexible and powerful business graphics function through a menu-driven interface. Users can create, modify, store, display, print, and plot business graphics using data from a keyboard or database file. Exercise and tutorial materials are supplied in the *BGU User's Guide* to provide the necessary familiarization.	
Extensive options provided by BGU offer users considerable flexibility in creating computer-generated charts. Font style, font size, font color, line styles, legend type, legend position, annotation, and grid line construction are a few of the many options. A chart management facility provides convenient storage, retrieval, deletion, modifications, renaming, and copying of charts.	
Minimum operating system level	OS/400 V5R1
Program size	6.3 MB
HIPO	1027
Availability	25 May 2001
Software type	Software Subscription 5733-SW1 or 5733-SW3
Ordering	Shipped as a chargeable software group-based OS/400 LPO.
Installation prerequisites	None
Replaces product	IBM Business Graphics Utilities for AS/400 (5769-DS1)

IBM Infoprint Fonts for Multiplatforms V1.1 (5648-E77)

IBM Infoprint Fonts for Multiplatforms V1.1 (5648-E77)

IBM Infoprint Fonts for Multiplatforms provides fonts that can be used by most Advanced Function Presentation products. It includes all the outline fonts in the IBM AFP Font Collection V2.1, with these enhancements:

- ► Euro support for Eastern European and Asia Pacific languages
- ► SAP support for Asia Pacific languages
- ► GB18030 support for People's Republic of China
- ► JIS X0213 support for Japan
- ► An improved graphical user interface (GUI) with context-sensitive help for the Type Transformer
- ► An improved GUI for RMARK font data

In addition, the GUIs that were in the AFP Font collection are improved.

Some additional considerations for Infoprint Fonts are:

- ► Infoprint Fonts does not include the raster fonts included with the AFP Font Collection (5648-B45).
- ► If you currently have the AFP Font Collection and do not need the preceding functions, you do not need to migrate to Infoprint Fonts for Multiplatforms.

The AFP Font Collection is shipped automatically with PSF/400.

Minimum operating system level	OS/400 V5R1
HIPO	N/A
Availability	20 December 2002
Ordering	
Installation prerequisites	5722-SS1 Option 36, 37, or 38; PSF/400 is required
Related products	Infoprint Server, Infoprint Designer, Page Printer Formatting Aid, AFP Toolbox, iSeries Access
Replaces product	None
Further information	http://www.printers.ibm.com http://www.printers.ibm.com/R5PSC.NSF/web/as400overview

IBM Facsimile Support for iSeries (5798-FAX)

IBM Facsimile Support for iSeries (5798-FAX)	
Facsimile Support for iSeries enables your users and your applications to send and receive faxes. Combined with native integrated modem hardware solutions, it provides a convenient, cost efficient fax solution for your business. It provides users with direct fax capabilities, which help increase operational efficiency and productivity through rapid information dispersal. Cost savings may also be achieved through reduced human intervention time, paper cost, telephone charges, postage charges, and document delivery time. Also, there is an audit trail of both inbound and outbound activity to track the flow of your business data.	
Minimum operating system level	OS/400 V5R1
HIPO	N/A
Availability	23 April 2001
Software type	Software Subscription 5733-SW1 or 5733-SW3
Ordering	Shipped as a chargeable software group-based OS/400 LPO
Installation prerequisites	For hardware and software requirements, see: http://www-1.ibm.com/servers/eserver/iseries/fax400/
Related products	IBM Integrated Domino Fax (5733-FXD)
Replaces product	IBM Facsimile Support for AS/400 (5769-TBY)
Further information	http://www-1.ibm.com/servers/eserver/iseries/fax400/ http://www.ibm.com/eserver/iseries/infocenter http://www.redbooks.ibm.com

IBM Advanced Function Printing Fonts for AS/400 (5769-FNT)

IBM Advanced Function Printing Fonts for AS/400 (5769-FNT)	
This is a set of 240 dpi fonts that primarily is provided for compatibility with existing print applications. Unless you have applications that require these specific fonts, the standard font product for OS/400 is AFP Font Collection (5648-B45).	
Minimum operating system level	OS/400 V5R1
Program size	0.5 - 50 MB
HIPO	1520
Availability	25 May 2001
Software type	Software Subscription
Ordering	
Installation prerequisites	
Related products	Infoprint Server, Infoprint Designer, Advanced Print Utility, Page Printer Formatting Aid, AFP Toolbox, and iSeries Access
Replaces product	None
Further information	http://www.printers.ibm.com/internet/wwsites.nsf/vwwebpublished/main_ww

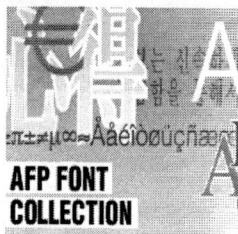

IBM Advanced Function Printing DBCS Fonts for AS/400 (5769-FN1)

IBM Advanced Function Printing DBCS Fonts for AS/400 (5769-FN1)	
IBM Advanced Function Printing DBCS Fonts for AS/400 is a rich selection of DBCS font families for use on 240 dots-per-inch, non-impact printers supported by AFP software integrated in the OS/400. This program includes: ▶ Japanese fonts ▶ Korean fonts ▶ Traditional Chinese fonts ▶ Simplified Chinese fonts ▶ Thai fonts AFP is designed to allow printing on page printers. These fonts allow clients more flexibility in printing. Some common uses for these families are for printing books, brochures, business plans, handbooks, magazines, manuals, operating schedules, price lists, presentation materials, headlines, subtitles, and reports. Some of the features of IBM Advanced Function Printing are: ▶ Provides a double-byte font library for use with 240 dots-per-inch, non-impact printers attached to an iSeries server ▶ Enhances system management flexibility with AFP resources transfer ▶ Allows for growth and flexibility in the use of AFP printers ▶ Enhances user productivity by printing the same object on AFP printers attached to an S/370™ or iSeries server	
Minimum operating system level	OS/400 V5R1
Program size	1 - 129 MB
HIPO	1535, 1536, 1537, 1538, 1539
Availability	25 May 2001
Software type	Software Subscription
Ordering	
Installation prerequisites	
Related products	Infoprint Server, Infoprint Designer, Advanced Print Utility, Page Printer Formatting Aid, AFP Toolbox, and iSeries Access
Replaces product	5716-FN1
Further information	http://www.printers.ibm.com/internet/wwsites.nsf/ vwwebpublished/main_ww

IBM Infoprint Designer for iSeries (5733-ID1)

IBM Infoprint Designer for iSeries (5733-ID1)	
Infoprint Designer for iSeries provides a fully-graphical document composition interface to the iSeries printing and e-output system. It supports the requirements of today's complex documents and reports to produce fully electronic documents combining data, text, electronic forms, graphics, image, barcoding, and typographic fonts. Infoprint Designer for iSeries can be used for the design of new output applications or the re-engineering of existing applications.	
Minimum operating system level	OS/400 V4R5
HIPO	N/A
Availability	25 May 2001
Software type	Software Subscription 5733-SW1 or 5733-SW3
Ordering	Shipped as a chargeable software group-based OS/400 LPO
Installation prerequisites	5722-SS1 and option 37, 38, or 39 are optional iSeries Access for Windows
Related products	Infoprint Server, iSeries Access, and PSF/400
Replaces product	IBM Advanced Function Printing Utilities for iSeries (5722-AF1)
Further information	http://www.printers.ibm.com/internet/wwsites.nsf/ vwwebpublished/main_ww

Infoprint Server for iSeries (5722-IP1)

Infoprint Server for iSeries (5722-IP1)		
The focus of Infoprint Server is to extend the considerable capabilities of the iSeries beyond printing to the management and dissemination of output. As business applications are re-engineered into applications for On Demand Business, the output of those applications may need to change and flow electronically to the consumer of that output. Infoprint Server provides for *multi-channel* delivery of communications that include print, e-mail, Web, and other options.		
For enterprise printing requirements, Infoprint Server delivers improved efficiency, improved reliability, and lower overall printing costs. It applies iSeries printing management and iSeries-attached printers to the task of handling all of the essential printing generated across the network.		
Minimum operating system level	OS/400 V5R1	
Program size	102 MB	
HIPO	1006	
Availability	25 May 2001	
Software type	Software Subscription 5733-SW1 or 5733-SW3	
Ordering	Shipped as a chargeable software group-based OS/400 LPO	
Prerequisites	OS/400 PASE, Option 33, is required for PostScript, PCL, or Portable Document Format (PDF) to AFPDS transforms	
Related products	PSF/400, Infoprint Designer, and Content Manager OnDemand	
Replaces product	None	
Further information	`http://www.printers.ibm.com/internet/wwsites.nsf/vwwebpublished/main_ww`	

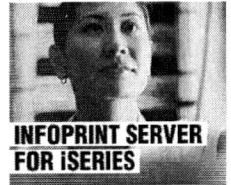

IBM Content Manager On Demand for iSeries (5722-RD1)

IBM Content Manager OnDemand for iSeries (5722-RD1)	
IBM Content Manager OnDemand for iSeries provides a powerful Enterprise Report Management solution to electronically capture and archive large volumes of computer-generated information. This includes customer statements, invoices, reports, scanned images, and e-mails. Content Manager OnDemand (OnDemand/400) supports electronic statement presentment solutions through robust, advanced client applications for both desktop and standard Web browsers, with advanced search and report mining capabilities. With OnDemand/400, enterprises can automatically organize printed output, and provide rapid, direct access to specific information, making more effective use of the massive amounts of information captured over time.	
Minimum operating system level	OS/400 V5R1
Installation prerequisites	None
Related products	IBM Content Manager for iSeries, Content Manager CommonStore for Lotus Domino, Enterprise Information Portal
Client code	Downloaded from `ftp://service.software.ibm.com/software/ondemand/fixes/v71/`
Replaces product	5769-RD1
Further information	`http://www.ibm.com/software/data/ondemand/400`

IBM Content Manager for iSeries (5722-VI1)

IBM Content Manager for iSeries (5722-VI1)		
IBM Content Manager for iSeries provides document imaging and workflow technology designed to replace cumbersome paper document processing with image processing to achieve greater productivity and process reliability. With *Advanced Workflow*, Content Manager provides a fast, efficient way to customize and automate business processes by automatically routing documents and folders through a business.		
Content Manager is highly scalable, from entry level to enterprise level needs. It extends the information infrastructure to manage unstructured content, integrate content with core business applications, and automate business processes.		
Minimum operating system level	OS/400 V5R1	
Program size	135.5 MB	
HIPO	1034	
Availability	25 May 2001	

Software type	Software Maintenance
	  ► One Year 5733-M81
	  ► Three Year 5733-M82	

Ordering		
Installation prerequisites	`http://www.ibm.com/software/data/ondemand/400/`	
Related products	Content Manager OnDemand, Content Manager CommonStore for Lotus Domino, Content Manager CommonStore for SAP, Enterprise Information Portal	
Replaces product	IBM Content Manager for AS/400 (5769-VI1)	
Further information	`http://www-3.ibm.com/software/data/cm/cmgr/400`	

IBM Print Services Facility for iSeries (5722-SS1 options 36, 37, 38)

IBM Print Services Facility for iSeries (PSF/400) (5722-SS1 options 36, 37, and 38)	
Print Services Facility for OS/400 (PSF/400), a feature of OS/400, provides support for high-function Advanced Function Presentation (AFP) electronic printing and print management of IPDS printers. With AFP, application output can be transformed into fully graphical documents with electronic forms, image, graphics, barcoding, lines, boxes, and text in a wide variety of fonts. This flexibility enables the production of electronic documents that are more effective and enables the re-engineering of business processes.	
Minimum operating system level	OS/400 V5R1
Program size	0.5 MB
HIPO	1501, 1502, or 1503
Availability	23 April 2001
Software type	Software Subscription
Ordering	Feature of OS/400
Installation prerequisites	None
Related products	Infoprint Server for iSeries, AFP Font Collection Type Transformer for Windows, Infoprint Designer for iSeries, and Facsimile Support for iSeries
Replaces product	PSF/400 (5769-SS1)
Further information	http://www.printers.ibm.com/internet/wwsites.nsf/ vwwebpublished/main_ww

34

Summary of earlier AS/400, AS/400e, and iSeries models

This chapter identifies resources and capacities for all AS/400e and iSeries processors that are no longer marketed by IBM. For the models most recently withdrawn from IBM marketing, processor and performance characteristics are included, along with the maximum capacities for main storage, disk, local area network (LAN), communication lines, workstations, tape devices, CD devices, and other input/output (I/O) components. Refer to other ITSO deliverables for the equivalent information for those processors withdrawn from IBM marketing at an earlier date.

You can find summary charts of iSeries processors currently marketed by IBM in Chapter 5, "Summary of today's iSeries" on page 79.

CISC systems

You can find resource and capacity information for the AS/400 CISC systems sold beginning in 1988 in *AS/400 CISC System Builder*, REDP-0042. This Redpaper covers the following AS/400 systems:

- ► 9401 Models P01, P02, P03 and 10S
- ► 9402 Models C04, C06, D02, D04, D06, E02, E04, E06, F02, F04, F06
- ► 9402 Model 200, 236
- ► 9402 Model 400
- ► 9402 Model 436
- ► 9404 Models B10, B20, C10, C20, C25, D10, D20, D25, E10, E20, E25, F10, F20, F25
- ► 9406 Models B30, B35, B40, B45, B50, B60, B70, D35, D45, D50, D60, D70, D80, E35, E45, E50, E60, E70, E80, E90, E95, F35, F45, F50, F60, F70, F80, F90, F95, F97
- ► 9406 Models 300, 310, 320
- ► Upgrades to 9406 Model 600, 620, 640, 650

RISC servers

You can find resource and capacity information for the AS/400e RISC servers sold beginning in 1996 in *AS/400e RISC System Builder*, REDP-0342. This Redpaper covers the following AS/400e servers:

- ► 9402 Model 436
- ► 9402 Server Model 100 and 9404 Server Models 135 and 140
- ► 9402 Server Model 20S and 9406 Server Model 30S
- ► 9402 Model 40S
- ► 9406 Model S10
- ► 9406 Model S20
- ► 9406 Model S30
- ► 9406 Model S40
- ► 9406 Models 50S and 53S
- ► 9406 Model SB1
- ► 9406 Model S30 and S40 Custom Mixed-Mode IBM @server
- ► 9401 Model 150
- ► 9402 2xx
- ► 9402 Model 400
- ► 9402 Model 40S
- ► 9406 Model S20 Custom Mixed-Mode Server
- ► 9406 Models 500, 510, 530
- ► 9406 Model 600, 620, 640, 650

Refer to the *IBM @server iSeries and AS/400e System Builder*, SG24-2155, for resource and capacity information for AS/400e RISC systems that is not found in *AS/400e RISC System Builder*, REDP-0342.

iSeries and AS/400e servers

This section presents resource and capacity information for the most recent *withdrawals from IBM marketing* and from the *IBM @server i5, iSeries, and AS/400e System Builder*, SG24-2155.

Refer to the *IBM @server i5, iSeries, and AS/400e System Builder*, SG24-2155, for resource and capacity information, and detailed information about supported features, for the following servers:

- ► 9406 Model 250
- ► 9406 Models SB2 and SB3

The following AS/400e and iSeries servers are found in this section:

- ► 9406 AS/400e Model 270
- ► 9406 AS/400e Model 720
- ► 9406 AS/400e Model 730
- ► 9406 AS/400e Model 740
- ► 9406 iSeries Model 820
- ► 9406 iSeries Model 830
- ► 9406 iSeries Model 840
- ► 9406 iSeries Model 890 (#0197, #0198, #2487, #2488)

9406 Model 270

Model	270			
Processor feature	#2248	#2250	#2252	#2253
Relative system performance [1,2]				
Processor CPW	150	370	950	2000
5250 CPW[5]				
Base #1516	-	0	0	0
#1517	25	-	-	-
#1518	-	30	-	-
#1519	-	-	50	-
#1520	-	-	-	70
Number/type/speed of processors	1/Pulsar/400 MHz	1/Pulsar/400 MHz	1/Pulsar/450 MHz	2/Pulsar/450 MHz
L2 Cache (MB)/processor	0	0	2	4
Main storage (MB min/max)	256 - 4096	256-4096	256-8192	256-8192
Main storage DIMMs (min/max)	2/8	2/8	2/16	2/16
Minimum operating system level	V4R5	V4R5	V4R5	V4R5
Software group [7]	P05	P10/P10	P05	P20/P20

Model	270 Dedicated Server for Domino		
Processor feature	#2422	#2423	#2424
Relative system performance (CPW) [1,2]			
Processor CPW	50	100	200
5250 CPW[5]	0	0	0
Simple Mail Users	2400	3860	7580
Mail and Calendaring Users	1600	2570	5050
Number/type/speed of processors	1/Pulsar/400 MHz	1/Pulsar/450 MHz	2/Pulsar/450 MHz
L2 Cache (MB)	0	2	4
Main storage (MB min/max)	256-4096	256-8192	256-8192
Main storage DIMMs (min/max)	2/8	2/16	2/16
Minimum operating system level	V4R5	V4R5	V4R5
Software group [7]	P05	P05	P10

	Model 270		
Processor feature	#2431	#2432	#2434
Relative system performance[1, 2]			
Processor CPW	465	1070	2350
5250 CPW[5]			
#1516 (Base)	-	0	0
#1517	-	-	-
#1518	30	-	-
#1519	-	50	-
#1520	-	-	70
Number/type/speed of processors	1/SSTAR/ 540 MHz	1/SSTAR/ 540 MHz	2/SSTAR/ 600 MHz
L2 Cache (MB)/processor	0	2	4
Main storage (MB min/max)	256 - 8192	256 - 8192	256 - 16384
Main storage DIMMs (min/max)	1/8	1/8	2/16
Minimum operating system level	V5R1	V5R1	V5R1
Software group[8]	P10	P10	P20

	Model 270 Dedicated Server for Domino	
Processor feature	#2452	#2454
Relative system performance[1, 2] Processor CPW	100	240
5250 CPW[5] Mail and Calendar Users[2]	0 3070	0 6660
Number/type/speed of processors	1/SSTAR/540 MHz	2/SSTAR/600 MHz
L2 Cache (MB)	2	4
Main storage (MB min/max)	256 - 8192	256 - 16384
Main storage DIMMs (min/max)	1/8	2/16
Minimum operating system level	V5R1	V5R1
Software group[8]	P05	P10

Processor feature	Model 270		
	#2431	#2432	#2434
Relative system performance[1, 2]			
Processor CPW	465	1070	2350
5250 CPW[5]			
#1516 (Base)	-	0	0
#1517	-	-	-
#1518	30	-	-
#1519	-	50	-
#1520	-	-	70
Number/type/speed of processors	1/SSTAR/ 540 MHz	1/SSTAR/ 540 MHz	2/SSTAR/ 600 MHz
L2 Cache (MB)/processor	0	2	4
Main storage (MB min/max)	256 - 8192	256 - 8192	256 - 16384
Main storage DIMMs (min/max)	1/8	1/8	2/16
Minimum operating system level	V5R1	V5R1	V5R1
Software group[8]	P10	P10	P20

Note 1	CPW is used to measure the performance of all iSeries and AS/400e processors announced from September 1996 onward. The CPW value is measured on maximum configurations. The type and number of disk devices, the number of workstation controllers, the amount of memory, the system model, other factors, and the application running determine what performance is achievable.
Note 2	Processor performance represents the relative performance (maximum capacity) of a processor feature running CPW in a client/server environment. Processor capacity is achievable when the commercial workload is not constrained by main storage and DASD. Interactive performance represents the relative performance available to perform host-centric workloads. The amount of interactive capacity consumed reduces the available processor capacity by the same amount. On the Dedicated Servers for Domino, the Processor CPW is an approximate value reflecting the maximum amount of non-Domino workload (10 to 15% of CPU) that can be supported.
Note 3	The total number of tape devices does not increase.
Note 4	One line is used if the #5544 System Console on Operations Console is used on a #9771 WAN adapter. One line might be used if the #5546 or #5548 System Console on LAN is selected and the #0367 Operations Console PCI Cable is connected.
Note 5	5250 online transaction processing (OLTP) CPW is an approximate value that reflects the amount of Processor CPW that can be used for workloads performing 5250-based tasks. Any task that uses a 5250 data stream is considered 5250 OLTP work and requires some amount of 5250 CPW to process no matter how the task was started. A task submitted through a 5250 session (5250 device or 5250 emulation) that does display or printer I/O requires 5250 CPW. A task submitted through a 5250 session (5250 device or 5250 emulation) as a "batch" job is not considered 5250 OLTP work and does not require any 5250 CPW unless the task does display or printer I/O. Limited 5250 CPW is available when 5250 Interactive CPW = 0, for a system administrator to use 5250 display device I/O to manage various aspects of the server. Multiple administrative jobs exceed this capability.
Note 6	There must be one CD-ROM or DVD-RAM per system.
Note 7	External DASD capacity maximum assumes 35.16 GB LUNs. External DASD cannot exceed the maximum system capacity or the maximum number of disk arms.
Note 8 Model 270	Software group is determined by a combination of the processor and interactive feature. The following table provides a cross reference.

Processor	Interactive feature	Processor feature	Software group
#2248	#1517	22A2	P05
#2250	#1516	22A4	P10
	#1518	22A5	P10
#2252	#1516	22A7	P10
	#1519	22A8	P10
#2253	#1516	22AA	P20
	#1520	22AB	P20
#2422	N/A	2422	P05
#2423	N/A	2423	P05
#2424	N/A	2424	P10

Summary	Base system	System Unit Expansion #7104	PCI Expansion Tower #5075/#5095	Total maximum	LPAR maximum
Disk storage (GB)					
Integrated minimum	17.56	-	-	8.58	-
Integrated maximum	210.9	421.9	210.9	843.9	843.9
External maximum[7]	808.7	-	808.7	808.7	808.7
Total maximum	843.9	421.9	808.7	843.9	843.9
DASD arms maximum	23	12	23	24	24
Arms internal	6	12	6/12	24	24
LUNs external	23	-	23	23	23
Physical packaging					
External HSL ports	2	-	-	2	2
External HSL loops	1	-	-	1	1
#5075 PCI Expansion Tower	1	-	-	1	1
#5095 PCI-X Expansion Tower	1	-	-	1	1
#5074 PCI Expansion Tower	-	-	-	-	-
External xSeries Servers supported	2	-	-	2	2
Embedded IOP	1	-	1	2	2
PCI card slots	7	-	8	15	15
Maximum PCI IOA cards	6	-	7	13	13
Communication lines[4]	26	-	34	50	50
LAN ports	3	-	5	8	8
Integrated xSeries Servers	1	-	2	3	3
Twinaxial workstation controllers	4	-	6	6	6
Twinaxial workstations	160	-	240	240	240
Internal/CD-ROM/DVD-RAM/tape[6]	2	-	-	2	2
External tape adapters	3	-	3	3	6
External CD-ROM/DVD-RAM[6]	3	-	3	3	6
Tape libraries[3]	3	-	3	3	6
Optical libraries	3	-	4	4	8
Diskettes (5 ¼-inch or 8-inch)	-	-	-	-	-
Cryptographic coprocessor	3	-	3	3	3

9406 Model 720

Model	720			
Processor feature	**#2061**	**#2062**	**#2063**	**#2064**
Relative system performance [1] Version 4 Release 3 and later Processor CPW	240	420	810	1600

Interactive CPW/system feature code
     #1500 (Base)
      #1501
      #1502
      #1503
      #1504
      #1505
	35/206A
	70/206B
	120/206C
	-
	-
	-
		35/206D
		70/206E
		120/206F
		240/207A
		-
		-
			35/207B
			-
			120/207C
			240/207D
			560/207E
			-
				35/207F
				-
				120/208A
				240/208B
				560/208C
				1050/208D

Number of processors	1	1	2	4
Main storage (MB)	256-2048	256-4096	256-8192	256-8192
Software group [7]	P10-P20	P10-P20	P20-P30	P20-P30

Numbers are for all processor features	Base system	SUE #9364 PCI (#9329) PCI (#9330)	SUE #9364 SPD (#9331)	#5065 Stg/PCI Exp Tower	Expansion tower	System maximum
		(note 4)	(note 4)			
Disk storage base (G)						
Maximum internal (G)	4.194	263.2	263.2	386.5	561.5	1625.9
Maximum external (G)	263.2		(note 2)		(note 2)	1595.3
Total maximum (G)	(note 5)					1625.9
External SPD bus		4	4		0	4
Maximum card slots-SPD	0	0	6	0	13	58
Maximum card slots-PCI	8	14	0	12	0	70
Communication lines [3]	18	0-40	0-36	0-42	0-78	128
LAN/ATM adapters	1-3	0-6	0-6	0-6	0-13	24
Maximum workstation controllers						
Twinaxial 6	5	11	18	12	39	66
ASCII [6]	0	0	6	0	13	58
Maximum workstations						
Twinaxial	188	440	720	480	1560	2628
ASCII	0	0	108	0	234	1044
¼-inch/8mm cartridge tape	1	3	3	3	4	17
CD-ROM	1	0-1	0	0-1	0-1	6
½-inch tape	1	2	8	3	8	8
Reel 9348	1	2	4	3	4	4
Reel 2440	0	0	4	0	4	4
Reel 9347	0	0	2	0	2	2
Cartridge 34xx, 35xx	1	2	8	3	8	8
Tape libraries maximum						
½-inch cartridge	1	2	8	3	8	8
8mm	1	2	4	3	4	4
8mm cartridge (external)	1	2	4	3	4	4
Optical libraries	1	2	13	3	14	14
Diskettes (5 ¼-inch or 8-inch)	0	0	2	0	2	2
LAN ports maximum	3	6	12	6	24	24
Wireless IOP maximum	0	0	3	0	3	3
FSIOP maximum	0	0	3	0	6	16
FSIOA (IPCS) maximum	1	1	0	0	0	2
PCI LAN maximum	3	6	0	6	0	9
Cryptographic processors	1	3	1	3	1	6
Fax adapters	0	0	6	0	13	32

Note 1	CPW is now being used to measure the performance of all iSeries and AS/400e processors. The CPW value is measured on maximum configurations. The type and number of disk devices, the number of workstation controllers, the amount of memory, the system model, other factors, and the application being run determine the performance that is achievable. All iSeries and AS/400e processors announced from September 1996 onward have only CPW performance measurements.
Note 2	External DASD can be attached using a System Products Division (SPD) card in the Expansion Unit.
Note 3	One line is used for Client Access Console or Operations Console if selected. The maximum is nine if Twinaxial Console is selected.
Note 4	The #9364 must be configured with #9329 /#9330 (PCI) or #9331 (SPD). Therefore, these columns are mutually exclusive.
Note 5	Maximum is 175.4 GB on the #2061 Processor.
Note 6	Any combination of Twinax or ASCII workstation controllers up to either maximum shown is allowed, Maximums are not additive.
Note 7 Model 720	Software group is determined by a combination of the processor and interactive feature. The following table provides a cross reference.

Processor	Interactive feature	System feature code	Software group
#2061	#1500	206A	P10
	#1501	206B	P20
	#1502	206C	P20
#2062	#1500	206D	P10
	#1501	206E	P20
	#1502	206F	P20
	#1503	207A	P20
#2063	#1500	207B	P20
	#1502	207C	P30
	#1503	207D	P30
	#1504	207E	P30
#2064	#1500	207F	P20
	#1502	208A	P30
	#1503	208B	P30
	#1504	208C	P30
	#1505	208D	P30

Note 8	The total number of internal tapes and CD-ROM per tower cannot exceed the maximum quantity shown for internal tapes. The system maximum for internal tapes and CD-ROMs is 18.

9406 Model 730

Model	730			
Processor feature	#2065	#2066	#2067	#2068
Relative system performance [1] Version 4 Release 3 and later Processor CPW	560	1050	2000	2890

Interactive CPW/system feature code
  #1506 (Base)
    #1507
    #1508
    #1509
    #1510
    #1511
	70/2A6A
	120/2A6B
	240/2A6C
	560/2A6D
	-
	-
		70/2A6E
		120/2A6F
		240/2B6A
		560/2B6B
		1050/2B6C
		-
			70/2B6D
			-
			240/2B6E
			560/2B6F
			1050/2C6A
			2000/2C6B
				70/2C6C
				-
				240/2C6D
				560/2C6E
				1050/2C6F
				2000/2D6A

Number of processors	1	2	4	8
Main storage (MB)	512-24576	512-24576	512-24576	1024-24576
Software group [4]	P20-P30	P20-P30	P30-P40	P30-P40

Numbers are for all processor features	System maximum

Disk storage
  Base (GB)
  Maximum internal (GB)
  Maximum external (GB)
  Total maximum (GB)
  Disk unit IOPs [2]
	
	4.19
	1683.6/2499.6 (V4R3/V4R4)
	1649.2/2473.9 (V4R3/V4R4)
	1683.6/2499.6 (V4R3/V4R4)
	1-37

Communication lines	1-250
Maximum workstation controllers	1-175

Maximum workstations
  Twinaxial
  ASCII
	
	7000
	3150

¼-inch/8mm cartridge tape (internal) [5]	0-18
CD-ROM (internal) [5]	1-18

½-inch tape [3]
  Reel 9348
  Reel 2440
  Reel 9347
	
	4
	4
	2

Cartridge 34XX, 35XX	8

Tape libraries maximum
  ½-inch cartridge
  8mm
	10
	4
	4

8mm cartridge (external)	4
Optical libraries	14
Diskettes (5 ¼-inch or 8-inch)	2
LAN/ATM ports maximum Wireless IOP maximum	1-48 3
IPCS maximum	16
Cryptographic processors	6
Fax IOPs (2 lines/IOP)	32

Note 1	CPW is now being used to measure the performance of all iSeries and AS/400e processors. The CPW value is measured on maximum configurations. The type and number of disk devices, the number of workstation controllers, the amount of memory, the system model, other factors, and the application being run determine the performance that is achievable. All iSeries and AS/400e processors announced from September 1996 onward have only CPW performance measurements.			
Note 2	This total includes the MFIOP. The combination of internal and external IOPs cannot exceed this number.			
Note 3	The maximum combination of 2440, 7208, or 9348 and Tape Libraries may not exceed four.			
Note 4 Model 730	The software group is determined by a combination of processor and interactive feature. The following table provides a cross reference.			
	Processor	**Interactive feature**	**System feature code**	**Software group**
	#2065	#1506	2A6A	P20
		#1507	2A6B	P30
		#1508	2A6C	P30
		#1509	2A6D	P30
	#2066	#1506	2A6E	P20
		#1507	2A6F	P30
		#1508	2B6A	P30
		#1509	2B6B	P30
		#1510	2B6C	P30
	#2067	#1506	2B6D	P30
		#1508	2B6E	P40
		#1509	2B6F	P40
		#1510	2C6A	P40
		#1511	2C6B	P40
	#2068	#1506	2C6C	P30
		#1508	2C6D	P40
		#1509	2C6E	P40
		#1510	2C6F	P40
		#1511	2D6A	P40
Note 5	The system maximum for internal tapes and CD-ROMs is 18.			

9406 Model 740

Model	740	
Processor feature	#2069	#2070

Relative system performance [1, 2] Version 4 Release 3 and later
   Processor CPW
 	
Interactive CPW/system feature code
   #1514 (Base)
   #1510
   #1511
   #1512
   #1513
	3660
	
	120/2D6B
	1050/2D6C
	2000/2D6D
	3660/2D6E
	-
		4550
		
		120/2E6A
		1050/2E6B
		2000/2E6C
		3660/2E6D
		4550/2E6E

Number of processors	8	12
Main storage (MB)	1024-40960	1020-40960
Software group [4]	P40-P50	P40-P50

Numbers are for all processor features	System maximum
Disk storage	
Base (GB)	4.19
Maximum internal (GB)	2095.9/4294.9 (V4R3/V4R4)
Maximum external (GB)	2061.3/4260.6 (V4R3/V4R4)
Total maximum (GB)	2095.9/4294.9 (V4R3/V4R4)
Disk unit IOPs [2]	1-37
SPD I/O bus	1-19
I/O card slots	3-237
Communication lines	1-300
Maximum workstation controllers	1-175
Maximum workstations	
Twinaxial	7000
ASCII	3150
¼-inch/8mm cartridge tape (internal) [5]	0-18
CD-ROM (internal) [5]	1-18
½-inch tape [3]	
Reel 9348	4
Reel 2440	4
Reel 9347	2
Cartridge 34XX, 35XX	8
Tape libraries maximum	14
½-inch cartridge	4
8mm	4
8mm cartridge (external)	4
Optical libraries	22
Diskettes (5 ¼-inch or 8-inch)	2
LAN/ATM ports maximum	1-72
Wireless IOP maximum	3
IPCS maximum	16
Cryptographic processors	6
Fax IOPs (2 lines/IOP)	32

Note 1	CPW is now being used to measure the performance of all iSeries and AS/400e processors. The CPW value is measured on maximum configurations. The type and number of disk devices, the number of workstation controllers, the amount of memory, the system model, other factors, and the application being run determine the performance that is achievable. All iSeries and AS/400e processors announced from September 1996 onward have only CPW performance measurements.
Note 2	This total includes the MFIOP. The combination of internal and external IOPs cannot exceed this number.
Note 3	The maximum combination of 2440, 7208, or 9348 and Tape Libraries may not exceed four.

Note 4 Model 740	Software group is determined by a combination of the processor and interactive feature. The following table provides a cross reference.

Processor	Interactive feature	System feature code	Software group
#2069	#1514	2D6B	P40
	#1510	2D6C	P50
	#1511	2D6D	P50
	#1512	2D6E	P50
#2070	#1514	2E6A	P40
	#1510	2E6B	P50
	#1511	2E6C	P50
	#1512	2E6D	P50
	#1513	2E6E	P50

Note 5	The system maximum for internal tapes and CD-ROMs is 18.

9406 Model 820

Model	820			
Processor feature	**#2395**	**#2396**	**#2397**	**#2398**
Relative system performance [1] Processor CPW	370	950	2000	3200
5250 CPW				
#1521	35	35	35	35
#1522	70	70	70	70
#1523	120	120	120	120
#1524	240	240	240	240
#1525	-	560	560	560
#1526	-	-	1050	1050
#1527	-	-	-	2000
Number/type/speed of processors	1/Pulsar/400 MHz	1/Pulsar/450 MHz	2/ISTAR/500 MHz	4/ISTAR/500 MHz
L2 Cache (MB)	0	2	4	4
Main storage (MB min/max)	256 - 4096	256-8192	256-16384	256-16384
Main storage DIMMs (min/max)	2/8	2/16	2/32	2/32
Minimum operating system level	V4R5	V4R5	V4R5	V4R5
Software group [11]	P10-P20	P20-P30	P20-P30	P30-P40

Model	820 Dedicated Server for Domino		
Processor feature	**#2425**	**#2426**	**#2427**
Relative system performance [1] Processor CPW	950	2000	3200
5250 CPW [8]	0	0	0
Simple Mail Users	4250	8000	14400
Mail and Calendaring Users	2570	5610	9890
Number/type/speed of processors	1/Pulsar/450 MHz	2/ISTAR/500 MHz	4/ISTAR/500 MHz
L2 Cache (MB)	2	4	4
Main storage (MB min/max)	256-8192	256-16384	256-16384
Main storage DIMMs (min/max)	2/16	2/32	2/32
Minimum operating system level	V4R5	V4R5	V4R5
Software group [11]	P05	P10	P10

	Model 820			
Processor feature	#2435	#2436	#2437	#2438
Relative system performance[1]				
Processor CPW	600	1100	2350	3700
5250 CPW[8]				
None	-	-	-	-
#1521	35	35	35	35
#1522	70	70	70	70
#1523	120	120	120	120
#1524	240	240	240	240
#1525	-	560	560	560
#1526	-	-	1050	1050
#1527	-	-	-	2000
Number/type/ speed of processors	1/SSTAR/ 600 MHz	1/SSTAR/ 600 MHz	2/SSTAR/ 600 MHz	4/SSTAR/ 600 MHz
L2 Cache (MB)	2	2	4	4
Main storage (MB min/max)	256 - 8192	256 - 16384	256 - 32768	256 - 32768
Main storage DIMMs	2/8	2/16	2/32	2/32
Minimum operating system level	V5R1	V5R1	V5R1	V5R1
Software group[11]	P10 or P20	P20 or P30	P20 or P30	P30 or P40

	Model 820 Dedicated Server for Domino		
Processor feature	#2456	#2457	#2458
Relative system performance[1]			
Processor CPW	1100	2350	3700
5250 CPW[8]	0	0	0
Mail and Calendar Users[1]	3110	6600	11810
Number/type/speed of processors	1/SSTAR/600 MHz	2/SSTAR/600 MHz	4/SSTAR/600 MHz
L2 Cache (MB)	2	4	4
Main storage (MB min/max)	256 - 16384	256 - 32768	256 - 32768
Main storage DIMMs (min/max)	2/16	2/32	2/32
Minimum operating system level	V5R1	V5R1	V5R1
Software group[11]	P05	P10	P10

Summary	Base system	#5075 PCI Expansion Tower	#5074 PCI Expansion Tower	Migrated total with #503x [5, 7]	New system max [6]	LPAR system max
Disk storage minimum (GB)	8.58				8.58	
Maximum internal (GB)	421.9	210.9	1582.4	1625.9	8334.1	
Maximum external (GB)[10]	4501.1	4501.1	6751.6	1595.3	8298.9	
Total maximum (GB)	4923.1	4712.1	8298.9	1625.9	8334.1	
DASD arms maximum	140	134	236		237	
Internal	12	6	45	210	237	
LUNs external	128	128	192	209	236	
Diskette (8 or 5 ¼-inch)	-	-	-	2	-	
Communication lines[3]	44	34	52	128	160	
Twinax workstation controllers	7	7	11	66	62	
Twinaxial devices	280	280	440	2628	2480	
Internal CD-ROM/DVD-RAM/tape[4]	2	-	2	18 [9]	12	
External CD-ROM/DVD-RAM [4]	7	7	8	8	8	18
External tape	7	7	8	8	8	18
Tape libraries maximum [2]	7	7	8	8	8	18
Optical libraries	7	7	14	14	14	18
Physical packaging						
External HSL ports	2	-	-	-	2	
External HSL loops	1	-	-	-	1	
#5074/#5075 Towers	5	-	-	-	5	
Integrated xSeries Adapter	8	-	-	-	8	
SPD towers supported	-	-	-	4	-	
Embedded IOPs	1	1	-	1	6	
PCI adapter card slots	12	8	14	86	82	
Maximum PCI IOA cards	9	7	11	70	63	
LAN ports maximum	7	5	8	24	30	
Maximum Integrated xSeries Server	2	2	2	16	12	
Cryptographic processor	7	7	8	3	8	

Processor feature	Model 820		
	#0150	#0151	#0152
Relative system performance[1] Processor CPW	1100	2350	3700
5250 CPW[8]			
None	0	0	0
#1521	-	-	-
#1522	-	-	-
#1523	-	-	-
#1524	-	-	-
#1525	-	-	-
#1526	-	-	-
#1527	-	-	-
Number/type/speed of processors	1/SSTAR/600 MHz	2/SSTAR/600 MHz	4/SSTAR/600 MHz
L2 Cache (MB)	2	4	4
Main storage (MB min/max)	256 - 16384	256 - 32768	256 - 32768
Main storage DIMMs	2/16	2/32	2/32
Minimum operating system level	V5R1	V5R1	V5R1
Software group[11]	P20	P20	P30

Note 1	CPW is used to measure the performance of all iSeries and AS/400e processors announced from September 1996 onward. The CPW value is measured on maximum configurations. The type and number of disk devices, the number of workstation controllers, the amount of memory, the system model, other factors, and the application running determine what performance is achievable. Processor performance represents the relative performance (maximum capacity) of a processor feature running CPW in a client/server environment. Processor capacity is achievable when the commercial workload is not constrained by main storage and DASD. Interactive performance represents the relative performance available to perform host-centric workloads. The amount of interactive capacity consumed reduces the available processor capacity by the same amount. On the Dedicated Servers for Domino, the Processor CPW is an approximate value reflecting the maximum amount of non-Domino workload (10 to 15% of CPU) that can be supported.
Note 2	Total number of tape devices does not increase.
Note 3	One line is used if the #5544 System Console on Operations Console is used on a #9771 WAN adapter. One line might be used if #5546 or #5548 System Console on LAN is selected and the #0367 Operations Console PCI Cable is connected.
Note 4	There must be one CD-ROM or DVD-RAM per system.
Note 5	Includes the #503x Migration Tower and all SPD bus towers attached to the #503x.

Note 6	New systems only. Does not apply to migrated systems.
Note 7	This column does not apply to Dedicated Domino Servers.
Note 8	5250 OLTP CPW is an approximate value that reflects the amount of Processor CPW that can be used for workloads performing 5250-based tasks. Any task that uses a 5250 data stream is considered 5250 OLTP work and requires some amount of 5250 CPW to process no matter how the task was started. A task submitted through a 5250 session (5250 device or 5250 emulation) that does display or printer I/O requires 5250 CPW. A task submitted through a 5250 session (5250 device or 5250 emulation) as a "batch" job is not considered 5250 OLTP work and does not require any 5250 CPW unless the task does display or printer I/O. Limited 5250 CPW is available when 5250 Interactive CPW = 0, for a system administrator to use 5250 display device I/O to manage various aspects of the server. Multiple administrative jobs exceed this capability.
Note 9	Includes a base CD-ROM in the migration tower (no feature code).
Note 10	External DASD capacity maximum assumes 35.16 GB LUNs. External DASD cannot exceed the maximum system capacity or the maximum number of disk arms.

Note 11 Model 820

Software group is determined by a combination of the processor and interactive feature. The following table provides a cross reference.

Processor	Interactive feature	Processor feature	Software group
#2396	#1521	23A9	P20
	#1522	23AA	P30
	#1523	23AB	P30
	#1524	23AC	P30
	#1525	23AD	P30
#2397	#1521	23B1	P20
	#1522	23B2	P30
	#1523	23B3	P30
	#1524	23B4	P30
	#1525	23B5	P30
	#1526	23B6	P30
#2398	#1521	23B8	P30
	#1522	23B9	P40
	#1523	23BA	P40
	#1524	23BB	P40
	#1525	23BC	P40
	#1526	23BD	P40
	#1527	23BE	P40

9406 Model 830

Model	830	
Processor feature	**#2402**	**#2403**
Relative system performance [1] Processor CPW	4200	7350
5250 CPW		
#1531 (Base)	70	70
#1532	120	120
#1533	240	240
#1534	560	560
#1535	1050	1050
#1536	2000	2000
#1537	-	4550
Number/type/speed of processors	4/ISTAR/540 MHz	8/ISTAR/540 MHz
L2 Cache (MB)	4	4
Main storage (GB min/max)	1-64	1-64
Main storage DIMMs (min/max)	8/64	8/64
Minimum operating system level	V4R5	V4R5
Software group [9]	P30-P40	P40-P50

	Model 830		
Processor feature	**#0153**	**#2349**	**#2400**
Relative system performance[1] Processor CPW	7350	4200/7350	1850
5250 CPW[9]	0		
#1531 (Base)		70	70
#1532		120	120
#1533		240	240
#1534		560	560
#1535		1050	1050
#1536		2000	-
#1537		4550	-
Number/type/speed of processors	8/ISTAR/540 MHz	4/8/ISTAR/540 MHz	2/ISTAR/400 MHz
L2 Cache (MB)	4	4	2
Main storage (GB min-max)	1 - 64	1 - 64	1 - 64
Main storage DIMMs (min/max)	8/64	8/64	8/64
Minimum operating system level	V5R1	V5R1	V4R5
Software group[11]	P30	P30 or P40	P20 or P30

Numbers are for all processor features	Base System #9074	PCI Exp Tower #5074	Migrated total with #5034, #5035 [5]	Migrated total with #5077 [6]	New system maximum [7]	LPAR system maximum
Disk storage minimum (GB)	8.58	-	-	-	8.58	
Maximum internal (GB)	1582.4	1582.4	1625.9	4294.9	22153.9	
Maximum external (GB)	5626.4	6751.6	1595.3	4260.9	22118.8	
Total maximum (GB) [10]	7208.8	8298.9	1625.9	4294.9	22153.9	
DASD arms maximum [10]	205	205		596	630	
Internal	45	45	210	596	630	
External LUNs	160	192	595	595	629	
Diskette (8 or 5 ¼-inch)	-	-	2	2	-	
Communication lines [4]	40	52	128	300	300	
Twinax workstation controllers	9	11	66	175	152	
Twinaxial devices	360	440	2628	7000	6080	
Internal CD-ROM/DVD-RAM [3]	2	2	18 [8]	18 [8]	18	28
Internal tape	1	2	17	17	17	28
External CD-ROM/DVD-RAM [3]	8	10	8	14	10	34
External tape (max/system)	8	10	8	14	10	34
Tape libraries maximum [2]	8	10	8	14	10	34
Optical libraries	8	11	14	22	22	34
Physical packaging				-		
External HSL ports	8	-	-	-	8	
External HSL loops	4	-	-	-	4	
#5074 Towers	13	-	-	18	13	
Integrated xSeries Adapter	16	-	-	-	16	
SPD towers supported	-	-	4	18	-	
Embedded IOPs	-	-	2		-	
PCI adapter card slots	14	14	86	270	196	
Maximum PCI IOA cards	11	11	70	216	154	
LAN ports maximum	6	8	24	72	72	
Maximum Integrated xSeries Server	2	2	16	16	16	
Cryptographic processors	3	3	3	3	3	

Note 1	CPW is used to measure the performance of all iSeries and AS/400e processors announced from September 1996 onward. The CPW value is measured on maximum configurations. The type and number of disk devices, the number of workstation controllers, the amount of memory, the system model, other factors, and the application running determine what performance is achievable.
Note 2	The total number of tape devices does not increase.
Note 3	There must be one CD-ROM or DVD-RAM per system.
Note 4	One line is used if the #5544 System Console on Operations Console is used on a #9771 WAN adapter. One line might be used if the #5546 or #5548 System Console on LAN is selected and the #0367 Operations Console PCI Cable is connected.
Note 5	Includes the #5034 or #5035 tower and all the SPD bus towers attached to the #5034 or #5035.
Note 6	Includes the #5077 tower and all the SPD bus towers attached to the #5077.
Note 7	New systems only, does not apply to migrated towers.
Note 8	Includes a base CD-ROM in the migration tower (no feature code).
Note 9	5250 OLTP CPW is an approximate value that reflects the amount of Processor CPW that can be used for workloads performing 5250-based tasks. Any task that uses a 5250 data stream is considered 5250 OLTP work and requires some amount of 5250 CPW to process no matter how the task was started. A task submitted through a 5250 session (5250 device or 5250 emulation) that does display or printer I/O requires 5250 CPW. A task submitted through a 5250 session (5250 device or 5250 emulation) as a "batch" job is not considered 5250 OLTP work and does not require any 5250 CPW unless the task does display or printer I/O. Limited 5250 CPW is available when 5250 Interactive CPW = 0, for a system administrator to use 5250 display device I/O to manage various aspects of the server. Multiple administrative jobs exceed this capability.
Note 10	External DASD capacity maximum assumes 35.16 GB LUNs. External DASD cannot exceed the maximum system capacity or the maximum number of disk arms.
Note 11 Model 830	Software group is determined by a combination of the processor and interactive feature. The following table provides a cross reference.

Processor	Interactive feature	Processor feature	Software group
#2402	#1531	23D1	P30
	#1532	23D2	P40
	#1533	23D3	P40
	#1534	23D4	P40
	#1535	23D5	P40
	#1536	23D6	P40

Note 11 (cont.)	#2403	#1531	23D8	P40
		#1532	23D9	P50
		#1533	23DA	P50
		#1534	23DB	P50
		#1535	23DC	P50
		#1536	23DD	P50
		#1537	23DE	P50

9406 Model 840

Processor feature	Model 840				
	#0158	#0159	#2352	#2353	#2354
Relative system performance[1] Processor CPW 5250 CPW[8] #1540 (Base) #1541 #1542 #1543 #1544 #1545 #1546 #1547 #1548	12000 0	20200 0	9000-12000 120 240 560 1050 2000 4550 10000 - -	12000-16500 120 240 560 1050 2000 4550 10000 16500 -	16500-20200 120 240 560 1050 2000 4550 10000 16500 20200
Number/type/ speed of processors	12/SSTAR/ 600 MHz	24/SSTAR/ 600 MHz	8 - 12/ SSTAR/ 600 MHz	12 - 18/ SSTAR/ 600 MHz	18 - 24/ SSTAR/ 600 MHz
L2 Cache (MB)	16x4	16x4	16x4	16x4	16x4
Main storage (GB min/max)	4/128	4/128	4/128	4/128	4/128
Main storage cards (min/max)	4/16	4/16	4/16	4/16	4/16
Minimum operating system level	V5R1	V5R1	V5R1	V5R1	V5R1
Software group[10]	P40	P40	P40 or P50	P40 or P50	P40 or P50

Numbers are for all processor features	#9079 Base I/O Tower	PCI Expansion Tower #5074	Migrated total with #5077 [5]	New system maximum [6]	LPAR maximum
Disk storage minimum (GB)	8.58	-	-		
Maximum internal (GB)	1582.4	1582.4	4294.9	37978.2	
Maximum external (GB)	5626.4	6751.6	4260.6	37943.0	
Total maximum (GB) [9]	7208.8	8298.9	4294.9	37978.2	
DASD arms maximum [9]	205	205		1080	
Internal	45	45	596	1080	
External LUNs	160	192	595	1079	
Diskette (8 or 5 ¼-inch)	-	-	2	-	
Communication lines [4]	40	52	300	400	
Twinax workstation controllers	9	11	175	175	
Twinaxial devices	360	440	7000	7000	
Internal CD-ROM/DVD-RAM [3]	2	2	18 [7]	24	34
Internal tape	1	2	17	26	34
External CD-ROM/DVD-RAM [3]	8	11	14	26	34
External tape (max/system)	8	11	14	26	34
Tape libraries maximum [2]	8	11	14	26	34
Optical libraries	8	11	22	26	34
Physical packaging					
External HSL ports	16	-	-	16	
External HSL loops	8	-	-	8	
#5074 Towers	23	-	-	23	
Integrated xSeries Adapter	32	-	-	32	
SPD towers supported	-	-	18	-	
PCI adapter card slots	14	14	270	336	
Maximum PCI IOA cards	11	11	216	264	
LAN ports maximum	6	8	72	96	
Maximum Integrated xSeries Server	2	2	16	16	
Cryptographic processor	3	3	3	3	

Model	840					
Processor feature	#2416	#2417	#2418	#2419	#2420	#2461
Relative system performance [1, 2]						
Processor CPW	10000	13200	10000	16500	16500	20200
5250 CPW						
#1540 (Base)	120	120	120	120	120	120
#1541	240	240	240	240	240	240
#1542	560	560	560	560	560	560
#1543	1050	1050	1050	1050	1050	1050
#1544	2000	2000	2000	2000	2000	2000
#1545	4550	4550	4550	4550	4550	4550
#1546	10000	10000	10000	10000	10000	10000
#1547	-	-	-	16500	16500	16500
#1548						20200
Number/ type/ speed of processors	8 to 12/ ISTAR/ 500 MHz	12 to 18/ ISTAR/ 500 MHz	12/ISTAR/ 500 MHz	18 to 24/ ISTAR/ 500 MHz	24/ISTAR/ 500 MHz	24/SSTAR/ 600 MHz
L2 Cache (MB)	8	8	8	8	8	16x4
Main storage (GB min/max)	4/128	4/128	4/128	4/128	4/128	4/128
Main storage cards (min/max)	4/16	4/16	4/16	4/16	4/16	4/16
Minimum operating system level	V4R5	V4R5	V4R5	V4R5	V4R5	V5R1
Software group [9]	P40-P50	P40-P50	P40-P50	P40-P50	P40-P50	P40-P50

Numbers are for all processor features	#9079 Base I/O Tower	PCI Expansion Tower #5074	Migrated total with #5077 [5]	New system maximum [6]	LPAR maximum
Disk storage minimum (GB)	8.58	-	-		
Maximum internal (GB)	1582.4	1582.4	4294.9	37978.2	
Maximum external (GB)	5626.4	6751.6	4260.6	37943.0	
Total maximum (GB) [9]	7208.8	8298.9	4294.9	37978.2	
DASD arms maximum [9]	205	205		1080	
Internal	45	45	596	1080	
External LUNs	160	192	595	1079	
Diskette (8 or 5 ¼-inch)	-	-	2	-	
Communication lines [4]	40	52	300	400	
Twinax workstation controllers	9	11	175	175	
Twinaxial devices	360	440	7000	7000	
Internal CD-ROM/DVD-RAM [3]	2	2	18 [7]	24	34
Internal tape	1	2	17	26	34
External CD-ROM/DVD-RAM [3]	8	11	14	26	34
External tape (max/system)	8	11	14	26	34
Tape libraries maximum [2]	8	11	14	26	34
Optical libraries	8	11	22	26	34
Physical packaging					
External HSL ports	16	-	-	16	
External HSL loops	8	-	-	8	
#5074 Towers	23	-	-	23	
Integrated xSeries Adapter	32	-	-	32	
SPD towers supported	-	-	18	-	
PCI adapter card slots	14	14	270	336	
Maximum PCI IOA cards	11	11	216	264	
LAN ports maximum	6	8	72	96	
Maximum Integrated xSeries Server	2	2	16	16	
Cryptographic processor	3	3	3	3	

Note 1	CPW is used to measure the performance of all iSeries and AS/400e processors announced from September 1996 onward. The CPW value is measured on maximum configurations. The type and number of disk devices, the number of workstation controllers, the amount of memory, the system model, other factors, and the application running determine what performance is achievable.
Note 2	The total number of tape devices does not increase.
Note 3	There must be one CD-ROM or DVD-RAM per system.
Note 4	One line is used if the #5544 System Console on Operations Console is used on a #9771 WAN adapter. One line might be used if the #5546 or #5548 System Console on LAN is selected and the #0367 Operations Console PCI Cable is connected.
Note 5	Includes the #5077 and all the SPD Bus towers attached to the #5077.
Note 6	New systems only. Does not apply to migrated system.
Note 7	Includes a base CD-ROM in the migration tower (no feature code).
Note 8	5250 OLTP CPW is an approximate value that reflects the amount of Processor CPW that can be used for workloads performing 5250-based tasks. ▶ Any task that uses a 5250 data stream is considered 5250 OLTP work and requires some amount of 5250 CPW to process no matter how the task was started. ▶ A task submitted through a 5250 session (5250 device or 5250 emulation) that does display or printer I/O requires 5250 CPW. ▶ A task submitted through a 5250 session (5250 device or 5250 emulation) as a "batch" job is not considered 5250 OLTP work and does not require any 5250 CPW unless the task does display or printer I/O. ▶ Limited 5250 CPW is available when 5250 Interactive CPW = 0, for a system administrator to use 5250 display device I/O to manage various aspects of the server. Multiple administrative jobs exceed this capability.
Note 9	External DASD capacity maximum assumes 35.16 GB LUNs. External DASD cannot exceed the maximum system capacity or the maximum number of disk arms.
Note 10a Model 840	Software group is determined by the combination of processor feature and edition feature. Display the QPRCFEAT system value or DSPHDWRSC TYPE(*AHW) to display the processor feature code value. This value is also shown for the Capacity Card CCIN value when using SST to perform a Capacity Upgrade on Demand.

Processor feature	Interactive feature	Software group	Processor feature code or QPRCFEAT value
#0158	N/A	P40	0158
#0159	N/A	P40	0159

Note 10a Model 840	#2352	#1540	P40	26B0
		#1541	P50	26B1
		#1542	P50	26B2
		#1543	P50	26B3
		#1544	P50	26B4
		#1545	P50	26B5
		#1546	P50	26B6
	#2353	#1540	P40	26B8
		#1541	P50	26B9
		#1542	P50	26BA
		#1543	P50	26BB
		#1544	P50	26BC
		#1545	P50	26BD
		#1546	P50	26BE
		#1547	P50	26BF
	#2354	#1540	P40	26C0
		#1541	P50	26C1
		#1542	P50	26C2
		#1543	P50	26C3
		#1544	P50	26C4
		#1545	P50	26C5
		#1546	P50	26C6
		#1547	P50	26C7
		#1548	P50	26C8

Note 10b Model 840	Software group is determined by a combination of the processor and interactive feature. The following table provides a cross reference.			
	Processor	Interactive feature	Processor feature	Software group
	#2416	#1540	#24C0	P40
		#1541	#24C1	P50
		#1542	#24C2	P50
		#1543	#24C3	P50
		#1544	#24C4	P50
		#1545	#24C5	P50
		#1546	#24C6	P50

Note 10b (cont.)	Software group is determined by a combination of the processor and interactive feature. The following table provides a cross reference.		

Processor	Interactive feature	Processor feature	Software group
#2417	#1540	#24C8	P40
	#1541	#24C9	P50
	#1542	#24CA	P50
	#1543	#24CB	P50
	#1544	#24CC	P50
	#1545	#24CD	P50
	#1546	#24CE	P50
#2418	#1540	#23E8	P40
	#1541	#23E9	P50
	#1542	#23EA	P50
	#1543	#23EB	P50
	#1544	#23EC	P50
	#1545	#23ED	P50
	#1546	#23EE	P50
#2419	#1540	#24D0	P40
	#1541	#24D1	P50
	#1542	#24D2	P50
	#1543	#24D3	P50
	#1544	#24D4	P50
	#1545	#24D5	P50
	#1546	#24D6	P50
	#1547	#24D7	P50
#2420	#1540	#23F8	P40
	#1541	#23F9	P50
	#1542	#23FA	P50
	#1543	#23FB	P50
	#1544	#23FC	P50
	#1545	#23FD	P50
	#1546	#23FE	P50
	#1547	#23FF	P50

Note 10b (cont.)	Software group is determined by a combination of the processor and interactive feature. The following table provides a cross reference.			
	Processor	**Interactive feature**	**Processor feature**	**Software group**
	#2461	#1540	#26D0	P40
		#1541	#26D1	P50
		#1542	#26D2	P50
		#1543	#26D3	P50
		#1544	#26D4	P50
		#1545	#26D5	P50
		#1546	#26D6	P50
		#1547	#26D7	P50
		#1548	#26D8	P50

9406 Model 890

	Model 890			
Processor feature	**#0197**	**#0198**	**#2487**	**#2488**

Relative system performance[1]
  Processor CPW
  5250 CPW[5]
    #1576 (Base)
    #1577
    #1578
    #1579
    #1581
    #1583
    #1585
    #1587
    #1588
    #1591
	29300
	0
		37400
		0
			20200 - 29300
			
			120
			240
			560
			1050
			2000
			4550
			10000
			16500
			20200
			--- 	
				29300 - 37400
				
				120
				240
				560
				1050
				2000
				4550
				10000
				16500
				20200
				37400

Number/type/speed of processor	24/POWER4/ 1.3 GHz	32/POWER4/ 1.3 GHz	16 - 24/POWER4/ 1.3 GHz	24 - 32/POWER4/ 1.3 GHz
L2 Cache (MB)	1.5 MB/chip set	1.5 MB/chip set	1.5 MB/chip set	1.5 MB/chip set
L2 and L3 Cache (MB/processor)	16.72	16.72	16.72	16.72
Main storage (GB min-max)	16 - 192	24 - 256	16 - 192	24 - 256
Main storage cards (min/max)	2/6	4/8	2/6	4/8
Minimum operating system level[7]	OS/400 V5R2	OS/400 V5R2	OS/400 V5R2	OS/400 V5R2
Software group[6]	P50	P50	P50-P60	P50-P60

Numbers are for all 890 processor features	Base Tower #9094	PCI-X Expansion Tower #5095/#0595	PCI-X Expansion Tower #5094	Total maximum	LPAR system maximum
Disk storage (GB)					
Integrated minimum	17.5	17.5	17.5		
Integrated maximum	3175.2	846.7	3175.2	144446	144446
External maximum[4]	11290	3175	13548	144375	144375
Total maximum	14462	4021	16720	144446	144446
DASD arms maximum					
Arms internal	45	12	45	2047	2047
LUNs external	160	127	192	2046	2046
Physical packaging					
External HSL/HSL-2 ports	-/24	-	-	-/24	-/24
External HSL/HSL-2 loops	-/12	-	-	-/12	-/12
PCI/PCI-X Expansion Towers	47	-	-	47	47
External xSeries Servers	60	-	-	60	60
Embedded IOP	-	-	-	-	-
Embedded IOA	-	-	-	-	-
PCI card slots	14	7	14	672	672
Maximum PCI IOA cards	11	5	11	528	528
Communication lines[3]	38	20	44	480	480
LAN ports	7	5	8	128	128
Integrated xSeries Servers	2	1	3	48	48
Twinaxial workstation controllers	9	5	11	180	180
Twinaxial workstations	360	200	440	7200	7200
Internal CD-ROM/DVD-RAM/tape[2]	2	-	2	26	48
External tape/optical/CD/DVD	9	5	11	26	48
Cryptographic coprocessor	8	3	8	32	32
Cryptographic accelerator	4	4	4	8	8

Note 1	CPW is used to measure the performance of all iSeries and AS/400e processors announced from September 1996 onward. The CPW value is measured on maximum configurations. The type and number of disk devices, the number of workstation controllers, the amount of memory, the system model, other factors, and the application running determine what performance is achievable.
Note 2	There must be one DVD-RAM or DVD-ROM in the #9094 Base PCI I/O Enclosure.
Note 3	One line is used if #5544 System Console on Operations Console is used. One line might be used if the #5546 or #5548 System Console on LAN is selected and the #0367 Operations Console PCI Cable must be connected.
Note 4	External DASD capacity assumes 70.56 GB LUNs. External DASD cannot exceed the maximum new system capacity or the maximum number of disk arms.
Note 5	5250 CPW (Interactive) is an approximate value that reflects the amount of Processor CPW that can be used for workloads performing 5250-based tasks. The iSeries Enterprise Edition provides maximum 5250 CPW support (up to 100% of the capacity of the active processor CPW).Remember that: ▶ Any task that uses a 5250 data stream is considered 5250 online transaction processing (OLTP) work and requires some amount of 5250 CPW to process regardless of how the task was started. ▶ A task submitted through a 5250 session (5250 device or 5250 emulation) that does display or printer I/O requires 5250 CPW. ▶ A task submitted through a 5250 session (5250 device or 5250 emulation) as a "batch" job is not considered 5250 OLTP work and does not require any 5250 CPW unless the task does display or printer I/O. ▶ Limited 5250 CPW is available with the Standard Edition for a system administrator who wants to use 5250 display device I/O to manage various aspects of the server. Multiple administrative jobs exceed this capability. ▶ Maximum 5250 CPW is equivalent to the Processor CPW for the active processor.

Note 6 Model 890

Software group is determined by the combination of processor feature and edition feature. Display the QPRCFEAT system value or DSPHDWRSC TYPE(*AHW) to display the processor feature code value. This value is also shown for the Capacity Card CCIN value when using SST to perform a Capacity Upgrade on Demand.

Processor feature and server feature	Edition feature	Software group	Processor feature code or QPRCFEAT value
#0197		P50	25D3
#0198		P50	25D5
#2487	#1576	P50	2AF0
	#1577	P60	2AF1
	#1578	P60	2AF2
	#1579	P60	2AF3
	#1581	P60	2AF5
	#1583	P60	2AF7
	#1585	P60	2AF9
	#1587	P60	2AFB
	#1588	P60	2AFC

Note 6 Model 890	#2488	#1576	P50	2AD0
		#1577	P60	2AD1
		#1578	P60	2AD2
		#1579	P60	2AD3
		#1581	P60	2AD5
		#1583	P60	2AD7
		#1585	P60	2AD9
		#1587	P60	2ADB
		#1588	P60	2ADC
		#1591	P60	2ADF
Note 7	OS/400 V5R2 with the February 2003 level of LIC and Cumulative PTF package C3021520.			

Notes for all summary tables

Notes:

► Commercial processing workload (CPW) values give a relative performance rating of all iSeries processors.

► The capacities shown may require prerequisites. Some combinations of features are not valid.

1. CPW is used to measure the performance of all iSeries and AS/400e processors. The CPW value is measured on maximum configurations. The type and number of disk devices, the number of workstation controllers, the amount of memory, the system model, other factors, and the application being run determine what performance is achievable. For more details, see "Commercial processing workload" on page 40.

2. The 9404 Model B10 with 16M main storage and 945M of Disk assigned value of 1.0. All data for 70% system utilization and maximum configurations. IBM RAMP-C workload. Client results may vary.

3. There are particular limitations within SSP, which means that quoted minimums and maximums are often with OS/400 installed.

4. RSP CPW 5.5/17.1 refers to interactive and client/server environments respectively on the 9401 Server 10S. RSP RAMP-C of 1.9/5.9 also refers to these two environments in the same order.

5. Three LANs are allowed when running IBM Firewall for AS/400 (5769-FW1).

6. One tape is required.

7. Does not include Operations Console.

8. These cards may have one or two LAN ports. The #6617 SPD Integrated PC Server can have up to three ports.

9. V4R2 or later is a prerequisite for optical library support.

10. Either #9329 (PCI cards) or #9331 (SPD cards) must be chosen on a #5064/#9364. Therefore, columns two and three below this point are mutually exclusive.

11. The lower figure is for #2175, #2179, and #2180 processors. The higher number is for the #2181 and #2182 processors.

12. External DASD can be attached through an SPD disk controller in this unit.

13. Maximums are:

   12 of #6500
   20 of #6501
    9 of #6502, #6512, #6530, #6532, #6533

These maximums may be limited when used in combination with other disk controllers.

14. With V4R1, a maximum of two workstation controllers is supported.

15. The combined maximum of local and remote displays attached to ASCII and Twinax is seven with V4R1 and 28 with V4R2 and V4R3.

16. The lower number is for the #2161 processor. The higher number is for #2163, #2165, and #2166 processors.

17. If there is no workstation controller specified, the console must be specified by #9721.

18. One line is used for Operations Console. The maximum is nine if there is a Twinaxial System Console.

19. For systems shipped between October 1997 and February 1998, maximum storage is 2048M.

21. The maximum reflects the usage of two slot wide IPCS. If using a three slot wide IPCS, Integrated Netfinity Server, or Integrated xSeries Server, the maximum is two.

22. The maximum reflects the usage of two slot wide IPCS. If using a three slot wide IPCS, Integrated Netfinity Server, or Integrated xSeries Server, the maximum is four.

23. Requires V4R2 or later.

24. On the 9401 Model 150, the processor is the same on both the Twinaxial and Server Models, and therefore, the performance figures are the same.

25. The performance figures shown are for a "constrained" workload due to memory and disk limitations on the 9401 Model 150. If these limitations are lifted, the "unconstrained" CPW measurements in the following table apply.

Processor	Interactive	Client/server
#0591 and #0593	13.8	27.0
#0592 and #0592	20.6	35.0

26. The system also includes a CD-ROM for IBM software.

27. The 9401 Model 150 includes BasePak software in the hardware cost. This includes OS/400, Client Access Family for Windows, Query, SQL, Facsimile Support, and PSF/400. Additional programs have to be purchased.

28. Two of these PCI I/O card slots are reserved for the Integrated Netfinity Server. Three are driven by the multifunction I/O processor.

29. Six lines in total, but one is reserved for Operations Console.

30. A maximum of one LAN can be driven off the multifunction I/O processor. If Integrated Netfinity Server is installed, no LANs are supported on the MFIOP.

† This processor was announced in September 1996 when IBM introduced CPW as the new method of measuring the performance of AS/400e processors. For this and future processor announcements, CPW values only are quoted.

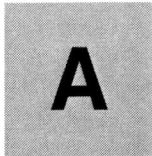

Referenced lists

This appendix accommodates lists and details that are considered pertinent to you, as referred to within the context of this publication. The details are presented in this appendix to improve the readability of the base information.

Options included in OS/400 V5R2

Note: Those product and product options identified with an asterisk (*) are preloaded on all new system orders.

- ► Option 1 OS/400 - Extended Base Support*
- ► Option 2 OS/400 - Online Information*
- ► Option 3 OS/400 - Extended Base Directory Support*
- ► Option 4 OS/400 - S/36 and S/38 Migration
- ► Option 5 OS/400 - System/36 Environment
- ► Option 6 OS/400 - System/38 Environment
- ► Option 7 OS/400 - Example Tools Library
- ► Option 8 OS/400 - AFP Compatibility Fonts
- ► Option 9 OS/400 - *PRV CL Compiler Support
- ► Option 11 OS/400 - S/36 Migration Assistant
- ► Option 12 OS/400 - Host Servers*
- ► Option 13 OS/400 - System Openness Includes
- ► Option 14 OS/400 - GDDM
- ► Option 16 OS/400 - Ultimedia System Facilities
- ► Option 21 OS/400 - Extended NLS Support
- ► Option 22 OS/400 - ObjectConnect
- ► Option 25 OS/400 - NetWare Enhanced Integration
- ► Option 29 OS/400 - iSeries Integration for Windows Server
- ► Option 30 OS/400 - Qshell*
- ► Option 31 OS/400 - Domain Name System
- ► Option 33 OS/400 - Portable Application Solutions Environment*
- ► Option 34 OS/400 - Digital Certificate Manager*
- ► Option 35 OS/400 - CCA Crypto Service Provider
- ► Option 39 OS/400 - International Components for Unicode
- ► Option 43 OS/400 - Additional Fonts

The following are included with all OS/400 V5R2 shipments:

- ► V5R2 HTTP Server*
- ► V5R2 Toolbox for Java*
- ► V5R2 Developer Kit for Java*

    - – Option 3 Java Developer Kit 1.2
    - – Option 4 Java Developer Kit 1.1.8
    - – Option 5 Java Developer Kit 1.3*
    - – Option 6 Java Developer Kit 1.4

- ► V3R7 Tivoli Management Agent*
- ► V5R2 Electronic Service Agent*
- ► V5R2 TCP/IP Utilities*

- ► V5R2 Integration for Windows Server*
- ► V5R2 iSeries Access for Windows*
- ► V5R2 iSeries Access for Wireless

All of the previously listed software is included in the software order.

Communication references

These networks, communication facilities, and protocols are supported on the iSeries.

Supported communication networks

Network types supported on the iSeries are:

- ► 1 Gbps Ethernet
- ► 100/10 Mbps Fast Ethernet
- ► IBM Token-Ring 4/16/100 Mbps Network (IEEE 802.5 and 802.2)
- ► Asynchronous Transfer Mode (ATM) 155 Mbps LAN
- ► X.21
- ► X.25
- ► ISDN Data Link Control (IDLC)*
- ► T1/E1/J1 and Fractional T1 Networks (high bandwidth)
- ► Asynchronous
- ► Binary synchronous
- ► Synchronous Data Link Control (SDLC)
- ► Ethernet Version 2 or IEEE 802.3
- ► FDDI/SDDI LANs (100 Mbps medium)

> **Note:** For the items marked with an asterisk (*), the #2750, #2751, #4750, and #4751 ISDN adapters are no longer supported at V5R2. For alternate solutions, see:
>
> http://www.ibm.com/servers/eserver/iseries/support/planning/isdnalt.htm

Supported communication facilities

The iSeries offers the following facilities:

- ► Simple Network Management Protocol (SNMP) in TCP/IP Networks
- ► Alerts support to NetView, iSeries, System/36, and System/38
- ► IBM Token-Ring Network Management Support
- ► Distributed Host Command Facility (DHCF)
- ► Link Problem Determination Aid (LPDA)
- ► Distributed System Node Executive (DSNX)

Supported communication protocols

The protocols that are supported by the iSeries are:

- ► Advanced Peer-to-Peer Networking (APPN)
- ► Advanced Program-to-Program Communication (APPC)
- ► ATM LAN Emulation (see note in the following section)
- ► Autodial Support
- ► Binary Synchronous Communications Equivalence Link (BSCEL)
- ► Dependent Logical Unit Requester (DLUR)
- ► Display Station Pass-through
- ► Distributed Data Management (DDM)
- ► Distributed Relational Database Support
- ► File Transfer Support
- ► IBM Network Routing Facility (NRF) Support/400
- ► ICF Retail Communications Support
- ► ICF Finance Communications Support
- ► Intersystem Communications Function
- ► Interactive Terminal Facility (ITF)
- ► ISDN Support
- ► Non-ICF Finance Communications Support
- ► Object Distribution Facility (ODF)
- ► Remote Workstation Support
- ► SNA Distribution Services (SNADS)
- ► SNA Primary Logical Unit 2 Support
- ► SNA/Management Services Transport
- ► SNA Pass-through
- ► SNA Upline Facility to System/370™ IMS™ and CICS Hosts
- ► Systems Application Architecture (SAA) Common Programming Interface for Communications (CPI-C)
- ► TCP/IP support
- ► X.21 Shorthold Mode (SHM) and multiple port sharing (MPS)
- ► 3270 Device Emulation
- ► 3270 SNA API Support for IBM 3278 Model 3, 4, and 5
- ► 3x74 Remote Attach
- ► 5x94 Remote Attach
- ► 5394/5494 SNA Backbone Support

ATM adapters not supported with i5/OS V5R3

ATM adapters not supported with i5/OS V5R3 include:

- ► #2811 PCI 25 Mbps UTP ATM IOA
- ► #2812 PCI 45 Mbps Coax T3/DS3 ATM IOA
- ► #2815 PCI 155 Mbps UTP OC3 ATM IOA
- ► #2816 PCI 155 Mbps MMF ATM IOA
- ► #2817 PCI 155 Mbps MMF ATM IOA
- ► #2818 PCI 155 Mbps SMF OC3 ATM IOA
- ► #2819 PCI 34 Mbps Coax E3 ATM IOA
- ► #4815 PCI ATM 155 Mbps UTP OC3
- ► #4816 PCI ATM 155 Mbps MMF
- ► #4818 PCI ATM 155 Mbps SMF OC3

ATM with SNA	ATM with TCP/IP
#2838	#2838
#2849	#2743, #2760

Note: OS/400 V5R2 is the final release to support the ATM networking technology and ATM adapters. The #5700, #5701, #2838, #2849, or #4838 10/100 Fast Ethernet with required infrastructure changes to the network as applicable (switches, routers, and so on) are recommended replacements. The #5706 and #5705 are also recommended replacements.

Gigabit Ethernet supports TCP/IP only. Therefore, Systems Network Architecture (SNA) Traffic requires using ANYNET as SNA over TCP/IP. 10/100 Fast Ethernet supports both SNA and TCP/IP. Although the Fast Ethernet adapter is limited to Unshielded Twisted Pair (UTP) cable, an external transceiver may be used to convert to multimode fiber (compatible with ATM fiber).

Features and devices not supported with OS/400 V5R1

The following features are not supported with OS/400 V5R1 or later:

- ► #2620 Full Cryptographic Processor
- ► #2628 Limited Cryptographic Processor
- ► #2851 Integrated PC Server
- ► #2854 PCI Integrated PC Server
- ► #6509 Additional 16 MS FSIOP Memory
- ► #6516 16 MB One-Port FSIOP
- ► #6517 32 MB One-Port FSIOP
- ► #6518 48 MB One-Port FSIOP
- ► #6519 64 MB One-Port FSIOP
- ► #6520 Upgrade 1 to 2 Port FSIOP
- ► #6526 16 MB Two-Port FSIOP
- ► #6527 32 MB Two-Port FSIOP
- ► #6528 48 MB Two-Port FSIOP
- ► #6529 64 MB Two-Port FSIOP
- ► #6616 Integrated PC Server
- ► #8716 Optional 16 MB One-Port FSIOP
- ► #8717 Optional 32 MB One-Port FSIOP
- ► #8718 Optional 48 MB One-Port FSIOP
- ► #8719 Optional 64 MB One-Port FSIOP
- ► #8726 Optional 16 MB Two-Port FSIOP
- ► #8727 Optional 32 MB Two-Port FSIOP
- ► #8728 Optional 48 MB Two-Port FSIOP
- ► #8729 Optional 64 MB Two-Port FSIOP

The following devices are not supported with OS/400 V5R1 or later:

- ► 2440
- ► 3422
- ► 3430
- ► 3995: Models 042, 043, 142, 143, A43
- ► 3995: All models connected via a #2621 are no longer supported
- ► 9347
- ► 9331: Models 001 and 002

The #2664 FAX IOP support is withdrawn at V5R1. See the following Web site for alternate solutions:

http://www.ibm.com/servers/eserver/iseries/support/planning/v5r1hardware.html

Some hardware features are supported with OS/400 V5R1 but are not supported on all iSeries models. Refer to the Planning Web site for more information:

http://www-1.ibm.com/servers/eserver/iseries/support/planning/v5r1hardware.html

Products and features no longer marketed by IBM

As products and features are withdrawn from marketing, they are removed from the published edition of the handbook. The tables in this section identify such products.

The currently available features are listed in this book, which may assist with providing a replacement. Refer to the iSeries Planning Web site for further information:

`http://www.ibm.com/servers/eserver/support/iseries/planning`

You can find alternate solutions for features no longer supported at V5R2 and V5R3 on the Web at:

`http://www.ibm.com/servers/eserver/iseries/support/planning/v5r2hardware.html`
`http://www.ibm.com/servers/eserver/iseries/support/planning/v5r3hardware.html`

Hardware no longer marketed by IBM

This section presents that hardware that is no longer marketed by IBM.

SPD technology

The following functions that are supported with SPD technology do not have equivalent function PCI cards for @server i5 and iSeries models:

- ASCII Adapter
- V.25 Autocall cable
- Select standby mode
- X.21 switched wide area network (WAN) dial-up or shorthold mode WAN
- Asynchronous communication speeds of less than 300 bps
- Data Rate Select signal on the EIA 232/V.24 interface

  This function is used by some older 2400 bps modems to reduce the speed to 1200 bps.
- LPDA-1 (Link Problem Determination Aids)

  This is a diagnostic function supported by some (primarily older IBM) modems.
- V.54 local and remote loopback (diagnostics functions supported by some modems)

PCI adapters also do not support X.21 switched WAN dial-up or shorthold mode WAN.

Hardware withdrawn from marketing

The hardware products and features shown in the following table are now withdrawn from marketing.

Product or feature	Withdrawal date	Recommended replacement
2105 Model B09 Versatile Storage Server (VSS)	24 November 1999	2105-800
2105 Models Exx IBM TotalStorage Enterprise Storage Server (ESS)	29 September 2000	2105-800
2105 Model F10 ESS	22 November 2000	2105-800
2105 Model F20 ESS	31 December 2003	2105-800
2109 Mod S08 S16 SAN Fibre Channel Switch	30 January 2003	3534 Model F08, 2109 Model F16
2422 ½-inch Reel Tape Drive		3580, 3590
2440 Magnetic Tape Subsystem (½-inch Reel Tape Drive)	20 January 1992	3580, 3590
2480 Wireless LAN Access Point (2480-RS0)	13 January 1999	N/A
2480 Wireless LAN Access Point (2480-E00, -EB0, -TR0, -TB0)	24 May 1999	N/A
2482 AS/400 Wireless Portable Transaction Computer (PTC)	24 May 1999	N/A
2483 Integrated Laser PTC for AS/400 Wireless Network	24 May 1999	N/A
2484 Industrial PTC for AS/400 Wireless Network	24 May 1999	N/A
2486 IBM PTC	24 May 1999	N/A
3430 Magnetic Tape Subsystem (½-in. Reel Tape Drive)	19 December 1989	3580, 3590
3490E Models F00 F01, F11, F1A, FC0 Magnetic Tape	28 June 2002	3580, 3590
3494 - L10, D10 IBM TotalStorage Enterprise Tape Library	27 December 2002	3494 L12, D12
3499 All Model Media	26 December 2003	N/A
3534 Model 1RU SAN Fibre Channel Managed Hub	14 February 2003	3534-F08
3570 Models Bxx Magstar® MP (Multi-Purpose) Tape Library	31 December 1999	3580. 3581, 3582
3570 Models Cxx Magstar MP (Multi-Purpose) Tape Library	27 December 2002	3580, 3581, 3582
3575 Models Lxx Magstar MP (Multi-Purpose) Tape Library Dataserver	28 June 2002	3583, 3584
3584-D42 UltraScalable Tape Library	25 April 2003	N/A
3995 Models A43, 043 143, 042, 142 Optical library	06 December 1996	3995 C40, C42, C44, C48

Product or feature	Withdrawal date	Recommended replacement
3995 Models C20, C22, C24, C26, C28 Optical Library, LAN attached	31 January 2002	N/A
5308 ASCII to 5250 Connection	21 December 1999	N/A
5494 Remote Control Unit	21 December 1999	N/A
5500 Express IP Control Unit	21 December 1999	N/A
6299 Midrange Hub	01 September 1999	N/A
7210-020 External CD ROM	29 June 2001	7210-025
7208-342 External 8mm Tape Drive	27 June 2003	7208-345
7852-40Z AS/400 Data/Fax Modem V.34	12 March 2002	#0032 Modem
7852-400 External V.34 Data/Fax Modem	01 November 2003	#0032 Modem
8361 -100 Network Station® series 100 Ethernet	14 October 1999	Neoware Eon Thin Client
8361 - 200 Network Station series 100 Token-Ring	14 October 1999	Neoware Eon Thin Client
8361 - 210 Network Station series 300 Token-Ring	31 December 1999	Neoware Eon Thin Client
8361 - 341 Network Station series 300 Twinax	31 December 1999	Neoware Eon Thin Client
9309 1.6m Rack Enclosure	01 October 2002	#0551 iSeries Tower
#9331 Expansion Unit for SPD Cards- 001 and 002 Diskette drive	25 October 1995	N/A
#9331 Expansion Unit for SPD Cards- 011 and 011 Diskette drive	15 September 1998	N/A
9347 Tape drive	31 October 2000	3580
9348 Magnetic tape device	26 February 1999	3580
Model 150 - System and features	31 October 2000	Model 520
Model 236 - Model upgrades from Model 236 to Model 436	25 February 2000	N/A
Model 436 Processor upgrades within the Model 436	25 February 2000	N/A
Model 170 - All models	31 May 2002	Model 520
Model 170 - All processor upgrades	28 December 2001	Model 520
Model 250- All models	16 June 2004	Model 520
Model 270 - All models, new model sales	21 November 2003	Model 520
Model 4xx - Model upgrades from 4xx to 7xx	30 June 2000	N/A

Product or feature	Withdrawal date	Recommended replacement
Model 5xx - Model upgrades from 5xx to 7xx	30 June 2000	N/A
Model 6xx - Model 600, 620, 640, and 650	31 May 1999	Model 520
Model 6xx - Model upgrades from 6xx to 6xx and processor feature conversions within 6xx models	31 May 2000	N/A
Model 6xx/Sxx - Model upgrades from 6xx/Sxx to 7xx/8xx	28 September 2001	N/A
Model 7xx - All models, new model sales Model 720 Model 730 Model 740	28 December 2001	Model 520 Model 520, 550 Model 550, 570
Model 7xx to 7xx model upgrades	28 December 2001	N/A
Model 7xx - Processor and interactive feature upgrades within 7xx models	02 July 2002	N/A
Model 7xx to 820, 830, 840 model upgrades	08 October 2003	N/A
Model 820 - #2396, #2397, #2398, #2425, #2426, and #2427 Model 820 processors	21 November 2003	Model 520, 550
Model 830 - #2402 and #2403 Model 830 processors	21 November 2003	Model 550, 570
Model 840 - #2416, #2417, #2418, #2419, #2420, and #2461 Model 840 processors	21 November 2003	Model 570
Model 890 - #0197, #0198, #2487, and #2488 Model 890 processors	07 May 2003	Model 570, 595
Model SB1 System	29 December 2000	Model 550, 570
Model SB2 System	03 December 2002	Model 550, 570
Model SB3 System	03 December 2002	Model 570
Model Sxx - Model S10, S20, S30, S40	31 May 1999	Model 520, 550
Model Sxx - Model upgrades from Sxx to Sxx and processor feature conversions within Sxx	31 May 2000	N/A
Model Sxx - Model upgrades from Sxx to 7xx/8xx	28 September 2001	N/A
#0001 - MES Bulk Order	02 July 2002	N/A
#0018 - 2440-xxx Local Source Rack Mount	30 June 2000	N/A
#0029 - 9347-xx Local Source Rack Mount	31 October 2000	N/A
#0034 - Red Covers	31 October 2000	N/A
#0046 - OptiConnect system	28 December 2001	N/A

Product or feature	Withdrawal date	Recommended replacement
#0059 - Transition Data Link	31 May 2000	N/A
#0086 - Optimize 3590 Performance	31 May 1999	N/A
#0088 - OptiConnect Cluster Specify	28 December 2001	N/A
#0123 - #5074 Lower Unit in Rack	03 December 2002	N/A
#0150 - 820 Base Processor	21 November 2003	Model 520, 550
#0151 - 820 Base Processor	01 October 2004	Model 520, 550
#0152 - 820 Base Processor	01 October 2004	Model 520, 550
#0153 - 830 8-way Processor	21 November 2003	Model 550, 570
#0158 - 840 12-way Processor	21 November 2003	Model 570
#0159 - 840 24-way Processor	21 November 2003	Model 570
#0185 - Performance Enhancement Model 150	31 October 2000	N/A
#0197 - Model 890 24-way processor	07 May 2003	Model 595
#0198 - Model 890 24-way processor	07 May 2003	Model 595
#0121 - 270 Lower Unit in a Rack	21 November 2003	N/A
#0122 - 270 Upper Unit in a Rack	21 November 2003	N/A
#0202 - Staged Upgrade Offering	31 May 1999	N/A
#0203 - Side-by-Side Install	02 July 2002	N/A
#0204 - Staged Side-by-Side Upgrade	31 May 1999	N/A
#0220 - Token ring on IPCS		#0223
#0221 - Ethernet on IPCS		#0224, #0225
#0295 - Performance Enhancement/28WS	31 October 2000	N/A
#0297 - Model 250 Package	16 June 2004	Model 520
#0298 - Model 250 Package	16 June 2004	Model 520
#0328 - Operations Console Cable	21 November 2003	#0367
#0362 - 20-ft. Communications Console Cable	31 January 2001	#0367
#0366 - Optical Bus Cable 20m	28 December 2001	N/A
#0380, #0381 Remote Control Panel Cable, #0382 Remote Control Panel Cable	02 July 2002	Virtual Control Panel, see Info APAR II13117

Product or feature	Withdrawal date	Recommended replacement
#0398 - Operations Console Package	02 July 2002	#9771
#0399 - 4 Port Twinaxial Expansion	30 June 2000	N/A
#0399 - Model 150 4 port Twinaxial Expansion	31 May 2000	N/A
#0578 PCI Expansion Unit in Rack	01 October 2004	N/A
#0591 - Entry Twinaxial Package V4R4 (type 9401)	31 October 2000	Model 520
#0592 - Growth Twinaxial Package V4R4 (type 9401)	31 October 2000	Model 520
#0593 - Entry Server Package V4R4 (type 9401)	31 October 2000	Model 520
#0594 - Growth Server Package V4R4 (type 9401)	31 October 2000	Model 520
#0601 - Direct Attach - #2743 PCI 1 Gbps Ethernet IOA (new orders only)	01 October 2004	#0620
#0602 - Direct Attach - #2760 PCI 1 Gbps Ethernet UTP IOA (new orders only)	01 October 2004	#0621
#0604 - Direct Attach - #2763 PCI RAID Disk Unit Controller (new orders only. Conversions to feature remain available)	21 November 2003	#0618
#0605 - Direct Attach - #4748 PCI RAID Disk Unit Controller (new orders only. Conversions to feature remain available)	02 July 2002	#0606
#0606 - Direct Attach - #4778 PCI RAID Disk Unit Controller New orders only. Conversions to feature remain available.)	19 November 2004	
#1312 - 1-Byte 1.03 GB Disk Unit Kit	31 October 2000	N/A
#1313 - 1-Byte 1.96 GB Disk Unit Kit	31 October 2000	N/A
#1322 - 2-Byte 1.03 GB Disk Unit Kit	31 October 2000	N/A
#1323 - 2-Byte 1.96 GB Disk Unit Kit	31 October 2000	N/A
#1325 - 2-Byte 1.03 GB Disk Unit Kit	31 October 2000	N/A
#1326 - 2-Byte 1.96 GB Disk Unit Kit	31 October 2000	N/A
#1327 - 2-Byte 4.19 GB Disk Unit Kit	31 October 2000	N/A
#1333 - 2-Byte 8.58 GB Disk Unit Kit	31 October 2000	N/A
#1334 - 2-Byte 17.54 GB Disk Unit Kit	31 October 2000	N/A
#1336 - 2-Byte 1.96 GB Disk Unit Kit	31 October 2000	N/A
#1337 - 2-Byte 4.19 GB Disk Unit Kit	31 October 2000	N/A
#1349 - 1.2 GB ¼-inch Tape Kit	31 October 2000	#4582

Product or feature	Withdrawal date	Recommended replacement
#1350 - 2.5 GB ¼-inch Tape Kit	31 October 2000	#4582
#1355 - 13.0 GB ¼-inch Tape Kit	31 October 2000	#4583
#1360 7.0 GB 8mm Cartridge Tape Kit	31 October 2000	7208-345 8mm
#1471 - 30m Optical HSL Cable	21 November 2003	#1472
#1490 to #1496 - Interactive Capacity Specify	02 July 2002	Enterprise Edition iSeries
#1500 to #1514 - Interactive Capacity Cards	02 July 2002	Enterprise Edition iSeries
#1517 to #1527, #1531 to #1547 - Interactive Capacity Cards	01 October 2004	Enterprise Edition iSeries
#1576 - Interactive Capacity Card	21 November 2004	Enterprise Edition iSeries
#1577 to #1578 - Interactive Capacity Card	01 October 2004	Enterprise Edition iSeries
#1579, #1581, #1583, #1585, #1587, #1591 - Interactive Capacity Card	21 November 2003	Enterprise Edition iSeries
#2061 - Model 720 Processor	28 December 2001	Model 520
#2062 - Model 720 Processor	02 July 2002	Model 520
#2063 - Model 720 2-way Processor	02 July 2002	Model 520
#2064 - Model 720 4-way Processor	02 July 2002	Model 520
#2065 - Model 730 Processor	28 December 2001	Model 520, 550
#2066 - Model 730 2-way Processor	02 July 2002	Model 520, 550
#2067 - Model 730 4-way Processor	02 July 2002	Model 520, 550
#2068 - Model 730 8-way Processor	02 July 2002	Model 520, 550
#2069 - Model 740 Processor	28 December 2001	Model 570
#2070 - Model 740 12-way Processor	02 July 2002	Model 570
#2159 - Model 170 Processor	February 2000	Model 520
#2248 - Model 270 Processor	21 November 2003	Model 520
#2250 - Model 270 Processor	03 December 2002	Model 520
#2252 - Model 270 Processor	03 December 2002	Model 520
#2253 - Model 270 2-way Processor	03 December 2002	Model 520
#2289 - Model 170 Processor	31 May 2002	Model 520
#2295 - Model 250 Processor	02 July 2002	Model 520

Product or feature	Withdrawal date	Recommended replacement
#2296 - Model 250 Processor	02 July 2002	Model 520
#2310 - Model SB1 8-way Processor	25 July 2000	Model 550, 570
#2311 - Model SB1 12-way Processor	25 July 2000	Model 550, 570
#2312 - Model SB1 8-way Processor	25 July 2000	Model 550, 570
#2313 - Model SB1 12-way Processor	25 July 2000	Model 550, 570
#2315 - Model SB2 8-way Processor	03 December 2002	Model 550, 570
#2316 - Model SB3 12-way Processor	03 December 2002	Model 570
#2318 - Model SB3 24-way Processor	03 December 2002	Model 570
#2349 - Model 830 4/8-way Processor	01 October 2004	Model 550, 570
#2351 Model 830 1/8-way (POD)	21 November 2003	Model 550, 570
#2352 Model 840 8/12-way (POD)	21 November 2003	Model 570
#2353 Model 840 12/18-way	01 October 2004	Model 570
#2354 Model 840 18/24-way	01 October 2004	Model 570
#2395 Model 820 Processor	21 November 2003	Model 520, 550
#2396 Model 820 Processor	03 December 2002	Model 520, 550
#2397 Model 820 2-way Processor	03 December 2002	Model 520, 550
#2398 Model 820 4-way Processor	03 December 2002	Model 520, 550
#2400 Model 830 2-way Processor	21 November 2003	Model 550, 570
#2402 Model 830 4-way Processor	03 December 2002	Model 550 570
#2403 Model 830 8-way Processor	03 December 2002	Model 550, 570
#2407 Model 170 Dedicated Domino Processor	31 May 2002	Model 520
#2416 Model 840 8/12-way	03 December 2002	Model 570
#2417 Model 840 12/18-way	03 December 2002	Model 570
#2418 Model 840 12-way Processor	03 December 2002	Model 570
#2419 Model 840 18/24-way	03 December 2002	Model 570
#2420 Model 840 24-way Processor	03 December 2002	Model 570
#2422 Dedicated Domino Processor	03 December 2002	Model 520
#2423 Dedicated Domino Processor	03 December 2002	Model 520

Product or feature	Withdrawal date	Recommended replacement
#2424 Dedicated Domino 2-way Processor	03 December 2002	Model 520
#2425 Dedicated Domino Processor	03 December 2002	
#2426 Dedicated Domino 2-way Processor	03 December 2002	
#2427 Dedicated Domino 4-way Processor	03 December 2002	
#2431 9406 Model 270 Processor	01 October 2004	Model 520
#2432 9406 Model 270 Processor	01 October 2004	Model 520
#2434 9406 Model 270 Processor	01 October 2004	Model 520
#2435 9406 820 Processor	01 October 2004	Model 520, 550
#2436 9406 820 Processor	01 October 2004	Model 520, 550
#2437 9406 820 2-way Processor	01 October 2004	Model 520, 550
#2438 9406 820 4-way Processor	01 October 2004	Model 520, 550
#2452 9406 Model 270 Processor	01 October 2004	Model 520
#2454 9406 Model 270 Processor	01 October 2004	Model 520
#2461 9406 Model 840 24-way Processor	03 December 2002	Model 570
#2487 Model 890 16/24-way Processor	07 May 2003	Model 570, 595
#2488 Model 890 24/32-way Processor	07 May 2003	Model 595
#2605 ISDN Basic Rate Interface Adapter	31 December 1999	#2742
#2609 EIA 232/V.24 Two-Line Adapter	31 March 1999	#2742
#2610 EIA 232/V.24 Two-Line Adapter	31 March 1999	#2742, #2772, #2773, #2805, #2806
#2612 EIA 232/V.24 One-Line Adapter	31 March 1999	#2742, #2793, #2794
#2613 V.35 One-Line Adapter	31 March 1999	#2742, #2793, #2794
#2614 X.21 One-Line Interface Adapter	31 March 1999	#2742, #2793, #2794
#2617 Ethernet/IEEE 802.3 Adapter/HP	31 March 1999	#2744, #2849, #4838, #5700, #5701, #5706, #5707
#2618 Fiber Distributed Data Interface Adapter	31 August 1998	N/A
#2619 LAN/WAN/Workstation IOA	31 March 1999	#2744
#2620 Full Cryptographic Processor	31 December 1999	#4801
#2621 Storage Device Controller	30 June 2000	#5702, #2749

Product or feature	Withdrawal date	Recommended replacement
#2623 Six-Line Communications Controller	31 December 1999	#2742
#2624 Storage Device Controller	28 December 2001	N/A
#2626 16/4 Mbps Token Ring Adapter/A	01 July 1997	#2744
#2628 Limited Cryptographic Processor	31 December 1999	#4801
#2629 LAN/WAN/Workstation IOP	31 May 2002	#2844
#2644 Magnetic Tape Attachment Card/HP	31 March 1999	#2749
#2654 EIA 232/V.24 Two-Line IOA	31 August 1998	#2742
#2655 EIA 232/V.24 20	31 August 1998	#2742
#2656 X.21 Two line 20	31 August 1998	#2742
#2657 EIA 232/V.24 50E	31 August 1998	#2742
#2658 EIA 232/V.24 50	31 August 1998	#2742
#2659 X.21 Two line 50	31 August 1998	#2742
#2664 Integrated Fax Adapter	31 December 1999	#2742 with #0032
#2665 Copper distributed data interface	31 August 1998	#2849, #2744, #5701
#2666 High-Speed Communications Adapter		#2742
#2668 Wireless LAN Adapter	31 August 1998	N/A
#2669 Shared bus interface card	28 December 2001	N/A
#2673 Optical Bus Adapter	30 June 2000	N/A
#2674 Optical Bus Adapter	30 June 2000	N/A
#2680 Optical bus receiver - 266 Mbps	28 December 2001	N/A
#2683 266 Mbps OptiConnect receiver	28 December 2001	N/A
#2685 1063 Mbps OptiConnect receiver	28 December 2001	#2792
#2686 Optical Link Processor	28 December 2001	#2842, #2843
#2688 Optical Link Processor	01 October 2004	#2842, #2843
#2695 Optical Bus Adapter	01 October 2004	N/A
#2699 Two-Line WAN IOA	28 December 2001	N/A
#2718 PCI Magnetic Media Controller	02 July 2002	#5702
#2720 Base PCI WAN/Twinaxial IOA	02 July 2002	#4746 and #2742

Product or feature	Withdrawal date	Recommended replacement
#2721 PCI Two-Line WAN IOA	31 October 2000	#2742
#2722 Twinaxial Workstation IOA	31 July 2001	#4746
#2723 PCI Ethernet IOA	28 December 2001	#2849, #4838, #5701, #5706
#2724 PCI 16/4 Mbps Token Ring IOA	31 July 2001	#2744
#2726 PCI RAID Disk Unit Controller	30 June 2000	#2757
#2729 PCI Magnetic Media Controller	02 July 2002	#2749
#2730 Programmable Regulator	01 October 2004	N/A
#2738 HSL ports - 8 copper	07 May 2003	N/A
#2740 PCI RAID Disk Unit Controller	31 May 2002	#2757
#2741 PCI RAID Disk Unit Controller	31 May 2002	#2757
#2743 1 Gbps PCI Ethernet IOA	16 June 2004	#5700, #5701, #5707
#2745 PCI Two-Line WAN IOA	01 October 2004	#2742
#2746 PCI Twinaxial Workstation IOA	01 October 2004	#4746
#2748 PCI RAID Disk Unit Controller	08 July 2003	#2757
#2749 PCI Ultra Magnetic Media Controller	01 October 2004	N/A
#2760 PCI 1 Gbps Ethernet UTP Adapter	01 October 2004	#5701, #5706
#2761 Integrated Analog Modem	02 July 2002	#2772, #2773
#2763 PCI RAID Disk Unit Controller	21 November 2003	#5703
#2766 PCI Fibre Channel Disk Controller	01 October 2004	#2787
#2768 PCI Magnetic Media Controller	01 October 2004	#5702
#2778 PCI RAID Disk Unit Controller	01 October 2004	#2757
#2782 PCI-X RAID Disk Unit Controller	01 January 2004	#5703
#2790 PCI Integrated Netfinity Server	31 May 2002	#4810
#2791 PCI Integrated xSeries Server	03 December 2002	#4810
#2799 PCI Integrated xSeries Server	21 November 2003	#4810
#2809 PCI LAN/WAN/Workstation IOP	31 May 2002	#2844
#2810 LAN/WAN IOP	31 May 2002	#2844
#2811 PCI 25 Mbps UTP ATM IOA	31 May 1999	N/A

Product or feature	Withdrawal date	Recommended replacement
#2812 PCI 45 Mbps Coax T3/DS3 ATM IOA	31 May 1999	N/A
#2815 PCI 155 Mbps UTP OC3 ATM IOA	31 May 2002	#2849, #4838, #5700, #5701, #5706, #5707
#2816 PCI 155 Mbps MMF ATM IOA	28 December 2001	#2849, #4838, #5700, #5701, #5706, #5707
#2817 PCI 155 Mbps MMF ATM IOA	03 December 2002	#2849, #4838, #5700, #5701, #5706, #5707
#2818 PCI 155 Mbps SMF OC3 ATM IOA	31 May 2002	#2849, #4838, #5700, #5701, #5706, #5707
#2819 PCI 34 Mbps Coax E3 ATM IOA	31 May 1999	N/A
#2824 PCI Feature Controller	28 December 2001	N/A
#2838 PCI 100/10 Mbps Ethernet IOA	21 November 2003	#2849, #4838, #5701, #5706
#2842 PCI IOP	21 November 2003	#2844
#2843 PCI IOP	01 October 2004	#2844
#2850 Integrated PC Server	31 March 1999	#4710, #4810
#2851 Integrated PC Server	31 March 1999	#4710, #4810
#2852 Integrated PC Server	30 June 2000	#4710, #4810
#2854 PCI Integrated PC Server	31 May 1999	#4710, #4810
#2857 Integrated PC Server	31 May 1999	#4710, #4810
#2858 FSIOA 128 MB memory, keyboard and mouse	30 June 2000	N/A
#2860 Integrated PC Server Memory	31 March 1999	N/A
#2861 32 MB IOP memory	28 December 2001	
#2862 128 MB IOP memory	28 December 2001	N/A
#2865 PCI Integrated Netfinity Server	02 July 2002	N/A
#2866 PCI Integrated Netfinity Server	02 July 2002	N/A
#2867 - 256 MB IOP memory	02 July 2002	N/A
#2868 Integrated Netfinity Server	31 October 2000	N/A
#2890 PCI Integrated Netfinity Server	31 May 2002	N/A
#2891 PCI Integrated xSeries Server	03 December 2002	N/A
#2892 PCI Integrated xSeries Server	01 January 2004	N/A

Product or feature	Withdrawal date	Recommended replacement
#2899 PCI Integrated xSeries Server	21 November 2003	N/A
#3000, #3002, #3004, #3006, #3007, #3009 Memory features (various)	01 October 2004	#3614
#3001, #3003, #3005 Memory features	31 May 2002	#3612
#3032 to #3034 Memory features	01 October 2004	#3613
#3025 512 MB main storage	03 December 2002	N/A
#3065 512 MB main storage	03 December 2002	N/A
#3103 32 MB main storage	31 March 1999	N/A
#3104 64 MB main storage	31 March 1999	N/A
#3110 64 MB main storage	30 March 2001	N/A
#3117, #3120, #3121 8 MB main storage	31 March 1999	N/A
#3118 16 MB main storage	31 March 1999	N/A
#3122 32 MB main storage	31 March 1999	N/A
#3133 64 MB main storage	31 March 1999	N/A
#3134 128 MB main storage	31 March 1999	N/A
#3135 256 MB main storage	31 March 1999	N/A
#3136 256 MB main storage	31 March 1999	N/A
#3138 64 MB main storage	31 March 1999	N/A
#3144 8 MB main storage	31 March 1999	N/A
#3145 16 MB main storage	31 March 1999	N/A
#3146 32 MB main storage	31 March 1999	N/A
#3147 32 MB main storage	31 March 1999	N/A
#3149 128 MB main storage	31 March 1999	N/A
#3172 32 MB main storage (two SIMMS)	31 March 1999	N/A
#3179 256 MB main storage	03 December 2002	N/A
#3180 512 MB main storage	03 December 2002	N/A
#3182 32 MB main storage	31 May 2002	N/A
#3189 128 MB main storage	03 December 2002	N/A

Product or feature	Withdrawal date	Recommended replacement
#3190 256 MB main storage	03 December 2002	N/A
#3191 512 MB main storage	03 December 2002	N/A
#3192 1024 MB main storage	03 December 2002	N/A
#3193 2048 MB main storage	03 December 2002	N/A
#3195 4096 MB main storage	03 December 2002	N/A
#3197 1024 MB main storage	03 December 2002	N/A
#3198 2048 MB main storage	03 December 2002	N/A
#4308 4.19 GB disk unit	29 December 2000	#4326
#4314 8.58 GB Disk Unit	23 October 2000	#4326
#4317 8.58 GB 10k RPM Disk Unit Feature conversions remain available	03 December 2002	#4326
#4318 17.54 GB 10k RPM Disk Unit	01 June 2004	#4326
#4324 17.54 GB Disk Unit	23 October 2000	#4326
#4425 CD-ROM	21 November 2003	#4625
#4430 DVD-RAM	01 January 2004	#4630
#4482 4 GB ¼-inch Cartridge Tape Device	01 January 2004	#4682
#4483 16 GB ¼-inch Cartridge Tape Device	03 December 2002	#4684
#4486 25 GB ¼-inch Cartridge Tape Device	03 December 2002	#4684
#4487 50 GB ¼-inch Cartridge Tape Device	01 January 2004	#4687
#4525 CD-ROM	21 November 2003	#4625
#4583 16 GB ¼-inch Cartridge Tape Device	03 December 2002	#4584
#4586 25 GB ¼-inch Cartridge Tape Device	03 December 2002	#4584
#4723 PCI 10 Mbps Ethernet Adapter	28 December 2001	#2849, #4838, #5701, #5706
#4748 PCI RAID Disk Unit Controller Feature conversions available	21 November 2003	#2757
#4761 PCI Integrated Analog Modem	02 July 2002	#2772, #2773, #2805 or #2806
#4800 PCI Cryptographic Processor	29 December 2000	#4801
#4802 PCI Cryptographic Processor	21 November 2003	#4801

Product or feature	Withdrawal date	Recommended replacement
#4815 PCI ATM 155 Mbps UTP OC3	28 December 2001	#2849, #4838, #5700, #5701, #5706, #5707
#4816 PCI ATM 155 Mbps MMF	28 December 2001	#2849, #4838, #5700, #5701, #5706, #5707
#4818 PCI ATM 155 Mbps SMF OC3	28 December 2001	#2849, #4838, #5700, #5701, #5706, #5707
#5033 Migration Tower I	07 May 2003	N/A
#5034 Migration Tower I	21 November 2003	N/A
#5035 Migration Tower I	21 November 2003	N/A
#5043 Convert primary rack to secondary rack	31 March 1999	N/A
#5044 System Unit Expansion Rack	31 March 1999	#5094, #5294
#5051 Storage Expansion Unit for System Unit	30 June 2000	#5108, #7127
#5052 Storage Expansion Unit	31 May 2002	#5108, #7127
#5055 Storage Expansion Unit	31 May 2002	#5108, #7127
#5057 Storage Expansion Unit Feature conversions available	02 July 2002	#5108, #7127
#5058 Storage Expansion Unit	31 May 2002	#5108, #7127
#5062 OptiConnect in tower	28 December 2001	N/A
#5063 OptiConnect in system unit tower	28 December 2001	N/A
#5064 System Unit Expansion	28 December 2001	N/A
#5065 Storage/PCI Expansion Tower	21 November 2003	#5094
#5066 1.8 M I/O Tower	21 November 2003	#5294
#5070 266 Mbps System Unit Expansion Tower	30 June 2000	#5088, #0588
#5071 266 Mbps System Unit Expansion Tower	02 July 2002	#5088, #0588
#5073 1063 Mbps System Unit Expansion Tower	28 December 2001	#5088, #0588
#5075 PCI Expansion Tower	21 November 2003	#5095 / #0595
#5080 266 Mbps Storage Expansion Tower	30 June 2000	#5088, #0588
#5081 266 Mbps Storage Expansion Tower	02 July 2002	#5094 with #5108
#5082 Storage Expansion Tower	30 June 2000	#5094 with #5108
#5083 Storage Expansion Tower	28 December 2001	#5094 with #5108

Product or feature	Withdrawal date	Recommended replacement
#5117 30-Disk Expansion with Dual Line Cord	07 May 2003	
#5135 Feature Power Supply	30 June 2000	N/A
#5143 Power Supply	02 July 2002	N/A
#5150 Battery Backup	20 November 2001	N/A
	02 July 2002	N/A
#5151 Power Supply	02 July 2002	N/A
#5153 Redundant Power Supplies	02 July 2002	N/A
#5155 Redundant Power and Cooling	01 October 2004	N/A
#5157 Feature Power Supply	01 October 2004	N/A
#5518 Alt IPL Spec 13 GB Tape	31 October 2000	N/A
#5543 Sys Console on comm	29 December 2000	N/A
#5601 OptiConnect in Rack	28 December 2001	N/A
#6050 Enhanced Twinaxial Workstation Controller	31 May 2002	#4746
#6140 Twinaxial Workstation Controller	27 March 1998	#4746
#6141 ASCII Workstation Controller	31 March 1999	N/A
#6142 ASCII 12-Port Workstation Attachment	31 March 1999	N/A
#6148 Eight-Port Twinaxial Expansion	30 June 2000	#4746
#6149 16/4 Mbps Token Ring IOA	31 May 2002	#2744
#6151 X.21 One-line adapter	31 August 998	#2742
#6152 EIA 232/V.24 adapter	31 October 1996	#2742
#6153 V.35 One-line adapter	31 August 1998	#2742
#6173 V.35 One-line adapter 50 foot	31 August 1998	#2742
#6180 Twinaxial workstation IOA	31 July 2001	#4746
#6181 Ethernet IOA	31 July 2001	#2849, #4838, #5701, #5706
#6325 CD-ROM New orders withdrawn Feature conversions available	02 July 2002	#4525, #4625
#6380 2.5 GB ¼-inch Cartridge Tape Unit	30 June 2000	#4582, #4682
#6381 2.5 GB ¼-inch Cartridge Tape	29 December 2000	#4582, #4682

Product or feature	Withdrawal date	Recommended replacement
#6382 4 GB ¼-inch Cartridge Tape Unit	03 December 2002	#4582, #4682
#6383 16 GB ¼-inch Cartridge Tape Unit	03 December 2002	#4583, #4683
#6384 30 GB ¼-inch Cartridge Tape Unit	21 November 2003	#4584, #4684
#6385 13 GB ¼-inch Cartridge Tape Unit	31 May 2000	#4583, #4683
#6386 25 GB ¼-inch Cartridge Tape Unit	03 December 2002	#4584, #4684
#6425 CD-ROM	02 July 2002	#4525, #4625
#6480 2.5 GB ¼-inch Cartridge Tape Unit	02 July 2002	#4582, #4682
#6481 2.5 GB ¼-inch Cartridge Tape Unit	29 December 2000	#4582, #4682
#6482 4 GB ¼-inch Cartridge Tape Unit	03 December 2002	#4582, #4682
#6483 16 GB ¼-inch Cartridge Tape Unit	03 December 2002	#4583, #4683
#6484 30 GB ¼-inch Cartridge Tape Unit	21 November 2004	#4584, #4684
#6485 13 GB ¼-inch Cartridge Tape Unit	31 May 2000	#4583, #4683
#6486 25 GB ¼-inch Cartridge Tape Unit	03 December 2002	#4584, #4684
#6501 Tape/Disk Device Controller	31 July 2001	#2787 for Disk #2749 for Tape
#6502 High Performance Controller	02 November 1997	#2757
#6512 High Performance Controller	30 June 2000	#2757
#6513 Internal Tape Device Controller	01 October 1999	#2749 or #5702
#6522 Disk unit controller for RAID	30 June 2000	#2757
#6523 Storage Device Controller	30 June 2000	#2757
#6530 Disk Unit Controller No Cache	31 March 1999	#2757
#6532 RAID Disk Unit Controller	30 June 2000	#2757
#6533 RAID Disk Unit Controller	31 May 2002	#4317
#6534 Magnetic Media Controller	31 May 2002	#2749
#6607 4.19 GB Additional Two-byte Disk Unit	29 December 2000	#4326
#6616 Integrated PC Server	31 March 1999	#4710, #4810
#6617 Integrated PC Server	31 May 1999	#4710, #4810
#6618 Integrated Netfinity Server	28 December 2001	#4710, #4810

Product or feature	Withdrawal date	Recommended replacement
#6713 8.58 GB Disk Unit (new features, feature conversions withdrawn)	23 October 2000 02 July 2002	#4326
#6714 17.54 GB Disk Unit	23 October 2000	#4326
#6717 8.58 GB 10k RPM Disk Unit (new orders withdrawn, feature conversions remain available)	03 December 2002	#4326
#6718 17.54 GB 10k RPM Disk Unit	03 December 2002	#4326
#6807 4.19 GB Additoinal Two byte Disk Unit	29 December 2000	#4326
#6813 8.58 GB Additional Two-byte Disk Unit	23 October 2000	#4326
#6817 8.58 GB 10k RPM Disk Unit	03 December 2002	#4326
#6818 17.54 GB 10k RPM Disk Unit	01 June 2004	#4326
#6824 17.54 GB Disk Unit	23 October 2000	#4326
#6907 4.19 GB Additional Two-byte Disk unit	29 December 2000	#4326
#7000 Panel Keylock	30 June 2000	N/A
#7101 System Expansion Unit	31 May 2002	N/A
#7102 System Expansion Unit	02 July 2002	N/A
#7108 Expansion Gate	30 June 2000	N/A
#7117 Integrated Expansion Unit	30 June 2000	N/A
#7123 DASD Expansion Unit	01 October 2004	N/A
#7127 DASD Expansion Unit	01 October 2004	N/A
#7128 DASD Expansion Unit	01 October 2004	N/A
#7130 Expansion Unit Tape Cage	02 July 2002	N/A
#7174 Ethernet IEEE 802.3 Adapter	31 August 1998	#2849, #4838, #5701, #5706
#7175 16/4 Mbps Token-ring Adapter	31 August 1998	#2744
#8079 Optional Base 1.8 M I/O Rack	21 November 2003	#5294
#8093 Optional 1.8 M I/O Rack	07 May 2003	#8094
#8180 Opt. Base 512 MB main storage	28 December 2001	N/A
#8191 Opt. Base 512 MB main storage	28 December 2001	N/A
#8192 Opt. Base 1024 MB main storage	28 December 2001	N/A
#8193 Opt. Base 2048 MB main storage	28 December 2001	N/A

Product or feature	Withdrawal date	Recommended replacement
#8617 Opt. Base 8.58 Gb 10k RPM Disk Unit	28 December 2001	#4326
#8618 Opt. Base 17.54 Gb 10k RPM Disk Unit	28 December 2001	#4326
#8713 Opt Base 8.58 GB Disk Unit new orders withdrawn feature conversions withdrawn	31 January 2001 02 July 2002	#4326
#8714 Opt Base 17.54 GB Disk Unit (7200 RPM) new orders withdrawn feature conversions withdrawn	31 January 2001 02 July 2002	#4326
#8809 EIA 232/V.24 Two line adapter		#2745
#8813 Opt Base 8.58 GB Disk Unit	23 October 2000	#4326
#8813 Opt Base 8.58 GB Disk Unit (7200 RPM)	31 January 2001	#4326
#8817 8.58 GB Optional Base Two-byte Disk Unit 10k RPM	28 December 2001	#4326
#8818 17.54 GB Optional Base Two-byte Disk Unit 10k RPM	28 December 2001	#4326
#8824 Opt Base 17.54 GB Disk Unit	23 October 2000	#4326
#8824 Opt Base 17.54 GB Disk Unit (7200 RPM)	31 January 2001	#4326
#8863 EIA 232/V.24 Two line adapter	31 May 2001	#2745
#8866 EIA 232/V.24 Two line adapter (50-foot)	31 May 2001	#2745
#8917 8.58 GB Optional Base 10 k RPM Disk Unit	02 July 2002	#4326
#8918 17.54 GB Optional Base 10 k RPM Disk Unit	02 July 2002	#4326
#8924 17.54 GB Optional Base Two-byte Disk Unit	23 October 2000	#4326
#8924 17.54 GB Optional Base Two-byte Disk Unit (7200RPM)	31 January 2001	#4326
#9052 Standard Storage Expansion Unit (16 disk)	02 July 2002	N/A
#9080 Watertight Line Cord	02 July 2002	N/A
#9082 120/240V 14-ft. Line Cord	02 July 2002	N/A
#9083 Locking Line Cord Plug	02 July 2002	N/A
#9116 High Performance CD Enable	02 July 2002	N/A
#9119 Migrated DASD	02 July 2002	N/A
#9174 Ethernet/IEEE 802.3 Adapter		#2849, #4838, #5701, #5706
#9175 16/4 Mbps Token-ring Adapter		#2744

Product or feature	Withdrawal date	Recommended replacement
#9179 Base 256 MB main storage	02 July 2002	N/A
#9180 Line Cord Specify	02 July 2002	N/A
#9182 14-ft. Line Cord Specify	02 July 2002	N/A
#9183 Locking Line Cord Plug	02 July 2002	N/A
#9190 Base 256 MB main storage	31 May 2002	N/A
#9240 Base 400 W Power Supply	30 June 2000	N/A
#9243 400 W Power Supply	30 June 2000	N/A
#9244 Expansion Unit 320 W Power Supply	30 June 2000	N/A
#9245 Base Battery Backup	30 June 2000	N/A
#9249 Base 16/4 Mbps Token Ring IOA	31 May 2002	#2744
#9251 Base I/O Tower	02 July 2002	N/A
#9280 Base Twinaxial Workstation Controller	28 December 2001	#2746 or #9746
#9313 8.58 GB Base Two-byte Disk Unit	23 October 2000	#4326
#9313 8.58 GB Base Two-byte Disk Unit	31 January 2001	#4326
#9329 PCI Card Expansion Unit	31 May 2002	N/A
#9330 PCI Integrated Expansion Unit New orders withdrawn Feature conversions remain available	02 July 2002	N/A
#9331 Expansion Unit for SPD Cards	28 December 2001	N/A
#9347 Local Source Rack Mount	31 October 2000	N/A
#9364 System Unit Expansion	28 December 2001	N/A
#9381 Base Ethernet IEEE 802.3 IOA	28 December 2001	#2849, #4838, #5701, #5706
#9699 Base Two-Line WAN IOA	28 December 2001	#2742
#9707 4.19 GB Base Two-byte Disk Unit (Ultra SCSI)	29 December 2000	#4326
#9720 Base PCI WAN/Twinaxial IOA	02 July 2002	#4746 and #2742
#9721 Base PCI Two-Line WAN IOA	31 October 2000	#2742
#9723 PCI Ethernet IOA	02 July 2002	#2849, #4838, #5701, #5706
#9724 PCI Token Ring IOA	02 July 2002	#2744
#9728 Base Disk Unit Controller	02 July 2002	#2757

Product or feature	Withdrawal date	Recommended replacement
#9738 PCI 100/10 Mbps Ethernet IOA	02 July 2002	#2849, #4838, #5701, #5706
#9740 Base RAID Disk Unit Controller	02 July 2002	#2757
#9745 Base PCI Two-Line WAN IOA	02 July 2002	#2742
#9748 Base PCI RAID Disk Unit Controller	08 July 2003	#2757
#9751 Base MFIOP with RAID (Models 640, 650, S30, S40, SB1)	31 May 1999	N/A
#9754 MFIOP with RAID	28 December 2001	N/A
#9778 Base PCI RAID Disk Unit Controller	21 November 2003	#2757
#9789 Base HSL Ports - 4 Optical	07 May 2003	#9710
#9792 Base PCI Integrated xSeries Server	01 January 2004	N/A
#9902 - Do not integrate	02 July 2002	N/A
#9907 - Base 4.19 GB Disk Unit	29 December 2000	#4326

Abbreviations and acronyms

Measurements

K	1,024 bytes
M	1,000,000 bytes
M	1,048,576 bytes
G	1,000M bytes
T	1,000G bytes
bps	bits per second
Kbps	1,024 bps
Mbps	1,048,576 bps
lpm	lines per minute
lpi	lines per inch
cps	characters per second
cpi	characters per inch
bpi	bits per inch
cpl	characters per line
ips	inches per second
dpi	dots per inch
ipm	impressions per minute

Keywords

ACD	Automated Call Director
ACL	Auto Cartridge Loader
ADCS	Advanced Data Communications for Stores
ADM	Application Development Manager
ADS	Application Dictionary Services
ADSM	ADSTAR Distributed Storage Manager
AFP	Advanced Function Printing
APAR	Authorized Program Analysis Report
API	application programming interface

APPC	Advanced Program to Program Communication
APPN	Advanced Peer to Peer Network
APW	Advanced Print Writer
ARP	Address Resolution Protocol
ASMI	Advanced System Management Interface
ASP	Application Solution Provider
ASP	auxiliary storage pool
ATM	asynchronous transfer mode
AUI	Attachment Interface Unit
AWT	Abstract Windowing Toolkit
B2B	business to business
B2C	business to consumer
B2E	business to employee
BBU	Battery Backup Unit
BGU	Business Graphics Utility
BI	Business Intelligence
BIOS	Basic Input Output System
BLOB	binary large object
BMS	Basic Mapping Support
BPC	Bulk Power Controller
BRI	Basic Rate Interface
BRMS	Backup and Recovery Media Services
BSC	bisynchronous
BSF	Bean Scripting Framework
CBU	Capacity Backup
CBX	computerized
CCA	Common Cryptographic Architecture
CCIN	Custom Card Identification Number
CCSID	Coded Character Set ID

CCW	Continuous Composite Worm	DDE	Dynamic Data Exchange
CDMF	Commercial Data Masking Facility	DDL	Database Definition Language
CEC	Central Electronics Complex	DDM	Data Directory Manager
CEMT	CICS Master Terminal	DDM	Distributed Data Management
CGI	Common Gateway Interface	DDM	disk drive module
CICS	Customer Information Control System	DDS	Data Description Specification
CIF	Customer Install Feature	DECS	Domino Enterprise Connection Services
CIFS	Common Internet File System	DES	Data Encryption Standard
CIM	Complex Impedance Matching	DFU	Data File Utility
CISC	Complex Instruction Set Computing	DHCF	Distributed Host Command Facility
CL	Control Language	DIMM	Dual Inline Memory Module
CLI	Call Level Interface	DLL	Dynamic Link Library
CLOB	Character Large Object	DMZ	Demilitarized Zone
CODE	Cooperative Development Environment	DOLS	Domino Off-Line Services
COLD	Computer Output to Laser Disk	DOM	Document Object Model
CORBA	Common Object Request Broker Architecture	DRDA	Distributed Relational Database Architecture
CPA	Common Programming APIs	DSD	Dedicated Server Domino
CPM	continuously powered main storage	DSL	Digital Subscriber Line
CPW	commercial processing workload	DSNX	Distributed System Node Executive
CRG	Cluster Resource Group	DSP	Digital Signal processing
CRM	customer relationship management	DST	Dedicated Service Tools
CSA	Callpath Services Architecture	DTD	Document Type Definition
CSP	Common Service Processor	DUOW	Distributed Unit of Work
CSU	Customer Setup	EADS	A term used to represent the Multi-Adapter Bridge Boundary
CSV	comma separated variable	EAI	Enterprise Application Integration
CUoD	Capacity Upgrade on Demand	ECM	error correction mode
DASD	direct access storage device	ECS	Electronic Customer Support
DBCS	double byte character set	EDF	Execution Diagnostic Facility
DBLOB	double-byte large object	EGL	Enterprise Generation Language
DCA	Distributed Converter Assembly	EIM	Enterprise Identity Mapping
DCA	Document Content Architecture	EIP	Enterprise Information Portal
DCE	Distributed Computing Environment	EIS	Executive Information System
DCM	Digital Certificate Manager	EJB	Enterprise JavaBeans
DCM	Dual Chip Module	EJS	Enterprise JavaServer

EMU	European Monetary Unit	IASP	independent auxiliary storage pool
ePoE	Electronic Proof of Entitlement	IBM	International Business Machines
ERP	Enterprise Resource Planning	ICA	Integrated Computing Architecture
ESP	Extreme Support Through Personalization	ICC	Information Catalog Center
		ICM	Information Catalog Manager
ESS	Enterprise Storage Server	ICMP	Internet Control Message Protocol
EVI	encoded-vector index	ICSS	Internet Connection Secure Server
FCMU	File Compose and Merge Utility	IDLC	ISDN Datalink Control
FFDC	first failure data capture	IDRC	improved data recording capability
FFT	Final Form Text	IGP	Intelligent Graphics Processor
FACT	Find and Compare Tool	IIOP	Internet Inter-ORB Protocol
FIFO	First In First Out	IKE	Internet Key Exchange
FIPS	Federal Information Processing Standard	ILE	Integrated Language Environment
		IMAP	Internet Message Access Protocol
FRCA	Fast Response Cache Accelerator	IMPI	Internal Machine Program Instruction
FSIOP	File Serving Input Output Processor		
FSB	front side bus	IMPI	Internal microprogram instruction
FTP	File Transfer Protocol	INS	Integrated Netfinity Server
FULIC	Featured User Licensed Internal Complex	IOA	Input Output Adapter
		IOP	Input Output Processor
GDDM	Graphical Data Display Manager	IPCS	Integrated PC Server
GUI	graphical user interface	IPDS	Intelligent Printer Data Stream
HACP	Host Access Client Package	IPL	initial program load
HATS	Host Access Transformation Services	IPLA	International Program License Agreement
HCP	Host Command Processor	IPP	Internet Printing Protocol
HMC	Hardware Management Console	IPS	IP over SNA Snackets
HMT	hardware multithreading	IPSec	IP Security Protocol
HOLAP	hybrid online analytical processing	IPX	Internet Packet exchange
HPOFS	High Performance Optical File System	ISA	Industry Standard Architecture
		ISDB	Interactive Source Debugger
HPT	Host Print Transform	ISDN	Integrated Services Digital Network
HSL	high-speed link	ISL	Inter Switch Link
HSM	Hierarchical Storage Manager	ISV	independent software vendor
HTML	Hypertext Markup Language	ITF	Interactive Terminal Facility
HTTP	Hypertext Transfer Protocol	ITU	International Telecommunication Union
HVD	High Voltage Differential		

IXA	Integrated xSeries Adapter	**LPR**	line printer requester
IXS	Integrated xSeries Server for iSeries	**LPO**	Licensed Program Offering
J2EE	Java 2 Platform, Enterprise Edition	**LPP**	licensed program product
J2SDK	Java 2 Software Developer Kit	**LTO**	Linear Tape Open
J2SE	Java 2 Platform, Standard Edition	**LUN**	Logical Unit Number
JAF	JavaBean Activation Framework	**LVD**	Low Voltage Differential
JAXP	Java API for XML parsing	**LZ1**	Lempel Ziv 1
JCE	Java Cryptographic Extension	**MABB**	Multi-Adapter Bridge Boundary
JDBC	Java Database Connection	**MAC**	Media Access Control
JDBC	Java Database Connectivity	**MBPS**	Megabytes Per Second
JDK	Java Developer Kit	**MCM**	Multi Chip Module
JFC	Java Foundation Class	**MCU**	Mail and Calendaring Users
JIT	Just in Time (Java compiler)	**MDI**	Microsoft Data Interchange
JMS	Java Messaging Service	**MES**	Miscellaneous Equipment Specification
JMX	Java Management Extension		
JNDI	Java Naming and Directory Interface	**MFIOP**	multifunction input/output processor
		MIB	Management Information Base
JSF	JavaServer Faces	**MMF**	Multi Mode Fiber
JSP	JavaServer Pages	**MO**	Magneto-Optical
JSSE	Java Secure Socket Extension	**MOLAP**	multidimensional online analytical processing
JVM	Java virtual machine		
KDC	key distribution center	**MQI**	Message Queue Interface
L2TP	Level 2 Tunneling protocol	**MQT**	Materialized Query Table
LAN	local area network	**MRI**	machine-readable information
LDAP	Lightweight Directory Access Protocol	**MSF**	Mail Services Framework
		MSS	Managed System Services
LEI	Lotus Enterprise Integrator	**MTS**	Microsoft Transaction Server
LIC	Licensed Internal Code	**MULIC**	Machine User License Internal Code
LID	License Information Document		
LLC	Logical Link Control	**MVS**	Multiple Virtual Storage
LMB	logical memory block	**NAT**	Network Address Translation
LOB	Large Object	**NAWT**	Native Abstract Window Toolkit
LOB	line of business	**NC**	Network Computer
LPAR	logical partition	**NDMP**	Network Data Management Protocol
LPD	line printer daemon		
LPDA	Link Problem Determination Aid	**NFS**	Network File System

NIST	National Institute of Standards & Technology	**PIN**	Personal Identification Number
NLM	Network Loadable Module	**PING**	Packet Internet Groper
NLS	national language support	**PLIC**	Partition Licensed Internal Code
NNTP	Net News Transfer Protocol	**POD**	Processor on Demand
NRF	Network Routing Facility	**POE**	Proof of Entitlement
NSM	Network Station Manager	**POP**	Post Office Protocol
NTAP	Windows NT Application Processors	**PPP**	Point-to-Point Protocol
ODBC	Open Database Connectivity	**PRPQ**	Programming Request for Price Quotation
ODF	Object Distribution Facility	**PSF**	Printing Support Facility
OGSA	Open Grid Services Architecture	**PSP**	preventive service planning
OIA	Operator Information Area	**PTF**	program temporary fix
OLAP	Online Asynchronous Processing	**PVC**	Private Virtual Circuit
OLE	Object Link Embedded	**QIC**	Quarter Inch Cartridge
OLP	Optical Link Processor	**QMF**	Query Management Facility
OLTP	online transaction processing	**R/DARS**	Report Data Archive and Retrieval System
ORB	Object Request Broker	**RAD**	Rapid Application Development
OSF	Open Software Foundation	**RAID**	Redundant Array of Independent Disks
OS/400	Operating System/400	**RAS**	reliability, availability, serviceability
PASE	Portable Application Solutions Environment	**RAS**	Remote Access Service
PBX	Private Branch Exchange	**RCD**	Read Cache Device
PCI	Peripheral Component Interconnect	**RDBMS**	relational database management system
PCL	Printer Control Language	**REXEC**	Remote Execution
PCML	Program Call Markup Language	**RF**	Radio Frequency
PDA	personal digital assistant	**RFC**	Request for Comments
PDF	Portable Document Format	**RFT**	Revisable Form Text
PDM	Programming Development Manager	**RIP**	Routing Information Protocol
PDML	Panel Definition Markup Language	**RISC**	Reduced Instruction Set Computing
PDPA	Physical Device Placement Assistant	**RJE**	Remote Job Entry
PDU	power distribution unit	**RLU**	Report Layout Utility
pHyp	POWER Hypervisor	**RMI**	remote method invocation
PICS	Platform for Internet Content Selection	**ROLAP**	relational online analytical processing
PIM	personal information management	**RPG**	Report Program Generator

RPO	Record Purpose Only	**SPCN**	System Power Control Network
RPQ	Request for Price Quotation	**SPD**	System Products Division
RPR	Relative Performance Rating	**SQL**	Structured Query Language
RSP	relative system performance	**SSL**	Secure Sockets Layer
RTAS	Run-Time Abstraction Services	**SSO**	single signon
SAA	Systems Application Architecture	**SSP**	System Support Program
SAN	storage area network	**SST**	System Service Tools
SCM	Single Chip Module	**SUE**	System Unit Expansion
SCM	Software Configuration Management	**SVC**	Switched Virtual Circuit
SCSI	Small Computer System Interface	**SVG**	Scalable Vector Graphing
SDA	Screen Design Aid	**SWA**	Save-while-active
SDF	Server Definition File	**TCP/IP**	Transmission Control Protocol/Internet Protocol
SDK	Software Developer Kit	**TIMI**	Technology Independent Machine Interface
SDLC	Synchronous Datalink Control		
SEU	System Expansion Unit Source Entry Utility	**TMA**	Tivoli Management Agent
		UDB	Universal Database
SHM	Short Hold Mode	**UDDI**	Universal Description, Discovery, and Integration
SIMM	Single Online Memory Module		
SLIC	System Licensed Internal Code	**UDF**	user defined functions
SLIP	Serial Line Internet Protocol	**UDFS**	user-defined file system
SLM	Software Licensed Management	**UDO**	Ultra Density Optical
SMAPP	System Managed Access Path Protection	**UDP**	User Datagram Protocol
		UDT	user defined types
SMF	Single Mode Fiber	**UIM**	User Interface Manager
SML	SQL Markup Language	**UOW**	Unit of Work
SMP	symmetric multiprocessing	**UPS**	uninterruptible power supply
SMT	simultaneous multithreading	**URL**	Universal Resource Locator
SMTP	Simple Mail Transfer Protocol	**URL**	Uniform Resource Locator
SMU	Simple Mail Users	**USF**	Ultimedia System Facility
SNA	Systems Network Architecture	**UTP**	Unshielded Twisted Pair
SNADS	SNA Distribution Services	**VLAN**	Virtual LAN
SNMP	Simple Network Management Protocol	**VM**	Virtual Machine
		VPN	virtual private network
SOAP	Simple Object Access Protocol	**VRU**	Voice Response Unit
SOI	Silicon On Insulator	**VSE**	Virtual Storage Extended
SP	Service Processor	**W3**	World Wide Web

WAF	Workfolder Application Facility
WAN	Wide Area Network
WLE	IBM @server Workload Estimator
WML	Wireless Markup Language
WORF	Web Services Object Runtime Framework
WORM	Write-Once-Read-Many
WSDL	Web Service Description Language
WWW	World Wide Web
WYSIWYG	What You See Is What You Get
XPCML	Extensible Program Call Markup Language
XSL	Extensible Stylesheet Language
XSLT	XSL transformation
XSM	cross-site mirroring
XML	Extensible Markup Language

Related publications

The publications listed in this section are considered particularly suitable for a more detailed discussion about the topics covered in this redbook.

IBM Redbooks

For information about ordering these publications, see "How to get IBM Redbooks" on page 791.

- ▶ *IBM @server i5 and iSeries System Handbook*, GA19-5486

  The latest update to this Handbook is always available in soft copy on the World Wide Web. You can also view, search, or download in PDF or HTML formats of this book from the Redbooks Web site. Simply enter iSeries Handbook or GA19-5486 in the search parameter on the Web site.

  You can find the final, edited edition of the Handbook directly at:

  http://www.redbooks.ibm.com/pubs/pdfs/redbooks/ga195486.pdf

  Prior to availability of the final edited edition, you can find the draft edition at:

  http://www.redbooks.ibm.com/redpieces/pdfs/ga195486.pdf

- ▶ *IBM @server iSeries and AS/400e System Builder*, SG24-2155
- ▶ *IBM Web-to-Host Integration Solutions*, SG24-5237
- ▶ *Developing an e-business Application for the IBM WebSphere Application Server*, SG24-5423
- ▶ *WebSphere Application Servers: Standard and Advanced Editions*, SG24-5460
- ▶ *Web Enabling AS/400 Applications with IBM WebSphere Studio*, SG24-5634
- ▶ *iSeries e-business Handbook: A Technology and Product Reference*, SG24-5694
- ▶ *IBM @server iSeries Migration: System Migration and Upgrades at V5R1 and V5R2*, SG24-6055
- ▶ *WebSphere Scalability: WLM and Clustering Using WebSphere Application Server Advanced Edition*, SG24-6153
- ▶ *WebSphere Personalization Solutions Guide*, SG24-6214
- ▶ *IBM @server iSeries in Storage Area Networks: Implementing Fibre Channel Disk and Tape with iSeries*, SG24-6220 (Redbook Draft)

785

- *IBM @server iSeries IP Networks: Dynamic!*, SG24-6718

- *IBM @server iSeries Independent ASPs: A Guide to Moving Applications to IASPs*, SG24-6802

- *IBM TotalStorage Tape Selection and Differentiation Guide*, SG24-6946

- *Integrating Backup Recovery and Media Services and IBM Tivoli Storage Manager on the IBM @server iSeries Server*, SG24-7031

- *Logical Partitions on the IBM PowerPC: A Guide to Working with LPAR on POWER5 for IBM @server i5 Servers*, SG24-8000

- *OS/400 Maximum Capacities V5R2*, REDP-0204

- *WebSphere for IBM @server iSeries Server Buying and Selling Guide*, REDP-3646

- *Lotus Domino for the IBM @server iSeries Server Buying and Selling Guide*, REDP-3845

- *iSeries Model 825 High-speed Link Loop*, TIPS-0297

- *Twinaxial Attached Device Throughput for Twinaxial Devices*, TIPS-0358

Other resources

These publications are also relevant as further information sources:

- Soltis, Frank G. *Fortress Rochester: The Inside Story of the IBM @server iSeries*. 29th Street Press, July 2001. ISBN 1583040838.

- *IBM TotalStorage Enterprise Tape System 3590 Introduction and Planning Guide*, GA32-0329

- *AS/400 Road Map for Changing to PowerPC Technology*, SA41-5150

- *iSeries Performance Capabilities Reference*, SC41-0607

  http://publib.boulder.ibm.com/infocenter/iseries/v5r3/ic2924/books/sc410607.pdf

- *System/36 Migration Planning*, SC41-4152

- *System/38 Migration Planning*, SC41-4153

- *Tips and Tools for Securing Your iSeries*, SC41-5300

- *Backup Recovery and Media Services for iSeries*, SC41-5345

- *IBM AS/400 Integration for Windows Server – Setup*, SC41-5439

- *Client Access Express for Windows – Setup*, SC41-5507

- *Operations Console Setup*, SC41-5508

- *System API Reference*, SC41-5801

► *Physical Planning Quick Reference*

You can find this document in the iSeries Information Center at:

`http://www.ibm.com/eserver/iseries/infocenter`

For OS/400 V5R2, select *your language* and **V5R2**. Then select **Plan for hardware and software** →**Planning reference**.

For i5/OS V5R3, select *your language* and **V5R3**. Then select **Planning**.

Referenced Web sites

These Web sites are also relevant as further information sources:

► Redbooks home page

`http://www.redbooks.ibm.com/`
`http://w3.itso.ibm.com`

► iSeries Information Center

`http://www.ibm.com/eserver/iseries/infocenter`
`http://publib.boulder.ibm.com/pubs/html/as400/v5r2/ic2924/index.htm`

► iSeries and AS/400 publications: "What's new" by release

`http://publib.boulder.ibm.com/pubs/html/as400/online/chgfrm.htm`

► IBM @server iSeries Resource Library

`http://www.ibm.com/eserver/iseries/library`

► IBM @server iSeries Support: Software Knowledge Base

`http://www.as400service.ibm.com/supporthome.nsf/Document/10000051`

► iSeries Technical articles and white papers

`http://www.ibm.com/servers/enable/resources/index.html`

► i5/OS V5R3 Console Positioning white paper

`http://www-1.ibm.com/servers/eserver/iseries/literature/index.html`

► IBM @server Hardware Management Console

`http://publib.boulder.ibm.com/infocenter/eserver/v1r2s/en_US/info/iphal/`
`hardwaremanagementconsolehmc.htm`

► IBM Product Publications

`http://www.elink.ibmlink.ibm.com/public/applications/publications/`
`cgibin/pbi.cgi`

► IBM Publications Center (intranet site)

`http://w3.ehone.ibm.com/public/applications/publications/cgibin/pbi.cgi`

► iSeries Nation

  http://www-1.ibm.com/servers/eserver/iseries/nation/

► Partnerworld for Developers - IBM @server iSeries

  http://www.iseries.ibm.com/developer/index.html

► IBM @server iSeries server site

  http://www-1.ibm.com/servers/eserver/iseries/

► iSeries software

  http://www.ibm.com/eserver/iseries/software

► ibm.com/software site

  http://www.software.ibm.com

► iSeries Planning

  http://www.ibm.com/servers/eserver/support/iseries/planning

► iSeries Upgrade Planning for OS/400 V5R2

  http://www-1.ibm.com/servers/eserver/iseries/support/planning/
  v5r2software.html

► iSeries Upgrade Planning for i5/OS V5R3

  http://www-1.ibm.com/servers/eserver/iseries/support/planning/
  v5r3software.html

► Product Previews, Statements of Direction, Planning for withdrawn products

  http://www.ibm.com/servers/eserver/iseries/support/planning/v5r3direct.html

► IBM @server Solution Connection

  http://www-1.ibm.com/servers/solutions/finder/
  CSFServlet.wss?mvcid=main&packageid=1000&ca=oiesc_uk&me=W

► Performance Center

  http://www.iseries.ibm.com/developer/performance/index.html

► Performance ratings for @server p5 and pSeries servers

  http://www-1.ibm.com/servers/eserver/pseries/hardware/rperf.html

► IBM @server Workload Estimator

  http://www-912.ibm.com/wle/EstimatorServlet

► Sizing IBM @server i5 servers for AIX 5L applications

  http://www-1.ibm.com/servers/eserver/iseries/aix/index.html

► iSeries technical support overview

  http://www.as400service.ibm.com/supporthome.nsf/document/20965550

- Storage networking home page

  `http://www.storage.ibm.com/ibmsan/index.html`

- IBM @server iSeries Support

  `http://www.ibm.com/iseries400/support`

- iSeries hardware editions

  `http://www-1.ibm.com/servers/eserver/iseries/hardware/editions`

- BRMS application client performance

  `http://www-1.ibm.com/servers/eserver/iseries/service/brms/adsmperf.htm`

- CICS

  `http://www.ibm.com/software/ts/cics/`

- IBM Connect for iSeries

  `http://www.ibm.com/eserver/iseries/btob/connect`

- iSeries Navigator for Wireless: Offers information and helpful links about Management Central-Pervasive

  `http://www-1.ibm.com/servers/eserver/iseries/navigator/pervasive.html`

- 5250 Emulation Products

  `http://www.networking.ibm.com/525`

- IBM @server Capacity Upgrade on Demand (CUoD)

  `http://www.ibm.com/eserver/iseries/ondemand`

- Windows integration (with iSeries)

  `http://www.iseries.ibm.com/windowsintegration`

- Electronic Support Access

  `http://www.iseries.ibm.com/tstudio/planning/esa/esa.htm`

- Ultrium Linear Tape-Open benefits

  `http://www.storage.ibm.com/hardsoft/tape/lto/prod_data/ultrium.html`

- IBM NetVista

  `http://www.pc.ibm.com/ww/netvista/index.html`

- Application Factory - OS/400 PASE

  `http://www.iseries.ibm.com/developer/factory/pase`

- Linux for IBM @server iSeries

  `http://www.ibm.com/eserver/iseries/linux`

- Eclipse platform

  `http://www.eclipse.org/`

- ► The Apache Software Foundation

  http://www.apache.org
- ► Logical partitioning

  http://www.ibm.com/servers/eserver/iseries/lpar
- ► VisualAge Generator

  http://www-4.ibm.com/software/ad/visgen
- ► IBM Toolbox for Java

  http://www.ibm.com/servers/eserver/iseries/toolbox
- ► IBM Electronic Services for iSeries and AS/400e

  http://www.ibm.com/services/electronic
- ► DB2 Content Manager

  http://www.ibm.com/software/data/cm/cmgr
- ► Backup Recovery and Media Services

  http://www.ibm.com/servers/eserver/iseries/service/brms.htm
- ► Facsimile Support for iSeries

  http://www.ibm.com/servers/eserver/iseries/fax400
- ► Lotus SmartSuite®

  http://www.lotus.com/smartsuite
- ► Lotus Domino

  http://www.lotus.com/domino
- ► Lotus Domino Support

  http://www.ibm.com/servers/eserver/iseries/domino/support
- ► Lotus Messaging

  http://www.lotus.com/messaging
- ► Lotus Enterprise Integration

  http://www.edge.lotus.com
- ► The ATM Forum

  http://www.atmforum.com
- ► Baan home page

  http://www.baan.com
- ► SAP home page

  http://www.sap.com

How to get IBM Redbooks

You can search for, view, or download Redbooks, Redpapers, Hints and Tips, draft publications and Additional materials, as well as order hardcopy Redbooks or CD-ROMs, at this Web site:

    ibm.com/redbooks

Help from IBM

IBM Support and downloads

    ibm.com/support

IBM Global Services

    ibm.com/services

Index

Symbols

Q

QMF Distributed Edition for Multiplaforms V8.1   602
QPRCMLTTSK   63
Query for iSeries   601
Query Governor   522
Query Manager   601
query tuning   522

R

racks   261
ragged SWA   532
RAID-5   383
record protocol   514
Redbooks Web site   791
    Contact us   xxviii
redundant power supply   153
referenced lists   749
referential integrity   517
remote control panel   676
required features
    Model 520   123
    Model 550   139
    Model 570   154
    Model 595   170
    Model 800   189
    Model 810   201
    Model 825   213
    Model 870   225
    Model 890   244
Reserve Capacity on Demand   46
RISC to RISC Data Migration (#0205)   318
rPerf   43
RPQ
    843977 disk unit conversion   381
    847102   382
    847102 10K DASD Mounting   382
    847102 10K DASD to PCI Tower/270/8xx   382
RPQ 847192   313

S

S/36 environment   566
S/38 environment   566
SAN (storage area network)   425
SB2 Model 9406   713
SB3 Model 9406   713
scalability   522
schematics   273
    expansion tower   267, 271, 276, 281, 283, 286,

288
    Model 520   130
    Model 550   143
    Model 570   161
    Model 595   180
    Model 800   194
    Model 810   206
    Model 825   218
    Model 870   233
    Model 890   253
secondary language   551
security   513
    features   514
server code distribution   399
Server feature   40
server structure   40
server virtualization   27
Silicon On Insulator (SOI)   18
Simple Cluster Management GUI   578
simultaneous multithreading   17
single address   42
single system reliability   24
single-level storage   9–10
single-step upgrades   321
single-system availability management   24
SLIC (System Licensed Internal Code)   11
SLM/400   588
soft rules   339
software end of support dates   322
software keys for LPAR system upgrades   593
Software License Manager/400   588
Software Maintenance   582
software no longer marketed by IBM   322, 756
Software Subscription   582–583
software terms   581
software upgrade paths   581
software upgrades   582
SOI (Silicon On Insulator)   18
Solution Edition   57
SPD Expansion Towers   262
SQL Development Kit   601
SQL optimizer   521
SQL query support   519
SSTAR technology   19
Standard Edition   56
standby processor   44
startup processor   48
Statement of Direction   70
storage area network (SAN) components   425